Tort Law in Bangladesh

This book explores the use of tort law in Bangladesh, outlining critical studies and cases on key concepts such as nuisance, intentional torts, negligence, and liability.

Drawing from case studies in the UK, USA, Canada, Australia, and India, the volume comparatively analyses various aspects of tort law including its efficacy, issues of determination, and monetary considerations. It scrutinizes academic literature and prominent cases such as *Bangladesh Beverage Industries Ltd v Rowshan Akhter* and *Children Charity Bangladesh Foundation v Government of Bangladesh*, among others, to examine the objective and use of tort law in Bangladesh. It also explores fundamental misconceptions related to the use of torts, protection of public and private rights, formalization of tort cases in courts, types of legal remedies for injuries, and more.

Lucid and topical, this book will be an essential read for scholars of law, tort law, constitutional law, civil and criminal law as well as for legal professionals, especially those concerned with Bangladesh.

Sakif Alam is a former professor of North South University in Dhaka, Bangladesh. He completed his undergraduate and graduate degrees from Carleton University, where he was a Deans' List law student, ranked among the top 15 Oralists at the Osgoode Cup, graduated with High Honours, and received a distinction in his master's thesis. Apart from tort law, his areas of interest include intellectual property, international trade, and private international law. He's interested in seeing an intergovernmental organization, similar to the Dispute Settlement Body of the World Trade Organization, established to address compensatory issues related to victims of corporate misconduct, who often don't receive any compensation from parent companies because of legal technicalities, such as *forum non conveniens* and *lex loci delicti*. In the near future, however, Sakif wants to practise personal injury law in Ontario and continue to teach and pursue research in his areas of interest.

Tort Law in Bangladesh
Applications and Challenges

Sakif Alam

LONDON AND NEW YORK

First published 2022
by Routledge
2 Park Square, Milton Park, Abingdon, Oxon OX14 4RN

and by Routledge
605 Third Avenue, New York, NY 10158

Routledge is an imprint of the Taylor & Francis Group, an informa business

© 2022 Sakif Alam

The right of Sakif Alam to be identified as authors of this work has been asserted in accordance with sections 77 and 78 of the Copyright, Designs and Patents Act 1988.

All rights reserved. No part of this book may be reprinted or reproduced or utilised in any form or by any electronic, mechanical, or other means, now known or hereafter invented, including photocopying and recording, or in any information storage or retrieval system, without permission in writing from the publishers.

Trademark notice: Product or corporate names may be trademarks or registered trademarks, and are used only for identification and explanation without intent to infringe.

British Library Cataloguing-in-Publication Data
A catalogue record for this book is available from the British Library

Library of Congress Cataloging-in-Publication Data
A catalog record has been requested for this book

ISBN: 978-1-032-07761-1 (hbk)
ISBN: 978-1-032-14927-1 (pbk)
ISBN: 978-1-003-24178-2 (ebk)

DOI: 10.4324/9781003241782

Typeset in Sabon
by SPi Technologies India Pvt Ltd (Straive)

To my father, *Brigadier General Md. Zahur-ul Alam, ndc, psc (Retd)*, and mother, *Anju Alam*.

My father, who is a loving parent, grandfather, husband (as I am sure my mother would agree), and human being, is the raising Commanding Officer of the 1 Para-Commando Battalion, which is the elite forces, of the Bangladesh Army.

My mother is the bedrock of the Alam household. You are my inspiration, my counsellor, and the reason I wish to be a better, and a more learned, person every day.

I wish I could someday be a mix of the two of you. I am proud and honoured to call you my parents.

I love you.

Contents

Preface		viii
Acknowledgements		ix
Abbreviations		xi
List of Legal Cases		xiv
1	Overview of torts	1
2	The development of tort law in Bangladesh	10
3	Nuisance	20
4	Intentional torts	63
5	Negligence	164
6	Strict liability	303
	Index	328

Preface

When I began teaching law at North South University, I was a little surprised by the fact that there was no book on tort law in Bangladesh. However, every other book (e.g. *inter alia*, contracts, constitutional law, administrative law, criminal law, criminal procedure, and civil procedure) used to teach law was written *about* Bangladesh.

We must understand that law is unlike any other subject. That is to say, you can teach engineering and medicine using books that were written abroad, as the symptoms of a heart attack in Bangladesh would be similar to that in England. Law, however, is sui generis and a different ballgame altogether because every country's laws are unique and somewhat different.

For example, in Bangladesh, adultery is a criminal offence, but that is not the case in Canada; in Milan, Italy, it is illegal to frown in public, unless you are at a funeral or are visiting someone at the hospital; and in some parts of Switzerland, it is illegal to flush the toilet in apartment buildings after 10:00 pm.

I hope these illustrations have proved my point.

Therefore, I set out on a protracted and tortuous journey to write this book in the context of Bangladesh, and after three long years, it has fructified.

Acknowledgements

It is my belief that a book, especially a textbook such as this one, is like a movie (minus the entertainment factor) in the sense that there are many people working behind-the-scenes to bring it to life. Here, I would like to acknowledge those dedicated and hardworking individuals without whom this book would not have been possible.

First and foremost, I thank my intelligent, loving, and beautiful lawyer-wife, *Muniza Kabir*. I remember sitting at a café with you in Dhaka when the idea of writing this book came to mind. You supported me unwaveringly throughout this three-year arduous writing process. Moreover, I ran many ideas and legal analyses by you and you never lost your patience; rather, you always found the time in your busy schedule to listen to me prattle and provided valuable insight and much-needed direction.

Even more impressive is that you gave me the time and space to resume working on this book three months after our wedding. For this, and everything else, I will always remain grateful.

Second, my mother, *Anju Alam*, is my everything. Your encouragement and confidence in this project kept me going even when I thought this was never-ending. Though a direct effect is that my clothes no longer fit, your cooking and baked goods provided the necessary fuel in completing this book. I hope that you will someday be as proud of me as I am of you.

Next, my father, *Brigadier General Md. Zahur-ul Alam, ndc, psc (Retd)*, is the hardest working, and the most disciplined, man I know. You have sacrificed everything for us and never asked for anything in return (including giving up golf during COVID-19). If more people were as magnanimous and altruistic as you, I am sure the world would have been a better place. Please always remain who you are.

Fourth, my brother, *Ariq Alam*, has been a constant source of support. Even though you were in a different country while I was writing this book, your words of encouragement and FaceTime calls greatly facilitated the research and writing processes.

Then, *Helal Uddin Nagari* always kept me going. Our conversations and prognostications about US politics were both enlightening and inspiring.

May you rest in peace.

x *Acknowledgements*

Sixth, *Nafiz Ahmed* and *Md. Fahmedul Islam Dewan*, the two Teaching Assistants at the Department of Law, were instrumental in completing this book. I remember texting Nafiz, who is now a graduate student at the University of Cambridge, at the oddest hours with complete disregard to the time-difference. You never expressed any irritation (or, maybe you did, and I did not understand it) and always provided the necessary material immediately.

Similarly, Fahmed, though a very busy law student who is also involved in many extracurricular activities, sent all of the necessary material as and when required – even when I commented on your Instagram stories about research I needed help with in a chapter.

Next, the editorial team at Routledge (Taylor & Francis Group) was fantastic, extremely helpful, and indispensable to getting this book passed the finish line, particularly *Antara Ray Chaudhury*, the Development Editor, and *Shloka Chauhan*, my Editorial Assistant. Though Shloka became involved later in the project, I remember emailing both of you incessantly, and every time I did, I was reminded of your kindness and attention to detail. Without the two of you and your guidance, I would never have been able to finish this book.

Lastly, *Fabia Rahman, Shajahan Kabir, Aniatus Saqa, Saif Ansari, Rabita Kabir*, and *Ifaz Kabir*, I thank you for your constant encouragement. And, of course, *Elara R Alam* and *Sofia R Ansari*, thank you for being the cutest kids and always making me smile.

Abbreviations

Adv Q	Advocates' Quarterly
African J of Intl & Comparative L	African Journal of International and Comparative Law
Alb L Rev	Albany Law Review
Am J Comp L	American Journal of Comparative Law
Am L Reg	The American Law Register
Art Ant & L	Art Antiquity and Law
Bangladesh Ins Leg Dev	Bangladesh Institute of Legal Development
Bangladesh J L	Bangladesh Journal of Law
Baylor L Rev	Baylor Law Review
Cal L Rev	California Law Review
Cambridge LJ	Cambridge Law Journal
Campbell L Rev	Campbell Law Review
Can B Rev	The Canadian Bar Review
Can Community LJ	Canadian Business Law Journal
Colum L Rev	Columbia Law Review
Conn L Rev	Connecticut Law Review
DePaul L Rev	DePaul Law Review
Fordham L Rev	Fordham Law Review
Geo LJ	Georgetown Law Journal
Harv L Rev	Harvard Law Review
Harv Negot L Rev	Harvard Negotiation Law Review
Int'l Fam Plan Pers	International Family Planning Perspectives
Int'l Pers Sexual & Rep Health	International Perspectives on Sexual and Reproductive Health
Iowa L Rev	Iowa Law Review
Issues in Leg Scholarship	Issues in Legal Scholarship
J Air L & Com	Journal of Air Law & Commerce
J Bone Miner Res	The Journal of Bone & Mineral Research
J Contemp L	Journal of Contemporary Law

xii *Abbreviations*

J for Contemporary Roman-Dutch L	Journal for Contemporary Roman-Dutch Law
J L & Econ	The Journal of Law & Economics
J Leg Stud	Journal of Legal Studies
J Small & Emerging Bus	Journal of Small & Emerging Business Law
L Q Rev	Law Quarterly Review
La L Rev	Louisiana Law Review
Law Q Rev	Law Quarterly Review
Loy L A L Rev	Loyola of Los Angeles Law Review
Marq L Rev	Marquette Law Review
McGill JL & Health	McGill Health Law Publication
Md L Rev	Maryland Law Review
Mich L Rev	Michigan Law Review
Miss LJ	Mississippi Law Journal
Mo L Rev	Missouri Law Review
Modern L Rev	Modern Law Review
NDL Rev	North Dakota Law Review
Neb L Rev	Nebraska Law Review
NYUL Rev	New York University Law Review
Or L Rev	Oregon Law Review
Oxford J Leg Stud	Oxford Journal of Legal Studies
SALJ	South African Law Journal
SCB	Supreme Court of Bangladesh
Sing JLS	Singapore Journal of Legal Studies
St. Mary's LJ	St. Mary's Law Journal
Stan L Rev	Stanford Law Review
Sw L Rev	Southwestern Law Review
Sydney L Rev	Sydney Law Review
Tex L Rev	Texas Law Review
U Chi L Rev Dialogue	University of Chicago Law Review Dialogue
U Colo L Rev	University of Colorado Law Review
U Pa L Rev	University of Pennsylvania Law Review
U Tol L Rev	University of Toledo Law Review
UBC L Rev	University of British Columbia Law Review
UC Davis L Rev	University of California Davis Law Review
UTLJ	University of Toronto Law Journal
Va L Rev	Virginia Law Review
Vand L Rev	Vanderbilt Law Review
VUWLR	Victoria University of Wellington Law Review
Wash L Rev	Washington Law Review

Wash ULO	Washington University Law Quarterly
Wi-Fi	Wireless Fidelity
Wis L Rev	Wisconsin Law Review
Yale JL & Human	Yale Journal of Law & the Humanities
Yale LJ	Yale Law Journal

List of Legal Cases

Abel v Eli Lilly & Co 238
Ad-Lib Club Ltd v Granville 124
Agar v Canning 84
Agdeppa v Glougie 175
Agni v Wenshall (in re City of New York) 180
Alderson v Booth 65
Allaire v St. Luke's Hospital 211
Allan et al v New Mount Sinai Hospital 91
Allen v Flood 129
Amann v Faidy 211
America Online, Inc v National Health Care Discount, Inc ... 110
American Surety Co v Pryor 68
Andreae v Selfridge & Co Ltd 45
Anns v Merton London Borough Council 204
Antrim Truck Centre Ltd v Ontario
(Minister of Transportation) 22, 25, 28, 43
Appleby v Erie Tobacco Co 21, 27, 33, 45, 187
Arkwright v Newbold 113
Armstrong v Warner Brothers Theatres Inc 177
Arndt v Smith 100
Ashby v White 77
Athey v Leonati 231, 234
Aubry v Éditions Vice-Versa 79
Babiuk v Trann 102
Bailey et al v Warner 68
Baker v Market Harborough Industrial Society Ltd 193
Baker v Willoughby 222
Balcom v Independence 177
Baltimore v Thompson 175
Bamford v Turnley 38
Bangladesh Beverage Industries Ltd v Rowshan Akhter 10
Bangladesh National Women Lawyers' Association v
The Government of Bangladesh 88
Barbour v University of British Columbia 112

List of Legal Cases xv

Barnett v Chelsea & Kensington Hospital Management
Committee 216
Barry v Third Avenue R R Co 68
Bazley v Curry 315
Belcher v City of San Francisco 174
Bellizia v Meares 193
Berstein of Leigh (Baron) v Skyviews and General Ltd 109
Biletski v University of Regina 276
Bird v Jones 65
Blackstock v Foster 235
Blackwater v Plint 321
Blunk v Atchison 68
Bocardo SA v Energy UK Onshore Ltd 109
Bollinger v Costa Brava Wine Company Ltd 124
Bolton v Stone 178
Bolton v Vellines 68
Bonbrest v Kotz 211
Boomer v Atlantic Cement Co 52
Borgstede v Waldbauer 176
Bourgoin v Leamington (Municipality) 275
Bradford v Kanellos 265
Bradford Corporation v Pickles 31
Bradley v Bath 279
Bristol Conservatories Ltd v Conservatories Custom Built Ltd 124
Brown v Swift & Co 175
Brune v De Benedetty 175
Burnett v Amalgamated Phosphate Co 175
Burnie Port Authority v General Jones Pty Ltd 310
Bury v Pope 28
Butterfield v Forrester 275
Byrne v Boadle 197
C(JS) v Wren 95
Caltagirone v Scozzari-Cloutier 81–2
Cambell v MGN Ltd 82
Cambridge Water Co Ltd v Eastern Counties Leather Plc 310
Canada Paper Company v Brown 23, 52
Canadian Foundation for Children, Youth and the Law v Canada
(Attorney General) 102
Carroll v New York Pie Baking Co 20
Carter v Canada (Attorney General) 74
Carter v Yardley & Co 175
Catherine Masud et al v Md Kashed Miah et al 12, 200
Century 21 Canada Ltd Partnership v Rogers
Communications Inc 109
Central of Georgia R Co v Robertson 175

xvi   *List of Legal Cases*

Chaproniere v Mason 193
Children Charity Bangladesh Foundation v Government
of Bangladesh 14, 194
Ciarlariello v Schacter 92
Ciba-Geigy Canada Ltd v Apotex Inc 119
Cincinnati Railroad Company v The Commonwealth 47
Clark v Canada (TD) 77
Clay v A J Crump & Sons Ltd 200
Comanche Duke Oil Co v Texas Pacific Coal & Oil Co 175
CompuServe Inc v Cyber Promotions Inc 109–10
Cook v Lewis 239, 244, 246
Cooper v Hobart 204
Cope v Sharpe 107
Coppins v Jefferson 175
Corrie v Gilbert 257
Cortlandt v The New York Central Railroad Company 47
Cotic v Gray 255
Crawford Adjusters (Cayman) Ltd v Sagicor General
Insurance (Cayman) Ltd 66
Crofter Hand Woven Harris Tweed Co Ltd v Veitch 130
Crossman v Thurlow 69
Das v George Weston Ltd 15
Daughtry v Blanket State Bank et al 68
Davidson v Toronto Blue Jays Baseball Ltd 106
Davies v Mann 279
Davies v Swan Motor Co (Swansea) Ltd 275
Davis v Boston MRR 174
Denfield v O'Callaghan et al 31
Derry v Peek 113
Diamond State Telephone Co v Hunter 177
Dick Bentley Productions v Harold Smith (Motors) Ltd 114
Didow v Alberta Power Ltd 108
Dietrich v Northampton 211
Dillenberger v Weingartner 175
Dobson (Litigation Guardian of) v Dobson 201
Doherty v Arcade Hotel 174
Donathan v McConnell 176
Donoghue v Stevenson 197
Doughty v Turner Manufacturing Co Ltd 260
Dow v Brown 176
Du Bois v Decker 2
Dube v Labar 279
Dulieu v White & Sons 224, 252
Duval et al v Seguin et al 206
Dwyer v Staunton 106

List of Legal Cases xvii

Dyk v De Young 69
EB v Order of the Oblates of Mary Immaculate in the Province
of British Columbia 320
Edwards v Sutton London Borough 187
Ernst v EnCana Corp 310
Estabrooks v New Brunswick Real Estate Association 66
Evaniuk v 79846 Manitoba Inc 106
Evansville v Blue 175
Fairchild v Glenhaven Funeral Services Ltd 241
Faulkinbury v Shaw 175
Faulkner v Keffalinos 234
Femling v Star Publishing Company 175
Fevold et al v Board of Supervisors of Webster County et al 35
Fisher v Carrousel Motor Hotel, Inc 69
Fitzpatrick v Cooper 197
Fontaine v British Columbia (Official Administrator) 197
Fontainebleau Hotel Corp v Forty-Five Twenty-Five, Inc 28, 33, 45
Fouldes v Willoughby 111
Foy v Winston 177
Froom et al v Butcher 273
Gambriell v Caparelli 102–3
Gates v Hoston & M Railroad 175
Geist v Moore 178
General & Finance Facilities Ltd v Cooks Cars (Romford) Ltd 110
Gifford v Dent 108
Glanzer v Shepard 115
Grand Restaurants of Canada Ltd v Toronto (City) 117
Grant v Australian Knitting Mills Ltd 176
Graves v Shattuck et al 47
Green v Atlanta Charlotte Air Line Railway Company et al 174
Green v TA Shoemaker & Co 77
Gobrecht v Beckwith 175
Goff v Hubbard 176
Gould v Slater Woolen Co 176
Gould Estate v Stoddart Publishing Co Ltd 127
Gregg v Scott 230
H S Leyman Company v Short 68
Hanson v Hall et al 47
Harr v Ward 68
Hay v Cohoes Co 31
Hay v Platinum Equities Inc 126
Haynes v G Harwood & Son 212, 215, 269, 278
Heckert v 5470 Investments Ltd 79
Hedley Byrne & Co Ltd v Heller & Partners Ltd 114
Henderson v Public Transport Commission of New South Wales 177

xviii   *List of Legal Cases*

Hesse v National Casket Co 175
Hogg v Ward 68
Holcombe v Whitaker 65
Holland v Pitocchelli 176
Hollis v Dow Corning Corp 96
Hollywood Silver Fox Farm Ltd v Emmett 28
Hope v Full Brook Coal Co 174
Hopper v Reeve 69
Houston v Town of Waverly 175
Hughes v Lord Advocate 257
Hunter v Canary Wharf Ltd 33
Huntingburgh v First 175
Hurst v Picture Theatres Ltd 106
Hymowitz v Eli Lilly & Co 238
Jacobi v Griffiths 315
James v Hayward 47
Jennings v Tacoma R & M Co 283
Jobling v Associated Dairies Ltd 220, 225
Johnson v Rulon 174
Johnson v St. Paul City Railway Co 178
Jones v Festiniog Railway Company 310
Jones v Hart 314
Jordan v Atchison Topeka & Santa Fe Railway Co 224
Kamloops v Nielson 204
Kathleen K v Robert B 90
Keith v Worcester and Blackstone Valley Street Railway Co 177
Kelemen v El-Homeira 114
*Kelsen v Imperial Tobacco Co (of Great Britain and
Ireland) Ltd* 108
Kennaway v Thompson 27, 42, 46
Kenney v Wong Len 77
Keys v Alamo City Baseball Co 175
Keys v Mistahia Regional Health Authority 206
Kingston v Chicago Northwestern Railway Company 242
Krouse v Chrysler Canada Ltd et al 126
KVP Co Ltd v Mckie et al 52
La Lievre v Gould 215
Laing v St. Thomas Dragway 27, 46
Lambert v Lastoplex Chemicals Co 276
Lamereaux v Tula 47
Landau v The City of New York 47
Latimer v AEC Ltd 182, 186, 253
Laws v Florinplace Ltd 36
Le Vonas v Acme Paper Board Company 175
Leigh v London Ambulance Service NHS Trust 246

List of Legal Cases xix

Levesley v Thomas Firth and John Brown Ltd 184
Lewvest Ltd v Scotia Towers Ltd 108
Lexington & E R Co v White 175
Linnehan v Sampson 175
Lipiec v Borsa 79
Lister et al v Hesley Hall Ltd 321
Lloyd (Litigation Guardian of) v Rotter 279
Lobert v Pack 177
London Borough of Southwark v Williams 107
London Drugs Ltd v Kuehne & Nagel International Ltd.................... 314
Lord v Canada (Attorney General).. 82
Losee v Buchanan 304
Louisville & Nashville Railroad Co v Perry's Administrator 176
Lumley v Gye... 129, 135
Lynch v Knight... 76
Macleay v Tait... 117
Magill v Magill... 113
Malette v Shulman 69
Manitoba Free Press Co Ltd v Nagy 118
Mann v Saulnier.. 104
Mansfield v Weetabix Ltd 166, 174
Marks' Adm'r v Petersburg Railroad Co 177
Martin v McNamara Construction Company Limited......................... 266
Mattel Inc v 3894207 Canada Inc... 118
Mazza v Greenstein.. 176
McCarty v Pheasant Run, Inc... 180
McErlean v Sarel et al 170
McGhee v National Coal Board... 230
McHale v Watson... 166
McIntyre v Pope.. 175
McLaughlin v Griffin 177
McMillen v Steele 175
Meering v Grahame-White Aviation Co 65
Miller v Jackson 26, 37, 40, 45, 105, 181
Milner v Manufacturer's Life Insurance Co 82
Missouri P R Co v Vinson 175
Mitchell v Rochester Railway Company... 77
Montreal Tramways Co v Léveillé 206, 211
Mogul Steamship Co v McGregor, Gow & Co.................................... 130
M/S Islamia Automatic Rice Mills Ltd v Bangladesh
Shilpa Rin Sangstha et al 176
Mullen v Barr & Co... 199
Munn & Co v The Sir John Crosbie 304
Murphy v Pere Marquette Railroad Co 175
Murray v Ministry of Defence 65, 68

xx   *List of Legal Cases*

Musgrove v Pandelis 310
NB v Hôtel-Dieu de Québec 74
Nelles v Ontario 66
Nilabati Behera v State of Orissa 75
Non-Marine Underwriters, Lloyds of London v Scalera 73
Norberg v Wynrib 84
O'Brien v Cunard SS Co 92
OBG Ltd v Allan 111
Oran v Kraft-Phenix Cheese Corp 174
Orkin Exterminating Co Inc v Pestco Co of Canada Ltd et al 126
Osborn v Leuffgen 175
Overseas Tankship (UK) Ltd v Morts Dock & Engineering
Co Ltd 247
Palsgraf v Long Island Railroad Company 263
Parker v New Brunswick Power Corp 310
Parrot v Wells 175
Parton v Phillips Petroleum Co 175
Pasley (and another) v Freeman 113
Peck v United Kingdom 82
Pelletier v Ontario 278
People v Wolf 31
Pennsylvania Coal Company v Mahon et al 47
Peppler Estate v Lee 74
Perlmutter v Greene 31
Phillips & Co v The State 47
Ploof v Putnam 106, 307
Polsue and Alfieri Limited v Rushmer 23
Prah v Maretti 29
Queen v Cognos Inc 115
Quinn v Leathem 131
R v B 90
R v Barnard 113
R v Cuerrier 88
R v Dudley and Stephens 107
R v Hill 170
R v J A 88
R v Mabior 91
R v Mwai 90
R v Vantandillo 37
R v W (RE) 171
Rajkot Municipal Corp v Manjulben Jayantilal 270
Ramos v Service Bros 175
Randolph's Admr v Snyder 2
Ray Plastics Ltd v Dustbane Products Ltd 122
Re Polemis and Furness, Withy & Co, Ltd 250

List of Legal Cases xxi

Read v J Lyons & Co Ltd 310
Reaver v Martin Theatres of Florida Inc....................................... 29
Reckitt and Colman Products Ltd v Borden Inc............................ 122
Reddaway & Co Ltd v Banham & Co Ltd 122
Redgrave v Hurd 114
Regina v Maurantonio.. 90
Reibl v Hughes... 90
Remmenga v Selk 178
Renslow v Mennonite Hospital 209
Resurface Corp v Hanke 246
Reynolds v Pierson... 69
Rickards v Lothian... 310
Rigby and another v Chief Constable of Northamptonshire.................. 107
Risk v Rose Bruford College 184
Roberts v Buster's Auto Towing Service Ltd................................. 67
Rodgers v Cox 176
Rodriquez v Patti... 211
Rogers v Elliot 24, 33, 45
Rohit Talwar et al v Municipal Corporation of Delhi...................... 42
Rookes v Barnard 133
Rozell v Rozell 170
Ryan et al v Hickson et al.. 172
Rylands v Fletcher 307, 310–11
Rzeszewski v Barth 174
Saccone v Orr 79
Sadhu Singh Hamdard Trust v Navsun Holdings Ltd...................... 124
Scott v London and St. Katherine Docks Co 195
Seattle Electric Co v Hovden.. 178
Seigle v Bromley... 47
Shelfer v City of London Electric Co.................................... 24, 50
Shibamoto & Co v Western Fish Producers Inc (Trustee of)................ 111
Shuttleworth v Vancouver General Hospital................................. 34
Sirajul Islam Chowdhury et al v Md Jainal Abedin et al 104
Simeon Groot v Florian Hitz... 80
Simone v The Rhode Island Company... 77
Sindell v Abbott Laboratories... 236
Singh (Litigation Guardian of) v Chini.. 304
Smillie v Continental Oil Company.. 47
Smith v City of Sedalia 47
Smith v Inco.. 310
Smith v Leech Brain & Co Ltd.. 251, 257
Smithline v Hadigrian 174
Snell v Farrell 246
Somwar v McDonald's Restaurants of Canada Ltd 81
South Australia Asset Management Corp v York Montague Ltd........... 251

xxii   *List of Legal Cases*

Spade v Lynn and Boston Railroad Company 77
Spring v Guardian Assurance PLC and Others 117
Spur Industries, Inc v Del E. Webb Development Co 50
St. Louis Gunning Advertisement Co v St. Louis 31
Standard Oil Co v Davis 68
State ex rel Wear v Springfield Gas & Electric Co 47
State of North Dakota v Hooker 47
Stephens v Myers 64
Stephenson v Waite Tileman Ltd 255
Stoleson v United States 224
Sturges v Bridgman 39
Swan v Salisbury Construction Co Ltd 193
Swinamer v Nova Scotia (Attorney General) 272
T.H. Critelli Ltd v Lincoln Trust and Savings Co et al 31
Temple v Hallem 83
ter Neuzen v Korn 190
Teva Canada Ltd v TD Canada Trust 111
Texaco Inc v Pennzoil Inc 136
The TJ Hooper 187
Thomas Cusack Co v Chicago 31
Thompson-Schwab v Costaki 36
Tomlinson v Congleton Borough Council 184, 253
Transco PLC v Stockport Metropolitan Borough Council 310
Transcontinental Gas Pipe Line Corp v Gault et al 47
Tremblay v Daigle 204
Tucker v Tucker 178
Uber BV and others v Aslam and others 321
Ultramares Corp v Touche, Niven & Co 115
United States v Carroll Towing 41, 180
United States v Ortega 69
Urbanski v Patel 266
Vandry v Quebec Railway, Light, Heat and Power Co 306
Vaughan v Menlove 165, 173
Vigneault v Dr. Hewson Dental Co 176
Vincent v Lake Eerie Transportation Co 307
Vosburg v Putney 224, 255
Wackett v Calder 101
Wagner v International Railway Company 269
Walker v Pioneer Construction Co Ltd 46
Wallace v Kam 100
Walter v Selfe 22
Waters v Wong 74
Wandsworth Board of Works v United Telephone Co 108
Wasserman v Hall 79
Waters v Pacific Coast Dairy Inc 177

List of Legal Cases xxiii

Wawrzyniak v Livingstone 74
Weare v Fitchburg 175
Weis v Superior Court of the County of San Diego 47
Wellman v Fordson Coal Company 175
Westjet Airlines Ltd v Air Canada 66
White v Mellin 117
White v Turner 99
Wilkinson v Downton 77
Williams v Ballard Lumber Co 175
Wilsher v Essex Area Health Authority 244
*Winter Garden Theatre (London) Ltd v Millenium
Productions Ltd* 106
Winterbottom v Wright 199
Winteringham v Rae et al 257
Woollerton & Wilson Ltd v Richard Costain Ltd 108
Wright v Cambridge Medical Group 225
XY Inc v International Newtech Development Inc 131
Ybarra v Spangard et al 195, 238

1 Overview of torts

"Tort" is derived from the Latin word *tortus*, which means "twisted," and it was imported into the English language from the French, who still use the word to mean "wrong."[1] In common law jurisdictions, such as Bangladesh, a tort is a civil wrong, as opposed to a criminal wrong, and permits the claimant to seek monetary compensation from the tortfeasor – who is the person whose action, or inaction, has caused a foreseeable injury.

Unlike criminal law, or other branches of civil law, torts are not governed by legislation.[2] Rather, torts are common law offences, which are formulated by judges to compensate an innocent victim. Nonetheless, this may engender the question as to why someone would institute proceedings against another under tort and not criminal or contract law. As will become evident, the result that the injured party may derive is different based on how he proceeds with litigation.

1.1 Fundamental misconception

Before proceeding further, I must address a fundamental misconception pervasive in Bangladesh. It is not uncommon to hear that tort law does not apply in this country. However, as I have mentioned in the previous paragraph (and I shall examine this again later in this chapter), torts are common law offences. This means that *any* aggrieved party in *any* common law country can institute proceedings under the principles adumbrated by the law of torts to avail its remedies. Furthermore, *The Constitution of the People's Republic of Bangladesh* (hereinafter "*Constitution of Bangladesh*") contains 153 sections and none of which prohibits one from bringing an action in tort.[3] Rather, Section 24(2) of *The Trademarks Act, 2009* (hereinafter "*Trademarks Act*") permits one to bring an action for passing-off, which is a tortious claim, if the injured party does not have a registered trademark.[4] To further explain, in order to institute proceedings for trademark infringement, the *condicio sine qua non* is that a trademark must be registered, and if it is not, then the aggrieved party cannot bring an action against the purported transgressor. However, in the absence of registration, tort law accords protection so that one cannot "pass-off" his goods as that

DOI: 10.4324/9781003241782-1

2 Overview of torts

of another's, as it may create confusion in the marketplace and injure consumers and businesses.[5]

While an action for passing-off has been codified by the *Trademarks Act*, even if it were not, this would not mean that one would not be able to bring such an action. For example, Explanation 1 of section 299 of *The Penal Code, 1860* (hereinafter "*Penal Code*") says that if someone causes bodily injury to one who has a disease or "bodily infirmity," and the infliction of the injury accelerates the latter's death, it will be held as though the injury caused the death. As in, it would not matter that the perpetrator did not know of the decedent's infirmity, or "thin skull," which is actually a common law doctrine[6] and is applicable in Bangladesh. Therefore, since we are a common law country, and principles of it can be applied, it is illogical to assert that tort law is inapplicable in Bangladesh.

1.2 Contract law and tort law

The primary difference between contract and tort law lies in how protection is provided.[7] For example, in contract, there is an interest in having promises performed because parties have provided consent. However, the obligation to carry out those promises is owed only to those named in the contract.[8] This also means that if there is a breach of contract, damages can only be claimed by, again, those that are party to the contract.

On the other hand, tort law casts a broader net of protection that is based not solely on individual will or intention (in other words, contractual relations), but social policy. Moreover, and as we will learn throughout this book, the duty to conduct oneself, or an activity, reasonably is so as not to harm a *group of people* – not just an individual with whom one has a contract.[9]

This means that relationships can give rise to a claim in contract, if a contract exists, and in tort. However, the outcome, based on how the claimant chooses to proceed, will be different. The primary objective of contract law is to place the claimant in the position he would have been in had the contract been performed. In tort law, the primary objective is to place the claimant in the position he would have been in had he not suffered the injury.[10] This means that tort law provides more monetary compensation than contract law (more on this later).

Suppose you entered into an agreement with someone to have him come over to your bungalow on 10 February and build a porch for a fee of ৳50,000. The next day, you find an advertisement whereby Woodswork Ltd. said it would do the same for ৳40,000, which is a promotional offer. The advertisement further says that the order for construction must be placed by 9 February even if the porch will be constructed a few weeks later, as otherwise, it will cost the usual price of ৳55,000. Though it would have saved you ৳10,000, since you have already entered into a prior agreement, you decide not to breach your original agreement. However, on 10 February, the gentleman informs you that he can no longer build the porch. Furious, not only because he is not constructing the porch, but also

Overview of torts 3

because you can no longer avail Woodswork's promotion, you sue him for breach of contract. In this case, a court would perhaps award you damages of ৳5,000 because that is the difference between (a) Woodswork's price of construction and (b) the amount you were originally willing to pay so that you can have the porch built and enjoy it.

Now suppose that the gentleman comes over on 10 February and constructs the porch, but does so negligently. Three days later, as you are drinking coffee on the porch, it crumbles and you suffer a broken leg and hand as a result thereof. If you bring proceedings under tort, the court will award damages for the injury and its associated costs. As in, because of the injury, if your hospital fees are ৳50,000, the court will order the defendant to pay the full amount.

Notice that there is a marked difference between damages in contract and tort law. In the first scenario, you would perhaps only receive ৳5,000, as it would meet the objective of contract law, which, again, is to place the party in the position he would have been in had the contract been performed. However, the amount of damages is nominal. In the second scenario, you would receive a significantly larger sum, because in order to place the party he would have been in had he not been injured, the negligent actor must compensate the injured party in full. In this manner, tort law would be more beneficial than filing a case for breach of contract.

1.3 Criminal law and tort law

When a pedestrian is struck and killed by a motor vehicle, the state can institute proceedings criminally under section 304B of the *Penal Code*, or his family members can do so civilly under tort law.[11] However, similar to contract law, the resulting remedy would be entirely different.[12] In fact, there are three differences between criminal law and tort law. First, prosecution of criminal law is the responsibility of the state; that is, if someone is accused of theft, it is the state that brings the action and not the individual whose property was stolen. The reason the government is involved is due to their desire for maintaining peace and public order. However, tort litigation is brought at the personal initiative and expense of the aggrieved party.[13]

Second, the standard of proof in criminal law is significantly higher than in tort. In criminal law, one must adduce evidence of the guilt of the accused "beyond a reasonable doubt," whereas, in tort, since it is a civil wrong, the standard of proof is "balance of probabilities." This means that a judge (or jury) must be convinced of the defendant's guilt on a preponderance of evidence, which is considerably lower than the standard in criminal litigation. As in, it is considerably more difficult to prove the accused's guilt in criminal law.

Third, in criminal law, the focus is on punishing the offender in order to prevent him from committing the same, or similar, offence again. However, in tort law, the focus is on the person who has suffered the injury and meeting his desire to receive monetary compensation; that is, the function of tort law is to (1) monetarily compensate the aggrieved party by correcting the injustice, (2) punish the offender by holding him accountable, (3) deter the offender

4   *Overview of torts*

and others from committing similar offences, (4) appease the plaintiff's anger, (5) provide a forum for vengeance, and (6) educate the public.

Criminal law's remedy is imprisoning the offender; tort law's remedy, however, is to award monetary compensation. The court punishes the defendant by ordering him to pay damages to the aggrieved party, which informs the public that similar sentences may be imposed for like offences, begetting the probability that others will not engage in such misconduct. For example, if someone cuts your hair sans permission, he would be guilty of assault, which, pursuant to section 352 of the *Penal Code*, would authorize a court to imprison the accused for up to three months. However, incarceration of the accused for intentionally cutting your hair without your permission may not be to your complete satisfaction; that is, you may have been growing your hair for the past three years because you view long hair as an important element of your beauty and the non-consensual interference will now militate against it. Therefore, you may want something more, or other, than the defendant's imprisonment.

This is where tort law can help in dispensing with an alternative remedy. Through tort, the victim – in our case, the lady with the long hair – can seek monetary compensation for the wrong suffered. While monetary compensation may not thoroughly satisfy someone's distress, it is a substitute to the remedy familiar to criminal law and the victim has the option of choosing whether to proceed criminally or civilly.

Additionally, since criminal law is governed by statute – *Penal Code* – it may occasionally be insufficient in according protection to another. While one is protected against, *inter alia*, trespass, assault, and theft, what protection is accorded to a person whose neighbour installs a CCTV camera outside his apartment and it periodically captures footage of activity happening inside the former's apartment when he opens his door? Alternatively, what statute protects a woman's privacy if her estranged lover begins informing others that she underwent an abortion?

The infelicitous truth is that the aforementioned scenarios fall into a lacuna of the *Penal Code*, whereby the statute is incapable of providing protection, rendering plaintiffs helpless. However, since torts are common law offences, judges, albeit not officiously, have identified actions, or inactions, to be wrong, which may not be criminally punishable; that is, even if no statute prohibits an action, if the plaintiff has sustained an injury because of the defendant's misconduct, it is the position of courts that barring the former to recover damages from the latter would be unjust. Therefore, the ambit of protection in tort law is wider than criminal law, as it protects persons in the presence and absence of statute.

1.4 Source of tort law

Though I have already mentioned this before, I reiterate that tort law is a common law offence, which means it is judges that have made what they perceive to be wrong compensable. Otherwise, a person can injure another

Overview of torts 5

with impunity and the innocent party will have no remedy because statutes are silent regarding that particular wrong. This does not mean that judges see every wrong as compensable; rather, they compensate the victim based on pragmatic considerations and, what will become evident throughout this book, a wrong in one country may not be a wrong in another.[14]

1.5 Elements of a tort

Tort law is about conduct and its consequences. Therefore, since tort law is premised on fairness, it examines the nature of the defendant's conduct and holds him liable only for the loss caused by his *wrongful* act, and not for loss caused by an accident. To this end, tort law classifies conduct into the following three categories: (1) intentional, (2) negligent, and (3) accidental.[15]

Intentional conduct is when the defendant desires its consequences. For example, a person who wilfully takes a cellphone, or one who spits on another, or who discloses embarrassing secrets about a former lover is *intentionally* causing damage to the property, person, or reputation of another. Conduct is negligent when the defendant has created a reasonably foreseeable and substantial risk of harm. As in, a storeowner who has, in order to clean the floor of his store, wiped it with a wet mop, but failed to warn customers, and as a result, someone slips and injures himself, has *negligently* caused damage to another. Conduct is accidental when the defendant neither desires its consequences nor creates a reasonably foreseeable and substantial risk of harm. For example, a person who is driving within the speed limit, but collides with a child who darted in front of the vehicle has injured the latter *accidentally*, for which the driver will not be held liable (unless factors warrant otherwise).

Once the conduct of the defendant has been probed, tort law then focuses on its consequences and usually compensates loss resulting from intentional and negligent conduct. However, not all misconduct, even if it is intentional or negligent, is compensable and the nature of the plaintiff's loss must be explored in order to determine whether damages should be awarded. As in, it is more justifiable to award damages to someone who was subjected to battery, rather than the person who felt humiliated because his mother intentionally told others that he used to wet the bed until the age of 16. Therefore, even though conduct is intentional, tort law must distinguish between compensable and non-compensable injuries.

1.6 Objectives of tort law

1.6.1 The moralist perspective

Tort law is influenced by moralists and instrumentalists. The moralists say that it is imperative to personally hold one accountable for the injury he has caused another. To not do so would run afoul the foundations of a

6   Overview of torts

civilized, stable, and humane society. This would permit the tortfeasor to incessantly engage in misconduct without apprehension of penalty, leading to the inexorable result of disorder. Therefore, tort law is designed to rectify this wrong and maintain balance in society.[16]

1.6.2 The instrumentalist perspective

Alternatively, instrumentalists proclaim that the most important function of tort law is to compensate the plaintiff for the loss he has suffered as a result of the defendant's conduct, which the courts view as being below social standards. Essentially, this means that there is conduct that courts view as acceptable because it is not anomalous to social norms. Therefore, if one's conduct falls below the acceptable standard and it causes injury to another, courts will direct the tortfeasor to correct the wrongdoing by paying damages to the aggrieved party. In this way, tort law is designed to place the plaintiff in the position he would have been in had the injury not occurred. For example, if you are walking on the sidewalk and, to no fault of your own, a car driven negligently hits you from the back, and you suffer a broken hand and a punctured leg due to the collision, and if the hospital fees for treatment is ৳75,000, tort law will order the driver of the vehicle to pay the said quantum; that is, you will be fully indemnified for the loss you have suffered.

By ordering the tortfeasor to pay damages, tort law also punishes him – in our case, the driver of the vehicle. As in, while damages compensate the victim, it concurrently expresses society's reproachfulness to conduct falling below social standards and operates as a sanction. One may have the proclivity to ask how paying damages punishes the defendant. The answer is simple – if the driver drove carefully, he would not have lost ৳75,000. Thus, saddling upon him an order of damages punishes him and will also deter him and others from engaging in similar conduct; that is, once the driver is ordered to pay damages, he is informed that his conduct was unacceptable, and not dissimilarly, others will now espouse safe practices (e.g. drive in a more careful fashion) to avoid tort liability. This also educates the public, as they will now be apprised of what reasonable standards of conduct are, which can aim to make society safer.[17]

Let me reuse the example of the pedestrian being struck by an automobile in the context of Bangladesh. If such a situation transpires, it would not be uncommon to see scores of people surround the vehicle and demand the driver to alight. If the latter acquiesces, the usual remedy dispensed by the public would be to slap and/or punch him. However, by doing so, members of the public have also now committed assault (or battery in tort, but more on this in chapter 4). As in, injuring the pedestrian is a wrongful act of the chauffeur and assaulting the latter thereafter is incorrect as well. Thence, this would give rise to the following two lawsuits: (1) the pedestrian would seek damages from the chauffeur,[18] and (2) the chauffeur would seek damages from members of the public.

Rather than acting chaotically, tort law can provide a forum for legally seeking vengeance by permitting the aggrieved party to attain monetary compensation from the tortfeasor. In this way, the law of torts placates one's (or, the public's) anger, makes the defendant personally accountable, and allows for disputes to be settled in a non-violent manner.[19]

Notes

1 Philip Osborne, *The Law of Torts*, 5th ed (Toronto: Irwin Law Inc, 2015) at 1 [Osborne]; Also see John G Fleming, *The Law of Torts*, 9th ed (Sydney: LBC Information Services, 1998) at 3 [Fleming].
2 In fact, there is no exact definition of "tort." However, there is consensus among scholars that it is a wrong because of a breach of duty of care and not because it is an infraction of the law or contract, at Arthur Underhill et al, *The Law of Torts*, 9th ed (London: Butterworth & Co, 1912) at 7–8 [Underhill]. In simpler terms, as will become evident throughout this book, a "tort" is a civil wrong that is not a breach of contract or has not yet been proscribed by law.
3 *The Constitution of the People's Republic of Bangladesh* (Bangladesh), Act of 1972 [*Constitution of Bangladesh*].
4 *The Trademarks Act*, 2009 (Bangladesh), Act No XIX of 2009, s 24(2).
5 For a cursory overview of the action, see Osborne, *supra* note 1 at 336–339; Also see Sakif Alam, "Takeout(s) Ltd: Trademark Infringement and/or Passing-off?" *The Daily Star* (9 January 2018), online: The Daily Star https://www.thedailystar.net/law-our-rights/law-analysis/takeouts-ltd-trademark-infringement-andor-passing-1516951. [16/03/2021]. Moreover, I have thoroughly examined passing-off in Chapter 4.
6 *The Penal Code*, 1860 (Bangladesh), Act No XLV of 1860, s 299 [*Penal Code*]. See generally Allen M Linden, "Down with Foreseeability: Of Thin Skulls and Rescuers" (1969) 47:4 Can B Rev 545; Stanley McQuade, "The Eggshell Skull Rule and Related Problems in Recovery for Mental Harm in the Law of Torts" (2001) 24:1 Campbell L Rev 1; Gary L Bahr & Bruce N Graham, "The Thin Skull Plaintiff Concept: Evasive or Persuasive" (1982) 15:3 Loy LA L Rev 409.
7 William L Prosser, *Handbook of The Law of Torts*, 4th ed (St. Paul, Minnesota: West Publishing Co, 1971) at 613 [Prosser].
8 *Ibid*; Also see Percy H Winfield, *The Province of the Law of Tort* (New York: Cambridge University Press, 1931) at 40.
9 Prosser, *supra* note 7; For example, see *Randolph's Admr v Snyder*, [1910] 139 Ky 159, 129 SW 562, where a doctor, who has contracted to treat a family for a year, but refused when summoned, was held liable for breach of contract. However, if he came in to treat the family, but provided medical attention without proper care, then he could be held liable under tort, at *Du Bois v Decker*, [1891] 130 NY 325, 1891 NY LEXIS 1274.
10 See Thomas Cooley, *Law of Torts*, 2nd ed (Chicago: Callaghan & Co, 1888) at 2; Also see Fleming, *supra* note 1.
11 William L Prosser, "Private Action for Public Nuisance" (1966) 52:6 Va L Rev 997 at 997. Essentially, what this means is that an action can give rise to both criminal and civil proceedings.
12 *Penal Code*, *supra* note 6 at s 304B. Section 304B stipulates the following:
Whoever causes the death of any person by rash or negligent driving of any vehicle or riding on any public way not amounting to culpable homicide shall be punished with imprisonment of either description for a term which may extend to three years, or with fine, or with both.

8   *Overview of torts*

However, in tort law, the remedy would not be imprisonment, but would be an award of damages to make reparations for the injury caused.

13 Osborne, *supra* note 1 at 3; Also see Fleming, *supra* note 1 at 3–5 and Vivienne Harpwood, *Principles of Tort Law*, 4th ed (London: Cavendish Publishing Limited, 2000) at 1–3 [Harpwood].

14 Harpwood, *ibid* at 9–10.

15 Osborne, *supra* note 1 at 8–12.

16 *Ibid* at 12–18. Also see Harpwood, *supra* note 13 at 13–15; See generally Gary T Schwartz, "Mixed Theories of Tort Law: Affirming Both Deterrence and Corrective Justice" (1996–1997) 75:7 Tex L Rev 1801. This is similar to what Justinian said: "The maxim of law are these: To live honestly, to hurt no man, and to give every one his due." At Underhill, *supra* note 2 at 3.

17 See generally Duncan Kennedy, "Distributive and Paternalist Motives in Contract and Tort Law, with Special Reference to Compulsory Terms and Unequal Bargaining Power" (1982) 41:4 MD L Rev 563.

18 If the chauffeur is not a man of means, then the pedestrian may also seek damages from his employer through the doctrine of vicarious liability. I shall explore this doctrine more extensively in Chapter 6.

19 See Fleming, *supra* note 1 at 8–14.

References

Legislation

The Constitution of the People's Republic of Bangladesh (Bangladesh), Act of 1972.
The Penal Code, 1860 (Bangladesh), Act No XLV of 1860.
The Trademarks Act, 2009 (Bangladesh), Act No XIX of 2009.

Caselaw

Du Bois v Decker, [1891] 130 NY 325, 1891 NY LEXIS 1274.
Randolph's Admr v Snyder, [1910] 139 Ky 159, 129 SW 562.

Secondary Material: Books

Cooley, Thomas, *Law of Torts*, 2nd ed (Chicago: Callaghan & Co, 1888).
Fleming, John G, *The Law of Torts*, 9th ed (Sydney: LBC Information Services, 1998).
Harpwood, Vivienne, *Principles of Tort Law*, 4th ed (London: Cavendish Publishing Limited, 2000).
Osborne, Philip, *The Law of Torts*, 5th ed (Toronto: Irwin Law Inc, 2015).
Prosser, William L, *Handbook of The Law of Torts*, 4th ed (St. Paul, Minnesota: West Publishing Co, 1971).
Underhill, Arthur, Pease, J. G. & Tremeear, W. J., *The Law of Torts*, 9th ed (London: Butterworth & Co, 1912).
Winfield, Percy H, *The Province of the Law of Tort* (New York: Cambridge University Press, 1931).

Secondary Material: Journal Articles

Bahr, Gary L & Graham, Bruce N, "The Thin Skull Plaintiff Concept: Evasive or Persuasive" (1982) 15:3 Loy LA L Rev 409.

Kennedy, Duncan, "Distributive and Paternalist Motives in Contract and Tort Law, with Special Reference to Compulsory Terms and Unequal Bargaining Power" (1982) 41:4 MD L Rev 563.

Linden, Allen M, "Down with Foreseeability: Of Thin Skulls and Rescuers" (1969) 47:4 Can B Rev 545.

McQuade, Stanley, "The Eggshell Skull Rule and Related Problems in Recovery for Mental Harm in the Law of Torts" (2001) 24:1 Campbell L Rev 1.

Prosser, William L, "Private Action for Public Nuisance" (1966) 52:6 Va L Rev 997.

Schwartz, Gary T, "Mixed Theories of Tort Law: Affirming Both Deterrence and Corrective Justice" (1996–1997) 75:7 Tex L Rev 1801.

Secondary Material: Websites

Alam, Sakif, "Takeout(s) Ltd: Trademark Infringement and/or Passing-off?" *The Daily Star* (9 January 2018), online: The Daily Star https://www.thedailystar.net/law-our-rights/law-analysis/takeouts-ltd-trademark-infringement-andor-passing-1516951.

2 The development of tort law in Bangladesh

If a person skims through the leading textbooks[1] on tort law, he/she will quickly learn that a dedicated chapter on the development of this branch of the law for a particular country does not exist. However, as I have mentioned in the Preface to this book, the law is sui generis, and therefore, a country's legal system, existing statutes, and contemporary scholarly work must be taken into consideration to provide a holistic and comprehensive view of the law and, in the context of Bangladesh, where it is headed.

In this chapter, I will outline the recent developments of tort law in Bangladesh by drawing on a triumvirate of cases and scholarly work. This, I am of the opinion, will lay the framework for the remaining part, which is really the heart, of the book.

2.1 The case that started it all

Bangladesh Beverage Industries Ltd v Rowshan Akhter[2]

On 3 December 1989, Mozammel Hossain, who was a well-known journalist, playwright, and poet, was crossing the road when a van, which was owned by Bangladesh Beverage Industries Ltd (hereinafter "Bangladesh Beverage") and was being driven on the wrong side of the road, hit him and fled. He was quickly rushed to the hospital. Unfortunately, however, as the accident shattered his skull, Mr. Hossain succumbed to his injuries. Holding Bangladesh Beverage vicariously liable, the court said,

> The word 'tort' is of French origin, which in English is wrong, derived from [the] Latin term ['*tortus*,' which] means twist and implies twisted [...] conduct[.] [The] essentials [of an action in tort] are (i) there must be some act or omission on the part of [the] defendant, not being a breach of some duty undertaken by contract, (ii) the act or omission complained of must not be authorized by law and (iii) the wrongful act or omission complained of must inflict injury special, private and peculiar to the plaintiff. Torts are infinitely vicious, not limited or confined until lawful jurisdiction is available from [the] defendant, [and] the plaintiff is entitled to sue in tort if there is definite injury to him, his property, his reputation.

DOI: 10.4324/9781003241782-2

The development of tort law in Bangladesh 11

This is a case on [tortious] liability of a person. This law is in our country more or less on book, not in practice. We have seen in daily newspapers that on each day several accidents [take] place causing death of passersby, passengers, driver[s,] but either for ignorance of law or for some other purpose, i.e. 'since death has occurred what will [we] do in getting compensation', no one come[s] forward for invoking this law and since this law has not been practiced, as a result, we are unable to protect the lives and properties of the citizens who lost their lives in different types of accidents. If this law be practiced, then it is our considered view that, at least, the death on accident may be minimized. [...]

On a reading of different authorities, particularly Salmond and Heuston, Lord Templeman, Winfield and ED Pitchfork, law of torts stands as in any society of people living together numerous conflicts of interest will arise and that the actions of one man or group of men will from time to time cause damage to others i.e. injury to the person, physical damage to property, damage to financial interests, injury to reputation and so on and whenever a man suffers damage he is inclined to look to the law for redress. [...]

As will be seen, much of the law of tort is concerned with the problem of accidental injury to the person or damage to property, and the general approach of the law of tort[s] to this problem rests on two broad principles. Both are subject to a number of exceptions and qualifications but by and large it is the case first that the victim of accidental injury or damage is entitled to redress through the law of tort[s] if, and only if, his loss was caused by the fault of the defendant or of those for whose fault the defendant must answer, and secondly that the redress due from the defendant whose liability is established should, as nearly as possible, be equivalent in value to the plaintiff's loss.

Recognition by the law that one person may have to answer for the fault of another, that is, the principle of "vicarious liability" (i.e. the case in our hand) has its most important manifestation in the rule that an employer is liable for the torts of his employees done in the course of their employment, and this means that in the majority of accident cases it is not the person at fault who is the defendant but his employer. [...]

A master is jointly and severally liable for any tort committed by his servant while acting in the course of his employment. [...] Vicarious liability means that one person takes or supplies the place of another so far as liability is concerned. In short, vicarious liability is based on social convenience and rough justice. This is an adequate explanation of the doctrine, subject to the qualification that the master may be liable even though the act or default is not for his benefit, and even though he has expressly prohibited it. In all this there is no doubt that the courts have been much influenced by the fact that the master is usually more able than the servant to satisfy claims by injured persons and can pass on the burden of liability by way of insurance. There is also some evidence to show that the imposition of strict liability on the master

12 *The development of tort law in Bangladesh*

results in the prevention of accidents as the master takes more care than he would otherwise have done.

Notes

We must take note of two important developments from this case. First, because tort law is little practised, and therefore, relatively unknown, in Bangladesh, the court provided an overview of torts, starting from the etymology of the word itself. Second, the court held Bangladesh Beverage vicariously liable for the misconduct of their employee and said that this may persuade employers to hire more competent drivers in the future.

Though primarily discussing the doctrine of vicarious liability,[3] *Bangladesh Beverage* was the first case in Bangladesh to be decided on the principles of tort law.[4] Essentially, this means, as I have mentioned in the previous chapter and I will do so again later in this chapter, since torts are common law offences, they readily apply in Bangladesh and victims should be awarded compensation for harm suffered.

2.2 The cases that followed

Catherine Masud et al v Md Kashed Miah et al[5]

Tareque Masud, who was a well-known filmmaker in Bangladesh, was married to Catherine Masud and they jointly owned a production house named Audiovision. Mr. Masud wanted to make a new film titled *Kagojer Phool*, and on 13 August 2011, along with nine others, he boarded his van in Dhaka and headed to a village in Manikganj to scope a site for shooting the movie. On their way back the same day, as the van arrived at Joka on the Dhaka-Aricha Highway, it collided head-on with a passenger bus, which killed Mr. Masud and four others immediately.

As the bus was being driven on the wrong side of the road, Mrs. Masud claimed compensation for the death of her husband. Finding the defendants liable, and on the importance of tort law, the court said,

> We also note that the petitioner's claim raises questions as to application of the law of tort in Bangladesh. As part of the English Common law, the law of tort[s] has become part of the law in India, as it is not considered contrary to "justice, equity, and good conscience" […]. It has also become part of the law in many other Commonwealth countries. However, law of tort[s] is not [an] integral part of the legal structure of Bangladesh. This is primarily because the subordinate courts do not feel empowered to determine a tortious claim unless the tortious claim is purely statutory. For that reason, we do not see rulings of the subordinate courts on medical negligence, vicarious liability etc. We were unable to provide guidelines since we were not called upon to review the issues relating to tort in entirety. In our opinion, the time has come for us to review the law of tort[s] and consider whether [the] law

The development of tort law in Bangladesh 13

of tort[s] should be incorporated in Bangladesh law so that claims arising from negligence, be it medical or otherwise, are properly dealt with.

Dr. Hossain pointed out that the measure of damages in tortious claim is different from the measure of damages arising out of, for instance, contractual claim. Dr. Hossain further pointed out that while the judgments of the apex courts of different jurisdictions, including India, Pakistan and Sri Lanka are highly persuasive, without a comprehensive judgment from our apex courts, the subordinate courts feel reluctant to take those into consideration. Under the current trend, the subordinate courts use the judgment of the apex courts of other jurisdiction if the Supreme Court of Bangladesh has reviewed the issue, partly or fully. We agree with his observation. Accordingly, we feel that a comprehensive judgment should come from [the] Supreme Court of Bangladesh which extensively deals with the tortious concept and clarifies how tort laws should be interpreted. We are inclined to take the view that an appropriately empowered Division Bench of the Supreme Court of Bangladesh should show how tortious claim be dealt with. If this is not done, social injustice that we see would not be cured and cases of negligence would go unpunished. We feel time has come for us to recognize the concept of duty of care, the applicable standard of care owed which would be instrumental in determining whether there has been negligence.

Notes

While *Bangladesh Beverage* was the first case to discuss tort law, I am of the opinion that *Catherine Masud* was more important.

We should not forget that the two cases were decided only four years apart. However, perhaps emboldened by its own precedent, in *Catherine Masud*, the SCB expressly said,

> In our opinion, the time has come for us to review the law of tort[s] and consider whether [the] law of tort[s] should be incorporated in Bangladesh law so that claims arising from negligence, be it medical or otherwise, are properly dealt with. [...] Accordingly, we feel that a comprehensive judgment should come from [the] Supreme Court of Bangladesh which extensively deals with the tortious concept and clarifies how tort laws should be interpreted. [...] If this is not done, social injustice that we see would not be cured and cases of negligence would go unpunished. We feel time has come for us to recognize the concept of duty of care, the applicable standard of care owed which would be instrumental in determining whether there has been negligence.

This displays a deliberate willingness of the highest court in Bangladesh to accept complaints filed on tortious principles. That is to say, moving forward, courts *should* be less reluctant to accept tortious complaints *only if* the SCB stipulates guidelines for lower courts to follow.

14 *The development of tort law in Bangladesh*

Children Charity Bangladesh Foundation v Government of Bangladesh[6]

On 26 December 2014, Jihad, a four-year-old boy, was playing at the Shahjahanpur Railway Colony. Unfortunately, at about 3:30 pm, he fell into a 16-inch wide tube well shaft that was left uncovered by Bangladesh Railway and Water Supply and Sewerage Authority (hereinafter "WASA"). When word spread that Jihad fell into the shaft, Bangladesh Railway and WASA launched a rescue effort by first sending cameras down to locate the boy. Their endeavour went on for about 10–12 hours and when they discovered it was fruitless, they abandoned their mission. Shortly thereafter, a group of five young men pulled up Jihad's dead body.

On behalf of Jihad's family, Children Charity Bangladesh Foundation brought an action against, *inter alia*, Bangladesh Railway, WASA, and Fire Service and Civil Defence. Finding the defendants liable, the court said,

> The word "negligence" is defined as the breach of a duty caused by the omission to do something which a reasonable man would do or doing something which a prudent and reasonable man would not do. In other words, negligence may arise from nonfeasance or from misfeasance.
>
> An action for negligence proceeds upon the idea of an obligation or duty on the part of the person concern to use care, a breach whereof results in the injury of the aggrieved person.
>
> However, the standard or degree of care which a man is required to use in a particular situation varies with the obviousness of the risk. If the danger of doing injury to the person or property of another in pursuance of a certain line of conduct is great, great care is necessary. If the danger is slight, only a slight amount of care is required. The care that will be required of them will be the care that an ordinary prudent man is bound to exercise. But, persons who profess to have special skill, or who have voluntarily undertaken a higher degree of duty, are bound to exercise more care than an ordinary prudent man.
>
> In order to succeed in an action for negligence, the aggrieved person must prove the following: 1. that the other party was under a legal duty to exercise due care and skill; 2. that the duty was towards [the] aggrieved person; 3. that in the circumstances of the case, the other party failed to perform that duty; 4. that the breach of such duty was the *causa causans* i.e., the direct and proximate cause, of the damage complained of; and 5. that the injury is caused on account of this breach of duty.
>
> As a general rule, the onus of proving negligence is on the aggrieved person. He must not merely establish the facts of the other parties' negligence and of his own injury, but must show that the one was the effect of the other.
>
> However, in an action of negligence the affected person must affirmatively prove negligence but may find hardship in cases where the aggrieved person can prove the accident, but cannot show how it

The development of tort law in Bangladesh 15

happened, the fact being solely outside his knowledge and within the knowledge of the other party who causes it. In such cases, it is sufficient for the aggrieved person to prove the accident and nothing more, for, there is a presumption of negligence according to the maxim "*res ipsa loquitur*" (the thing speaks for itself). Such [a] presumption arises when the cause of the mischief was apparently under the control of the other person or his servants. The accident itself constitutes reasonable evidence of negligence in the particular circumstances.

Thus, the following are the essential requirements for [the] application of the said maxim: (i) The thing causing the damage must be under the control of the other party or his servants; (ii) the accident must be such as would not, in the ordinary course of things, have happened without negligence and (iii) there must be no evidence of the actual cause of the accident.

2.3 The way forward

Collectively, these three cases have paved the way for tort law to reform liability in Bangladesh.[7] Unfortunately, this has not meant that cases are now filed on a daily basis under tortious principles, but that it *could*.[8] A lot, however, still needs to be done to make tort law more accessible to victims.

For example, and first, in *Catherine Masud*, the SCB said that formal legislation is necessary to recognize and incorporate tort law in Bangladesh, which is, as I have mentioned in the previous chapter, what happened with the tort of passing-off.[9] This, however, seems impractical, as torts are common law offences, and since Bangladesh is a common law country, formal legislation recognizing torts is unwarranted. That is to say, I believe judges are in the best position to accept tortious complaints and further expound its principles. Therefore, if lower courts are unwilling to accept complaints based on principles of tort law, then the SCB, in line with *Catherine Masud*, is in the best position to provide thorough guidelines and should do so forthwith. As Taqbir Huda has said,

> It is high time we recognized the potential of tort law to promote ethical and conscientious behaviour in a country teeming with cases of negligence, where there is wanton disregard for human life and the potentially injurious consequences of our actions (or inactions) on others.

Second, in *Das v George Weston Ltd*,[10] where victims of the Rana Plaza disaster filed a civil lawsuit in Ontario against George Weston Ltd, the Ontario Superior Court of Justice dismissed their claim because of, *inter alia*, *lex loci delicti*, which is a common law principle meaning "law of the land where the tort was committed." To further explain, since the disaster happened in Bangladesh, and by definition, the tort did as well, the applicable law is of Bangladesh and not Canada. Furthermore, and more importantly, the court added,

16   *The development of tort law in Bangladesh*

Their characterization of the law in Bangladesh as nascent is patently incorrect. The *Bangladesh Beverage Industries Ltd v Rowshan Akhter* decision may be the first fulsome treatment by an appellate court in Bangladesh of the *Limitation Act, 1908* with comments about tort law generally, but Bangladesh has a fully developed tort law jurisprudence about personal injury claims and wrongful death claims.

The bench and the bar in Bangladesh are well-educated, and there is the normal body of judicial literature comprised of reported judgments. As a matter of substantive law, the *Bangladesh Beverage Industries Ltd v Rowshan Akhter* decision reveals a sophisticated understanding of tort law reflecting the English common law roots of tort law in Bangladesh. Not surprisingly, the Bangladesh Beverage decision refers to numerous Bangladesh reported decisions about tort law.

This means that, even if we do not believe it, Bangladesh's legal system is sufficiently developed to entertain tortious claims. It is just that courts are not taking the first step, but are rather waiting for the legislature to act first.[11] However, as I have mentioned earlier, since torts are common law offences, it is the courts that are best-positioned to handle, adumbrate, and expound principles of tort law.

Notes

1 Please note that I am referring to books, such as, John G Fleming, *The Law of Torts*, 9th ed (Sydney: LBC Information Services, 1998); R F V Heuston & R A Buckley, *Salmond and Heuston on the Law of Torts*, 19th ed (London: Sweet & Maxwell, 1987); Allen M Linden & Bruce Feldthusen, *Canadian Tort Law*, 9th ed (Markham, ON: LexisNexis Canada Inc, 2011); William L Prosser, *Handbook of The Law of Torts*, 4th ed (St. Paul, Minnesota: West Publishing Co, 1971); Ernest J Weinrib, *Tort Law: Cases and Materials*, 4th ed (Toronto: Emond Montgomery Publications Limited, 2014); Philip Osborne, *The Law of Torts*, 5th ed (Toronto: Irwin Law Inc, 2015); Lewis Klar, *Tort Law*, 5th ed (Toronto: Carswell, 2012); and Patrick Atiyah, *Accidents, Compensation, and the Law*, 2nd ed (London: Weidenfeld and Nicolson, 1975).

   I am not unaware that there are many scholars whose books I did not mention. However, the aforementioned list should not be considered exhaustive, as, given the global development of scholarly work in this area of the law, it would be inexpedient to provide one. Nonetheless, the list of books is sufficient to arm anyone with a working knowledge of tort law.

2 *Bangladesh Beverage Industries Ltd v Rowshan Akhter*, [2010] 62 DLR 483 [*Bangladesh Beverage*].

3 In this chapter, I will not explain the doctrine of vicarious liability, which is a form of strict, or no-fault, liability. For a detailed analysis of this doctrine, please see Chapter 6 of this book.

4 However, it is worth noting that the Joint District Court awarded damages of ৳35,297,000, which the High Court Division of the Supreme Court of Bangladesh (hereinafter "SCB") reduced to ৳20,147,008. See generally Taqbir Huda, "Vicarious Liability of Employers in the Law of Tort: Deciphering *Bangladesh Beverage Industries vs Roswan Akhter and Others*" (2016) 16:2 Bangladesh J L 119 at 128 [Huda]; Also see "Symposium on Tort Law Judgments Held at

The development of tort law in Bangladesh 17

BILIA" *The Daily Star* (22 October 2017), online: The Daily Star https://www.thedailystar.net/law-our-rights/symposium-recent-tort-law-judgments-held-bilia-1480180. [24/03/2021].

Please note that the name of the case "*Bangladesh Beverage Industries Ltd v Rowshan Akhter*" has been spelled differently in different places, including in the title of Taqbir Huda's paper and in the article published by *The Daily Star*. I mention this in the hopes that this does not create any confusion and the case I have mentioned on page 10 should be understood as that mentioned in the articles of this footnote. Moreover, I have decided to spell the disputed portion of the case as "Rowshan Akhter" because that is how the SCB has recorded it and that is also how it has been spelled by the Ontario Superior Court of Justice in *Das v George Weston Ltd*, [2018] OJ No 6742, 2018 ONCA 1053.

5 *Catherine Masud et al v Md Kashed Miah et al*, [2014] 67 DLR 523 [*Catherine Masud*].

6 *Children Charity Bangladesh Foundation v Government of Bangladesh*, [2017] 5 CLR 278.

7 See Huda, *supra* note 4; Also see Farhana H Mehtab & Ali Mashraf, "Decoding *Children's Charity Bangladesh (CCB) Foundation v Government of Bangladesh*: The First Ever Public Law Compensation Case in Bangladesh and the Way Forward" (2019) 4:2 Bangladesh Ins Leg Dev 9.

8 See, for example, Taqbir Huda, "Beyond Criminal Justice: Towards Tort Liability for Sexual Violence Against Women" (2017) 17:1&2 Bangladesh J L 201, where the author argues using tort law as means of redress for victims of sexual assault.

9 See *The Trademarks Act, 2009* (Bangladesh), Act No XIX of 2009, s 24(2).

10 *Das v George Weston Ltd*, [2017] OJ No 3542, 2017 ONSC 4129 at paras 283–284.

11 Here, I add that, similar to the Dispute Settlement Body (hereinafter "DSB") of the World Trade Organization (hereinafter "WTO"), global powers should work harmoniously to develop the International Board for Corporate Governance (hereinafter "IBCG"), which would be an intergovernmental organization governing corporations.

In 1916, John Hobson suggested the "utilization of the economic resources of the world for the benefit of the world," demanding opening doors for trade, capital, and labor, at John Hobson, *Towards International Government* (New York: MacMillan Company, 1916) at 142. As the Second World War devastated Europe's economy and the United States emerged as the most powerful economy and country, its liberal economic policies were accepted, without hesitation, by Europe, at Peter Van den Bossche, *The Law and Policy of the World Trade Organization: Text, Cases and Materials* (New York: Cambridge University Press, 2005) at 78–79 and Joseph Stiglitz, *Globalization and its Discontents* (New York: W.W. Norton & Co, 2002) at 11. Eventually, this engendered the rise of the International Monetary Fund, the World Bank, and the *General Agreement on Tariffs and Trade*, which evolved into the WTO on 1 January 1995.

Because of these institutions and neoliberal policies, multinational enterprises (hereinafter "MNE") and global trade proliferated, at Peter Muchlinski, *Multinational Enterprises and the Law*, 2nd ed (New York: Oxford University Press, 2007) at 8–9, 10–12 & 15–16. This, however, gave rise to a pressing question and problem – who governs MNEs, as international law does not apply to them? The answer is domestic law, at Rosalyn Higgins, *Problems and Process: International Law and How We Use it* (New York: Oxford University Press, 1994) at 39–40. This, however, begets another problem.

For example, if an MNE is headquartered in Ontario, Canada, but has a subsidiary operating in Dhaka, Bangladesh, and if its subsidiary's misconduct injures Bangladeshi people, then it is the laws of Bangladesh that will apply to

18 *The development of tort law in Bangladesh*

the subsidiary. Frequently, however, domestic law is incapable of dispensing compensation, or, more often than not, the subsidiary says it does not have money to provide reparation. At this point, victims often file a case against the parent company, but because of the doctrine of separate legal personality and *forum non conveniens*, they are unable to extract any fruit.

In order to avoid these problems, an organization, such as the IBCG and similar to the DSB, can be set up to ensure that victims of MNE misconduct always have a forum to file complaints and receive adequate compensation.

References

Legislation

The Trademarks Act, 2009, (Bangladesh), Act No XIX of 2009

Caselaw

Bangladesh Beverage Industries Ltd v Rowshan Akhter, [2010] 62 DLR 483
Catherine Masud et al v Md Kashed Miah et al, [2014] 67 DLR 523
Children Charity Bangladesh Foundation v Government of Bangladesh, [2017] 5 CLR 278
Das v George Weston Ltd, [2017] OJ No 3542, 2017 ONSC 4129
Das v George Weston Ltd, [2018] OJ No 6742, 2018 ONCA 1053

Secondary Material: Books

Atiyah, Patrick, *Accidents, Compensation, and the Law*, 2nd ed (London: Weidenfeld and Nicolson, 1975)
Bossche, Peter Van den, *The Law and Policy of the World Trade Organization: Text, Cases and Materials* (New York: Cambridge University Press, 2005)
Fleming, John G, *The Law of Torts*, 9th ed (Sydney: LBC Information Services, 1998)
Heuston, R F V & Buckley, R A, *Salmond and Heuston on the Law of Torts*, 19th ed (London: Sweet & Maxwell, 1987)
Higgins, Rosalyn, *Problems and Process: International Law and How We Use it* (New York: Oxford University Press, 1994)
Hobson, John, *Towards International Government* (New York: MacMillan Company, 1916)
Klar, Lewis, *Tort Law*, 5th ed (Toronto: Carswell, 2012)
Linden, Allen M & Feldthusen, Bruce, *Canadian Tort Law*, 9th ed (Markham, ON: LexisNexis Canada Inc., 2011)
Muchlinski, Peter, *Multinational Enterprises and the Law*, 2nd ed (New York: Oxford University Press Inc, 2007)
Osborne, Philip, *The Law of Torts*, 5th ed (Toronto: Irwin Law Inc., 2015)
Prosser, William L, *Handbook of The Law of Torts*, 4th ed (St. Paul, Minnesota: West Publishing Co, 1971)
Stiglitz, Joseph, *Globalization and its Discontents* (New York: W.W. Norton & Co, 2002)
Weinrib, Ernest J, *Tort Law: Cases and Materials*, 4th ed (Toronto: Emond Montgomery Publications Limited, 2014))

Secondary Material: Journal Articles

Huda, Taqbir, "Vicarious Liability of Employers in the Law of Tort: Deciphering *Bangladesh Beverage Industries vs Roswan Akhter and Others*" (2016) 16:2 Bangladesh J L 119

Huda, Taqbir, "Beyond Criminal Justice: Towards Tort Liability for Sexual Violence Against Women" (2017) 17:1&2 Bangladesh J L 201

Mehtab, Farhana H & Mashraf, Ali "Decoding *Children's Charity Bangladesh (CCB) Foundation v Government of Bangladesh*: The First Ever Public Law Compensation Case in Bangladesh and the Way Forward" (2019) 4:2 Bangladesh Ins Leg Dev 9

Secondary Material: Websites

"Symposium on Tort Law Judgments Held at BILIA" *The Daily Star* (22 October 2017), online: The Daily Star https://www.thedailystar.net/law-our-rights/symposium-recent-tort-law-judgments-held-bilia-1480180

3 Nuisance

As I have mentioned in the first chapter, certain actions do not qualify as offences simply because a statute does not prohibit them. For example, imagine you live on the seventh floor of a building in Dhanmondi. It is now 11:45 pm and you are trying to sleep as you have class at 8:00 am. Unfortunately, you cannot because the person living on the eighth floor is playing deafeningly loud music. While you can go upstairs and ask him to reduce the volume, what can you do if he flouts your request? I will rephrase that question: is there anything you can *legally* do to have him desist from playing music in a manner that causes you material discomfort? While you can file a claim under *The Penal Code, 1860*[1] (hereinafter "*Penal Code*"), recall that the standard of proof is significantly higher in criminal law, and therefore, it would be more propitious if you institute proceedings under tort.

Assuming, however, you proceed criminally, you can seek an injunction, which is one of the two remedies dispensed by civil courts as well. However, what if the impugned nuisance is an oil spill that contaminates the water in your lake, which you rely on for bathing, drinking, or feeding your cattle, and kills marine life?[2] Though you can seek an injunction, which will proscribe the company from spilling oil in the future, thereby preventing future injuries, how is the injury already suffered supposed to be mitigated? Under the *Penal Code*, you can claim monetary compensation of up to ৳200,[3] which is hopelessly inadequate for an injury with an estimated possible monetary equivalent of ৳2,000,000. Therefore, not only is the standard of proof in tort law lower, but also the compensation one can receive is considerably higher.

Nuisance, which is a very vague term, is a French word meaning "harm" or "annoyance."[4] Perhaps no other word has vexed the English language as much as "nuisance," since it has meant anything from an alarming advertisement to a cockroach baked in a cake.[5] However, there is agreement among scholars, lawyers, and judges that the word is incapable of a precise definition. Nonetheless, from its provenance, nuisance has been, and is, an interference with the use and enjoyment of one's land. This action was (and is) different from trespass in that there is no direct entrance onto a person's property, but it causes disturbance to the enjoyment of the aggrieved party's

DOI: 10.4324/9781003241782-3

Nuisance   21

land. The example in the first paragraph is illustrative, as the person never entered your apartment uninvited and played loud music; rather, he was playing loud music on *his* property, which obstructed your enjoyment of your property.

There are two kinds of nuisance – private and public – and I shall probe both in this chapter. A private nuisance is anything that interferes with the enjoyment of an individual's property, such as, *inter alia*, smell, noise, or dust. A public nuisance is anything that interferes with the rights of the community, which could range from blocking a public highway to indecently exposing oneself to another.[6] Nonetheless, as will become evident in this chapter, courts have provided guidelines as to what actions constitute nuisance, and similarly, what actions, though *prima facie* annoying, are not nuisances.[7]

3.1 Actions giving rise to lability

Appleby v Erie Tobacco Co[8]

Erie Tobacco Company (hereinafter "Erie") operated in a town near Appleby's place of business and manufactured plug tobacco, which is tobacco leaves pressed together to create a brick-like mass for the purposes of chewing. The process of producing plug tobacco involves steaming, steeping, and stewing tobacco leaves. It is then added to a mixture of sugar, liquorice, and other ingredients, which are first boiled together. However, this process produces an odour that has been described as a "most sickening," "very bad," "very, very offensive," and "very nauseating" smell, which causes vertigo and dizziness. Nonetheless, Erie is doing their best to contain the smell so that others are not detrimentally affected and have produced witnesses who say the smell is "not unhealthy" and one person has even said that it is "just splendid." Since people were disturbed by the activity at Erie, the question submitted before the court was whether the smell resulting from the manufacture of plug tobacco constituted a nuisance. The court held it to be a nuisance and said:

> In *Fleming v Hislop* [...] the Earl of Serborne states his view of the law thus:
> What causes material discomfort and annoyance for the ordinary purposes of life to a man's house or to his property, is to be restrained [...] although the evidence does not go to the length of proving that health is in danger [...] What makes life less comfortable and causes sensible discomfort and annoyance is a proper subject of injunction.
> [In *Colls v Home and Colonial Stores Limited*, Lord Halsbury said,]
> A dweller in towns cannot expect to have as pure air, as free from smoke, smell, and noise as if he lived in the country, and distant from other dwellings, and yet an excess of smoke, smell and noise may give a cause of action, but in each of such cases it becomes a question of

22 *Nuisance*

degree, and the question is in each case whether it is a nuisance which will give right of action. [...]

It is plain, in this case, that the defendants' manufactory does constitute a nuisance. The odours do cause material discomfort and annoyance and render the plaintiff's premises less fit for the ordinary purposes of life, even making all possible allowances for the local standard of the neighbourhood. [...]

The injunction should, therefore, go, restraining the defendants from so operating their works as to cause a nuisance to the plaintiff by reason of the offensive odours arising from the [...] manufacture of tobacco: the operation of this injunction to be stayed for six months to allow the defendants to abate the nuisance if they can do so, or to make arrangements for the removal of that part of the business causing the odour.

Notes

From *Appleby*, the following two points must be understood: (1) What constitutes nuisance, and (2) what is its proper remedy?

Firstly, a nuisance is anything that causes "material discomfort and annoyance for the ordinary purposes of life." Additionally, as was identified in *Antrim Truck Centre Ltd v Ontario (Minister of Transportation)*,[9] the focus is on whether the interference the claimant suffers is unreasonable, and not on whether the defendant's conduct is unreasonable. Therefore, regardless of whether the impugned irritant is noise or smell, if it causes "material discomfort" and is unreasonable to the plaintiff, he would have a right to bring a complaint against its creator. Does this mean that you will have a case against your neighbour if he is cooking dry fish and its smell is pungently odious and bothersome? While you may think you do, the correct answer is to the contrary.

In the preceding case, the court also referred to *Walter v Selfe*,[10] where the defendant was a brick-maker and the nuisance complained of was the smoke. The court said,

> Ought this inconvenience to be considered in fact as more than fanciful, more than one of mere delicacy or fastidiousness, as an inconvenience materially interfering with the ordinary comfort physically of human existence, not merely according to the elegant or dainty modes and habits of living, but according to plain and sober and simple notions among the English people? [...] As far as the human frame in an average state of health at least is concerned, mere insalubrity, mere unwholesomeness, may possibly [...] be out of the case [...] A smell may be sickening though not in a medical sense [...] A man's body may be in a state of chronic discomfort, still retaining its health [...] The defendant's intended proceedings will, if prosecuted, abridge and diminish seriously and materially the ordinary comfort of existence to the occupier and inmates of the plaintiff's house.

Nuisance 23

Therefore, your neighbour cooking dry fish would be considered a "mere insalubrity" and would not interfere with the "ordinary comfort" to one's life (more on this later). This is not to suggest that one must have a recognizable medical illness resulting from the smell in order for it to be considered nuisance. In fact, an activity can be a nuisance even if it does not harm (by this, I mean a recognizable medical condition) others, but it must cause "material discomfort." However, in an urban area, we impliedly consent to such smells or noise and are subject to louder noises and perhaps harsher smells than rural areas; that is, courts will consider the characteristics of a neighbourhood before declaring whether the impugned activity constitutes a nuisance. For example, construction of an apartment building at Mirpur DOHS carried on at 1:00 am may be a nuisance in 2021, since the area is inhabited and replete with residents. However, with the same facts, it may not have been a nuisance in 2008 when the area was mostly vacant. Furthermore, what can constitute nuisance in a rural area may not be so in an urban area. For example, playing loud music in Bagmara, Rajshahi, which is a rural area, at 9:00 pm may constitute a nuisance, whereas doing the same in Gulshan, Dhaka, may not be so.

Moreover, smell discharged by a factory operating in a designated residential area would constitute a nuisance; whereas, a person, who buys property close to a commercial area and is thereafter sickened by a factory's smell, would have no remedy.[11] However, this does not mean that a manufacturer can engage in any type of activity in a commercial area, cause annoyance to residents in the vicinity, and not be subject to legal action.[12] As in, if you buy property near a commercial area, you impliedly consent to less clean air and more noise than if you had purchased property in a residential area. Nonetheless, imagine you have lived close to the said commercial area for nearly five years and you have experienced smoke and odours from the manufacture of a tobacco company, to which you did not – because you could not – complain. Yet, a company has now opened a waste management facility in that commercial area and the smell generated from its operation is pungent and sickening. Are you without remedy because you live near a commercial area and you must consent to whatever smell or noise that may be generated?

Fortunately, that would not be the case, as the House of Lords said in *Polsue and Alfieri Limited v Rushmer*:[13]

> [A] person living in a district specially devoted to a particular trade cannot complain of any nuisance by noise caused by the carrying on of any branch of that trade without carelessness and in a reasonable person. I cannot assent to this argument. A resident in such a neighbourhood must put up with a certain amount of noise. The standard of comfort differs according to the situation of the property and the class of people who inhabit it [...] But whatever the standard of comfort in a particular district may be, I think the addition of a fresh noise caused by the defendant's works may be so substantial as to cause a legal nuisance.

24 Nuisance

> It does not follow that because I live, say, in the manufacturing part of Sheffield, I cannot complain if a steam-hammer is introduced next door, and so worked as to render sleep at night almost impossible, although previous to its introduction my house was a reasonably comfortable abode, having regard to the local standard; and it would be no answer to say that the steam-hammer is of the most modern approved pattern and is reasonably worked. In short [...] it is no answer to say that the neighbourhood is noisy, and that the defendant's machinery is of first-class character.

Essentially, this means that even if you live near a commercial area, the introduction of a new smell can constitute a nuisance so long as it interferes with the "ordinary comfort" of your life. Simply because an area is commercial does not mean that every activity – whether new or old – can persist. Nonetheless, preferences are given to old activities in the case of commercial areas and proving that it constitutes a nuisance would be difficult, but not insurmountable. While it is true that you have implicitly submitted to lesser clean air and more noise by electing to live near a commercial area, it does not mean that you have consented to *every* type of noise or smell. Thus, the waste management facility, if it is a "material discomfort" to daily life, could be declared a nuisance even though it has opened in a commercial area.[14] Notice that in this instance, you had been living near a commercial area *prior* to the opening of the waste management facility and this will also affect the court's verdict (as we will see later in this chapter).

Secondly, the remedy for the nuisance of smell is an injunction, which proscribes a person from engaging in the activity. As was said in *Shelfer v City of London Electric Co*,[15] no one should submit to an annoyance resulting from noxious odour for a "small money payment"; that is, if an activity incommodes others, permitting its continuation in exchange for paying damages is nonsensical. For example, it would be preposterous to ask residents of a neighbourhood, where a restaurant has recently opened generating a cacophony of noise to accept money as compensation in exchange for allowing the restaurant's operations to continue. Therefore, the most common remedy meted out by courts in reference to the nuisance of smell or noise is an injunction, which terminates the activity.

Rogers v Elliot[16]

Mr. Elliot was a custodian and manager of the Roman Catholic Church, which was constructed inside a residential area, and as part of his duties, he rang a large church bell daily. Mr. Rogers, who lived across the street from the church, was recovering from a severe sunstroke. When Mr. Elliot rang the bell one day, Mr. Rogers suffered convulsions, and the latter's physician believed it was due to the noise generated from ringing the bell at the church. Mr. Elliot was informed of Mr. Rogers' condition and was requested to stop ringing the bell. However, he disregarded the plea, rang the bell the following day, and Mr. Rogers again suffered convulsions.

Nuisance 25

He then brought an action to have the ringing of the church bell declared and sought an injunction. Dismissing Mr. Rogers' claim, the court said:

> [A] fundamental question is, by what standard, as against the interests of a neighbour, is one's right to use his real estate to be measured. In densely populated communities the use of property in many ways which are legitimate and proper necessity affects in greater or less degree the property or persons of others in the vicinity. In such cases the inquiry always is, when rights are called in question, what is reasonable under the circumstances. If a use of property is objectionable solely on account of the noise which it makes, it is a nuisance, if at all, by reason of its effect upon the health or comfort of those who are within hearing. The right to make a noise for a proper purpose must be measured in reference to the degree of annoyance which others may reasonably be required to submit to. In connection with the importance of the business from which it proceeds, that must be determined by the effect of noise upon people generally, and not upon those, on the one hand, who are peculiarly susceptible to it, or those, on the other, who by long experience have learned to endure it without inconvenience; not upon those whose strong nerves and robust health enable them to endure the greatest disturbances without suffering, nor upon those whose mental or physical condition makes them painfully sensitive to everything about them.
>
> If one's right to use his property were to depend upon the effect of the use upon a person of peculiar temperament or disposition, or upon one suffering from an uncommon disease, the standard for measuring it would be so uncertain and fluctuating as to paralyze industrial enterprises. The owner of a factory containing noisy machinery, with dwelling houses all about it, might find his business lawful as to all but one of the tenants of the houses, and as to that one, who dwelt no nearer than the others, it might be a nuisance. The character of his business might change from legal to illegal, or illegal to legal, with every change of tenants of an adjacent estate, or with an arrival or departure of a guest or boarder at a house near by; or even with the wakefulness or the tranquil repose of an invalid neighbour on a particular night. Legal rights to the use of property cannot be left to such uncertainty. When an act is of such a nature as to extend its influence to those in the vicinity, and its legal quality depends upon the effect of that influence, it is as important that the rightfulness of it should be tried by the experience of ordinary people, as it is, in determining a question as to negligence, that the test should be the common care of persons of ordinary prudence, without regard to the peculiarities of him whose conduct is on trial.
>
> In the case at bar it is not contended that the ringing of the bell for church services in the manner shown by the evidence materially affected the health or comfort of ordinary people in the vicinity, but

26 Nuisance

the plaintiff's claim rests upon the injury done him on account of his peculiar condition.

Notes

Rogers refused to consider the peculiarities of a person when determining whether noise – or, using the same logic, smell – is a nuisance. This means that if a person is particularly sensitive to a noise, or smell, he will have no legal remedy, as the courts will consider what is unacceptable and "unreasonable" to a reasonable person[17] and not the person with the eccentricity. If courts were to consider one's peculiar characteristics, then it would stymie the growth of business and the efficacy of the law would be lost. However, by the same logic, it follows that if the preponderance of people were adversely affected by the ringing of the church bell, it could be declared a nuisance.

I do not wish to assume, but I trust that people in Bangladesh are accustomed to hearing the Azan five times per day. This means that if a person has an adverse reaction – even a medical one – to the noise generated by the Azan, he cannot legally have it declared a nuisance. However, what would happen if the majority of people living in the vicinity of a mosque is disturbed by the Azan? Will the court issue an injunction prohibiting the mosque from reciting it? While a *prima facie* glance at *Rogers* makes it seem as though an injunction will be ordered, it actually will not.

It is pertinent to note that the court said that whether something constitutes a nuisance will depend on what is "reasonable under the circumstances." Section 8 of the *Constitution of Bangladesh* holds secularism to be a fundamental principle, but Section 2A declares Islam to be the state religion.[18] Therefore, this means that there is a high probability – perhaps 99% – that the Azan will not be considered a nuisance even if everyone in a neighbourhood complains. By contrast, the Azan in the United States of America or Australia could be a nuisance due to the reason that it would not be reasonable under the circumstances. As in, in the aforementioned countries, the Azan is uncommon and it would take years for society to accept such a loud call for prayer five times per day.

However, what would happen if the mosque was close to a hospital and it disturbed patients that needed sleep? Since the court considers what is "reasonable under the circumstances," the Azan *might* be a nuisance. As we will see in *Miller v Jackson*,[19] it will also depend on whether the mosque or the hospital was there first. If the hospital was there first, then the Azan *might* be a nuisance, but if the mosque was there first, then the law would assume that the hospital impliedly consented to the noise and the Azan would not constitute a nuisance. Why, though, would the Azan in a residential area not be a nuisance, yet it may be so if near a hospital?

The difference is that people go to hospitals when they are despondent and ill with the expectation that doctors will properly diagnose and remedy the problem. Imagine you were involved in a car accident, which required the doctor to administer nine stitches, and after the successful completion of the procedure, you have been taken into a cabin for rest. However, though you have been injected with morphine, within an hour, you are awakened by the Azan. This may militate against recovery as you are required to sleep. In this situation, the Azan may be declared a nuisance if it disturbs not just you, but others inside the hospital. Nonetheless, if the Azan was being recited and the power to control its volume was given to hospital authority, particularly to each doctor overseeing a cabin, and there was no loud central speaker, then it probably would not be considered a nuisance as it was within the ambit of the doctor's power to either turn it off entirely or maintain a low volume. To further explain, imagine that a doctor was incharge of a cabin, where there was a patient. The said doctor was also given a volume-control button inside the cabin from where he could toggle the volume of the Azan. In this situation, since the power to control the volume was given to the doctor, the Azan would probably not be considered a nuisance.

As we will see from *Kennaway v Thompson*,[20] even if the Azan is considered a nuisance, the court would perhaps simply order the mosque to reduce its central volume, as opposed to stopping it altogether. Alternatively, the court could also order that the mosque not recite the Azan in the early mornings on Fridays and Saturdays since they are holidays in Bangladesh.[21]

It is also important to keep in mind that the preponderance of people in Bangladesh are Muslim, and therefore, I have said that the Azan recited in close proximity to a hospital *could* be a nuisance and not that it *would* be one. To simplify, the latter statement contains a greater degree of certainty than the former, and I have chosen to deliberately remain equivocal as I cannot glean how a court would rule if such a situation presented itself. However, premised on the current social milieu, I am of the opinion that the Azan would *not* be considered a nuisance even if it disturbs patients inside a hospital, as the fact that the majority of persons are Muslim would outweigh the concern for patients.

Furthermore, the court will examine the motive of the noisemaker and inquire for what purpose the noise was made. As was identified in *Appleby*, courts consider the characteristics of a neighbourhood before declaring an activity to be a nuisance. Therefore, two scenarios warrant discussion and both involve you residing on the fifth floor of an eight-story building. First, at 2:00 am, while you are sleeping, you are awakened by a clamouring noise, which you later discover was caused when the tenant on the sixth floor accidentally dropped a wok and spatula on the floor while cooking a late-night meal. Second, you are repeatedly awakened at 2:00 am because the same tenant is creating a cacophony of sounds by slamming a wok on the floor simply because he wishes to do it.

The first situation would not be a nuisance because we expect noise of this nature to happen in an urban setting. As in, it is not unlikely that a person cooking will inadvertently drop a pan or any other object from his hands. However, the second situation is a nuisance since the tenant is deliberately engaging in an activity that ultimately disturbs others even if that was not his intention. As in, the tenant may argue that his motive was not to annoy others; rather, it was art. Imagine that instead of banging a wok

28 *Nuisance*

on the floor, the tenant was playing drums at 2:00 am. This would certainly be considered a nuisance since it is unreasonable to play drums at 2:00 am in both rural and densely populated urban areas even if you are doing so on your land. For example, in *Hollywood Silver Fox Farm Ltd v Emmett*,[22] on their land, Hollywood Silver Fox Farm carried on the business of breeding silver foxes, which requires quiet during mating season, as otherwise, they will not mate, or they may miscarry or eat their cubs. After a dispute with the adjacent landowner, the latter fired multiple bird-scaring cartridges on his land, but near the vixens' breeding pens, which resulted in one vixen not mating and the other to eat her cubs. The plaintiff sought damages in nuisance. Finding in his favour, the court, citing *Keeble v Hickeringill*, said,

> No proprietor has an absolute right to create noises upon his own land, because any right which the law gives him is qualified by the condition that it must not be exercised to the nuisance of his neighbours or of the public. If he violates that condition he commits a legal wrong, and if he does so intentionally, he is guilty of a malicious wrong, in its strict legal sense.

Essentially, this means that while one has the right to use his property, it is not absolute; rather, it is conditional in the sense that if the interference he causes to another is unreasonable, then his conduct would constitute a nuisance.[23]

Similarly, what if you are constantly awakened at 3:00 am because the tenant on the sixth floor has, during the month of Ramadan, generated noise in the kitchen from cooking by dropping frypans to scuttling? In this situation, you would be unsuccessful in suing the tenant under a claim for nuisance, as we – living in Bangladesh – expect the level of noise to slightly escalate during *Sahūr* in Ramadan. Nonetheless, this does not mean that one can play drums at 3:00 am during Ramadan simply because others would be up for *Sahūr*, and therefore, it would not be a disturbance. Rather, this simply means that one can expect reasonable increases in volume (e.g. speaking, scuttling, and other noise generated from working in the kitchen) during the said time, and unreasonable increases from unreasonable activities (e.g. playing drums at 3:00 am) would still constitute nuisance even if you are doing an otherwise lawful activity on your land.

Fontainebleau Hotel Corp v Forty-Five Twenty-Five, Inc[24]

Fontainebleau Hotel Corp (hereinafter "Fontainebleau") and Forty-Five Twenty-Five, Inc owned contiguous luxury hotels facing the Atlantic Ocean. Fontainebleau constructed the hotel in 1954 and Forty-Five Twenty-Five erected the Eden Roc Hotel (hereinafter "Eden Roc") in 1955. Fontainebleau now wishes to construct a further 14-story tower, which will be 160 feet in height, near its north property line. Unfortunately, the tower will cast a shadow over the swimming pool and sunbathing areas of the Eden Roc post 2:00 pm, rendering the said areas wholly unfit for use. Therefore, when

Nuisance 29

the tower was approximately eight-stories high, Forty-Five Twenty-Five filed for an injunction to restrain its development.

In dismissing Forty-Five Twenty-Five's claim, the court applied the maxim *sic utere tuo ut alienum non laedas*, which means that one should use his property so that another's lawful rights are not impaired. The court relied on *Reaver v Martin Theatres of Florida Inc*[25] and said that a landowner can lawfully use his property for any purpose so long as it is not a nuisance and he does not impinge upon an adjoining landowner's legally recognized and protected rights. Furthermore, the court said,

> There being, then, no legal right to the free flow of light and air from the adjoining land, it is universally held that where a structure serves a useful and beneficial purpose, it does not give rise to a cause of action, either for damages or for an injunction under the maxim *sic utere tuo ut alienum non laedas*, even though it causes injury to another by cutting off the light and air interfering with the view that would otherwise be available over adjoining land in its natural state, regardless of the fact that the structure may have been erected party for spite [...]

Notes

The common law does not recognize and protect one's right to air and light from a neighbour's property. Since said right is not legally recognized and protected, one can construct a tall building on his property, and even if it obstructs sunlight on yours, you will have no remedy. For example, if you lived in Gulshan or Banani DOHS in the 1980s, you would perhaps have resided in a bungalow or a duplex. However, due to societal demands, such structures have been demolished and tall buildings have taken their place. Nonetheless, if you opposed construction due to the reason that it will disrupt the flow of air and hinder sunlight on your property, the court would not rule in your favour, as the common law does not recognize such a right. Yet, what would happen if your complaint alleged that you needed the sunlight for a solar heated or powered residence?[26]

In *Prah v Maretti*,[27] Glenn Prah harnessed solar energy by placing solar panels on the rooftop of his house to supply heat and hot water throughout his residence. Richard Maretti bought an adjoining plot to construct a house. When Prah discovered where Maretti wants to construct the said house, he requested that the latter choose a different location, as otherwise it would obstruct sunlight from reaching the former's solar panels, which would considerably reduce efficiency. However, Marreti proceeded with construction and Prah successfully sought an injunction enjoining construction.

The court subscribed to the following view of William L Prosser:

> Most of the litigation as to private nuisance has dealt with the conflicting interests of landowners and the question of the reasonableness of the defendant's conduct: The defendant's privilege of making a

30 *Nuisance*

reasonable use of his own property for his own benefit and conducting his affairs in his own way is no less important than the plaintiff's right to use and enjoy his premises. The two are correlative and interdependent, and neither is entitled to prevail entirely, at the expense of the other. Some balance must be struck between the two. The plaintiff must be expected to endure some inconvenience rather than curtail the defendant's freedom of action, and the defendant must so use his own property that he causes no unreasonable harm to the plaintiff. The law of private nuisance is very largely a series of adjustments to limit the reciprocal rights and privileges of both. In every case the court must make a comparative evaluation of the conflicting interests according to objective legal standards, and the gravity of the harm to the plaintiff must be weighed against the utility of the defendant's conduct.

The court then added:

This court's reluctance in the nineteenth and early part of the twentieth century to provide broader protection for a landowner's access to sunlight was premised on three policy considerations. First, the right of landowners to use their property as they wished, as long as they did not cause physical damage to a neighbour, was jealously guarded [...] Second, sunlight was valued only for aesthetic enjoyment or as illumination. Since artificial light could be used for illumination, loss of sunlight was at most a personal annoyance which was given little, if any, weight by society. Third, society had a significant interest in not restricting or impeding land development.

These three policies are no longer fully accepted or applicable. They reflect factual circumstances and social priorities that are now obsolete. First, society has increasingly regulated the use of land by the landowner for the general welfare [...] Second, access to sunlight has taken on a new significance in recent years. In this case the plaintiff seeks to protect access to sunlight, not for aesthetic reasons or as a source of illumination but as a source of energy. Access to sunlight as an energy source is of significance both to the landowner who invests in solar collectors and to a society which has an interest in developing alternative sources of energy [...] Third, the policy of favouring unhindered private development in an expanding economy is no longer in harmony with the realities of our society [...] The need for easy and rapid development is not as great today as it once was, while our perception of the value of sunlight as a source of energy has increased significantly. Courts should not implement obsolete policies that have lost their vigour over the course of the years. The law of private nuisance is better suited to resolve landowners' dispute about property development in the 1980s than is a rigid rule which does not recognize a landowner's interest in access to sunlight [...]

Let me now reimport a previous example. Remember you opposed construction of your neighbour's building in Gulshan alleging you required sunlight for your solar-powered – albeit not fully solar-powered – residence? You can actually seek injunctive relief from the court to proscribe construction. However, as Prosser said, "Some balance must be struck between the two." To this end, the following was said in *Hay v Cohoes Co*:

> It is an elementary principle with reference to private rights, that every individual is entitled to the undisturbed possession and lawful enjoyment of his own property. The mode of enjoyment is necessarily limited by the rights of others – otherwise it might be made destructive of their rights altogether [...] The defendants had the right to dig the canal. The plaintiff had the right to the undisturbed possession of his property. If these rights conflict, the former must yield to the latter, as the more important of the two, since, upon grounds of public policy, it is better that one man should surrender a particular use of his land than that another should be deprived of the beneficial use of his property altogether, which might be the consequence if the privilege of the former should be wholly restricted. The case before us illustrates this principle. For if the defendants in excavating their canal, in itself a lawful use of their land, could, in the manner mentioned by the witness, demolish the stoop of the plaintiff with impunity, they might, for the same purpose, on the exercise of reasonable care, demolish his house, and thus deprive him of all use of his property.[28]

Therefore, it is equally important to understand the principle in reverse. Let us assume you own the house but reside in Canada and do not rent to a tenant. In this situation, the court, upon balancing conflicting rights, would view construction more favourably as the extent of injury upon you would be less than prohibiting construction; that is, since you do not live in the house or rent to a tenant, your neighbour has *more of a right* to construct the building, obstructing sunlight on your property, even though you require it for solar power. In other words, since it is about balancing competing rights, rather than permitting one to prevail absolutely at the expense of another, you would be unable to argue your requirement of sunlight for solar power if you are not there to actually use it.[29]

Bradford Corporation v Pickles[30]

Edward Pickles owned a tract of land on a hill, beneath which was a natural reservoir. This water flowed in an undefined stream and accumulated under land owned by Bradford Corporation's (hereinafter "the plaintiff") land, which was on the lower part of the hillside. For the past 40 years, the plaintiff, through statutory powers, collected and supplied water to the town of Bradford. Suddenly, Mr. Pickles sank a shaft down in his own land (and he was going to sink more), which disrupted the flow of water and reduced the amount that usually accumulated underneath the plaintiff's property. Therefore, the plaintiff could no longer supply Bradford with

32 *Nuisance*

water. Strangely, Mr. Pickles sank the shaft and did nothing to extract the water. The plaintiff alleges that Mr. Pickles' motive in sinking the shaft on his land was to compel them to buy his property. Thus, they seek an injunction to prohibit the defendant from continuing his work.

The court, holding that even if Mr. Pickles did nothing further to abstract the water, sinking a shaft onto his land is a lawful act and it cannot be prohibited, said,

> The appellants endeavoured to construe the prohibitory clause as effecting a virtual confiscation in their favour of all water rights in or connected with the respondent's land lying to the west of Trooper Farm. It appears to me to be exceedingly improbable that the legislature should have intended to deprive a landowner of part of his property for the benefit of a commercial company without any provision for compensating him for his loss. But it is not necessary to rely upon probabilities, because, in my opinion, the language of the clause is incapable of bearing such an interpretation. I think that the plain object of the statutory prohibition, which has two distinct branches, was to give protection to the supply of water which had been acquired by or belonged to the company for the time being, and that it was not meant to forbid, and does not prevent, any legitimate use made by a neighbouring proprietor of water running upon or percolating below his land before it reached the company's supply and became part of their undertaking. The first branch makes it unlawful for any person other than the company to divert, alter, or appropriate any of the "waters now supplying" the Many Wells springs, which appear to include sources of supply existing upon lands adjacent to Trooper Farm. Had the prohibition been absolute, it would have struck against the operations of the respondent; but it is subject to the qualification that the respondent, or any landowner similarly situated, may lawfully divert those waters which ultimately feed the Many Wells springs, so long as he does so in any manner which is not in excess of his common law rights. The respondent's operations, of which the appellants' complain, are within his proprietary right, and are, therefore, not obnoxious to that part of the prohibition. The second branch, which prohibits the sinking of wells and other operations, has no reference to outside waters, more or less distant, which might ultimately find their way to the Many Wells springs. It relates to "the waters of the said springs," an expression which, in my opinion, can only denote the waters which have actually reached the Many Wells springs, or some channel or reservoir which has been prepared for their reception upon their issuing from those springs. The prohibition gives effectual protection against the withdrawal or diminution, either by an adjacent proprietor or any other person, of waters which have come within the dominion of the appellants. But it does not prevent the diversion or impounding by an adjacent proprietor of water in his

own land which has never reached that point, so long as his operations are such as the law permits.

Notes

This case must be understood in juxtaposition to the others discussed *ad nunc*. The common law confers broad rights to property holders – including ownership of everything on and below the parcel of land to which you have title – which means that you may use your property in a manner that you wish.[31] However, we have learned from *Appleby*, *Rogers*, and particularly *Fontainebleau*, that there are limitations to one's use of property. Therefore, the correct statement is that you may use your property in a manner that you wish so long as it does not create "material discomfort" to others and that your action does not unreasonably interfere with the enjoyment of another's property. To further simplify, in accordance with Prosser's statement, if there is a conflict between competing rights, a balance must always be struck.

What needs to be understood is why noise or smell generated from one's property could be a nuisance, but not so if one, by doing something on his property, disrupts the flow of water on your land. In *Hunter v Canary Wharf Ltd*,[32] the House of Lords said,

> [F]or an action in private nuisance to lie in respect of interference with the plaintiff's enjoyment of his land, it will generally arise from something emanating from the defendant's land. Such an emanation may take many forms – noise, dirt, fumes, a noxious smell, vibrations, and suchlike.

The difference is that noise or smell would create "material discomfort" to one's life, as they can, *inter alia*, prevent sleep and cause or exacerbate illnesses, and most importantly, it is something that *emanates* from one's land. However, how does the disruption of the flow of water cause "material discomfort" to one's life? Simply put, it does not even though it is an activity that emanates from one's land, its *effects* are different from other cases. That is to say, the disruption of water will not cause "material discomfort" in the sense of rendering one to lose sleep or causing or aggravating illnesses as one can go out and buy water. Nonetheless, while the aggrieved party could contest that he is disturbed because he relies on the water for cleaning, cooking, and drinking, it would be insufficient to have someone's lawful activity declared a nuisance.

Upon balancing competing rights – (a) right to sink a shaft into one's own land and (b) right to water beneath one's property that flows from another's – it is not difficult to see that the latter right weighs less than the former. To further explain, even though you rely on the water, its disruption is not a wrongful activity, since the only reason you enjoyed it was because of the other property holder's omission in extracting it heretofore; that is, the water did not naturally accumulate under your property, but beneath another's, and thus, your right to the water is outweighed by the true

34 Nuisance

owner of the property (who has a greater right to the water). Nonetheless, what would be wrong is if the reservoir was under your land and another abstracted its water, which would allow you to hold him liable in trespass.[33]

However, common law rights must be balanced against any domestic statutory rights, and if any rights are guaranteed by legislation, then the statutory right prevails so long as it is not inconsistent with any provisions of the *Constitution*. Section 143(1)(a) of the *Constitution* says that minerals and "things of value" underneath land are the property of Bangladesh.[34] This means that if the owner of land finds gold or diamonds underneath his land, it would be the property of Bangladesh. This also means that water, which is considered a public resource, is also the property of Bangladesh. However, similar to how one has the right to use public highways, he also has the right to extract water from beneath his land, which people do using tube wells or other mechanized methods. What one would be unable to do is implant a tube well on his land and extract subterranean water from an adjacent landowner. However, if you plant a tube well on your land and it disrupts the flow and accumulation of water on your neighbour's land, he cannot sue you under nuisance. Similarly, in *Bradford*, even though pickles did not ultimately abstract subterranean water, he did nothing wrong on his property (by sinking a shaft) for which the plaintiffs could seek an injunction.

Shuttleworth v Vancouver General Hospital[35]

Vancouver General Hospital has carried on activities for many years at the Vancouver Civil Hospital and, on Block 418, which is an adjacent plot to the main block of the hospital, constructed a new building to treat infectious diseases (hereinafter "Isolation Hospital"). One end of the Isolation Hospital faces 13th Avenue, which is directly across Shuttleworth's residence with a distance of approximately 110 feet. From the upper windows of his house, the rooms of the Isolation Hospital can be seen, but the patients in their cots cannot. For this, the plaintiff seeks a *quia timet* injunction, whereby an injunction is granted not for wrongs already committed, but for wrongs a party has reason to fear will result from the operation of the activity. He alleges, first, that crying child patients will make it a nuisance; second, when persons inside his house see into the rooms of the Isolation Hospital, they will sympathize with human suffering to an extent where their comfort would be seriously impaired; and third, members of his house would be susceptible to infection.

In dismissing the claim, the court said, first, that the proper time to seek an injunction would be when child patients *actually* cry and it creates an annoyance because there may not be child patients whatsoever or that, if there are, there may be so few that it does not disturb others. Second, the objection to the operation of the Isolation Hospital based on perceived human sentiment is insufficient for an award of injunction. Third, the court said,

> [T]he onus is on plaintiff to prove a well-founded apprehension of injury, proof of actual and real danger. What plaintiff has in fact done

Nuisance 35

is to call evidence to show that members of his household and his neighbours entertain a real fear of such infection. I am quite prepared to believe they do. He has also sought to establish, mainly by cross-examination, that fear of infection from an Isolation Hospital, given the facts as to proximity proven herein, is widely held by people in general and even by members of the medical profession. No direct testimony that medical men do entertain such fear was led by him. Again, I am prepared to accept the contention that such fear under the given conditions would be widely entertained by laymen. In the absence of direct testimony, I cannot impute belief of the likelihood of infection to members of the plaintiff's household to any qualified physician. But the cases cited show plaintiff must go further and prove not only widespread belief but that such belief must be well founded in fact [...]

Evidence was led by plaintiff to show that, in the opinion of real estate men, the value of the plaintiff's property has been depreciated by the erection of the Isolation Hospital. But if depreciation has taken place the only reason given before me is the existence of the fear of infection. It being my view that does not *per se* constitute a ground for an action such as this, it follows that such depreciation — assuming it proven — has not been occasioned by any legal wrong. The mere fact of depreciation cannot found an action.

Notes

I will not explore the first claim, as I am of the opinion that it is self-explanatory. The second claim, however, requires a rudimentary discussion. Here, I add that while one's emotion may be inundated with sadness at the sight of the rooms of a hospital, another may be indifferent. It will be difficult to identify who would and would not be affected. Moreover, what if no one in your household is upset and disturbed by such sight? In this situation, ordering the hospital to cease operations would be a gross disservice to all the patients who require treatment.

Lastly, and most importantly, the gravamen of Shuttleworth's argument was that there was a fear of infection from the operation of the Isolation Hospital owing to its proximity to his house. However, even this did not warrant injunctive relief. Therefore, if Evercare Hospital (hereinafter "Evercare") in Bashundhara constructed a new building to treat infectious diseases opposite a person's residence, the latter would not be entitled to seek a remedy from the courts to have their operations ceased, unless the fear was well-founded and evidence was adduced that there exists a real chance of infection. For example, AIDS is an infectious disease and if Evercare wished to open a new facility to treat infected patients, you would have no legal remedy, as it is primarily transmitted to others through sexual, or other intimate, contact. However, if Evercare wished to treat patients with Ebola Virus Disease (hereinafter "Ebola") in the said facility, the courts may be more inclined to entertain your complaint.[36]

36 Nuisance

Ebola was first discovered in 1976 and the World Health Organization says more research is required to understand the risks of sexual transmission, which means that it would not be incorrect to hold that we are currently not fully apprised of all the necessary facts of this disease, including its transmission.[37] However, people can be infected by other humans[38] through direct contact with broken skin, blood, or touching an infected person's clothing provided the article of clothing is contaminated by said fluids. In fact, health care workers have been infected while treating patients, as have persons burying the decedent.

As of 2020, we do not thoroughly understand Ebola, and therefore, its treatment in a facility in the vicinity of other human beings would perhaps be a nuisance. However, this is subject to change when advances are made to medical knowledge so that we can treat infected patients without fear of transmission. Essentially, what must be understood is that whether the treatment of patients in a hospital with respect to infectious diseases is a nuisance will depend on the facts and circumstances of each case. Hence, I will provide no blanket statement as to whether said construction would be a nuisance. Nonetheless, in order to avoid legal problems, it is probably best to construct hospitals at a reasonable distance from residential areas.

Moreover, if the construction of a new wing at a hospital depreciates the value of nearby land owned by another, it is still insufficient to warrant an injunction. Let us eliminate the hospital and imagine that, for the preceding five years, you have owned an apartment in Bashundhara on the top floor of a seven-story building. You have leased the apartment to a tenant who has enjoyed an unimpeded view of the airport, which is approximately 15 kilometres away, so that he could see airplanes land and take-off. However, the adjoining landowner has decided to construct a ten-story building, which will certainly obstruct your tenant's view of the airport, and thus, he has left. You have found a new tenant, but she is unwilling to pay the requested amount in rent since she has no unobstructed view. As in, the value of your apartment has declined because of the development of your neighbour's property, but this depreciation is expected in our daily lives in a metropolitan city, and therefore, you would have no legal remedy. Similarly, a hospital's decision to construct a new building to treat infectious diseases on land owned by the hospital, but in close proximity to your residence, which results in your property being devalued, will not permit you to seek the help of courts, as it is not a nuisance, unless of course, the above elements are met.

While a hospital is, therefore, at liberty to carry on operations, what would happen if an apartment in Baridhara was rented to a woman known to be a prostitute, who would use the premises to entertain clients? Prostitution is legal in Bangladesh;[39] hence, you cannot seek the help of the criminal law. However, you may be able to have her desist from the activity by having it declared a nuisance even though the activity is occurring on her premises. In *Laws v Florinplace Ltd*,[40] residents successfully sought an injunction against a store in their neighbourhood that was selling hardcore

Nuisance   37

pornography videos. The court said that there can be nuisance where the use of the property, though legal, is an affront to the ordinary sensibilities of humans. As in, even if the woman carries on her activities discreetly, and though the activity is legal, its nature would be apparent, and if it offends society, a remedy can be sought.[41]

3.2 Public rights and private rights

Miller v Jackson[42]

People played cricket for 70 years at the Lintz Cricket Club (hereinafter "the Club"), which was located in the village of Lintz at County Durham and was built on land leased to the club owned by the National Coal Board (hereinafter "NCB"). The NCB also owned the adjacent property and sold it to the Stanley Urban District Council who further sold the land to George Wimpey for development of residential houses. One house was bought by John and Brenda Miller (hereinafter "the Millers"), which was approximately 100 feet away from the nearest batting pitch. Between 1972 and 1974, several balls have come onto their property and, when this occurred, players walked to the Millers' property to retrieve the ball, which irritated Mrs. Miller. She has said,

> When the balls come over, they the cricketers, either ring or come around in twos and threes and ask if they can have the ball back, and they never ask properly. They just ask if they can have the ball back, and that's it. They have been very rude, very arrogant and very ignorant, and very deceitful [...] to get away from any problems we make a point of going out on Wednesdays, Fridays and the weekends.

In 1975, at the beginning of the cricket season, the Club increased the height of its protective fence from 6 feet to 15 feet, and they could not raise it any higher due to strong winds. They also instructed batsmen to hit balls low for fours and to not hit sixes whatsoever. Despite such protective measures, a few balls still went over onto the Millers' property. In 1975, 13,326 balls were bowled, and of them, 120 were sixes. Of these sixes, only six went over the fence. In 1976, 15,696 balls were bowled, and of them, 160 were sixes and only nine went over the fence. A few of these balls have damaged the Millers' roof and the Club has offered to pay all expenses with respect to repairs. Furthermore, the Club has also offered to supply and fit unbreakable glass and shutters onto the Millers' residence and to fit a safety net over the latter's garden whenever cricket is being played.

Though the Club has taken extensive precautionary steps to ensure the Millers are not disturbed, Mrs. Miller seeks an injunction to stop the Club's operations. In dismissing her claim, the court has said,

> I would, therefore, adopt this test: is the use by the cricket club of this ground for playing cricket a reasonable use of it? To my mind it is a

38 Nuisance

most reasonable use. Just consider the circumstances. For over 70 years the game of cricket has been played on this ground the great benefit of the community as a whole, and to the injury of none. No one could suggest that it was a nuisance to the neighbouring owners simply because an enthusiastic batsman occasionally hit a ball out of the ground for six to the approval of the admiring onlookers. Then I would ask: does it suddenly become a nuisance because one of the neighbours chooses to build a house on the very edge of the ground, in such a position that it may well be struck by the ball on the rare occasion when there is a hit for six? To my mind the answer is plainly No. The building of the house does not convert the playing of cricket into a nuisance when it was not so before. If an insofar as any damage is caused to the house or anyone in it, it is because of the position in which it was built [...]

[N]owadays it is a matter of balancing the conflicting interests of the two neighbours. That was made clear by Lord Wright in *Sedleigh-Denfield v O'Callagan*, when he said: "A balance has to be maintained between the right of the occupier to do what he likes with his own and the right of his neighbour not to be interfered with." In this case it is our task to balance the right of the cricket club to continue playing cricket on their cricket ground, as against the right of the householder not to be interfered with. On taking the balance, I would give priority to the right of the cricket club to continue playing cricket on the ground, as they have done for the last 70 years. It takes precedence over the right of the newcomer to sit in his garden undisturbed. After all he bought the house four years ago in mid-summer when the cricket season was at its height. He might have guessed that there was a risk that a hit for six might possibly land on his property.

Bamford v Turnley[43]

Mr. Turnley made a kiln on his land to make (with the use of fire) bricks, which generated noxious fumes that carried onto Mr. Bamford's land, even though the kilns were placed as far away as possible from the latter's property. The smoke interfered with Mr. Bamford's enjoyment of his property, as it made him and his servants ill. Therefore, he sought an injunction to prohibit Mr. Turnley's activities. However, Mr. Turnley contends that since he made bricks for the public benefit, which would be used to make roads and houses, his activity is not a nuisance. In finding for the plaintiff, the court said,

But it is said that [...] it is lawful because it is for the public benefit. Now, in the first place, that law to my mind is a bad one which, for the public benefit, inflicts loss on an individual without compensation. But further, with great respect, I think this consideration misapplied in this and in many other cases. The public consists of all the individuals of it, and a thing is only for the public benefit when it is productive of good to those individuals on the balance of loss and gain to all. So that if all the loss and all the gain were borne and received by one individual, he on the whole would be a gainer. But whenever this is the case – whenever a thing is for the public benefit, properly understood – the loss to the individuals of the public who lose will bear compensation out of the gains of those who gain. It is for the public benefit there should be railways, but it would not be unless the gain of having the railway was sufficient to compensate the loss occasioned by the use of the land required for its site; and accordingly no one thinks it would be right to take an individual's land without compensation to make a railway.

Sturges v Bridgman[44]

Mr. Bridgman, a confectioner by profession, lives in a house on Wimpole Street. The back of the house contained a kitchen with two large mortars where meat and other products for his business were pounded for the past 20 years. Mr. Sturges is a physician who also occupies a house on Wimpole Street. The back of his house had a garden, which was contiguous to Mr. Bridgman's backyard. Mr. Sturges recently constructed a consulting-room on his garden (where, again, his property meets Mr. Bridgman's) for private practice, but is greatly disturbed by the noise generated by Mr. Bridgman's mortars. Therefore, he seeks an injunction to have Mr. Bridgman's operations ceased. In finding for the plaintiff, the court said,

> It is said that if this principle is applied in cases like the present, and were carried out to its logical consequences, it would result in the most serious practical inconveniences, for a man might go – say into the midst of the tanneries of Bermondsey, or into any other locality devoted to a particular trade or manufacture of a noisy or unsavoury character, and, by building a private residence upon a vacant piece of land, put a stop to such trade or manufacture altogether. The case also is put of a blacksmith's forge built away from all habitations, but to which, in course of time, habitations approach. We do not think that either of these hypothetical cases presents any real difficulty. As regards the first, it may be answered that whether anything is a nuisance or not is a question to be determined, not merely by an abstract consideration of the thing itself, but in reference to its circumstances; what would be a nuisance in Belgrave Square would not necessarily be so in Bermondsey; and where a locality is devoted to a particular trade or manufacture carried on by the traders or manufacturers in a particular and established manner not constituting a public nuisance, Judges and juries would be justified in finding, and may be trusted to find, that the trade or manufacture so carried on in that locality is not a private or actionable wrong. As regards the blacksmith's forge, that is really an idem per idem case with the present. It would be on the one hand in a very high degree unreasonable and undesirable that there should be a right of action for acts which are not in the present condition of the adjoining land, and possibly never will be any annoyance or inconvenience to either its owner or occupier; and it would be on the other hand in an equally degree unjust,

40 *Nuisance*

and, from a public point of view, inexpedient that the use and value of the adjoining land should, for all time and under all circumstances, be restricted and diminished by reason of the continuance of acts incapable of physical interruption, and which the law gives no power to prevent. The smith in the case supposed might protect himself by taking a sufficient curtilage to ensure what he does from being at any time an annoyance to his neighbour, but the neighbour himself would be powerless in the matter. Individual cases of hardship may occur in the strict carrying out of the principle upon which we found our judgment, but the negation of the principle would lead even more to individual hardship, and would at the same time produce a prejudicial effect upon the development of land for residential purposes.

Notes

The reason my commentary succeeds three cases, as opposed to one, is because the principles of the cases must be discussed in tandem. In *Bamford* and *Sturges*, private rights prevailed, as Mr. Turnley was ordered to stop manufacturing bricks and Mr. Bridgman was ordered to stop using his mortars for commercial purposes, respectively. However, in *Miller*, private rights yielded to the public interest and Lintz Cricket Club was allowed to operate. The question that arises is, "why"?

The guiding principle of the courts was the pressing need to strike a balance between public and private rights. For the sake of convenience, I shall discuss the cases in *seriatim*. Firstly, in *Miller*, the court found that between 1975 and 1976, only 5.3% of balls struck as sixes went over the fence. Additionally, the Club did everything possible to ensure that the Millers were not adversely affected from cricket being played at the Club. More importantly, the Club operated for 70 years without disturbing anyone and the Millers bought a house nearby in the middle of summer, which is the peak of the cricket season. This means that, firstly, since the Club was there first, it has *more of a right* to continue playing cricket than the Millers do in having its activities stopped; and secondly, since the Millers bought a house nearby the Club, they knew, or ought to have known, that cricket would be played, which means they tacitly consented to a bit of disturbance.

Suppose you own a plot of land in Nasirabad, Chittagong, and have constructed a ten-story building. On the rooftop, you have placed a basketball rim and have told prospective tenants that you will play basketball between 4:00 pm and 6:00 pm on a daily basis. Therefore, when tenants move in and are disturbed by the noise, they would be precluded from bringing an action in nuisance because they were already aware that you would play. However, this does not mean that you can play basketball at 10:00 pm. Rather, since you have stipulated the time, you should play within that designated time, as otherwise an injunction may be granted.

Similarly, as I have briefly mentioned above, when the Millers purchased their house, they knew that cricket would be played. As in, if I see an empty field and a cricket pitch within that field, the natural and reasonable presumption would be that people have played cricket and there is a likelihood that they will do so in the future. For example, Mirpur DOHS has a few fields where people play football, cricket, and badminton throughout the year. One such field is surrounded by apartments on three sides, and a mosque on the fourth. It would not be unreasonable to assume that, while playing cricket, a few balls have gone over onto another's property and it may have caused damage. However, residents would not have a case against the players, as they knew, or ought to have known, that there was a probability of this happening. Similarly, if you are driving by the field and a cricket ball strikes and shatters your windshield when it was hit by a batsman, you would also not be able to seek the help of the court as you knew, or ought to have known, that this could occur.

Let me use another example. Kurmitola Golf Club (hereinafter "KGC") has been at its present location since 1966 and it is nearby Banani DOHS, which is a residential area.[45] It would not be incorrect to assume that a novice golfer may have hit a ball that found its way onto a land owner's property – perhaps breaking a window or injuring someone. However, the person that rents, or buys, an apartment in the vicinity of KGC will not be successful in stopping golfers from playing, as it will be assumed that he knew, or ought to have known, that such incidents could happen before he moved in; that is, if he did not wish to be disturbed by the rare occasions of a golfball interfering with his property, he should have bought a house where the probability of interference was *de minimis* – e.g. at a part of Banani DOHS away from KGC or at a place outside of Banani DOHS altogether. It is also important to note that the tenant, or landlord, does not need to expressly consent to such interference, as the law will imply consent through the act of the tenant moving in, or the landlord purchasing the property, or to speak of the example in the preceding paragraph, the person driving by the field at Mirpur DOHS.

I am not unaware that this may lead to the confusion that a person would not be able to acquire a remedy if someone intentionally throws a golf or cricket ball and destroys his property. However, this is not true. In the examples I have used, while a person has intentionally hit a ball, they have not done so *with the intention of destroying your property or injuring you*. Rather, that person has hit the ball in order to play the game and the injury you sustained was inadvertent. Therefore, these cases do not preclude you from bringing an action against someone who has *intentionally* caused damage by, for example, aiming and deliberately throwing a ball, which breaks your apartment's window or injures you.

However, there is a crucial point for us to understand. The court's decision to not issue an injunction is not solely based on the fact that the Club operated for 70 years without any complaints, but also because of the low probability of cricket balls (5.3%) going over the fence and the Club's decision to increase the fence's height to 15 feet. This means they took all the precautionary measures that are legally required.[46] Furthermore, this intimates that KGC and the field at Mirpur DOHS, where football, cricket, and

42 Nuisance

badminton is played, must also build protective fences so that balls do not frequently leave the field and land on another's property.

On a slightly different note, while you consented – either expressly or impliedly – to a modicum of cricket balls coming onto your property at Mirpur DOHS, what if the field is used regularly to host concerts until 11:00 pm? Would you still be barred from bringing an action in nuisance? In *Kennaway v Thompson*,[47] Mary Kennaway inherited land, which was near a lake, from her father. On the lake, a club organized motor boat races and waterskiing since the 1960s. Kennaway was fully aware of the club's activities, but decided to construct a house on the land in 1969. However, she could not enjoy the property, as the noise from racing and waterskiing became louder and more frequent; thus, she sought an injunction against the club to stop the excessive noise and keep its activities restricted to specific times. The court awarded an injunction and provided, (1) only one large boat race can occur annually over a period of three days, (2) the maximum number of boats simultaneously in the water can be six, and (3) the maximum level of noise can be 75 decibels on all other occasions. Therefore, to put *Kennaway* into the perspective of Mirpur DOHS, even though you perhaps consent to a few cricket balls landing on your property, you do not consent to excessive noise or excessive interference with your property from concerts.

Secondly, while public rights prevailed in *Miller*, private rights triumphed in *Bamford* and *Sturges*.[48] In *Sturges*, the court ruled against Mr. Bridgman because he was carrying on a commercial activity in a residential area. Simply put, if a person carries on commercial activity in a residential area, it will be declared a nuisance even if the commercial activity existed first. Unlike *Miller*, where the court emphasized on who was there first and decided against the Millers because the Club had operated for 70 years and the Millers moved in afterwards, this does not matter in a residential area, as a commercial activity will not be permitted to continue. For example, imagine that a carpenter rented an apartment at Mirpur DOHS, which is a residential area. He used the apartment to manufacture chairs to sell to the public and he has done so for the past 15 years. Recently, you have moved in as his neighbour and the noise generated from his apartment is interfering with the enjoyment of your property – perhaps preventing sound sleep. You can seek an injunction to prohibit the carpenter's work on the grounds that he should not carry on commercial activity in a residential area. Even if you knowingly rent an apartment next to the carpenter, it is no defence for him to claim that you consented to the noise as you knew that he would carry on such activities inside his apartment. Similarly, though I shall not dedicate much time to this case, in *Bamford*, Mr. Turnley was also carrying on a commercial activity in a residential area, and therefore, Mr. Bamford was successful in seeking an injunction.

Antrim Truck Centre Ltd v Ontario (Minister of Transportation)[49]

The Camerons owned and operated the Antrim Truck Centre Ltd, which is a truck shop on Highway 17, in the province of Ontario. In 2004, for reasons of public safety, Ontario decided to construct Highway 417.

Nuisance 43

This rerouted traffic away from Highway 17 and had the effect of putting the Camerons' shop out of business, as clients could reach Antrim only through a circuitous route. Therefore, the Camerons seek damages under the *Expropriations Act*, alleging that the project has substantially interfered with the enjoyment of their property.

In finding for the Camerons, the court balanced the private rights of the Camerons against the public interest in having roads constructed. The court said,

> The main question here is how reasonableness should be assessed when the activity causing the interference is carried out by a public authority for the greater public good. As in other private nuisance cases, the reasonableness of the interference must be assessed in light of all of the relevant circumstances. The focus of that balancing exercise, however, is on whether the interference is such that it would be unreasonable in all of the circumstances to require the claimant to suffer it without compensation.
>
> In the traditional law of private nuisance, the courts assess, in broad terms, whether the interference is unreasonable by balancing the gravity of the harm against the utility of the defendant's conduct in all of the circumstances [...] In relation to the gravity of the harm, the courts have considered factors such as the severity of the interference, the character of the neighbourhood and the sensitivity of the plaintiff [...]
>
> The first point is that there is a distinction between the utility of the conduct, which focuses on its purpose, such as construction of a highway, and the nature of the defendant's conduct, which focuses on how that purpose is carried out. Generally, the focus in nuisance is on whether the interference suffered by the claimant is unreasonable, not on whether the nature of the defendant's conduct is unreasonable [...]
>
> The nature of the defendant's conduct is not, however, an irrelevant consideration. Where the conduct is either malicious or careless, that will be a significant factor in the reasonableness analysis [...] Moreover, where the defendant can establish that his or her conduct was reasonable, that can be a relevant consideration, particularly in cases where a claim is brought against a public authority. A finding of reasonable conduct will not, however, necessarily preclude a finding of liability. The editors of *Fleming's The Law of Torts* put this point well [...]

> > [U]nreasonableness in nuisance relates primarily to the character and extent of the harm caused rather than that threatened [...] [T]he "duty" not to expose one's neighbours to a nuisance is not necessarily discharged by exercising reasonable care or even all possible care. In that sense, therefore, liability is strict. At the same time, evidence that the defendant has taken all possible precaution to avoid harm is not immaterial, because it has a bearing on whether he subjected the plaintiff to an unreasonable interference, and is decisive in those cases where the offensive activity is carried on under

44   *Nuisance*

statutory authority [...] [I]n nuisance it is up to the defendant to exculpate himself, once a *prima facie* infringement has been established, for example, by proving that his own use was "natural" and not unreasonable.

The second point is that the utility of the defendant's conduct is especially significant in claims against public authorities. Even where a public authority is involved, however, the utility of its conduct is always considered in light of the other relevant factors in the reasonableness analysis; it is not, by itself, an answer to the reasonableness inquiry. Moreover, in the reasonableness analysis, the severity of the harm and the public utility of the impugned activity are not equally weighted considerations. If they were, an important public purpose would always override even very significant harm caused by carrying it out. As the editors of *Fleming's The Law of Torts* put it, the utility consideration "must not be pushed too far [...] [A] defendant cannot simply justify his infliction of great harm upon the plaintiff by urging that a greater benefit to the public at large has accrued from his conduct" [...]

Generally speaking, the acts of a public authority will be of significant utility. If simply put in the balance with the private interest, public utility will generally outweigh even very significant interferences with the claimant's land. That sort of simple balancing of public utility against private harm undercuts the purpose of providing compensation for injurious affection. That purpose is to ensure that individual members of the public do not have to bear a disproportionate share of the cost of procuring the public benefit. This purpose is fulfilled, however, if the focus of the reasonableness analysis is kept on whether it is reasonable for the individual to bear the interference without compensation, not on whether it was reasonable for the statutory authority to undertake the work. In short, the question is whether the damage flowing from the interference should be properly viewed as a cost of "running the system" and therefore borne by the public generally, or as the type of interference that should properly be accepted by an individual as part of the cost of living in organized society [...]

Of course, not every substantial interference arising from a public work will be unreasonable. The reasonableness analysis should favour the public authority where the harm to property interests, considered in light of its severity, the nature of the neighbourhood, its duration, the sensitivity of the plaintiff and other relevant factors, is such that the harm cannot reasonably be viewed as more than the claimant's fair share of the costs associated with providing a public benefit. This outcome is particularly appropriate where the public authority has made all reasonable efforts to reduce the impact of its works on neighbouring properties. [...]

To sum up on this point, my view is that in considering the reasonableness of an interference that arises from an activity that furthers the public good, the question is whether, in light of all of the circumstances,

Nuisance 45

it is unreasonable to expect the claimant to bear the interference without compensation.

Notes

Similar to *Fontainebleau*, *Miller*, *Bamford*, and *Sturges*, a balance was struck between public and private rights. If the government constructs roads, it is doing so for the benefit of the public. However, this does not mean that they can inflict injury upon a person without compensating him. For example, if the construction of the Jamuna Bridge led to a ferry operator becoming insolvent, then, though it facilitates road-travel between Dhaka and the northern part of Bangladesh, the operator would nevertheless need to be compensated. Generally, whenever the government constructs roads, bridges, and the like, it will benefit the public, which means the utility of the government's conduct will usually outweigh any injury suffered by an individual. However, if this results in unreasonable interference with one's interests, then the government's action can be declared a nuisance and damages can be sought.

We have already learned that courts consider the characteristics of a neighbourhood, the sensitivity of the claimant, and the degree of injury sustained in deciding whether an activity is a nuisance.[50] In *Antrim*, we find that courts will also consider the duration of the injury to the plaintiff in deciding whether an activity is a nuisance. Does this mean that the construction of the 20.1-kilometre Mass Rapid Transit (let us assume it is being constructed by the government) is a nuisance because residents in the vicinity of construction are subject to copious amounts of dust and noise? In *Andreae v Selfridge & Co Ltd* (hereinafter "*Andreae*"),[51] it was said,

> [W]hen one is dealing with temporary operations, such as demolition and rebuilding, everybody has to put up with a certain amount of discomfort, because operations of that kind cannot be carried on at all without a certain amount of noise and a certain amount of dust. Therefore, the rule with regard to interference must be read subject to this qualification [...] that in respect of operations of this character, such as demolition and building, if they are reasonably carried on and all proper and reasonable steps are taken to ensure that no undue inconvenience is caused to the neighbours, whether from noise, dust, or other reasons, the neighbours must put up with it.

Thus, to answer the question posed, premised on *Andreae*, it is not. What we must understand is that in *Antrim*, the plaintiff suffered a permanent injury, which could be remedied by an award of damages. Similarly, and by the same logic, if the injury is ephemeral, then there is a lower probability of him receiving compensation — in fact, due to *Appleby*, *Rogers*, *Miller*, and *Andreae*, he probably would have no remedy whatsoever.

As we are aware, courts will consider the characteristics of a neighbourhood. Therefore, a person living in Dhaka knows, or ought to know,

46   Nuisance

that the city may begin construction of bridges, roads, or buildings at any moment. This means that, prior to taking residence anywhere in the city, he has either explicitly or implicitly consented to being disturbed by noise, dust, or any other inconvenience that is reasonable under the circumstances. Nonetheless, there are times when construction, in general, could constitute nuisance.

Firstly, though a resident of Dhaka consented to disturbance from construction of the MRT, he has not agreed to be disturbed *at all times*. As in, if construction is carried on at 1:00 am for a week, or a month, or several months, then a resident could seek the help of the courts in having it limited to a specified time – e.g. 8:00 am to 6:00 pm – but perhaps not have it stopped altogether.[52] Hence, even though construction is carried on for the benefit of the public, it cannot be unreasonable. As in, it is reasonable to expect that a resident near the MRT has consented to be disturbed by the corollary of construction, which could range from higher levels of noise and dust to taking an alternative route home because traffic has been rerouted. However, it is unreasonable to expect that he has consented to the aforementioned disturbances at 1:00 am, as we generally dedicate that time to sleep.[53]

Let us assume, though, that everyone nearby construction works from 8:00 pm to 4:00 am and that is the reason construction was carried on until 1:00 am. If a resident moves out and another, who works from 8:00 am to 4:00 pm, moves in, though he may feel disturbed, he would have no remedy, as he knew, or ought to have known, that construction in this neighbourhood is carried on at unconventional hours. Keep in mind that this would also mean that construction would remain stopped throughout the day, as that would be the time when residents would rest.[54] As in, in this particular neighbourhood, its characteristic would allow construction at hours different from others.

Secondly, as was identified in *Rogers*, courts will also consider the sensitivity of the claimant. Since, however, I have scrupulously probed this element in my text earlier, I shall eschew doing so again. Briefly put, though, even if a resident is allergic to dust and the construction of the MRT is causing him "material discomfort," he would not be able to get an injunction.[55] As in, even if he is extensively injured by construction (perhaps suffering a heart attack because he is hypersensitive to noise), it would not be a nuisance.

Lastly, and perhaps most importantly, courts will consider the duration of injury, which means exactly what common sense dictates – for how long will the plaintiff suffer the injury/for how long has he suffered the injury? For example, the construction of the MRT began on 26 June 2016, with a portion slated to be completed by 2019 (Uttara North to Agargaon), and it will be fully operational in 2020 (Uttara North to Motijheel).[56] For railway that is 20.1 kilometres, four years can be accepted as reasonable. Therefore, the resident suffering during this time would have no remedy. However, if construction of the same MRT lasted 20 years, there is a probability that it could be declared a nuisance.[57]

3.3 Public nuisance

A public nuisance is anything that interferes with the rights of the community. Unlike a private nuisance, it is not enough that it affects only one individual even if that person is prevented from using and/or enjoying his property.[58] However, it is also not necessary that the entire community is affected. Rather, what is required is that it interferes with persons that are exercising a public right.[59] Therefore, when a river is polluted and it affects the rights of riparian owners, it is a private nuisance,[60] but if it kills the fish, it then becomes public.[61] However, similar to a private nuisance, it is necessary that the interference is substantial and offends the reasonable man. Therefore, a bad smell on the highway that is objectionable to one or two persons,[62] or blocking access to a river or a road that people could not use anyway are not public nuisances.[63]

It is often said that for nuisance to be considered public, it must also be recurring. To further simplify, this means that the activity must happen for a considerable period of time.[64] Therefore, the keeping of a hog-pen,[65] or keeping diseased animals,[66] or providing a premises for indecent exhibitions,[67] or bad odours, smoke, dust, and vibrations that interfere with public comfort have been held to be public nuisances.[68] Moreover, if the harm is minimal and the nature of the conduct is reasonable, then a claim for nuisance would not succeed. For example, if a highway is temporarily obstructed due to a moving house, it is not a public nuisance.[69] However, shooting fireworks in the streets, obstructing a highway, or creating a condition that makes travel unsafe have been held to be public nuisances.[70] In short, a public nuisance is any invasion into the interests of another who is exercising a public right, and if it affects the community at large, even if the activity occurs only once, or multiple times, so long as the harm it creates is more than minimal, it is a public nuisance.

Cincinnati Railroad Company v The Commonwealth[71]

On 16 October 1880, the defendant intentionally parked his handcar on an intersection where a track and road cross, creating an obstruction, for which horses and others using the road could not pass. Ruling it to be a public nuisance, the court said,

> A public road is a way established and adopted by proper authority for the use of the public, and over which every person has a right to pass, and to use for all purposes of travel or transportation to which it is adapted and devoted; "and though any temporary use of a highway or street that is rendered absolutely necessary from the necessities of trade or erection of buildings that do not unnecessarily or unreasonably obstruct the same is lawful, and temporary obstructions arising from accidental causes do not render a person liable for a nuisance, provided no unreasonable or unnecessary delay is permitted, still no cause whatever will justify any unreasonable use of a public road or street" […]

48 *Nuisance*

To secure the free use and enjoyment of a public road, it is necessary that it be always open and unobstructed. The offence of obstructing it is not therefore determined necessarily by the length of time the thing that worketh hurt, inconvenience, or damage to the public continues, or by the number of times it may be repeated; nor is it necessary, in order to constitute the offence, that actual injury be suffered by any person. It is no more necessary that a public road shall be repeatedly, continuously, or habitually obstructed by a person to render him guilty of the offence of a public nuisance than that any other violation of law shall be in order to make the offence complete. But, subject to the exemptions arising from absolute necessity and accidental causes before mentioned, the offence is committed when by actual obstruction or impediment a public road is rendered by any person inconvenient or dangerous to pass.

To secure the reasonable and proper use and enjoyment of the public road by the public, and of the railroad by its owners, each must be required to observe the maxim of law that every person is restricted against using his property to the prejudice of others. And as it is plain that the railroad and the public road cannot at the crossing place both be occupied and used at the same time, even partially, the law, for manifest reasons, makes it the duty of persons traveling upon the public road to stop until an approaching train or car passes that point. But the public, on the other hand, is entitled to the unobstructed use of the public road at the crossing place when it is not actually occupied, or about to be occupied, by moving trains or cars.

To concede to the owners of railways the right to stop their trains or cars at the place the public road crosses the railroad would not merely render the latter inconvenient and dangerous, but, in many cases, useless. Not even business necessities will authorize the owners of railroads to thus obstruct the public roads.

Notes

From *Cincinnati*, we should know, firstly, that a public road is a highway that every member of the public has the right to use. Secondly, because it is a public road, it must always remain open and unobstructed, unless it has otherwise been closed on grounds that are reasonable under the circumstances. Lastly, while everyone has the right to use a public highway, they cannot do it in a manner that interferes with another's rights. Against this backdrop, a question apt to Bangladesh can be asked – since copious amounts of ink has been spilled expressing discontent about halting traffic for dignitary movement in Dhaka, which makes life in a congested city further unbearable,[72] does this amount to nuisance? No, but under certain circumstances, it could.

3.4 Public roads and balancing of rights

Though public roads must remain open and unobstructed, there are exceptions. Firstly, if a vehicle collides with another at a busy intersection, which

Nuisance 49

causes gridlock traffic, this would not amount to nuisance, as the obstruction is not intentional. However, if the driver stops his vehicle in the middle of the road and goes to buy a packet of cigarettes thereby causing congestion, this would be a nuisance. Similarly, if a driver momentarily stops his vehicle to let passengers alight, this would not be a nuisance, but if he parks his vehicle outside Pink City preventing others from passing, this would be a nuisance.[73]

Secondly, traffic, under section 41 of *The Road Transport Act, 2018*, can be halted or diverted by the police, or any other institution delegated with the authority to regulate traffic. This can happen for a host of reasons that can range from construction to emergencies to letting dignitaries pass.[74] For example, imagine a conflagration at a building, and, for public safety, police divert traffic away from the site. Even if this aggravates congestion and interferes with one exercising a public right, the safety of the public outweighs the public right to use the road. Essentially, this means that the police are empowered to stop traffic, but their authority is not plenary. As in, simply because something is permitted by statute does not mean that it cannot be prohibited or become a nuisance. For example, a public servant is allowed to associate with whomever he pleases, but if he engages in malversation, he can be imprisoned or fined or both.[75] That is to say, as we have learned from *Miller*, *Bamford*, and *Sturges*, a balance must be struck between public and private rights, or between two competing private rights, or two competing public rights. This means that one's right to use a public road is not absolute and it must be balanced against other interests in society, and in the case of stopping traffic to let dignitaries pass, the safety of the principal.

3.5 Reasonableness in halting traffic

Police stopping traffic to let dignitaries pass is not a nuisance unless it amounts to an "unreasonable use of a public road." In society, while we accept that our rights to use a public road is not absolute and that some receive greater protection from law enforcement than others, this also means that a police's right to close a road and a dignitary's need for safety are not absolute either. That is to say, there must be a balance between (a) the right to use a public road, and (b) a dignitary's need for safety. Therefore, if a road has been blocked for 15 to 30 minutes, or even an hour, it would not be a nuisance because we must accept such disturbances in a city.[76] However, if traffic is stopped for five to six hours, it may amount to nuisance because that would be unreasonable. Moreover, what if a person suffered a heart attack and requires immediate medical attention, but he reaches the hospital two hours later because he was stuck in traffic, which was stopped for dignitary movement? Furthermore, the doctor said that there would have been an 80% chance of survival had he received treatment an hour ago.[77] Here, stopping traffic would certainly constitute nuisance.[78]

Overall, what should become abundantly clear is that whether a private or a public right, a balance must always be struck so that one person's right

50 Nuisance

does not always prevail at the expense of another's. This allows the law of nuisance to maintain peace and harmony in society and also meet the objective of tort law.

3.6 Remedies

Shelfer v City of London Electrical Lighting Co[79]

Meux's Brewery Company (hereinafter "Meaux's Brewery") owned the Waterman's Arms, which was a house that they leased to Shelfer. The City of London Electrical Lighting Company (hereinafter "London ELC") had powerful engines on land near Meux's Brewery that was used to carry on its work. However, the noise and vibrations from the engines became unbearable for Shelfer. In fact, the vibrations of the engines damaged the structure of the house Shelfer leased. Therefore, Meux's Brewery and Shelfer bring an action for damages and seek an injunction to have London ELC's activity stopped. Awarding an injunction, the court said,

> So again, whether the case be for a mandatory injunction or to restrain a continuing nuisance, the appropriate remedy may be damages in lieu of an injunction, assuming a case for an injunction to be made out. In my opinion, it may be stated as a good working rule that (i) if the injury to the plaintiff's legal right is small; (ii) and is one which is capable of being estimated in money; (iii) and is one which can be adequately compensated by a small money payment; (iv) and the case is one in which it would be oppressive to the defendant to grant an injunction, damages in lieu of an injunction may be awarded. If these four requirements are found in combination in a case, then damages in substitution for an injunction may be given. There may also be cases in which, though the four above-mentioned requirements exist, the defendant, by his conduct, as, for instance, hurrying up his buildings so as, if possible, to avoid an injunction, or otherwise acting with a reckless disregard to the plaintiff's rights, has disentitled himself from asking that damages may be assessed in substitution for an injunction. It is impossible to lay down any rule as to what, under the differing circumstances of each case, constitute either small injury, or what can be estimated in money, or what is a small money payment or an adequate compensation, or what would be oppressive to the defendant. This must be left to the good sense of the tribunal which deals with each case as it comes up for adjudication.

Spur Industries, Inc v Del E. Webb Development Co[80]

Spur Industries, Inc (hereinafter "Spur") operated a cattle feedlot in an agricultural district that was approximately 15 miles west of Phoenix, Arizona. Del E. Webb Development Co (hereinafter "Del Webb") purchased land near Spur and began developing a retirement community named Sun City. As Del Webb's development grew, it came closer to Spur's feedlot, who was now feeding between 20,000 and 30,000 cattle. Even though Spur practised

Nuisance 51

good housekeeping, 30,000 cattle produced about one million pounds of wet manure per day (or, 35 to 40 pounds per cattle per day), and the smell and flies from the manure prevented Del Webb's sale of property. Additionally, the persons who bought property in Sun City were also unable to enjoy outdoor living. Therefore, Del Webb seeks an injunction to enjoin Spur's operations. Granting the injunction, the court said,

> There was no indication in the instant case at the time Spur and its predecessors located in western Maricopa County that a new city would spring up, full-blown, alongside the feeding operation and that the developer of that city would ask the court to order Spur to move because of the new city. Spur is required to move not because of any wrongdoing on the part of Spur, but because of a proper and legitimate regard of the courts for the rights and interests of the public.
>
> Del Webb, on the other hand, is entitled to the relief prayed for (a permanent injunction), not because Webb is blameless, but because of the damage to the people who have been encouraged to purchase homes in Sun City. It does not equitably or legally follow, however, that Webb, being entitled to the injunction, is then free of any liability to Spur if Webb has in fact been the cause of the damage Spur has sustained. It does not seem harsh to require a developer, who has taken advantage of the lesser land values in a rural area as well as the availability of large tracts of land on which to build and develop a new town or city in the area, to indemnify those who are forced to leave as a result.
>
> Having brought people to the nuisance to the foreseeable detriment of Spur, Webb must indemnify Spur for a reasonable amount of the cost of moving or shutting down. It should be noted that this relief to Spur is limited to a case wherein a developer has, with foreseeability, brought into a previously agricultural or industrial area the population which makes necessary the granting of an injunction against a lawful business and for which the business has no adequate relief.
>
> It is therefore the decision of this court that the matter be remanded to the trial court for a hearing upon the damages sustained by the defendant Spur as a reasonable and direct result of the granting of the permanent injunction. Since the result of the appeal may appear novel and both sides have obtained a measure of relief, it is ordered that each side will bear its own costs.

Notes

While the usual remedy for nuisance is an injunction, as per *Shelfer*, damages, instead of an injunction, can be awarded if the following four conditions are met: the injury (1) suffered is small, (2) can be estimated by money, (3) can be properly compensated by money, and (4) if an injunction is granted, it would be oppressive to the party carrying on the activity. Additionally, if the event that causes the injury did not happen more than once, then damages, again, would be the right remedy.[81] For example, recall that

52 Nuisance

if you buy or rent an apartment in Mirpur DOHS close to a field known to be used for playing cricket, you are held to implicitly consent to higher levels of noise during certain hours of the day. Imagine that during a game, a player strikes a ball so hard that it breaks your window, which would cost about ৳15,000 to replace.

Firstly, the sum of ৳15,000 is small. However, this does not mean that only if the injury is ৳15,000 or less will a court award damages instead of an injunction. Therefore, so long as the amount is small, which can be a different amount in different jurisdictions, damages can be awarded, provided the other three conditions are met. Secondly, as I have done without difficulty, the quantum of damage can be estimated by money, and thirdly, since the injury can be estimated by money, the aggrieved party can also be accordingly compensated through a money payment. Lastly, prohibiting others from playing cricket would be oppressive because (1) you knew, or ought to have known, that cricket would be played, and (2) since the injury can be compensated by money, damages can be awarded instead of an injunction.[82] However, how do you calculate the amount of damage to be compensated by money if a person is disturbed by noise or smell? The obvious answer is you probably cannot, and therefore, it is in those instances that injunctions are awarded.

Recall from *Polsue* and *Canada Paper* that even if a person lives near a commercial area, in which case he is held to have impliedly consented to higher levels of noise and other similar activities, he can bring an action under nuisance if a new activity generates noise, smell, or some other analogous disturbance that did not exist before. As in, no person's right is absolute, and as I have tried to explicate throughout this chapter, the law of nuisance tries to strike a balance between competing rights. Similarly, in *Spur Industries*, even though the feedlot was there first, the complainants were successful in having the business relocated.

Notes

1 *The Penal Code*, 1860 (Bangladesh), Act No XLV of 1860, s 268 [*Penal Code*], which stipulates, "A person is guilty of a public nuisance who does any act or is guilty of an illegal omission which causes any common injury, danger or annoyance to the public or to the people in general who dwell or occupy property in the vicinity, or which must necessarily cause injury, obstruction, dangers or annoyance to persons who may have occasion to use any public right. A common nuisance is not excused on the ground that it causes some convenience or advantage."

2 For a similar case, see Nathaniel Rich, "The Lawyer Who Became DuPont's Worst Nightmare" *The New York Times* (6 January 2016), online: The New York Times Company https://www.nytimes.com/2016/01/10/magazine/the-lawyer-who-became-duponts-worst-nightmare.html. [16/03/2021].

3 Section 290 of the *Penal Code*, *supra* note 1, provides, "Whoever commits a public nuisance in any case not otherwise punishable by this Code, shall be punished with fine which may extend to two hundred taka."

4 In fact, it is distantly derived from the Latin word "*nocumentum*," at footnote 7 of William L Prosser, *Handbook of The Law of Torts*, 4th ed (St. Paul, Minnesota: West Publishing Co, 1971) at 571 [Prosser].

Nuisance 53

5 *Ibid*; Also see *Carroll v New York Pie Baking Co*, [1926] 215 AD 240, 1926 NY App Div LEXIS 10942.

6 William L Prosser, "Private Action for Public Nuisance" (1966) 52:6 Va L Rev 997 at 997 [Prosser: PAPN].

7 *Ibid* at 999; See generally John W Salmond, *Law of Torts*, 16th ed (London: Sweet & Maxwell, 1973).

8 *Appleby v Erie Tobacco Co*, [1910] OJ No 64, 22 OLR 533 [*Appleby*]; Also see Ernest J Weinrib, *Tort Law: Cases and Materials*, 4th ed (Toronto: Emond Montgomery Publications Limited, 2014) at 2–3 [Weinrib].

9 *Antrim Truck Centre Ltd v Ontario (Minister of Transportation)*, [2013] 1 SCR 594, [2013] SCJ No 13 [*Antrim*]; Also see Prosser, *supra* note 4 at 572–573.

10 *Walter v Selfe*, [1851] 20 LJ Ch 433, 64 ER 849.

11 See Robert Abrams & Val Washington, "The Misunderstood Law of Public Nuisance: A Comparison with Private Nuisance Twenty Years After *Boomer*" (1990) 54:2 Alb L Rev 359 and Ronald J Rychlak, "Common-Law Remedies for Environmental Wrongs: The Role of Private Nuisance" (1989) 59:3 Miss LJ 657.

12 See generally, *Canada Paper Company v Brown*, [1922] 63 SCR 243, [1922] SCJ No 7 [*Canada Paper*].

13 *Polsue and Alfieri Limited v Rushmer*, [1904–7] All ER Rep 586, [1907] AC 121 [*Polsue*]; Also see *ibid*.

14 See generally *Canada Paper*, *supra* note 12. The opposite would likewise be true. That is to say, if there is a tennis court in your neighbourhood where people play between 3:00 pm to 9:00 pm, and suddenly people began playing tennis until 2:00 am, which generated loud noise, this could be declared a nuisance and an injunction limiting the time of play could be ordered.

15 *Shelfer v City of London Electric Co*, [1891–4] All ER Rep 838, [1895] 1 Ch 287 [*Shelfer*].

16 *Rogers v Elliot*, [1888] 146 Mass 349, 1888 Mass LEXIS 260 [*Rogers*]; Also see Weinrib, *supra* note 8 at 4–7.

17 *Antrim*, *supra* note 9. See Chapter 5 for an exhaustive discussion on what constitutes a "reasonable person"; Also see Prosser, *supra* note 4 at 149–166.

18 *The Constitution of the People's Republic of Bangladesh* (Bangladesh), Act of 1972, ss 2A and 8 [*Constitution of Bangladesh*]. Section 2A stipulates, "The state religion of the Republic is Islam, but the State shall ensure equal status and equal right in the practice of the Hindu, Buddhist, Christian and other religions." This also means that if a church, synagogue, or a temple generates noise in exercise of religion, then others would be unable to complain even if they (the aggrieved party) are the majority in a neighbourhood.

   The relevant part of section 8 states, "The principles of nationalism, socialism, democracy and secularism, together with the principles derived from those as set out in this Part, shall constitute the fundamental principles of state policy."

19 *Miller v Jackson*, [1977] 3 All ER 778, [1977] QB 966 [*Miller*].

20 *Kennaway v Thompson*, [1980] 3 All ER 329, [1981] QB 88 [*Kennaway*].

21 *Laing v St. Thomas Dragway*, [2005] OJ No 254, [2005] ILR para G-1827 [*Laing*], where the court took into consideration that people sleep late on weekends, and therefore, church bells should not be rung until 9:00 am. However, though an injunction was granted in Australia, I do not see that a similar situation would transpire in Bangladesh. I am of the opinion that society would have to be made over in order for the court to order the Azan not be recited before a certain time on weekends even if people in Bangladesh, much like Australia, sleep late on weekends.

   Moreover, I feel compelled to say that my intention is not to offend the sensibilities of religion or society in Bangladesh. Rather, the purpose of this discussion is purely academic and to bring to attention common law doctrines, and if anyone is offended, it is wholly inadvertent.

54   Nuisance

22 *Hollywood Silver Fox Farm Ltd v Emmett*, [1936] 1 All ER 825, [1936] 2 KB 468 [*Hollywood Farm*].

23 *Ibid*. Also see *Antrim, supra* note 9. More on the principle of conditional enjoyment of one's property *infra*.

24 *Fontainebleau Hotel Corp v Forty-Five Twenty-Five, Inc*, [1959] 1 14 So 2d 357. See *Bury v Pope*, [1586] Cro Eliz 118, 74 ER 115, which is purportedly the first case that dealt with the issue of sunlight from neighbouring property.

25 *Reaver v Martin Theatres of Florida Inc*, [1951] 52 So 2d 682, 1951 Fla LEXIS 1351.

26 See generally Ralph Becker Jr, "Common Law Sun Rights: An Obstacle to Solar Heating and Cooling?" (1976) 3:1 J Contemp L 19, where he argues that a person should have the right to sunlight if it is for the purposes of solar heating and cooling.

27 *Prah v Maretti*, [1982] 321 NW 2d 182, 108 Wis 2d 223. Also see Lee J Hollis, "A Private Nuisance Remedy for Obstruction of Solar Access" (1983) 48:3 Mo L Rev 769.

28 *Hay v Cohoes Co*, [1849] 2 NY 159, 1849 NY LEXIS 5. Also see Weinrib, *supra* note 8 at 8-12; Jeff L Lewin, "Boomer and the American Law of Nuisance: Past, Present, and Future" (1990) 54:2 Alb L Rev 189; Franklin Gevurtz, "Obstruction of Sunlight as a Private Nuisance" (1977) 65:1 Cal L Rev 94.

29 See *T.H. Critelli Ltd v Lincoln Trust and Savings Co et al*, [1978] 20 OR (2D) 81, where, subscribing to *Denfield v O'Callaghan et al*, it was said, "A balance has to be maintained between the right of the occupier to do what he likes with his own, and the right of his neighbour not to be interfered with. It is impossible to give any precise or universal formula, but it may broadly be said that a useful test is perhaps what is reasonable according to the ordinary usages of mankind living in society, or more correctly in a particular society."

Putting up billboards on your property is an area of tort law that is not wholly clear, but courts have been generally reluctant to declare it as a nuisance, see Robert W Pearson, "Billboard Laws Today – Reaction or Solution" (1972) 24:1 Baylor L Rev 86. Nonetheless, whether you can post a billboard on your property will depend on city laws and whether it is a source of danger, an obstruction to motorists, and propriety, see generally *Thomas Cusack Co v Chicago*, [1917] 242 US 546, 1917 US LEXIS 2171, *Perlmutter v Greene*, [1932] 259 NY 327, 1932 NY LEXIS 945, *St. Louis Gunning Advertisement Co v St. Louis*, [1911] 235 Mo 99, 1911 Mo LEXIS 84, and *People v Wolf*, [1927] 220 AD 71, 220 NYS 656.

30 *Bradford Corporation v Pickles*, [1895–99] All ER Rep 984, [1895] AC 587 [*Bradford*].

31 I am not unaware of the fact that, pursuant to section 143(1)(a) of the *Constitution*, one does not have ownership of land. Rather, they have *title*, and it is the Government that has ownership. However, for the sake of convenience, I shall refer to it as "ownership" of land throughout this book, as opposed to saying they have "title."

32 *Hunter v Canary Wharf Ltd*, [1997] 2 All ER 426, [1997] AC 655.

33 Philip Osborne, *The Law of Torts*, 5th ed (Toronto: Irwin Law Inc, 2015) at 316–318 [Osborne].

34 The wording of the section is the following: "[A]ll minerals and other things of value underlying any land of Bangladesh" is the property of Bangladesh, at *Constitution of Bangladesh, supra* note 18 at s 143(1)(a). Though I speak briefly of property law, I shall eschew an exploration of the topic, as it is beyond the scope of this book.

35 *Shuttleworth v Vancouver General Hospital*, [1927] 2 DLR 573, [1927] BCJ No 71; Also see John G Fleming, *The Law of Torts*, 9th ed (Sydney: LBC Information Services, 1998) at 475–476 [Fleming].

Nuisance   55

36 *Fevold et al v Board of Supervisors of Webster County et al*, [1926] 202 Iowa 1019, 210 NW 1019 [*Fevold*].

37 "Ebola Virus Disease" *World Health Organization* (10 February 2020), online: World Health Organization https://www.who.int/news-room/fact-sheets/detail/ebola-virus-disease. Also see information on COVID-19 at "WHO Timeline - COVID-19" *World Health Organization* (27 April 2020), online: World Health Organization https://www.who.int/news-room/detail/27-04-2020-who-time-line---covid-19 (this URL is updating on a rolling basis and was last updated on 27 April); Also see "Coronavirus disease (COVID-19): What parents should know" *UNICEF* (2020), online: United Nations Children's Fund https://www.unicef.org/bangladesh/en/coronavirus-disease-covid-19-what-parents-should-know. [All 16/03/2021].

38 As of the time of writing, the World Health Organization says that there is no risk of contracting COVID-19 from dead bodies. See "Are there disease risks from dead bodies and what should be done for safe disposal?" *World Health Organization* (2020), online: World Health Organization https://www.who.int/water_sanitation_health/emergencies/qa/emergencies_qa8/en/. [16/03/2021].

39 With the exception of buying and selling minors, who is anyone under the age of 18, into prostitution. See ss 372–373 of *Penal Code, supra* note 1.

40 *Laws v Florinplace Ltd*, [1981] 1 All ER 659. Also see *Thompson-Schwab v Costaki*, [1956] 1 All ER 652, [1956] 1 WLR 335, where a residential house used for prostitution was held to be a nuisance due to the vehicular traffic and the number of undesirable persons it attracted. Therefore, I am of the opinion that a woman carrying on the legal profession of prostitution in her apartment at Baridhara would be a nuisance because of the conservative nature of Bangladesh. Furthermore, I predict that it would take eons for Bangladeshis to accept prostitution as a legitimate profession. Alternatively, it could also be that prostitution may be a nuisance in Baridhara, but not so in Nasirabad, Chittagong. As in, based on *Appleby* and *Rogers*, we know that courts will consider the characteristics of each neighbourhood before deciding whether an activity is a nuisance, and thus, my prediction may also be incorrect.

41 See *R v Vantandillo*, [1815] 4 M&S 73, 105 ER 762. Also see Oliver W Holmes Jr, "Privilege, Malice, and Intent" (1894) 8:1 Harv L Rev 1 and Jamie Cassels, "Prostitution and Public Nuisance: Desperate Measures and the Limits of Civil Adjudication" (1985) 63:4 Can Bar Rev 764.

For an interesting discussion on prostitution in America, Netherlands, Belgium, and Germany, see Ronald Weitzer, *Legalizing Prostitution: From Illicit Vice to Lawful Business* (New York: New York University Press, 2012). Also see Peter C Hennigan, "Property War: Prostitution, Red-Light Districts, and the Transformation of Public Nuisance Law in the Progressive Era" (2004) 16:1 Yale JL & Human 123.

42 *Miller, supra* note 19; Also see Prosser, *supra* note 4 at 573 where the author says, "A public or common nuisance, on the other hand, is a species of catch-all criminal offence, consisting of an interference with the rights of the community at large [...]"

43 *Bamford v Turnley*, [1861–73] All ER Rep 706, [1862] 122 ER 27 (Exch); Also see Fleming, *supra* note 35 at 488–490 and R F V Heuston & R A Buckley, *Salmond and Heuston on the Law of Torts*, 19th ed (London: Sweet & Maxwell, 1987) at 78-84 [Heuston & Buckley].

44 *Sturges v Bridgman*, [1879] 11 Ch D 852; See Fleming, *supra* note 35 at 459–463.

45 "History of KGC" (2020) *KGC*, online: KGC https://kgc-bd.com/history-of-kurmitola-golf-club/. [16/03/2021].

46 The precautionary measure is the "Hand Formula," which states that if the probability of the harm (P) and the gravity of the loss (L) is greater than the burden

56 Nuisance

of taking precautions (*B*), then liability will be imposed (with the opposite equation being equally true), at *United States v Carroll Towing*, [1947] 159 F 2d 169, 1947 US App LEXIS 3226. I will discuss this more thoroughly in Chapter 5.

47 *Kennaway, supra* note 20.

48 For an interesting perspective on *Sturges*, see Ronald Coase, "The Problem of Social Cost" (2013) 56:4 J L & Econ 837 (reprinted from 1960), where he says at 844–845,

> The court's decision established that the doctor had the right to prevent the confectioner from using his machinery. But, of course, it would have been possible to modify the arrangements envisaged in the legal ruling by means of a bargain between the parties. The doctor would have been willing to waive his right and allow the machinery to continue in operation if the confectioner would have paid him a sum of money which was greater than the loss of income which he would suffer from having to move to a more costly or less convenient location or from having to curtail his activities at this location or, as was suggested as a possibility, from having to build a separate wall which would deaden the noise and vibration. The confectioner would have been willing to do this if the amount he would have to pay the doctor was less than the fall in income he would suffer if he had to change his mode of operation at this location, abandon his operation or move his confectionery business to some other location. The solution of the problem depends essentially on whether the continued use of the machinery adds more to the confectioner's income than it subtracts from the doctor's. But now consider the situation if the confectioner had won the case. The confectioner would then have had the right to continue operating his noise and vibration-generating machinery without having to pay anything to the doctor. The boot would have been on the other foot: the doctor would have had to pay the confectioner to induce him to stop using the machinery. [Footnotes omitted].

Also see Patrick Atiyah, *Accidents, Compensation, and the Law*, 2nd ed (London: Weidenfeld and Nicolson, 1975), where it was said at 532–533,

> [*Sturges*] is criticized by Professor Coase on the ground that the real question facing the court in an action of this sort, is the economic question, namely which of the services which have to be sacrificed here are more valuable to society? But he also points out that since the parties could have modified the court's ruling by subsequent agreement between themselves, the ruling did not, in fact, greatly matter from the economic point of view. Thus if, for instance, the additional value to the confectioner of the use of his machinery was [...] £500 a year, while the additional value to the doctor of the use of his consulting room at the end of his garden was [...] £200 a year, it would plainly have been in the interest of both parties for the confectioner to resume using his machinery, and to pay the doctor anything between £200 and £500 a year. In the economic world in which all men are economic men, this is just what would have happened so that the court's original decision to grant an injunction would not have stopped the confectioner using his machinery. Equally, if the doctor's loss of income for his inability to use his consulting room as £500 a year, and the confectioner's loss from inability to use his machinery was only £200, and the court had refused an injunction, it would have been profitable for the doctor to pay the confectioner anything between £200 and £500 a year not to use the machinery, and it would have been profitable for the confectioner to take it. Thus, once again, there is no misallocation of resources, whatever result the law arrives it. If it places the risk on the party who should bear it in order to optimize the allocation of resources, the risk will remain there whereas if the law places the risk on the wrong party, the parties will correct the law's mistakes by a bargain.

Nuisance 57

See Richard A Epstein, "A Theory of Strict Liability" (1973) 2:1 J Leg Stud 151 where he criticizes Ronald Coase's approach in *Sturges*; Also see *Rohit Talwar et al v Municipal Corporation of Delhi*, [1992] 24 DRJ 473.

49 *Antrim*, *supra* note 9; Also see Prosser, *supra* note 4 at 583–591 and Heuston & Buckley, *supra* note 43 at 69–71 & 93–100.

50 See *Appleby*, *Rogers*, and *Miller*.

51 *Andreae v Selfridge & Co Ltd*, [1937] 3 All ER 355, [1938] Ch 1; See generally Heuston & Buckley, *supra* note 43 at 59–61 & 90–93.

52 See *Kennaway*, *supra* note 20.

53 See, for example, *Walker v Pioneer Construction Co Ltd*, [1975] 8 OR (2d) 35, where noise was held to be a nuisance at night, but not during the day.

54 See *Miller*, *supra* note 19. Also see *Laing*, *supra* note 21, where the court took into consideration that people sleep late on weekends, and therefore, church bells should not be rung until 9:00 am.

55 See Maria Mansfield, "When Private Rights Meet Public Rights: The Problems of Labeling and Regulatory Takings" (1994) 65:2 U Colo L Rev 193.

56 "Fact Box: All You Need to Know About Bangladesh Metro Rail Project" *The Daily Star* (30 April 2018), online: The Daily Star https://www.thedailystar.net/country/dhaka-metro-rail-project-in-bangladesh-fact-box-all-you-need-to-know-about-this-1569868. [16/03/2021]. For the sake of convenience, even though construction will be completed in three to four years, I shall say it will be completed in four years.

57 The outbreak of COVID-19, which has brought the global economy to a grinding halt, can render some contracts impossible to perform, and therefore, the construction of the MRT may become suspended during the pandemic. Moreover, this may mean that it will take longer than 2020 to complete construction and residents must accept it, at Emily Palmer, "'Nothing Like Normal': Covering an Infected Global Economy" *The New York Times* (17 March 2020), online: The New York Times Company https://www.nytimes.com/2020/03/17/reader-center/coronavirus-economy-reporter.html. [16/03/2021]. Also see Barry Nicholas, "Force Majeure and Frustration" (1979) 27:2 & 3 Am J Comp L 231.

58 *Pennsylvania Coal Company v Mahon et al*, [1922] 43 S CT 158, 67 L Ed 22; *The City of Phoenix v Will Johnson*, [1938] 51 Ariz 115. Also see Prosser: PAPN, *supra* note 6 at 1001. In this case, it would be a private nuisance.

59 *State of North Dakota v Hooker*, [1957] 87 NW 2d 337, 1957 ND LEXIS 182 [*Hooker*]. Also see Prosser: PAPN, *ibid* at 1001-1002.

60 *Smith v City of Sedalia*, [1899] 152 Mo 283, 53 SW 907.

61 *State ex rel Wear v Springfield Gas & Electric Co*, [1918] 204 SW 942, 1918 Mo App LEXIS 477.

62 *Phillips & Co v The State*, [1874] 66 Tenn 151, 1874 Tenn LEXIS 96.

63 *Cortlandt v The New York Central Railroad Company*, [1934] 265 NY 249, 1934 NY LEXIS 1023; Also see Heuston & Buckley, *supra* note 43 at 60 where it was said, "[Public nuisance] is an act or omission which materially affects the reasonable comfort and convenience of life of a class of Her Majesty's subjects. It is not necessary to establish that every member of the public, as distinct from a representative cross-section, has been affected."

64 *Smillie v Continental Oil Company*, [1954] 127 F Supp 508, 1954 US Dist LEXIS 2403. Again, this element is also similar to a private nuisance.

65 *Seigle v Bromley*, [1912] 22 Colo App 189, 1912 Colo App LEXIS 18.

66 *Fevold*, *supra* note 36.

67 *Weis v Superior Court of the County of San Diego*, [1916] 30 Cal App 730, 1916 Cal App LEXIS 468. This could range from operating a strip-club to a known swingers club.

68 *Transcontinental Gas Pipe Line Corp v Gault et al*, [1952] 198 F2d 196, 1952 US App LEXIS 3163; Also see *Appleby*, *supra* note 8.

58 Nuisance

69 *Graves v Shattuck et al*, [1857] 35 NH 257, 1857 NH LEXIS 68.

70 *Landau v The City of New York*, [1904] 180 NY 48, 1904 NY LEXIS 1293, *James v Hayward*, [1630] Cro Car 184, W Jo 221, and *Lamereaux v Tula*, [1942] 312 Mass 359, 44 NE 2d 789 respectively.

71 *Cincinnati Railroad Company v The Commonwealth*, [1882] 80 Ky 137, 1882 Ky LEXIS 27 [*Cincinnati*]; Also see *Hanson v Hall et al*, [1938] 202 Minn 381, Prosser: PAPN, *supra* note 6 at 1003, and Heuston & Buckley, *supra* note 43 at 60–61.

72 Akim Rahman, "Dhaka's Traffic Agony" *The Daily Star* (28 January 2018), online: The Daily Star https://www.thedailystar.net/opinion/dhakas-traffic-agony-1525948; Dhrubo Alam & Arfar Razi, "Why Dhaka's Livability is only Worsening" *The Daily Star* (1 January 2018), online: The Daily Star https://www.thedailystar.net/supplements/unpacking-2017/why-dhakas-liveability-only-worsening-1512988; "2 and a Half Hours and Still on the Road" *The Daily Star* (24 July 2017), online: The Daily Star https://www.thedailystar.net/city/dhaka-traffic-jam-alert-public-suffering-2-and-half-hours-and-still-the-road-1437955. [All 16/03/2021].

73 *The Dhaka Metropolitan Police Ordinance*, 1976 (Bangladesh), Ordinance No III of 1976, s 72 [*DMPO*], which only, however, applies to Dhaka.

74 *The Road Transport Act, 2018* (Bangladesh), Act No XLVII of 2018, s 41, which stipulates, "সরকার বা তৎকর্তৃক ক্ষমতাপ্রাপ্ত কোনো প্রতিষ্ঠান বা সংস্থা ট্রাফিক চলাচল নিয়ন্ত্রণ এবং সড়ক নিরাপত্তা বিধানে মোটরযানের ব্যবহার, গতিসীমা, পার্কিং এলাকা, ট্রাফিক সাইন ও সংকেত ব্যবহার, চলাচল ইত্যাদি নির্ধারিত পদ্ধতিতে নিয়ন্ত্রণ করিতে পারিবে।" This translates into "The government or any institution or body empowered by it may control the movement of traffic and control the use of motor vehicles, speed limit, parking areas, use of traffic signs and signals, movement etc. in the prescribed manner under the road safety provisions."

   The Road Transport Act, 2018 replaced the *The Motor Vehicles Ordinance, 1983* (Bangladesh), Act No LV of 1983, which stipulates at s 102(1)(a), "The driver of a motor vehicle shall cause the vehicle to stop and remain stationary so long as may reasonably be necessary [...] when required to do so by any police officer in uniform, or any Inspector of Motor Vehicles, or any person authorized in this behalf by the Government [...]." Also see *DMPO*, *ibid* at s 30.

75 *Penal Code*, *supra* 1 at s 161; Also see the *Anti-Corruption Commission Act*, 2004 (Bangladesh), Act No V of 2004.

76 For example, the President of the United States has an extensive security detail from the Secret Service, whereby bridges and roads are shut down in preparation for his arrival, at Stephanie Susskind, "President Trump in Town for Thanksgiving" *Fox 29 WFLX* (19 November 2018), online: Fox 29 WFLX http://www.wflx.com/2018/11/19/president-trump-visit-palm-beach-tuesday/; Also see "USSS History" *Department of Homeland Security* (2018), online: Department of Homeland Security https://www.secretservice.gov/about/history/events/. [All 16/03/2021].

77 For this, an argument could be propounded under section 32 of the *Constitution of Bangladesh*, *supra* note 18, which stipulates, "No person shall be deprived of life or personal liberty save in accordance with law," that the halting of traffic deprived one to the right to life. Also see Jeremiah Smith, "Private Action for Obstruction to Public Right of Passage" (1915) 15:2 Colum L Rev 142 and Ann Woolhandler, "Public Rights, Private Rights, and Statutory Retroactivity" (2006) 94:4 Geo LJ 1015.

78 By now, it is apparent that this book does not discuss procedure. However, I should clarify here that the Attorney General, or "two or more persons having obtained the consent in writing of the" Attorney General can institute proceedings for public nuisance in Bangladesh, at *The Code of Civil Procedure*, 1908 (Bangladesh), Act No V of 1908, s 91(1).

Nuisance   59

Essentially, this means that if the Attorney General, who is appointed by the President of Bangladesh, does not provide written consent, citizens of Bangladesh cannot file a claim under public nuisance.

79 *Shelfer*, *supra* note 15.
80 *Spur Industries, Inc v Del E. Webb Development Co*, [1972] 108 Ariz 178, 1972 Ariz LEXIS 274 [*Spur Industries*].
81 See *Hollywood Farm*, *supra* note 22.
82 See Jeff Lewin, "Compensated Injunctions and the Evolution of Nuisance Law" (1986) 71:3 Iowa L Rev 775, where he comments on *Spur Industries* at 792,

On remand, discovery was commenced on the issue of Spur's cost of moving, but the case was settled without a hearing. Although the terms of the settlement were not made public, they involved Spur moving the feedlot to a new location, with payment of an undisclosed sum of money by Del Webb to Spur [...] The lawsuit of the residents was settled after the settlement of Del Webb's suit against Spur with the payment of undisclosed sums to the individual plaintiffs.

Also see *Boomer v Atlantic Cement Co*, [1970] 26 NY 2d 219, 257 NE 2d 870, where the defendant operated a large cement factory and neighbouring residents brought actions for an injunction and damages for injury caused by dirt, smoke, and vibration. However, the court would not grant an injunction, but did award damages, because the surrounding area was economically dependent on the cement factory. For a similar outcome, see *KVP Co Ltd v Mckie et al*, [1949] SCR 698, [1949] 4 DLR 497.

References

Legislation

Anti-Corruption Commission Act, 2004 (Bangladesh), Act No V of 2004
The Code of Civil Procedure, 1908 (Bangladesh), Act No V of 1908
The Constitution of the People's Republic of Bangladesh (Bangladesh), Act of 1972
The Dhaka Metropolitan Police Ordinance, 1976 (Bangladesh), Ordinance No III of 1976
The Motor Vehicles Ordinance, 1983 (Bangladesh), Act No LV of 1983
The Penal Code, 1860 (Bangladesh), Act No XLV of 1860
The Road Transport Act, 2018 (Bangladesh), Act No XLVII of 2018

Caselaw

Andreae v Selfridge & Co Ltd, [1937] 3 All ER 355, [1938] Ch 1
Antrim Truck Centre Ltd v Ontario (Minister of Transportation), [2013] 1 SCR 594, [2013] SCJ No 13
Appleby v Erie Tobacco Co, [1910] OJ No 64, 22 OLR 533
Bamford v Turnley, [1861–73] All ER Rep 706, [1862] 122 ER 27 (Exch)
Bradford Corporation, [1895–99] All ER Rep 984, [1895] AC 587
Bury v Pope, [1586] Cro Eliz 118, 74 ER 115
Canada Paper Company v Brown, [1922] 63 SCR 243, [1922] SCJ No 7
Carroll v New York Pie Baking Co, [1926] 215 AD 240, 1926 NY App Div LEXIS 10942
Cincinnati Railroad Company v The Commonwealth, [1882] 80 Ky 137, 1882 Ky LEXIS 27
Cortlandt v The New York Central Railroad Company, [1934] 265 NY 249, 1934 NY LEXIS 1023

60   Nuisance

Fevold et al v Board of Supervisors of Webster County et al, [1926] 202 Iowa 1019, 210 NW 1019

Fontainebleau Hotel Corp v Forty-Five Twenty-Five, Inc, [1959] 1 14 So 2d 357

Graves v Shattuck et al, [1857] 35 NH 257, 1857 NH LEXIS 68

Hanson v Hall et al, [1938] 202 Minn 381

Hay v Cohoes Co, [1849] 2 NY 159, 1849 NY LEXIS 5

Hollywood Silver Fox Farm Ltd v Emmett, [1936] 1 All ER 825, [1936] 2 KB 468

Hunter v Canary Wharf Ltd, [1997] 2 All ER 426, [1997] AC 655

James v Hayward, [1630] Cro Car 184, W Jo 221

Kennaway v Thompson, [1980] 3 All ER 329, [1981] QB 88

KVP Co Ltd v Mckie et al, [1949] SCR 698, [1949] 4 DLR 497

Laing v St. Thomas Dragway, [2005] OJ No 254, [2005] ILR

Lamereaux v Tula, [1942] 312 Mass 359, 44 NE 2d 789

Landau v The City of New York, [1904] 180 NY 48, 1904 NY LEXIS 1293

Laws v Florinplace Ltd, [1981] 1 All ER 659

Miller v Jackson, [1977] 3 All ER 778, [1977] QB 966

Pennsylvania Coal Company v Mahon et al, [1922] 43 S CT 158, 67 L Ed 22

People v Wolf, [1927] 220 AD 71, 220 NYS 656

Perlmutter v Greene, [1932] 259 NY 327, 1932 NY LEXIS 945

Phillips & Co v The State, [1874] 66 Tenn 151, 1874 Tenn LEXIS 96

Polsue and Alfieri Limited v Rushmer, [1904–7] All ER Rep 586, [1907] AC 121

Prah v Maretti, [1982] 321 NW 2d 182, 108 Wis 2d 223

R v Vantandillo, [1815] 4 M&S 73, 105 ER 762

Reaver v Martin Theatres of Florida Inc, [1951] 52 So 2d 682, 1951 Fla LEXIS 1351

Rogers v Elliot, [1888] 146 Mass 349, 1888 Mass LEXIS 260

Rohit Talwar et al v Municipal Corporation of Delhi, [1992] 24 DRJ 473

Seigle v Bromley, [1912] 22 Colo App 189, 1912 Colo App LEXIS 18

Shelfer v City of London Electric Co, [1891-4] All ER Rep 838, [1895] 1 Ch 287

Shuttleworth v Vancouver General Hospital, [1927] 2 DLR 573, [1927] BCJ No 71

Smillie v Continental Oil Company, [1954] 127 F Supp 508, 1954 US Dist LEXIS 2403

Smith v City of Sedalia, [1899] 152 Mo 283, 53 SW 907

Spur Industries, Inc v Del E. Webb Development Co, [1972] 108 Ariz 178, 1972 Ariz LEXIS 274

St. Louis Gunning Advertisement Co v St. Louis, [1911] 235 Mo 99, 1911 Mo LEXIS 84

State ex rel Wear v Springfield Gas & Electric Co, [1918] 204 SW 942, 1918 Mo App LEXIS 477

State of North Dakota v Hooker, [1957] 87 NW 2d 337, 1957 ND LEXIS 182

Sturges v Bridgman, [1879] 11 Ch D 852

T. H. Critelli Ltd v Lincoln Trust and Savings Co et al, [1978] 20 OR (2D) 81

The City of Phoenix v Will Johnson, [1938] 51 Ariz 115

Thomas Cusack Co v Chicago, [1917] 242 US 546, 1917 US LEXIS 2171

Thompson-Schwab v Costaki, [1956] 1 All ER 652, [1956] 1 WLR 335

Transcontinental Gas Pipe Line Corp v Gault et al, [1952] 198 F2d 196, 1952 US App LEXIS 3163

Walter v Selfe, [1851] 20 LJ Ch 433, 64 ER 849

Walker v Pioneer Construction Co Ltd, [1975] 8 OR (2d) 35

Weis v Superior Court of the County of San Diego, [1916] 30 Cal App 730, 1916 Cal App LEXIS 468

United States v Carroll Towing, [1947] 159 F 2d 169, 1947 US App LEXIS 3226

Secondary Material: Books

Atiyah, Patrick, *Accidents, Compensation, and the Law*, 2nd ed (London: Weidenfeld and Nicolson, 1975)

Fleming, John G, *The Law of Torts*, 9th ed (Sydney: LBC Information Services, 1998)

Heuston, Robert F V & Buckley, Richard A, *Salmond and Heuston on the Law of Torts*, 19th ed (London: Sweet & Maxwell, 1987)

Osborne, Philip, *The Law of Torts*, 5th ed (Toronto: Irwin Law Inc, 2015)

Prosser, William L, *Handbook of The Law of Torts*, 4th ed (St. Paul, Minnesota: West Publishing Co, 1971)

Salmond, John W, *Law of Torts*, 16th ed (London: Sweet & Maxwell, 1973).

Weinrib, Ernest J, *Tort Law: Cases and Materials*, 4th ed (Toronto: Emond Montgomery Publications Limited, 2014)

Weitzer, Ronald, *Legalizing Prostitution: From Illicit Vice to Lawful Business* (New York: New York University Press, 2012)

Secondary Material: Journal Articles

Abrams, Robert & Washington, Val, "The Misunderstood Law of Public Nuisance: A Comparison with Private Nuisance Twenty Years After Boomer" (1990) 54:2 Alb L Rev 359

Becker Jr, Ralph, "Common Law Sun Rights: An Obstacle to Solar Heating and Cooling?" (1976) 3:1 J Contemp L 19

Cassels, Jamie, "Prostitution and Public Nuisance: Desperate Measures and the Limits of Civil Adjudication" (1985) 63:4 Can Bar Rev 764

Coase, Ronald, "The Problem of Social Cost" (2013) 56:4 J L & Econ 837 (reprinted from 1960)

Epstein, Richard A, "A Theory of Strict Liability" (1973) 2:1 J Leg Stud 151

Gevurtz, Franklin, "Obstruction of Sunlight as a Private Nuisance" (1977) 65:1 Cal L Rev 94

Hennigan, Peter C, "Property War: Prostitution, Red-Light Districts, and the Transformation of Public Nuisance Law in the Progressive Era" (2004) 16:1 Yale JL & Human 123

Hollis, Lee J, "A Private Nuisance Remedy for Obstruction of Solar Access" (1983) 48:3 Mo L Rev 769

Holmes Jr, Oliver W, "Privilege, Malice, and Intent" (1894) 8:1 Harv L Rev 1

Lewin, Jeff L, "Compensated Injunctions and the Evolution of Nuisance Law" (1986) 71:3 Iowa L Rev 775

Lewin, Jeff L, "Boomer and the American Law of Nuisance: Past, Present, and Future" (1990) 54:2 Alb L Rev 189

Mansfield, Maria, "When Private Rights Meet Public Rights: The Problems of Labeling and Regulatory Takings" (1994) 65:2 U Colo L Rev 193

Nicholas, Barry, "Force Majeure and Frustration" (1979) 27:2 & 3 Am J Comp L 231

Pearson, Robert W, "Billboard Laws Today – Reaction or Solution" (1972) 24:1 Baylor L Rev 86

Prosser, William L, "Private Action for Public Nuisance" (1966) 52: 6 Va L Rev 997

Rychlak, Ronald J, "Common-Law Remedies for Environmental Wrongs: The Role of Private Nuisance" (1989) 59: 3 Miss LJ 657

62   Nuisance

Smith, Jeremiah, "Private Action for Obstruction to Public Right of Passage" (1915) 15:2 Colum L Rev 142

Woolhandler, Ann, "Public Rights, Private Rights, and Statutory Retroactivity" (2006) 94:4 Geo LJ 1015.

Secondary Material: Websites

"2 and a Half Hours and Still on the Road" *The Daily Star* (24 July 2017), online: The Daily Star https://www.thedailystar.net/city/dhaka-traffic-jam-alert-public-suffering-2-and-half-hours-and-still-the-road-1437955

Alam, Dhrubo & Razi, Arfar, "Why Dhaka's Livability is only Worsening" *The Daily Star* (1 January 2018), online: The Daily Star https://www.thedailystar.net/supplements/unpacking-2017/why-dhakas-liveability-only-worsening-1512988

"Are there disease risks from dead bodies and what should be done for safe disposal?" *World Health Organization* (2020), online: World Health Organization https://www.who.int/water_sanitation_health/emergencies/qa/emergencies_qa8/en/

"Coronavirus disease (COVID-19): What parents should know" *UNICEF* (2020), online: United Nations Children's Fund https://www.unicef.org/bangladesh/en/coronavirus-disease-covid-19-what-parents-should-know

"Ebola Virus Disease" *World Health Organization* (10 February 2020), online: World Health Organization https://www.who.int/news-room/fact-sheets/detail/ebola-virus-disease

"Fact Box: All You Need to Know About Bangladesh Metro Rail Project" *The Daily Star* (30 April 2018), online: The Daily Star https://www.thedailystar.net/country/dhaka-metro-rail-project-in-bangladesh-fact-box-all-you-need-to-know-about-this-1569868

"History of KGC" (2020) *KGC, online: KGC* https://kgc-bd.com/history-of-kurmitola-golf-club/

Palmer, Emily, "'Nothing Like Normal': Covering an Infected Global Economy" *The New York Times* (17 March 2020), online: The New York Times Company https://www.nytimes.com/2020/03/17/reader-center/coronavirus-economy-reporter.html

Rahman, Akim, "Dhaka's Traffic Agony" *The Daily Star* (28 January 2018), online: The Daily Star https://www.thedailystar.net/opinion/dhakas-traffic-agony-1525948

Rich, Nathaniel, "The Lawyer Who Became DuPont's Worst Nightmare" *The New York Times* (6 January 2016), online: The New York Times Company https://www.nytimes.com/2016/01/10/magazine/the-lawyer-who-became-duponts-worst-nightmare.html

Susskind, Stephanie, "President Trump in Town for Thanksgiving" *Fox 29 WFLX* (19 November 2018), online: Fox 29 WFLX http://www.wflx.com/2018/11/19/president-trump-visit-palm-beach-tuesday/

"USSS History" *Department of Homeland Security* (2018), online: Department of Homeland Security https://www.secretservice.gov/about/history/events/

"WHO Timeline – COVID-19" *World Health Organization* (27 April 2020), online: World Health Organization https://www.who.int/news-room/detail/27-04-2020-who-timeline---covid-19

4 Intentional torts

Imagine that you have gone out to jog one afternoon, near the lake at Dhanmondi, and someone spits on you. What can you *legally* do? Can you bring proceedings against him under *The Penal Code* or any other legislation? Similarly, recall from the previous chapter that playing cricket at the field inside Mirpur DOHS does not constitute nuisance. However, imagine that a player hits a ball that eventually lands on someone's lawn, and when he goes to retrieve it, the landlord refuses to return it, picks up the ball, and takes it inside his home. Has the landlord done anything wrong? Alternatively, what if someone crashed into you with his bicycle, or walks into your house uninvited, or takes your cellphone to make a phone call without your permission, or copies and uses your company's logo, or points a gun at you, but does not shoot? Are any of the enumerated wrong, and if so, which statute, if any, prohibits such conduct?

In this chapter, I shall focus on intentional torts, which hails from the writ of trespass (known as *quare clausum fregit*) that emerged in thirteenth-century England to deal with breaches of the King's peace.[1] In fact, trespass originally had a criminal character and was concerned with the gravest breaches of the King's peace. Therefore, royal courts accepted jurisdiction, and once the defendant was convicted, he was fined and would be imprisoned only if he could not pay that fine.[2] Historians generally agree that this was the beginning of awarding damages to the injured plaintiff.[3]

A case for intentional tort will be successful if the plaintiff can prove that the defendant's misconduct was deliberate and he desired its consequences.[4] Intentional torts are generally divided into four categories: (1) interference with the person, (2) interference with realty, (3) interference with chattel, and (4) interference with economic interests, and I will explore all of them in *seriatim*. I remain optimistic that by the end of this chapter, you will be able to answer all of the questions posed in the first paragraph.

DOI: 10.4324/9781003241782-4

64   *Intentional torts*

4.1 Interference with the person

4.1.1 Assault

In torts, *sensu stricto*, assault is any intentional act that causes another to fear that a battery is imminent.[5] Therefore, if someone points a gun at you and threatens to shoot, it is an assault, but not battery. Only if the person subsequently fires the gun and the bullet actually hits you does a battery occur. Similarly, if he fires the gun and the bullet does not hit you, then there is, again, assault, but no battery. Additionally, if someone punches your back, and before being hit, you did not see him advance towards you with a clenched fist, then there is battery, but no assault. As in, for an act to constitute assault, it is essential that the plaintiff apprehend an immediate battery to his person. For example, in *Stephens v Myers*,[6] at a parish meeting, the defendant advanced towards the plaintiff in a threatening manner so that if he was not stopped and restrained by others, he would have been able to strike the plaintiff, as he had already made his way to the chair next to the latter. The court held that an assault had been committed because the threat of battery was imminent.

Imagine, however, a different scenario. You currently live in Dhaka and an old enemy calls. He mentions that he is in Chittagong, will reach Dhaka in about 8 hours, and he will come to your house and shoot you. In this case, there is no assault, as the threat of battery is not imminent; that is, 8 hours is sufficient time for a reasonable person to go to the police and file a complaint.[7] Nonetheless, if the same person calls and, rather than telling you that he will reach your house in 8 hours and shoot you, he says that there is a bomb in your apartment, then this would constitute assault, as the threat of battery is imminent. Here, it is not necessary for him to mention *when* the bomb will explode, as it is probable that it could detonate before the timer lapses (furthermore, no reasonable person would consent to having a bomb planted on his premises; therefore, if one conceals an explosive device on another's home, the former would be guilty of interference with the latter's land).

It is of paramount importance to understand the two conditions precedent for the tort of assault. First, there must be a real threat that the battery could be executed immediately. Therefore, if someone knows that a threat cannot be acted upon with celerity, then there is no assault. Second, the plaintiff must take the threat seriously. As in, if my brother, who is also my best friend, calls and informs me that he has planted a bomb in my apartment and I do not take his statement seriously, then there is no assault. Similarly, if my friend, whom I know for 20 years, tells me over lunch that he will punch me, there is no assault provided I do not take his threat seriously. However, if my brother or my friend is estranged and I perceive their threats to be real (in that they could execute their threats), then there could be an assault. For example, during the course of a domestic dispute, if one says, "I will kill you if you take me to court," then there is an assault, as the threat of violence is imminent, in that one requires the other to buy their safety

Intentional torts   65

through an immediate promise.[8] Nonetheless, it would not be an assault if, for example, one spouse asks the other for the newspaper, coupled with a threat (e.g. "pass me the newspaper or I will throw this spoon at you") that the other knows is a joke. Simply put, whether a threat constitutes an assault will depend on the facts and circumstances of each case.[9]

4.1.2 False imprisonment

The word "false" implies one doing something without lawful authority, and "imprisonment" is any direct and intentional action that completely curtails another's liberty.[10] Therefore, false imprisonment is when one, without lawful authority, directly, intentionally, and completely restricts another's liberty, which is actionable without proof of damage. This means, though, that if the police have reasonable grounds to take someone into custody, which would restrict the latter's liberty entirely, there would be no false imprisonment, as law enforcement has the right to lawfully detain someone. However, this also means that if the police lack reasonable grounds to detain someone, perhaps because of scant evidence, then false imprisonment could result.[11]

A partial obstruction, however, is insufficient to constitute the tort. For example, in *Bird v Jones*, the plaintiff was partially obstructed from crossing a bridge, but since nothing prevented him from circumventing the impediment, there was no false imprisonment.[12] Therefore, if someone throws you inside a room and locks the door and windows, thereby precluding your escape, there is imprisonment. However, if a person leaves you inside a room, walks out, and emphatically orders you to not leave, but does not lock the door or the windows, then there is no imprisonment because you have an opportunity of escape.

The tort of false imprisonment is not limited to being confined in a room. For example, you can be imprisoned inside, *inter alia*, a vehicle, aircraft, ship, or submarine. Nonetheless, simply because you are inside any of the enumerated does not mean that there is imprisonment so long as you have voluntarily entered the vessel and nothing prevents exit. However, this also does not mean you are imprisoned if you wilfully board a plane, but wish to disembark halfway through the journey and are now prohibited. For example, assume you are flying from Dhaka to Chittagong and 30 minutes into the flight, while cruising at 22,000 feet, you inform an air-hostess that you wish to deplane, which she prohibits. This would not amount to false imprisonment because of the following reasons: firstly, the act of buying a ticket to fly to Chittagong imports consent, and therefore, in the absence of evidence to the contrary, you have voluntarily bought a ticket and boarded the flight.[13]

Secondly, and perhaps more importantly, an aircraft is different from other vessels in the sense that it cannot stop everywhere; rather, runways are designed specifically for that purpose. Therefore, even if your wish to deplane midair is denied, no imprisonment exists as the airline already has

66   *Intentional torts*

prior consent (e.g. ticket) in taking you to Chittagong. However, what could constitute false imprisonment is if cabin crew refuses to let you leave upon landing without just cause. As in, if the crew delays disembarkation due to a potential hazard, such as a fire or tempest, or any other justifiable reason, then there is no false imprisonment. But, if they refuse exit simply because they want to keep you inside the aircraft, which curtails your liberty entirely, then there could be false imprisonment.

While I have used the example of an airplane, it is important to note that the situation would be different if you were inside a vehicle. For example, if you are travelling from Gulshan to Dhanmondi by Uber and you request to be let out halfway through the journey, the driver would be compelled to adhere to your request unless to do so would violate applicable statute.[14]

4.1.3 Malicious prosecution

The tort of malicious prosecution seeks to balance two competing, but equally important, rights: first, the private interest in protecting the individual's reputation from baseless criminal proceedings, and second, the public interest in prosecuting criminal behaviour. Though public interests usually prevail, malicious prosecution favours private rights if litigation is brought maliciously. In order to prove malicious prosecution, the plaintiff must adduce evidence that the (1) defendant initiated proceedings, (2) the proceedings ended in his favour, (3) there was no probable cause for bringing proceedings, (4) there was malice on the part of the defendant, and (5) the plaintiff suffered damage.[15]

4.1.3.1 Defendant initiated proceedings

Malicious prosecution applies only to criminal proceedings because of the inherent possibility of one's liberty being curtailed.[16] In order to institute proceedings under this tort, the defendant must have been instrumental in bringing a case against the plaintiff. Therefore, providing information to the police is generally insufficient unless one deliberately furnishes a false report, which begets a wrongful prosecution. For example, and one that I will use throughout this section, let us assume that the police are looking for a suspect believed to have committed murder. Since they do not have much information, they conscript the help of the public and inform them that the murder was committed between 9:00 pm and 11:30 pm on Tuesday, and that if anyone has information that can lead to the apprehension of the suspect, they should notify the police. For security purposes, you have CCTV cameras outside your apartment. Your neighbour is a misanthrope who lives by himself and there is enmity between the two of you. Therefore, you doctor footage showing your neighbour exiting the elevator at 10:45 pm on Tuesday and submit it to the police. Relying solely on this video and no other culpable evidence, if the police press charges, and if the proceedings terminate in your neighbour's favour, and arrest

Intentional torts 67

your neighbour, he would have grounds to bring litigation under malicious prosecution.

4.1.3.2 Proceedings end in plaintiff's favour

The second requirement for bringing proceedings under malicious prosecution is that the original proceedings must end in the plaintiff's favour; that is, even if the police arrested your neighbour based on the doctored video and other evidence, assume they searched his premises and found forensic evidence linking him to the crime with which his guilt is proven beyond a reasonable doubt at trial. Thence, even though you fabricated a video pointing to his guilt, since he is actually found guilty, he cannot institute proceedings for malicious prosecution.[17]

4.1.3.3 Lack of reasonable grounds

There must be reasonable and probable grounds to bring proceedings against your neighbour, which involve subjective and objective elements. As in, it is imperative that the police either genuinely believe in your neighbour's guilt (subjective element), or that they harbour a rational reason for holding said belief (objective element). For example, if the police rely upon the doctored video, and are incognizant of its fabrication, then it can be said that they either genuinely believe in your neighbour's guilt, or have a rational basis for their belief (or both).[18] Consequently, if the proceedings end in your neighbour's favour, he would be barred from bringing an action for malicious prosecution against the police because they had either a genuine belief (e.g. videotape) in your neighbour's guilt, or a rational basis for holding that belief (e.g. videotape). However, he would not be precluded from bringing an action against you, as you were the one who doctored the video, and by doing so, you became instrumental to the prosecution.

4.1.3.4 Malice

As the tort suggests, the defendant's actions must have been malicious, which is any act ranging from spite, vengeance, ill will, to any other improper purpose. The object of prosecution is the enforcement of criminal law and dispensing justice for both the offender and the victim.[19] Therefore, instituting proceedings for any purpose other than the aforesaid may constitute malice. For example, when you fabricate a video showing your neighbour exiting your apartment's elevator at 10:45 pm on Tuesday, even if it was done as a practical joke, it may constitute malice because it is an improper purpose.

4.1.3.5 Damage

The last element the plaintiff must establish is damage, which can be an injury, *inter alia*, to his reputation, financial loss, or the loss of liberty.

68 Intentional torts

Malicious prosecution is not actionable without proof of damage.[20] For example, let us, again, assume that the video you doctored is relied upon to press charges, and as is your neighbour's constitutional right, he retains a lawyer. However, during proceedings, he is kept in prison and his employer suspends him. If the lawsuit ends in his favour, he can bring litigation against you for the injury he has suffered, *videlicet* (1) monetary loss from retaining a lawyer; (2) monetary loss from being suspended by his employer, which can also be tantamount to an injury to his reputation; and (3) the constraint on his liberty.

4.1.3.6 *False imprisonment and malicious prosecution*

While false imprisonment and malicious prosecution are similar, they are, in fact, distinct. False imprisonment arises when the plaintiff is *directly* imprisoned by the defendant whereby his liberty is completely restricted. However, malicious prosecution seeks relief from *indirect* acts.[21] For example, the person who locks you inside a room is *directly* imprisoning you, which is false imprisonment.[22] However, the person who doctors a video and submits it to the police, upon which the latter relies and presses charges, is not directly imprisoning you, but is *indirectly* and adversely affecting your interests, such as your reputation, liberty, or other financial loss, which is malicious prosecution.[23] Moreover, as I have said before, if one is sleeping and unaware that another has locked the door, thereby preventing his escape, he can still bring proceedings under false imprisonment.[24]

Malicious prosecution, on the other hand, and as I have said before, requires the commencement of judicial proceedings and proof of injury (such as to reputation, financial loss, or loss of liberty).[25] However, this begets the question of whether a person, who provides information to the police upon request, can be held liable for malicious prosecution. Fortunately, he cannot. For example, if the police ask you for information, and you provide details that you honestly believe is true, which leads to the apprehension of the suspect, then you will not be liable for the proceedings instituted by the police even if it is later proven that your information was incorrect. Nonetheless, if the police ask for information and you doctor a video, which ultimately leads to the apprehension of the suspect, but the proceedings end in the defendant's favour and it is proven that your video was a fabrication, then litigation can be brought against you under malicious prosecution, as you were instrumental in the proceedings. To simplify, there is a marked difference between the person who fabricates a video and one who provides information that he honestly believes is true. Furthermore, the common law holds that the public are a credible source and law enforcement can ask for, and rely on, information provided by them.[26] However, if the circumstances reveal that the information is not credible, then the police are bound to not act on it, but the person who provided the details would not be liable unless he deliberately engaged in wrongful activity and injected himself into the investigation.[27]

Intentional torts 69

4.1.4 Battery

In Bangladesh, battery in tort law is "force" or "criminal force" in criminal law. Battery, which is actionable without proof of damage, is any physical, direct, intentional, and non-consensual interference with the bodily integrity of another person that is offensive or harmful.[28] For example, punching, stabbing, shooting, cutting someone's hair, and spitting on someone without their consent constitute battery. Additionally, it is not necessary that the interference be with the person of another. To further explain, if you yank someone's clothes or remove a hat they are wearing without their permission, you have committed battery.[29] However, if an action is not offensive or harmful, then no battery results. For example, gently tapping someone's shoulder to get their attention or patting someone on the back is not battery, as it is ordinarily accepted for the purposes of daily life.[30] Nonetheless, as I will delineate in Section 4.1.7.1, the line between gently patting someone on the back and battery depends on the facts and circumstances of each case.

Malette v Shulman[31]

On 30 June 1979, Mrs. Georgette Malette, who was the passenger, and her husband, who was driving the vehicle, were involved in a car accident. Upon a head-on collision with a truck, her husband was instantly killed and Mrs. Malette suffered serious injuries that rendered her unconscious. She was rushed to the Kirkland and District Hospital in Kirkland Lake, Ontario, where she was initially examined by Dr. David Shulman. He discovered that Mrs. Malette, *inter alia*, had severe head and face injuries, was suffering from incipient shock due to profuse bleeding, and ordered the administration of intravenous glucose followed by Ringer's Lactate. If she did not respond to the treatment, then Dr. Shulman recommended blood transfusion to facilitate the transmission of oxygen to tissues, thereby preventing damage to vital organs. At this time, however, a nurse found a card inside Mrs. Malette's purse, which stipulated the following:

No Blood Transfusion!

> As one of Jehovah's Witnesses with firm religious convictions, I request that no blood or blood products be administered to me under any circumstances. I full realize the implications of this position, but I have resolutely decided to obey the Bible command: "Keep abstaining [...] from blood." (Acts 15:28, 29). However, I have no religious objection to use the non-blood alternatives, such as Dextran, Haemaccel, PVP, Ringer's Lactate or saline solution.

Dr. Shulman was advised forthwith of the content of the card.

Mrs. Malette was then examined by another surgeon, who, similar to Dr. Shulman, recommended that her blood volume be maintained in order to prevent irreversible shock. He then transferred Mrs. Malette to the X-ray department for X-rays of her skull, pelvis, and chest. However, before the X-rays could be completed, Mrs. Malette's condition worsened, as her blood

70   *Intentional torts*

pressure dropped severely and her respiration became more distressed. At this point, Dr. Shulman decided to transfuse blood to preserve her life and health and personally administered the transfusion in spite of being aware of Mrs. Malette's religious beliefs.

Approximately 3 hours after transfusion began, Celine Bisson, who is Mrs. Malette's daughter, arrived at the hospital with her husband and a local church elder and vociferously objected to the procedure. She informed Dr. Shulman of her mother's faith and signed a document prohibiting transfusion and a release of liability of the latter if her mother does not survive. However, Dr. Shulman, to execute his professional responsibility as a doctor, refused to comply with Mrs. Bisson's instructions.

By midnight, Mrs. Malette's condition stabilized. The next day, she was transferred to Toronto General Hospital by air ambulance. She required no further transfusions, and on 11 August 1979, she was discharged from the hospital and made a full recovery. In June 1980, Mrs. Malette brought an action against Dr. Shulman for battery because he transfused blood while being fully apprised of her objection even though the procedure was necessary to preserve her life and health. Finding the doctor liable, the court said,

> The right of a person to control his or her own body is a concept that has long been recognized at common law. The tort of battery has traditionally protected the interest in bodily security from unwanted physical interference. Basically, any intentional non-consensual touching which is harmful or offensive to a person's reasonable sense of dignity is actionable. Of course, a person may choose to waive this protection and consent to the intentional invasion of this interest, in which case an action for battery will not be maintainable. No special exceptions are made for medical care, other than in emergency situations, and the general rules governing actions for battery are applicable to the doctor–patient relationship. Thus, a matter of common law, a medical intervention in which a doctor touches the body of a patient would constitute a battery if the patient did not consent to the intervention. Patients have the decisive role in the medical decision-making process. Their right of self-determination is recognized and protected by the law. As Justice Cardozo proclaimed in his classic statement: "Every human being of adult years and sound mind has a right to determine what shall be done with his own body; and a surgeon who performs an operation without his patient's consent commits an assault, for which he is liable in damages" [...]
>
> The doctrine of informed consent has developed in the law as the primary means of protecting a patient's right to control his or her medical treatment. Under the doctrine, no medical procedure may be undertaken without the patient's consent obtained after the patient has been provided with sufficient information to evaluate the risks and benefits of the proposed treatment and other available options. The doctrine presupposes the patient's capacity to make a subjective treatment decision based on her understanding of the necessary medical facts

Intentional torts 71

provided by the doctor and on her assessment of her own personal circumstances. A doctor who performs a medical procedure without having first furnished the patient with the information needed to obtain an informed consent will have infringed the patient's right to control the course of her medical care, and will be liable in battery even though the procedure was performed with a high degree of skill and actually benefitted the patient.

The right of self-determination which underlies the doctrine of informed consent also obviously encompasses the right to refuse medical treatment. A competent adult is generally entitled to reject a specific treatment or all treatment, or to select an alternate form of treatment, even if the decision may entail risks as serious as death and may appear mistaken in the eyes of the medical profession or of the community. Regardless of the doctor's opinion, it is the patient who has the final say on whether to undergo the treatment. The patient is free to decide, for instance, not to be operated on or not to undergo therapy or, by the same token, not to have blood transfusion. If a doctor were to proceed in the face of a decision to reject the treatment, he would be civilly liable for his unauthorized conduct notwithstanding his justifiable belief that what he did was necessary to preserve the patient's life or health. The doctrine of informed consent is plainly intended to ensure the freedom of individuals to make choices concerning their medical care. For this freedom to be meaningful, people must have the right to make choices that accord with their own values regardless of how unwise or foolish those choices may appear to others [...]

The emergency situation is an exception to the general rule requiring a patient's prior consent. When immediate medical treatment is necessary to save the life or preserve the health of a person who, by reason of unconsciousness or extreme illness, is incapable of either giving or withholding consent, the doctor may proceed without the patient's consent. The delivery of medical services is rendered lawful in such circumstance either on the rationale that the doctor has implied consent from the patient to give emergency aid or, more accurately in my view, on the rationale that the doctor is privileged by reason of necessity in giving the aid and is not to be held liable for so doing. On either basis, in an emergency the law sets aside the requirement of consent on the assumption that the patient, as a reasonable person, would want emergency aid to be rendered if she were capable of giving instructions. As Prosser & Keeton [...] state:

> The touching of another that would ordinarily be a battery in the absence of the consent of either the person touched or his legal agent can sometimes be justified in an emergency. Thus, it has often been asserted that a physician or other provider of health care has implied consent to deliver medical services, including surgical procedures, to a patient in an emergency. But such lawful action is more

72 *Intentional torts*

satisfactorily explained as a privilege. There are several requirements: (1) the patient must be unconscious or without capacity to
make a decision, while no one legally authorized to act as agent for
the patient is available; (2) time must be of the essence, in the sense
that it must reasonably appear that delay until such time as an effective consent could be obtained would subject the patient to a risk of
a serious bodily injury or death which prompt action would avoid;
and (3) under the circumstances, a reasonable person would consent,
and the probabilities are that the patient, would consent [...]

A doctor is not free to disregard a patient's advance instructions any
more than he would be free to disregard instructions given at the time
of the emergency. The law does not prohibit a patient from withholding consent to emergency medical treatment, nor does the law prohibit
a doctor from following his patient's instructions. While the law may
disregard the absence of consent in limited emergency circumstances,
it otherwise supports the right of competent adults to make decisions
concerning their own health care by imposing civil liability on those
who perform medical treatment without consent.

The patient's decision to refuse blood in the situation I have posed
was made prior to and in anticipation of the emergency. While the doctor would have had the opportunity to dissuade her on the basis of his
medical advice, her refusal to accept his advice or her unwillingness
to discuss or consider the subject would not relieve him of his obligation to follow her instructions. The principles of self-determination and
individual autonomy compel the conclusion that the patient may reject
blood transfusions even if harmful consequences may result and even if
the decisions are generally regarded as foolhardy. Her decision in this
instance would be operative after she lapsed into unconsciousness, and
the doctor's conduct would be unauthorized. To transfuse a Jehovah's
Witness in the face of her explicit instructions to the contrary would, in
my opinion, violate her right to control her own body and show disre-
spect for the religious values by which she has chosen to live her life [...]

One further point should be mentioned. The appellant argues that to
uphold the trial decision places a doctor on the horns of a dilemma, in
that, on the one hand, if the doctor administers blood in this situation
and saves the patient's life, the patient may hold him liable in battery
while, on the other hand, if the doctor follows the patient's instructions
and, as a consequence, the patient dies, the doctor may face an action
by dependents alleging that, notwithstanding the card, the deceased
would, if conscious, have accepted blood in the face of imminent death
and the doctor was negligent in failing to administer the transfusions.
In my view, that result cannot conceivably follow. The doctor cannot be
held to have violated either his legal duty or professional responsibility
towards the patient or the patient's dependents when he honours the
Jehovah's Witness card and respects the patient's right to control her

Intentional torts   73

own body in accordance with the dictates of her conscience. The onus is clearly on the patient. When members of the Jehovah's Witness faith choose to carry cards intended to notify doctors and other providers of health care that they reject blood transfusions in an emergency, they must accept the consequences of their decision. Neither they nor their dependents can later be heard to say that the card did not reflect their true wishes. If harmful consequences ensue, the responsibility for those consequences is entirely theirs and not the doctor's.

Notes

I should clarify that Dr. Shulman was not found liable for negligence; rather, he transfused blood and provided treatment in a competent and professional manner and was indispensable to Mrs. Malette's survival and recovery. However, in so doing, he violated the plaintiff's right to autonomy, and therefore, he was liable for battery.

Recall that a battery is any physical, direct, and intentional interference with the bodily integrity of another person and is actionable without proof of damage.[32] In this case, not only was there no damage, but, as I have said, Dr. Shulman was vital to Mrs. Malette's recovery. The common law places a high level of importance on the protection of a person's bodily integrity, and any interference with it that is offensive is actionable.[33] However, this engenders the question of "how can a doctor, who saved a patient's life by transfusing blood, be held to have offended the patient's bodily integrity"?

Imagine you are a staunch Muslim woman and usually wear a veil whenever you exit the house. You are married, eight months into your pregnancy and are treated by a female obstetrician at United Hospital. At 1:30 am, as you and your husband are driving back home, he collides with another vehicle, which destroys your cellphones and renders both of you unconscious from severe head trauma. You and your husband are rushed to the nearest hospital, which is Evercare, where the doctor at the Emergency, who is also an obstetrician, is male. Upon an initial examination, he discovers that in order to save you and the foetus' life, he must immediately administer a Caesarean section. However, a nurse then discovers a note from inside a pocket of your veil that stipulates, "TO BE TREATED BY FEMALE NURSES AND DOCTORS ONLY." Essentially, this means you are unwilling to be treated by a male doctor, but since this was an emergency, and necessary to save your, and your foetus' life, the doctor decides to begin the operation.

Fortunately, the operation ended successfully. You regain consciousness at 6:30 am, and the doctor, who administered the operation, enters your cabin at 6:50 am and informs you that you have given birth to a healthy and beautiful daughter, and that your husband's condition has stabilized. Though inebriated by drugs, you are startled by the sight of a male doctor and petrified when you discover he was the doctor that administered the operation. Within a month, the three of you make a full recovery and are discharged from the hospital. You can subsequently bring an action against

74 Intentional torts

the doctor for battery because you had a note that the doctor discovered prior to the operation, which prohibited male persons from treating you. As in, similar to *Malette*, the offending action is not in providing treatment without proper care for which your condition deteriorated, but the treatment itself. That is to say, you did not consent to being treated by a person of the opposite gender, and therefore, when the doctor, being apprised of your choice, treated you, he committed battery, even though it was the treatment that saved your and the baby's life.

Two additional points warrant discussion. First, let us assume that upon discovery of the note, the doctor decided against the operation, which culminated in the baby's death and inflicted permanent injury on your uterus, causing you to become incapable of conceiving in the future. While he tried to contact a female obstetrician, it was to no avail. When you regain consciousness, you cannot bring an action against the doctor for failing to provide medical care in an emergency, as he was honouring your express prohibitory instructions. As in, even if it were true that you would have changed your mind in the face of apparent danger had you been conscious, since the note proscribed male doctors from treating you, the law will assume that you have accepted all of the consequences of your choice, even if it results in death.

However, a note does not mean that you would be precluded from consenting to treatment by a male doctor had you been conscious. As in, assume that after the accident, you were conscious and of sound mind when brought to the hospital. Then, a nurse discovers the note and shows it to the doctor, and if the doctor refuses to treat you on the basis of the note even though you are now conscious and consenting to treatment, then you can bring an action against the doctor for failing to provide medical care. In simpler words, later consent will negate prior prohibitory instructions, but in the absence of consent, the note will take precedence, and any actions in transgression of the note will constitute battery.[34]

Second, assume, again, that the accident rendered you unconscious, but that you carried no prohibitory note. Ordinarily, while any kind of interference with the bodily integrity of another constitutes battery, touching can be justified in cases of emergency, as the law implies consent. According to William Prosser and Page Keaton, if three requirements are met, then the person who touches or treats an unconscious individual will not be liable. Firstly, the doctor must seek permission to treat the patient from an authorized agent, which can be any person of adult years. However, if an agent is unavailable, it does not mean that treatment cannot be administered (so long as the other two elements are met). Secondly, time must be of the essence in the sense that if there is a delay in treatment, the patient may suffer irreversible harm, such as to the liver or other vital organs, or death. Lastly, under the circumstances, there is a probability that the patient, if conscious, would consent to treatment. That is to say, if you were conscious and were informed of the attendant risks of refusing treatment, if it is more

Intentional torts 75

probable than not that you would have consented to treatment, then the law would imply consent when unconscious.[35]

Nilabati Behera v State of Orissa[36]

Nilabati Behera's son, Suman Behera, who was about 22 years old, was taken into custody by police in Sundergarh, Odisha (formerly "Orissa"), at about 8:00 am on 12 January 1987. That same night, Ms. Behera and her mother brought food to Suman at the police station, which the latter had for dinner. The women subsequently left. Around 2:00 pm the following day, Ms. Behera was informed that her son died and that his dead body was found near the railway tracks at Jeraikela Railway Station. There were multiple injuries found on the deceased's body, including, *inter alia*, lacerations on the forehead, left thigh and knee joint, bruises on the neck, right scapula, right shoulder, and multiple fractures including the skull. Ms. Behera then brought proceedings against the police for custodial death under Article 32 of the *Constitution of India*. Holding the police liable and awarding compensation, the court said,

> The admitted facts are, that Suman Behera was taken in police custody on 1.12.1987 at 8 a.m. and he was found dead the next day on the railway track near the Police Outpost Jeraikela, without being released from custody, and his death was unnatural caused by multiple injuries sustained by him. The burden is, therefore, clearly on the respondents to explain how Suman Behera sustained those injuries which caused his death. Unless a plausible explanation is given by the respondents which is consistent with their innocence, the obvious inference is that the fatal injuries were inflicted to Suman Behera in police custody resulting in his death, for which the respondents are responsible and liable. [...] Shri M.S. Ganesh, who appeared as *amicus curiae* for the petitioner, however, contended that the evidence adduced during the inquiry does not support the defence of [the] respondents and there is no reason to reject the finding of the learned District Judge that Suman Behera died in police custody as a result of injuries inflicted to him. [...]
>
> The doctor deposed that all the injuries were caused by hard and blunt objects; the injuries on the face and left temporal region were postmortem while the rest were ante-mortem. The doctor excluded the possibility of the injuries resulting from dragging of the body by a running train and stated that all the ante-mortem injuries could be caused by *lathi* blows. It was further stated by the doctor that while all the injuries could not be caused in a train accident, it was possible to cause all the injuries by *lathi* blows. Thus, the medical evidence comprising the testimony of the doctor, who conducted the postmortem, excludes the possibility of all the injuries to Suman Behera being caused in a train accident while indicating that all of them could result from the merciless beating given to him. [...]

76 *Intentional torts*

It follows that "a claim in public law for compensation" for contravention of human rights and fundamental freedoms, the protection of which is guaranteed in the *Constitution*, is an acknowledged remedy for enforcement and protection of such rights, and such a claim based on strict liability made by resorting to a constitutional remedy provided for the enforcement of a fundamental right is "distinct from, and in addition to, the remedy in private law for damages for the tort" resulting from the contravention of the fundamental right. [...]

We respectfully concur with the view that the court is not helpless and the wide powers given to this Court by Article 32, which itself is a fundamental right, imposes a constitutional obligation on this Court to forge such new tools, which may be necessary for doing complete justice and enforcing the fundamental rights guaranteed in the *Constitution*, which enable the award of monetary compensation in appropriate cases, where that is the only mode of redress available.

Notes

While constitutional torts drew their nascent breaths in the 1980s in India, it was cemented by *Nilabati*,[37] which essentially said two things. First, the State cannot act with impunity, and second, constitutional torts, or tortious claims in general, can be brought against the State for breaches of duty of care. Here, the Supreme Court of India (hereinafter "SCI") acknowledged that even though Article 32 of the *Constitution of India* does not explicitly permit the SCI to provide monetary compensation, nothing in the provision precludes the court to "forge such new tools" when it "is the only mode of redress available."[38]

A perusal of the case will allow one to deduce that the case was one of battery causing death and that monetary compensation was awarded based on principles of tort law, especially because the SCI was not statutorily empowered to dispense such a remedy. This is similar to Bangladesh as the High Court Division of the Supreme Court of Bangladesh[39] recognized that it must, as a moral imperative, award compensation to victims when there is no other redress available, even when the perpetrator is the State.

4.1.5 *Intentional infliction of nervous shock*

For a long time, courts had been unwilling to provide compensation to victims of mental injuries, primarily on the grounds of measuring the damage.[40] For example, in *Lynch v Knight*,[41] the court said,

Mental pain and anxiety the law cannot value and does not pretend to redress, when the unlawful act complained of causes that only; though, where a material damage occurs connected with it, it is impossible a jury, in estimating it, should altogether overlook the feelings of the party interested. For instance, where a daughter is seduced, however deeply the feelings of the parent may be affected by the wicked act of

Intentional torts   77

the seducer, the law gives no redress, unless the daughter is also a servant, the loss of whose service is a material damage which a jury has to
estimate, and they usually cannot avoid considering the injured honour
and wounded feelings of the parent in making that estimate.

Furthermore, courts have also expressed concern over the veracity of claims
made in connection with mental injuries and were unequivocal in saying
that it is easy to lie about what goes on inside one's head.[42] However, in
Ashby v White,[43] the court said,

> If plaintiff has a right he must of necessity have a means to vindicate
> and maintain it, and a remedy if he is injured in the exercise and enjoy-
> ment of it; indeed, it is a vain thing to imagine a right without a rem-
> edy, for want of right and remedy are reciprocal. Every injury imports
> a damage though it does not cost the party one farthing; if men will
> multiply injuries, actions must be multiplied too, for every man that is
> injured ought to have his recompense.

Therefore, with the passage of time, courts realized that it would be a miscarriage of justice to deny compensation to one who has genuinely suffered
mental injury, and therefore, gradually began recognizing it as a tortious
offence.[44]

Wilkinson v Downton[45]

Being fully apprised that the information is false, the defendant, as a means
of practical joke, told Mrs. Lavinia Wilkinson that her husband – Thomas
Wilkinson – was involved in an accident and was lying at the Elms-public
house with both of his legs broken and that she was to go and see him
immediately. This provoked a violent shock to Mrs. Wilkinson's nervous
system whereby she persistently vomited and became incapacitated for several weeks. Seeking reparation for fraudulent and malicious misrepresentation, Mr. and Mrs. Wilkinson sued the defendant. The court said,

> One question is whether the defendant's act was so plainly calculated
> to produce some effect of the kind which was produced, that an inten-
> tion to produce it ought to be imputed to the defendant regard being
> had to the fact that the effect was produced on a person proved to
> be in an ordinary state of health and mind. I think that it was. It is
> difficult to imagine that such a statement, made suddenly and with
> apparent seriousness, could fail to produce grave effects under the
> circumstances upon any but an exceptionally indifferent person, and
> therefore an intention to produce such an effect must be imputed,
> and it is no answer in law to say that more harm was done than was
> anticipated, for that is commonly the case with all wrongs. The other
> question is whether the effect was, to use the ordinary phrase, too
> remote to be in law regarded as a consequence for which the defend-
> ant is answerable. Apart from authority I should give the same answer,

78 *Intentional torts*

and on the same grounds, as to the last question, and say that it was not too remote.

Notes

The tort of intentional infliction of nervous shock has three elements. First, there must be some form of outrageous or extreme conduct, such as the dissemination of shocking information known to the defendant to be false. Second, there must be actual, or constructive, intent to cause harm of the kind suffered by the plaintiff. Third, once the first two elements are proven, the plaintiff must then prove that he has suffered nervous shock, which is a recognizable psychiatric illness or physical harm.[46]

To illustrate, firstly, knowing it to be false, if I approach and tell you that your husband was involved in a car accident and that he lost his eyesight, then the first element has been met. If I, however, did not know that the information was false, meaning I thought it was true, then I cannot be held liable. Next, upon hearing the news, if you experience a heart attack, then the third element has been met, as you have suffered physical harm.[47] However, it is the second element that is slightly confusing, but can nevertheless be proven. That is, when I informed you of your husband's condition, had I intended that you suffer a heart attack or another similar injury, then *actual* intent has been proven. Nonetheless, if I contest that I did not intend that you have a heart attack, then *constructive* intent can be inferred, which is when there is less than a substantial certainty that an injury may result. To further explain, as was said in *Wilkinson*, it is difficult to imagine a situation where such an outrageous statement delivered with sufficient seriousness will not produce a grave and significant result – in our case, a heart attack. Therefore, if one, knowing it to be false, provides infelicitous information with a serious demeanour, and you sustain an injury as a result thereof, he will be held liable even if he actually did not intend that you suffer any harm.

4.1.6 *Privacy*

Section 43 of the *Constitution of Bangladesh*[48] stipulates the following:

> Every citizen shall have the right, subject to any reasonable restrictions imposed by law in the interests of the security of the State, public order, public morality or public health:
>
> [T]o be secured in his home against entry, search and seizure; and
> [T]o the privacy of his correspondence and other means of communication.

This means that the security of a person's home, correspondence, "[A]nd other means of communication" are protected by the *Constitution of Bangladesh*. However, as we have learned in the previous chapter, no right is

Intentional torts   79

absolute and it must always be balanced against competing interests. Here, the balance is between interests in privacy and freedom of information.[49] For example, if one had absolute right to privacy in communication, what would prevent him from disseminating intimate pictures of an estranged lover?

Section 8(3) of *The Pornography Control Act*, 2012,[50] stipulates,

> Any person who supplies pornographic material through the use of the Internet, or website, or mobile phone, or any other electronic communication device, shall be said to have committed a crime and shall be punished with rigorous imprisonment for a term which may extend to a maximum of 5 (five) years and with a fine not exceeding ৳200,000.
> (two hundred thousand)

This means that the circulation of material that is amatory in nature is prohibited and a person's privacy concerning intimate pictures is protected by law. However, which statute prevents one from pointing a CCTV camera at another's house? For example, imagine you live on the fifth floor of an apartment building at Banani DOHS and each floor houses two apartments. Your neighbour installed a CCTV camera outside his apartment door, which, if your main door is open, can also capture footage inside your apartment. Is there anything you can legally do to require your neighbour to readjust the position of the camera? Though there are 511 sections in the *Penal Code*, none of its provisions prohibit one from pointing a CCTV camera towards your home.[51]

However, the answer does not lie in statute, but in the common law. Recall I had said in the first chapter that the lacuna left by legislation is often filled by tort law. Thence, in this scenario, tort law will require your neighbour to reposition the camera so that it cannot capture footage from inside your home.[52] Alternatively, the mere fact that the camera is directed at your house, even if it cannot view into your home, is actionable in and of itself.[53]

The tort of "intrusion upon seclusion," which is a relatively new tort, protects the privacy interests of individuals.[54] There are three elements of the tort. First, the intrusion must be intentional or reckless. Second, the intrusion must relate to private matters and is without lawful justification, and third, the intrusion is one that a reasonable person would find grossly offensive.

Saccone v Orr[55]

Augustine Saccone and Robert Orr were good friends. As was not uncommon, they had a private telephone conversation, which the latter recorded. When Mr. Saccone heard of this tape, he went to Mr. Orr's office. However, Mr. Orr was not at work, and therefore, Mr. Saccone told a woman, who was working there, that Mr. Orr was to abstain from using the tape. Later that night, Mr. Orr called Mr. Saccone and assured him that there was no such tape, to which the latter replied, "If you have a tape, don't use it or I'll have to sue you." Unfortunately, Mr. Orr played the tape a few days later at

80 *Intentional torts*

a council meeting to vindicate himself of an accusation and the content of the tape was then printed in *The Niagara Falls Review*. Mr. Saccone sued for invasion of privacy. Finding for Mr. Saccone, the court said,

> Our Courts, and law in general, have an obligation to protect those who for whatever reason cannot protect themselves [because,] [i]n a very real sense the law belongs to the people and [...] they must have access to the forum of their choice without fear that even though vindicated in principle they will suffer financially. [...]
>
> The whole case of the plaintiff, therefore, falls on a question of invasion of privacy in the plane of a recorded private telephone conversation between the plaintiff and the defendant. There is no doubt that the telephone conversation was recorded without the plaintiff's knowledge or consent. There was also no doubt that Orr denied the existence of the tape, after which he played it at a council meeting, despite being told by the plaintiff that, if the tape existed, he wasn't to use it and that, if he did use it, he would be sued.
>
> It also appears to me quite clear that the defendant's purpose was to vindicate himself and to prove that he was not a liar and that he didn't break confidences. But, in fact, as it turns out, he broke the confidence of Mr. Saccone, firstly the taping the conversation without Mr. Saccone's knowledge and, secondly, by denying the existence of the tape. [...]
>
> Be that as it may, it's my opinion that certainly a person must have the right to make such a claim as a result of a taping of a private conversation without his knowledge and, also, as against the publication of the conversation against his will or without his consent.
>
> Certainly, for want of a better description as to what happened, this is an invasion of privacy and, despite the very able argument of defendant's counsel that no such action exists, I have come to the conclusion that the plaintiff must be given some right of recovery for what the defendant has in this case done.

Notes

As *Saccone* clarifies, divulging private telephone conversations can constitute intrusion upon seclusion.[56] Similarly, disclosing private conversations that happened on social media would also likely be tortious. For example, if one carries on a conversation on Facebook or Instagram that, by nature, is private, then disclosing that conversation would allow the aggrieved party to seek injunctive relief and perhaps compensation. Assume, however, that you are texting a friend and the two of you joke about Donald Trump. Approximately 20 minutes later, you find that your friend took a screenshot of the conversation and posted it on Facebook, whereby your name is visible to anyone viewing the picture. Even though you did not anticipate that your friend would publicly exhibit your conversation, this would not be actionable as the texts were not of a "private nature." What, then, constitutes "private nature?"

Intentional torts 81

In *Caltagirone v Scozzari-Cloutier*,[57] the court adumbrated the following guideline:

1. Is the information acquired, collected, disclosed, or published of a kind that a reasonable person would consider private?
2. Has the Plaintiff consented to acquisition or collection of the information?
3. If not, has the information been acquired or collected for a legal process or public interest reason? If so, what is that reason?
4. Has the Plaintiff consented to disclosure or publication of the information?
5. If not, has the information been disclosed or published for a legal process or public interest reason? If so, what is that reason?
6. Is the legal process or public interest reason put forward for acquisition, collection, disclosure, or publication one that a reasonable person would consider outweighs the interest of the individual in keeping the information private?

Therefore, for example, if the conversation between you and your friend was of your sexual orientation, it would be actionable *only if* you kept your orientation secret. As in, assume you are homosexual and you did not disclose this to anyone. You then confided in your friend through a text message who took a screenshot of it and posted it for public viewing. This could be actionable as information that is private in nature, which is your sexual orientation, has been divulged without consent. However, if you were openly homosexual, then your friend's action of posting the screenshot would not be tortious, even though you may feel betrayed or embarrassed.

Similarly, imagine two estranged lovers who, during their relationship, shared sensual texts and pictures. We have already learned that disseminating intimate pictures, but not private texts, is prohibited under the *PCA*. However, if you take a screenshot of a conversation, whose language and context is amorous, and post it online for public viewing, then it could be actionable under the tortious offence of intrusion upon seclusion.

Imagine a different scenario. You have gone to dinner with friends, and after ordering food, you text your girlfriend to tell her you miss her. Then, you place your phone on the table and go to the bathroom. While you are in the washroom, your girlfriend sexts. The notification illuminates and displays the text on your phone's screen, and the person in the next seat views it, but does not touch or unlock your phone. If your friend discloses the content of the text, your girlfriend, who is the aggrieved party, cannot bring an action against him because phones, particularly smartphones, allow the recipient to choose how they wish to be notified.

For example, you can either elect to have a preview of the text displayed on your home screen, which would allow you, or someone nearby, to read the text from the home screen without unlocking it, or to see only

82 *Intentional torts*

a "notification" whereby you are informed of the name of the sender and not the content of the text. In the latter option, you would subsequently be required to unlock your phone and view the text message. Therefore, since you allowed the preview to be displayed, which means you have implicitly accepted the inherent risk of the wandering eye to view and read your text, kept your phone facing up on the table, and your friend did not touch or otherwise interfere with the phone, he did not do anything to invade your privacy. However, had your friend picked up the cellphone, unlocked it, viewed the text, and then discussed it with your friends, the outcome would be different.

For public places, the consideration of privacy is different.[58] Imagine you have gone to a park and taken a picture of a bird, yet, a stranger was also captured in the photograph. You then post the photo on your Instagram profile, which is public. The stranger, who also uses Instagram, finds the photo on her "Explore" feature and is livid when she sees a picture of her posted on your profile, which she believes is an invasion of her privacy as you posted it without her consent. Since there is a diminished expectation of privacy in public places, your action of posting the photo may not be tortious.[59] However, this does not mean that you can go to any public place, take a picture of a person, and post it without fear of penalty. As was said in *Cambell v MGN Ltd*,[60]

> Accordingly, in deciding what was the ambit of an individual's 'private life' in particular circumstances courts need to be on guard against using as a touchstone a test which brings into account considerations which should more properly be considered at the later stage of proportionality. Essentially the touchstone of private life is whether in respect of the disclosed facts the person in question had a reasonable expectation of privacy.

This means that even if the space is public, if the person had a reasonable expectation of privacy, then posting her photo would be actionable. For example, imagine you have gone out for coffee with your friend and you see a woman breastfeeding her baby. Even though she is in a public place, she still has an expectation of privacy, and if you take a picture and post it online, then she can bring proceedings against you. However, had she only been sitting there with her baby, and you took a selfie, which also captured her in the photo, and posted it online, then it would not be actionable. Similarly, having a video camera inside a fitting room or a bathroom at a restaurant (or any other establishment) would be actionable, as though the person is in a public space, he would have a reasonable expectation of privacy inside those particular rooms. Overall, what amounts to an invasion of privacy will depend on the facts and circumstances of each case.[61]

4.1.7 Complete defences

An allegation of intentional interference with the person is not without defence. Therefore, the defendant is permitted to adduce evidence that the

Intentional torts 83

plaintiff, *inter alia*, consented to the interference, or that he acted out of self-defence, or that he was defending his property, or that he was disciplining the plaintiff.

4.1.7.1 Consent

Since battery is any physical, direct, intentional, and non-consensual interference with the bodily integrity of another person that is offensive or harmful, if there is consent to the interference, then there is no battery. For example, while it is battery to cut someone's hair without their permission, there is no battery if they consent to it.

Consent can be express or implied.[62] For example, with long hair and no facial hair, if you go to a barber and sit on the barber chair, consent is implied and the barber may begin cutting your hair. However, the conduct that implies consent must be of a nature whereby a reasonable person would be led to believe that you consent. As in, using the same example, if you go to a barber and sit on the barber chair, and the barber inexplicably begins cutting your t-shirt, then he is guilty of battery, as you had gone to him for tonsorial, and not tailoring, services. Similarly, if you go to a dentist, sit on the dental chair, and open your mouth, the reasonable inference is that you consent to the dentist operating on your teeth. However, if the dentist begins cutting your hair, it would constitute battery.

4.1.7.2 Contact sports

An inherent characteristic of playing sports is the intentional interference with the person of another. If this form of contact happens outside of the game, one would have a case for battery. However, as a general rule, it has been held that during the game, there is implied consent to all battery that is reasonable under the circumstances.

For example, imagine you are playing cricket. You have struck a ball, and you and your teammate begin running to opposite sets of wickets for runs. After an opponent brings the ball under his control, he throws it towards a set of wickets to knock them down prior to you reaching the crease. Unfortunately, as you approach the crease, the ball hits your chest, causing you to become unconscious. Though you are injured, you will not be able to bring an action against the opponent who threw the ball as it is accepted that you have impliedly consented to such battery.[63] To further explain, the possibility of being struck by a cricket ball during the game while one is trying to reach the opposite set of wickets is not uncommon or unreasonable, and therefore, it does not constitute battery.

Alternatively, visualize a different scenario. While playing cricket, you, as the batsman, did not strike the ball and it is now in the possession of the wicketkeeper. The usual practice is that the wicketkeeper will then toss the ball back to the bowler so that the game can recrudesce. However, instead of giving the ball back to the bowler, he intentionally throws it towards

84 Intentional torts

you and strikes your head. This will constitute battery, as it is an aberration from the usual and accepted rules of the game; that is to say, any action that is not concomitant to playing the sport will constitute battery.[64]

For example, in football, to recover the ball from his opponent, a defensive player may slide towards the ball (similar to a tackle). Occasionally, the tackle may not be clean and the defender may inadvertently strike the offensive player's shinbone or ankle, causing him to lose balance and concede the ball, or perhaps injuring him. Depending on the extent of contact, the referee may caution or expel the tackling player from the game. However, even if the offensive player suffers an injury, he cannot bring an action against the defender for battery, as it is assumed that the former has consented to such forms of interference. Nonetheless, the infamous act of Zinedine Zidane head-butting Marco Materazzi in the 2006 World Cup Final is battery because that is not a usual practice in the game of football.[65]

4.1.7.3 Sexual relationships

Any kind of sexual, or other intimate, contact is battery unless there is free consent.[66] This means that your girlfriend or spouse must consent to you touching her (with the obverse being equally important as well). Nonetheless, this does not mean that you require explicit permission every time before engaging in an intimate act.[67] As in, let us assume that you and your girlfriend have been dating for a year and the both of you have engaged in consensual carnal activities with one another. Therefore, when you meet your girlfriend, you do not need to ask, "May I kiss you?" prior to kissing her if you are on affable terms, as doing so would be quite unconventional and bizarre. Not dissimilarly, if the two of you are in bed and conscious, you do not need to ask whether you can kiss her so long as she does not thwart your advances, such as moving your hands away or otherwise prohibiting such acts. However, if the two of you are at the nadir of your relationship and she has expressly prohibited you from touching her, then doing so could constitute battery. In simpler terms, whether your girlfriend or spouse has consented to the activity will depend on the facts and circumstances of each case.

While consent is a defence to battery (in reference to sexual contact), if it is acquired by force or minacious language, then it could be invalid. As in, even if someone consented to the sexual act, a case of battery could nevertheless succeed. Furthermore, consent could also be vitiated if there is a gross inequality of power between parties and evidence is adduced that the stronger party exploited the weakness of the vulnerable party.

Norberg v Wynrib[68]

Laura Norberg was a young woman undergoing treatment through prescription pain-killers for an abscessed tooth. Unfortunately, by the time her dental problem healed, she became addicted to the drug Fiorinal, which contained codeine (opiate) and butalbital (barbiturate), and her physicians did

Intentional torts 85

nothing to gradually help her withdraw from the medicine. Since Fiorinal was illegal, and therefore, could only be lawfully obtained through prescriptions, the best method to acquire Fiorinal was through doctors. The doctor that provided her sister with prescription medicine was a fructuous source, but after he retired, the replacement doctor refused to provide prescriptions.

It is then that she went to Dr. Morris Wynrib and regaled him with a story of a painful ankle and the latter issued a prescription. When she repeatedly visited his practice for the medicine, Dr. Wynrib realized that she was addicted to the drug and said, "If you're good to me, I will be good to you," as he pointed upstairs to where he resided. Ms. Norberg refused and left, but had a difficult time acquiring Fiorinal from other sources, and she soon became "desperate" for the drug. Consequently, she returned to Dr. Wynrib for the prescription and gave him what he wanted – sexual favours. At one point, she begged Dr. Wynrib for help, to which he responded, "Quit," but did not advise any treatment. Soon thereafter, on her own initiative, she went to a rehabilitation centre for drug addiction, and upon successfully completing its program, was discharged, and brought an action against Dr. Wynrib for battery.

Finding Dr. Wynrib liable, the court said that in the law of contracts, an unconscionable transaction requires, firstly, proof of inequality between parties, and secondly, proof of an improvident or imprudent bargain. Similarly, in torts, evidence must be submitted regarding, firstly, inequality between parties, such as the relationship of doctor and patient or lawyer and client; and secondly, exploitation of a party by the other. The court then added,

> It seems clear to me that there was a marked inequality in the respective powers of the parties. The appellant was a young woman with limited education. More important, she was addicted to the heavy use of tranquilizers and painkillers. On this ground alone, it can be said that there was an inequality in the position of the parties arising out of the appellant's need. The appellant's drug dependence diminished her ability to make a real choice. Although she did not wish to engage in sexual activity with Dr. Wynrib, her reluctance was overwhelmed by the driving force of her addiction and the unsettling prospect of a painful, unsupervised chemical withdrawal [...]
>
> On the other side of the equation was an elderly, male professional – the appellant's doctor. An unequal distribution of power is frequently a part of the doctor-patient relationship. As it is stated in *The Final Report of the Task Force on Sexual Abuse of Patients, An Independent Task Force Commissioned by the College of Physicians and Surgeons of Ontario* [...]:
>
> > Patients seek the help of doctors when they are in a vulnerable state – when they are sick, when they are needy, when they are uncertain about what needs to be done.

86 *Intentional torts*

> The unequal distribution of power in the physician-patient relationship makes opportunities for sexual exploitation more possible than in other relationships. This vulnerability gives physicians the power to exact sexual compliance. Physical force or weapons are not necessary because the physician's power comes from having the knowledge and being trusted by patients.

In this case, Dr. Wynrib knew that the appellant was vulnerable and driven by the compulsion for drugs. It is likely that he knew or at least strongly suspected that she was dependent upon Fiorinal before she admitted her addiction to him. It was he who ferreted out that she was addicted to drugs. As a doctor, the respondent knew how to assist the appellant medically and he knew (or should have known) that she could not "just quit" taking drugs without treatment [...] The respondent's medical knowledge and knowledge of the appellant's addiction, combined with his authority to prescribe drugs, gave him power over her. It was he who suggested the sex-for-drugs arrangement.

However, it must still be asked if there was exploitation. In my opinion, there was. Dr. Herbert [Department of Family Practice, Faculty of Medicine, University of British Columbia] expressed the opinion that "a reasonable practitioner would have taken steps to attempt to help Ms. Norberg end her addiction by, for example, suggesting drug counselling, or at the very least, by discontinuing her prescriptions of Fiorinal." However, Dr. Wynrib did not use his medical knowledge and expertise to address the appellant's addiction. Instead, he abused his power over her and exploited the information he obtained concerning her weakness to pursue his own personal interests. [...]

Notes

What *Norberg* elucidates is that consent, even when provided, can be vitiated and a case of sexual battery can subsequently be established. As in, if someone holds a gun to another's head and demands sex, then the other will have no choice but to comply, which, however, would allow the victim to file criminal charges for rape as consent would be lacking.[69] However, imagine a different scenario. You are a student pursuing tertiary education and are registered in four courses. You have gone to your professors to explain that you require a "B" in your courses, as you are on probation, and any grade lower than the aforesaid in any course may result in expulsion. While you have done well in three courses, you have performed poorly on the midterm in one course, and unless you score a 70% on the final exam, you will not be able to attain your desired grade. When the final is graded, the professor – in whose class you have performed poorly – informs you that you have received a score of 62%, which means your overall grade will be a "C+." Seeing your disappointment, he tells you that your grade could be raised if you meet him at his house at 8:00 pm tonight. While his salacious intentions become clear, you think not with reason and visit his

Intentional torts 87

house. The two of you have sex and then he drops you off home. While you consented to have sex with your professor, a claim of battery can nonetheless be instituted. As in, though having sex with your professor was consensual, your consent could be argued to have been vitiated if, firstly, it can be demonstrated that there is an inequality of bargaining power between you and your professor, and secondly, the powerful party exploited the weakness or vulnerability of the weaker party.

First, it is indisputable that there is an inequality of bargaining power between a doctor and patient, a lawyer and client, an employer and employee, and similarly, a teacher and student.[70] That is, the latter persons are usually at the mercy of the former to an extent that they feel helpless in contesting unreasonable acts. For example, a client, if accosted, may have sex with her lawyer because she believes he will expend more resources to help her; or an employee may sleep with her boss due to the mistaken belief that if she does not do so, she will not be promoted. Not dissimilarly, when your professor asked you to meet him at his residence, you acquiesced because you desperately required the grade. That is to say, your professor has the ability to affect your future (e.g. expulsion from school), which can influence your actions. Therefore, even though you knew that his request was lascivious and unreasonable, since he could adversely affect your life, you could not reject his offer, which establishes inequality of bargaining power between you and your professor.[71]

Second, did the person with power (your professor) exploit the weakness or vulnerability of the weaker party (you)? In other words, did the teacher use his authority to extort something from the student? The answer *prima facie* is negative because the professor did not coerce the student to have sex by saying, for example, "If you do not come to mine and have sex with me, I will kill you." Rather, he said that if you wish to get a better grade (meaning the choice is yours), you should meet him at his house at 8:00 pm, to which you voluntarily acceded. As in, you went to your professor's house by election; not by the lack thereof. Furthermore, at his house, your professor did not hold a gun to your head and demand sex; thus, there was no fear of loss of life or limb in disobeying. Therefore, having sex with your professor was a choice – not a command.

However, simply because your professor did not threaten you with bodily harm to have sex does not mean that he did not exploit your weakness. A person's level of education and position (since he has the ability to affect your future) in relation to another is sufficient to establish exploitation even if there is no threat of physical harm. As in, you felt as though you had no choice but to have sex with your professor in order to receive a higher grade so that you can remain in school. That is to say, you were driven by the compulsion of avoiding expulsion, and as such, you slept with your professor.

Furthermore, while you went over to your professor's house voluntarily, it was restricted to choosing only one activity, which is tantamount to having no choice whatsoever. To further explain, your professor did not provide two options whereby you chose one and forwent the other; rather, the only

88   *Intentional torts*

thing you could do to raise your grade was to have sex with him. Therefore, your consent, though given with volition, could be argued to have been vitiated on the grounds that you had no other choice but to concede to his amorous request. Moreover, in *Bangladesh National Women Lawyers' Association v The Government of Bangladesh*, the High Court Division of the Supreme Court of Bangladesh said, *inter alia*, that the demand for sexual favours constitutes sexual harassment.[72]

For further protection against sexual offences, one may also invoke the *Penal Code*, which, unfortunately, is inadequate, as it punishes rape, which requires penetration, and not the broader offence of sexual assault.[73] Therefore, if someone touches a woman's breasts without her consent, though the act is sexual in nature, the perpetrator will not be penalized unless he also penetrates her.[74] However, if one has sex with someone who was unconscious during the time of the act, then it amounts to rape under the *Penal Code*, as she could not consent to the activity.[75] Nonetheless, in this particular case, the gap left by the *Penal Code* is filled both by the common law (under the tort of battery) and a different statute, as one can bring proceedings under section 10 of *The Nari-O-Shishu Nirjaton Domon Ain*, 2000 for sexual assault.[76] While it is now clear that there is statutory and common law protection for rape and sexual assault in Bangladesh, what happens if you consent to having sex with someone you met on Tinder, and only after the act does he mention that he is HIV-positive?

R v Cuerrier[77]

Henry Cuerrier tested to be HIV-positive in August 1992 and a public health nurse instructed him to use protection during sexual intercourse and to inform prospective sexual partners of his HIV-positive status. However, he rejected her advice, and three weeks later, entered into a relationship with a woman with whom he had unprotected sex for about 100 times. Their relationship ended in May 1994, at which point, Mr. Cuerrier began dating another woman and had sex with her approximately ten times, mostly without protection. Both women have testified that they would not have had sex with Mr. Cuerrier had they known that he was HIV-positive. Therefore, the issue became whether the consent of the women was vitiated on account of Mr. Cuerrier's failure, or refusal, to disclose his HIV-positive status. Finding Mr. Cuerrier liable, the court said,

> The first requirement of fraud is proof of dishonesty. In light of the provisions of s. 265, the dishonest action or behaviour must be related to the obtaining of consent to engage in sexual intercourse, in this case unprotected intercourse. The actions of the accused must be assessed objectively to determine whether a reasonable person would find them to be dishonest. The dishonest act consists of either deliberate deceit respecting HIV status or nondisclosure of that status. It cannot be forgotten that the act of intercourse is usually far more than the mere manifestation of the drive to reproduce. It can be the culminating

Intentional torts 89

demonstration of love, admiration and respect. It is the most intimate of physical relations and what actions and reactions led to mutual consent to undertake it will in retrospect be complex. It would be pointless to speculate whether consent would more readily follow deliberate falsehoods than failure to disclose. The possible consequence of engaging in unprotected intercourse with an HIV-positive partner is death. In these circumstances there can be no basis for distinguishing between lies and a deliberate failure to disclose.

Without disclosure of HIV status there cannot be a true consent. The consent cannot simply be to have sexual intercourse. Rather it must be consent to have intercourse with a partner who is HIV-positive. True consent cannot be given if there has not been a disclosure by the accused of his HIV-positive status. A consent that is not based upon knowledge of the significant relevant factors is not a valid consent. The extent of the duty to disclose will increase with the risks attendant upon the act of intercourse. To put it in the context of fraud, the greater the risk of deprivation the higher the duty of disclosure. The failure to disclose HIV-positive status can lead to a devastating illness with fatal consequences. In those circumstances, there exists a positive duty to disclose. The nature and extent of the duty to disclose, if any, will always have to be considered in the context of the particular facts presented.

The second requirement of fraud is that the dishonesty results in deprivation, which may consist of actual harm or simply a risk of harm. Yet it cannot be any trivial harm or risk of harm that will satisfy this requirement in sexual assault cases where the activity would have been consensual if the consent had not been obtained by fraud. For example, the risk of minor scratches or of catching cold would not suffice to establish deprivation. What then should be required? In my view, the Crown will have to establish that the dishonest act (either falsehoods or failure to disclose) had the effect of exposing the person consenting to a significant risk of serious bodily harm. The risk of contracting AIDS as a result of engaging in unprotected intercourse would clearly meet that test. In this case the complainants were exposed to a significant risk of serious harm to their health. Indeed their very survival was placed in jeopardy. It is difficult to imagine a more significant risk or a more grievous bodily harm. As Holland, [...] wrote:

> The consequences of transmission are grave: at the moment there is no "cure," a person infected with HIV is considered to be infected for life. The most pessimistic view is that without a cure all people infected with the virus will eventually develop AIDS and die prematurely.

To have intercourse with a person who is HIV-positive will always present risks. Absolutely safe sex may be impossible. Yet the careful use of condoms might be found to so reduce the risk of harm that it could no longer be considered significant so that there might not be either deprivation or risk of deprivation. To repeat, in circumstances such as those

90 *Intentional torts*

presented in this case, there must be a significant risk of serious bodily harm before the section can be satisfied. In the absence of those criteria, the duty to disclose will not arise. [...]

It must be remembered that what is being considered is a consensual sexual activity which would not constitute assault were it not for the effect of fraud. Obviously if the act of intercourse or other sexual activity was consensual it could not be an assault. It is only because the consent was obtained by fraud that it is vitiated. Aggravated assault is a very serious offence. Indeed, a conviction for any sexual assault has grave consequences. The gravity of those offences makes it essential that the conduct merit the consequences of conviction.

Notes

Cuerrier makes clear that even if sex is consensual, consent can be vitiated if (1) one party has a condition that has the potential to cause serious bodily harm to his partner, but (2) he does not disclose his condition to his partner, as this can amount to fraud. In the context of dating, if one's partner, whether man or woman, does not disclose that he is HIV-positive, or has any other analogous condition, then even if his girlfriend has consensual sex with him, her consent can be argued to have been vitiated, as the consent is not true. This does not mean that she did not consent to having sex with her boyfriend, but that she did not consent to having sex with her boyfriend *who is HIV-positive.*[78]

Moreover, the partner's condition must have the potential to inflict serious bodily harm on the other. For example, since one can ultimately succumb to HIV or suffer heart disease, or maybe even death, from gonorrhoea, they are diseases whose nondisclosure is actionable.[79] However, if one has a common cold, but does not exhibit any symptoms, and a day after having sex, his partner contracts it, she cannot bring an allegation of battery against her boyfriend, as the consequences of a cold is not serious bodily harm.[80]

Let us assume you have met someone at a café, and during your conversation, you mention that you are the heir to a company worth more than a billion dollars. You then tell her that you want to take her home with you, to which she agrees. The two of you have sex and then fall asleep. The next morning, however, you tell her that you are not the heir to a billion-dollar company, but that you are the Vice President of Finance at *Pathao*. Since you fraudulently misrepresented information about your identity, she can bring an action under battery.

Fraud consists of two elements: (1) there must exist some form of deceit or lie and (2) there must be a deprivation (injury), or a risk of deprivation, to the life of another from the deceit or lie.[81] However, we must understand that there is a difference between (a) fraud regarding the nature of the offence, which vitiates consent, and (b) fraud regarding ancillary matters, which does not vitiate consent. While it can be argued that the woman, to whom you told you are the heir to a billion-dollar company, would not suffer physical harm from the fraudulent misrepresentation, the approach

Intentional torts 91

courts now take is that if the fraud exploits a person, then there arises a case for battery. For example, in *R v Mabior*, the court said,

> The *Charter* values of equality, autonomy, liberty, privacy and human dignity are particularly relevant to the interpretation of fraud vitiating consent to sexual relations. The formerly narrow view of consent has been replaced by a view that respects each sexual partner as an autonomous, equal and free person. Our modern understanding of sexual assault is based on the preservation of the right to refuse sexual intercourse: sexual assault is wrong because it denies the victim's dignity as a human being. Fraud in s. 265(3) (c) of the *Criminal Code* must be interpreted in light of these values. [...]
>
> In keeping with the *Charter* values of equality and autonomy, we now see sexual assault not only as a crime associated with emotional and physical harm to the victim, but as the wrongful exploitation of another human being. To engage in sexual acts without the consent of another person is to treat him or her as an object and negate his or her human dignity.[82]

Essentially, sexual battery is no longer restricted to physical harm, as there is a growing concern on protecting the dignity of the individual.[83]

4.1.7.4 *Medical treatment*

Medical treatment of any kind is battery unless the patient consents.[84] Every competent adult has the right to accept treatment, reject treatment, provide conditional consent to treatment, or revoke consent to treatment already provided.

Allan et al v New Mount Sinai Hospital[85]

On 2 November 1972, Mrs. Venita Allan, who would undergo a dilation and curettage operation, met Dr. Kurt Hellman, who is an anaesthetist and had been assigned to perform the anaesthesia on her, outside of the operating room. She said to him, "Please don't touch my left arm. You'll have nothing but trouble there," to which Dr. Hellman purportedly responded, "We know what we are doing." Unfortunately, Dr. Hellman inserted the needle into Mrs. Allan's left arm, and during the course of the surgery, it was dislodged, resulting in the anaesthesia interstitially leaking into her tissue, from which she suffered a severe allergic reaction. Holding Dr. Hellman liable, the court said,

> Without a consent, either written or oral, no surgery may be performed. This is not a mere formality; it is an important individual right to have control over one's own body, even where medical treatment is involved. It is the patient, not the doctor, who decides whether surgery will be performed, where it will be done, when it will be done and by whom it will be done. Dr. Hellman, when told by Mrs. Allan not to use her left

92   *Intentional torts*

arm, had an obligation to comply with her wishes. If he thought it inadvisable, it was his duty to discuss the matter with her and try to convince her to change her mind. The expert evidence of Dr. Renwick was to the effect that this would be the usual thing to do. Dr. Hellman was not entitled to say that he knew what he was doing, and proceed to inject the needle into Mrs. Allan's left arm contrary to her express wishes.

Notes

We must not forget that before surgery, or any medical procedure, we provide consent to the doctor to treat us, and as we have learned throughout this section, any non-consensual medical treatment constitutes battery.[86] Therefore, doctors remain careful and seek consent, most commonly through a written form, before performing surgery. Moreover, the consent form must be understood by the patient. For example, if the patient does not speak or understand English, then seeking consent through a form written in English is not true consent, unless the procedure and its attendant risks are subsequently explained in a language understood by the patient.[87]

Ciarlariello v Schacter[88]

Mrs. Giovanna Ciarlariello was diagnosed with subarachnoid haemorrhage, for which she required two cerebral angiograms. The general procedure for this type of angiogram is that a catheter is inserted into the patient's groin and pushed up to the neck, where a dye is then injected into the blood vessels leading to the head, so that an X-ray image can be taken to precisely locate the problem area. The first angiogram posed no difficulties. The second angiogram, performed on 29 December 1980, however, caused discomfort and Mrs. Ciarlariello began moaning and yelling, which Dr. Greco and Dr. Keller concluded resulted from tetany that had been caused by hyperventilation. Dr. Keller then explained to the patient that another area needed to be examined and asked whether they can complete the test, to which Mrs. Ciarlariello responded, "Please go ahead." Unfortunately, when the dye was injected, she suffered an immediate reaction, which rendered her quadriplegic and she brought a suit against the doctor for battery. Finding for the doctor, the court said,

> Whether or not there has been a withdrawal of consent will always be a question of fact. The words used by a patient may be ambiguous. Even if they are apparently clear, the circumstances under which they were spoken may render them ambiguous. On some occasions, the doctors conducting the process may reasonably take the words spoken by the patient to be an expression of pain rather than a withdrawal of consent. Obviously, these are questions of fact which will have to be resolved by the trial judge. [...]
>
> It should not be forgotten that every patient has a right to bodily integrity. This encompasses the right to determine what medical procedures will be accepted and the extent to which they will be accepted.

Everyone has the right to decide what is to be done to one's own body. This includes the right to be free from medical treatment to which the individual does not consent. This concept of individual autonomy is fundamental to the common law and is the basis for the requirement that disclosure be made to a patient. If, during the course of a medical procedure a patient withdraws the consent to that procedure, then the doctors must halt the process. This duty to stop does no more than recognize every individual's basic right to make decisions concerning his or her own body. [...]

An individual's right to determine what medical procedures will be accepted must include the right to stop a procedure. It is not beyond the realm of possibility that the patient is better able to gauge the level of pain or discomfort that can be accepted or that the patients premonitions of tragedy or mortality may have a basis in reality. In any event, the patient's right to bodily integrity provides the basis for the withdrawal of a consent to a medical procedure even while it is underway. Thus, if it is found that the consent is effectively withdrawn during the course of the proceeding then it must be terminated. This must be the result except in those circumstances where the medical evidence suggests that to terminate the process would be either life threatening or pose immediate and serious problems to the health of the patient.

The issue as to whether or not a consent has been withdrawn during the course of a procedure may require the trial judge to make difficult findings of fact. If sedatives or other medication were administered to the patient then it must be determined if the patient was so sedated or so affected by the medication that consent to the procedure could not effectively have been withdrawn. The question whether a patient is capable of withdrawing consent will depend on the circumstances of each case. Expert medical evidence will undoubtedly be relevant, but it will not necessarily be determinative of the issue. Indeed, in cases such as this where the patient must be conscious and cooperative in order for the procedure to be performed, it may well be beyond doubt that the patient was capable of withdrawing consent. [...]

When a patient withdraws consent during a procedure to its continuation, the procedure must be stopped unless to do so would seriously endanger the patient. However, the patient may still consent to the renewal or continuation of the process. That consent must also be informed. Although it may not be necessary that the doctors review with the patient all the risks involved in the procedure, the patient must be advised of any material change in the risks which has arisen and would be involved in continuing the process. In addition, the patient must be informed of any material change in the circumstances which could alter his or her assessment of the costs or benefits of continuing the procedure. Here, there had been no material change in the circumstances and a valid consent was given to the continuation of the process.

94   *Intentional torts*

Notes

From *Allen*, we learn that patients provide consent before surgery, or any medical procedure, is performed, and if the patient does not consent, but the doctor administers treatment, then he is liable for battery. *Ciarlariello* goes one step further and tells us that during surgery, a patient has the right to revoke consent he has already provided. For example, if you go to a dentist for a root-canal, and halfway through the procedure, you instruct him to stop, then the dentist must stop the operation. However, if, in the opinion of the doctor, terminating the procedure would be life threatening to the patient, then he can disregard the patient's instruction and continue the operation. As in, if you instruct the dentist to stop, but he continues the operation because he believes that if the bacteria is not removed from underneath your tooth, your pain will exacerbate, then he is liable for battery, as stopping the operation will not endanger your life.

Imagine another scenario. While chopping an onion, you punctured your left index finger. Since the wound is deep, you go to the hospital because you recognize that you will need stitches. The doctor informs you that you will need five stitches, but the wound is at a place where he cannot administer anaesthesia, which means you will feel the needle repeatedly piercing through your skin. Reluctantly, you consent to treatment. However, because of the excruciating pain, as no anaesthesia was injected, you instruct the doctor to stop after three stitches. The doctor explains that if he stops now, the area may become infected and they may have to amputate your finger. Informed, you tell the doctor to stop the operation anyway. If he continues the procedure, he will be liable for battery because you revoked consent. As in, even if there is a 99% chance that your finger would have to be amputated if the operation is stopped, since it would not endanger your life, the doctor has to adhere to the patient's instruction.

Imagine, now, another scenario. While a woman is giving birth through normal delivery, a complication arises. The obstetrician informs the patient that in order to save her, and the foetus', life, he needs to perform a Caesarean section, as otherwise there is a very high probability that she will die. The patient does not consent to surgery. If the doctor disregards the patient's instruction and performs the procedure, he will not be liable for battery as the operation is necessary to save her life. This scenario is different from the previous two examples in the sense that, here, there is a danger to the patient's life if the doctor stops the operation. Therefore, and as was identified in *Ciarlariello*, the doctor can disregard the patient's instruction and continue the operation only if stopping a medical procedure will endanger the patient's life.

It is pertinent to understand that *Ciarlariello* does not reduce the patient's power to revoke consent. Rather, it clarifies that a doctor must, at all times, seek consent from the patient before performing any medical procedure, and the only time a doctor can disregard the patient's lack of consent to treatment is if it endangers the latter's life. The law is stringent in protecting the autonomy of the patient and *Ciarlariello* should not be misconstrued to be an attempt to whittle this position down.[89]

Intentional torts 95

Furthermore, it is the patient, and no one else, unless the patient is temporarily incapacitated, who can provide consent even if she is under the age of adulthood in that jurisdiction. For example, in *C(JS) v Wren*,[90] the parents of a 16-year-old tried to unsuccessfully prevent their daughter from terminating her pregnancy. However, the court held that she was a mature-minor and had the right to control her medical treatment. Additionally, the court said,

> The real thrust of argument before us was that children should obey their parents and the courts should intervene to prevent others from interfering with parental control of those children who are committed to their custody and control. That is not quite the suit that has been brought here today, but we will deal with the issue. Parental rights (and obligations) clearly do exist and they do not wholly disappear until the age of majority. The modern law, however, is that the courts will exercise increasing restraint in that regard as a child grows to and through adolescence. The law and the development of the law in this respect was analyzed in detail by Lord Scarman in the *Gillick* case. He analyzes the law back to Blackstone and extracts this principle:
>
>> The principle is that parental right or power of control of the person and property of his child exists primarily to enable the parent to discharge his duty of maintenance, protection and eduction until he reaches such an age as to be able to look after himself and make his own decisions. [...]
>
> He then reviews the application of that principle in cases over the past century, especially in the "age of discretion" cases. He says:
>
>> The "age of discretion" cases are cases in which a parent or guardian (usually the father) has applied for *habeas corpus* to secure the return of his child who has left home without his consent. The courts would refuse an order if the child had attained the age of discretion, which came to be regarded as 14 for boys and 16 for girls, and did not wish to return. The principle underlying them was plainly that an order would be refused if the child had sufficient intelligence and understanding to make up his own mind. [...]
>
> We infer from the circumstances detailed in argument here that this expectant mother and her parents had fully discussed the ethical issues involved and, most regrettably, disagreed. We cannot infer from that disagreement that this expectant mother did not have sufficient intelligence and understanding to make up her own mind. Meanwhile, it is conceded that she is a "normal intelligent 16 year old." We infer that she did have sufficient intelligence and understanding to make up her own mind and did so. At her age and level of understanding, the law is that she is to be permitted to do so.

96 Intentional torts

As in, even if the age of maturity is eighteen, if a 15-year-old demonstrates intelligence that she can look after her interests, then it is her consent that is required for medical treatment and not her guardian's.[91] However, a doctor will need to adhere to the guardian's order if, for example, the patient is 12 years old and does not understand the complications and the mental and physical burden of continuing a pregnancy. Overall, when read in tandem, *Malette, Ciarlariello*, and *C(JS)* confers broad rights to patients to exercise control over their bodies even if they are under the age of majority.

Hollis v Dow Corning Corp[92]

In June 1983, Susan Hollis went to Dr. Ken Mills for a complete physical examination. Dr. Mills determined that Ms. Hollis suffered from "tubular breasts," which produced a cylinder-like shape in the breasts and collected blood near the nipples, causing the areolae to be larger than usual. Dr. Mills recommended that she see Dr. Birch with whom she met in July. Dr. Birch determined that her congenital deformity could be corrected by implants and explained the surgical procedure, confirming that she would not be able to feel the implants after the operation and that it would not prevent her from breast-feeding. However, he mentioned nothing about post-surgical rupture.

On 21 October 1983, Ms. Hollis underwent surgery for implanting "gel-filled, low profile round" Silastic implants, which were manufactured by Dow Corning Corporation (hereinafter "Dow"). However, by January 1985, she had developed lumps near her right breast, which caused her acute pain, and on 19 March 1985, she underwent surgery to have the implants removed. It was then discovered that the Silastic implant on the right-breast ruptured – allowing the gel to accumulate on the breast cavity, which caused severe pain. She then brought actions against, *inter alia*, Dow and Dr. Birch, and the pivotal issue was whether Dow can be held liable for failing to adequately warn of post-surgical complications of Silastic to the operating surgeon. Holding Dow liable, the court said,

> It is well established in Canadian law that a manufacturer of a product has a duty in tort to warn consumers of dangers inherent in the use of its product of which it has knowledge or ought to have knowledge [...] The duty to warn is a continuing duty, requiring manufacturers to warn not only of dangers known at the time of sale, but also of dangers discovered after the product has been sold and delivered [...] All warnings must be reasonably communicated, and must clearly describe any specific dangers that arise from the ordinary use of the product [...]
>
> In the case of medical products such as the breast implants at issue in this appeal, the standard of care to be met by manufacturers in ensuring that consumers are properly warned is necessarily high. Medical products are often designed for bodily ingestion or implantation, and the risks created by their improper use are obviously substantial. The courts in this country have long recognized that manufacturers of products that are ingested, consumed or otherwise placed in the body, and thereby have a great capacity to cause injury to consumers, are subject

to a correspondingly high standard of care under the law of negligence [...] Given the intimate relationship between medical products and the consumer's body, and the resulting risk created to the consumer, there will almost always be a heavy onus on manufacturers of medical products to provide clear, complete and current information concerning the dangers inherent in the ordinary use of their product.

I pause at this point to observe that there is an important analogy to be drawn in this context between the manufacturer's duty to warn and the doctrine of "informed consent" developed by this Court in recent years with respect to the doctor-patient relationship [...] The doctrine of "informed consent" dictates that every individual has a right to know what risks are involved in undergoing or foregoing medical treatment and a concomitant right to make meaningful decisions based on a full understanding of those risks [...]

In my view, the principles underlying the doctrine of "informed consent" are equally, if not more, applicable to the relationship between manufacturers of medical products and consumers than to the doctor-patient relationship. The doctrine of "informed consent" was developed as a judicial attempt to redress the inequality of information that characterizes a doctor-patient relationship. An even greater relationship of inequality pertains both between the manufacturer of medical products and the consumer and, to a lesser degree, between the manufacturer and the doctor. In contrast to the doctor-patient relationship, where the patient can question the doctor with respect to the risks and benefits of particular procedures and where doctors can tailor their warnings to the needs and abilities of the individual patients, the manufacturer-consumer relationship is characterized primarily by a lack of direct communication or dialogue [...]

As a general rule, the duty to warn is owed directly by the manufacturer to the ultimate consumer. However, in exceptional circumstances, a manufacturer may satisfy its informational duty to the consumer by providing a warning to what the American courts have, in recent years, termed a "learned intermediary" [...]

While the "learned intermediary" rule was originally intended to reflect, through an equitable distribution of tort duties, the tripartite informational relationship between drug manufacturers, physicians and patients, the rationale for the rule is clearly applicable in other contexts. Indeed, the "learned intermediary" rule is less a "rule" than a specific application of the long-established common law principles of intermediate examination and intervening cause developed in *Donoghue v Stevenson*, [...] and subsequent cases; see, for example, *Holmes v Ashford*, [...] Generally, the rule is applicable either where a product is highly technical in nature and is intended to be used only under the supervision of experts, or where the nature of the product is such that the consumer will not realistically receive a direct warning from the manufacturer before using the product. In such cases, where an intermediate inspection of the product is anticipated or where a consumer is placing primary reliance on the judgment of a "learned intermediary" and not the manufacturer, a warning to the ultimate consumer may not be necessary and the manufacturer may satisfy its duty to warn the ultimate consumer by warning the learned intermediary of the risks inherent in the use of the product.

However, it is important to keep in mind that the "learned intermediary" rule is merely an exception to the general manufacturer's duty to warn the consumer. The rule operates to discharge the manufacturer's duty not to the learned intermediary, but to the ultimate consumer, who has a right to full and current information about any risks inherent in the ordinary use of the product. Thus, the rule presumes that the intermediary is "learned," that is to say, fully apprised of the risks associated with the use of the product. Accordingly, the manufacturer can only be said to have discharged its duty to the consumer when the intermediary's knowledge approximates that of the manufacturer. To allow manufacturers to claim the benefit of the rule where they have not fully warned the physician would undermine the policy rationale for the duty to warn, which is to ensure that the consumer is fully informed of all risks. Since the manufacturer is in the best position to know the risks attendant upon the use of its product and is also in the best position to ensure that the product is safe for normal use, the primary duty to give a clear, complete, and current warning must fall on its shoulders [...]

However, the mere fact that the "learned intermediary" rule is applicable in this context does not absolve Dow of liability. As I mentioned earlier, the "learned intermediary" rule presumes that the intermediary is fully apprised of the risks, and can only provide shelter to the manufacturer where it has taken adequate steps to ensure that the intermediary's knowledge of the risks in fact approximates that of the manufacturer. Thus, the second, and more important, question to be resolved is whether Dow fulfilled its duty to Ms. Hollis by adequately warning Dr. Birch of the risk of post-surgical rupture of the implant [...]

In my view, Dow had a duty to convey its findings concerning both the "unexplained" rupture phenomenon and the possible harm caused by loose gel inside the body to the medical community much sooner than it did. In light of the fact that implants are surgically placed inside the human body, and that any defects in these products will obviously have a highly injurious effect on the user, the onus on Dow to be forthcoming with information was extremely high throughout the relevant period. Despite this fact, for over six years Dow took no action to express its concerns to the medical community. Given Dow's knowledge of the potential harm caused by loose gel in the body, this lag time is simply unacceptable. The duty to warn is a continuing one and manufacturers of potentially hazardous products have an obligation to keep doctors abreast of developments even if they do not consider those developments to be conclusive [...]

Ms. Hollis, it will be remembered, demonstrated that Dow had breached its duty to warn her of the risk of rupture, that she would not have undergone the medical procedure if she had been fully informed of the risks, and that she suffered injury from the rupture. Had Dr. Birch been adequately warned but had not passed on the information to Ms. Hollis, Dow would, it is true, have been absolved of liability by virtue of the learned intermediary doctrine. But I fail to see how one can reason from this that, for Dow to be liable, Ms. Hollis must now establish that Dr. Birch would have informed her if he had known. To require her to do so would be to ask her to prove a hypothetical situation relating to her doctor's conduct, one, moreover, brought about by Dow's failure to perform its duty.

Notes

Medical products are intimate in the sense that they are occasionally ingested or placed inside a patient's body. If the patient does not understand the nature of the medical procedure, or the product, he cannot be held to have truly consented to the treatment. Therefore, not only can the doctor be held liable in battery for failing to acquire the patient's consent, but the manufacturer can be held liable as well even if the latter never communicates directly with the patient. However, as was said in *White v Turner*,[93]

It is clear that Canadian doctors are obligated to disclose to their patients "the nature of the proposed operation, its gravity, any material risks and any special or unusual risks attendant upon the performance of the operation" [...] It is also clear [...] that these problems are to be analyzed with negligence law theory, rather than with the law of battery. Further, the language of "informed consent" should be avoided in these cases, since it spawns confusion between these two distinct theories of liability.

The law of battery is to be used no longer in cases involving the adequacy of information about risks that is given to these patients, but it remains available where there is no consent to the operation, where the treatment given goes beyond the consent, or where the consent is obtained by fraud or misrepresentation [...]

The future use of battery is, therefore, to be limited to cases involving a real lack of consent. Where there has been a basic consent to the treatment, there is no place left for discussions of battery. The problems associated with inadequacy of information about risks are to be handled with negligence theory. [...]

Further, in analyzing the quality and quantity of the information given to a patient under negligence principles, the test to be employed is no longer the professional medical standard, heretofore used by our Courts, but rather the reasonable patient standard. This is a major shift heralded by the Supreme Court of Canada in *Reibl v Hughes* [...] No longer does the medical profession alone collectively determine, by its

100   *Intentional torts*

own practices, the amount of information a patient should have in order to decide whether to undergo an operation. From now on, the Court also has a voice in deciding the appropriate level of information that must be conveyed to a patient in the circumstances as a question of fact. [...]

In my view, material risks are significant risks that pose a real threat to the patients' life, health or comfort. In considering whether a risk is material or immaterial, one must balance the severity of the potential result and the likelihood of its occurring. Even if there is only a small chance of serious injury or death, the risk may be considered material. On the other hand, if there is a significant chance of slight injury this too may be held to be material. As always in negligence law, what is a material risk will have to depend on the specific facts of each case.

Essentially, this means that the failure to disclose attendant risks of an operation should now be covered under negligence law. On the other hand, cases of battery are to be limited to whether the doctor left "the patient with a substantial misunderstanding as to the general nature and character of the touching which the patient was to undergo."[94] As in, if the patient understands the treatment, consents, and is subsequently injured, then the doctor is not liable for battery, but can be liable under negligence if he does not carry on the operation with due care. However, if the doctor fails to disclose the risks of the operation, then he can be liable in negligence so long as the plaintiff can prove that had he been aware of the attendant risks, he would not have submitted to the medical procedure.[95]

Nonetheless, from *Hollis*, we must understand that, in the medical world, the law imposes two distinct duties upon two separate parties. Firstly, a duty is imposed on the manufacturer to disclose risks of their products to the ultimate consumer, who is often the patient. Secondly, a duty is imposed on the doctor to divulge all the attendant risks of a medical procedure and products. However, since the manufacturer does not always communicate directly with the ultimate consumer, he relies on the "learned intermediary," who is a person between the patient and the manufacturer, such as a doctor. Therefore, once the manufacturer informs the doctor of the attendant risks of a medical product, the former is held to have discharged his obligation to inform the ultimate user of all risks associated with using that particular device. That is to say, it is then the doctor who will be liable for failing to disclose material risks of the medical procedure or product, unless (1) there is a defect in the product itself or (2) the manufacturer did not inform the doctor of the risks of using his product.

4.1.7.5 Self-defence

The common law, in conjunction with the *Penal Code*, recognizes one's right to defend his person, property, and another. Since there is extensive overlap between tort and the criminal law in relation to defence, I shall speak of them concurrently.[96]

Intentional torts   101

Section 96 of the *Penal Code* stipulates, "Nothing is an offence which is done in the exercise of the right of private defence."[97] Furthermore, section 97 says,[98]

> Every person has a right, subject to the restrictions contained in section 99 to defend,
> Firstly, his own body, and the body of any other person against any offence affecting the human body;
> Secondly, the property, whether moveable or immovable, of himself or of any other person, against any act which is an offence falling under the definition of theft, robbery, mischief, or criminal trespass, or which is an attempt to commit theft, robbery, mischief or criminal trespass.

Additionally, section 99 provides,[99]

> There is no right of private defence against an act which does not reasonably cause the apprehension of death or of grievous hurt, if done, or attempted to be done by a public servant acting in good faith under colour of his office, though that act may not be strictly justifiable by law.
> There is no right of private defence against an act which does not reasonably cause the apprehension of death or of grievous hurt, if done, or attempted to be done, by the direction of a public servant acting in good faith under colour of his office, though that act may not be strictly justifiable by law.
> There is no right of private defence in cases in which there is time to have recourse to the protection of the public authorities.

A person has the right to use "reasonable force" to repel an attack. What this means is, *inter alia*, the age, height, weight, weapons used by the assailant, and the imminence of the attack are important factors in determining whether the person defending himself used reasonable force.[100] For example, imagine that the attacker is 5', 14 years old, weighs 42 kgs, and is approaching to attack you without a weapon; you are 5' 10", 28 years old, and weigh 72 kgs. If you repel his attack with a knife, and while doing so, stab him, you are using excessive force, as you are, firstly, bigger than him, secondly, using a knife, and thirdly, he is not using a weapon. That is to say, when defending oneself, his property, or another person, one cannot use more force than is necessary to subdue his assailant.

Imagine a similar scenario, but with the characteristics of the assailant and the victim reversed. Since you are younger, shorter, and weaker than the attacker, you can restrain him by using a weapon, such as a glass bottle. However, after you have neutralized him, if you strap him onto a chair, strike him repeatedly until he loses a tooth, and break his finger, then it is no longer reasonable; rather, you have committed battery.[101] Nonetheless, if, for example, you require only four strikes to subdue the assailant, but you hit him seven times, thereby causing more injury than is necessary, the law

102 *Intentional torts*

is not going to measure reasonableness stringently.[102] That is, in moments of peril, we cannot properly calculate what would be reasonable under the circumstances – so long as what we do is not patently unreasonable (e.g. after negating the threat, we break his finger).

The situation would be entirely different if, however, the threat was not imminent. For example, suppose you are in Dhaka while the assailant is in Chittagong. He calls to inform you that he will reach Dhaka in approximately 6 hours and beat you senseless. Fearing for your safety, you load your gun and await his arrival. When he enters your house 7 hours later, you shoot his leg so that he cannot attack you. Here, your act was unreasonable, as firstly, the threat was not imminent, and secondly, you had ample time to report the threat to the police, who have the lawful right to address this issue. Therefore, self-defence would be inapplicable.

4.1.7.6 *Defence of another person*

Similar to how the law permits a person to use reasonable force to protect himself from an imminent attack, it also allows him to protect another. For example, in *Gambriell v Caparelli*, Mrs. Caparelli's son and the plaintiff were embroiled in a fight. When Mrs. Caparelli, who was 57 years old, approached the scene, she saw the plaintiff choking her son. Fearing that he could die, she grabbed a weapon, which was a garden cultivator, and hit the plaintiff a total of four times – thrice on the shoulder, which did not prevent his ability to fight, and once on the head, which caused him to bleed and eventually stop fighting. Mrs. Caparelli was not liable in battery as she was defending another person from an ongoing attack even though she hit the plaintiff a total of four times in order to subdue him.[103]

While *Gambriell* sees one defending another who is a family member, defence of another person can also extend to protecting a person who is not a family member.[104] Additionally, the attack does not have to be ongoing, but, similar to self-defence, so long as it is imminent, one can use reasonable force to defend another.

4.1.7.7 *Discipline*

When a parent disciplines his child through the application of force, he is committing battery. However, the law does not punish the parent so long as the force is corrective, transitory, and trifling. This means that a parent can use force to *correct*, what a parent otherwise perceives to be, a child's *incorrect* behaviour. This means that if the parent had a bad day at work, he cannot come back home and beat up his child as catharsis. Furthermore, the force must be transitory and trifling, which means that a parent cannot, *inter alia*, tie up the child's hands and legs to a closet-door, as this would restrict the child's mobility and be excessive.[105]

Intentional torts 103

The defence of discipline is also granted to those that are temporary custodians of the child, such as a babysitter or a teacher. However, force applied must, again, be corrective, transitory, and trifling. As in, if I am babysitting my brother's daughter, I can use force of a transitory and trifling nature to correct my niece's behaviour. However, in Bangladesh, teachers previously had untrammelled power to impart corporal punishment upon children, who would then require medical attention. In order to prevent such abominable conduct, the legislature[106] and the High Court[107] intervened, and therefore, a teacher can no longer use corrective force to discipline a child in Bangladesh.

4.1.8 Partial defences

Not all actions constitute a complete defence to interference with the person. For example, while, *inter alia*, consent, self-defence, defence of another, and discipline will be a full defence, which means the person will be exonerated absolutely, provocation and contributory negligence are partial defences, whereby the defendant is nevertheless liable, but the extent of his liability is reduced.[108]

4.1.8.1 Provocation

Provocation relates to temporal closeness between the tortfeasor's comment and the plaintiff's conduct. Provocative conduct can include, *inter alia*, insults, blasphemous language, racial epithets, and obscene gestures.[109] For example, suppose you are a 12th-grade Muslim student and there is a gentleman named Kumar Roy, who is Hindu, in your class. One day, you tell him that Hindus smell bad because they do not shower for weeks. You then tell him that his mom, dad, and younger sister are malodorous and that if they wish to smell more pleasant, they should accept Islam. At this point, Kumar loses his temper and punches you. While, if you proceed civilly, you can charge Kumar with battery, the extent of his liability would be reduced because of your provocative conduct.

More importantly, though, we must understand that Kumar's punch was very closely related in time to your insult. As in, if you taunt him and he punches you an hour later, he cannot argue the defence of provocation, as there was a significant gap between your insult and his punch. Additionally, your statement was so insensitive that it caused, and would cause, a reasonable person to lose self-control. That is to say, if someone is known to be mercurial, and you call him an idiot and he punches you, he cannot argue provocation because the comment would not make a reasonable person lose his/her self-control.[110] Simply put, the defence of provocation can be argued only when (1) there is little to no time between the tortfeasor's and plaintiff's conduct, and (2) the comment must be of a nature that would make a reasonable person lose their temper.

104 *Intentional torts*

4.2 Interference with realty

4.2.1 Interference with land

Any direct, intentional or negligent, and physical interference with land owned by another is actionable even if there is no damage. Interference with land, which is commonly known as trespass, is committed, firstly, when a person enters land owned by another without the latter's permission; secondly, when one places an object on land owned by another; and thirdly, when someone enters your property with permission, but does not leave within a reasonable time at your request.

Mann v Saulnier[111]

The plaintiff and defendant shared contiguous property, on which the defendant constructed a fence throughout the length of the boundary. Upon completion, the fence was "as straight as a die," but three years later, it was discovered that there were portions of the fence that leaned approximately 1.75 inches to 3.75 inches over the plaintiff's land. While the plaintiff alleged trespass to land, his claim failed as the interference was not direct or due to the negligence of construction. The court said,

> Trespass to land is the act of entering upon land, in the possession of another, or placing or throwing or erecting some material object thereon without the legal right to do so. In Salmond on Torts [...] there is the following statement: "In all such cases, in order to be actionable as a trespass, the injury must be direct, within the meaning of the distinction between direct and consequential injuries [...] It is a trespass, and therefore actionable *per se*, directly to place material objects upon another's land; it is not a trespass, but at the most a nuisance or other wrong actionable only on proof of damage, to do an act which consequentially results in the entry of such objects. To throw stones upon one's neighbour's premises is the wrong of trespass; to allow stones from a ruinous chimney to fall upon those premises is the wrong of nuisance."

Notes

For an action in trespass to land to arise, the interference must be direct, physical, and intentional or negligent. That is, entering someone's premises without permission is a direct, physical, and intentional interference with the land of the possessor, and therefore, constitutes trespass.[112] However, if the interference is indirect, then there is no trespass. In fact, in *Sirajul Islam Chowdhury et al v Md Jainal Abedin et al*,[113] the Appellate Division of the Supreme Court of Bangladesh said,

> Trespass is a wrong in tort to another's possession and it is actionable per se without proof of actual or special damage, because every person's land is presumed to be surrounded by a fence, and the law encircles the land with an imaginary enclosure the violation of which is essentially an injury to the possessory right inhering in the plaintiff.

Intentional torts 105

Let us use another example. Suppose your neighbour planted an apple tree on his property, but very close to the contiguous boundary he shares with you, and it fructified five years later. By natural reasons, if an apple falls onto your property, then, while the interference is direct and physical, no action in trespass arises, as it was not intentional or negligent. However, if your neighbour shakes a branch of the tree with veritable force and an apple falls on your property, then an action in trespass could lie because the interference was either intentional (your neighbour shook a branch of the tree with the intention that an apple fall onto your property) or negligent (your neighbour shook a branch of the tree without reasonable care as to whether an apple could fall onto your property).

In *Mann*, though the fence leaned over onto neighbouring property, no trespass was found because the slant occurred by natural reasons and not because of intentional or negligent construction. While trespass can arise from negligent interference, in practice, it is restricted to intentional conduct; whereas, negligent interference is generally dealt with under the tort of negligence. Therefore, for example, imagine you constructed a three-story house on your land, and on the second floor, there is a bay window that protrudes onto neighbouring property. This will constitute trespass (albeit to airspace), as you have intentionally constructed a bay window that traverses the boundary line. Furthermore, it does not matter that your neighbour did not suffer any damage; rather, any interference, regardless of how trivial it may be, is trespass.[114]

Recall, from the previous chapter, that the playing of cricket at Lintz Cricket Club (hereinafter "the Club") was not a nuisance in *Miller v Jackson*, because, since the Club was there first, the law presumes that residents implicitly consented to being disturbed by the occasional cricket ball landing on their property.[115] Similarly, if you live at Banani DOHS and find golf balls hit onto your property, since Kurmitola Golf Club has been at its location before you moved in, it would not be a nuisance. However, is it trespass? Simply put, no, because a player has not intentionally hit the golf ball onto your property. Nonetheless, had someone stood in front of your house and intentionally threw a ball, or any other object, into your premises, then it would constitute trespass.

Moreover, the intrusion upon one's land must be physical; that is, personally entering someone's premises or placing an object on another's property is trespass, as the interference is physical. However, if the object is not physical, then there is no trespass. For example, smog, smoke, noise, odour, and vibrations from nearby construction is not trespass, as the interference is not physical. Perhaps the simplest way to understand physical intrusion is that the interference must be something *tangible*.[116] As in, if you can touch and hold on to the intruding object, such as a cellphone, rock, or a golf ball, then there is trespass. However, if the intruding object cannot be touched and held, such as vibration or smoke, then, even though it can be felt and cause disturbance, it is not trespass.

106　*Intentional torts*

I must also clarify that if you are in possession of the premises, then you have the right to bring an action for trespass. As in, if you rent an apartment, then though you are not the owner, you can bring an action for trespass for any unauthorized intrusions.[117]

4.2.2 Defences

4.2.2.1 Consent

If one permits another to enter his land, then there is no trespass. For example, if you invite your friend to your house for coffee, then your friend entering your premises is not trespass. However, suppose your friend has stayed at your house for 4 hours and you then ask him to leave because you need to sleep. If he refuses, after a reasonable amount of time, he is a trespasser and the law allows you to use reasonable force to eject him.[118] Nonetheless, what constitutes "reasonable amount of time" will depend on the facts and circumstances of each case. To illustrate, assume a person is on the fifth floor of Jamuna Future Park, and because he was smoking inside the mall, which is prohibited, guards have asked him to leave. If he does not have a disability that would otherwise interfere with his capacity to walk, then reasonable amount of time would perhaps be 20–30 minutes, due to the size of the establishment. However, if it were your house, which is only 2,000 square feet, and if the person does not have a disability, then reasonable amount of time would perhaps be 10–15 minutes.

Furthermore, when you permit another to enter your land, it is known as a *license*, which is divided into the following two categories: gratuitous and contractual. A gratuitous license, to use the previous example, is the one you have provided to your friend so that he can lawfully enter your house, and it is revocable at the inviter's will. As in, similar to how you have the freedom to invite your friend into your house, you have a corresponding right to ask him to leave at any time you wish. However, a contractual license, which is supported by consideration, is somewhat irrevocable; that is, when you purchase a ticket to watch a movie at Cineplex, your license to remain inside Cineplex is irrevocable until the movie ends or unless you breach a fundamental condition of the license.[119] This means that once the movie ends, you must leave Cineplex, or during the movie, if you sell cocaine to another viewer, or punch another licensee, then Cineplex can revoke your license and eject you from their premises.[120]

4.2.2.2 Necessity

Trespass to land can be justified if a situation of danger or emergency arises whereby a person trespasses to prevent harm to himself, a third party, the possessor of land, or the public. For example, firstly, if you are being chased through the street by an armed person, and you enter another's land without permission to take shelter, it is justified on the grounds of saving your life and limb.[121] Next, if you see a person being threatened with a knife

Intentional torts 107

on private property, and you trespass to save the victim's life, it is justified because you are trying to prevent harm to a third party. Thirdly, if you trespass to extinguish a fire, which, if left ignited, would cause further damage, then it is justified because you are trying to prevent destruction to the possessor's land.[122] Lastly, again, if you see a fire on one's land and trespass to destroy three full cords of wood, which would have otherwise ignited, created a conflagration, and spread the fire onto public area, then even though you have trespassed and destroyed someone else's property (e.g. three cords of wood), it is justified because you were trying to contain the fire and prevent harm to the public.[123]

However, simply because one is permitted to trespass on the four aforesaid grounds does not mean that the right is plenary. For example, in *London Borough of Southwark v Williams*,[124] due to a severe housing shortage and the approaching winter, homeless persons entered and began dwelling in empty houses owned by the Borough Council, and when the latter applied for eviction, the squatters relied on the defence of necessity. Siding with the Borough Council, the court said,

> [I]f hunger were once allowed to be an excuse for stealing, it would open a way through which all kinds of disorder and lawlessness would pass. So here, if homelessness were once admitted as a defence to trespass, no one's house could be safe. Necessity would open a door which no man could shut. It would not only be those in extreme need who would enter. There would be others who would imagine that they were in need, or would invent a need, so as to gain entry. Each man would say his need was greater than the next man's. The plea would be an excuse for all sorts of wrongdoing. So the courts must, for the sake of law and order, take a firm stand. They must refuse to admit the plea of necessity to the hungry and homeless: and trust that their distress will be relieved by the charitable and the good.

Similarly, regardless of the magnitude of the emergency, you cannot unlawfully enter another's premises for food, because, if this were allowed, society would precipitate into disorder, lawlessness, and no house would be safe from intrusion.[125] As in, even though food is required for survival, which could be an emergency, one cannot unlawfully enter another's premises for it. Therefore, overall, it is important to understand that while trespass is allowed, one can only do so if (1) there is imminent peril, (2) there are no reasonable alternatives available, and (3) the benefits of the unlawful act outweighs the probable harm.[126]

4.2.2.3 Legal authorization

A person is permitted to trespass when it is authorized by law. For example, entering someone's land to execute a search warrant is when entrance is authorized by law, even though the possessor of land may prohibit it

108 *Intentional torts*

(it is important to note that the search warrant would prevail over his prohibition).[127] As in, if the possessor permits entrance, then it is not trespass, as the person entering the property is doing so with prior approval. However, and as is common, if the possessor proscribes admission, then it is trespass, but is nevertheless justified on the grounds of legal authorization. To further simplify, authorization by law would prevail over the possessor's rights.

4.2.3 Interference with airspace

The Latin maxim *cujus est solum ejus est usque ad coelum*, which hails from the common law, says that a person who owns land has a corresponding right to everything that lies below the surface and the airspace above.[128] However, it was not until the advent of air travel that there arose a pressing need to balance the interests between (a) landowners in the use of the airspace above the surface of their land and (b) persons with a legitimate interest in using the airspace above another's land.[129] Nonetheless, there is consensus that there are three kinds of interference with airspace, *videlicet*, permanent intrusion into airspace at a moderately low height, transient intrusion into airspace by an object other than aircraft, and temporary intrusion by airplane. Similar to trespass to land, interference with airspace is actionable without proof of damage.

First, permanent intrusions into airspace at a relatively low height, which is the most common, occurs when a portion of a billboard, or a sign, or electrical wires, or even a building projects over another's land. For example, if you have constructed a duplex, and on the second floor, there is a bay window that protrudes onto your neighbour's property, then you have interfered with your neighbour's airspace, for which he can seek a remedy.[130]

Second, a temporary intrusion by an object other than an aircraft occurs when, for example, the sheaves of a crane project over someone's property. To illustrate, suppose your neighbour is constructing a bungalow on his land, and while a crane is kept on his land and is being used in the construction process, its sheaves have frequently swung through your airspace. Here, your neighbour could secure a license from you, which would permit his machinery to enter your airspace for the duration of construction. However, if negotiation fails and your neighbour's machinery enters your airspace, then there is trespass, for which you can seek a remedy. However, remedies have been variegated, as some courts have issued an injunction to immediately stop the trespass,[131] while others have waited to enjoin the trespass until after construction ends.[132]

Third, it is trespass to airspace if a plane passes over one's land without the permission of the landowner. However, as I have mentioned earlier, not every intrusion into the airspace of another is trespass, as the landowner's use of the airspace above his land must be balanced against the legitimate interests of others to also use the same space. Therefore, it is not trespass

Intentional torts 109

unless the plane flies through the landowner's zone of "effective possession," which is

> [T]he height above the land as [is] necessary for the ordinary use and enjoyment of the land and the structures on it, and above that height the owner [has] no greater rights in the airspace than any other member of the public.[133]

Here, we must understand that, firstly, there is currently no legislation circumscribing the extent of a landowner's airspace in Bangladesh, and secondly, the zone of effective possession is generally held to be a few hundred feet above the tallest structure of one's land. Therefore, if you have constructed an eight-story building on your land, your zone of effective possession starts from the top of the building, while your neighbour's, whose land is barren, zone of effective possession would begin from the surface of his land.

4.3 Interference with chattel

4.3.1 Trespass to chattel

Any direct and intentional interference with chattel, which is movable property, in the possession of another is actionable.[134] For example, and one I will use repeatedly, if your friend touches and dislocates your cellphone without your permission, then he has trespassed to chattel (the cellular phone). Moreover, similar to trespass to land, the tort of trespass to chattel protects possessory rights – not ownership. As in, if you allow your friend to use your cellphone, and while he is using the phone, if another grabs or otherwise interferes with it, then it is your friend, and not you, who has an action for trespass to chattel.

While views differ, trespass to chattel is generally available in the absence of damage.[135] That is to say, if one touches chattel that is in your possession without your consent, then it is actionable even if there is no injury to the property. For example, touching a painting at a museum, though without *malum* and causing no damage, can constitute trespass to chattel;[136] or, if your friend, without your permission, grabs your phone and places a call, even if there is no damage to your cellphone, you nevertheless have an action for trespass to chattel;[137] or, if someone posts a sticker on your car without your permission, though there may not be any damage, an action for trespass to chattel would arise.

4.3.1.1 Wireless piggybacking

I will briefly discuss a contemporary issue. I am quite certain that those reading this book have used, or will use, the Internet. However, what many of you may not have experienced are dial-up connections of the 1990s,

110 *Intentional torts*

whereby the computer was tethered, and no other device except that particular computer had access, to the Internet.[138] Nonetheless, with the evolution of technology, we can now access the Internet wirelessly, which is known as Wireless Fidelity (hereinafter "Wi-Fi"), through multiple devices (e.g. phones, tablets, laptops, desktops, and TVs).[139] This, however, has begotten another problem.

Imagine you are in your home at Baridhara and, through your smartphone, are trying to post a 5-second story on Instagram. Ten minutes have passed and you cannot post the story because your internet is hopelessly slow, which is odd because your parents are at work and no one else, except you, is at home using the Internet. You then login to your router, or modem, and discover that your neighbour is using your Wi-Fi.

This is commonly known as "wireless piggybacking," where a person accesses the Internet through your Wi-Fi network without your permission.[140] This can constitute trespass to chattel, as a person has *directly* and *intentionally* interfered with your router or modem, which is movable property under your possession.[141] Moreover, in Bangladesh, such an action is also prohibited under section 18 of *The Digital Security Act*, 2018, whereby a person can be imprisoned for six months, or fined ৳300,000, for a first-time offence, and be imprisoned for three years, or fined ৳1,000,000, for a repeat-offence.[142]

4.3.2 *Detinue*

Detinue, which is an uncommon and rare action, is the refusal to return chattel to the rightful owner upon request.[143] For example, imagine you own a PlayStation 4 Pro and you invite your friend over to play FIFA 2020. While the two of you thoroughly enjoy the game, before leaving, your friend requests to borrow it and promises to return the game tomorrow. You accept his offer. If your friend does not return the game the following day and you demand he does, then an action in detinue arises. However, if your friend does not return the game the following day, and you did not request that he does, then there is no action in detinue, but an action would arise in trespass to chattel, as his possession of the game is unauthorized.[144] As in, the two essential conditions for an action in detinue are, firstly, a demand by the rightful owner for the return of the chattel, and secondly, the refusal to hand it back.

4.3.3 *Conversion*

While conversion is similar to trespass to chattel and detinue, the difference is that it requires an act that severely and seriously interferes with the rights of the owner.[145] For example, imagine you have allowed your friend to use your cellphone to place a phone call – with an implied understanding that he will return the phone back to you once he is done using it. However, instead of returning the phone, if your friend sells it to another person,

Intentional torts 111

then he is liable for conversion because the act of sale seriously interferes with your rights as the owner. Similarly, if your friend destroys or pledges the cellphone to another person after use, then there also arises a case for conversion. Overall, it is important to understand that in trespass to chattel and detinue, you may be able to retrieve the chattel, even though one has otherwise interfered with it. However, in conversion, the asportation is so extensively inconsistent with your ownership rights (e.g. destroyed, sold, or pledged) that you may not be able to retrieve the chattel.[146]

Fouldes v Willoughby[147]

The plaintiff boarded a ferry from Birkenhead to Liverpool with two of his horses. The defendant, who operated the ferry, was made aware that the plaintiff had behaved improperly, and therefore, told the plaintiff that he would not carry his horses over the water and that he must keep the horses ashore. However, the plaintiff refused, and the defendant then took control of the horses and left them on shore in the care of the defendant's brother, who operated a hotel. The plaintiff remained on board and was transported to Liverpool. He then brought an action for conversion. Not finding conversion, Lord Abinger said,

> It is a proposition familiar to all lawyers, that a simple asportation of a chattel, without any intention of making any further use of it, although it may be a sufficient foundation for an action of trespass, is not sufficient to establish a conversion. It has never yet been held that the single act of removal of a chattel, independent of any claim over it, either in favour of the party himself or anyone else, amounts to a conversion of the chattel.

Notes

In *Fouldes*, since the plaintiff's right to recover the chattel was not lost (as the defendant left the horses with his brother), the defendant's conduct did not amount to conversion. As in, if the plaintiff who momentarily lost the chattel because of the defendant's unlawful interference, can nevertheless recover it, then the latter's misconduct could be trespass to chattel or detinue (provided the plaintiff demanded its return and the defendant refused). However, it will not constitute conversion, as the action of the defendant did not seriously interfere with the ownership interests of the plaintiff.

If one converts another's chattel, the usual remedy is a forced sale, whereby the defendant pays money to the plaintiff as if he has bought it. However, this applies only if the defendant destroyed the chattel. If he has sold it and the buyer knew that the good was not the property of the seller, then the actual owner can (1) bring an action against the seller for conversion and (2) bring an action against the buyer to recover the good.[148] If, however, the buyer did not know that the seller had no authority to sell, then the true owner cannot sue the buyer directly, but can nonetheless bring an action against the seller to recover the chattel.[149] Here, it is important to understand that even though you may be able to recover the chattel, since

112 *Intentional torts*

the defendant extensively interfered with your rights by selling it to another, a case for conversion would nevertheless arise.

4.3.4 *Distress damage feasant*

While, depending on the degree of intervention, unlawful interference with chattel can give rise to an action in trespass, detinue, or conversion, there are times when a party can refuse to deliver chattel to its rightful owner (or to one with the right to immediate possession). For example, imagine your neighbour's cattle has trespassed onto your land and destroyed your crops. In order to recover money for the injury caused, you can keep the animal captive until payment is made.[150] As in, even if the owner of the cattle demands its return, you have the right to withhold delivery, and the owner would not be able to bring an action in detinue for your refusal to return his cattle. However, it is essential that the trespassing chattel has caused, or is causing, damage to your property, as otherwise, you cannot hold the animal captive.[151]

Additionally, you can keep the chattel only if you were able to capture it while it was still on your land;[152] that is, if the chattel trespassed, destroyed your property, but *left* your land and then you captured it, then you could be liable for interference with chattel. Furthermore, you have the right to only keep *possession* of the chattel in order to recover compensation. This means that if you sell or pledge the chattel, then you can subsequently be held liable for conversion.[153] In other words, simply because a chattel finds its way onto your property does not mean that you are now its owner.

4.4 Interference with economic interests

While a free market invites healthy competition, the law of torts has prohibited actions that detrimentally interfere with the economic interests of others.[154] As in, though narrowly defined, any serious or grave misconduct that obstructs the efficient operation of business in the market will allow the aggrieved party to seek a remedy under economic torts, which are divided into, firstly, deceptive practices, and secondly, improper market practices.

4.4.1 *Deceptive practices*

The underlying rationale protecting one against deceptive practices is the moral proposition that one should not be able to advance his business interests through lies.[155] As in, competition in the marketplace must be fair and if one unjustly enriches himself at the expense of another, the former, as a principle of fairness, ought to compensate the latter. Moreover, protection against deceptive practices is granted not only to businessmen, but to consumers as well.

4.4.1.1 Deceit

Deceit, which is a misrepresentation made about the nature or quality of the product or the subject matter of the contract,[156] is established when a person makes a fraudulent misrepresentation to another and the latter relies on it to his detriment.[157] Therefore, there are four elements of deceit: misrepresentation, fraud, reliance, and injury. I shall delineate each component in *seriatim*.

First, deceit requires misrepresentation, which is a false statement made by a party either verbally, in writing, or through conduct. However, even if the statement is false, if it is unreasonable, or one that a reasonable person would be expected to know is untrue, then there is no misrepresentation; rather, the statement would be considered a mere "puff" (as in, a sales commendation). For example, suppose you went to buy a car and the salesman, while pointing to one, tells you that if you purchase this particular vehicle, you will "fly through the city." Relying on his statement, you buy the car, but to your disappointment, it does not "fly through the city." While you are upset by his false representation, there is no deceit since a reasonable person would be expected to know that a car cannot fly.

Second, the person who made the representation must have done so fraudulently. As in, not only must the statement be false, but the person must also have either, (a) known that it was false at the time of making the statement, or (b) made it recklessly without knowing whether it is true, and therefore, without belief in its truth. For example, imagine that you are married. You and your wife are fourth-year law students and want to buy an apartment. You tell the real estate agent that you want a quiet neighbourhood because the two of you must study for your finals, and subsequently, the Bar Exams. The agent shows you an apartment at Mohakhali DOHS and informs you that every resident owns their apartment, are above 60 and that the overall ambience is serene. You ask the agent whether anyone is likely to renovate their apartment within the next year, to which he responds "Nobody will," even though he knows that the resident upstairs will be renovating his apartment next month. A few days later, you buy the apartment. Unfortunately, your upstairs neighbour began replacing his floor tiles, which has created clamorous noise. Since the real estate agent, at the time of telling you, knew that renovation would begin next month, his statement is fraudulent.

Alternatively, even if the agent did not know that renovation would begin within a month, but made the statement without knowing whether it is true, his representation can amount to fraud. As in, the position of tort law is that when one makes a statement with the intention that another will rely on it, which is usually the case in commercial contracts, such as buying a car or apartment, then the maker of the statement has a duty to make disclosures that are true; that is, if the agent does not know whether renovation will begin, he should say so, or he can find out and furnish truthful information. What he should not do is speculate and provide an uninformed response.[158]

114   *Intentional torts*

Third, the person making the representation must intend that the person, to whom the statement was made, will rely on it, which establishes causation.[159] Moreover, the latter must actually rely on the statement. For example, and to use the previous illustration, when the real estate agent said that no construction would happen within the next year, he must have intended that you will rely on the statement.[160] Moreover, he will subsequently be barred from disclaiming liability on the grounds that he did not intend that you will rely on his representation, as courts now hold otherwise.[161]

Hedley Byrne & Co Ltd v Heller & Partners Ltd[162]

Hedley Byrne (hereinafter "Byrne") was an advertising agent that placed orders on behalf of clients on credit, with the promise that it would be personally liable should the client default. Easipower Limited (hereinafter "Easipower") placed a large order and Byrne wanted to examine the company's financial position before placing the order, and therefore, asked the National Provincial Bank to get a record from Easipower's bank – Heller & Partners Ltd (hereinafter "Heller"). Upon inquiry, Heller responded saying Easipower was "[C]onsidered good for its ordinary business engagements," but also added that they have provided the information, "without responsibility" on their part. A few months later, Easipower was liquidated and Byrne lost £17,000 in contracts. Consequently, Byrne sued Heller for negligent misrepresentation, alleging that the information provided was misleading. However, Heller responded by saying that they did not owe a duty of care to Byrne and that even if they did, they were exempt from liability because of the disclaimer. Finding for Heller, the House of Lords said,

> I consider that it follows and that it should now be regarded as settled that if someone possessed of a special skill undertakes, quite irrespective of contract, to apply that skill for the assistance of another person who relies on such skill, a duty of care will arise. The fact that the service is to be given by means of, or by the instrumentality of, words can make no difference. Furthermore if, in a sphere in which a person is so placed that others could reasonably rely on his judgment or his skill or on his ability to make careful inquiry, a person takes it on himself to give information or advice to, or allows his information or advice to be passed on to, another person who, as he knows or should know, will place reliance on it, then a duty of care will arise. [...]
>
> [I]n my judgment the bank in the present case, by the words which they employed, effectively disclaimed any assumption of a duty of care. They stated that they only responded to the inquiry on the basis that their reply was without responsibility. If the inquirers chose to receive and act upon the reply they cannot disregard the definite terms upon which it was given. They cannot accept a reply given with a stipulation and then reject the *stipulati* present case, by the words which they employed, effectively disclaimed any assumption of a duty of care. They stated that they only responded to the inquiry on the basis that their reply was without responsibility. If the inquirers chose to receive and

Intentional torts   115

act upon the reply they cannot disregard the definite terms upon which it was given. They cannot accept a reply given with a stipulation and then reject the stipulation. Furthermore, within accepted principles.

(as illustrated in *Rutter v Palmer* the words employed were apt to exclude any liability for negligence)

However, the House of Lords said that a party could seek compensation for economic loss if these four conditions are met: (1) a fiduciary relationship exists between parties; (2) the party preparing the information has voluntarily assumed the risk; (3) the party relied on the information; and (4) the reliance on information was reasonable in the circumstances.

Notes

Therefore, as we can see from *Hedley Byrne*, you must actually rely on the representation in making the purchase, which, in our example, is the apartment; that is, even if the real estate agent told you that there would be no construction within the next year, but instead of relying on his statement, you reached the same conclusion based on your own research by, for example, using the Internet, then reliance is not established.[163]

Fourth, the plaintiff must suffer damage. Let us, again, revisit the example of the real estate agent. While he knew that renovations would begin the following week, he said that there would be no construction within a year, and you bought the apartment relying on his statement. While, as we have established, his misrepresentation is fraudulent, if it is not to your detriment, then there is no deceit. For example, imagine that you bought the apartment, moved in, but before your neighbour began renovations, your mother calls to inform you that your father was in a car accident and is hospitalized. You and your wife immediately visit your parents in Khulshi, Chittagong, and decide to stay with them during your father's convalescence. He recovers in approximately six months and then the two of you decide to move back to your apartment. While you were away, your neighbour finished renovating, but unfortunately, you dropped two semesters and could not finish school that year.

Here, though the real estate agent fraudulently misrepresented information (telling you there would be no construction within a year even when he knew it to be false), since you did not suffer any injury because of it (as you were not able to finish school because you stayed with your parents for six months, and not because of disturbance from construction), you cannot seek compensation from him. That is to say, you must have suffered an injury as a result of the statement. For example, in *Queen v Cognos Inc*,[164] during a job interview, the defendant told the plaintiff that the project was lucrative and that if he was the successful candidate, he would play an important role. Relying on this statement, the plaintiff left his relatively well-paid and secure job to accept a position with the defendant. However, what the defendant never mentioned was that funding for the project was not yet secured, and shortly afterwards, the defendant scaled down the project and eliminated

116 *Intentional torts*

the plaintiff's position. The plaintiff brought an action under negligent misrepresentation. Finding in his favour, the court said,

> The respondent concedes that it itself and its representative, Mr. Johnston, owed a duty of care towards the six job applicants being interviewed, including the appellant, not to make negligent misrepresentations as to Cognos and the nature and permanence of the job being offered. In so doing, it accepts as correct the findings of both the trial judge and the Court of Appeal that there existed between the parties a "special relationship" within the meaning of *Hedley Byrne*, supra.
>
> In my view, this concession is a sensible one. Without a doubt, when all the circumstances of this case are taken into account, the respondent and Mr. Johnston were under an obligation to exercise due diligence throughout the hiring interview with respect to the representations made to the appellant about Cognos and the nature and existence of the employment opportunity.
>
> There is some debate in academic circles, fuelled by various judicial pronouncements, about the proper test that should be applied to determine when a "special relationship" exists between the representor and the representee which will give rise to a duty of care. Some have suggested that "foreseeable and reasonable reliance" on the representations is the key element to the analysis, while others speak of "voluntary assumption of responsibility" on the part of the representor. [...]
>
> For my part, I find it unnecessary – and unwise in view of the respondent's concession – to take part in this debate. Regardless of the test applied, the result which the circumstances of this case dictate would be the same. It was foreseeable that the appellant would be relying on the information given during the hiring interview in order to make his career decision. It was reasonable for the appellant to rely on said representations. There is nothing before this Court that suggests that the respondent was not, at the time of the interview or shortly thereafter, assuming responsibility for what was being represented to the appellant by Mr. Johnston. As noted by the trial judge, Mr. Johnston discussed the Multiview project in an unqualified manner, without making any relevant caveats. The alleged disclaimers of responsibility are provisions of a contract signed more than two weeks after the interview. For reasons that I give in the last part of this analysis, these provisions are not valid disclaimers. They do not negate the duty of care owed to the appellant or prevent it from arising as in *Hedley Byrne* and *Carman Construction*, supra. It was foreseeable to the respondent and its representative that the appellant would sustain damages should the representations relied on prove to be false and negligently made. There was, undoubtedly, a relationship of proximity between the parties at all material times. Finally, it is not unreasonable to impose a duty of care in all the circumstances of this case; quite the contrary, it would be unreasonable not to impose such a duty. In short, therefore, there existed

Intentional torts   117

between the parties a "special relationship" at the time of the interview. The respondent and its representative Mr. Johnston were under a duty of care during the pre-employment interview to exercise reasonable care and diligence in making representations as to the employer and the employment opportunity being offered.[165]

4.4.1.2 Injurious falsehood

Injurious falsehood is the successor to slander of title and slander of goods and protects one from false statements that injure his business to the extent where others abstain from trading with him.[166] Slander of title is when one makes a false statement to another that the plaintiff is not the owner of the goods he is trying to sell, thereby precluding sale;[167] slander of goods is when one makes a false statement to another about the quality of the plaintiff's goods, which also prevents him from selling his products. In order to demonstrate injurious falsehood, four elements must be proven: (1) A false statement must be made about the person's business, (2) the statement must be communicated to a third person, (3) the person making the false statement must have done so with malice, and (4) the injured party must suffer pecuniary loss as a result of the statement.[168]

Since the first and second elements are inextricably intertwined, I will delineate them together. First, a person must publish a false statement, which can relate to the quality of the products or services another sells or provides, his competence, or even the legality or existence of his business or property. For example, and second, telling someone that a particular doctor is incompetent or that the restaurateur operates his drug empire from an office at the back of his restaurant, are actionable because the statements may prevent others from doing business with the person about whom the representations are made.[169]

Moreover, it is important that the false statement is communicated to a third party, which establishes cause and effect. That is, the essence of injurious falsehood is a misrepresentation that leads others to not transact business with a person. Therefore, if one does not know of a false statement, but he decides to not visit a particular doctor or restaurant, then his decision has not been influenced by your representation, and the loss they suffer cannot be ascribed to you.

Third, the person making the false statement must have done so maliciously, which is interpreted as ill will, spite, or the intention to inflict damage.[170] For example, if John tells Jacob that Tiffany is an incompetent doctor, which is false, and Tiffany loses Jacob as a client because of the statement, then an action for injurious falsehood can be brought against John only if he acted with malice; that is, if John's intention was that Tiffany lose Jacob as a client, then malice can be proven. However, if John claims that he was trying to be humorous, then proving malice could be insuperable;[171] that is, it is not uncommon to inveigh a restaurant because of its food or service, or to say that a doctor or teacher is incompetent, or that an airline

118   *Intentional torts*

is horrible, or a host of other disparaging statements that adversely affect one's business. However, such representations, albeit tendentious, are not actionable unless maliciously said because one is allowed to express subjective thought. As in, food at a particular restaurant may not match your palette, or a professor's style of teaching may not be to your liking, and if you express an honest opinion, even if it influences another, you are not committing a tortious offence.

Essentially, to prove malice, the question is whether the person making the representation knew his statement was false or was reckless with its truth.[172] Therefore, if you have tried food at a restaurant and disliked it, there is no problem dissuading someone from going there, or even if you did not have food at the restaurant, it is still not actionable to be reproachful. However, for example, assume a friend asks whether you recommend Regent Bistro, which is a restaurant that serves French cuisine, but instead of directly responding to the question, you tell him that you do not go there because the owner uses the restaurant's proceeds to fund terrorism. If the statement is true, then no action for injurious falsehood arises. Nonetheless, if it is false, and you knew it, then an action could arise if your friend relied on the statement and did not visit the restaurant.[173]

Fourth, regardless of how false and malicious one's conduct is, if there is no damage to another's business, an action under injurious falsehood does not arise. As in, while you, knowing it to be false, lied about Regent Bistro to your friend and advised him to not visit the restaurant, if your friend flouts your recommendation and tries food there, an action for injurious falsehood would not arise because there was no injury stemming from your misrepresentation. That is to say, even if your conduct is wholly motivated by malice, if there is no damage to the business of Regent Bistro, then no action would arise under injurious falsehood.

4.4.1.3 Passing-off

In Bangladesh, *The Trademarks Act*, 2009 governs the registration and protection of trademarks, which is a name, words, a combination of colours, or any distinctive mark indicating a connection between the goods and services provided and the proprietor entitled to use that mark.[174] The purpose of a trademark is to prevent one from selling his goods and services as that of another. For example, since Roll Xpress is a restaurant in Bangladesh that caters to the public, any restaurant using the same name, logo, or any distinctive mark the former is exclusively entitled to use, will be infringing on its trademark, for which Roll Xpress can institute proceedings.[175] However, in order to begin a case for trademark infringement, whereby an injunction would be granted to prevent the copycat's operations, the trademark must be registered with the Trademarks Registry Wing of the Department of Patents, Designs and Trademarks.[176] This begets the question of what protection, if any, is granted to the proprietor of an *unregistered* trademark?

Intentional torts 119

Ciba-Geigy Canada Ltd v Apotex Inc[177]

Ciba-Geigy Canada Limited (hereinafter "Ciba-Geigy") is a pharmaceutical laboratory that has manufactured and sold metoprolol tartrate (hereinafter "metoprolol") in Canada, since 1977, under the trade-name "Lopresor," which has been prescribed in Ontario, and Canada, to treat low to moderate hypertension. Lopresor is produced in two doses: (1) 50 milligrams, which is oblong-shaped and pink, and (2) 100 milligrams, which, similar to the earlier, is oblong-shaped, but blue.

From July 1984 to June 1986, Apotex Inc.'s (hereinafter "Apotex") metoprolol, which was sold under the trade-name "Apo-metoprolol," was white, circular, biconvex, and was offered at 50 and 100 milligrams. However, from June 1986, Apo-metoprolol adopted the same shape, size, and colour of Lopresor. Novopharm Limited (hereinafter "Novopharm"), who is the second respondent, also manufactured metoprolol under the trade-name "Novo-metoprolol," offered them in 50 and 100 milligram doses, and adopted the same shape, size, and colour of Lopresor since 1986. Therefore, in June 1986, Ciba-Geigy brought an action for passing-off against Apotex and Novopharm, claiming that Lopresor has a unique "get-up" (shape, size, and colour), and that the respondents' metoprolol tablets, since they are similar to Ciba-Geigy's, have the ability to confuse consumers into thinking they are purchasing – even though the impugned tablets were only available through prescription – Lopresor. Finding the respondents liable, the court said,

> The three necessary components of a passing-off action are thus: the existence of goodwill, deception of the public due to a misrepresentation and actual or potential damage to the plaintiff. [...]
>
> A manufacturer must therefore avoid creating confusion in the public mind, whether deliberately or not, by a get-up identical to that of a product which has acquired a secondary meaning by reason of its get-up. [...]
>
> [The protection of manufacturers] corresponds to the third point mentioned by Lord Oliver. The right to be protected against the "pirating" of a brand, trade name or the appearance of a product is linked to a kind of "ownership" which the manufacturer has acquired in that name, brand and appearance by using them.
>
> [As John Drysdale and Michael Silverleaf have said]: In countries with a free market system the proper functioning of the economy depends upon competition between rival trading enterprises. It is the mechanism of competition which controls the price, quality and availability of goods and services to the public. However, merchants must observe certain rules which, quite apart from being legal, are ethical at the least: Just as an effort made to dislodge an opponent from the position he occupies, to attract sales to oneself by offering better goods on better terms, is legitimate when only fair methods are used, so such

120 *Intentional torts*

conduct is objectionable when it infringes the rules of honesty and good faith that underlie commercial transactions. [...]

The purpose of the passing-off action is thus also to prevent unfair competition. One does not have to be a fanatical moralist to understand how appropriating another person's work, as that is certainly what is involved, is a breach of good faith.

Finally, another more apparent, more palpable aspect, a consequence of the preceding one, must also be mentioned. The "pirated" manufacturer is very likely to experience a reduction in sales volume and therefore in his turnover because of the breaking up of his market. When such a situation occurs in the ordinary course of business between rival manufacturers that is what one might call one of the rules of the game, but when the rivalry involves the use of dishonest practices, the law must intervene. [...]

[I]t should never be overlooked that [...] unfair competition cases are affected with a public interest. A dealer's good will is protected, not merely for his profit, but in order that the purchasing public may not be enticed into buying A's product when it wants B's product [...] Accordingly, the power of the court in such cases is exercised, not only to do individual justice, but to safeguard the interests of the public [...] The ordinary customer, the consumer, is at the heart of the matter here. [...]

The customer expects to receive a given product when he asks for it and should not be deceived. It often happens that products are interchangeable and that a substitution will have little effect. However, the customer may count on having a specific product. There are many reasons for such a choice: habit, satisfaction, another person's recommendation, the desire for change, and so on. I have no hesitation in using the classic saying, taken from popular imagery: "the customer is always right." Merchants must respect his wishes, choices and preferences as far as possible. Where this is simply not possible, no substitution must be made without his knowledge. That is the minimum degree of respect which manufacturers and merchants, who we should remember depend on their customers, should show. [...]

The look, the appearance, the get-up of a product play a crucial role in the purchase process since they are the chief means at the manufacturer's disposal to attract customers. The importance of visual impact is well known: what appeals to the eye is crucial.

The product's appearance or its packaging – shape, size or colour – may be characteristic of a particular manufacturer and have the effect of marking out the product or making it recognizable as his own. In the mind of the customer appearance is not always linked to a trademark, that is, the consumer may rely on the appearance rather than the trademark to indicate the use of the product. For example, when he needs removable self-stick notes, he will look for small blocks of yellow paper. He may not know the name of the product or manufacturer, but he does not need to in order to recognize what he wants to buy. What

Intentional torts   121

he has noticed and what he has retained is the specific colour of the merchandise; or he will know that a particular product contained in a tin with an exotic bird on the lid is polish, without necessarily having to know the trade name or brand, and when he wishes to purchase that polish it is the image of the bird on the packaging that will assist him in recognizing the product. With a few exceptions, the external features of a product are not sought for themselves, but because they are the means of recognizing the satisfactory product, for example. They are a source of information associated with reputation for a consumer or a group of customers. Appearance is thus useful not only in product recognition but also to distinguish one product from another with the same uses. [...]

The question now is as to who lies beyond the product, that is who must be protected, who must not be confused by manufacturers, for example, by a similar appearance. As business is organized at present, it is very seldom that an individual deals directly with the manufacturer or producer: he is not generally the immediate customer. The route taken by a product between the time of its manufacture, to use a broad term, and the time it reaches the consumer can be compared to a chain made up of several links which must all be there and be in a particular order. Manufacturer, wholesaler, retailer and consumer are all links in this chain.

The first person who buys the product is not generally the one for whom it is ultimately intended. Assuming that there are three links in the chain, with the producer and the consumer at the two ends, the "retailer" (grocer, bookseller, garage owner and so on) is an intermediary between the producer and the consumer. I would without hesitation describe him as a "trade customer," that is a person who obtains a product not for his own use but with a view to passing it on to a third person in the course of his business. There is little need to dwell at length on the case of such merchant intermediaries, who are in fact part of the manufacturer's or producer's clientele. There may at times be some question whether the passing-off action really affects them as customers. The closer they are, that is the more direct contact they have with the manufacturer or producer, the less likely they are to be misled.

There is no question that confusion, which is the essence of the tort of passing-off, must be avoided in the minds of all customers, whether direct – here one thinks of the retailers – or indirect – in that case the consumers. Proof of reputation or secondary meaning and of misrepresentation has never been limited by the courts to direct customers of the person claiming a right.

Notes

Passing-off is protection the common law accords to an unregistered trademark. That is to say, it is the same as trademark infringement when the trademark is not registered.[178] Interestingly, and as I had mentioned in the

122 *Intentional torts*

first chapter, section 24(2) of the *Trademarks Act*[179] has codified the tort of passing-off, stipulating,

> [n]othing in this Act shall be deemed to affect [the] rights of [an] action against any person for passing-off goods or services as the goods or services, as the case may be, of another person or the remedies in respect thereof.

In order to succeed in an action for passing-off, the plaintiff must prove the following three elements: (1) The existence of goodwill, (2) a misrepresentation by the defendant, and (3) actual or potential damage to the plaintiff.[180]

First, the plaintiff must establish goodwill, which is the ability to attract and retain customers.[181] It is obtained by repeatedly providing quality goods and services that are identified through a mark, such as, *inter alia*, a name, symbol, logo, images, or other distinctive features that are, in the minds of the consumer, connected to the plaintiff's goods.[182] For example, take a few seconds to think of a chocolate – including its packaging – that is triangular. Are you done? If so and if your response is "Toblerone," then your answer and mine matches. Notice that I did not say whether the chocolate contains nuts or fruits; rather, and most probably, it is the distinctive feature of its *triangular* shape that led you to think of Toblerone immediately.

However, let us try the same exercise with the original question slightly altered. Other than Toblerone, think of a chocolate – including its packaging – that is triangular. If you are bemused at this quandary, it is because no other chocolate with the distinct triangular shape exists (or if one does, it is beyond the ambit of my knowledge). To further explain, Mondelēz International Inc., which produces Toblerone chocolates, has trademarked the triangular shape; therefore, if any other chocolatier uses the same shape, they would be infringing Mondelēz's trademark.[183]

Toblerone may not be the paradigm example, as its shape has been trademarked, which means it is registered. Passing-off, however, is the protection of unregistered trademarks. Therefore, let us use another example. Imagine that there is a restaurant called "Silver Table," which has been serving the best gourmet burgers in Dhaka for the past three years and has developed a set of loyal customers. Its logo is a distinct silver "S" and "T" enclosed in a maroon circle, which consumers immediately associate with the restaurant. Although its name is registered with the Office of the Registrar of Joint Stock Companies and Firms, its logo has not been trademarked. Recently, a new bistro opened with the name "Silver Table 2.0" and, while it also serves gourmet burgers, its logo is a silver "S" and "T" encompassed by a maroon box. Is this a problem or can both restaurants operate simultaneously?

Reddaway & Co Ltd v Banham & Co Ltd[184]

For many years, Frank Reddaway manufactured machine belting, and in October 1892, he converted his business into a company titled, "F. Reddaway & Co Ltd" (hereinafter "Reddaway Ltd"). From 1877, he began making belts from yarn, which was similar to those used in making carpets and

Intentional torts 123

principally consisted of wool or hair, as he discovered that belts made from yarn were of superior quality. However, as other companies, primarily Lancashire Belting Co Ltd, were also manufacturing belts with similar fabrics, in order to differentiate his company, Reddaway began marketing his products as "Camel-Hair Belting" from 1879.

George Banham was an employee of Reddaway Ltd, but he left in 1889 and began manufacturing belts similar to the latter. However, in 1891, he began marketing his products as "Camel-Hair Belting," and Reddaway sought an injunction to stop Banham's operations. Finding a case for passing-off, the court said,

> For myself, I believe the principle of law may be very plainly stated, and that is that nobody has any right to represent his goods as the goods of somebody else. How far the use of particular words, signs, or pictures does or does not come up to the proposition which I have enunciated, in each particular case must always be a question of evidence, and the more simple the phraseology, the more a mere description of the article sold comes to be nearer to or far from a representation of the goods of the rival manufacturer, the greater becomes the difficulty of proof, but if the proof establishes the fact, the legal consequence appears to follow. [...]
>
> [A] manufacturer might obtain the right to prevent a person using a name which would be understood as his, and the use of which would thus interfere with his trade, but that, though this was the fundamental proposition, you could not restrain a man from telling the simple truth, and that this was all the respondents had done when they called their belting "camel hair belting." It must be taken, if the findings of the jury are to stand, on which I shall have a word or two to say presently, that the description by the respondents of their belting as "camel hair belting" would deceive purchasers into the belief that they were getting something which they were not getting, namely, belting made by Reddaway. If they would be thus deceived by the respondents' statement, there must surely be some fallacy in saying that they have told the simple truth. I will state presently where I think the fallacy lurks. [...]
>
> But, there was ample evidence to justify the finding that among those who were the purchasers of such goods the words "camel hair" were not applied to belting made of that material in general – that, in short, it did not mean in the market belting made of a particular material, but meant belting made by a particular manufacturer. [...]
>
> I cannot help saying that, if the respondents are entitled to lead purchasers to believe that they are getting the appellants' manufacture when they are not, and thus to cheat the appellants of some of their legitimate trade, I should regret to find that the law was powerless to enforce the most elementary principles of commercial morality.

Notes

It is important to understand that the phrase "Camel-Hair Belting" developed a secondary meaning that customers associated with Reddaway's

124   *Intentional torts*

goods. Therefore, if a similar phraseology is used, a case for passing-off can arise.

Similarly, concerning our example, to understand why Silver Table and Silver Table 2.0 cannot concurrently operate, we must understand two things. Firstly, naming a restaurant "Silver Table 2.0," which also serves burgers in the same geographic region (more on this later) and uses a similar logo, is known as *source misrepresentation* if the restaurants are unrelated.[185] That is to say, if the owners are the same, then using a similar name and logo is allowed, but if they are different, then it is prohibited because this can create confusion in the mind of the casual customer. To further explain, the law of passing-off is not concerned with the vigilant consumer who will peruse every document before buying a product to figure out, for example, whether Silver Table 2.0 is related to Silver Table. Rather, it is about whether the casual customer, who is somewhat in a hurry, will be confused and led to believe that Silver Table 2.0 is the same as Silver Table.[186]

Secondly, it is the similar name (e.g. Silver Table 2.0) and logo (e.g. silver "S" and "T" enclosed in a maroon box), itself, that is the misrepresentation, which has the ability to create confusion in the mind of the casual customer. It is not necessary for Silver Table 2.0 to announce that they are related to Silver Table.

Thirdly, there must be damage, actual or threatened, to the plaintiff; that is, if customers visit Silver Table 2.0 because they assume it is related to Silver Table, then there is actual damage, which is pecuniary, as consumers have been diverted. However, it is not required that the plaintiff actually suffer an injury; rather, if there is a probability that Silver Table *will* be harmed, then they can institute proceedings under passing-off. Nonetheless, if there is actual harm, then Silver Table will be awarded either damages or account of profits, based on its monetary loss from the diversion of customers, and an injunction to stop Silver Table 2.0's operations.[187] If, however, the harm is threatened, then only an injunction will be granted. However, while both Silver Table and Silver Table 2.0 operated in Bangladesh, would a case for passing-off succeed if the former operated in Bangladesh and the latter in the United States?

Sadhu Singh Hamdard Trust v Navsun Holdings Ltd[188]

Since 1955, Hamdard Trust has owned and published the "Ajit Daily," which is a Punjabi-language newspaper, in India, and has made an online version available from 2002. Moreover, the paper has become popular among the Punjabi-community in India. While a modicum of subscriptions have been sold in Canada, several people in Canada have confirmed that they are aware of the paper's existence and importance in India.

Navsun Holdings Ltd (hereinafter "Navsun") has published the "Ajit Weekly," which is a free, Punjabi-language newspaper, in Canada since 1993, and has made an online version available from 1998. However, Hamdard Trust claims that the name "Ajit," along with a similar depiction of it on Ajit Weekly's masthead, can create confusion in the marketplace and alleges that Navsun has tried to pass-off its newspaper as that of Hamdard Trust's. Finding in favour of the plaintiff, the court said,

> Here, there was evidence before the Federal Court to indicate that the Ajit Daily enjoyed a reputation in the eyes of several affiants in Canada as a well-known Punjabi-language newspaper published in India. There was also evidence that a number of Canadians accessed the Ajit Daily's online version by visiting its website. It was incumbent on the Federal Court to evaluate this evidence to determine whether it was sufficient to establish that the Ajit Daily had garnered a reputation among a wider group in Canada than the few subscribers who bought the paper. Had such a wider reputation been established, it would have been sufficient to establish the requisite goodwill to meet the first step in the tripartite test for passing-off. The Federal Court, however, did not engage in this analysis as it erroneously viewed the issue of goodwill from the vantage point of the few Canadian subscribers who were shown to have purchased the Ajit Daily in Canada. [...]
>
> The evidence before the Federal Court indicated that the stylized version of the word "Ajit" that appears on the masthead of the Ajit Daily was developed by an employee of Hamdard Trust and that the copyright for the *Nanak*-heavy font was acquired only in 1995, two years *after* the Ajit Weekly had begun using the Ajit Daily logo in Canada. These facts support the originality of the stylized Ajit Daily trademark. If the trademark were original, its use by the Bains Defendants is more likely to have been a result of a deliberate attempt to copy the Ajit Daily trademark, which may well have led to confusion. Moreover, in assessing the issue of distinctiveness, the Federal Court failed to consider the evidence as to the reputation that the Ajit Daily enjoyed, which may have contributed to the mark's acquiring distinctiveness. The Federal Court committed a palpable and overriding error in failing to consider these factors, which are central to the issue of distinctiveness. [...]

Notes

Essentially, *Hamdard Trust* tells us that an action for passing-off can succeed in a geographic region other than where the plaintiff does business. However, the difficult, but not impossible, task would be adducing evidence of goodwill in the region where the remedy is sought. For example, "Mr. Twist," which is manufactured by Bombay Sweets, is a popular brand of potato chips in Bangladesh.[189] Therefore, if another company in Bangladesh wants to use a similar name and logo, then Bombay Sweets can institute proceedings for trademark infringement (if the mark is registered) or passing-off (if the mark is unregistered).

If a person, however, in California, United States, does not know of Mr. Twist, then he can use the name (he would think he has concocted it) to sell potato chips only if others in that region do not confuse his product with that of Bombay Sweets.[190] That is to say, if there are people who are

126 *Intentional torts*

Bangladeshi or are otherwise familiar with Bombay Sweets, then the name "Mr. Twist" cannot be used, or if it is, then a case for passing-off would arise and it would not matter whether Bombay Sweets sold Mr. Twist in the United States.[191]

4.4.1.4 *Misappropriation of personality*

Misappropriation of personality is the right of a person to prevent the unauthorized exploitation of his name for commercial purposes.[192] While the tort primarily protects celebrities and public figures, whereby a defendant tries to promote his goods by deceiving the public into thinking that a celebrity or public figure has endorsed them, it also provides protection to ordinary persons.[193] There are three elements to the tort: (1) the intentional use of the plaintiff's image or likeness, (2) the unauthorized use of his image or likeness for commercial purposes, and (3) damage.

Since the first and second elements are similar, I will speak of them together. If a person uses another's image to promote his goods, then the first element is met. For example, if Regent Bistro uses an image of Michael Jordan next to its name, and secondly, if the use of his image is unauthorized, then Jordan would have grounds to institute proceedings so long as damage is proven (more on this later). As in, the use of Jordan's image may confuse customers into thinking that he recommends this particular restaurant, which, in reality, is false. To elaborate, it is not uncommon for us to purchase a product or try a restaurant simply because a celebrity has endorsed it.[194] However, an endorsement implies that the person whose image is being used to promote the product is aware of its use and has authorized it in exchange for a fee. Therefore, without consent, any use of a person's image or likeness to him is misappropriation of personality.[195]

Third, there must be damage to the person whose image or likeness is being used without consent.[196] However, in our example, it seems that using Jordan's image to promote Regent Bistro is harmless. Nonetheless, what if Jordan dislikes French cuisine, or the name "Regent," or the owners of the restaurant because they are rumoured to be associated with organized crime, or what if he likes French food, but the quality at Regent is substandard? If I have still failed to convince you that this could be injurious to Jordan, then imagine that instead of Regent using his picture, Exxotica, which is a gentlemen's club, used the same to promote their store?

One question, however, remains unanswered, and that is, as we are now aware that it is misappropriation of personality to use another's image to promote one's product, then are newspapers also liable when they publish information about a celebrity or public figure? As in, let us assume that a politician has declared his candidacy to be the Prime Minister of Bangladesh, and *The Bangladesh Herald*, which is a daily newspaper, printed an image of him and provided a conspectus of his biography. Would this be tantamount to misappropriation of personality because many Bangladeshis may buy the newspaper simply to learn about him?

Intentional torts 127

Gould Estate v Stoddart Publishing Co Ltd[197]

In 1956, Jock Carroll interviewed Glenn Gould, who was a pianist, for an article in the *Weekend Magazine*. The two of them spoke on multiple occasions and Carroll even accompanied Gould on a trip to the Bahamas, where the former took meticulous notes, recorded some of their conversations, and took approximately 400 photographs of Gould. A modicum of the photographs and Gould's comments were used in Carroll's article. Then, in 1982, Mr. Gould died.

In 1995, Carroll, through Stoddart Publishing Co Limited, published a book entitled *Glenn Gould: Some Portraits of the Artist as a Young Man*, whereby 70 of the original 400 photographs taken in 1956 were used. The book also extensively incorporated conversations that happened between Carroll and Gould from the same year. The estate of Mr. Gould then brought an action for misappropriation of personality against the publishers. Finding in favour of the publishers, the court said,

> While at first glance this decision may seem to support the present defendants' broad interpretation of commercialization, the decision is consistent with the endorsement context. *Athans* was a situation where an identifiable "representational image" was utilized by a waterskiing school in the school's promotional brochure. Therefore, on the basis of these Canadian authorities it would seem open to the court to conclude, on a contextual basis, that the tort of appropriation of personality is restricted to endorsement-type situations.
>
> More broadly, it also seems clear that in articulating this tort the court must be mindful of the public interest. In *Krouse, supra*, the Ontario Court of Appeal explicitly stated [...]

> > Progress in the law is not served by the recognition of a right which, while helpful to some persons or classes of persons, turns out to be unreasonable disruption to the community at large and to the conduct of its commerce. [...]

> The US courts have similarly recognized the necessity of limits on the right of personality. These limits are usually discussed in terms of First Amendment considerations: "the scope of the right of publicity should be measured or balanced against societal interests in free expression" [...] In *Presley, supra*, the United States District Court [...] stated [...]

> > Thus, the purpose of the portrayal in question must be examined to determine if it predominantly serves a social function valued by the protection of free speech. If the portrayal merely serves the purpose of contributing information, which is not false or defamatory, to the public debate of political or social issues or of providing the free expression of creative talent which contributes to society's cultural enrichment, then the portrayal generally will be immune from liability. If, however, the portrayal functions primarily as a means of commercial exploitation, then such immunity will not be granted.

128 *Intentional torts*

Accordingly, the right of publicity has not been successfully invoked in cases where the activity in question consists of thoughts, ideas, newsworthy events or matters of public interest. In this regard, it is important to note that:

> The scope of the subject matter which falls within the protected area of the 'newsworthy' or of 'public interest' extends far beyond the dissemination of news in the sense of current events and includes all types of factual, educational and historical data, or even entertainment and amusement. [...]

Conversely, the right of publicity has been upheld in situations where famous names or likeness are used 'predominately in connection with the sale of consumer merchandise or solely for purposes of trade – e.g. merely to attract attention' [...] As a result, Elvis Presley posters, pewter replicas of a statue of Elvis Presley, a "Howard Hughes" game which included Hughes' name and other biographical information, and a board game utilizing the names and biographies of famous golfers, have all been found to infringe the right of publicity [...] All were found to be commercial products which were not vehicles through which ideas and opinions are regularly disseminated. [...]

In the end then, and perhaps at the risk of over simplifying, it seems that the courts have drawn a 'sales vs subject' distinction. Sales constitute commercial exploitation and invoke the tort of appropriation of personality. The identity of the celebrity is merely being used in some fashion. The activity cannot be said to be about the celebrity. This is in contrast to situations in which the celebrity is the actual subject of the work or enterprise, with biographies perhaps being the clearest example. These activities would not be within the ambit of the tort. To take a more concrete example, in endorsement situations, posters and board games, the essence of the activity is not the celebrity. It is the use of some attributes of the celebrity for another purpose. Biographies, other books, plays, and satirical skits are by their nature different. The subject of the activity is the celebrity and the work is an attempt to provide some insights about that celebrity.

Notes

We can see from *Gould* that courts distinguish between "sale" and "subject," and that only the former is actionable; that is, if Regent Bistro uses an image of Jordan, then the reasonable interpretation is that he has endorsed the restaurant, which can facilitate Regent's sales. To further explain, it can be said that Regent is using Jordan's celebrity-status to promote its restaurant, which, in the absence of evidence to the contrary, is tortious. However, if *The Bangladesh Herald* publishes an article and an image of the candidate for Prime Minister of Bangladesh, then there is no misappropriation of personality, as he is the *subject* of the article. While one can argue that the credit for the newspaper's sales can be redounded to the candidate's picture, it is foremost an informative piece, which the public have an interest in receiving.

Intentional torts 129

4.4.2 *Improper market practices*

Allen v Flood[198]

Flood was a shipwright whose employment contract expired every 24 hours (in other words, he was employed by the company on a daily basis). Unfortunately, other employees objected to Flood's employment, as the latter had worked at a rival company. Allen, who was a trade union representative for the disgruntled employees, approached the employer and informed them that if they do not dismiss Flood immediately, then the other employees would go on strike.

Apprehensive of what may ensue, the employer subsequently relieved Flood of his duties and the latter brought an action against Allen for maliciously inducing a breach of contract (between the employer and Flood). Dismissing his claim, the court said,

> I accept for the present purpose without comment the doctrine laid down in *Lumley v Gye* [...] and *Bowen v Hall* [...] that maliciously to induce one to break a contract of exclusive personal service with an employer to the injury of that employer is actionable. But a perusal of the judgments delivered by the learned judges in *Lumley v Gye* [...] shows that, in their opinion at any rate, it was vital to the plaintiff's case that there was a subsisting contract of service. An employer may discharge a workman (with whom he has no contract) or may refuse to employ one from the most mistaken, capricious, malicious, or morally reprehensible motives that can be conceived; but the workman has no right of action against him. It seems to me strange to say that the principal who does the act is under no liability, but the accessory who has advised him to do so without any wrongful act is under liability. To persuade a person to do or abstain from doing what that person is entitled at his own will to do or abstain from doing is lawful and in some cases meritorious, although the result of the advice may be damage to another. This is not a case of conspiracy. I do not say whether, if it were, it would or would not make an essential difference. But I do say that I am not aware of any authority binding on this House for holding, and it humbly appears to me to be against sound principle to hold, that the additional ingredient of malice should give a right of action against an individual for an act which, if done without malice, would not be wrongful, although it results in damage to a third person.

4.4.2.1 *Conspiracy*

Conspiracy, which is divided into simple conspiracy and conspiracy to injure by unlawful means, arises when two or more persons have entered into an agreement and acted in concert to cause economic loss to another. It would then seem that there was conspiracy, in *Allen*, between Mr. Allen and the employer when they agreed to, and subsequently did, dismiss

130   *Intentional torts*

Mr. Flood from employment, which would cause economic harm to the latter. However, it is pertinent to note that, firstly, *Allen* was decided in 1898 when the nominate tort of conspiracy did not exist;[199] secondly and more importantly, Mr. Flood was employed on a daily basis, which means that even though his employer discharged and refused to hire him at the advice (or behest) of Mr. Allen, there was no breach of contract between the employer and Mr. Flood. As in, if a company renews an employment contract on a daily basis, then electing to forgo renewal is their prerogative and no amount of ingenuity will make the company liable for an otherwise lawful act. Nonetheless, I will now delineate simple conspiracy and revisit *Allen* again to further expound why the court found no conspiracy.

4.4.2.2 *Simple conspiracy*

Simple conspiracy is when two or more persons have agreed and used lawful means for the predominant purpose of causing economic injury to the plaintiff.[200] While the agreement can be express or implied, formal or informal, it must demonstrate an intention to act together to economically harm the plaintiff. However, this does not mean that a company cannot aggressively compete with another; rather, simple conspiracy prevents two or more companies agreeing and acting on their agreement, to cause economic loss to another.

Crofter Hand Woven Harris Tweed Co Ltd v Veitch[201]

At the Island of Lewis, the plaintiffs, who were producers of Harris Tweed, gained a competitive advantage over other businesses by importing yarn, as opposed to relying on local crofters. However, local crofters, with the assistance of Mr. Veitch, who was the Scottish Area Secretary of the Transport and General Workers' Union, were able to foist an embargo on the import of yarn, which brought the plaintiff's business to a complete halt, and they consequently brought an action for conspiracy. Finding no conspiracy, the court said,

> Conspiracy, when regarded as a crime, is the agreement of two or more persons to effect any unlawful purpose, whether as their ultimate aim, or only as a means to it, and the crime is complete if there is such agreement, even though nothing is done in pursuance of it (I am omitting consideration of those cases on the borderland of illegality, where the combination was held to amount to a criminal conspiracy because the purpose aimed at, though not perhaps specifically illegal, was one which would undermine principles of commercial or moral conduct). The crime consists in the agreement, though in most cases overt acts done in pursuance of the combination are available to prove the fact of agreement. But the tort of conspiracy is constituted only if the agreed combination is carried into effect in a greater or less degree and damage to the Plaintiff is thereby produced. [...]

Intentional torts 131

[I]t is to be borne in mind that there may be cases where the combination has more than one "object" or "purpose." The combiners may feel that they are killing two birds with one stone, and, even though their main purpose may be to protect their own legitimate interests notwithstanding that this involves damage to the Plaintiffs, they may also find a further inducement to do what they are doing by feeling that it serves the Plaintiffs right. The analysis of human impulses soon leads us into the quagmire of mixed motives, and even if we avoid the word "motive," there may be more than a single "purpose" or "object." It is enough to say that if there is more than one purpose actuating a combination, liability must depend on ascertaining the predominant purpose. If that predominant purpose is to damage another person and damage results, that is tortious conspiracy. If the predominant purpose is the lawful protection or promotion of any lawful interest of the combiners (no illegal means being employed), it is not a tortious conspiracy, even though it causes damage to another person.

Notes

It would not be unreasonable to say that *Allen* and *Crofter* presage that courts balk at finding conspiracy. This is so because there is no conspiracy unless causing economic injury is the parties' predominant purpose.[202] As in, *Crofter* tells us that this may seem like the parties are "killing two birds with one stone," whereby their primary motive could be to preserve or enhance their business, but its corollary is that it causes economic injury to another. In such a scenario, conspiracy would not arise because the tort is concerned with the parties' *predominant purpose* and not with its repercussions.[203] Thence, against the backdrop of *Crofter*, *Allen* now makes more sense because the company's decision to dismiss Mr. Flood was based on its interest in preventing its employees from going on strike, thereby preserving its business. However, if evidence could be adduced that the primary purpose of Mr. Allen and the company was to cause economic harm to Mr. Flood, then conspiracy would exist, but proving such a case seems well-nigh impossible, as parties can claim that their purpose was to preserve their business – not cause economic injury.[204]

4.4.2.3 *Conspiracy to injure by unlawful means*

XY Inc v International Newtech Development Inc[205]

XY, LLC Inc. (hereinafter "XY") licensed its technology to JingJing Genetic Inc. (hereinafter "JingJing"), whereby the "X" and "Y" chromosomes in bovine spermatozoa could be separated, which would allow scientists to produce calves of their desired gender. Unfortunately, it was discovered that JingJing falsified reports regarding its revenue from the use of XY's technology, thus, underpaid royalties to XY, concealed documents from XY, and violated its confidentiality provisions of their contract. Moreover, JingJing's decision to do the above stemmed from Mr. Jesse Zhu, who was

132 *Intentional torts*

the controlling shareholder of the "IND Group" and the controlling mind of JingJing. At trial, it was proven that Mr. Zhu conspired with Ms. Jin Tang and Ms. Selen Zhou to cause economic harm to XY by misusing the latter's technology amounting to a gross breach of confidence. On appeal, the court said,

> I certainly agree that the acts of the defendants must be causally related to loss or damage to the plaintiff for purposes of establishing a civil conspiracy. As stated in *Lombardo v Caiazzo* [...] "A conspiracy that does not result in damages is not actionable" [...] The fact that the plaintiff must have suffered loss as a result of the conspiracy, however, does not mean it must have changed its position or relied to its detriment on misconduct of the defendant. In *Canada Cement LaFarge*, for example, the defendants were alleged to have conspired to drive the plaintiff aggregate manufacturer out of business through marketing arrangements aimed at dividing the concrete products market in British Columbia between two of the defendants. Although the plaintiff's claim ultimately failed, no issue arose concerning the sustainability in theory of the plaintiff's claim to loss of the "benefits of a free market" as a result of the alleged conspiracy. [...]
>
> There is not a great deal of caselaw in Canada on the meaning of "unlawful means" or "unlawful act" in the context of civil conspiracy. In 1961, in *Gagnon v Foundation Maritime Ltd* [...], the Court referred in this context to "means [...] [that] were prohibited, and this of itself supplies the ingredient necessary to change a lawful agreement which would not give rise to a cause of action into a tortious conspiracy [...]" [...] More recently, the Ontario Court of Appeal considered the issue in *Agribrands Purina Canada Inc v Kasamekas*, [...] in connection with a claim of intentional inference with economic relations. The Court referred to *Bank of Montreal v Tortora*, [...] in which it was said [...] that for conspiracy to lie, the plaintiff must show unlawful conduct by each conspirator. After considering the specific context of intentional interference cases, the Court in *Agribrands* continued:
>
>> [R]ather than automatically adopting the meaning of unlawful conduct given in the intentional interference tort cases, I think the better course is to use those cases as a guide, but also consider the kind of conduct that the jurisprudence has found to be unlawful conduct for the purposes of the conspiracy tort.
>
> It is clear from that jurisprudence that quasi-criminal conduct, when undertaken in concert, is sufficient to constitute unlawful conduct for the purposes of the conspiracy tort, even though that conduct is not actionable in a private law sense by a third party. The seminal case of *Canada Cement LaFarge* is an example. So too is conduct that is in breach of the *Criminal Code*. These examples of "unlawful conduct" are not actionable in themselves, but they have been held to constitute conduct that is wrongful in law and therefore sufficient to be considered

Intentional torts   133

"unlawful conduct" within the meaning of civil conspiracy. There are also many examples of conduct found to be unlawful for the purposes of this tort simply because the conduct is actionable as a matter of private law. In Peter Burns & Joost Blom, *Economic Interests in Canadian Tort Law* [...], the authors say [...]:

> Examples of conspiracies involving tortious conduct include inducing breach of contract, wrongful interference with contractual rights, nuisance, intimidation, and defamation. Of course, a breach of contract itself will support an action in civil conspiracy and, as one Australian court has held, the categories of "unlawful means" are not closed. [...]

What is required, therefore, to meet the "unlawful conduct" element of the conspiracy tort is that the defendants engage, in concert, in acts that are wrong in law, whether actionable at private law or not. In the commercial world, even highly competitive activity, provided it is otherwise lawful, does not qualify as "unlawful conduct" for the purposes of this tort. [...]

Notes

When two or more persons agree and act on their agreement, or act unlawfully to cause economic harm to the plaintiff, or if they knew or ought to have known that their unlawful conduct was going to harm the plaintiff, then conspiracy to injure by unlawful means arises. For example, assume you have garnered a great deal of wealth from developing real estate. You wish to invest your money, but are unaware of where to invest, and therefore, consult an investment banker, James Smith. James, on your behalf, will invest your money, and, from the profits derived, keep 10% in commission. However, unbeknownst to you, James has a younger brother, Allan Smith, who works with him. Allan dislikes you because you used to date his wife. Therefore, after you leave, Allan approaches James and persuades him to conceal 8% of the profits, whereby you will be paid less than the actual return. Since suppressing profits is unlawful, James and Allan's agreement to cause economic harm would be conspiracy to injure by unlawful means.[206]

4.4.2.4 Intimidation

Rookes v Barnard[207]

Until November 1955, Douglas Rookes was a draughtsman working at British Overseas Airways Corporation (hereinafter "BOAC") and was a union member of the Association of Engineering and Shipbuilding Draughtsman (hereinafter "AESD"). Unfortunately, due to disagreement with AESD, Rookes resigned his membership in November 1955. BOAC and AESD had an agreement that the former would only hire persons who were union members, that members would not go on strike, and if a dispute arose, the matter would be negotiated. Furthermore, the enumerated constituted part

134   *Intentional torts*

of the composite employment contract between each member of AESD with BOAC. However, on 10 January 1956, BOAC was informed that if they did not dismiss Rookes by 4:00 pm on 13 January 1956, members of AESD (who were also employees at BOAC) would go on strike. Rookes was subsequently dismissed and he brought an action against AESD for threatening BOAC with unlawful means to terminate his employment. Ruling in his favour, the court said,

> There is at common law a tort of intimidation by a threat to a person other than plaintiff to do an unlawful act, made with the intention of damnifying plaintiff, whereby loss accrues to him, and for the purposes of constituting the tort there is no distinction between a threat to do a tortious act to, and a threat to break a contract with, the person threatened.

Notes

Intimidation arises when either, (a) a person threatens a third party with unlawful means and coerces him to harm the plaintiff, or (b) a person threatens the plaintiff to act to his detriment.[208] Therefore, when AESD threatened BOAC with strike if they do not terminate Douglas Rookes, they engaged in three-party intimidation. As in, because their contract prohibited strikes, the threat of it transformed an otherwise lawful activity (e.g. strike) into an unlawful one, and since it coerced BOAC to harm Rookes, intimidation resulted. However, had AESD not threatened strike, then there would be no intimidation, as BOAC was contractually obligated only to hire members of AESD, and since Rookes resigned his membership, he would have been dismissed anyway.

Two-party intimidation can arise when, for example, you are amid constructing a hotel in Cox's Bazar and, because you submitted the lowest bid of ৳15,000,000, you have been selected to construct a five-kilometre flyover in Dhaka. However, two months into the construction of the flyover, an officer from the Ministry of Road Transport and Bridges informs you that the Ministry can only pay you ৳5,000,000 for the flyover and that if you do not accept their revised offer, then water, electricity, and gas will not be supplied to your hotel in Cox's Bazar. While you explain to the officer that the contract was formed for ৳15,000,000 and that you will suffer a gross loss at ৳5,000,000, he is obstinate in his position. Though you can seek relief from courts, you realize that if you launch a complaint against the Ministry, there may be unforeseeable consequences, and therefore, you accept their revised offer. However, once you fully appreciate the magnitude of your loss after the project has completed, you nevertheless pursue legal action.

You can either, (a) have the contract set aside due to lack of consent, which would be a contractual remedy, or (b) file a case under the tort of intimidation. If you seek a remedy under contracts, then a court will set the contract aside without awarding damages because the purpose of a contractual remedy is to place the party in the position he would have been

Intentional torts 135

in *had the contract been performed* (or alternatively, *not been breached*). Therefore, since the issue is not about performance or breach, a court can only set the contract aside at the request of the innocent party.[209]

However, if you pursue litigation under the tort of intimidation, damages will be awarded for the injury suffered. To further explain, dissimilar from contracts, the purpose of a tortious remedy is to place the party in the position he would have been in *had the tort not been committed*. Therefore, the question is "what was the tort?" and the answer is the threat by the officer of the Government that if you do not accept the amended offer, which will cause you economic harm, your hotel in Cox's Bazar would not be supplied with water, electricity, or gas. As in, pursuing litigation through the tort of intimidation would permit you to extract the deficient amount of ৳10,000,000 (or, the original price contractually bargained for).[210]

4.4.2.5 Inducement to breach a contract

The primary means of transacting business is through contracts, and therefore, as discussed earlier, tort law supplements the law of contracts by according protection to parties in contractual relationships. Therefore, directly inducing one to breach a contract – whose essential elements are (1) direct inducement to breach a contract, (2) defendant's knowledge on the existence of a contract, (3) intention to secure breach, and (4) damage – is actionable.[211]

Lumley v Gye[212]

Johanna Wagner was in a contract with Benjamin Lumley, who owned Her Majesty's Theatre, to sing exclusively at the said theatre for three months. By offering to pay her more, Frederick Gye, who operated the Covent Garden Theatre, successfully persuaded Ms. Wagner to breach her contract with Mr. Lumley and sing at his theatre. Mr. Lumley then brought an action against Mr. Gye for damages for loss of income. Holding Mr. Gye liable, the court said,

> It was laid down broadly, as a general proposition of law, that no action will lie for procuring a person to break a contract, although such procuring is with a malicious intention and causes great and immediate injury. The law as to enticing servants was said to be contrary to the general rule and principle of law, to be anomalous, and probably to have had its origin from the state of society when serfdom existed and to be founded upon, or upon the equity of, the Statute of Labourers. It was said that it would be dangerous to hold that an action was maintainable for persuading a third party to break a contract unless some boundary or limits could be pointed out; that the remedy for enticing away servants was confined to cases where the relation of master and servant, in a strict sense, subsisted between the parties; and that, in all other cases of contract, the only remedy was against the party breaking the contract.

136   *Intentional torts*

Whatever may have been the origin or foundation of the law as to enticing of servants, and whether it be, as contended by the plaintiff, an instance and branch of a wider rule, or, as contended by the defendant, an anomaly and an exception from the general rule of law on such subjects, it must now be considered clear law that a person who wrongfully and maliciously, or, which is the same thing, with notice, interrupts the relation subsisting between master and servant by procuring the servant to depart from the master's service, or by harbouring and keeping him as servant after he has quitted it and during the time stipulated for as the period of service, whereby the master is injured, commits a wrongful act for which he is responsible at law. I think that the rule applies wherever the wrongful interruption operates to prevent the service during the time for which the parties have contracted that the service shall continue, and I think that the relation of master and servant subsists, sufficiently for the purpose of such action, during the time for which there is in existence a binding contract of hiring and service between the parties.

Notes

While the court found Gye liable for inducing Wagner to breach her contract, it is pertinent to note that not every conversation with a person involved in a contract amounts to tortious liability. That is, in *Lumley*, all of the four essential elements were met: (1) Gye induced Wagner to breach her contract with Lumley by offering to pay her more money; (2) Gye was aware of Wagner and Lumley's contract; (3) by offering to pay her more money, not only did Gye induce Wagner to breach her contract, but he also intended to make sure she breached her contract because of the inducement; and (4) while Lumley would have earned money through Wagner's performances at his theatre, he was precluded from earning money on account of the contractual breach.[213]

However, let us assume that you are the Chief Executive Officer of the Dhaka Stock Exchange (hereinafter "DSE") receiving a salary of ৳600,000 on a monthly basis. Your employment contract is from January 2019 to December 2022. In November 2020, while golfing with the Chair of the Board of Directors (hereinafter "Chair") of Grey Limited (hereinafter "Grey"), which is the most profitable company in Bangladesh, he mentions that a person of your caliber would receive, *inter alia*, ৳900,000 per month at Grey and a full-time chauffeur-driven vehicle. Though he knows you work at DSE, he is unaware of your contractual obligation to work until December 2022. Nonetheless, relying on his statement, you resign from DSE and begin working at Grey from January 2021.

Since you have breached your contract with DSE, they can hold you accountable. However, they will have no case against the Chair of Grey for inducing you to breach your contract, as the latter could contend that he never intended that you breach your contract with DSE.[214] Furthermore, it would not matter that he did not know for how long you were supposed to work at DSE because specific knowledge regarding the terms of the contract are irrelevant. Rather, he could claim that he advised you of options and you chose to leave DSE voluntarily, which would mean that the third element of the tort (intention to secure breach) is unmet, and therefore, litigation cannot be pursued against the Chair.[215] Simply put, it is extremely difficult to prove that one intended to secure a breach of contract even if an inducement is provided and injury results from the breach of contract.

Notes

1 R F V Heuston & R A Buckley, *Salmond and Heuston on the Law of Torts*, 19th ed (London: Sweet & Maxwell, 1987) at 46 [Heuston & Buckley]. "*Quare clausum fregit*" means a writ for land trespass.

2 William L Prosser, *Handbook of The Law of Torts*, 4th ed (St. Paul, Minnesota: West Publishing Co, 1971) at 28 [Prosser].

3 *Ibid*. See generally George F Deiser, "The Development of Principle of Trespass" (1917) 27:2 Yale LJ 220 and George E Woodbine, "The Origins of the Action of Trespass" (1924) 33:8 Yale LJ 799; Also see John G Fleming, *The Law of Torts*, 9th ed (Sydney: LBC Information Services, 1998) where he says at 45 [Fleming],

    In the course of its history, this action of trespass came to be used for a number of different purposes which have left their mark on its conditions of liability. In origin, trespass was a remedy for forcible breach of the King's peace, aimed against acts of intentional aggression. This early association with the maintenance of public order explains why the action lies only for interference with an occupier's *actual* possession. Its proprietary aspect became more dominant when it was later used for the purpose of settling boundary disputes, quieting title and preventing the acquisition of easements by prescriptive user. These latter functions account for the rule that the plaintiff is not required to prove material loss, and that a mistaken belief by the defendant that the land was his affords no excuse. [Footnotes omitted].

4 Ernest J Weinrib, *Tort Law: Cases and Materials*, 4th ed (Toronto: Emond Montgomery Publications Limited, 2014) at 469 [Weinrib]; Philip Osborne, *The Law of Torts*, 5th ed (Toronto: Irwin Law Inc, 2015) at 264 [Osborne].

5 In Bangladesh, "assault" is statutorily prohibited and is an offence punishable by the criminal law, at *The Penal Code*, 1860 (Bangladesh), Act No XLV of 1860, s 351 [*Penal Code*]. Battery is any form of intentional, direct, and non-consensual interference with the bodily integrity of another that is offensive or harmful, see Osborne, *ibid*.

6 *Stephens v Myers*, [1830] 172 ER 735, 4 Car & P 349; Also see Osborne, *ibid*. at 270. See generally Francis Trindade, "Intentional Torts: Some Thoughts on Assault and Battery" (1982) 2:2 Oxford J Leg Stud 211.

7 Subject to proof, the person delivering the threat can perhaps be charged under section 503 of the *Penal Code*, which stipulates, "Whoever threatens another with any injury to his person, reputation or property, or to the person or reputation of any one in whom that person is interested, with intent to cause to alarm to that person, or to cause that person to do any act which he is not legally bound to do, or to omit to do any act which that person is legally entitled to do, as the means of avoiding the execution of such threat, commits criminal intimidation [...]" at *Penal Code, supra* note 5 at s 503.

8 *Holcombe v Whitaker*, [1975] 318 So 2d 289, 294 Ala 430; Also see Osborne, *supra* note 4 at 271.

138   *Intentional torts*

9   Fleming, *supra* note 3 at 33; Also see Jesse Elvin, "Liability of Schools for Bullying" (2002) 61:2 Cambridge LJ 239, for the usage of the tort of assault to address bullying in schools.

10 Osborne, *supra* note 4 at 272; Also see *Penal Code, supra* note 5 at ss 339–340, which speak of wrongful restraint and wrongful confinement, respectively.

11 *Alderson v Booth*, [1969] 2 All ER 271, [1969] 2 QB 216.

12 *Bird v Jones*, [1845] 7 QBR 742, 115 ER 668; Also Fleming, *supra* note 3 at 34.

13 See generally William L Prosser, "False Imprisonment: Consciousness of Confinement" (1955) 55:6 Colum L Rev 847 for a discussion on whether it is necessary that the person is aware of his imprisonment. For example, in *Meering v Grahame-White Aviation Co*, [1918–19] All ER Rep Ext 1490, 122 LT 44, Lord Atkin said, at 848:

> It appears to me that a person could be imprisoned without his knowing it. I think a person can be imprisoned while he is asleep, while he is in a state of drunkenness, while he is unconscious, and while he is a lunatic. So a man might in fact […] be imprisoned by having the key of a door turned against him so that he is imprisoned in a room in fact although he does not know that the key has been turned […] Of course the damages might be diminished and would be affected by the question whether he was conscious of it or not.

> However, it is highly likely that being apprised of the imprisonment is not necessary to prove false imprisonment, see *Murray v Ministry of Defence*, [1988] 2 All ER 521, [1988] 1 WLR 692 [*Murray*]. As in, if you are sleeping inside your room and someone locks its door from outside, the person who locked the door would be guilty of false imprisonment even though you have no knowledge of his action.

14 See *Burton v Davies*, [1953] St R QD 26.

15 Osborne, *supra* note 4 at 273–274. Also see *Nelles v Ontario*, [1989] 2 SCR 170, [1989] SCJ No 86.

16 See *Estabrooks v New Brunswick Real Estate Association*, [2014] NBCA 48, [2014] NBJ No 186, where the New Brunswick Court of Appeal held that malicious prosecution is not available in civil litigation. However, in England, the Privy Council said malicious prosecution does extend to civil litigation, *Crawford Adjusters (Cayman) Ltd v Sagicor General Insurance (Cayman) Ltd*, [2013] 4 All ER 8, [2013] UKPC 17.

> The civil equivalent, the topic of which I shall eschew writing, is abuse of process. Briefly put, since the plaintiff is not required to establish that (1) the proceedings ended in his favour or (2) that there was a lack of reasonable grounds to bring the action, abuse of process is often easier to establish. See Osborne, *supra* note 4 at 278–279; Also see *Westjet Airlines Ltd v Air Canada*, [2005] OJ No 2310, 2005 CarswellOnt 2101.

17 However, if the plaintiff is found guilty at trial, is imprisoned, but new evidence surfaces that later exonerates him, he can then institute proceedings for malicious prosecution, at Osborne, *supra* note 4 at 274–275. It is important to note that if the police rely solely on the doctored video to acquire a search warrant of his premises, and it is later proven that the video was fabricated, then the evidence found in his premises, which was gathered from a search warrant authorized by a judge as a result of the video, may become inadmissible in court, and your neighbour may subsequently be able to institute proceedings under malicious prosecution.

18 *Ibid* at 275; Also see *Roberts v Buster's Auto Towing Service Ltd*, [1976] 70 DLR (3d) 716, [1976] BCJ No 1386.

19 Osborne, *ibid*. Also see Don Stuart, Steve Coughlan & Ronald Delisle, *Learning Canadian Criminal Law*, 12th ed (Toronto: Thompson Reuters

Intentional torts 139

Canada Limited, 2014) at 1; See generally Mark Kelman, "Interpretive Construction in the Substantive Criminal Law" (1981) 33:4 Stan L Rev 591.

20 Osborne, *supra* note 4 at 276. Also see *Blunk v Atchison*, [1889] 38 F 311, 1889 US App LEXIS 2820, where the plaintiff was able to recover expenses incurred during criminal prosecution; Also see *Harr v Ward*, [1904] 73 Ark 437 84 SW 496, for the same; See *H S Leyman Company v Short*, [1926] 214 Ky 272, 283 SW 96, for loss of position. Then see *Daughtry v Blanket State Bank et al.*, [1931] 41 SW 2d 527, 1931 Tex App LEXIS 1373, for the injury to the plaintiff's future earning power.

21 Fowler Harper, "Malicious Prosecution, False Imprisonment and Defamation" (1937) 15:2 Tex L Rev 157 at 163 [Harper].

22 See *Bolton v* Vellines, [1897] 94 Va 393, 26 SE 847 and *Bailey et al v Warner*, [1902] 118 F 395, 1902 US App LEXIS 4535.

23 In *Standard Oil Co v Davis*, [1922] 208 Ala 565, [1922] Ala LEXIS 353, it was said,

> The inquiry with regard to a charge of false imprisonment is: (1) Whether or not the defendant or his agent directed, commanded, or in any way instigated the arrest; and (2) whether such conduct, if shown, was a material factor in causing the officer to make the arrest. Of course if the officer acts solely upon his own judgment and initiative, the defendant would not be responsible even though he had directed or requested such action, and even though he were actuated by malice or other improper motive.

24 *Murray, supra* note 13.

25 In *Barry v Third Avenue R R Co*, [1900] 51 AD 385, 64 NYS 615, it was said at 386:

> [T]he mere fact of an illegal arrest and detention is not sufficient to sustain an action for malicious prosecution. The essential element of that action is that a judicial proceeding has been begun and carried on maliciously and without probable cause and has resulted in the discharge of the plaintiff. Unless the arrest is followed by some sort of a judicial proceeding there can be no malicious prosecution, and the plaintiff must seek his remedy in an action for false imprisonment.

Also see Harper, *supra* note 21 at footnote 17.

26 In *American Surety Co v Pryor*, [1927] 217 Ala 244, 115 So 176, the court said at 179:

> The general rule has been declared, based upon considerations of public policy and supported by many authorities, that, where a person gives information to the state's prosecuting officer charged by law with the duty of enforcing the criminal law, or the investigation and prosecution of probably committed crime, and that information tends to connect another with the commission of crime or the violation of the criminal law, and the informant states all the material facts bearing thereon within his knowledge, and leaves that officer to a discharge of his official duty and the exercise of his own judgment and responsibility, or, where such informant disclaims personal knowledge of the incriminating facts, or does not state the facts as of his own knowledge, and the officer thereafter brings the matter to the attention of the grand jury for their investigation of the facts upon probable cause in the premises, without more, the informant is not liable in an action for malicious prosecution under an indictment returned by that grand jury.

27 For example, in *Hogg v Ward*, it was said:

140 *Intentional torts*

If a person comes to a constable and says of another simplicitor 'I charge this man with felony,' that is a reasonable ground, and the constable ought to take the person charged into custody. But if from the circumstances it appears to be an unfounded charge, the constable is not only not bound to act upon it, but he is responsible for so doing. See Harper, *supra* note 21 at footnote 16.

28 Osborne, *supra* note 4 at 266; Also see *Penal Code, supra* note 5 at ss 349–350.

29 *United States v Ortega*, [1825] 27 F Cas 359, 1825 US App LEXIS 262; Also see *Dyk v De Young*, [1889] 35 Ill App 138, 1889 Ill App LEXIS 517 (battery to interfere with someone's paper); *Fisher v Carrousel Motor Hotel, Inc*, [1967] 424 SW 2d 627, 1967 Tex LEXIS 267 (battery to interfere with anything one is holding in their hands); *Hopper v Reeve*, [1817] 7 Taunt 698, 129 ER 278 (battery to interfere with the chair on which someone is seated); *Crossman v Thurlow*, [1957] 336 Mass 252, 1957 Mass LEXIS 622 (battery to interfere with the car someone is riding or driving); *Reynolds v Pierson*, [1902] 29 Ind App 273, 1902 Ind App LEXIS 136 (battery to interfere with the person against whom one is leaning).

Overall, it is important to understand that the tort of battery covers a wide range of interferences with the person, and that it is not limited to contact *only* *with* the person.

30 See generally Prosser, *supra* note 2 at 34–37.

31 *Malette v Shulman*, [1990] OJ No 350, 72 OR (2d) 417 [*Malette*]; Also see Weinrib, *supra* note 4 at 470–476.

32 A useful discussion of battery can be found at *Non-Marine Underwriters, Lloyds of London v Scalera*, [2000] 1 SCR 551, [2000] SCJ No 26.

33 See generally George J Annas & Joan E Densberger, "Competence to Refuse Medical Treatment: Autonomy vs. Paternalism" (1984) 15:2 U Tol L Rev 561.

34 In *NB v Hôtel-Dieu de Québec*, [1992] JQ No 1, 86 DLR (4th) 385, a patient, who was suffering from an incurable disease that completely incapacitated her, was on a respirator, which was keeping her alive. She instructed the doctor to remove her from the respirator, which the latter refused. She then sought the help of the court where it was held that the patient's right to autonomy prevailed and the doctor was required to remove her from the respirator. Though this case was not about assisted suicide, I mention here that readers should also see *Carter v Canada (Attorney General)*, [2015] 1 SCR 331, [2015] SCJ No 5, where the Supreme Court of Canada permitted assisted suicide and adumbrated guidelines as to when it can be done. Also see *Wawrzyniak v Livingstone*, [2019] OJ No 4291, 2019 ONSC 4900; *Peppler Estate v Lee*, [2019] AJ No 249, 2019 ABQB 144; *Waters v Wong*, [2019] AJ No 50, 2019 ABQB 51.

35 Also see Alan Meisel, "The Exceptions to the Informed Consent Doctrine: Striking a Balance between Competing Values in Medical Decisionmaking" (1979) 1979:2 Wis L Rev 413 and Peter H Schuck, "Rethinking Informed Consent" (1994) 103:4 Yale LJ 899.

36 *Nilabati Behera v State of Orissa*, [1993] AIR 1960, 1993 SCR (2) 581 [*Nilabati*].

37 Usha Ramanathan, "Tort Law in India" *IELRC* (2002), online: International Environmental Law Research Centre http://www.ielrc.org/Content/a0206. pdf. [17/03/2021].

38 For reference, Article 32 of the *Constitution of India* stipulates the following:

(1) The right to move the Supreme Court by appropriate proceedings for the enforcement of the rights conferred by this Part is guaranteed; (2) The Supreme Court shall have power to issue directions or orders or writs, including writs

in the nature of *habeas corpus*, *mandamus*, prohibition, *quo warranto* and *certiorari*, whichever may be appropriate, for the enforcement of any of the rights conferred by this Part; (3) Without prejudice to the powers conferred on the Supreme Court by clauses (1) and (2), Parliament may by law empower any other court to exercise within the local limits of its jurisdiction all or any of the powers exercisable by the Supreme Court under clause (2); (4) The right guaranteed by this article shall not be suspended except as otherwise provided for by this Constitution.

At *Constitution of India* (India), Act of 1950 at s 32. This provision of the *Constitution of India* is analogous to s 102 of *The Constitution of the People's Republic of Bangladesh* (Bangladesh), Act of 1972 [*Constitution of Bangladesh*].

39 See generally Taqbir Huda, "State Liability to Pay Compensation for Rape: A Necessary Ruling" *The Daily Star* (15 March 2019), online: The Daily Star https://www.thedailystar.net/opinion/law/news/state-liability-pay-compensation-rape-necessary-ruling-1715395; Also see Taqbir Huda, "US-Bangla Air Crash: A Tort Law Perspective" *The Daily Star* (27 March 2018a), online: The Daily Star https://www.thedailystar.net/law-our-rights/tort-law-perspective-1553911; Taqbir Huda, "Judicial Activism for Constitutional Torts" *The Daily Star* (7 August 2018b), online: The Daily Star https://www.thedailystar.net/news/law-our-rights/judicial-activism-constitutional-torts-1616731; "Compensation Ordered in only 7pc Rape Cases" *The Daily Star* (8 March 2021), online: The Daily Star: https://www.thedailystar.net/city/news/compensation-ordered-only-7pc-rape-cases-2056673. [17/03/2021].

40 William L Prosser, "Intentional Infliction of Mental Suffering: A New Tort" (1939) 37:6 Mich L Rev 874 at 875 [Prosser: A New Tort]; Also see Francis H Bohlen, "Right to Recover for Injury Resulting from Negligence without Impact" (1902) 50:3 Am L Reg 141 and Archibald H Throckmorton, "Damages for Fright" (1921) 34:3 Harv L Rev 260. See generally Prosser, *supra* note 2 at 49–62.

41 *Lynch v Knight*, [1861] All ER Rep Ext 2344, 9 HL Cas 577 at 2360.

42 See *Mitchell v Rochester Railway Company*, [1896] 151 NY 107, 45 NE 354, where the court held that the plaintiff could not recover for fright even if it led to a miscarriage; Also see *Spade v Lynn and Boston Railroad Company*, [1897] 168 Mass 285, 47 NE 88, where the court held that the plaintiff could not recover for mental anguish simply because she viewed an altercation between the railway conductor and a passenger.

43 *Ashby v White*, [1703] 2 Ld Raym 938, 1 ER 417, 92 ER 710.

44 *Simone v The Rhode Island Company*, [1907] 28 RI 186, 66 A 202; *Green v TA Shoemaker & Co*, [1909] 111 Md 69, 73 A 688; *Kenney v Wong Len*, [1925] 81 NH 427, 128 A 343; *Clark v Canada (TD)*, [1994] 3 FC 323, [1994] FCJ No 576.

45 *Wilkinson v Downton*, [1897] All ER Rep 267, 2 QB 57.

46 Prosser: A New Tort, *supra* note 40; Also see Osborne, *supra* note 4 at 279–281.

47 Also see Harvey Teff, "Liability for Psychiatric Illness after Hillsborough" (1992) 12:3 Oxford J Leg Stud 440.

48 *Constitution of Bangladesh*, *supra* note 38 at s 43.

49 See *Caltagirone v Scozzari-Cloutier*, [2007] OJ No 4003, [*Caltagirone*], where it was said at para 14, "Anything which involves the regulation of information flow also involves a balance between competing private and public interests. Even the most private of information (e.g. one's HIV-positive status) must sometimes be disclosed (e.g. to a public health agency) in the service of a

142   *Intentional torts*

broader public good." Also see *Aubry v Éditions Vice-Versa*, [1998] 1 SCR 591, [1998] SCJ No 30.

Since the two aforesaid cases are from Canada, I will also mention that Canada amended the *Criminal Code* and added section 162.1, which makes the non-consensual publishing, distributing, transmitting, selling, or advertising intimate images of a person a criminal offence, whereby the offender can be punished with imprisonment for up to five years, at *Criminal Code*, RSC 1985, c C-46, s 162.1 [*Criminal Code*].

50 *The Pornography Control Act, 2012* (Bangladesh), Act No IX of 2012, at s 8(3) [*PCA*]. The *PCA* has been written and published in Bengali. Thus, in the event my translation is incorrect, I am providing the original text as reference: "কোন ব্যক্তি ইন্টারনেট বা ওয়েবসাইট বা মোবাইল ফোন বা অন্য কোন ইলেকট্রনিক ডিভাইসের মাধ্যমে পর্নোগ্রাফি সরবরাহ করিলে তিনি অপরাধ করিয়াছেন বলিয়া গণ্য হইবেন এবং উক্তরূপ অপরাধের জন্য তিনি সর্বোচ্চ ৫ (পাঁচ) বৎসর পর্যন্ত সশ্রম কারাদণ্ড এবং ২,০০,০০০ (দুই লক্ষ) টাকা পর্যন্ত অর্থদণ্ডে দণ্ডিত হইবেন।" Please note that the penalty is both imprisonment and a fine, which is unusual in the sense that parliamentarians generally allow the "either/or" punishment. However, due to the severity of the offence, Bangladesh deemed it best to impose both imprisonment and a substantial fine.

51 *Penal Code, supra* note 5.

52 *Lipiec v Borsa*, [1996] OJ No 3819, 17 OTC 64; Also see *Wasserman v Hall*, [2009] BCJ No 1932, 2009 BCSC 1318.

53 *Heckert v 5470 Investments Ltd*, [2008] BCJ No 1854, [2008] 62 CCLT (3d) 249. Also see Eli A Meltz, "No Harm, No Foul: Attempted Invasion of Privacy and the Tort of Intrusion upon Seclusion" (2015) 83:6 Fordham L Rev 3431.

54 However, some provinces in Canada have promulgated statute to protect privacy. For example, see *Privacy Act*, RSBC 1996, c 373 (British Columbia); *The Privacy Act*, RSM 1987, c P125 (Manitoba); *Privacy Act*, RSNL 1990, c P-22 (Newfoundland and Labrador); and *Privacy Act*, RSS 1978, c P-24 (Saskatchewan). Also see Adam J Tutaj, "Intrusion upon Seclusion: Bringing an Otherwise Valid Cause of Action into the 21st Century" (1999) 82:3 Marq L Rev 665. Similar to Canada, Bangladesh can also deliberate promulgating legislation that protects one's privacy. For an interesting discussion on protecting online privacy, see Tigran Palyan, "Common Law Privacy in a Not So Common World: Prospects for the Tort of Intrusion upon Seclusion in Virtual Worlds" (2008) 38:1 Sw L Rev 167.

55 *Saccone v Orr*, [1982] 34 OR (2d) 317 [*Saccone*].

56 Also see Samuel D Warren & Louis D Brandeis, "The Right to Privacy" (1890) 4:5 Harv L Rev 193. Moreover, as early as 1884, there were calls for the law to remedy the unauthorized distribution of pictures of private citizens, see *Simeon Groot v Florian Hitz*, [1884] 12 Wash L Rep 353.

57 Caltagirone, supra note 49 at para 21. In this case, the defendants were liable for disclosing to family members that the plaintiff was HIV-positive without his consent; Also see *Somwar v McDonald's Restaurants of Canada Ltd*, [2006] OJ No 64, 79 OR (3d) 172; See generally Allen M Linden & Bruce Feldthusen, *Canadian Tort Law*, 9th ed (Markham, ON: LexisNexis Canada Inc, 2011) at 59–64 [Linden & Feldthusen].

58 See generally Richard G Wilkins, "Defining the Reasonable Expectation of Privacy: An Emerging Tripartite Analysis" (1987) 40:5 Vand L Rev 1077; Also see Christopher Slobogin, "Public Privacy: Camera Surveillance of Public Places and the Right to Anonymity" (2002) 72:1 Miss LJ 213.

59 *Lord v Canada (Attorney General)*, [2000] 50 CCLT (2d) 206, 2000 BCSC 750. Also see *Milner v Manufacturer's Life Insurance Co*, [2006] BCJ No 2787, 2006 BCSC 1571, where it was held to not be an intrusion upon seclusion to conduct video surveillance of the insured's home by the insurer; *Peck v United Kingdom*, [2003] ECHR 44647/98, [2003] All ER (D) 255 (Jan). For

Intentional torts 143

an excellent discussion of privacy law, see Nicole A Moreham, "Privacy in Public Places" (2006) 65:3 Cambridge LJ 606.

60 *Cambell v MGN Ltd*, [2004] 2 All ER 995, [2004] 2 AC 457 at para 21.
61 Linden & Feldthusen, *supra* note 57 at 61–62.
62 Osborne, *supra* note 4 at 293–294.
63 In *Temple v Hallem*, [1989] MJ No 203, [1989] 58 DLR (4th) 541, the plaintiff, who was guarding home plate, was injured when the defendant slid into her, as he was trying to score a run in a mixed-league softball game. The court held that since the game allowed sliding and the defendant did so professionally, there was not battery.
64 *Agar v Canning*, [1965] MJ No 24, [1965] 54 WWR 302. Notice that when the player threw the ball in an attempt to strike the wickets, but failed, and rather, the ball hit you, it is not battery, as it is not unreasonable for such contact to occur in the game of cricket. However, it is battery if an opponent deliberately throws the ball towards you and hits you, instead of handing the ball back to the bowler, which is the usual practice.
65 Rob Hughes, "Suspensions in World Cup Head-Butting Incident" *The New York Times* (21 July 2006), online: The New York Times Company https://www.nytimes.com/2006/07/21/sports/soccer/21soccer.html. [17/03/2021]. Arguments similar to the ones propounded could be made about any sport, for example, *inter alia*, boxing, basketball, baseball, volleyball, rugby, and football (American).
66 I am not unaware that this is a sensitive and delicate issue. I, therefore, shall try to elucidate the tort without being tendentious. Some may argue that you should always explicitly seek your partner's permission prior to engaging in any sexual relationship with them. I am not opposing this view, but I am saying that there are times when consent of one's partner could be implied from the circumstances so long as the said circumstances under which consent is inferred is reasonable.
67 However, see Elizabeth Adjin-Tettey, "Protecting the Dignity and Autonomy of Women: Rethinking the Place of Constructive Consent in the Tort of Sexual Battery" (2006) 39:1 UBC L Rev 3, where she argues that consent must be *affirmative*, as opposed to *constructive*.
68 *Norberg v Wynrib*, [1992] 2 SCR 226, [1992] SCJ No 60; Also see Weinrib, *supra* note 4 at 477–486.
69 *Penal Code, supra* note 5 at s 375.
70 Though primarily discussing contract law, for an excellent disquisition on inequality of bargaining power, see Daniel D Barnhizer, "Inequality of Bargaining Power" (2005) 76:1 U Colo L Rev 139.
71 According to Robert Dahl, "That some people have more power than others is one of the most palpable facts of human existence. Because of this, the concept of power is as ancient and ubiquitous as any that social theory can boast. If these assertions needed any documentation, one could set up an endless parade of great names from Plato and Aristotle through Machiavelli and Hobbes to Pareto and Weber to demonstrate that a large number of seminal social theorists have devoted a good deal of attention to power and the phenomena associated with it." At Robert Dahl, "The Concept of Power," (1957) 2:3 J Soc Gen Systems Research 201 at 201. See generally Robert S Adler & Elliot M Silverstein, "When David Meets Goliath: Dealing with Power Differentials in Negotiations" (2000) 5 Harv Negot L Rev 1.
72 *Bangladesh National Women Lawyers' Association v The Government of Bangladesh*, [2011] 31 BLD 324 at 334. Moreover, the High Court also provided a list of behaviours and actions that constitute sexual harassment. To further explain, even if the illustrated scenario is not battery (which, I ratiocinate, will not be the case), it will, at least, be sexual harassment in Bangladesh.

144 *Intentional torts*

For the sake of simplicity, the case can be found here: https://www.blast.org.
bd/content/judgement/BNWLA-VS-Bangladesh2.pdf and https://uniteforre-
prorights.org/wp-content/uploads/2018/01/BNWLA-Bangladesh-2009.pdf.
[All 17/03/2021].

73 *Penal Code, supra* note 5 at s 375. For the sake of convenience, I shall quote
the wording of the provision:
   A man is said to commit 'rape' who except in the case hereinafter excepted,
has sexual intercourse with a woman under circumstances falling under any of
the five following descriptions:

> Firstly. Against her will.
> Secondly. Without her consent.
> Thirdly. With her consent, when her consent has been obtained by putting
> her in fear of death, or of hurt.
> Fourthly. With her consent, when the man knows that he is not her husband,
> and that her consent is given because she believes that he is another
> man to whom she is or believes herself to be lawfully married.
> Fifthly. With or without her consent, when she is under fourteen years of
> age.
> Explanation. Penetration is sufficient to constitute the sexual intercourse
> necessary to the offence of rape.
> Exception. Sexual intercourse by a man with his own wife, the wife not
> being under 13 years of age, is not rape.

Punishment for rape, which is imprisonment for 10 years or life imprisonment
and a fine, can be found in s 376 of the *Penal Code*.

74 This is a gross deficiency in our *Penal Code*, but see, for example, Canada's
Criminal Code, where the punishment for the offence of sexual assault is
included in the statute, at *Criminal Code, supra* note 49 at s 271.

75 Also see *R v J A*, [2011] 2 SCR 440, [2011] SCJ No 28. Here, however, I must
add that there is an exception in s 375 of the *Penal Code*, whereby it declares
that a man having sex with his wife – even if it is against her will or she has
not consented – is not rape so long as she is not below the age of thirteen.
While I will not opine on the said exception, I will add that this would constitute rape between persons who are not married even if they are both of adult
years.
   However, also see section 354 of the *Penal Code, supra* note 5, which stipulates, "Whoever assaults or uses criminal force to any woman, intending to
outrage or knowing it to be likely that he will thereby outrage her modesty,
shall be punished with imprisonment of either description for a term which
may extend to two years, or with fine, or with both."

76 *The Nari-O-Shishu Nirjaton Domon Ain*, 2000 (Bangladesh), Act No VIII of
2000. Translated, the title of the law is *Preventing the Repression of Women
and Children Act*, 2000.
   Section 10 stipulates, "If any person, to satisfy his sexual urge or desire,
unlawfully touches the sexual organs or any other organ or bodily part of a
woman or child, through any organ of his body or with any other substance,
or violates the modesty of any woman or child, he shall be said to have committed sexual oppression and shall be punished with rigorous imprisonment,
which shall not be less than 3 years and may extend up to 10 years, and shall
also be fined."
   In the event my translation is incorrect, I am providing the original text as
reference: "যদি কোন ব্যক্তি অবৈধভাবে তাহার যৌন কামনা চরিতার্থ করার উদ্দেশ্যে তাহার শরীরের যে
কোন অঙ্গ বা কোন বস্তু দ্বারা কোন নারী বা শিশুর যৌন অঙ্গ বা অন্য কোন অঙ্গ স্পর্শ করেন বা কোন নারীর

শ্লীলতাহানি করেন তাহা হইলে তাহার এই কাজ হইবে যৌন পীড়ন এবং তজ্জন্য উক্ত ব্যক্তি অনধিক দশ বত্সর কিন্তু অন্যূন তিন বত্সর সশ্রম কারাদণ্ডে দণ্ডনীয় হইবেন এবং ইহার অতিরিক্ত অর্থদণ্ডেও দণ্ডনীয় হইবেন৷"

Also see sections 75–76 of The Dhaka Metropolitan Police Ordinance, 1976 (Bangladesh), Act No III of 1976 [*DMPO*], and s 509 of the *Penal Code*, *supra* note 5.

77 *R v Cuerrier*, [1998] 2 SCR 371, [1998] SCJ No 64. [Cuerrier]. It should be noted that this is a criminal case, but I am discussing it to demonstrate that to have consensual sex with a person without disclosing whether one has a sexually transmitted disease is actionable. Also see *R v Mabior*, [2012] 2 SCR 584, [2012] SCJ No 47 [*Mabior*].

78 See generally *Reibl v Hughes*, [1980] 2 SCR 880, [1980] SCJ No 105 [*Reibl*]. As we will see later in this chapter, if one is not fully apprised of the risks of an activity, whether it is a medical procedure or having sexual intercourse, then the law holds that the person did not, because they could not, provide true consent.

However, in *R v B*, [2006] EWCA Crim 2945, [2006] All ER (D) 173 (Oct), the English courts held that exposure to HIV is insufficient and what is required to be an actionable offence is transmission; Also see *R v Mwai*, [1995] 3 NZLR 149, (1995) 13 CRNZ 273. However, I cannot subscribe to the English and New Zealander view. If a person represents himself to be a doctor, but he is not, and if I consent to his treatment, then it is battery whether there is damage or otherwise because the consent I provided is not true as I did not have all the material information; that is to say, I did not know that he was not a doctor, and therefore, my consent is vitiated. See *Regina v Maurantonio*, [1968] 1 OR 145.

79 See *Kathleen K v Robert B*, [1984] 150 Cal App 3d 992, 1984 Cal App LEXIS 1510.

80 However, it should be noted that as of date of authoring this book, COVID-19 does not have a cure or a vaccine. Therefore, if one has the disease and does not disclose it to his partner, then it can constitute battery as the woman, or anyone, can contract it simply by being in close proximity to him.

81 *Reibl, supra* note 78 at para 114.

82 *Mabior, supra* note 77 at paras 45 and 48.

83 See Deana P Sacks, "Intentional Sex Torts" (2008) 77:3 Fordham L Rev 1051; Also see Lorne Wolfson & Andrea Himel, "Broken Promises, Broken Hearts: Intrafamilial Tort and Contract Claims" (2002) 25:4 Adv Q 441.

84 Osborne, *supra* note 4 at 297–300; Also see Heuston & Buckley, *supra* note 1 at 133–134 and Fleming, *supra* note 3 at 29–31.

85 *Allan et al. v New Mount Sinai Hospital*, [1980] OJ No 3095, 28 OR (2d) 356 [*Allan*].

86 Also see *The Bangladesh Medical and Dental Council Act*, 2010 (Bangladesh), Act No LXI of 2010, at ss 28–29. While the said sections do not penalize doctors or dentists for battery (e.g. wrongful surgery in the face of express instructions of the patient), it does provide sanctions for fraudulently misrepresenting that one is a doctor and for using false titles, respectively.

87 *O'Brien v Cunard SS Co*, [1891] 154 Mass 272, 28 NE 266; Also see Prosser, *supra* note 2 at 101–103.

88 *Ciarlariello v Schacter*, [1993] 2 SCR 119, [1993] SCJ No 46 [*Ciarlariello*].

89 It should also be noted that a patient can imply consent through gestures. For example, during a root-canal, if the doctor asks whether he can continue with the procedure and you respond with a thumbs-up, then that is sufficient consent and you cannot subsequently bring an action against the doctor for battery because he continued the operation without express consent.

146   *Intentional torts*

90   *C(JS) v Wren*, [1986] AJ No 1166, 76 AR 115.
91   For example, in Bangladesh, the age of majority is eighteen years, at *The Majority Act, 1875* (Bangladesh), Act No IX of 1875, at s 3; Also see Marjorie Maguire Shultz, "From Informed Consent to Patient Choice: A New Protected Interest" (1985) 95:2 Yale LJ 219.
92   *Hollis v Dow Corning Corp*, [1995] 4 SCR 634, [1995] SCJ No 104 [*Hollis*]; Also see Fleming, *supra* note 3 at 86–91.
93   *White v Turner*, [1981] OJ NO 2498, 120 DLR (3d) 269, at paras 43–45 and 47.
94   Marcus L Plante, "An Analysis of Informed Consent" (1968) 36:4 Fordham L Rev 639 at 657. Plante further says at 666–667, "The essence of a legal wrong to the plaintiff in a battery case is the touching itself which, standing alone, entitles him to substantial damages. Thus the issues of causation and damages are simple. All that need be shown is that what was done differed substantially from that which consent was given. That cause of action is then complete [...] In Medical negligence cases, however, the issue of causation is more complex in theory and practice. Plaintiff must show that if he had been fully advised as to the collateral risk he would not have submitted to the procedure. This is a sort of "but for" rule. There must be a cause-in-fact relationship between the plaintiff's ignorance of the risk and his willingness to go forward with the operation. The converse is also true, i.e., if it appears that the plaintiff knew of the risk all the time, the failure of the physician to disclose it would have no causal connection with the injury."
        Also see Izhak England, *The Philosophy of Tort Law* (Aldershot, UK: Dartmouth, 1992) at 162 where he states, "The retreat from doctrine of battery has been explained by the discomfort of treating doctors who genuinely care for the well-being of the patient, under a doctrine aimed at sanctioning anti-social conduct, usually perpetrated with the worst kind of intentions. Courts were reluctant to stigmatize physicians with the label of having committed battery, lumping them into the same category as murderers, robbers, and bar-room brawlers."
95   In *Wallace v Kam*, [2013] 297 ALR 383, [2013] HCA 19, though the doctor did not disclose the attendant risks of the operation and the patient subsequently suffered an injury, the doctor was not liable because the patient would have elected surgery even if he was informed of the risks, as that was the only way to treat his condition. However, I draw discord with this case because even if this was the only treatment available to the patient, it could be argued that had he been informed of the risks, he would not have submitted to treatment whatsoever. As in, a doctor cannot be exonerated when he fails to discharge his duty to disclose material risks to the patient on the grounds that even if he had done so, the patient would have consented to treatment anyway.
        Also see *Arndt v Smith*, [1997] 2 SCR 539, [1997] SCJ No 65; Gerald Robertson, "Informed Consent Ten Years Later: The Impact of Reibl v Hughes" (1991) 70:3 Can Bar Rev 423; Nonetheless, I will provide an exposition of medical negligence in the following chapter.
96   I note here that I will only stipulate ss 96, 97, and 99 in this section even though the defence is applicable for the defence of person, another person, and property (which I shall delineate later). Therefore, though the reader may be on the sections infra, he may need to view this page repeatedly for the sake of convenience and understanding.
97   *Penal Code, supra* note 5 at s 96.
98   *Ibid* at s 97.
99   *Ibid* at s 99.
100 See generally *Wackett v Calder*, [1965] BCJ No 129, 51 DLR (2d) 598.

Intentional torts   147

101 Or, your attacker can then perhaps charge you criminally under ss 339, 340, 349, and 350 of the *Penal Code*.

102 *Gambriell v Caparelli*, [1974] OJ No 2243, [1974] 7 OR (2d) 205 [*Gambriell*].

103 *Gambriell, supra* note 102. Furthermore, it is also worth noting that the court mentioned that Mrs. Caparelli was weaker than the plaintiff, and therefore, using a garden cultivator was justified, as even though she hit the plaintiff in the head, the wound was only a laceration and nothing deep that it required stitches.

104 For example, see *Babiuk v Trann*, [2005] SJ No 41, 248 DLR (4th) 530.

105 *Canadian Foundation for Children, Youth and the Law v Canada (Attorney General)*, [2004] 1 SCR 76.

106 Parliament promulgated the *Shishu Act*, 2013 (in English, it translates into *The Children Act*, 2013), which replaced *The Children Act*, 1974. Section 70 stipulates, "If any person, who has custody, charge, or care of any child, assaults, ill-treats, neglects, abandons, or exposes such child or causes such child to be assaulted, ill-treated, neglected, abandoned, or exposed in a manner likely to cause such child unnecessary suffering or injury to his health, including loss of sight or hearing, or injury to limb or organ of the body, or any other mental derangement, such person shall be punishable with imprisonment for a term which may extend to 5 (five) years, or with fine which may extend to ৳1 (one) lac, or with both."

In the event my translation is incorrect, I am providing the original text as reference: "কোন ব্যক্তি যদি তাহার হেফাজতে, দায়িত্বে বা পরিচর্যায় থাকা কোন শিশুকে আঘাত, উৎপীড়ন, অবহেলা, বর্জন, অরক্ষিত অবস্থায় পরিত্যাগ ব্যক্তিগত পরিচর্যার কাজে ব্যবহার বা অশালীনভাবে প্রদর্শন করে এবং এইরূপভাবে আঘাত, উৎপীড়ন, অবহেলা, বর্জন, পরিত্যাগ ব্যক্তিগত পরিচর্যা বা প্রদর্শনের ফলে উক্ত শিশুর অহেতুক দুর্ভোগ সৃষ্টি হয় বা স্বাস্থ্যের এইরূপ ক্ষতি হয়, যাহাতে সংশ্লিষ্ট শিশুর দৃষ্টিশক্তি বা শ্রবণশক্তি নষ্ট হয়, শরীরের কোন অঙ্গ বা ইন্দ্রিয়ের ক্ষতি হয় বা কোন মানসিক বিকৃতি ঘটে, তাহা হইলে তিনি এই আইনের অধীন অপরাধ করিয়াছেন বলিয়া গণ্য হইবে এবং উক্ত অপরাধের জন্য তিনি অনধিক ৫ (পাঁচ) বৎসর কারাদণ্ড অথবা অনধিক ১ (এক) লক্ষ টাকা অর্থদণ্ড অথবা উভয় দণ্ডে দণ্ডিত হইবেন।"

107 See Bangladesh Legal Aid and Services Trust v Secretary, Ministry of Education (Bangladesh), at "Bangladesh Legal Aid and Services Trust v Secretary, Ministry of Education (Bangladesh)" BLAST (13 January 2011), online: BLAST https://www.blast.org.bd/content/judgement/wp_5684of2010.pdf. [17/03/2021].

108 Remedies in tort are dispersed throughout the book.

109 Osborne, *supra* note 4 at 307.

110 However, there are certain words or phrases that, owing to history or contemporary sentiment, would make a reasonable person lose control even though it may seem trivial or innocuous to others. For example, the word "negro" may make a person of African descent lose control, but not one who is Bangladeshi; or, telling a Jewish person that the Holocaust is fabricated or that what Adolf Hitler did was correct; or telling Muslims that they are all terrorists may make them lose self-control. Therefore, as is not unusual in law, whether a person can argue provocation will depend on the facts and circumstances of each case.

The other partial defence is 'contributory negligence.' However, since contributory negligence relates primarily to negligence, I will delineate it in Chapter 5.

111 *Mann v Saulnier*, [1959] NBJ No 12, 19 DLR (2d) 130 [*Mann*].

112 See ss 441–458 of the *Penal Code*, which makes trespass a criminal offence and prescribes punishment thereof. Section 442 stipulates, "Whoever commits criminal trespass by entering into or remaining in any building, tent or vessel used as a human dwelling or any building used as a place for worship, or as a place for the custody of property, is said to commit 'house trespass.' [...]," at *Penal Code, supra* note 5 at s 442. Also see *DMPO, supra* note 76 at s 84.

148 *Intentional torts*

113 *Sirajul Islam Chowdhury et al. v Md Jainal Abedin et al,* [1997] 49 DLR (AD) 164. For those unfamiliar with the court structure in Bangladesh, the country has two divisions in its Supreme Court. The lower body is the High Court Division and the upper, which is the final court in Bangladesh, is the Appellate Division, at *Constitution of Bangladesh, supra* note 38 at ss 94, 101 and 103.

114 I will discuss trespass to airspace in Section 4.2.3. See *Basely v Clarkson,* [1681] 3 Lev 37, 83 ER 565, where the defendant was held liable in trespass for mowing his neighbour's grass in the innocent belief that it was his; Also see Osborne, *supra* note 4 at 312.

115 *Miller v Jackson,* [1977] 3 All ER 778, [1977] QB 966 [*Miller*]. However, please also remember that the court's decision to not issue an injunction also rested on the low probability (5.3%) of cricket balls landing on the Millers' property, and the Club's precautionary measures, which is based on the 'Hand Formula' and is something I will delineate more scrupulously in the following chapter. The consideration for Kurmitola Golf Club would also be the same.

116 Thomas W Merrill, "Trespass, Nuisance, and the Costs of Determining Property Rights" (1985) 14:1 J Leg Stud 13 at 14–15.

117 "Intentional intrusions subject to the rule of trespass are governed by a standard of care which is 'exceptionally simple and exceptionally rigorous.' In order to establish an actionable trespass, all that A need show is that B is responsible for an invasion of the column of space that defines A's possessory interest under the ad coelum rule. No weighing or balancing of costs and benefits is involved. Thus, one who commits an act which qualifies as an intentional trespass is subject to liability whether or not the benefits of the interfering act – either to B or to the community at large – are greater than the harm imposed on A." *Ibid* at 16.

118 See *Evaniuk v 79846 Manitoba Inc,* [1990] MJ No 584, 68 Man R (2d) 306. This case is also an excellent illustration of what constitutes 'reasonable force.' However, the force that is reasonable under the circumstances will be commensurate with the force permitted to be used to repel an attack under self-defence, *supra* at 4.1.7.5, and since I have elucidated 'reasonable force' earlier, I shall eschew doing so again.

119 *Hurst v Picture Theatres Ltd,* [1914–1915] All ER Rep 837, [1915] 1 KB 1. Also see *Winter Garden Theatre (London) Ltd v Millenium Productions Ltd,* [1947] 2 All ER 331, [1948] AC 173, where it was said at 335–336, "There is yet a third variant of a license for value which constantly occurs, as in the sale of a ticket to enter premises and witness a particular event, such as a ticket for a seat at a particular performance at a theatre or for entering private ground to witness a day's sport. In this last class of case, the implication of the arrangement, however it may be classified in law, plainly is that the ticket entitles the purchaser to enter and, if he behaves himself, to remain on the premises until the end of the event which he has paid his money to witness. Such, for example, was the situation which gave rise to the decision of the Court of Appeal in Hurst v Picture Theatres Ltd. I regard this case as rightly decided, and repudiate the view that a licensor who is paid for granting his licensee to enter premises in order to view a particular event, can nevertheless, although the licensee is behaving properly, terminate the license before the event is over, turn the licensee out, and leave him to an action for the return of the price of his ticket. The license in such a case is granted under contractual conditions, one of which is that a well-behaved licensee shall not be treated as a trespasser until the event which he has paid to see is over, and until he has reasonable time thereafter to depart, and in Hurst's case, where the plaintiff was forced to leave prematurely, substantial damages for assault and false imprisonment rightly resulted."

Intentional torts 149

120 *Davidson v Toronto Blue Jays Baseball Ltd*, [1999] OJ No 692, 170 DLR (4th) 559. Furthermore, the court said at para 36, "There is however an implied term to show a ticket, whether it is a SkyClub ticket, or any other category of ticket, in certain circumstances. The plaintiff has been a season ticket holder at the SkyDome since its inception in 1989. He has always willingly shown his ticket upon admission, or upon being seated. It is a reasonable implied term to show a ticket (if personnel are present to verify a ticket) upon entering the SkyDome. It is reasonable to show a ticket to an usher or usherette to facilitate seating at the beginning of a game, or when a ticket holder first arrives to a designated area. It is reasonable to show a ticket if at any time two patrons are disputing entitlement to sit in a specific seat. It is not reasonable once a sporting event has begun for management to demand to see a ticket when they deem it appropriate. Granting to management such a broad right could result in abuse, as occurred in this case, as well as the disruption to fans in the area. It appears that the limited implied contractual term that I have outlined accords with the reasonable expectation of the contracting parties, and it ensures that the principles of reserve seating with differing price structures are respected."

Essentially, this means that unless there are reasonable grounds (e.g. dispute regarding seat or when first being seated), management of property, such as Cineplex, cannot approach and ask to see your ticket at any time they wish.

121 For example, see *Ploof v Putnam*, [1908] 81 Vt 471, 71 A 188, where it was held that even though there was trespass (by the Ploof family entering and mooring their boat on Mr. Putnam's dock), it was justified on the grounds of necessity, as the sudden tempest threatened Mr. Ploof and his family's life; Also see *Dwyer v Staunton*, [1947] AJ No 59, 4 DLR 393, where it was held not to be trespass when the defendant drove through the plaintiff's property because the public highway was impassable.

122 See *Cope v Sharpe*, [1911–1913] All ER Rep Ext 1212, [1912] 1 KB 496, 81 LJKB 346, where it was held that the setting of fire on the plaintiff's land was a necessity to keep another fire from destroying the plaintiff's property and nesting pheasants.

123 See *Rigby and another v Chief Constable of Northamptonshire*, [1985] 2 All ER 985, [1985] 1 WLR 1242, which, however, speaks of public necessity, but is nonetheless comparable. Also see John A Cohan, "Private and Public Necessity and the Violation of Property Rights" (2007) 83:2 NDL Rev 651.

124 *London Borough of Southwark v Williams*, [1971] 2 All ER 175, [1971] 2 WLR 467 at 179.

125 For example, see *R v Dudley and Stephens*, [1881–1885] All ER Rep 61, 14 QBC 273.

126 Lewis Klar, *Tort Law*, 5th ed (Toronto: Carswell, 2012) at 159; Also see Lewis Klar, "The Defence of Private Necessity in Canadian Tort Law" (2005) 5:2 Issues in Leg Scholarship 1.

127 See generally *The Code of Criminal Procedure*, 1898 (Bangladesh), Act No V of 1898, s 47; *The Building Construction Act*, 1952 (Bangladesh), Act No II of 1953, s 10, which, after providing reasonable notice, permits an Authorized Officer to enter one's premises to carry out the purposes of the Act; the *Food Safety Act, 2013* (Bangladesh), Act No XLII of 2013, s 53, which permits an Inspector to enter any food establishment to ascertain whether anything in violation of the Act is being carried out.

128 Osborne, *supra* note 4 at 318; Also see Heuston & Buckley, *supra* note 1 at 46–51 and Prosser, supra note 2 at 63–71; See also *The Constitution of the People's Republic of Bangladesh* (Bangladesh), Act of 1972, s 143, which stipulates that property for, "[A]ll minerals and other things of value underlying any land of Bangladesh" vests in the Government of Bangladesh.

150 *Intentional torts*

129 See *Wandsworth Board of Works v United Telephone Co*, [1884] 13 QBD 904, 48 JP 676; *Corbett v Hill*, [1870] LR 9 Eq 671, 39 LJ Ch 547. Both cases confirmed a landowner's right to airspace above the surface. Also see Roderick B Anderson, "Some Aspects of Airpsace Trespass" (1960) 27:4 J Air L & Com 341.

130 Earlier, I had used the same example and mentioned that it constitutes trespass. I now clarify that it is trespass to airspace; Also see *Kelsen v Imperial Tobacco Co (of Great Britain and Ireland) Ltd*, [1957] 2 All ER 343, [1957] 2 QB 334; *Didow v Alberta Power Ltd*, [1988] AJ No 620, 88 AR 250; In *Gifford v Dent*, [1926] WN 336, 71 Sol Jo 83, it was said at p 336, "If he was right in the conclusion to which he had come that the plaintiffs were tenants of the forecourt and were accordingly tenants of the space above the forecourt usque ad coelum, it seemed to him that the projection was clearly a trespass upon the property of the plaintiffs."

131 *Lewvest Ltd v Scotia Towers Ltd*, [1981] NJ No 220, [1981] 126 DLR (3d) 239.

132 *Woollerton & Wilson Ltd v Richard Costain Ltd*, [1970] 1 All ER 483, [1970] 1 WLR 411.

133 *Berstein of Leigh (Baron) v Skyviews and General Ltd*, [1977] 2 All ER 902, [1978] QB 479; Also see *Bocardo SA v Energy UK Onshore Ltd*, [2010] 3 All ER 975, [2011] 1 AC 380.

134 Osborne, *supra* note 4 at 321; Also see *Penal Code*, *supra* note 5 at s 378, which stipulates, "Whoever, intending to take dishonestly any moveable property out of the possession of any person without that person's consent, moves that property in order to such taking, is said to commit theft."

135 See Dan L Burk, "The Trouble with Trespass" (2000) 4:1 J Small & Emerging Bus L 27, where the opposite view is expressed.

136 See *Century 21 Canada Ltd Partnership v Rogers Communications Inc*, [2011] BCJ No 1679, [2011] BCSC 1196, which stipulates that a person does not have possessory rights on the server of an Internet Service Provider; See *CompuServe Inc v Cyber Promotions Inc*, [1997] 962 F Supp 1015, 1997 US Dist LEXIS 1997 [*CompuServe*].

137 Trespass to chattel is different from the criminal offence of theft as the latter requires evidence of an intention to take and keep the property, whereas the earlier does not. As in, simply moving a painting at a museum can give rise to an action in trespass to chattel even if there was never an intention to keep the property. However, a criminal action in theft would not lie unless the person had an intention to move and keep the painting in his possession. Alternatively, no action for theft arises if you accidentally left your cellphone at your friend's house. Nonetheless, if you demand its return and he refuses, then an action would arise in detinue.

138 Ken Belson, "Dial-Up Internet Going the Way of Rotary Phones" The New York Times (21 June 2005), online: The New York Times Company https://www.nytimes.com/2005/06/21/technology/dialup-internet-going-the-way-of-rotary-phones.html. [17/03/2021].

139 Ned Snow, "Accessing the Internet through the Neighbor's Wireless Internet Connection: Physical Trespass in Virtual Reality" (2005) 84:4 Neb L Rev 1226 at 1227 [Snow].

140 Grant J Guillot, "Trespassing Through Cyberspace: Should Wireless Piggybacking Constitute a Crime or Tort Under Louisiana Law?" (2009) 69:2 La L Rev 389 at 390. This is also known as "war driving" and "joyriding." However, the term "war driving" is usually used when one drives from place-to-place in search of an unsecured Wi-Fi network.

141 Snow, *supra* note 139 at 1235–1239. Also see *CompuServe*, *supra* note 136 and *America Online, Inc v National Health Care Discount, Inc*, [2000] 121 F

Intentional torts 151

Supp 2d 1255, 2000 US Dist LEXIS 17055, where it was held that sending mass unsolicited e-mails constituted trespass to chattel.

142 *The Digital Security Act*, 2018 (Bangladesh), Act No XLVI of 2018, at s 18.

143 Osborne, *supra* note 4 at 323–324; Also see Nicholas Queree, "Detinue: Gone but Not Forgotten: Schwarzschild v. Harrods Ltd" (2008) 13:2 Art Ant & L 203 and Remigius N Nwabueze & Polycarp C Okorie, "Flexibility of Damages for Conversion and Detinue" (2009) 17:1 African J of Intl & Comparative L 102.

144 Similarly, if you rent a car from Enterprise on Tuesday with a promise that you will return it on Thursday and you fail to do so, unless Enterprise calls and demands you return the vehicle, no action in detinue would arise; rather, the company can saddle a fine upon you for breach of contract. Thence, the refusal to return the chattel is indispensable for an action in detinue, as it is at that time that there is an interference with the rights of the owner.
The most common remedy for an action in detinue is an order to return the chattel. However, sometimes, a court may order its return and award damages for its detention, see *General & Finance Facilities Ltd v Cooks Cars (Romford) Ltd*, [1963] 2 All ER 314, [1963] 1 WLR 644.

145 John R Jr Faust, "Distinction between Conversion and Trespass to Chattel" (1958) 37:3 Or L Rev 256.

146 Carolyn Sappideen & Prue Vines, eds, *Fleming's Law of Torts*, 10th ed (Sydney: Law Book Co, 2002) at 66–67; Also see Fleming, *supra* note 3 at 60–61.

147 *Fouldes v Willoughby*, [1841] 10 LJ Ex 364, 151 ER 1153 [*Fouldes*]; Also see *Shibamoto & Co v Western Fish Producers Inc (Trustee of)*, [1991] FCJ No 243, [1991] 3 FC 214.

148 See *OBG Ltd v Allan*, [2005] 2 All ER 602, [2005] QB 762 [*OBG*] and *Teva Canada Ltd v TD Canada Trust*, [2017] SCJ No 51, [2017] 2 SCR 317.

149 See *The Sale of Goods Act*, 1930 (Bangladesh), Act No III of 1930, s 27 [*Sale of Goods*], which stipulates, "Subject to the provisions of this Act and of any other law for the time being in force, where goods are sold by a person who is not the owner thereof and who does not sell them under the authority or with the consent of the owner, the buyer acquires no better title of the goods than the seller had, unless the owner of the goods is by his conduct precluded from denying the seller's authority to sell [...]" In simpler terms, you can bring an action against the buyer for the return of the chattel only if the buyer had knowledge that the seller was not the rightful owner of the good. Nonetheless, regardless of the buyer's knowledge, his title to the good is defective.

150 Osborne, *supra* note 4 at 330.

151 Also see *DMPO*, *supra* note 76 at s 23.

152 The right to refuse delivery is not limited only to trespassing cattle, but extends to any chattel that has intentionally interfered with the occupier's rights. For example, if one drives his vehicle onto your property and causes damage, then you have the right to keep the vehicle on your property until reparations are made; See *Barbour v University of British Columbia*, [2009] BCJ No 617, 310 DLR (4th) 130; Also see Fleming, *supra* note 3 at 100.

153 Recall from Section 4.2.1 the example of the golfball finding its way onto your property at Banani DOHS. Since the ball was not struck with an intention that it enters your premises, no action would lie in trespass to land. If you then request the landowner to return the ball and he refuses, you would have an action against him for detinue. However, if the ball caused damage to the landowner's premises, then he retains the right to withhold delivery until compensation is fairly made, but he cannot pledge or sell the golfball.
Also see *replevin* and *recaption of chattels*, which address when one with the right to immediate possession of the chattel can forcibly take back the chattel, at Osborne, *supra* note 4 at 329.

152   Intentional torts

154 See generally Peter Burns & Joost Blom, *Economic Interests in Canadian Tort Law*, 2nd ed (Markham, ON: LexisNexis Canada, 2009).

155 Osborne, *supra* note 4 at 331.

156 *Ibid.*

157 *Pasley (and another) v Freeman*, [1775–1802] All ER Rep 31, 100 ER 450 [*Pasley*]. In fact, Pasley was the case that established the tort of deceit; See also *Magill v Magill*, [2006] HCA 51, [2006] 231 ALR 277, for a discussion on the extent to which deceit can be relied upon in a family matter involving a wife telling her husband that their kids were fathered by him.

158 Proving fraud is perhaps the most difficult element in deceit as the person making the representation can claim in defence that when he made the statement, he honestly believed it to be true. As in, if one genuinely believes something is true, then the question of fraud does not arise, because what must be proved is that either the person knowingly furnished false information or recklessly made a statement without knowing whether it is true; See *Derry v Peek*, [1886–1890] All ER Rep 1, 58 LJ Ch 864. However, in the simplest form, it is fraudulent to get goods on credit at Oxford University by wearing an undergraduate gown and cap, at *R v Barnard*, [1837] 173 ER 342, 7 C&P 784. Also see *Arkwright v Newbold*, [1881] 50 LJ Ch 372, 17 Ch D 301.

159 *Kelemen v El-Homeira*, [1999] AJ No 1279, 250 AR 67.

160 See generally Heuston & Buckley, *supra* note 1 at 434–440.

161 It is now commonly held that statements made during contractual negotiations are usually done so to induce the other party to enter into a contract. That is to say, the presumption is that a party makes representations during contractual negotiations with the intention that the other will rely on it, and it would be difficult – but not impossible – to rebut said presumption. For example, see *Dick Bentley Productions v Harold Smith (Motors) Ltd*, [1965] 2 All ER 65, [1965] 1 WLR 623, where it was said, "[I]t seems to me that if a representation is made in the course of dealings for a contract for the very purpose of inducing the other party to act on it, and it actually induces him to act on it by entering into the contract, that is prima facie ground for inferring that the representation was intended as a warranty. It is not necessary to speak of it as being collateral. Suffice it that the representation was intended to be acted on and was in fact acted on. But the maker of the representation can rebut this inference if he can show that it really was an innocent misrepresentation, in that he was in fact innocent of fault in making it, and that it would not be reasonable in the circumstances for him to be bound by it," at 67; Also see *Redgrave v Hurd*, [1881–1885] All ER Rep 77, 51 LJ Ch 113.

162 *Hedley Byrne & Co Ltd v Heller & Partners Ltd*, [1963] 2 All ER 575, [1964] AC 465 [*Hedley Byrne*].

163 Also see *Ultramares Corp v Touche, Niven & Co*, [1931] 255 NY 170, 174 NE 441; Contrast this case to *Glanzer v Shepard*, [1921] 233 NY 236, 135 NE 275.

164 *Queen v Cognos Inc*, [1993] 1 SCR 87, [1993] SCJ No 3 at paras 43–46.

165 Moreover, in *Spring v Guardian Assurance PLC and Others*, [1994] 3 All ER 129, [1995] 2 AC 296, the House of Lords held that negligent misrepresentation can be relied upon for compensation where a defendant has assumed responsibility of performing professional services (providing a letter of reference), but has harmed the plaintiff while doing so because of their mistake; Also see *Grand Restaurants of Canada Ltd v Toronto (City)*, [1981] OJ No 2503, 32 OR (2d) 757, where the plaintiff, who had been in the restaurant business for a while, was held contributorily negligent when he relied on the defendant's fraudulent misrepresentation to his detriment; See generally *Macleay v Tait*, [1906] AC 24, 75 LJ Ch 90.

Intentional torts 153

166 See Jeremiah Smith, "Disparagement of Property" (1913) 13:1 Colum L Rev 13. Moreover, injurious falsehood has had many names in the past, such as disparagement of title, disparagement of goods, trade libel, unfair competition, and interference with prospective advantage.

167 Recall from earlier that if the seller is not the owner of the goods, then the buyer's title to the goods is subsequently defective, at *Sale of Goods, supra* note 149.

168 See William L Prosser, "Injurious Falsehood: The Basis of Liability" (1959) 59:3 Colum L Rev 425 at 425–428 [Prosser: Injurious Falsehood]. Also see Edwin R Fischer & Leo A Huard, "Injurious Falsehood – An Expanding Tort" (1945) 33:2 Geo LJ 213.

169 However, if one trader tells a customer that his products are better than his competitor's (even if it is not), then no action will lie against him. This is an exception to injurious falsehood to prevent traders from using litigation as a way of advertising their business. At *White v Mellin*, [1895] AC 154, 64 LJ Ch 308; Also see Heuston & Buckley, *supra* note 1 at 447.

170 This is where injurious falsehood differs from defamation. While the two actions have significant overlap, firstly, defamation protects the reputation of a person, whereas injurious falsehood protects one's business interests. Secondly, an action in injurious falsehood requires proof of malice (in conjunction with the requirement of proving the falsity of the statement and injury). However, in defamation, injury to the plaintiff is presumed and he does not need to prove malice on the part of the defendant. Thence, it is more advantageous to frame an action in defamation, as opposed to injurious falsehood.

171 Prosser: Injurious Falsehood, *supra* note 168 at 429–433.

172 *Manitoba Free Press Co Ltd v Nagy*, [1907] 39 SCR 340.

173 However, difficulty arises when one is facetious; that is, what if, knowing it to be false, you told your friend about Regent's support for terrorism with a somber tone, but were actually joking, and since your friend is credulous, he relied on your statement and abstained from trying their food? Therefore, I am of the opinion that the success of a case for injurious falsehood is considerably tenuous due to the requirement of proving malice; Also see William L Prosser, "Misrepresentation and Third Persons" (1966) 19:2 Vand L Rev 231.

174 *The Trademarks Act*, 2009 (Bangladesh), Act No XIX of 2009, s 2(8) [*Trademarks Act*].

175 *Ibid* at s 24(1); However, see *Mattel Inc v 3894207 Canada Inc*, [2006] 1 SCR 772, [2006] SCJ No 23, where it was held that a restaurant called "Barbie's" could be registered and used even though Mattel Inc. trademarked the name "Barbie," primarily because the former catered to adult persons, whereas the latter sold dolls to 3 to 11-year-old girls [Mattel].

176 *Trademarks Act, supra* note 174 at s 3(1).

177 *Ciba-Geigy Canada Ltd v Apotex Inc*, [1992] 3 SCR 120, [1992] SCJ No 83 [Emphasis removed].

178 Greg Hagen et al, *Canadian Intellectual Property Law: Cases and Materials*, 2nd ed (Toronto: Emond Montgomery Publications Limited, 2018) at[317] [Hagen et al].

179 *Trademarks Act, supra* note 174 at s 24(2).

180 See Heuston & Buckley, *supra* note 1 at 449–452.

181 See *Reckitt and Colman Products Ltd v Borden Inc*, [1990] 1 All ER 873, [1990]1 WLR 491, where it was said at 880, "The law of passing-off can be summarized in one short general proposition, no man may pass off his goods as those of another. More specifically, it may be expressed in terms of the elements which the plaintiff in such an action has to prove in order to succeed. These are three in number. First, he must establish a goodwill or reputation attached to the goods or services which he supplies in the mind of the

154   *Intentional torts*

purchasing public by association with the identifying 'get-up' (whether it consists simply of a brand name or a trade description, or the individual features of labelling or packaging) under which his particular goods or services are offered to the public, such that the get-up is recognized by the public as distinctive specifically of the plaintiff's goods or services. Second, he must demonstrate a misrepresentation by the defendant to the public (whether or not intentional) leading or likely to lead the public to believe that goods or services offered by him are the goods or services of the plaintiff. Whether the public is aware of the plaintiff's identity as the manufacturer or supplier of the goods or services is immaterial, as long as they are identified with a particular source which is in fact the plaintiff. For example, if the public is accustomed to rely on a particular brand name in purchasing goods of a particular description, it matters not at all that there is little or no public awareness of the identity of the proprietor of the brand name. Third, he must demonstrate that he suffers or, in a quia timet action, that he is likely to suffer damage by reason of the erroneous belief engendered by the defendant's misrepresentation that the source of the defendant's goods or services is the same as the source of those offered by the plaintiff." Also see W L Morison, "Unfair Competition and Passing-off - The Flexibility of a Formula" (1956) 2:1 Sydney L Rev 50.

182   Hagen et al, *supra* note 178.

183   Kameron Virk, "Kit-Kat Case: The Food and Drinks with Trademarked Shapes" BBC (25 July 2018), online: BBC https://www.bbc.com/news/newsbeat-44953460. [17/03/2021].

184   *Reddaway & Co Ltd v Banham & Co Ltd*, [1895–1899] All ER Rep 133, [1896] AC 199, 65 LJQB 381; Also see *Ray Plastics Ltd v Dustbane Products Ltd*, [1994] OJ No 2050, 57 CPR (3d) 474.

185   See *Bristol Conservatories Ltd v Conservatories Custom Built Ltd*, [1989] RPC 455.

186   *Mattel, supra* note 175; Also see *Bollinger v Costa Brava Wine Company Ltd*, [1961] 1 All ER 561, 1 WLR 277, where the plaintiffs were successful in seeking an injunction to have the defendant company stop producing "Spanish Champagne," as "Champagne" is actually a drink that is produced in Champagne – a region in France – which had acquired a distinctive meaning associated with quality. I import this case to illustrate that passing-off can also be used to protect geographic place names in conjunction with source misrepresentation.

187   Also see *Ad-Lib Club Ltd v Granville*, [1971] 2 All ER 300, 115 Sol Jo 74, where the court confirmed that a case for passing-off can arise even if the loss is in relation to one's business reputation.

188   *Sadhu Singh Hamdard Trust v Navsun Holdings Ltd*, [2016] FCJ No 239, 483 NR 33 [*Hamdard Trust*].

189   "Bombay Sweets Chips" (2020) Bombay Sweets Bangladesh, online: Bombay Sweets & Co Ltd https://www.bombaysweetsbd.com/chips.php. [17/03/2021].

190   It is for this reason that you probably may have seen stores with similar names in Malaysia and Thailand, or Russia and France, or Vietnam and Bangladesh; See generally Graeme W Austin, "The Consumer in Cross-Border Passing off Cases" (2016) 47:2 VUWLR 209; Also see Fleming, supra note 3 at 782–784.

191   See *Orkin Exterminating Co Inc v Pestco Co of Canada Ltd et al*, [1985] 50 OR (2d) 726, where it was said, "[A] plaintiff does not have to be in direct competition with the defendant to suffer injury from the use of its trade name by the defendant. If the plaintiff's trade name has a reputation in the defendant's jurisdiction, such that the public associates it with services provided by the plaintiff, then the defendant's use of it means that the plaintiff

Intentional torts 155

has lost control over the impact of its trade name in the defendant's jurisdiction."

However, selling Mr. Twist brand of potato chips in the United States would assist Bombay Sweets in establishing goodwill in that particular region. Nonetheless, there are companies that are so monolithic that goodwill would be easy to establish. For example, Nike, McDonald's, Apple, and Google are companies that may not sell products at a particular region, but can adduce evidence of goodwill in that location.

192 Osborne, *supra* note 4 at 339–340.
193 See *Hay v Platinum Equities Inc*, [2012] ABQB 204, 538 AR 68, where the successful plaintiff was not a celebrity or a public figure, but an accountant.
194 For example, Michael Jordan and Nike, or David Beckham and H&M, or Leonardo DiCaprio and TAG Heuer, or Scarlett Johansson and Mango, or Jennifer Aniston and Smartwater.
195 See *Krouse v Chrysler Canada Ltd et al.*, [1973] OJ No 2157, 1 OR (2d) 225.
196 See generally Susan H Abramovitch, "Misappropriation of Personality" (2000) 33:2 Can Community LJ 230.
197 *Gould Estate v Stoddart Publishing Co Ltd*, [1996] OJ No 3288, 14 OTC 136.
198 *Allen v Flood*, [1895–1899] All ER Rep 52, 46 WR 258 [*Allen*].
199 While the tort of conspiracy's roots can be traced to the reign of Edward I, it truly gained prominence through industrial disputes in the nineteenth century, at Heuston & Buckley, *supra* note 1 at 414; Also see *Mogul Steamship Co v McGregor, Gow & Co*, [1891–4] All ER Rep 263, 56 JP 101.
200 Osborne, *supra* note 4 at 342.
201 *Crofter Hand Woven Harris Tweed Co Ltd v Veitch*, [1942] 1 All ER 142, [1942] AC 435 [*Crofter*].
202 See Philip Sales, "The Tort of Conspiracy and Civil Secondary Liability" (1990) 49:3 Cambridge LJ 491; Also see *Quinn v Leathem*, [1901] All ER Rep 1, [1901] AC 495, where the House of Lords invented the tort of simple conspiracy.
203 G J Hughes, "The Tort of Conspiracy" (1952) 15:2 Modern L Rev 209 at 209–211; Also see J Charlesworth, "Conspiracy as a Ground of Liability in Tort" (1920) 36:1 Law Q Rev 38.
204 Gary Chan Kok Yew, "Intention and Unlawful Means in the Tort of Conspiracy" (2005) 2005:1 Sing JLS 261.
205 *XY Inc v International Newtech Development Inc*, [2013] BCCA 352, 366 DLR (4th) 443.
206 See generally Janet O'Sullivan, "Unlawful Means Conspiracy in the House of Lords" (2008) 67:3 Cambridge LJ 459; Also see *OBG, supra* note 148.
207 *Rookes v Barnard*, [1964] 1 All ER 367, [1964] AC 1129 [*Rookes*].
208 The former is known as "three-party intimidation" and the latter is "two-party intimidation"; See generally Osborne, *supra* note 4 at 345–346; See generally D W Smith, "The Tort of Intimidation in English Law" (1966) 29:1 Tydskrif vir Hedendaagse Romeins-Hollandse Reg (J for Contemporary Roman-Dutch L) 21; Also see Heuston & Buckley, *supra* note 1 at 421–425.
209 To further clarify, a court would order damages for breach of contract. However, here, the question of breach does not arise, as you accepted the revised offer. Rather, if you did not originally accept the amended offer, then you would have been successful in attaining damages for breach of contract had they refused to pay upon completion of the project.
210 See K.W. Wedderburn, "Intimidation and the Right to Strike" (1964) 27:3 Modern L Rev 257.

156   *Intentional torts*

211   See generally Francis Bowes Sayre, "Inducing Breach of Contract (1922–1923) 36:6 Harv L Rev 663.
212   *Lumley v Gye*, [1843–1860] All ER Rep 208, 2 E & B 216, 22 LJQB 463 [*Lumley*].
213   Also see *Texaco Inc v Pennzoil Inc*, [1986] 784 F 2d 133, 1986 US App LEXIS 22524.
214   See Heuston & Buckley, *supra* note 1 at 404–414; Also see Fleming, *supra* note 3 at 756–765.
215   See generally Richard A Epstein, "Inducement of Breach of Contract as a Problem of Ostensible Ownership" (1987) 16:1 J Leg Stud 1.

References

Legislation

Constitution of India (India), Act of 1950
Criminal Code, RSC 1985, c C-46
Privacy Act, RSBC 1996, c 373 (British Columbia)
Privacy Act, RSNL 1990, c P-22 (Newfoundland and Labrador)
Privacy Act, RSS 1978, c P-24 (Saskatchewan)
The Bangladesh Medical and Dental Council Act, 2010 (Bangladesh), Act No LXI of 2010
The Building Construction Act, 1952 (Bangladesh), Act No II of 1953
The Code of Criminal Procedure, 1898 (Bangladesh), Act No V of 1898
The Constitution of the People's Republic of Bangladesh (Bangladesh), Act of 1972
The Dhaka Metropolitan Police Ordinance, 1976 (Bangladesh), Act No III of 1976
The Digital Security Act, 2018 (Bangladesh), Act No XLVI of 2018
The Food Safety Act, 2013 (Bangladesh), Act No XLII of 2013
The Majority Act, 1875 (Bangladesh), Act No IX of 1875
The Nari-O-Shishu Nirjaton Domon Ain, 2000 (Bangladesh), Act No VIII of 2000
The Penal Code, 1860 (Bangladesh), Act No XLV of 1860
The Pornography Control Act, 2012 (Bangladesh), Act No IX of 2012
The Privacy Act, RSM 1987, c P125 (Manitoba)
The Sale of Goods Act, 1930 (Bangladesh), Act No III of 1930
The Trademarks Act, 2009 (Bangladesh), Act No XIX of 2009

Caselaw

Ad-Lib Club Ltd v Granville, [1971] 2 All ER 300, 115 Sol Jo 74
Agar v Canning, [1965] MJ No 24, [1965] 54 WWR 302
Alderson v Booth, [1969] 2 All ER 271, [1969] 2 QB 216
Allan et al v New Mount Sinai Hospital, [1980] OJ No 3095, 28 OR (2d) 356
Allen v Flood, [1895–1899] All ER Rep 52, 46 WR 258
America Online, Inc v National Health Care Discount, Inc, [2000] 121 F Supp 2d 1255, 2000 US Dist LEXIS 17055
American Surety Co v Pryor, [1927] 217 Ala 244, 115 So 176
Arkwright v Newbold, [1881] 50 LJ Ch 372, 17 Ch D 301
Arndt v Smith, [1997] 2 SCR 539, [1997] SCJ No 65
Ashby v White, [1703] 2 Ld Raym 938, 1 ER 417, 92 ER 710
Aubry v Éditions Vice-Versa, [1998] 1 SCR 591, [1998] SCJ No 30

Intentional torts   157

Babiuk v Trann, [2005] SJ No 41, 248 DLR (4th) 530
Bailey et al v Warner, [1902] 118 F 395, 1902 US App LEXIS 4535
Bangladesh National Women Lawyers' Association v The Government of Bangladesh, [2011] 31 BLD 324
Barbour v University of British Columbia, [2009] BCJ No 617, 310 DLR (4th) 130
Barry v Third Avenue R R Co, [1900] 51 AD 385, 64 NYS 615
Basely v Clarkson, [1681] 3 Lev 37, 83 ER 565
Berstein of Leigh (Baron) v Skyviews and General Ltd, [1977] 2 All ER 902, [1978] QB 479
Bird v Jones, [1845] 7 QBR 742, 115 ER 668
Blunk v Atchison, [1889] 38 F 311, 1889 US App LEXIS 2820
Bocardo SA v Energy UK Onshore Ltd, [2010] 3 All ER 975, [2011] 1 AC 380
Bollinger v Costa Brava Wine Company Ltd, [1961] 1 All ER 561, 1 WLR 277
Bolton v Vellines, [1897] 94 Va 393, 26 SE 847
Bristol Conservatories Ltd v Conservatories Custom Built Ltd, [1989] RPC 455
Burton v Davies, [1953] St R QD 26
Caltagirone v Scozzari-Cloutier, [2007] OJ No 4003
Cambell v MGN Ltd, [2004] 2 All ER 995, [2004] 2 AC 457
Canadian Foundation for Children, Youth and the Law v Canada (Attorney General), [2004] 1 SCR 76
Carter v Canada (Attorney General), [2015] 1 SCR 331, [2015] SCJ No 5
Century 21 Canada Ltd Partnership v Rogers Communications Inc, [2011] BCJ No 1679, [2011] BCSC 1196
Ciarlariello v Schacter, [1993] 2 SCR 119, [1993] SCJ No 46
Ciba-Geigy Canada Ltd v Apotex Inc, [1992] 3 SCR 120, [1992] SCJ No 83
C(JS) v Wren, [1986] AJ No 1166, 76 AR 115
Clark v Canada (TD), [1994] 3 FC 323, [1994] FCJ No 576
CompuServe Inc v Cyber Promotions Inc, [1997] 962 F Supp 1015, 1997 US Dist LEXIS 1997
Cope v Sharpe, [1911–1913] All ER Rep Ext 1212, [1912] 1 KB 496, 81 LJKB 346
Corbett v Hill, [1870] LR 9 Eq 671, 39 LJ Ch 547
Crawford Adjusters (Cayman) Ltd v Sagicor General Insurance (Cayman) Ltd, [2013] 4 All ER 8, [2013] UKPC 17
Crofter Hand Woven Harris Tweed Co Ltd v Veitch, [1942] 1 All ER 142, [1942] AC 435
Crossman v Thurlow, [1957] 336 Mass 252, 1957 Mass LEXIS 622
Davidson v Toronto Blue Jays Baseball Ltd, [1999] OJ No 692, 170 DLR (4th) 559
Daughtry v Blanket State Bank et al, [1931] 41 SW 2d 527, 1931 Tex App LEXIS 1373
Derry v Peek, [1886–1890] All ER Rep 1, 58 LJ Ch 864
Dick Bentley Productions v Harold Smith (Motors) Ltd, [1965] 2 All ER 65, [1965] 1 WLR 623
Didow v Alberta Power Ltd, [1988] AJ No 620, 88 AR 250
Dwyer v Staunton, [1947] AJ No 59, 4 DLR 393
Dyk v De Young, [1889] 35 Ill App 138, 1889 Ill App LEXIS 517
Estabrooks v New Brunswick Real Estate Association, [2014] NBCA 48, [2014] NBJ No 186
Evaniuk v 79846 Manitoba Inc, [1990] MJ No 584, 68 Man R (2d) 306
Fisher v Carrousel Motor Hotel, Inc, [1967] 424 SW 2d 627, 1967 Tex LEXIS 267
Fouldes v Willoughby, [1841] 10 LJ Ex 364, 151 ER 1153

158 *Intentional torts*

Gambriell v Caparelli, [1974] OJ No 2243, [1974] 7 OR (2d) 205

General & Finance Facilities Ltd v Cooks Cars (Romford) Ltd, [1963] 2 All ER 314, [1963] 1 WLR 644

Gifford v Dent, [1926] WN 336, 71 Sol Jo 83

Glanzer v Shepard, [1921] 233 NY 236, 135 NE 275

Gould Estate v Stoddart Publishing Co Ltd, [1996] OJ No 3288, 14 OTC 136

Grand Restaurants of Canada Ltd v Toronto (City), [1981] OJ No 2503, 32 OR (2d) 757

Green v TA Shoemaker & Co, [1909] 111 Md 69, 73 A 688

Harr v Ward, [1904] 73 Ark 437 84 SW 496

Hay v Platinum Equities Inc, [2012] ABQB 204, 538 AR 68

Heckert v 5470 Investments Ltd, [2008] BCJ No 1854, [2008] 62 CCLT (3d) 249

Hedley Byrne & Co Ltd v Heller & Partners Ltd, [1963] 2 All ER 575, [1964] AC 465

Holcombe v Whitaker, [1975] 318 So 2d 289, 294 Ala 430

Hollis v Dow Corning Corp, [1995] 4 SCR 634, [1995] SCJ No 104

Hopper v Reeve, [1817] 7 Taunt 698, 129 ER 278

H S Leyman Company v Short, [1926] 214 Ky 272, 283 SW 96

Hurst v Picture Theatres Ltd, [1914–1915] All ER Rep 837, [1915] 1 KB 1

Kathleen K v Robert B, [1984] 150 Cal App 3d 992, 1984 Cal App LEXIS 1510

Kelemen v El-Homeira, [1999] AJ No 1279, 250 AR 67

Kelsen v Imperial Tobacco Co (of Great Britain and Ireland) Ltd, [1957] 2 All ER 343, [1957] 2 QB 334

Kenney v Wong Len, [1925] 81 NH 427, 128 A 343

Krouse v Chrysler Canada Ltd et al, [1973] OJ No 2157, *1 OR (2d) 225*

Lewvest Ltd v Scotia Towers Ltd, [1981] NJ No 220, [1981] 126 DLR (3d) 239

Lipiec v Borsa, [1996] OJ No 3819, 17 OTC 64

London Borough of Southwark v Williams, [1971] 2 All ER 175, [1971] 2 WLR 467

Lord v Canada (Attorney General), [2000] 50 CCLT (2d) 206, 2000 BCSC 750

Lumley v Gye, [1843–1860] All ER Rep 208, 2 E & B 216, 22 LJQB 463

Lynch v Knight, [1861] All ER Rep Ext 2344, 9 HL Cas 577

Macleay v Tait, [1906] AC 24, 75 LJ Ch 90

Magill v Magill, [2006] HCA 51, [2006] 231 ALR 277

Malette v Shulman, [1990] OJ No 350, 72 OR (2d) 417

Manitoba Free Press Co Ltd v Nagy, [1907] 39 SCR 340

Mann v Saulnier, [1959] NBJ No 12, 19 DLR (2d) 130

Mattel Inc v 3894207 Canada Inc, [2006] 1 SCR 772, [2006] SCJ No 23

Meering v Grahame-White Aviation Co, [1918–19] All ER Rep Ext 1490, 122 LT 44

Miller v Jackson, [1977] 3 All ER 778, [1977] QB 966

Milner v Manufacturer's Life Insurance Co, [2006] BCJ No 2787, 2006 BCSC 1571

Mitchell v Rochester Railway Company, [1896] 151 NY 107, 45 NE 354

Mogul Steamship Co v McGregor, Gow & Co, [1891–4] All ER Rep 263, 56 JP 101

Murray v Ministry of Defence, [1988] 2 All ER 521, [1988] 1 WLR 692

NB v Hôtel-Dieu de Québec, [1992] JQ No 1, 86 DLR (4th) 385

Nelles v Ontario, [1989] 2 SCR 170, [1989] SCJ No 86

Nilabati Behera v State of Orissa, [1993] AIR 1960, 1993 SCR (2) 581

Non-Marine Underwriters, Lloyds of London v Scalera, [2000] 1 SCR 551, [2000] SCJ No 26

Norberg v Wynrib, [1992] 2 SCR 226, [1992] SCJ No 60

Intentional torts 159

O'Brien v Cunard SS Co, [1891] 154 Mass 272, 28 NE 266
OBG Ltd v Allan, [2005] 2 All ER 602, [2005] QB 762
Orkin Exterminating Co Inc v Pestco Co of Canada Ltd et al, [1985] 50 OR (2d) 726
Pasley (and another) v Freeman, [1775–1802] All ER Rep 31, 100 ER 450
Peck v United Kingdom, [2003] ECHR 44647/98, [2003] All ER (D) 255 (Jan)
Peppler Estate v Lee, [2019] AJ No 249, 2019 ABQB 144
Ploof v Putnam, [1908] 81 Vt 471, 71 A 188
Queen v Cognos Inc, [1993] 1 SCR 87, [1993] SCJ No 3
Quinn v Leathem, [1901] All ER Rep 1, [1901] AC 495
R v B, [2006] EWCA Crim 2945, [2006] All ER (D) 173 (Oct)
R v Barnard, [1837] 173 ER 342, 7 C&P 784
R v Cuerrier, [1998] 2 SCR 371, [1998] SCJ No 64
R v Dudley and Stephens, [1881–1885] All ER Rep 61, 14 QBC 273
R v J A, [2011] 2 SCR 440, [2011] SCJ No 28
R v Mabior, [2012] 2 SCR 584, [2012] SCJ No 47
R v Mwai, [1995] 3 NZLR 149, [1995] 13 CRNZ 273
Ray Plastics Ltd v Dustbane Products Ltd, [1994] OJ No 2050, 57 CPR (3d) 474
Reckitt and Colman Products Ltd v Borden Inc, [1990] 1 All ER 873, [1990]1 WLR
    491
Reddaway & Co Ltd v Banham & Co Ltd, [1895–1899] All ER Rep 133, [1896]
    AC 199, 65 LJQB 381
Redgrave v Hurd, [1881–1885] All ER Rep 77, 51 LJ Ch 113
Regina v Maurantonio, [1968] 1 OR 145
Reibl v Hughes, [1980] 2 SCR 880, [1980] SCJ No 105
Reynolds v Pierson, [1902] 29 Ind App 273, 1902 Ind App LEXIS 136
Rigby and another v Chief Constable of Northamptonshire, [1985] 2 All ER 985,
    [1985] 1 WLR 1242
Roberts v Buster's Auto Towing Service Ltd, [1976] 70 DLR (3d) 716, [1976] BCJ
    No 1386
Rookes v Barnard, [1964] 1 All ER 367, [1964] AC 1129
Saccone v Orr, [1982] 34 OR (2d) 317
Sadhu Singh Hamdard Trust v Navsun Holdings Ltd, [2016] FCJ No 239, 483 NR
    33
Shibamoto & Co v Western Fish Producers Inc (Trustee of), [1991] FCJ No 243,
    [1991] 3 FC 214
Simeon Groot v Florian Hitz, [1884] 12 Wash L Rep 353
Simone v The Rhode Island Company, [1907] 28 RI 186, 66 A 202
Sirajul Islam Chowdhury et al v Md Jainal Abedin et al, [1997] 49 DLR (AD) 164
Somwar v McDonald's Restaurants of Canada Ltd, [2006] OJ No 64, 79 OR (3d)
    172
Spade v Lynn and Boston Railroad Company, [1897] 168 Mass 285, 47 NE 88
Spring v Guardian Assurance PLC and Others, [1994] 3 All ER 129, [1995] 2 AC
    296
Standard Oil Co v Davis, [1922] 208 Ala 565, [1922] Ala LEXIS 353
Stephens v Myers, [1830] 172 ER 735, 4 Car & P 349
Temple v Hallem, [1989] MJ No 203, [1989] 58 DLR (4th) 541
Teva Canada Ltd v TD Canada Trust, [2017] SCJ No 51, [2017] 2 SCR 317
Texaco Inc v Pennzoil Inc, [1986] 784 F 2d 133, 1986 US App LEXIS 22524
Ultramares Corp v Touche, Niven & Co, [1931] 255 NY 170, 174 NE 441
United States v Ortega, [1825] 27 F Cas 359, 1825 US App LEXIS 262

160   *Intentional torts*

Wackett v Calder, [1965] BCJ No 129, 51 DLR (2d) 598
Wallace v Kam, [2013] 297 ALR 383, [2013] HCA 19
Wandsworth Board of Works v United Telephone Co, [1884] 13 QBD 904, 48 JP 676
Wasserman v Hall, [2009] BCJ No 1932, 2009 BCSC 1318
Waters v Wong, [2019] AJ No 50, 2019 ABQB 51
Wawrzyniak v Livingstone, [2019] OJ No 4291, 2019 ONSC 4900
Westjet Airlines Ltd v Air Canada, [2005] OJ No 2310, 2005 CarswellOnt 2101
White v Mellin, [1895] AC 154, 64 LJ Ch 308
White v Turner, [1981] OJ NO 2498, 120 DLR (3d) 269
Wilkinson v Downton, [1897] All ER Rep 267, 2 QB 57
Winter Garden Theatre (London) Ltd v Millenium Productions Ltd, [1947] 2 All
    ER 331, [1948] AC 173
Woollerton & Wilson Ltd v Richard Costain Ltd, [1970] 1 All ER 483, [1970] 1
    WLR 411
XY Inc v International Newtech Development Inc, [2013] BCCA 352, 366 DLR
    (4th) 443

Secondary Material: Books

Burns, Peter & Blom, Joost, *Economic Interests in Canadian Tort Law*, 2nd ed
    (Markham, ON: LexisNexis Canada, 2009)
Englard, Izhak, *The Philosophy of Tort Law* (Aldershot, UK: Dartmouth, 1992)
Fleming, John G, *The Law of Torts*, 9th ed (Sydney: LBC Information Services,
    1998)
Hagen, Greg, Hutchison, Cameron, Lametti, David, Reynolds, Graham, Scassa,
    Teresa & Wilkinson, Margaret Ann, *Canadian Intellectual Property Law: Cases
    and Materials*, 2nd ed (Toronto: Emond Montgomery Publications Limited, 2018)
Heuston, Robert F V & Buckley, Richard A, *Salmond and Heuston on the Law of
    Torts*, 19th ed (London: Sweet & Maxwell, 1987)
Klar, Lewis, *Tort Law*, 5th ed (Toronto: Carswell, 2012)
Linden, Allen M & Feldthusen, Bruce, *Canadian Tort Law*, 9th ed (Markham, ON:
    LexisNexis Canada Inc, 2011)
Osborne, Philip, *The Law of Torts*, 5th ed (Toronto: Irwin Law Inc, 2015)
Prosser, William L, *Handbook of The Law of Torts*, 4th ed (St. Paul, Minnesota:
    West Publishing Co, 1971)
Sappideen, Carolyn & Vines, Prue, eds, *Fleming's Law of Torts*, 10th ed (Sydney:
    Law Book Co, 2002)
Stuart, Don, Coughlan, Steve & Delisle, Ronald, *Learning Canadian Criminal Law*,
    12th ed (Toronto: Thompson Reuters Canada Limited, 2014)
Weinrib, Ernest J, *Tort Law: Cases and Materials*, 4th ed (Toronto: Emond
    Montgomery Publications Limited, 2014)

Secondary Material: Journal Articles

Abramovitch, Susan H, "Misappropriation of Personality" (2000) 33:2 Can
    Community LJ 230
Adjin-Tettey, Elizabeth, "Protecting the Dignity and Autonomy of Women:
    Rethinking the Place of Constructive Consent in the Tort of Sexual Battery"
    (2006) 39:1 UBC L Rev 3

Adler, Robert S & Silverstein, Elliot M, "When David Meets Goliath: Dealing with Power Differentials in Negotiations" (2000) 5 Harv Negot L Rev 1

Anderson, Roderick B, "Some Aspects of Airpsace Trespass" (1960) 27:4 J Air L & Com 341

Annas, George J & Densberger, Joan E, "Competence to Refuse Medical Treatment: Autonomy vs. Paternalism" (1984) 15:2 U Tol L Rev 561

Austin, Graeme W, "The Consumer in Cross-Border Passing off Cases" (2016) 47:2 VUWLR 209

Barnhizer, Daniel D, "Inequality of Bargaining Power" (2005) 76:1 U Colo L Rev 139

Bohlen, Francis H, "Right to Recover for Injury Resulting from Negligence without Impact" (1902) 50:3 Am L Reg 141

Burk, Dan L, "The Trouble with Trespass" (2000) 4:1 J Small & Emerging Bus L 27

Charlesworth, J., "Conspiracy as a Ground of Liability in Tort" (1920) 36:1 Law Q Rev 38

Cohan, John A, "Private and Public Necessity and the Violation of Property Rights" (2007) 83:2 NDL Rev 651

Dahl, Robert, "The Concept of Power" (1957) 2:3 J Soc Gen Systems Research 201

Deiser, George F, "The Development of Principle of Trespass" (1917) 27:2 Yale LJ 220

Elvin, Jesse, "Liability of Schools for Bullying" (2002) 61:2 Cambridge LJ 239

Epstein, Richard A, "Inducement of Breach of Contract as a Problem of Ostensible Ownership" (1987) 16:1 J Leg Stud 1

Faust, John R Jr, "Distinction between Conversion and Trespass to Chattel" (1958) 37:3 Or L Rev 256

Fischer, Edwin R & Huard, Leo A, "Injurious Falsehood–An Expanding Tort" (1945) 33:2 Geo LJ 213

Guillot, Grant J, "Trespassing Through Cyberspace: Should Wireless Piggybacking Constitute a Crime or Tort Under Louisiana Law?" (2009) 69:2 La L Rev 389

Harper, Fowler, "Malicious Prosecution, False Imprisonment and Defamation" (1937) 15:2 Tex L Rev 157

Hughes, G. J., "The Tort of Conspiracy" (1952) 15:2 Modern L Rev 209

Kelman, Mark, "Interpretive Construction in the Substantive Criminal Law" (1981) 33:4 Stan L Rev 591

Klar, Lewis, "The Defence of Private Necessity in Canadian Tort Law" (2005) 5:2 Issues in Leg Scholarship 1

Meisel, Alan, "The Exceptions to the Informed Consent Doctrine: Striking a Balance between Competing Values in Medical Decisionmaking" (1979) 1979:2 Wis L Rev 413

Meltz, Eli A, "No Harm, No Foul: Attempted Invasion of Privacy and the Tort of Intrusion upon Seclusion" (2015) 83:6 Fordham L Rev 3431

Merrill, Thomas W, "Trespass, Nuisance, and the Costs of Determining Property Rights" (1985) 14:1 J Leg Stud 13

Moreham, Nicole A, "Privacy in Public Places" (2006) 65:3 Cambridge LJ 606

Morison, W. L., "Unfair Competition and Passing-off – The Flexibility of a Formula" (1956) 2:1 Sydney L Rev 50

Nwabueze, Remigius N, & Okorie, Polycarp C, "Flexibility of Damages for Conversion and Detinue" (2009) 17:1 African J of Intl & Comparative L 102

O'Sullivan, Janet, "Unlawful Means Conspiracy in the House of Lords" (2008) 67:3 Cambridge LJ 459

162   *Intentional torts*

Palyan, Tigran, "Common Law Privacy in a Not So Common World: Prospects for the Tort of Intrusion upon Seclusion in Virtual Worlds" (2008) 38:1 Sw L Rev 167

Plante, Marcus L, "An Analysis of Informed Consent" (1968) 36:4 Fordham L Rev 639

Prosser, William L, "Intentional Infliction of Mental Suffering: A New Tort" (1939) 37:6 Mich L Rev 874

Prosser, William L, "False Imprisonment: Consciousness of Confinement" (1955) 55:6 Colum L Rev 847

Prosser, William L, "Injurious Falsehood: The Basis of Liability" (1959) 59:3 Colum L Rev 425

Prosser, William L, "Misrepresentation and Third Persons" (1966) 19:2 Vand L Rev 231

Queree, Nicholas, "Detinue: Gone but Not Forgotten: Schwarzschild v. Harrods Ltd" (2008) 13:2 Art Ant & L 203

Robertson, Gerald, "Informed Consent Ten Years Later: The Impact of Reibl v Hughes" (1991) 70:3 Can Bar Rev 423

Sacks, Deana P, "Intentional Sex Torts" (2008) 77:3 Fordham L Rev 1051

Sales, Philip, "The Tort of Conspiracy and Civil Secondary Liability" (1990) 49:3 Cambridge LJ 491

Sayre, Francis B, "Inducing Breach of Contract" (1922–1923) 36:6 Harv L Rev 663

Schuck, Peter H, "Rethinking Informed Consent" (1994) 103:4 Yale LJ 899

Shultz, Marjorie Maguire, "From Informed Consent to Patient Choice: A New Protected Interest" (1985) 95:2 Yale LJ 219

Slobogin, Christopher, "Public Privacy: Camera Surveillance of Public Places and the Right to Anonymity" (2002) 72:1 Miss LJ 213

Smith, D. W., "The Tort of Intimidation in English Law" (1966) 29:1 Tydskrif vir Hedendaagse Romeins-Hollandse Reg (J for Contemporary Roman-Dutch L) 21

Smith, Jeremiah, "Disparagement of Property" (1913) 13:1 Colum L Rev *13*

Snow, Ned, "Accessing the Internet through the Neighbor's Wireless Internet Connection: Physical Trespass in Virtual Reality" (2005) 84:4 Neb L Rev 1226

Teff, Harvey, "Liability for Psychiatric Illness after Hillsborough" (1992) 12:3 Oxford J Leg Stud 440

Throckmorton, Archibald H, "Damages for Fright" (1921) 34:3 Harv L Rev 260

Trindade, Francis, "Intentional Torts: Some Thoughts on Assault and Battery" (1982) 2:2 Oxford J Leg Stud 211

Tutaj, Adam J, "Intrusion upon Seclusion: Bringing an Otherwise Valid Cause of Action into the 21st Century" (1999) 82:3 Marq L Rev 665

Warren, Samuel D & Brandeis, Louis D, "The Right to Privacy" (1890) 4:5 Harv L Rev 193

Wedderburn, K. W., "Intimidation and the Right to Strike" (1964) 27:3 Modern L Rev 257

Wilkins, Richard G, "Defining the Reasonable Expectation of Privacy: An Emerging Tripartite Analysis" (1987) 40:5 Vand L Rev 1077

Wolfson, Lorne & Himel, Andrea, "Broken Promises, Brokn Hearts: Intrafamilial Tort and Contract Claims" (2002) 25:4 Adv Q 441

Woodbine, George E, "The Origins of the Action of Trespass" (1924) 33:8 Yale LJ 799

Yew, Gary Chan Kok, "Intention and Unlawful Means in the Tort of Conspiracy" (2005) 2005:1 Sing JLS 261

Secondary Material: Websites

"Bangladesh Legal Aid and Services Trust v Secretary, Ministry of Education (Bangladesh)" *BLAST* (13 January 2011), online: BLAST https://www.blast.org.bd/content/judgement/wp_5684of2010.pdf

Belson, Ken, "Dial-Up Internet Going the Way of Rotary Phones" *The New York Times* (21 June 2005), online: The New York Times Company https://www.nytimes.com/2005/06/21/technology/dialup-internet-going-the-way-of-rotary-phones.html

"Bombay Sweets Chips" *Bombay Sweets Bangladesh* (2020), online: Bombay Sweets & Co Ltd https://www.bombaysweetsbd.com/chips.php

"Compensation Ordered in only 7pc Rape Cases" *The Daily Star* (8 March 2021), online: The Daily Star: https://www.thedailystar.net/city/news/compensation-ordered-only-7pc-rape-cases-2056673

Huda, Taqbir, "US-Bangla Air Crash: A Tort Law Perspective" *The Daily Star* (27 March 2018a), online: The Daily Star https://www.thedailystar.net/law-our-rights/tort-law-perspective-1553911

Huda, Taqbir, "Judicial Activism for Constitutional Torts" *The Daily Star* (7 August 2018b), online: The Daily Star https://www.thedailystar.net/news/law-our-rights/judicial-activism-constitutional-torts-1616731

Huda, Taqbir, "State Liability to Pay Compensation for Rape: A Necessary Ruling" *The Daily Star* (15 March 2019), online: The Daily Star https://www.thedailystar.net/opinion/law/news/state-liability-pay-compensation-rape-necessary-ruling-1715395

Hughes, Rob, "Suspensions in World Cup Head-Butting Incident" *The New York Times* (21 July 2006), online: The New York Times Company https://www.nytimes.com/2006/07/21/sports/soccer/21soccer.html

Ramanathan, Usha, "Tort Law in India" *IELRC* (2002), online: International Environmental Law Research Centre http://www.ielrc.org/Content/a0206.pdf

Virk, Kameron, "Kit-Kat Case: The Food and Drinks with Trademarked Shapes" *BBC* (25 July 2018), online: BBC https://www.bbc.com/news/newsbeat-44953460

5   Negligence

The origin of negligence liability is relatively recent.[1] As I have mentioned in the previous chapter, early common law was concerned with intentional acts and did not pay much attention to harm that was inadvertent. Even with the passage of time, as the writ system was overly formal and primarily focused on the nature of the plaintiff's injury, rather than the defendant's conduct, people could not speculate when one would be held liable.[2] This trend of generally not foisting liability in negligence lasted until the end of the 18th century.[3]

Then, in the first quarter of the 19th century, the embryonic concept of negligence began developing into a separate basis of tort liability. Broadly coinciding with the Industrial Revolution, which engendered machinery and urbanization, the law was not able to manage the countless new risks and losses by resorting to its archaic tort remedies. It was at this critical juncture (of social and economic transformation) that courts acceded to the calls of the people and found a new pattern to adjust losses (e.g. vehicular accidents, workplace injuries, medical malpractice, and the like) by focusing on the concept of negligence.[4]

In little more than a century, negligence has transformed, and became the most important basis of, tort liability.[5] At its most basic form, negligence is conduct that falls below the standard of care formulated by law to protect others from unreasonable risks of harm. In order to succeed in a claim for negligence, the plaintiff must prove, firstly, a *negligent act*; secondly, the *injury* that he has suffered; and thirdly, the injury must have been *caused* by the defendant's negligent conduct.[6] As in, while the objective of tort law is to compensate one for the injury suffered (in other words, placing the party in the position he would have been in had the tort not been committed), if there was no negligent act, or alternatively, if there was, but the misconduct did not cause the injury, or if the damage is too remote, then liability cannot be imposed on anyone.[7] For example, while walking on a sidewalk, if you trip, fall, and fracture your left-wrist, nobody can be held liable for your injury, as it was not caused by another's negligent act. Nonetheless, what if a passenger on a rickshaw saw your fall, became momentarily inattentive, fell off the rickshaw, and scraped her elbow. Would she be able to hold you liable on the grounds that had you not fallen, then she would not have injured herself?

DOI: 10.4324/9781003241782-5

Moreover, is the driver of a vehicle liable for colliding into a child, who darted in front of his car, and injuring him even though he was driving within the speed limit? Or, if you buy a can of an effervescent drink, take one sip, and pour the remaining contents into a transparent glass and see the remnants of a dead mouse, can you hold the manufacturer or the seller of the drink liable? Or, if you are a passenger in a vehicle and suffer an injury because the other driver was speeding and collided with your car, is the driver of the other car fully liable, or will his liability be diminished if there is evidence demonstrating that the extent of your injury could have been reduced had you been wearing a seatbelt?

As I will delineate in this chapter, not every negligent act causing injury is compensable, as otherwise a heavy burden would be placed upon every individual to be overly vigilant. As in, is it sensible to make a 7-month pregnant woman liable to her foetus for falling on ice and causing the subsequently born child to be quadriplegic? Therefore, in order to limit the kind of misconduct that is actionable, courts have employed the terms standard of care, duty of care, remoteness of damage, and proximate cause.

5.1 The standard of care

Vaughan v Menlove[8]

Mr. Menlove built a haystack on his land near the contiguous border he shared with Mr. Vaughan. In order to prevent the stack of hay from spontaneously igniting, he built a chimney (as in, a ventilation system). Over a period of five weeks, Mr. Vaughan repeatedly warned Mr. Menlove that, notwithstanding the ventilation, the construction of the haystack was dangerous and it could ignite, but Mr. Menlove said that he would "chance it." The hay soon ignited and the fire spread to Mr. Vaughan's land and destroyed several of his cottages, for which the latter seeks damages. However, Mr. Menlove contends that he is a man whose intelligence is not of the highest order, and therefore, he should not be held liable for damage he did not foresee. Rejecting Mr. Menlove's argument, the court said,

> Though, in some cases a greater degree of care is exacted than in others […] The care taken by a prudent man has always been the rule laid down; and as to the supposed difficulty of applying it, a jury has always been able to say, whether, taking that rule as their guide, there has been negligence on the occasion in question.
>
> Instead, therefore, of saying that the liability for negligence should be co-extensive with the judgment of each individual, which would be as variable as the length of the foot of each individual, we ought rather to adhere to the rule which requires in all cases a regard to caution such as a man of ordinary prudence would observe. That was, in substance, the criterion presented to the jury in this case and, therefore, the present rule must be discharged.

166　*Negligence*

Notes

Vaughan tells us that incorporating characteristics of every individual would require courts to consider *subjective* elements, which would erode the efficacy of the law. Therefore, the court adopted an *objective* test, which is that of a "reasonable person"; that is, the question in each case is not "would the defendant act differently if placed in a similar situation under similar circumstances"; rather, it is "would a reasonable person in the place of the defendant act differently under similar circumstances"? If yes, then liability can be imposed on the defendant. That is to say, if a reasonable person, under similar circumstances, would act differently than did the defendant, which means his action, or inaction would not cause injury, then the defendant's conduct has fallen below the standard of care (or, what I call acceptable behaviour) expected of a reasonable person in society, for which the injured party can claim compensation.[9]

While *Vaughan* is a landmark decision that introduces us to the concept of the "reasonable person,"[10] confusion regarding his characteristics did not dissipate immediately thereafter. For example, is the standard of care, which is a legal fiction used as a barometer against which all conduct is measured, expected of a 15-year-old the same as that of a 48-year-old; or, is the standard of care expected of an autistic person the same as that of a person who is not autistic; or, is the standard of care expected of a person experiencing a heart-attack the same as one who is not?[11] Perhaps more importantly, would it be unfair to hold any of the enumerated persons to the same standard of care – e.g. a 15-year-old to that of a 48-year-old? As will become evident, though the test of the reasonable person remains objective, courts have not been unwilling to provide different characteristics to the reasonable person in different situations.

McHale v Watson[12]

On the afternoon of 21 January 1957, Barry Watson, who was 12 years and 2 months, was playing tag with Susan McHale and two other girls – all three girls were slightly younger than Barry. Near the end of their game, Barry brought out a six-inch rod from his pocket with a sharpened edge (similar to a spear) and threw it towards a tree in front of him. Unfortunately, it ricocheted off of the tree and struck Susan in the right eye, which rendered her permanently blind. While the guardians of Susan brought an action against Barry, the court did not find him liable and said,

> It has been strongly urged for the plaintiff that, in considering whether Barry was negligent, I must judge what he did by the standard expected of a reasonable man, and that that standard is not graduated according to age. In one sense, of course, that is so; for the question whether conduct was negligent, in a legal sense, always depends on an objective standard. This has been generally recognized ever since [...] *Vaughan v Menlove* [...] In *Glasgow Corporation v Muir*, Lord Macmillan said: "The standard of foresight of the reasonable man is, in one sense, an impersonal test. It eliminates the personal equation and is independent

Negligence 167

of the idiosyncrasies of the particular person whose conduct is in question [...] The reasonable man is presumed to be free both from over-apprehension and from over-confidence, but there is a sense in which the standard of care of the reasonable man involves in its application a subjective element. It is still left to the judge to decide what, in the circumstances of the particular case, the reasonable man would have had in contemplation, and what accordingly the party sought to be made liable ought to have foreseen." That is the question I have to determine. It is a question of fact, a jury question, not a question of law. I have not to determine it by regarding the facts of other cases, but by regarding all the circumstances of the case. I do not think that I am required to disregard altogether the fact that the defendant Barry Watson was at the time only twelve years old. In remembering that I am not considering the "idiosyncrasies of the particular person." Childhood is not an idiosyncrasy. It may be that an adult, knowing the resistant qualities of hardwood and of the uncertainty that a spike, not properly balanced as a dart, will stick into wood when thrown, would foresee that it might fail to do so and perhaps go off at a tangent. A person who knew, or might reasonably be expected to know that might be held to be negligent if he were not more circumspect than was this infant defendant. [...]

There is ample American authority in favour of applying a lower standard of care in cases involving the primary negligence of young children. The American *Restatement of the Law of Tort* [...] divides infants into three categories for the purpose of discussing the standard of care applicable. The categories and the standards are as follows:

(a) Children who are so young as to be manifestly incapable of exercising any of the qualities necessary to the perception of risk. This group would comprise babies and children of very tender years and instead of formulating a standard of care for them it suffices to say that they are incapable of negligence;

(b) Infants who, although they have not yet attained majority, are capable as adults of foreseeing the probable consequences of their actions. In view of the capabilities of this class, the standard of care required of them is the same as that required of adults;

(c) Children who come between the extremes indicated in the above categories and whose capacities are infinitely various. The standard of care required of these children is that which it is reasonable to expect of children of like age, intelligence, and experience. [...]

In the present case we are concerned with a boy of the age of twelve years and two months. He was not, of course, a child of tender years. On the other hand, he was not grown up and, according to the evidence, he played as a child. I think it was right for the learned trial judge to refer

168   *Negligence*

to him in common with Susan and other playmates as young children. It cannot be laid down as an absolute proposition that a boy of twelve years of age can never be liable in negligence; nor that he would always be liable in the same manner as an adult in the case of that tort. The defendant's conduct in relation to this object which he threw, a useless piece of scrap metal, is symbolic of the tastes and simplicity of boyhood. He kept the object in his pocket after using it earlier in the day to scrape marine life off the rocks at the beach; after that he carried it around with him for the rest of the day until the accident happened. It was the type of thing that a wise parent would take from a boy if he thought the boy would play with it as a dart in the company of other children. The defendant on his way from the beach took the object from his pocket to show Susan and her companions, whom he met playing in a paddock, what he was doing at the beach – apparently he was proud of how he had transformed the piece of scrap metal by rubbing it on the rocks. The game of chasing having ended, the wooden corner post was an allurement or temptation to him to play with the object as a dart. If it had stuck into the post at the first throw, doubtless, he would not have been content with one throw. The evidence does not suggest that the defendant was other than a normal twelve-year-old-boy. His Honour considered that the defendant, being a boy of twelve years, did not have enough maturity of mind to foresee that the dart might glance off the post in the direction of Susan if he did not make it hit the post squarely, and that there was a possibility that he might not succeed in doing so. It seems to me that the present case comes down to a fine point, namely whether it was right for the trial judge to take into account Barry's age in considering whether he did foresee or ought to have foreseen that the so-called dart might not stick in the post but be deflected from it towards Susan who was in the area of danger in the event of such an occurrence. [...]

The standard of care being objective, it is no answer for him, any more than it is for an adult, to say that the harm he caused was due to his being abnormally slow-witted, quick-tempered, absent-minded or inexperienced. But it does not follow that he cannot rely in his defence upon a limitation upon the capacity for foresight or prudence, not as being personal to himself, but as being characteristic of humanity at his stage of development and in that sense normal. But doing so he appeals to a standard of ordinariness, to an objective and not a subjective standard. In regard to the things which pertain to foresight and prudence – experience, understanding of causes and effects, balance of judgment, thoughtfulness – it is absurd, indeed it is a misuse of language, to speak of normality in relation to persons of all ages taken together. In those things normality is, for children, something different from what normality is for adults; the very concept of normality is a concept is a concept of rising levels until "years of discretion" are attained. The law does not arbitrarily fix upon any particular age for this purpose, and tribunals of fact may well give effect to different views as to the age

Negligence 169

at which normal adult foresight and prudence are reasonably to be expected in relation to particular sets of circumstances. But up to that stage the normal capacity to exercise those two qualities necessarily means the capacity which is normal for a child of the relevant age; and it seems to me that it would be contrary to the fundamental principle that a person is liable for harm that he causes by falling short of an objective criterion of "propriety" in his conduct – propriety, that is to say, as determined by a comparison with the standard of care reasonably to be expected in the circumstances from the normal person – to hold that where a child's liability is in question the normal person to be considered is someone other than a child of corresponding age [...]

Notes

We are aware that the question in a case for negligence is "would a reasonable person in the place of the defendant act differently under similar circumstances". While this maintains objectivity in, and preserves the efficacy of, the law, the salient question is "who is a reasonable person against whom the conduct of a twelve-year-old should be measured?"; that is, is the standard of care expected of a 12-year-old the same as that of a 30-year-old adult with sufficient intelligence and maturity? To answer this question, the three categories of children outlined in the case need to be examined.

Firstly, there are children who are so young that they are incapable of perceiving risk, and therefore, cannot be held liable in negligence. For example, if a 2-year-old, who recently learned to walk, bumps into a vase, which falls on the head of, and injures, a 1-year-old, he cannot be held liable in negligence as he cannot foresee injury from colliding with the vase. As in, it is natural that a child of such tender years will scuttle with disregard to objects nearby, and if his collision with the vase injures another, since the child cannot understand the link between *his collision* and *injury*, he cannot be liable in negligence. However, if a person, who is 30 years of age with sufficient intelligence and maturity, bumps into the same vase and injures another, he could be held liable because an adult of the said disposition is held to foresee the risk of harm. Therefore, the standard of care expected of this group of children is different from that which is expected of an adult with sufficient intelligence and maturity.

Secondly, there are children who are not the age of majority,[13] but are capable of foreseeing the repercussions of their actions. For example, a 10-year-old child may have sufficient intelligence to understand that an unextinguished flame on a discarded match, which he used to light a candle, can ignite a fire and cause damage; or, an 11-year-old child is expected to know that tossing a knife in a direction where people are gathered can injure one of them; or, it is not unreasonable to expect a 12-year-old child to know that clogging a bathtub's drainage system, into which water is pouring, can cause water to overflow and damage property.[14] Here, the law is not concerned with whether the child can foresee the extent of damage, but only that damage could result.[15] Therefore, the standard of care expected of

170   *Negligence*

this group of children is the same as adults. As in, the general rule is that if the child is doing an activity common to adults, then the conduct expected of him is that of an adult.[16] As was said in *McErlean v Sarel et al*,[17]

> It is well-established that, as a general rule in determining negligence, children are not required to conform to the standard of conduct which may reasonably be expected of adults. Their conduct is judged by the standard to be expected of children of like age, intelligence and experience. This is essentially a subjective test which recognizes that the capacities of children are infinitely various and accordingly treats them on an individual basis and, out of a public interest in their welfare and protection, in a more lenient manner than adults. A child at one end of the scale may be of such tender years as to be manifestly incapable of exercising any of those qualities of intelligence and experience which are necessary to enable him or her to perceive a risk and realize its unreasonable character while a child at the other end may be quite as capable as an adult of exercising such qualities. In each case, the question is whether the child "exercised the care expected from a child of like age, intelligence and experience [...]" There are, however, exceptions to this general rule.
>
> Where a child engages in what may be classified as an "adult activity," he or she will not be accorded special treatment, and no allowance will be made for his or her immaturity. In those circumstances, the minor will be held to the same standard of care as an adult engaged in the same activity. This exception, which has been widely accepted in the United States [...] was recognized in this province [...]

Similarly, in *Rozell v Rozell*, Evelyn Rozell, a 16-year-old, was held liable for negligently operating an automobile and crashing into another vehicle, for which her 12-year-old brother, Ernest Rozell, who was a passenger in her vehicle, sustained injuries. The court said that since driving was an activity common to adults (and by extrapolation, uncommon to minors), Ms. Rozell should be judged as if she were an adult.[18]

Rozell is not anomalous to the *Children Act*, which governs, *inter alia*, criminal liability and sentencing of persons under the age of 18. While section 33(1) of the *Children Act* prohibits imposing imprisonment, life imprisonment, and the death sentence on a child, it provides an exception to the rule of not sentencing a child to prison and stipulates,

> Provided that when a child is found to have committed such a serious offence for which the detention provided under the Act is, in the opinion of the court, not sufficient or if the court is satisfied that the child is so unruly or of such depraved character that he cannot be committed to any certified institute and that none of the other methods in which the case may legally be dealt with is suitable, the Children's Court may sentence the child to imprisonment and may order him to be sent to prison[19] [...]

Negligence 171

This means that if the offence is "serious" or that if the "child is so unruly or of such depraved character," that the child's act or disposition merits imprisonment, then instead of ordering the child to be sent to a Child Development Centre under section 34(1), the court can order the child to be imprisoned. However, this begets the question of what kinds of acts are so serious, or behaviour so depraved, that imprisonment is to be imposed?

R v W (RE),[20] which is a case from the Ontario Court of Appeal, is illuminating. In *W (RE)*, a 14-year-old lived with Douglas Moore, who dealt drugs and was a violent criminal convicted of a homicide, but was not the minor's father. In the fall of 2003, Moore suspected that Robert Grewal and Guiseppe Manchisi stole his drugs and money, and therefore, killed them. Then, in the minor's presence, Moore dismembered the bodies and, with the minor's help, placed them in containers, transported them to the Montreal area, and buried them in several locations. At trial, the court sentenced the minor to prison, which was permitted under section 39(1)(d) of the *YCJA*, due to the "exceptional" nature of the crime. The court said,

> When the act is so monstrous, when the consequences are so horrid, how can defence counsel request me not to give this young man a sentence, a stricter sentence, a jail sentence?
>
> I have therefore not the slightest hesitation. The monstrosity of this act, the horror, in spite of the fact that this accused was a young person, cannot be negatived by the fact that he was young and that he was under the influence of somebody else. A very strong influence. I therefore agree with the suggestion made by the Crown. [...]
>
> Presumably the offence that would trigger the use of custody [...] would be so exceptionally aggravated that custody was the only proportionate consequence that would hold the youth accountable through the imposition of just sanctions, thereby contributing to the long-term protection of the public

On appeal, the court added that an example of an exceptional circumstance meriting imprisonment is when the facts of a case are so shocking that they offend "widely shared community values."

Interestingly, the language of section 39(1) of the *YCJA* is similar to section 33(1) of the *Children Act*. This means that, in Bangladesh, criminal law permits a minor to be dealt with like an adult if the circumstances are so serious and severe that they offend "widely shared community values" (e.g. when a minor assists another in disposing of a dismembered corpse, or when a minor is the mastermind of detonating a bomb on a busy public railway killing thousands, or other analogous grounds).[21] Furthermore, I add that, after examining the totality of the case, the need for public safety, because of the heinous and violent nature of the offence, must outweigh the rehabilitative needs of the youth, and only then should he be imprisoned.

While I have deviated onto, and perorated on, criminal law, I have done so to demonstrate that a minor can be treated like an adult if circumstances

172   *Negligence*

require.[22] In tort law, it is not about whether the act is so serious that it offends "widely shared community values"; rather, it is about whether the minor was engaged in an activity common to adults. Though the questions are different, the similarity is that both tort and criminal law (statutorily permitted under section 33(1) of the *Children Act*) allow a minor to be treated like an adult.[23] For example, in *Ryan et al v Hickson et al*,[24] James Cummings, a 12-year-old, and Michael Hickson, a 14-year-old, were both held civilly liable for injuring Steven Ryan, who was a 9-year-old, due to their negligent operation of snowmobiles. Similar to *Rozell*, The court added that since the minors were engaged in an activity common to adults, the standard of care expected of them is the same as adults and endorsed the view of Allen Linden,

> Special rules for children make sense, especially when they are plaintiffs; however, when a young person is engaged in an adult activity, which is normally insured, the policy of protecting the child from ruinous liability loses its force. Moreover, when the rights of adulthood are granted, the responsibilities of maturity should also accompany them. In addition, the legitimate expectations of the community are different when a youth is operating a motor vehicle than when he is playing ball. As one American court suggested, juvenile conduct may be expected from children at play, but "one cannot know whether the operator of an approaching automobile [...] is a minor or adult, and usually cannot protect himself against youthful imprudence even if warned." Consequently, there has been a movement toward holding children to the reasonable man standard when they engage in adult activities. A more lenient standard for young people in the operation of motor vehicles, for example, was thought to be "unrealistic" and "inimical to public safety." When a society permits young people of 15 or 16, *Highway Traffic Act*, [...] the privilege of operating a lethal weapon like an automobile on its highways, it should require of them the same caution it demands of all other drivers.

As in, expecting the same standard of care from a minor engaged in an "adult activity" forces him to accept greater responsibility, and by holding him to this higher standard of care, the law tries to make society safer. To further explain, it is more sensible that the law imposes a higher standard of care on the minor engaged in an activity common to adults, as opposed to asking all of society to be more cautious because it would make life excessively cumbersome by asking an already careful society to be even more prudent.[25]

Thirdly, there are children that do not fall into either category (they are so little that they are incapable of perceiving risk or that they are minors who are not engaged in an activity common to adults), and therefore, the standard of care expected of them is that of other children of like age and intelligence.[26] For example, a 9-year-old child may not be expected to know

Negligence 173

that an iron left on with its soleplate facing the iron table could ignite a fire. However, if this child's intelligence is higher than that of an average 9-year-old, then he could be held liable. That is to say, a 9-year-old is usually in third or fourth grade, but if this child is in seventh grade due to his superior intelligence, then the law will presume that he has the capacity, which others of his age lack, to perceive risk, and therefore, he can be held liable.

Overall, it is best to not be alarmed if you are confused. It is easy to identify the group of children of tender years that the law does not hold liable. Slightly more difficult is the third category of children whose capacity to foresee risk is infinite, which means complex calculations must be done about their age, maturity, and intelligence before imposing liability. However, perhaps the most complex is imposing liability on the second group of children because it depends on whether they were involved in an "adult activity," in conjunction with considering their age, maturity, and intelligence. For example, is a 10-year-old, who is using a knife to cut apples, considered an activity common to adults; or, is a 12-year-old fixing a home's wiring with pliers considered an activity common to adults; or is a 13-year-old dragging luggage across the airport considered an activity common to adults?

While it *prima facie* seems that imposing liability on a minor is unpredictable, a closer look reveals that if the potential harm is substantial and grave, then the activity will be considered as one common to adults, and the child will be held to the same standard as an adult. As in, a 13-year-old dragging luggage across the airport, albeit negligently and injuring five people, will not be considered an "adult activity" because the potential injury is not substantial and grave. However, a 10-year-old using a knife to cut an apple or a 12-year-old fixing a home's wiring will be considered an activity common to adults because the possibility of injury is substantial and grave.

5.2 Reasonable person

At the beginning of this chapter, I mentioned that negligence is conduct that falls below the standard of care established by law to protect others from unreasonable risks of harm.[27] However, not every negligent conduct that injures another is actionable, as the injury may not have been caused by one's negligence. Moreover, as was identified in *Vaughan*, the standard against which the negligent actor's conduct is measured is known as the "reasonable person," who is a mystical creature, and if the reasonable person would have acted differently in similar circumstances than did the defendant, then the latter will be liable. However, this engenders the obvious question of who is the "reasonable person"?

5.2.1 Moral qualities and knowledge

Firstly, a reasonable person's moral qualities are always examined. As in, a person is allowed to do business to make a profit, and while it could be successful, his business imports a risk of harm to others.[28] For example,

174 *Negligence*

assume that a person transports goods from Dhaka to Chittagong, which involves operating multiple motor vehicles. Simply because this business is, or could be, dangerous, as there may be accidents that can injure or kill others, does not mean that he cannot pursue it, as nearly every activity involves some degree of risk.[29] Therefore, tort law is not concerned with every risk-creating activity, but rather, only those that create an *unreasonable risk of harm*.[30]

Secondly, knowledge, which is condition precedent to liability in negligence, is the awareness of the existence of a fact.[31] The concept of negligence presumes that either the person, (a) could foresee an unreasonable risk of harm, but acted without due care and injured another, or (b) could have envisioned it had he acted more reasonably.[32] As in, the law presumes that a reasonable person has knowledge that a knife could create an incision, or that a firearm discharges projectiles that can pierce human tissue and bones, or that a dog may bite and injure another, or that gasoline can accelerate a fire. Therefore, the notion that the actor could foresee harm depends on his knowledge of the attendant risks connected to the activity.[33] Essentially, this means that a reasonable person ought to know that he should not throw a knife towards a group of people because it may injure someone, and that he should be cautious so as not to inadvertently pull the trigger of a firearm, and that he should remain alert so that his pet dog does not bite another, and that he should not light a cigarette at a gas station.

Furthermore, the law is concerned with the knowledge the person had, or ought to have had, at the time he engaged in the conduct.[34] Consequently, a reasonable person knows, or ought to know, that he may fall if he runs on a wet floor, and therefore, should exercise caution to avoid hydroplaning and injuring himself.[35] However, though prudent and careful, if he sustains an injury, he could hold the person, who spilled the water, liable if the water was not clearly visible and if there was no conspicuously placed cautionary sign.[36]

Moreover, a reasonable person is expected to know the characteristics of the road he has frequented, including speed bumps, sharp turns, and other eccentric qualities. Therefore, if he is speeding and forgets of a sharp turn, it is no defence when he loses control, hits another vehicle, and injures the driver, to claim that he did not remember the turn or that he did not see the sign signalling the turn.[37] To further explain, if the government has placed visible signs of a sharp turn, then, regardless of a momentary lapse of attention, a reasonable person is expected to notice it, and if it is a road the person has used before, then the law demands that he remain more careful, as he is supposed to be aware of the turn. Additionally, a reasonable person is expected to be attentive of his surroundings. For example, if he is walking down the stairs, which do not have handrails, he is expected to avoid the edges so that he does not fall; or, if a fire alarm of a building is ringing, he is expected to evacuate the premises immediately.[38]

The memory of an adult is also considered in negligence cases because he is expected to remember everything that would otherwise create a mark on the reasonable person.[39] While the general rule is that a person cannot be forgetful,[40] he is exonerated if he is startled or if the grounds of his distraction are reasonable.[41] For example, imagine that as you are driving out of Mirpur DOHS, which is something you have done multiple times before, you collide with another vehicle because you did not stop at a speed bump. While the bump is not marked with luminescent paint, it is no defence that you forgot about it or that the city council should have painted over it because the reasonable person is expected to remember the speed bump, as it is on a road he has used multiple times before.

The reasonable person is also supposed to be knowledgeable about common things. For example, he is supposed to know, albeit not extensively and rudimentary knowledge shall suffice, of the laws of gravity, the principles of leverage, that smoke suffocates, water drowns, and fire burns.[42] Furthermore, every person is presumed to have knowledge regarding his own characteristics, such as, *inter alia*, his ability and capacity to lift heavy objects, the amount of space he occupies, and the equilibrium of his body.[43] Therefore, if an adult cannot swim, he should not dive into the deep end of the swimming pool, and if he does and injures himself, he cannot recover from the occupier unless there is a fundamental problem with the pool or there is a dearth of cautionary signs.

A person living in Bangladesh is supposed to be apprised of facts common to his community, and as society evolves, more knowledge and prudence is, and will be, demanded of the reasonable person. For example, he is to be familiar with the winter-fog in Bangladesh and a stray dog's propensity to bite.[44] Thence, even if the speed limit is 50 km/h, the reasonable person is supposed to drive under the limit if the fog impairs his vision, and if he injures another on the road, he cannot disclaim liability by alleging negligence on the part of the government for their failure to clear the fog.

Additionally, the reasonable person is supposed to be familiar with the proclivities of children[45] and the inherent dangers of common sports.[46] He is also supposed to know of the dangerous nature of electricity, revolving instruments, chemicals and gasoline; the inherent perils in common modes of travel, firearms, and the intoxicating effect of alcohol.[47] This means that a reasonable person should not touch an exposed electrical wire, or try to stop a revolving fan with his hands, or light a cigarette at a gas station, or consume alcohol to absolute inebriation, and if he does the aforesaid, he cannot claim compensation even if there is a lack of cautionary signs, as the danger and ramifications from doing so are obvious.

While the reasonable person, as we have discovered, is supposed to be knowledgeable about the regular activities of life, he is also required to be aware of the peculiar characteristics of his surroundings and trade. For example, it is imperative that, (1) the occupier notifies guests of unnoticeable dangers; (2) the landlord inform his tenants about the risks of the appliances he has provided; (3) the carrier, who carries passengers, discover and rectify defects of his vessel; and (4) the manufacturer know of the inherent dangers of his products and their processes.[48]

176 *Negligence*

A corollary of advances in science (or any field) is the discovery, and subsequent avoidance, of risk. Persons affected by scientific advancement should remain abreast such discovery because the failure to adhere to the newly discovered standard will warrant liability. That is to say, excusable conduct today may transform into negligence tomorrow, and therefore, the law dictates that the reasonable person remain vigilant and exercise more caution as necessary. For example, manufacturers were not held liable for selling chrome mordanted stockings, which caused ulceration, in the 1800s, as it was not reasonable for manufacturers to know of its deleterious effects;[49] however, today the lack of such knowledge amounts to negligence.[50]

5.2.2 *Skill*

Thirdly, in addition to moral qualities and knowledge, the reasonable person may also have skill, which is a superior ability, unbeknown to others in society, to undertake certain activities due to experience and training.[51] If he possesses skill, the standard of care expected of him would be like that of others with similar skills. For example, the reasonable person must operate his vehicle like other competent drivers, and the failure to do so – even on account of his minority status – will not displace liability.[52] Moreover, if he is a doctor or engineer, he will be held to the same standard as other doctors or engineers.[53]

If the reasonable person does not have a particular set of skills, but is involved in an activity that otherwise requires it, the standard of care expected of him is like that of others who have that skill. For example, if he is driving, but does not have a license or does not know how to drive, he will be judged as though he has a license and knows how to drive like other competent drivers. This also means that if he is practising medicine or engineering, he will be judged as though he has the knowledge of being a doctor or an engineer even if he has never gone to school to study that field of academia.[54]

The problem, however, arises when it concerns the liability of a beginner. For example, a 38-year-old, who has been driving since the age of 18, will have more driving-experience than a 19-year-old who has only been driving for two weeks; thus, is the novice's liability lesser because of his inexperience? While this issue is contentious, it is important to understand that the beginner, since he is involved in an "adult activity," will be treated like an adult, but the standard of care expected of him will be less than that which is expected of an experienced driver.[55] Therefore, regarding the novice, the question would be "would a reasonable person act similarly in similar circumstances"; whereas, in reference to the experienced-driver, it would be "would a reasonable person *who has similar experience* act similarly in similar circumstances".

It is not incorrect to assume that a person accumulates experience by doing the same activity repeatedly, and therefore, it would not be unreasonable to

Negligence   177

expect that the experienced person conduct himself in a more careful manner, which the beginner would perhaps be unable to do. Though this means that the beginner will not be punished for not having esoteric knowledge of a particular activity, he will be required to know that, for example, before turning 90° at an intersection, he must significantly reduce the speed of his vehicle, as this is so basic that every reasonable driver ought to know it, and not knowing it, regardless of experience, will merit liability.

5.2.3 Physical and mental characteristics

Fourthly, while the reasonable person test is objective, subjective elements, such as a person's physical, mental, and emotional characteristics, are evaluated. As in, if a person has a physical disability, the conduct expected of him would be like that of others with the same, or similar, disability, as it would be inexpedient and unjust to expect his conduct to be the same as, or similar to, others without the disability.[56] However, the consensus is that the person with the disability must take extra caution to counterbalance his infirmity – something that would otherwise not be required of the reasonable person.[57] Nonetheless, this does not mean that a blind man will be required to see, but that he must use his other faculties with greater vigilance.[58] Here, two examples are warranted. First, premised on contemporary technology, a blind man driving constitutes negligence, regardless of whether he used his other senses to a more heightened state of awareness. However, if the vehicle is a self-driving one and the blind man was seated at the driver's seat, then he is not negligent because he is a passenger in an automobile that is operated by a computer. Second, if the city is repairing its roads, it has a common law duty to post cautionary signs and cordon the area. If the city has done so, then a blind man who trips on a pothole and breaks his ankle will be unable to recover from the city, as he should have taken reasonable steps, such as walking with another person or using a stick as assistance, to minimize his injury.[59]

Since negligence presupposes a voluntary act, a person who injures another while asleep cannot be held negligent.[60] As in, during an episode of sleepwalking, if a person spills water on the floor, he will not be liable if someone subsequently slips and injures himself. However, if a person falls asleep while doing something, then he could be held liable in negligence because, firstly, sleep does not befall one without warning, and secondly, he failed to notice it. For example, if one is driving and has become somnolent, but instead of pulling over, he continues to drive, falls asleep, and injures another, then the driver can be held liable in negligence, as he understood, or ought to have understood, that he was falling asleep, and for his failure to adhere to the warning.[61]

Moreover, a person, who is driving (or is involved in any activity that can create an unreasonable risk of harm), could be liable in negligence for continuing to drive and injuring another even when he shows signs of a seizure, provided he has experienced the symptoms before.[62] Similarly, it is

178   *Negligence*

important to know that a person will not be liable if he has previously not experienced the symptoms, as it would be impractical to impose liability on one who does not have knowledge that a particular sign presages imminent danger. Additionally, a person who is voluntarily intoxicated, such as from the wilful consumption of alcohol and other drugs, can be found liable in negligence if he subsequently injures another.[63]

5.2.4 Age and sanity

Lastly, since I have already provided an exposition of the liability of minors and adults,[64] I shall eschew discussing the age of the reasonable person. Nonetheless, a person who is *non compos mentis* by reason of nature will not be judged to the same standard as one who is. As in, if a person is schizophrenic, or suffers from other medically recognized and diagnosed diseases of the mind, then holding him to the same standard as that of others who do not suffer from the same, or similar, diseases, would be indefensible and inexpedient. Therefore, the standard of care expected of them is the same as the conduct expected of others with the same, or similar, condition.[65]

5.3 Reasonable care

Bolton v Stone[66]

On 9 August 1947, Ms. Stone was standing outside of her house on 10 Beckenham Road, Cheetham Hall, when a cricket ball, which was hit by a batsman for six playing at the Cheetham Cricket Ground, hit her. People have been playing cricket at the stadium, which has a 7-foot fence surrounding it, since 1864 and residents moved nearby after 1910, when a proper road was built. While the exact number of times balls, which have been hit out of the stadium, is unknown, witnesses corroborated that it has not happened more than 6 times in 30 years. Nonetheless, for her injuries, Ms. Stone brings an action against the cricket club under negligence for their failure to take steps to avoid balls being hit out of the stadium. Dismissing her appeal, Lord Porter said,

> Undoubtedly, they knew that the hitting of a cricket ball out of the ground was a possible event, and, therefore, that there was a conceivable possibility that someone would be hit by it, but so extreme an obligation of care cannot be imposed in all cases. If it were, no one could safely fly an aeroplane or drive a motor car since the possibility of an accident could not be overlooked, and, if it occurred, some stranger might well be injured. Cases of that kind, however, pre-suppose the happening of an event which the flyer or driver desires to do everything possible to avoid, whereas the hitting of a ball out of the ground is an incident in the game and, indeed, one which the batsman would wish to bring about. In order that the act may be negligent there must be not only a reasonable possibility of

Negligence   179

its happening, but also of injury being caused. In the words of Lord Thankerton [...] in *Bourhill v Young*, the duty is to exercise, "[...] such reasonable care as will avoid the risk of injury to such persons as he can reasonably foresee might be injured by failure to exercise such reasonable care." [...]

It is not enough that the event should be such as can reasonably be foreseen. The further result that injury is likely to follow must also be such as a reasonable man would contemplate before he can be convicted of actionable negligence. Nor is the remote possibility of injury occurring enough. There must be sufficient probability to lead a reasonable man to anticipate it. The existence of some risk is an ordinary incident of life, even when all due care has been, as it must be, taken.

It must be remembered, and cannot too often be repeated, that there are two different standards to be applied. When one is considering whether an appeal should be allowed or not, the first is whether the facts relied on are evidence from which negligence can in law be inferred; the second is whether, if negligence can be inferred, those facts do constitute negligence. The first is a question of law on which the judge must actually or inferentially rule; the second, a question of fact on which they jury, if there is one, or, if not, the judge, as judge of fact, must pronounce. Both to some extent, but more particularly the latter, depend on all the surrounding circumstances of the case. In the present instance the learned trial judge came to the conclusion that a reasonable man would not anticipate that injury would be likely to result to any person as a result of cricket being played in the field in question and I cannot say that that conclusion was unwarranted. In arriving at this result I have not forgotten the view entertained by Singleton LJ that the appellants knew that balls had been hit out of the ground into the road, though on very rare occasions – six were proved in about thirty years – and it is true that a repetition might at some time be anticipated. Its happening, however, would be a very exceptional circumstance, the road was obviously not greatly frequented, and no previous accident had occurred, nor do I think that the respondent improves her case by proving that a number of balls were hit into Mr. Brownson's garden. It is danger to persons in the road, not to Mr. Brownson or his visitors, which is being considered. In these circumstances I cannot say that as a matter of law the decider of fact, whether judge or jury, must have come to the conclusion that the possibility of injury should have been anticipated. I cannot accept the view that it would tend to exonerate the appellants if it were proved that they had considered the matter and decided that the risks were very small and that they need not do very much. In such a case I can imagine it being said that they entertained an altogether too optimistic outlook. They seem to me to be in a stronger position if the risk was so small that it never even occurred to them.

180 *Negligence*

Notes

It seems as though *Bolton* allows one to inadvertently injure another with impunity. However, that is incorrect. As Lord Porter said, since people play cricket at the stadium, there is a probability that a ball could be hit out of the stadium and injure someone. Nonetheless, to impose liability under negligence, three factors must be met: firstly, the probability that a ball could be hit out of the stadium; and secondly, the likelihood and gravity of the incident (which, in our case, is the cricket ball leaving the stadium) injuring others. As in, simply because a ball could be hit out of the stadium does not mean that liability will be imposed on someone, but what is also required is a high probability of the likelihood and gravity of the injury. In other words, the higher the likelihood of the ball leaving the stadium and causing serious injury, the more likely it is that liability will be imposed.

While *Bolton* is silent on the third factor, it is implicit throughout the decision. In *United States v Carroll Towing Co*,[67] Justice Learned Hand propounded three factors, which has since become known as the "Hand Formula," and is widely used in cases involving negligence.[68] He said,

> Since there are occasions when every vessel will break from her moorings, and since, if she does, she becomes a menace to those about her, the owner's duty, as in other similar situations, to provide against resulting injuries is a functioning of three variables: (1) The probability that she will break away; (2) the gravity of the resulting injury, if she does; (3) the burden of adequate precautions. Possibly it serves to bring this notion into relief to state it in algebraic terms: if the probability be called P; the injury, L; and the burden, B; liability depends upon whether B is less than L multiplied by P: i.e., whether B less than PL.

To apply it to *Bolton*, we see it is not enough that, (1) there is a probability of a ball being hit out of the stadium (P), but what is also required is, (2) the likelihood of it injuring another, the gravity of the resulting loss (L), and (3) the burden placed on the defendant of taking precautionary measures (B).

Perhaps a mathematical equation of the formula will make it easier to understand. If P and L are greater than B, then liability will be imposed; and if P and L are less than B, then liability will not be imposed.[69] Or, in simpler terms,

- $PL > B$ = liability will be imposed;
- $PL < B$ = liability will not be imposed.

That is to say, if the probability of the ball leaving the stadium and the gravity of the injury (from the ball leaving the stadium) is greater than the burden of taking precautions, then liability will be imposed. Let us now apply this formula to *Bolton* and understand why liability was not imposed on anyone.[70]

Whenever cricket is being played at a stadium, there is a probability that a ball may be hit with so much force that it may leave the stadium (P). In *Bolton*, we see that balls have been hit out of the stadium once every 5 years, which is a low probability. Nonetheless, even if we assume that this is a high probability, we see that the loss (L), resulting from balls leaving the stadium, is trivial – e.g. broken windows of houses or someone wounded. Generally, a person's wound is not insignificant. However, in comparison to a game that has been played in the area for 46 years before residents moved in nearby (in addition to the burden of taking precautions), a significant injury would be multiple, and not just one, maiming injuries or deaths. As in, the gravity of the loss (injuries sustained), in addition to the probability of it happening (balls being hit out of the stadium), was not sufficient to merit liability.

Again, if we assume that balls being hit out the stadium once every 5 years is a high probability and that the injuries it caused are severe, we will nevertheless need to consider the burden, which is anything that is provided as consideration in exchange for something else, of taking precautions (B). Here, the question is "if the injury-causing activity is to be continued (e.g. cricket), what is the burden (in other words, what needs to be surrendered) on the keeper of the stadium or its players"?

Recall that in *Miller v Jackson*,[71] playing cricket at the Lintz Cricket Club (hereinafter "the Club") was not a nuisance because, (1) cricket was played there for 70 years before residents moved nearby; (2) the Club raised its fences to 15 feet to preclude balls from going out of the stadium; (3) of the 29,022 balls bowled between 1975 and 1976, only 5.3% of them went over the fence; and (4) of those 1,539 balls that were hit out of the stadium, they caused minor damage, such as broken windows or roof-tiles. While I briefly mentioned the Hand Formula when discussing *Miller*, it cannot be refuted that it is inherent in the decision, where we see that the burden of taking precautions was either, (a) financial (elevating the height of the Club's fences to 15 feet), which the Club had done, or (b) desist from playing cricket altogether.

Similarly, in *Bolton*, the burden was also either, (a) financial (constructing fences around its boundaries, which they had done), or (b) stop playing cricket entirely. Since the burden (B) was higher than the probability of occurrence (P) and the gravity of the loss (L), in both cases, neither an injunction nor damages were awarded. As in, in *Bolton*, the stadium had fences surrounding it, which is everything they could have done to prevent balls from leaving the stadium. However, in order to completely eliminate the risk of injury, which, as we will see later, is not necessary, the only other option was to stop playing cricket at the stadium altogether. This is too high a burden.

Let us use another example. Imagine you live at Mirpur DOHS at the intersection of Avenue 3 and Road 4, next to an empty field where sports are usually played. One day, you hear a window in your apartment shatter. You frantically rush to discover the cause and find that it happened because

182 *Negligence*

of a cricket ball, which was hit for six by a batsman. While we know from *Miller* that playing cricket at the field, which has been designated for sports, will not constitute nuisance, is it negligence? As we have learned from *Bolton*, it is not so long as Mirpur DOHS *Porishod* has done enough to ensure that balls, especially those hit for six, do not leave the field and injure someone or their property. As in, if the *Porishod* has constructed a fence, or any other device to prevent balls from leaving the field, then liability cannot be imposed on the batsman or *Porishod*.[72]

Moreover, as I have mentioned earlier, nearly every activity entails a degree of risk, which can injure others. However, the panacea cannot be to stop the activity altogether. For example, there is a high probability, and frequency, that driving can cause death, but this does not mean that a court, or the legislature, should prohibit driving, for if that were the case, life would become unduly burdensome. Nonetheless, the government has prescribed safety measures, for example, you must reach a particular age to get a driver's license, or that you must maintain the fitness of your vehicle, or that you must obey traffic rules. As in, even though there is a high probability of vehicles causing injury (P), which may result in death (L), since the burden of prevention (B) would be considerably higher than the probability of injury and the gravity of the loss, driving cannot, or should not, be prohibited.

Latimer v AEC Ltd[73]

On 31 August 1950, there was a tempest between 12:00 pm and 3:00 pm in Southall, London, England, which flooded AEC Limited's (hereinafter "AEC") premises. Unfortunately, the water mixed with an oily liquid, known as mystic, which was collected in channels on the floor of the building to cool the machines. When the water subsided, it left an oily film on the surface of the floor, causing it to become slippery. AEC tried to dry, and decrease the slipperiness of, the floor by spreading sawdust. However, the flood affected a greater area than the sawdust could cover, and therefore, AEC also posted signs warning employees of the slippery floor. Mr. Latimer, who was employed by AEC as a horizontal milling machine operator, began his shift around 7:45 pm. At about 8:45 pm, as he was lifting a barrel, which contained handbrake levers and was quite heavy, with the help of a trolley, he slipped, fell on the floor, and the barrel fell and crushed his left ankle. He then brought an action in negligence against AEC for failing to close the factory. Dismissing his appeal, the court said,

> A number of complaints of negligence and breach of duty are set out in the statement of claim, but so far as common law negligence is concerned I can find no suggestion that the factory should have been closed [...] On the issue of common law negligence, as now presented, the direction which should be given is not in doubt. It is to determine what action, in the circumstances which have been proved, would a reasonably prudent man have taken. The probability of a workman slipping is one matter which must be borne in mind, but it must be remembered

Negligence 183

that no one else did so. Nor does the possibility seem to have occurred to anyone at the time. It is true that after the event Mr. Milne, one of the respondents' witnesses, expressed the opinion that he would not have gone on to the floor in the condition in which it was and that it would be too dangerous to do so. But this was after the event, and, though he was the respondents' safety engineer and was present until late that night, it seems never to have occurred to him that there was any danger or that any further steps than those actually taken were possible, or required for the safety of the employees. The seriousness of shutting down the works and sending the night shift home and the importance of carrying on the work on which the factory was engaged are all additional elements for consideration, and without adequate information on these matters it is impossible to express any final opinion. Moreover, owing to the course taken at the trial, there is no material for enabling one to judge whether a partial closing of the factory was possible, or the extent to which the cessation of the appellant's activities would have retarded the whole of the work being carried on. In my view, in these circumstances, the appellant has not established that a reasonably careful employer would have shut down the works, or that the respondents ought to have taken the drastic step of closing the factory. [...]

There was such evidence in the present case since the respondents themselves proved that the flooding of their factory was unprecedented: that, owing to their system of partially open mystic drains, oil in such circumstances would, and did, escape over the factory floor: that in view of this state of affairs they put forty men on specially to lay down all the sawdust they had on the floors and passages: that they kept twenty-four volunteers on to continue the work of cleaning the floors and passages, but that they did not stop the work of the factory but allowed the night shift to come on duty. Now, although it is true that no questions were put in cross-examination to the respondents' witnesses suggesting that they ought to have closed the factory, the point was raised by the judge during the argument and no application was made for an adjournment, or for an amendment of the pleadings [...] I come to the conclusion that the conduct of the respondents can, at the highest, be said to have been an error of judgment in circumstances of difficulty and such an error of judgment does not, in my opinion, amount to negligence.

Notes

Similar to *Bolton*, the Hand Formula is inherent in this case. Since Latimer was the only employee to have been injured, the probability that others would was low (P), and the gravity of the loss was relatively unknown (L). However, it would not be unreasonable for an employer to assume that while one could be injured, it would not be permanent and would not result in death. Moreover, AEC asked forty of its employees to cover the slippery floor with sawdust and posted cautionary signs, which means they did everything they could to diminish the possibility of injury (B). However, Latimer's contention was that

184 *Negligence*

AEC is negligent for not eliminating the risk of injury entirely, which, unfortunately or otherwise, is too high a burden – on anyone.

Let us revisit the example of driving. While it can cause injuries and deaths, if the government prohibits driving, the burden placed on people would be excessively high and life would have to be reconstructed for society to function. Therefore, a person does not need to eliminate the possibility of injury; rather, they are only required to *diminish the risk of injury*. For example, if a company has been contracted to do repairs on a road beset with potholes, they do not need to cover the effected area with wooden or metal slabs to eliminate the risk of injury; rather, so long as they post cautionary signs, cordon, and illuminate the section where repairs are being made, the law will hold that the company has done enough to warn users of the risk of injury.[74] That is to say, so long as one has done enough to diminish the risk of injury, he will not be held liable for another's injury.[75]

Tomlinson v Congleton Borough Council[76]

Congleton Borough Council (hereinafter "Congleton") owned, occupied, and managed a public park, where a lake was artificially formed by flooding an old sand quarry. The lake had sandy beaches, which became a popular recreational destination, where, *inter alia*, yachting and sub-aqua diving were allowed. However, swimming was prohibited and signs reading, "Dangerous Water: No Swimming" were posted. Unfortunately, that did not deter swimmers and the possibility of injury became a concern for Congleton. Therefore, they began to landscape the beaches from where visitors swam in an attempt to discourage, and completely stop, swimming.

On 6 May 1995, shortly after work began, John Tomlinson ran into the lake, dived, and struck his head at the bottom of the quarry with great force, causing him to become tetraplegic. Afterwards, he brought proceedings against Congleton under negligence for breaching their common law duty of care, which was eventually appealed to the House of Lords. Finding for Congleton, the court said,

> In my view the danger and risk of injury from diving in the lake where it was shallow were obvious. That is my conclusion on the evidence in the case [...] an occupier is not under a duty to warn against a risk which is obvious. But, if I take a step further and say that the history showed some protection was required because of the attractions of the lake, then I would hold that the signs were reasonable and sufficient steps to give warning of the danger and to discourage persons from incurring the risk. It can be said that despite the signs people continued to go into the water. That was a decision which they were free to make: they could choose to accept the risk. I do not think that the defendants' legal duty to the claimant in the circumstances required them to take the extreme measures which were completed after the accident involving the fencing off of the areas where people went into the water and the planting of the beaches with trees. I should add that I reject

Negligence   185

the submission that by putting the warning signs on the beaches the defendants were inviting swimming elsewhere. That is lacking in realism. If the water was dangerous off the beaches, it was plainly at least as dangerous elsewhere [...]

In this case there was a risk of injury being suffered by anyone entering the water because of the dangers due to the state of the premises, the premises being constituted by the configuration and contents of this pond created as it was from a disused sand-extraction pit. There was a risk of injury through drowning because of the dangers, among others, of the effect of cold water, being caught in weed, being stuck in the mud or plunging unexpectedly into deep water. There was the risk of injury through diving because of the dangers of diving too steeply in shallow water or into an obstruction. There may have been risks of other injury from other dangers, e.g. Weil's disease. These risks of injury arose as soon as one entered the water because one did not know what danger lurked, or where it lay hidden. The exact nature of the hazard may not much matter in the particular circumstances of this case [...]

The second criterion to establish whether a duty is owed is provided by s 1(3)(b), namely that the occupier knows or has reasonable grounds to believe that the other person is in the vicinity of the danger concerned. Again this has not been in dispute. The minutes I have cited establish that and there is more to like effect. It is quite clear that the park was a very popular venue and despite all efforts to impose the ban on swimming, it was known to the defendants that many entered the water and were in the vicinity of the dangers concerned.

The third, and in this case crucial, requirement laid down by s 1(3) (c) [under the *Occupiers' Liability Act, 1957*] is whether the risk was one against which, in all the circumstances of the case, the occupiers might reasonably be expected to offer the trespasser some protection. Analyzing that, the protection is against any such risk as is referred to in sub-s (1), the risk, that is, of the trespasser suffering injury by reason of the dangers lurking in the mere. The protection we are looking for is 'some protection'. The question is whether *some* protection might reasonably be expected to be offered. The question is *not* whether *reasonable* protection is to be expected [...]

In discharge of the common duty of care owed to the visitors [...] the authorities placed prominently signs which forbade swimming and warned of the 'dangerous water'. In entering the water against that prohibition, the claimant made himself a trespasser to whom a different duty was now owed. If the words on the noticeboard 'NO SWIMMING' qualified the use he was permitted to make of the facility, do the other words above or below that, 'DANGEROUS WATER' constitute some protection against the risk of injury if the person decides to take a swim? I think that maybe too narrow a view of a warning notice which serves a composite purpose of turning a visitor into a trespasser and also warning him of a danger. But this case does not rest there. The misuse

186　*Negligence*

of the facility, the extent of the unauthorized swimming, the history of accidents and the perceived risk of fatality was noted and acted upon by the occupiers over many years. They did not, as may have been the fact in some of the other decided cases, treat the notice as sufficient to discharge any duty that might be owed. Here, the authorities employed rangers whose duty it was to give oral warnings against swimming albeit that this met with mixed success and sometimes attracted abuse for their troubles. In addition to the oral warnings, the rangers would hand out safety leaflets which warned of the variable depth in the pond, the cold, the weeds, the absence of rescue services, waterborne diseases and the risk of accidents occurring. It seems to me that the rangers' patrols and advice and the handing out of these leaflets reinforced the ineffective message on the sign and constituted 'some protection' in fact given and reasonably expected to be offered in the case [...]

The fact that during the defendants' management of the site three accidents had occurred to people swimming in the mere cannot of itself impose a duty of care since swimming in open stretches of water is often an inherently dangerous activity. It would only be if the number of accidents was significantly above the norm that any duty could arise and that would then be because it would be possible to conclude that there was a particular hazard in relation to the stretch of water (even if the hazard might not at first be easily identifiable). Likewise, the fact that a local authority may responsibly seek to deter or prevent swimming does not to my mind give rise to any duty to an individual member of the public or the public at large to take steps to prevent people swimming, unless there is a particular hazard (over and above the ordinary risks of swimming) about which the public should know.

I should add that, for myself, I would have reached the same conclusion even if the claimant had not conceded that he was a trespasser. I find it odd that if there is a general licence to the public to come to a park for leisure activities but there are notices which prohibit swimming, someone who enters the water intending to swim becomes a trespasser. At what point does he become a trespasser? When he starts to paddle, intending thereafter to swim? There was no evidence that Mr. Tomlinson in fact swam at all. He dived from a position in which swimming was difficult, if not impossible. I would be troubled if the defendants' duty of care differed depending on the precise moment when a swim could be said to have begun.

Notes

Again, the Hand Formula is implicit in *Tomlinson*. In fact, the unifying principle in *Bolton*, *Latimer*, and *Tomlinson* is the Hand Formula where the courts found that since the burden of taking precautions (B) was greater than the probability (P) and gravity of injury (L), the defendants were not liable. In *Tomlinson*, since Congleton had posted conspicuous prohibitory signs about swimming, it is sufficient to avoid liability, as the reasonable

Negligence 187

person should have noticed it. Additionally, as was discovered in *Latimer*, nobody is required to *eliminate the risk of injury* entirely; instead, so long as one has does enough to *diminish the risk of injury* (in this case, posting signs forbidding swimming), liability will not be imposed.[77]

Reading *Latimer* and *Tomlinson*, one might ask "what would happen if the injured party is illiterate, and therefore, unable to read the warning signs that would otherwise have cautioned him"? Recall from *Appleby v Erie Tobacco Co* that courts consider the characteristics of a neighbourhood before deciding whether an activity constitutes a nuisance.[78] Similarly, whether a sign is sufficient to warn visitors, or employees, of danger will depend on the characteristics of that particular area. For example, if the cautionary sign is visible and placed at a lake in Dhaka, it is reasonable to assume that visitors would have minimum literacy to understand its content, and therefore, the city will not be held liable. However, if it were placed at a remote lake in Khagrachari, Chittagong, where literacy is scant, then it would be reasonable to assume that visitors will not understand its content and that the city should do more than just placing cautionary signs to warn visitors. That is to say, similar to other areas of tort law, liability will depend on the facts and circumstances of each case.

The TJ Hooper[79]

Northern Barge Corporation (hereinafter "Northern Barge") owned and operated Barges 17 and 30 (collectively, hereinafter "barges"). They loaded the barges with coal, which belonged to New England Coal & Coke Company (hereinafter "New England Coal"), in Norfolk, Virginia, to transport it to New York. Upon leaving the dock at Virginia, the barges were towed by two tugboats – the Montrose and the Hooper, which were owned by H.N. Hartwell & Son Incorporated (hereinafter "Hartwell"). During the tow, a storm with gales caused the barges and the tugboats to capsize, resulting in the total loss of cargo. New England Coal brought an action against Northern Barge for the loss of their cargo, and Northern Barge brought an action against Hartwell for their failure to equip the tugboats with radios and claim that had they done so, they could have been informed about the storm and taken an alternative route. In fact, four other boats were on the same route and avoided the storm because of reliable radios. Imposing liability on Northern Barge and Hartwell, the court said,

> The wind began to freshen in the morning of the ninth and rose to a gale before noon; by afternoon the second barge of the Hooper's tow was out of hand and signalled the tug, which found that not only this barge needed help, but that the No. 30 was aleak. Both barges anchored and the crew of the No. 30 rode out the storm until the afternoon of the tenth, when she sank, her crew having been meanwhile taken off. The No. 17 sprang a leak about the same time; she too anchored at the Montrose's command and sank on the next morning after her crew also had been rescued. The cargoes and the tugs maintain that the barges were not fit for their service; the cargoes and the barges that the tugs

188 *Negligence*

should have gone into the Delaware Breakwater, and besides, did not handle their tows properly.

The evidence of the condition of the barges was very extensive, the greater part being taken out of court. As to each, the fact remains that she foundered in weather that she was bound to withstand. A March gale is not unusual north of Hatteras; barges along the coast must be ready to meet one, and there is in the case at bar no adequate explanation for the result except that these were not well-found. [...]

A more difficult issue is as to the tugs. [...]

The weather bureau at Arlington broadcasts two predictions daily, at ten in the morning and ten in the evening. Apparently there are other reports floating about, which come at uncertain hours but which can also be picked up. The Arlington report of the morning read as follows: "Moderate north, shifting to east and southeast winds, increasing Friday, fair weather tonight." The substance of this, apparently from another source, reached a tow bound north to New York about noon, and, coupled with a falling glass, decided the master to put in to the Delaware Breakwater in the afternoon. The glass had not indeed fallen much and perhaps the tug was over cautious; nevertheless, although the appearances were all fair, he thought discretion the better part of valour. Three other tows followed him, the masters of two of which testified. Their decision was in part determined by example; but they too had received the Arlington report or its equivalent, and though it is doubtful whether alone it would have turned the scale, it is plain that it left them in an indecision which needed little to be resolved on the side of prudence; they preferred to take no chances, and chances they believed there were. Courts have not often such evidence of the opinion of impartial experts, formed in the very circumstances and confirmed by their own conduct at the time.

Moreover, the "Montrose" and the "Hooper" would have had the benefit of the evening report from Arlington had they had proper receiving sets. This predicted worse weather; it read: "Increasing east and southeast winds, becoming fresh to strong, Friday night and increasing cloudiness followed by rain Friday." The bare "increase" of the morning had become "fresh to strong." To be sure this scarcely foretold a gale of from forty to fifty miles for five hours or more, rising at one time to fifty-six; but if the four tows thought the first report enough, the second ought to have laid any doubts. The master of the "Montrose" himself, when asked what he would have done had he received a substantially similar report, said that he would certainly have put in. The master of the "Hooper" was also asked for his opinion, and said that he would have turned back also, but this admission is somewhat vitiated by the incorporation in the question of the statement that it was a "storm warning," which the witness seized upon in his answer. All this seems to us to support the conclusion of the judge that prudent masters, who had received the second warning, would have found the risk more than the exigency warranted; they would have been amply vindicated by what followed. To be sure the barges would, as we have said, probably have withstood the gale, had they been well found; but a master is not justified in putting his tow to every test which she will survive, if she be fit. There is a zone in which proper caution will avoid putting her capacity to the proof; a coefficient of prudence that he should not disregard. [...]

They did not, because their private radio receiving sets, which were on board, were not in working order. These belonged to them personally, and were partly a toy, partly a part of the equipment, but neither furnished by the owner, nor supervised by it. It is not fair to say that there was a general custom among coastwise carriers so as to equip their tugs. One line alone did it; as for the rest, they relied upon their crews, so far as they can be said to have relied at all. An adequate receiving set suitable for a coastwise tug can now be got at small cost and is reasonably reliable if kept up; obviously it is a source of great protection to their tows. Twice every day they can receive these predictions, based upon the widest possible information, available to every vessel within two or three hundred miles and more. Such a set is the ears of the tug to catch the spoken word, just as the master's binoculars are her eyes to see a storm signal ashore. Whatever may be said as to other vessels, tugs towing heavy coal laden barges, strung out for half a mile, have little power to maneuver, and do not, as this case proves, expose themselves to weather which would not turn back stauncher craft. They can have at hand protection against dangers of which they can learn in no other way.

Notes

While *The TJ Hooper* was decided 15 years before *Carroll Towing*, the Hand Formula is nevertheless present.[80] However, and more importantly, it is pertinent to note that even though it was not the industry standard to equip tugboats with radio receiving sets in the late 1920s, the court said that it was negligent to not have them, as it was an inexpensive way to avoid loss to cargo and life.[81] As in, the court said that the industry standard does not always determine whether reasonable care is used, or what constitutes reasonable in the circumstances; rather, it is the court that dictates what is reasonable in a particular industry.

For example, imagine a vehicle without wipers. Even if the industry does not require vehicles to be equipped with them, it would be no defence to a driver, who is driving through torrential rainfall, to claim that his vehicle did not have wipers, and therefore, he should not be liable for colliding with another car because he was not able to see him. Or alternatively, imagine a factory, which has 5,000 workers on the floor at any given time, without clearly outlined fire exits. Even if the government does not mandate them, it would be negligent on the part of management to not have visible fire exits. Or alternatively, if a manufacturer releases a television with silver, instead of copper, wires to conduct electricity, and it catches fire and scalds

190 *Negligence*

the customer because of its relatively low thermal resistance, it would be no defence to the manufacturer to claim that the industry uses silver wires, and therefore, he did nothing wrong. However, in each case, the other option – equipping the vehicle with wipers, clearly marking fire exits, and using copper wires, respectively – was safer than what the industry did, and, as we know, if the cost of the safety precaution is less than the probability and gravity of loss, then the courts will impose liability, which essentially would establish new industry standards.

ter Neuzen v Korn[82]

Dr. Gerald Korn is an obstetrician and gynaecologist and has been practising artificial insemination (hereinafter "AI") since 1974. Kobe ter Neuzen is a nurse who participated in 35 AI procedures, administered by Dr. Korn, from 1981 to 21 January 1985. Unfortunately, on that day, ter Neuzen became infected with human immunodeficiency virus (hereinafter "HIV"), which Dr. Korn did not warn her about, as a result of the procedure. However, Dr. Korn did not warn ter Neuzen about the risk of infection because it was not known to the medical world until 1986.[83] Ter Neuzen brought an action in negligence against Dr. Korn for the failure to warn her. Finding for Dr. Korn, the court said,

> It is well settled that physicians have a duty to conduct their practice in accordance with the conduct of a prudent and diligent doctor in the same circumstances. In the case of a specialist, such as a gynaecologist and obstetrician, the doctor's behaviour must be assessed in light of the conduct of other ordinary specialists, who possess a reasonable level of knowledge, competence and skill expected of professionals in Canada, in that field. A specialist, such as the respondent, who holds himself out as possessing a special degree of skill and knowledge, must exercise the degree of skill of an average specialist in his field [...]
>
> It is also particularly important to emphasize, in the context of this case, that the conduct of physicians must be judged in the light of the knowledge that ought to have been reasonably possessed at the time of the alleged act of negligence. As Denning L.J. eloquently stated in *Roe v Ministry of Health*, [...] "[w]e must not look at the 1947 accident with 1954 spectacles." That is, courts must not, with the benefit of hindsight, judge too harshly doctors who act in accordance with prevailing standards of professional knowledge. This point was also emphasized by this Court in *Lapointe* [*v Hôpital Le Gardeur*] [...]
>
> > [C]ourts should be careful not to rely upon the perfect vision afforded by hindsight. In order to evaluate a particular exercise of judgment fairly, the doctor's limited ability to foresee future events when determining a course of conduct must be borne in mind. Otherwise, the doctor will not be assessed according to the norms of the average doctor of reasonable ability in the same circumstances, but rather will be held accountable for mistakes that are apparent only after the fact. [...]

The evidence of standard practice on the first aspect of the case was based entirely on the state of knowledge required of the reasonable practitioner in 1985 and it would have been equally impossible for a jury acting judicially to have found that, given the state of knowledge, the reasonable practitioner ought to either have discontinued AI or warned the patients of the risk. It having been admitted that the respondent continued AI and did not warn his patients, there was no issue concerning his conformity with the standard practice. [...]

It is generally accepted that when a doctor acts in accordance with a recognized and respectable practice of the profession, he or she will not be found to be negligent. This is because courts do not ordinarily have the expertise to tell professionals that they are not behaving appropriately in their field. In a sense, the medical profession as a whole is assumed to have adopted procedures which are in the best interests of patients and are not inherently negligent. As L'Heureux-Dubé J. stated in *Lapointe*, in the context of the Quebec *Civil Code* [...]

> Given the number of available methods of treatment from which medical professionals must at times choose, and the distinction between error and fault, a doctor will not be found liable if the diagnosis and treatment given to a patient correspond to those recognized by medical science at the time, even in the face of competing theories. As expressed more eloquently by André Nadeau in "La responsabilité médicale" [...]

In *The Law of Torts* [...] Professor Fleming observed the following with respect to the role of standard practice [...]

> *Conformity* with general practice, on the other hand, usually dispels a charge of negligence. It tends to show what others in the same "business" considered sufficient, that the defendant could not have learnt how to avoid the accident by the example of others, that most probably no other practical precautions could have been taken, and that the impact of an adverse judgment (especially in cases involving industry or a profession) will be industry-wide and thus assume the function of a "test case." Finally, it underlines the need for caution against passing too cavalierly upon the conduct and decision of experts. [...]

With respect to the medical profession in particular, Professor Fleming noted [...]

> Common practice plays its most conspicuous role in medical negligence actions. Conscious at once of the layman's ignorance of medical science and apprehensive of the impact of jury bias on a peculiarly vulnerable profession, courts have resorted to the safeguard of insisting that negligence in diagnosis and treatment (including disclosure of risks) cannot ordinarily be established without the aid of expert testimony or in the

192 *Negligence*

teeth of conformity with accepted medical practice. However there is no categorical rule. Thus an accepted practice is open to censure by a jury (nor expert testimony required) at any rate in matters not involving diagnostic or clinical skills, on which an ordinary person may presume to pass judgment sensibly, like omission to inform the patient of risks, failure to remove a sponge, an explosion set-off by an admixture of ether vapour and oxygen or injury to a patient's body outside the area of treatment. [...]

It is evident from the foregoing passage that while conformity with common practice will generally exonerate physicians of any complaint of negligence, there are certain situations where the standard practice itself may be found to be negligent. However, this will only be where the standard practice is "fraught with obvious risks" such that anyone is capable of finding it negligent, without the necessity of judging matters requiring diagnostic or clinical expertise.

Notes

While *The TJ Hooper* told us that courts determine industry standards and whether its practices are in conformity with what is expected of a reasonable person, *ter Neuzen* says that if the issue is technical, then it is the industry, and not the courts, that will determine the correct standard, unless the standard is "fraught with obvious risks." As in, courts know that they cannot be well-informed of all matters, particularly those that require special training and knowledge, such as, *inter alia*, engineering and medicine. Therefore, if a practice is common among doctors and it does not display obvious risks, then courts will not impose liability even if the practice injures the patient. However, today, with advances made in medical science, a doctor is supposed to know that there is a risk of HIV-transmission through AI, and if the doctor does not inform the patient of this risk, then he can be held liable in negligence. Or, if the doctor has informed the patient of the risk, but then transfuses HIV-infected blood, then he can be held liable in negligence for his failure to first test the blood.

Earlier, I mentioned that scientific knowledge advances and those affected by newly discovered information should remain aware of the discovery because the failure to do so could be tantamount to negligence. In *ter Neuzen*, evidence suggests that Dr. Mascola reported the risk of transmission of STDs through AI 2 years before ter Neuzen was infected with HIV. This means that, premised on what I said earlier, Dr. Korn is supposed to be liable in negligence. However, Dr. Mascola's article was printed on a journal that, albeit prestigious, was not widely circulated. Think of it this way, you discovered the cure to cancer, but published your findings on ogrish.com, which is a now defunct website that did not generate many visitors anyway; or, you published it on your Instagram account, which is private and you only have three followers, none of whom are doctors, and therefore, not concerned about your discovery. That is to say, while scientific knowledge advances and people affected by its progress should remain aware of it,

Negligence 193

people can be informed only if the information is made public through a widely circulated medium, as otherwise, it would be unjust to impose liability because people cannot be expected to read every literature.

Overall, premised on *The TJ Hooper* and *ter Neuzen*, what needs to be understood is that the industry standard may not always be sufficient and courts will impose liability if the defendant's conduct was not reasonable under the circumstances. However, if the industry is one that requires special training and esoteric knowledge, then courts presume that the procedure used was reasonable, unless it is "fraught with obvious risks."

5.4 *Res Ipsa Loquitur*

In some, albeit rare, circumstances, an accident raises an inference of negligence. As lawyers know, a plaintiff is never obligated to provide direct evidence (though it helps) to prove his case, as circumstantial evidence shall suffice. Therefore, and as we will see below, based on common sense and observation, it occasionally happens that a "thing tells its own story."[84] For example, experience tells us that a crane does not collapse or a bale does not fall off of a truck unless some actor was negligent somewhere.[85]

Or, imagine that a person, who is male and married, is driving (let us refer to him as "driver 1") towards Chittagong, and another, who is also male and married, is driving (let us refer to him as "driver 2") towards Dhaka. Neither driver has any passengers on board. At 3:00 am, their vehicles collide at the centre of the road on N1 and both drivers are killed immediately. Unfortunately, there are no witnesses to, or video footage of, the accident. While *The Road Transport Act*, 2018[86] will try to impose liability, imprisonment will not be considered as both parties are dead. However, the wife of each driver wants damages; yet, which driver is liable – driver 1, driver 2, or both?

Baker v Market Harborough Industrial Society Ltd[87]

Two vehicles, which did not have any passengers, collided in the middle of a two-way street and killed both drivers. Unfortunately, there was a dearth of evidence about who may be at fault. Nonetheless, since the decedents were married, their wives wanted damages from the owner of the vehicle of the other driver. Holding both drivers equally liable, the court said,

> It is pertinent to ask, what would have been the position if there had been a passenger in the back of one of the vehicles who was injured in the collision? He could have brought an action against both vehicles. On proof of the collision in the centre of the road, the natural inference would be that one or other or both were to blame. If there was no other evidence given in the case, because both drivers were killed, would the court, simply because it could not say whether it was only one vehicle that was to blame or both of them, refuse to give the passenger any compensation? The practice of the courts is to the contrary. Every day, proof of the collision is held to be sufficient to call on the two

194   *Negligence*

defendants for an answer. Never do they both escape liability. One or other is held to blame, and sometimes both. If each of the drivers were alive and neither chose to give evidence, the court would unhesitatingly hold that both were to blame. They would not escape simply because the court had nothing by which to draw any distinction between them.

So, also, if they are both dead and cannot give evidence, the result must be the same. In the absence of any evidence enabling the court to draw a distinction between them, they must be held both to blame, and equally to blame.

Now take this case where there is no passenger, but both drivers are killed. The natural inference, again, is that one or other was, or both were, to blame. The court will not wash its hands of the case simply because it cannot say whether it was only one vehicle which was to blame or both. In the absence of any evidence enabling the court to draw a distinction between them, it should hold them both to blame, and equally to blame.

It is very different from a case where one or other only is to blame, but clearly not both. Then the judge ought to make up his mind between them [...] But when both may be to blame, the judge is under no such compulsion and can cast the blame equally on each.

So much seems clear on principle that it is unnecessary to go further; but I would like to say that the evidence to my mind makes it much more likely that both were to blame than that one only was to blame.

Notes

Res ipsa loquitur, which means "the thing speaks for itself," allows a court to deduce a defendant's negligence, but it does not incontrovertibly prove that the defendant *was* negligent. As in, while the literal translation is "the thing speaks for itself," it does not mean that the cause of an injury automatically proves that the defendant is guilty; rather, it simply means that in the absence of evidence to the contrary, the court can draw an inference that the defendant was probably at fault and apportion liability accordingly.[88] For example, in *Children Charity Bangladesh Foundation v The Government of Bangladesh*, the High Court Division of the Supreme Court of Bangladesh outlined its three essential requirements: (i) the thing that causes the injury must be under the control of the other party, (ii) the nature of the accident must be such that it would not have happened without negligence, and (iii) there must be no other evidence for the injury.[89]

As we see in *Baker*, (1) since the vehicles collided in the middle of a two-way street, (2) with no witnesses to testify about the accident, and (3) there was a lack of evidence, it is more probable than not that both parties were at fault. Therefore, in this case, the owner of each vehicle was the defendant, similar to how the wife of each driver was the plaintiff. However, if the vehicles crashed on one side of the road and killed both drivers, then the inference would have been that the driver, who was on the wrong side, was at fault. Moreover, simply because both drivers were dead and no witness,

Negligence   195

or evidence, was found, does not mean that neither driver can be held liable. Recall that the purpose of tort law is to compensate a victim for his injury. That is to say, to place him in the position he would have been in had the tort not been committed. This means that not compensating the wives of the decedents, from an accident that occurred in the middle of the street, simply due to a lack of evidence, would flout the objective of, and be an affront to, tort law.[90]

Additionally, it is important to recognize that both parties were held equally liable because the accident happened in the "middle of a two-way street." If the road were one-way, then the person who was driving in the wrong direction would have been held liable even if the accident happened in the middle of the road and killed both drivers; that is, for *res ipsa loquitur* to apply, there must be sufficient evidence for a reasonable person to conclude a posteriori that, on the whole, it is more probable than not that the accident was caused by negligence.[91]

Let us revisit the example used earlier in this section. Imagine that while the accident happened in the middle of N1, killing both drivers, driver 2's vehicle shows pronounced tire-marks on the road, which is evidence that he tried to either slow down or bring his vehicle to a complete stop. Driver 1's vehicle, on the other hand, demonstrates no such evidence. Though both drivers will be held liable, it will not be apportioned equally. Since driver 2 tried to slow his vehicle down, it is just that his liability is reduced and the preponderance of liability is imposed on driver 1, as he did not take reasonable care to slow down. All of this to say that the doctrine of *res ipsa loquitur* does not operate in a vacuum and will consider circumstantial evidence when determining liability in the absence of concrete evidence.

Ybarra v Spangard et al[92]

On 28 October 1939, Joseph Ybarra consulted Dr. Tilley who diagnosed his condition as appendicitis and arranged an appointment for an appendectomy, which was to be performed by Dr. Lawrence Spangard. At the operating room, Dr. Reser adjusted Mr. Ybarra for operation by pulling his body to the head of the operating table and placing him against two hard objects (near his shoulders). He then administered anaesthesia, whereby Mr. Ybarra lost consciousness. When he woke up, he felt an acute pain halfway between his neck and right shoulder, whose sequela became paralysis. Mr. Ybarra then consulted Dr. Wilfred Clark, who, based on an X-Ray, concluded that the area of diminished sensation was caused by trauma between his neck and right shoulder. For a second opinion, Mr. Ybarra also consulted Dr. Fernando Garduno, who said that the source of the injury was traumatic and not pathological. Armed with this information, Mr. Ybarra then brought proceedings against Dr. Spangard and others under negligence. Finding for Mr. Ybarra, the court said,

> The doctrine of *res ipsa loquitur* has three conditions: "(1) the accident must be of a kind which ordinarily does not occur in the absence of someone's negligence; (2) it must be caused by an agency or

196 *Negligence*

instrumentality within the exclusive control of the defendant; (3) it must not have been due to any voluntary action or contribution on the part of the plaintiff." [...]

The present case is of a type which comes within the reason and spirit of the doctrine more fully perhaps than any other. The passenger sitting awake in a railroad car at the time of a collision, the pedestrian walking along the street and struck by a falling object or the debris of an explosion, are surely not more entitled to an explanation than the unconscious patient on the operating table. Viewed from this aspect, it is difficult to see how the doctrine can, with any justification, be so restricted in its statement as to become inapplicable to a patient who submits himself to the care and custody of doctors and nurses, is rendered unconscious, and receives some injury from instrumentalities used in his treatment. Without the aid of the doctrine a patient who received permanent injuries of a serious character, obviously the result of someone's negligence, would be entirely unable to recover unless the doctors and nurses in attendance voluntarily chose to disclose the identity of the negligent person and the facts establishing liability. [...]

The condition that the injury must not have been due to the plaintiff's voluntary action is of course fully satisfied under the evidence produced herein; and the same is true of the condition that the accident must be one which ordinarily does not occur unless someone was negligent. We have here no problem of negligence in treatment, but of distinct injury to a healthy part of the body not the subject of treatment, nor within the area covered by the operation. The decisions in this state make it clear that such circumstances raise the inference of negligence, and call upon the defendant to explain the unusual result. [...]

The argument of defendants is simply that plaintiff has not shown an injury caused by an instrumentality under a defendant's control, because he has not shown which of the several instrumentalities that he came in contact with while in the hospital caused the injury; and he has not shown that any one defendant or his servants had exclusive control over any particular instrumentality. Defendants assert that some of them were not the employees of other defendants, that some did not stand in any permanent relationship from which liability in tort would follow, and that in view of the nature of the injury, the number of defendants and the different functions performed by each, they could not all be liable for the wrong, if any. [...]

Every defendant in whose custody the plaintiff was placed for any period was bound to exercise ordinary care to see that no unnecessary harm came to him and each would be liable for failure in this regard. Any defendant who negligently injured him, and any defendant charged with his care who so neglected him as to allow injury to occur, would be liable. The defendant employers would be liable for the neglect of their employees; and the doctor in charge of the operation would be

Negligence   197

liable for the negligence of those who became his temporary servants for the purpose of assisting in the operation.

Notes

Since Ybarra never complained of pain in the area between his neck and right shoulder before the operation, and since the side-effect of an appendectomy is not paralysis of the right arm, and since the paralysis was not congenital, but the result of trauma (as confirmed by two doctors), then in the absence of contrary evidence, an inference can be drawn that he was injured while unconscious. That is to say, as the plaintiff was unconscious, he cannot *directly* prove that he was injured during the operation; or, in other words, the guilt of the defendant.[93] However, if he can adduce evidence, which he has done, that (1) he did not experience any pain before the operation, and (2) the paralysis was the result of trauma, and not congenital, then the only logical explanation is that he suffered the injury *while he was unconscious*. Essentially, this means that he has *indirectly* proven the guilt of the defendant by eliminating other possibilities of injury.[94]

However, if the two doctors Ybarra consulted said that his paralysis was congenital, then the doctors would not be found liable because it would become evident that they did not breach their duty of care owed to him. As in, *res ipsa loquitur* is not an interloper; rather, she is a wise spectator and will intervene only when other possible explanations have been eliminated.[95] To further explain, the above excepted, there is nothing more an unconscious patient can do to prove guilt of the defendant, and as such, it is more probable than not that the doctors, or anyone who had custody of Ybarra while he was unconscious, were negligent.[96]

Overall, it should be noted that *res ipsa loquitur* does not ask the defendant to prove his innocence; rather, once the plaintiff has adduced evidence that the only reasonable explanation of his injury is the negligence of the defendant, then a tactical burden is placed on him to refute the evidence. Only if the defendant is unable to present evidence to the contrary will the court infer that the plaintiff's injury was caused by the defendant's negligence.

5.5 Duty of care

Donoghue v Stevenson[97]

On 26 August 1928, Mrs. Donoghue visited the Wellmeadow Café, which was owned by Mr. Francis Minghella, at Paisley, Renfrewshire, Scotland, with her friend, Mrs. Mary M'Alister. Mrs. M'Alister ordered a pear and ice for herself and an ice-cream float, which is a mixture of ice cream and a soft drink or flavoured syrup (in this case, it was ginger beer), for Mrs. Donoghue. Mr. Minghella brought over a tumbler of ice cream and poured ginger beer on it from a brown, opaque bottle. Mrs. Donoghue had a bit of the ice cream float, and when Mrs. M'Alister poured the rest of the ginger beer onto Mrs. Donoghue's tumbler, the remnants of a decomposed

198 *Negligence*

snail floated out of the bottle. Upon seeing the snail, Mrs. Donoghue began complaining of abdominal pain, consulted a doctor on 29 August, and was admitted to the Glasgow Royal Infirmary on 16 September. She was diagnosed with shock and severe gastroenteritis. Mrs. Donoghue then brought proceedings against Mr. David Stevenson, who was the manufacturer of the ginger beer, for breach of duty of care. Holding Mr. Stevenson liable, the court said,

> The sole question for determination in this case is legal. Do the averments made by the pursuer in her pleadings, if true, disclose a cause of action? [...] The question is whether the manufacturer of an article of drink sold by him to a distributor, in circumstances which prevent the distributor or the ultimate purchaser or consumer from discovering by inspection any defect, is under any legal duty to the ultimate purchaser or consumer to take reasonable care that the article is free from defect likely to cause injury to health. I do not think a more important problem has occupied your Lordships in your judicial capacity, important both because of its bearing on public health and because of the practical test which it applies to the system under which it arises. [...]
>
> In the present case we are not concerned with the breach of the duty; if a duty exists, that would be a question of fact which is sufficiently averred and for present purposes must be assumed. We are solely concerned with the question whether, as a matter of law in the circumstances alleged, the defender owed any duty to the pursuer to take care.
>
> It is remarkable how difficult it is to find in the English authorities statements of general application defining the relations between parties that give rise to the duty. The Courts are concerned with the particular relations which come before them in actual litigation, and it is sufficient to say whether the duty exists in those circumstances. The result is that the Courts have been engaged upon an elaborate classification of duties as they exist in respect of property, whether real or personal, with further divisions as to ownership, occupation, or control, and distinctions based on the particular relations of the one side or the other, whether manufacturer, salesman or landlord, customer, tenant, stranger, and so on. In this way it can be ascertained at any time whether the law recognizes a duty, but only where the case can be referred to some particular species which has been examined and classified. And yet the duty which is common to all the cases where liability is established must logically be based upon some element common to the cases where it is found to exist. To seek a complete logical definition of the general principle is probably to go beyond the function of the judge, for the more general the definition the more likely it is to omit essentials or to introduce non-essentials. [...]
>
> At present I content myself with pointing out that in English law there must be, and is, some general conception of relations giving rise to a duty of care, of which the particular cases found in the books are

Negligence   199

but instances. The liability for negligence, whether you style it such or treat it as in other systems as a species of 'culpa,' is no doubt based upon a general public sentiment of moral wrongdoing for which the offender must pay. But acts or omissions which any moral code would censure cannot, in a practical world, be treated so as to give a right to every person injured by them to demand relief. In this way rules of law arise which limit the range of complainants and the extent of their remedy. The rule that you are to love your neighbour becomes in law, you must not injure your neighbour; and the lawyer's question, Who is my neighbour? receives a restricted reply. You must take reasonable care to avoid acts or omissions which you can reasonably foresee would be likely to injure your neighbour. Who, then, in law, is my neighbour? The answer seems to be – persons who are so closely and directly affected by my act that I ought reasonably to have them in contemplation as being so affected when I am directing my mind to the acts or omissions which are called in question. [...]

If your Lordships accept the view that this pleading discloses a relevant cause of action, you will be affirming the proposition that by Scots and English law alike a manufacturer of products, which he sells in such a form as to show that he intends them to reach the ultimate consumer in the form in which they left him, with no reasonable possibility of intermediate examination, and with the knowledge that the absence of reasonable care in the preparation or putting up of the products will result in an injury to the consumer's life or property, owes a duty to the consumer to take that reasonable care.

Notes

Donoghue is a landmark case that upended, and forever changed, product liability under tort law.[98] Before 1932, a consumer was allowed to bring proceedings against a manufacturer for the *sale* of defective goods. This means a *contractual relationship* was required between parties. For example, in *Winterbottom v Wright*,[99] Mr. Winterbottom was employed by the Postmaster General to drive a mail coach from Hartford to Holyhead. The Postmaster General also employed Mr. Wright to maintain and keep the coach "fit, proper, safe, and secure." Unfortunately, Mr. Winterbottom was injured when the coach broke apart. While he brought an action against Mr. Wright and provided cogent evidence demonstrating negligence on his part in failing to maintain the coach, the court held that since there was no contract between Mr. Winterbottom and Mr. Wright, the latter cannot be held liable.

Similarly, in *Mullen v Barr & Co*,[100] John and Francis Mullen drank ginger beer, but found the taste to be rancid. When they poured the contents of the bottle into a glass, they discovered dead mice inside their bottles and became sick. They then brought an action against the manufacturer of the ginger beer. However, the court ruled against them and said that the manufacturer can be held liable by the ultimate consumer only if, (1) there was a contract between the consumer and the manufacturer; or (2) the product

200 *Negligence*

was inherently dangerous, such as a bomb, and this characteristic was withheld from the consumer. Therefore, since John and Francis were not in a contractual relationship with the manufacturer and since ginger beer is not inherently dangerous, they received no compensation.[101]

In *Donoghue*, Mrs. Donoghue was not in a contractual relationship with the manufacturer; rather, and for the sake of simplification, the equation of contracts was the following: (1) Mrs. M'Alister was in a contract with Wellmeadow Café (as she was the one who paid the bill), and (2) Wellmeadow Café was in a contract with the manufacturer. As in, Mrs. Donoghue was a third party and, similar to *Winterbottom* and *Mullen*, is supposed to be barred from bringing litigation against the manufacturer. However, the court entertained her complaint, flouted precedence, and imposed liability on the manufacturer propounding, and relying on, the "neighbour principle."

For reference, I quote again the seminal passage by Lord Atkin:

> The rule that you are to love your neighbour becomes in law, you must not injure your neighbour; and the lawyer's question, Who is my neighbour? receives a restricted reply. You must take reasonable care to avoid acts or omissions which you can reasonably foresee would be likely to injure your neighbour. Who, then, in law, is my neighbour? The answer seems to be – persons who are so closely and directly affected by my act that I ought reasonably to have them in contemplation as being so affected when I am directing my mind to the acts or omissions which are called in question.

A person owes a duty of care to his neighbour, which consists of a responsibility to not injure him.[102] As in, one must abstain from doing, or not doing, anything that can harm his neighbour. For example, if you live in an apartment building at Gulshan, your actions, or omissions, cannot harm those nearby; that is, if you spill oil on the landing of the second floor, and the tenant of the fifth floor slips on the oil and injures himself, then your action (spilling oil), or inaction (failing to clean up the spill), has injured your neighbour and you can be liable in negligence. However, would you be accountable if the injured party was not a tenant, but a *visitor*?

According to Lord Atkin, *anyone* can be your neighbour if your actions, or omissions, are capable of harming them;[103] that is, a neighbour, in the legal sense, is different from a neighbour in the social context. This means that a neighbour can be a person who is geographically far away. As in, if you live in Dhaka, Bangladesh, your neighbour can be a person who lives in Ottawa, Ontario, Canada. For example, imagine you have a factory in Gazipur, Bangladesh, where you manufacture canisters of aerosol and export them to Bali, Indonesia, which is approximately 4,470 kilometres away. However, none of the canisters contain a label warning users that it is flammable and that it must be kept away from direct sunlight. If a consumer buys the aerosol and places it in direct sunlight, which causes it to explode

Negligence 201

and injure him, then you, as the manufacturer, can be held liable under negligence for your failure to warn him of its inherent danger.

Essentially, *Donoghue* tells us that a contract is no longer required to bring an action against a blameworthy manufacturer. Again, to use the example above, though there is no contract between you and the consumer in Indonesia (the contract the consumer entered into was with the retailer from where he bought the aerosol, and the contract you entered into was with an importer in Indonesia, who probably entered into a separate contract with the retailer to supply the aerosol), since your action, or omission, is capable of harming him, you have, in law, become his neighbour and you owe him a duty of care. Therefore, you must now be careful so that your actions, or inactions, do not harm him, and if they do, then liability can be imposed on you under negligence for breaching that duty.[104]

However, simply because *Donoghue* expanded the scope of liability by introducing the neighbour principle does not mean that everyone can be held liable because they are your neighbour. In any proceeding brought under negligence, the first question courts ask is "does the defendant owe the plaintiff a duty of care," and if so, then the second question is "did the defendant breach that duty of care"? Remember that one only owes a duty of care to his neighbour, or to any person who can be affected by his actions, and if no duty is owed, then he is not liable under negligence. This means that, *inter alia*, a roommate owes a duty of care to his other roommates, a tenant to other members of the building, a driver to others on the road, and a manufacturer to the ultimate consumer. However, if a 7-month pregnant woman injures herself and her foetus while cooking, and the baby suffers from cerebral palsy thereafter when delivered prematurely, is the mother liable to the baby who was a foetus at the time of the injury?

Dobson (Litigation Guardian of) v Dobson[105]

On 14 March 1993, Cynthia Dobson, who was in the 27th week of her pregnancy, was driving her husband's vehicle towards Moncton in a snowstorm. Unfortunately, she lost control of her vehicle and struck oncoming traffic. Ryan Dobson, who was a foetus at the time of the accident, was injured *in utero* and delivered by Caesarean section later the same day. However, because of the injuries he sustained, Ryan suffers from permanent physical and mental injuries and has cerebral palsy. His maternal grandfather, and litigation guardian, Gerald Price, then launched a claim against Mrs. Dobson to recover money from Mr. Dobson's insurers, which insured him against damage caused by negligence of drivers of his motor vehicle. The court recognized that the relationship between Mrs. Dobson and Mr. Price was not acrimonious; rather, this claim was primarily about receiving compensation to pay Ryan's medical bills. Nonetheless, not holding the insurance company liable, the court said,

> Although increased medical knowledge makes the consequences of certain behaviour more foreseeable, and facilitates the establishment of a

202 *Negligence*

causative link in negligence suits, public policy must also be considered. Significant policy concerns militate against the imposition of maternal tort liability for prenatal negligence. These relate primarily to (1) the privacy and autonomy rights of women and (2) the difficulties inherent in articulating a judicial standard of conduct for pregnant women.

First and foremost, for reasons of public policy, the Court should not impose a duty of care upon a pregnant woman towards her fetus or subsequently born child. To do so would result in very extensive and unacceptable intrusions into the bodily integrity, privacy and autonomy rights of women. It is true that Canadian tort law presently allows a child born alive and viable to sue a third-party for injuries which were negligently inflicted while *in utero* [...] However, of fundamental importance to the public policy analysis is the particularly unique relationship that exists between a pregnant woman and the fetus she carries.

Pregnancy represents not only the hope of future generations but also the continuation of the species. It is difficult to imagine a human condition that is more important to society. From the dawn of history, the pregnant woman has represented fertility and hope. Biology decrees that it is only women who can bear children. Usually, a pregnant woman does all that is possible to protect the health and well-being of her fetus. On occasion, she may sacrifice her own health and well-being for the benefit of the fetus she carries. Yet it should not be forgotten that the pregnant woman – in addition to being the carrier of the fetus within her – is also an individual whose bodily integrity, privacy and autonomy rights must be protected.

The unique and special relationship between a mother-to-be and her fetus determines the outcome of this appeal. There is no other relationship in the realm of human existence which can serve as a basis for comparison. It is for this reason that there can be no analogy between a child's action for prenatal negligence brought against some third-party tortfeasor, on the one hand, and against his or her mother, on the other. The inseparable unity between an expectant woman and her fetus distinguishes the situation of the mother-to-be from that of a negligent third-party.

The unique relationship between a pregnant woman and her fetus is so very different from the relationship with third parties. Everything the pregnant woman does or fails to do may have a potentially detrimental impact on her fetus. Everything the pregnant woman eats or drinks, and every physical action she takes, may affect the fetus. Indeed, the fetus is entirely dependent upon its mother-to-be. Although the imposition of tort liability on a third party for prenatal negligence advances the interest of both mother and child, it does not significantly impair the right of third parties to control their lives. In contrast to the third-party defendant, a pregnant woman's every waking and sleeping moment, in essence, her entire existence, is connected to the fetus she may potentially harm. If a mother were to be held liable for prenatal

Negligence 203

negligence, this could render the most mundane decision [...] subject to the scrutiny of the courts.

Is she to be liable in tort for failing to regulate her diet to provide the best nutrients for the fetus? Is she to be required to abstain from smoking and all alcoholic beverages? Should she be found liable for failing to abstain from strenuous exercise or unprotected sexual activity to protect her fetus? Must she undertake frequent safety checks of her premises in order to avoid falling and causing injury to the fetus? There is no rational and principled limit to the types of claims which may be brought if such a tortious duty of care were imposed upon pregnant women.

Whether it be considered a life-giving miracle or a matter of harsh reality, it is the biology of the human race which decrees that a pregnant woman must stand in a uniquely different situation to her fetus than any third-party. The relationship between a pregnant woman and her fetus is of fundamental importance to the future mother and her born alive child, to their immediate family and to our society. So far as the fetus is concerned, this relationship is one of complete dependence. As to the pregnant woman, in most circumstances, the relationship is marked by her complete dedication to the well-being of her fetus. This dedication is profound and deep. It affects a pregnant woman physically, psychologically and emotionally. It is a very significant factor in this uniquely important relationship. The consequences of imposing tort liability on mothers for prenatal negligence raise vastly different considerations, and will have fundamentally different results, from the imposition of such liability on third parties. [...]

Whether it be in the household, on the roadways, or in the workplace, the imposition of a duty of care upon a pregnant woman towards her fetus or subsequently born child could render that woman liable in tort, even in situations where her conduct could not possibly affect a third-party. A mother could be held liable in tort for negligent acts or defaults, which occurred while she was pregnant and alone, and which subsequently caused damages to her born alive child. This could include the careless performance of household activities – such as preparing meals, carrying loads of laundry, or shovelling snow – while alone in the home. It could include the negligent operation of any motor vehicle – be it for personal, family or work-related purposes – even if no third-party could possibly be affected. A mother who injured her fetus in a careless fall, or who had unreasonable lapse of attention in the home, at work or in the roadways, could potentially be held liable in tort for the damages suffered by her born alive child. The imposition of tort liability in those circumstances would [...] undermine the privacy and autonomy rights of women. [...]

The imposition by courts of tort liability on mothers for prenatal negligence would restrict a pregnant woman's activities, reduce her autonomy to make decisions concerning her health, and have a negative

204 *Negligence*

impact upon her employment opportunities. It would have a profound effect upon every woman, who is pregnant or merely contemplating pregnancy, and upon Canadian society in general. Any imposition of such tort liability should be undertaken, not by the courts, but by the legislature after careful study and debate.

Moreover, the imposition of tort liability in this context would carry psychological and emotional repercussions for a mother who is sued in tort by her newborn child.

Notes

Recall that I mentioned earlier that at any time a tort case is filed under negligence, the first question the courts ask is "does the defendant owe the plaintiff a duty of care." The answer depends, to a large extent, on whether the parties were sufficiently close such that one party's actions, or inactions, can harm the other. In *Dobson*, the court said, "There is no other relationship in the realm of human existence which can serve as a basis for comparison" and that there is an "inseparable unity" between a pregnant woman and her foetus, which means the relationship between an expectant mother and her foetus is sufficiently close, as "[e]verything the pregnant woman does or fails to do may have a potentially detrimental impact on her fetus."[106] Essentially, this means that a pregnant woman owes a duty of care to her foetus.

Since the first question has been affirmatively answered, the second question is "did the defendant breach that duty of care." It is apodeictic that Mrs. Dobson did as she drove negligently and injured her foetus. This means that Ryan Dobson was supposed to be able to recover money from the insurance company because his mother was liable. However, that was not the case because, before imposing liability, courts ask a third question, and that is, "are there any policy reasons to negate or limit that duty?"[107] Here, the court decided against imposing liability on expectant mothers and said that if such a burdensome duty is to be imposed, it should be done by the legislature after deliberation and debate. While the relationship between a pregnant woman and the foetus is immensely close (or is of "inseparable unity"), imposing a duty on her towards her foetus would unduly and unjustifiably curtail her autonomy, as nearly every activity she does would then become scrutinized by courts, and this responsibility is one that courts are not willing to impose.[108]

For example, imagine that a 7-month pregnant woman is cooking in the kitchen. As she reaches for a can of mushrooms on the top-shelf, she slips and falls, which injures her foetus. Unfortunately, the subsequently born child suffers from cerebral palsy as a result of the injury. Should the child be allowed to bring an action against his mother for negligence during pregnancy? Alternatively, what if the same woman was walking up the stairs, fell, and injured the foetus who now suffers from a permanent physical impairment. Can the child bring an action against his mother for

Negligence 205

negligence? Thankfully, Alberta's *Maternal Tort Liability Act*[109] is illuminating, which stipulates,

> A mother may be liable to her child for injuries suffered by her child on or after birth that were caused by the mother's use or operation of an automobile during her pregnancy if, at the time of that use or operation, the mother was insured under a contract of automobile insurance evidenced by a motor vehicle liability policy.

Therefore, to answer the questions posed, no. It is also important to recognize that the *MTLA* imposes liability on a pregnant woman only if she is *negligent while driving*. This means that no other activity carried on negligently will make her liable to her foetus. Moreover, the *MTLA* also limits a mother's liability and says,[110]

> A mother's liability under section 4 is limited to the amount of insurance money payable under contracts of automobile insurance indemnifying the mother that the child can recover as a creditor under section 579 of the *Insurance Act*.

Essentially, common law's position is that while there is "inseparable unity" between a pregnant woman and her foetus, it will not impose a duty of care on her towards her foetus because of the restrictions it may impose on her liberty, and therefore, it has left that task to the legislature.[111] However, imagine that the woman fell, injured her abdominal area, and an X-Ray reveals that the foetus suffered trauma to the head, which doctors say will lead to cerebral palsy. While we know that the mother cannot be held negligent by the foetus, can she discontinue the pregnancy because she does not want to give birth to a child with a disability?

Dobson meets the *Penal Code* at a critical and interesting junction. Section 312 stipulates,[112]

> Whoever voluntarily causes a woman with child to miscarry, shall, if such miscarriage be not caused in good faith for the purpose of saving the life of the woman, be punished with imprisonment of either description for a term which may extend to three years, or with fine, or with both; and, if the woman be quick with child, shall be punished with imprisonment of either description for a term which may extend to seven years, and shall also be liable to fine.
>
> Explanation: A woman who causes herself to miscarry, is within the meaning of this section.

This means that abortion is a criminal offence in Bangladesh unless it is done to save the life of the mother.[113] In other words, if carrying the pregnancy poses a risk to the mother's health, she may terminate it. As in, if *Dobson* happened in Bangladesh and instead of giving birth to Ryan, Mrs.

206 *Negligence*

Dobson terminated her pregnancy after the accident because continuing the pregnancy may imperil her health, then she would not be charged with a criminal offence. However, if any other reason for the abortion is provided, then Mrs. Dobson could be criminally charged.

Nonetheless, it is important to understand that *Dobson* is not about abortion (even though it is not illogical that the question of abortion may arise); rather, it is about whether an expectant mother owes a duty of care to her foetus. One scenario asks whether a pregnant woman can terminate her pregnancy without fear of penalty, while the other asks whether she can be held liable in negligence by her child who was injured *in utero*. Therefore, if *Dobson*, or a similar case, arises in Bangladesh, I anticipate that courts would, and *should*, rule similarly.

Duval et al v Seguin et al[114]

At about 11:30 pm on 16 February 1969, Mr. Gaetan Duval was driving his car on Highway 34 in Ontario, Canada, which runs north to south (between Hawkesbury and Vankleek Hill). In his vehicle were Rosemary (his wife), Carol (his 2-year-old child), Huguette (his 19-year-old child), Maurice Duval (Mr. Duval's brother), Therese (Mr. Maurice Duval's wife and hereinafter "Mrs. Duval"), and Pierre (Mr. Maurice and Mrs. Therese Duval's 3-year-old son). Mrs. Duval was 31-weeks pregnant. As they approached an intersection, a vehicle driven by Mr. Gerard Seguin, whose wife and three kids were on board, crashed into Mr. Duval's vehicle. The collision destroyed the Duval-vehicle's headlights, and shortly thereafter, another vehicle, driven by Mr. Jean-Claude Blais, collided with Mr. Duval's vehicle. Both accidents injured passengers inside Mr. Duval's vehicle and evidence suggests that he was not at fault for either accident.

In the second accident, Mrs. Therese's pelvis was broken, and therefore, she was carefully monitored at the hospital. The foetus did not move for three days after the accident, and on 9 March 1969, Mrs. Therese gave birth prematurely to Ann Duval. At 6 months of age, Ann was examined and the doctor said that her progress was slow and that the suture, which ran from the front of her head to the back, was closing abnormally fast. She was 2 months behind normal development. On 15 June 1970, Ann's head was small and elongated, her gait was not normal, and her progress in talking was slow. Later that year, it was discovered that her IQ was between 60 and 70 and that it is highly improbable that she will ever be able to complete secondary school. It then becomes evident that Ann's disabilities resulted from the second accident, for which she brought an action against Mr. Blais. Finding for Ann, the court said,

> By the civil law, generally speaking, a child *en ventre sa mere* was considered as alive when to do so was for its benefit. In *Montreal Tramways Co v Leveille*, [...] an appeal from Quebec and in which the civil law was therefore applicable, a child *en ventre sa mere* was injured by the fault of the defendant [...] Two months later the child was born with club feet which, in the facts, was held to be attributable

Negligence 207

to injuries received in the accident and the defendant was held liable [...] In *Pinchin et al, N.O. v Santam Ins Co Ltd*, [...], the civil law was reviewed, including the *Leveille* case. After discussing the authorities, civilian, American and others, Hiemstra, J held that a child could recover damages for brain injury caused by the fault of the defendant while the plaintiff was *en ventre sa mere*.

In *Montreal Tramways Co v Leveille*, [...] Lamont, J said:

> If a child after birth has no right of action for prenatal injuries, we have a wrong inflicted for which there is no remedy, for, although the father may be entitled to compensation for the loss he has incurred and the mother for what she has suffered, yet there is a residuum of injury for which compensation cannot be had save at the suit of the child. If a right of action be denied to the child it will be compelled, without any fault on its part, to go through life carrying the seal of another's fault and bearing a very heavy burden of infirmity and inconvenience without any compensation therefor. To my mind it is but natural justice that a child, if born alive and viable, should be allowed to maintain an action in the courts for injuries wrongfully committed upon its person while in the womb of its mother. [...]
>
> There were two other matters to which our attention was called; the first was that cases similar to the present one must have arisen many times in the past, but that no decided case (or at most only one) has been found in which the child's right of action for pre-natal injuries has been maintained. The paucity of decided cases is far from conclusive, and may be largely accounted for by the inevitable difficulty or impossibility of establishing the existence of a causal relation between the fault complained of and the injury to the child. With the advance in medical science, however, that which may have been an insuperable difficulty in the past may now be found susceptible of legal proof. [...]

Ann's mother was plainly one of a class within the area of foreseeable risk and one to whom the defendants therefore owed a duty. Was Ann any the less so? I think not. Procreation is normal and necessary for the preservation of the race. If a driver drives on a highway without due care for other users it is foreseeable that some of the other users of the highway will be pregnant women and that a child *en ventre sa mere* may be injured. Such a child therefore falls well within the area of potential danger which the driver is required to foresee and take reasonable care to avoid.

In my opinion it is not necessary in the present case to consider whether the unborn child was a person in law or at which stage she became a person. For negligence to be a tort there must be damages. While it was the foetus or child *en ventre sa mere* who was injured, the damages sued for are the damages suffered by the plaintiff Ann since birth and which she will continue to suffer as a result of that injury. [...]

208   *Negligence*

To refuse to recognize such a right would be manifestly unjust and unreasonable. In my opinion, and for the reasons I have tried to formulate, such a refusal would not be consonant with relevant legal principles as they have developed and have been applied in the last 50 years. Under the doctrine of *M'Alister (or Donoghue) v Stevenson*, [...] and the cases cited, an unborn child is within the foreseeable risk incurred by a negligent motorist. When the unborn child becomes a living person and suffers damages as a result of prenatal injuries caused by the fault of the negligent motorist the cause of action is completed. A tortfeasor is as liable to a child who has suffered prenatal injury as to the victim with a thin skull or other physical defect. [...]

Notes

While *Dobson* tells us that a pregnant woman is not liable to her foetus for prenatal injuries caused by her negligence, *Duval* tells us that injuries a child suffers *en ventre sa mere*, because of a third party's negligence, is actionable. The principle is clear – a pregnant woman is not liable for negligence to her foetus because imposing liability would unjustifiably curtail her autonomy. However, this would not be the case for a third party, as the burden placed on him is not something in excess of what is already expected of him by law.

It is important to understand two things. First, as was said in *Donoghue*, people must act reasonably so that they do not injure their neighbours, and one's neighbour is anyone that can be affected by his actions or omissions. That is to say, if you are driving, anyone, which can be another driver, passenger, pedestrian, or vendor, who can be affected by your actions, or omissions, is your neighbour, and you owe a duty of care to them. This means that Blais' neighbours were others on the road, such as the Duval and Seguin families.

Second, if liability, arising from a breach of a duty of care, is imposed on a party for injuries he causes a child *en ventre sa mere*, on whom is this duty more cumbersome – (a) a pregnant woman, or (b) a third party? The correct answer is the former.[115] As was said in *Dobson*,

Is [a pregnant woman] to be liable in tort for failing to regulate her diet to provide the best nutrients for the fetus? Is she to be required to abstain from smoking and all alcoholic beverages? Should she be found liable for failing to abstain from strenuous exercise or unprotected sexual activity to protect her fetus? Must she undertake frequent safety checks of her premises in order to avoid falling and causing injury to the fetus? There is no rational and principled limit to the types of claims which may be brought if such a tortious duty of care were imposed upon pregnant women. [...]

Whether it be in the household, on the roadways, or in the workplace, the imposition of a duty of care upon a pregnant woman towards her fetus or subsequently born child could render that woman liable in tort, even in situations where her conduct could not possibly affect a third-party. A mother could be held liable in tort for negligent acts or defaults, which occurred while she was pregnant and alone, and which subsequently caused damages to her born alive child. This could include the careless performance of household activities – such as preparing meals, carrying loads of laundry, or shovelling snow – while alone in the home. It could include the negligent operation of any motor vehicle – be it for personal, family or work-related purposes – even if no third-party could possibly be affected. A mother who injured her fetus in a careless fall, or who had unreasonable lapse of attention in the home, at work or in the roadways, could potentially be held liable in tort for the damages suffered by her born alive child. The imposition of tort liability in those circumstances would significantly undermine the privacy and autonomy rights of women.

There should be no doubt that holding a pregnant woman liable in negligence for injuring her foetus is significantly more burdensome on her than holding a third party liable for injuring another's foetus. If the former were imposed, it would be tantamount to imprisoning her to a bedroom, as her slightest neglect would otherwise become actionable. However, the latter does not demand something in addition to what is already expected of him by law; that is, since a person owes a duty of care to his neighbour, he must already remain careful so as not to injure his neighbour. Therefore, imposing a duty of care on him does not require that he exercise *extra caution* around a pregnant woman, and does not demand that he does not cook, or shovel snow, or carry loads of laundry. Essentially, this means that his life does not become overly burdensome if a duty of care, towards a foetus, is imposed on him. The same cannot be said to be true for a pregnant woman.[116]

Renslow v Mennonite Hospital[117]

In October 1965, Emma Murphy (as she then was) was admitted to Mennonite Hospital, where she was treated by Dr. Hans Stroink. On 8 and 9 October, Emma was transfused 500 cubic centimetres of blood, which the hospital was in control of choosing, each day. Emma's blood type is A-RH negative. Unfortunately, the blood transfused was A-RH positive, which sensitized her blood. Neither Emma nor the hospital knew of the sensitization and it had no adverse effect on her. Then, in December 1973, Emma Renslow was pregnant and was asked to do a routine blood test, which revealed the sensitization of her blood. The doctors quickly diagnosed that the life of the foetus was in jeopardy, and therefore, on 25 March 1974, Emma was hospitalized, labour was induced, and she gave birth to Leah Ann Renslow prematurely. Since Emma's blood was sensitized, Leah Ann was born jaundiced, required a complete exchange transfusion of blood, and suffers from permanent damage to her nervous system and brain. Therefore, Emma brings an action for herself, and on behalf of Leah Ann, against the hospital

210 *Negligence*

for their negligence in transfusing the wrong type of blood, for which they both suffered injuries. Finding in their favour, the court said,

> The basic understanding of Rh-negative and Rh-positive effects upon hemolytic disease of the newborn has been a medical fact since the 1940's [...]. It has long been known that sensitization occurs in 90% of Rh-negative women who have received multiple transfusions of Rh- positive blood [...] and that about 85% of white Americans and a higher percentage of [African Americans] and Chinese are Rh-positive [...]. It has been likewise long known that the Rh-positive fetus of an Rh-negative woman previously sensitized is "at high risk." [...] Thus, it has been pointed out that "it must be an absolute rule that Rh-positive blood is never transfused to an Rh-negative female who is below the age of menopause." [...] For these reasons, routine Rh typing has been established practice since at least 1961. [...]
>
> In the case at bar, the wrongful conduct took place prior to plaintiff's conception; the plaintiff at the time of the conduct was in no sense a separate entity to whom the traditional duty of care could be owed. Plaintiff herein asks us to reexamine our notions of duty, and to find, in essence, a contingent prospective duty to a child not yet conceived but foreseeably harmed by a breach of duty to the child's mother. [...]
>
> We reaffirm the utility of the concept of duty as a means by which to direct and control the course of the common law. But examples of changing notions of legal duty in the area of products liability, as well as the progressive expansion of duty in prenatal cases already documented, demonstrate that duty is not a static concept.
>
> This court has long recognized that a duty may exist to one foreseeably harmed though he be unknown and remote in time and place. [...]
>
> The cases allowing relief to an infant for injuries incurred in its pre-viable state make it clear that a defendant may be held liable to a person whose existence was not apparent at the time of his act. We therefore find it illogical to bar relief for an act done prior to conception where the defendant would be liable for this same conduct had the child, unbeknownst to him, been conceived prior to his act. We believe that there is a right to be born free from prenatal injuries foreseeably caused by a breach of duty to the child's mother.
>
> The extension of duty in such a case is further supported by sound policy considerations. Medical science has developed various techniques which can mitigate or, in some cases, totally alleviate a child's prenatal harm. In light of these substantial medical advances it seems to us that sound social policy requires the extension of duty in this case. [...]
>
> While we are aware that there may be similar potential for perpetual claims arising from chemical accident or long-term radiation exposure [...] the case at bar is clearly distinguishable. The damage alleged is not, by its nature, self-perpetuating, nor is the plaintiff a remote descendant. We feel confident that when such a case is presented, the judiciary will

Negligence 211

effectively exercise its traditional role of drawing rational distinctions, consonant with current perceptions of justice, between harms which are compensable and those which are not.

Notes

While *Dobson* tells us that a pregnant woman cannot be held liable in negligence for injuring her foetus, and *Duval* tells us that a third party can be held liable in negligence for injuring another's foetus, *Renslow* goes a step further and tells us that a third party can be held liable in negligence for injuring another's foetus even if the action causing injury happened before the foetus was conceived. However, this begets the question of "why should a person be found liable to a fetus when the injuring action happened before he was conceived (as in, before he developed a heart, pulse, and a brain; or, in other words, before he was a foetus)"?

The court first examined the history of similar cases and found that actions of this nature were generally denied. For example, in *Dietrich v Northampton*, a woman who was 4- to 5-month pregnant slipped on a defect in the highway and subsequently gave birth to her child prematurely at the hospital. Unfortunately, the child was not sufficiently developed in fetal life to survive. When she brought an action in negligence, it was dismissed because the child died after birth.[118] Then, in *Allaire v St. Luke's Hospital*, a pregnant woman was injured by the hospital when she was receiving treatment, and after she gave birth, the child suffered permanent injuries as a result of the hospital's negligent treatment of the woman. While an action was brought on behalf of the child against the hospital, the court found for the hospital because it held that an action could not be maintained by a person who, at the time of the injury, was not a person separate from the mother.[119]

The trend of impunity, however, shifted in 1946 when, in *Bonbrest v Kotz*, the court said that a child who suffers injury *in utero* can hold a third party liable in tort because the unborn child is a separate person, from the mother, from the moment of conception.[120] Then, in *Amann v Faidy*, the court said that a third party can be held liable for injuring a child *in utero* if the injury happened when the uterus was sufficiently viable to survive outside of the mother's womb.[121] Both cases allowed the recovery of monetary compensation because the child died after birth as a result of the injuries he sustained *in utero*. It was then in *Rodriquez v Patti* that the court held that a child who was injured *en ventre sa mere* by a third party can hold the latter liable even if the injury does not result in the child's death.[122]

While history exhibits the intransigence of courts, it does demonstrate that, with the passage of time, courts overturned their own decisions and began recognizing the right of a foetus to hold a third party liable in negligence. This is not uncommon, as law and society exist in a symbiotic relationship and a change in one brings about a change in the other.[123] However, this does not mean that courts will overturn all of their decisions, or strike down fundamental provisions of legislation, simply because time

212 *Negligence*

has passed. I cannot envision a future when the Supreme Court of Bangladesh will strike down section 300, which is murder, of the *Penal Code*, for to do so would precipitate the country into chaos; or, a time when bigamy, which is prohibited under section 494 of the *Penal Code*, is legalized.[124] As in, rights and duties that are fundamental for the proper functioning of civilized life will not be changed, but ancillary rights (e.g. mother's duty to foetus, third party's duty to foetus, or abortion resulting from the victim of rape even if it does not harm the woman's health) can be changed, or if they already have, will remain constant for the foreseeable future.

Haynes v G Harwood & Son[125]

Mr. Bird was an employee of G Harwood & Son (hereinafter "Harwood"). On 24 August 1933, he went to Quiney's Wharf, Rotherhithe, England, on duty with a two-horse carriage, which was owned by Harwood, to unload goods. Once done, Mr. Bird needed to collect a receipt from the owners of the wharf. However, out of consideration to the owners, who wanted to unload more goods from other carriages, instead of leaving the carriage on the wharf, he brought it to Paradise Street, kept it there, and went back to the wharf to collect the receipt. The carriage was equipped with a chain, which operated as a drag on its rear wheels when properly fastened. However, Mr. Bird did not use the chain when he parked the carriage on Paradise Street. While Mr. Bird was away, two boys approached the carriage and one of them threw a stone at the horses, which – perhaps out of fear – caused them to run.

Mr. Haynes, who was a police constable, on duty and at the police station, saw the horses running towards a woman and a group of children. Realizing that they were in danger, he ran to the scene and interposed himself between the horses and the woman and children to try to control the horses. He was eventually successful. However, in the process, he injured himself when one of the horses fell on him, for which he brought an action against Harwood for negligence. Ruling in Haynes' favour, the court said,

> It is said that the plaintiff is in law without remedy. I should say, before dealing with the reasons given for that contention, that it would be a little surprising if a rational system of law did not provide, in the circumstances stated, any remedy for a F bravo man who had received his injuries through the original default of the defendants' servant. If the matter had concerned this case alone, and we had not dealt with some dicta in other cases, I should almost have been content to say that I agreed with the admirable judgment of the trial judge, but I do not think I ought to deal with it in that short way.
>
> With regard to the defences put forward, it was said, first, that there was no evidence of negligence on the part of the defendants' driver. Secondly, that, assuming some evidence of negligence, the accident happened through the intervention of some consciously acting persons between the wrongful conduct of the defendants' driver and the accident which resulted in the injuries from which the plaintiff suffered, and in respect of which he claims damages. As frequently happens

when precision of thought is not very helpful, this point was put into the language of Latin terms. It was said that here I there was a *novus actus interveniens*, and that by the law of this country once a *novus actus interveniens* is established the chain of causation between the cause of the accident and the damage is broken and the claim of the plaintiff cannot be sustained. The third point was that, quite apart from that question and independently of it – although it is very difficult to separate the second and third points – the plaintiff took on himself the risk which he ran, and that, therefore, he cannot recover because the damage he I suffered was the result of his own act. That, again, was put into the Latin phrase *volenti non fit injuria*. [...]

What is the negligence complained of here? It seems to me that counsel for the plaintiff was right in describing it as a failure to use reasonable care for the safety of others who were lawfully using the highway in which this van with the two horses was left unattended. I have no doubt that anyone, and still more a policeman, using the highway for the purpose of stopping a runaway horse, and thereby preventing serious accidents and possibly loss of life, is a person within the category of those lawfully using the highway. Accordingly, I think the first point fails. It does not follow that in all circumstances it ought to be held to be negligence to leave horses unattended in a highway; all the facts of the case must be considered. What, to me, makes it quite clear that the defendants' servant was guilty of a want of reasonable care in leaving his horses unattended is that this is a crowded street in which a great many people and a good many children are likely to be at the time when the horses were left and before the defendants' servant could get back to them. [...] Be that as it may, the neighbourhood was one in which he had frequently been before and he had often delivered goods at Quiney's Wharf. He must be taken to know something of the character of the neighbourhood. To leave horses unattended, even for such a short time as three minutes in a place where mischievous children may be about and where something may be done which may result in the horses running away, seems to me to be negligent having regard to all the proved circumstances of the case.

The next point to consider is the one called *novus actus interveniens*. It is not true to say that, in English law, where a plaintiff has suffered damage occasioned by a combination between the wrongful act of a defendant and some further conscious act by an intervening person, that necessarily of itself prevents the court from coming to a conclusion in his favour, if the accident was the natural and probable consequence of the wrongful act. That seems to me to be the necessary result of some of the decided cases which are accepted as authorities.

The third point is *volenti non fit iujuria*. Unfortunately, there is a dearth of authority in this country on the subject, and apparently a wealth of authority in the decisions of the courts of the United States, which are not binding on us. We must only act on principles accepted in

214 *Negligence*

this country. There is, unfortunately, an *obiter dictum* of SCRUTTON, LJ, in *Cutler v United Dairies (London) Ltd* [...] which has to be dealt with and explained, an observation which, I think, has been much misunderstood and misapplied in the argument put before us. [...]

I regard the law on the subject as being this. If what is relied, on as *novus actus interveniens* is the very kind of thing which is likely to happen if the want of care which is alleged in the case takes place, then it is no defence to say that there has been a *novus actus interveniens*. The whole question is whether or not, to use the words of the leading case, *Hadley v Baxendale* [...] the accident can be said to be the natural and probable result of the breach. If it is the very thing which ought to be anticipated by a man who was leaving his horses, or one of the things likely to arise as a consequence of his wrongful act, then it is no defence at all; it is only a step in the way of proving that the damage is really the result of the wrongful act.

In my judgment, there can be no doubt that in the present case the damage was the result of the wrongful act in the sense of being one of the natural and probable consequences of the wrongful act. It is not necessary to show that this particular accident and this particular damage were probable, but it is sufficient if it is of a class that might well be anticipated as one of the reasonable and probable results of the wrongful act. The third ground was treated as if it was a separate ground, namely, that the principle of *volenti non fit injuria* applied. [...] [T]here is a wealth of authority in the United States, and one of the cases cited before us, *Eckert v Long Island Railroad* [...] is quite sufficient to show what the American law is. The effect of the American cases, although we are not bound by them, is, I think, accurately stated in [Professor Goodhart's] article: [...] In summing up the American authorities and staling the result of *Eckert v Long Island Railroad* [...] the learned author says [...]

> The American rule is that the doctrine of the assumption of risk does not apply where the plaintiff has, under an exigency caused by the defendants' wrongful misconduct, consciously and deliberately faced a risk, often of death, to rescue another from imminent danger of personal injury or death, whether the person endangered is one to whom he owes a duty of protection, as a member of his family, or is a mere stranger to whom lie owes no such special duty.

In my judgment, that passage not only represents the law of the United States but also the law of this country. It is all the more applicable to this case because the man injured was a policeman who might readily be anticipated to do the very thing which he did, whereas the intervention of a more passer-by was not so probable.

Notes

As we know from *Donoghue*, we owe a duty of care to anyone who may be affected by our actions or omissions, which can be someone nearby or

Negligence 215

several thousand kilometres away. However, *Haynes* tells us that *novus actus interveniens* can preclude liability if the action causing injury is not the result of the original actor's negligence. As Harry Street said,[126]

> The question is whether the defendant is to be relieved of liability because some other circumstance actively operates in producing the harm complained of after he has committed his act of negligence.

This means that *novus actus interveniens* is when the original actor is negligent, but the injury happens because of the intervention of a new action.[127] For example, imagine you have driven your car to Sairu Hill Resort and parked on a hill without engaging the handbrake. If your vehicle rolls down and injures someone, you will be liable because you did not engage the handbrake, which is a general safety procedure used when parking one's vehicle, especially at an upward or downward slant. However, if you park your vehicle on the same hill and not engage the handbrake, but someone breaks into your car and this causes it to roll down and injure someone, you will not be liable, as the action causing injury was not the result of your negligence; rather, it was because of an intervening act (e.g. perhaps the sudden movement from breaking into your car) of a new action.

Overall, the concept of duty of care, in conjunction with tort law's objective of placing the party in the position he would have been in had the tort not been committed, tries to make society safer. Think of it this way, if you owe a duty of care to others on the road, would you not be more careful and engage the handbrake of your vehicle when parking at an upward or downward slant; or, if you, as a third party, owe a duty of care to a foetus, would you not be more careful to make sure that you do not injure the pregnant woman; or, if you manufacture cellphones and owe a duty of care to the ultimate consumer, would you not be more careful and produce a phone that does not inexplicably explode and injure someone? The answer is you would.

5.6 Cause in fact

We have learned, heretofore, that there is a standard of conduct that is expected of reasonable persons in society, and conduct that falls below that standard could be subject to tortious litigation. However, in order to institute proceedings, it must also be proven that the defendant owes a duty of care to the plaintiff, which he breached. Essentially, a person is entitled to act "as negligent as he pleases towards the whole world if he owe[s] no duty to them."[128] Nonetheless, even if the defendant owes a duty of care to the plaintiff and breaches that duty, thereby falling short of the conduct expected of him, if his misconduct does not cause the plaintiff's injury (in other words, the negligent conduct and the injury is remote and unconnected), then the defendant will not be held liable. That is to say, in order to impose liability on the defendant, it must also be proven that the plaintiff's negligence *caused* the former's injury.

216 *Negligence*

5.7 "But for"

Barnett v Chelsea & Kensington Hospital Management Committee[129]

William Barnett, Frederick Whittall, and Herbert Weighall work as watchmen at the Chelsea College of Sciences and Technology. On 31 December 1965, the three men began their duty at approximately 9:30 pm, and shortly thereafter, drank a few alcoholic beverages to welcome and celebrate the new year. At about 5:00 am on 1 January 1966, the three of them drank tea – some of it came from a thermos and some of it was freshly made in a teapot. Within a few minutes, William Barnett complained of the heat in the room and at approximately 5:20 am, all three men began vomiting persistently until about 8:00 am. At that time, guards, who are to be on duty from the morning, arrived and the three of them went to the casualty department at St. Stephen's Hospital.

Unfortunately, there was no receptionist at the casualty department, as she had not begun her duty that early. While Mr. Barnett walked over to an armless chair, sat down, and placed his head on his hands, Mr. Whittall and Mr. Weighall found Nurse Corbett who was, however, visibly hesitant about what should be done. Mr. Weighall told Nurse Corbett that they began vomiting after having tea, to which she responded, "[T]ea would not cause that." At this point, Mr. Weighall was livid and said, "I did [not] come here for nothing. We are ill. Can we or can we not see a doctor?"

Approximately ten minutes later, Nurse Corbett called Dr. Banerjee and said, "Is that Dr. Banerjee? There are three men complaining of vomiting after drinking tea," to which Dr. Banerjee responded, "Well, I [am] vomiting myself and I have not been drinking. Tell them to go home and go to bed and call in their own doctors [...]." Nurse Corbett then repeated the same to the three men, who thought it was final, and left. Mr. Barnett drove the three men back to Chelsea College, and he went inside a telephone room, lied down, and placed a pillow under his head. At about 9:10 am, Mr. Whitall asked if Mr. Barnett needed anything to which he replied, "Leave me alone, I [will] be alright." At approximately 1:30 pm, Mr. Barnett died, which was later discovered to be from arsenical poisoning.

Mrs. Barnett brought an action against the Chelsea & Kensington Hospital Management Committee (who oversaw St. Stephen's Hospital) under negligence, claiming that the hospital breached its duty of care to her husband by refusing to treat him. Finding, however, for the hospital, the court said,

> There are two main questions here: Has the plaintiff established, on the balance of probabilities, (i) that Dr. Banerjee was negligent, and, if so, (ii) that such negligence caused the death of the deceased?
>
>   The first of these questions can be divided into four other questions – (i) Should Dr. Banerjee have seen the deceased? (ii) Should he have examined the deceased? (iii) Should he have admitted the deceased

Negligence 217

to the wards? (iv) Should he have treated or caused to be treated the deceased?

The first two of those four questions can be answered together. It is not, in my judgment, the case that a casualty officer must always see the caller at his department. Casualty departments are misused from time to time. If the receptionist, for example, discovers that the visitor is already attending his own doctor and merely wants a second opinion, or if the caller has a small cut which the nurse can perfectly well dress herself, then the casualty officer need not be called. However, apart from such things as this, I find the opinion of Dr. Sydney Lockett entirely acceptable. He said [...]

> In my view, the duty of a casualty officer is in general to see and examine all patients who come to the casualty department of the hospital. [...] I cannot conceive that after a history of vomiting for three hours a doctor would leave the matter to a nurse, however experienced the nurse.

Without doubt Dr. Banerjee should have seen and examined the deceased. His failure to do either cannot be described as an excusable error as has been submitted, it was negligence. It is unfortunate that Dr. Banerjee was himself at the time a tired and unwell doctor, but there was no-one else to do that which it was his duty to do. Having examined the deceased I think that the first and provisional diagnosis would have been one of food poisoning.

The third question is should Dr. Banerjee have admitted the deceased to the wards? It is sufficient to say that I accept Dr. Lockett's opinion that, having regard to all the circumstances, it was Dr. Banerjee's duty to have admitted him.

The fourth question is should Dr. Banerjee have treated the deceased or caused him to be treated, and it is the case that, once admitted, the deceased's case could have gone to the medical registrar or to others if such was the desire. The immediate purpose of admission would be for observation and diagnosis. No one who has listened to the evidence can doubt that arsenical poisoning is extremely difficult to diagnose. Professor Camps accepted some figures which were put to him which were these, that out of six thousand deaths between 1955 and 1965 from poisoning, only five were due to arsenical poisoning. Again, that three or four million people are admitted to about five thousand hospitals in the course of a year and only sixty are cases of arsenical poisoning or potassium loss.

I conclude that after a period of observation and after taking the patient's blood pressure and subjecting him to other general tests, and on a reconsideration of the history, in particular the fact that vomiting had occurred within twenty minutes of drinking the tea and also finding loss of fluid, the doctor would have rejected the provisional diagnosis of food or staphylococcal poisoning and have decided that it might well have been a case of metallic poisoning. In any event, I

218 *Negligence*

am satisfied that the deceased's condition of dehydration and severe malaise was such that intravenous treatment should have been given. Further, I think it would have become plain that it was necessary to test a specimen of the deceased's blood and in the end to send certain other specimens away for analysis to discover what poison it was which was causing the deceased's condition.

Thus, it is that I find that under all four headings the defendants were negligent and in breach of their duty in that they or their servants or agents did not see and did not examine and did not admit and did not treat the deceased.

It remains to consider whether it is shown that the deceased's death was caused by this negligence or whether, as the defendants have said, the deceased must have died in any event. In his concluding submission counsel for the plaintiff submitted that Dr. Banerjee should have examined the deceased and, had he done so, he would have caused tests to be made which would have indicated the treatment required and that, since the defendants were at fault in these respects, therefore the onus of proof passed to the defendants to show that the appropriate treatment would have failed, and authorities were cited to me. I find myself unable to accept this argument and I am of the view that the onus of proof remains on the plaintiff, and I have in mind (without quoting it) the decision quoted by counsel for the defendants in *Bonnington Castings Ltd v Wardlaw*. However, were it otherwise and the onus did pass to the defendants, then I would find that they have discharged it, as I would proceed to show.

There has been put before me a timetable which, I think, is of much importance. The deceased attended at the casualty department at 8:05 or 8:10 am. If Dr. Banerjee had got up and dressed and come to see the three men and examined them and decided to admit them, the deceased (and Dr. Lockett agreed with this) could not have been in bed in a ward before 11:00 am. I accept Dr. Goulding's evidence that an intravenous drip would not have been set up before 12 noon, and if potassium loss was suspected it could not have been discovered until 12:30 [pm]. Dr. Lockett, dealing with this, said "If [the deceased] had not been treated until after 12 noon, the chances of survival were not good."

Without going in detail into the considerable volume of technical evidence which has been put before me, it seems to me to be the case that when death results from arsenical poisoning, it is brought about by two conditions; on the one hand dehydration and on the other disturbance of the enzyme processes. If the principal condition is one of enzyme disturbance – as I am of the view that it was here – then the only method of treatment which is likely to succeed is the use of the specific or antidote which is commonly called B.A.L. Dr. Gouding said this in the course of his evidence:

The only way to deal with this is to use the specific B.A.L. I see no reasonable prospect of the deceased being given B.A.L. before the time at which he died, [...] I feel that even if fluid loss had been

Negligence 219

discovered death would have been caused by the enzyme disturbance. Death might have occurred later.

For these reasons, I find that the plaintiff has failed to establish, on the grounds of probability, that the defendants' negligence caused the death of the deceased.

Notes

While *Barnett* seems to permit doctors to act as negligently as they want with impunity, the reality is significantly different. The court accepted that Dr. Banerjee was negligent in not treating Mr. Barnett, and that even if the former was sick (as he indeed was), it was his duty to treat Mr. Barnett and had he saw him, he would probably have admitted him to the hospital. However, simply because Dr. Banerjee was negligent in not treating Mr. Barnett does not mean that it caused Mr. Barnett's death, as the court, relying on expert evidence, found that the latter would have died anyway. As in, since Mr. Barnett would have died even if Dr. Banerjee treated him, his refusal to do so cannot be held to have *caused* Mr. Barnett's death.

An examination of the cases we have discussed heretofore will reveal that every time liability has been imposed for negligence, the defendant's conduct *caused* the plaintiff's injury. Here, the courts use the "but for" test to demonstrate causation; that is, if the plaintiff's injury would have happened "but for" the defendant's negligence, then the defendant's misconduct *did not cause* the injury, and therefore, he will not be liable.[130] Similarly, if the plaintiff's injury would not have happened "but for" the defendant's negligence, then the defendant's misconduct *caused* the injury, and therefore, he will be found liable. In simpler terms, the question is, "would the plaintiff have suffered the injury even if the defendant was not negligent" (or, in other words, if the defendant were more careful, would the plaintiff have suffered an injury)? If the plaintiff would have sustained an injury regardless of whether the defendant was negligent, then the defendant cannot be held liable, as the plaintiff would have been injured anyway, or that his injury is too remote from the type and character of the defendant's negligence.

The converse of the formula then is, since the plaintiff would not have been injured if the defendant were not negligent (or, in other words, if the defendant were more careful), then the defendant will be found liable.[131] As in, here, the plaintiff's injury was *caused by* the defendant's negligence and the plaintiff would otherwise not have been injured had the defendant not been negligent, and therefore, liability will be imposed on him.[132]

For example, imagine you are on board a Bangladesh Biman flight from Chittagong to Dhaka. The flight circles Dhaka airport for about thirty minutes because the landing gear has not engaged. Then, serendipitously and almost as if by divine intervention, the issue is resolved and the pilots successfully land the aircraft. While disembarking, however, you fall down the stairs and break your left elbow. It was later discovered that the problem with the landing gear was due to a lack of maintenance by Biman engineers.

220 *Negligence*

For your injury, you will not receive compensation from Biman because even though the airliner was negligent (e.g. failure to maintain the aircraft), your injury was not *caused by* their negligence. To further explain, the type of injuries that are "reasonably foreseeable" (a term I will delineate in the following section) from landing an airplane without the landing gear are, *inter alia*, injuries to the head from a dislodged valise kept improperly in the overhead cabin, or breaking your wrist from the sudden shock and force of the plane's fuselage touching the tarmac. However, the injury you suffered (e.g. broken left elbow) while disembarking the aircraft, which landed properly, was not the type and character of injuries one suffers from the kind of negligence at issue, which means it was not reasonably foreseeable, and therefore, not caused by Biman's negligence. Therefore, even if the airliner has conceded to being negligent, since they did not *cause* your injury, they cannot be held liable. In other words, your injury would have happened "but for" Biman's negligence (as in, even if they were more careful).

Similarly, in *Barnett*, we find that Mr. Barnett would have died even if Dr. Banerjee treated him because, *inter alia*, the former visited the hospital late and the hospital was not equipped to address his condition, which was arsenical poisoning. This means that while Dr. Banerjee was negligent in not treating Mr. Barnett, his death would have happened "but for" Dr. Banerjee's negligence. That is to say, he would have died anyway. Therefore, Dr. Banerjee's refusal to treat Mr. Barnett did not cause his death and he cannot be held liable.

Jobling v Associated Dairies Ltd[133]

Alexander Jobling was a manager at a butcher shop operated by Associated Dairies Limited (hereinafter "Associated Dairies"). Due to his employer's negligence and their breach of the *Office, Shops and Railways Premises Act, 1963* (by not having the floor free of substances likely to cause others to slip), in January 1973, Mr. Jobling fell inside a meat refrigerator and injured his back. He was subsequently reduced to only doing light work and his earning capacity decreased to 50%. Therefore, he brought an action against his employer under negligence, which eventually found its way to court in 1979.

However, in 1975, Mr. Jobling suffered another injury to his back, which was not connected to, and did not occur in the course of, his employment. Nonetheless, this reduced him to doing mostly sedentary work. By the end of 1976, he developed spondylotic myelopathy, which rendered him wholly unable to do work. Thence, not only does Mr. Jobling seek compensation from Associated Dairies for the initial injury, but he also claims damages for his complete incapacity. Finding Associated Dairies liable for only the initial injury (where Mr. Jobling saw his earnings reduced by 50%), the court said,

> Lord Reid later went on to distinguish the case where damages might properly fall to be diminished by reason of the death of the plaintiff before trial, on the basis that in such a case the supervening event had reduced the plaintiff's loss. He said [...]

Negligence 221

If the later injury suffered before the date of the trial either reduces the disabilities from the injury for which the defendant is liable, or shortens the period during which they will be suffered by the plaintiff then the defendant will have to pay less damages. But if the later injuries merely become a concurrent cause of the disabilities caused by the injury inflicted by the defendant, then in my view they cannot diminish the damages. Suppose that the plaintiff has to spend a month in bed before the trial because of some illness unconnected with the original injury, the defendant cannot say that he does not have to pay anything in respect of that month; during that month the original injuries and the new illness are concurrent causes of his inability to work and that does not reduce the damages.

It seems clear from this passage that the principle of concurrent causes which Lord Reid selected as the *ratio decidendi* of the case would, if sound, apply with the same force where the supervening event is natural disease, as in the present case, as it does where the supervening event is a tortious act.

Lord Pearson's main reason for rejecting the respondent's argument was that it would produce manifest injustice. He said [...]

The supervening event has not made the plaintiff less lame nor less disabled nor less deprived of amenities. It has not shortened the period over which he will be suffering. It has made him more lame, more disabled, more deprived of amenities. He should not have less damages through being worse off than might have been expected.

Lord Pearson went on to illustrate the nature of the injustice by pointing out that, where the supervening event was a tortious act, the later tortfeasor, on the principle that he takes his victim as he finds him, would be liable for damages in respect of loss of earnings only to the extent that the act had caused an additional diminution of earning capacity. If the earlier incapacity were treated, in a question with the first tortfeasor, as submerged by the later, the plaintiff would be left in the position of being unable to recover from anyone a substantial part of the loss suffered after the date of the second tort. So he would not be fully compensated in respect of the combined effects of both torts. It is to be observed that this was the consideration which had been principally urged in the argument for the appellant. [...]

The assessment of damages for personal injuries involves a process of *restitutio in integrum*. The object is to place the injured plaintiff in as good a position as he would have been in but for the accident. He is not to be placed in a better position. The process involves a comparison between the plaintiff's circumstances as regards capacity to enjoy the amenities of life and to earn a living as they would have been if the accident had not occurred and his actual circumstances in those respects following the accident. In considering how matters might have been

222 Negligence

expected to turn out if there had been no accident, the "vicissitudes" principle says that it is right to take into account events, such as illness, which not uncommonly occur in the ordinary course of human life. If such events are not taken into account, the damages may be greater than are required to compensate the plaintiff for the effects of the accident, and that result would be unfair to the defendant. Counsel for the appellant sought to draw a distinction between the case where the plaintiff, at the time of the tortious injury, is already suffering from a latent undetected condition which later develops into a disabling illness and the case where the inception of the illness occurs wholly at a later date. In the former case, so it was maintained, the illness would properly fall to be taken into account in diminution of damages, on the principle that the tortfeasor takes his victim as he finds him, but in the latter case it would not. There is no trace of the suggested distinction in any of the authorities, and in my opinion it is unsound and apt to lead to great practical difficulties, providing ample scope for disputation among medical men. What would be the position, it might be asked, of an individual having a constitutional weakness making him specially prone to illness generally, or an hereditary tendency to some specific disease? [...]

While it is logically correct to say that in both cases the original tort and the supervening event may be concurrent causes of incapacity, that does not necessarily, in my view, provide the correct solution. In the case of supervening illness, it is appropriate to keep in view that this is one of the ordinary vicissitudes of life, and when one is comparing the situation resulting from the accident with the situation, had there been no accident, to recognize that the illness would have overtaken the plaintiff in any event, so that it cannot be disregarded in arriving at proper compensation, and no more than proper compensation.

Additional considerations come into play when dealing with the problems arising where the plaintiff has suffered injuries from two or more successive and independent tortious acts. In that situation it is necessary to secure that the plaintiff is fully compensated for the aggregate effects of all his injuries. As Lord Pearson noted in *Baker v Willoughby* [...] it would clearly be unjust to reduce the damages awarded for the first tort because of the occurrence of the second tort, damages for which are to be assessed on the basis that the plaintiff is already partially incapacitated. I do not consider it necessary to formulate any precise juristic basis for dealing with this situation differently from the case of supervening illness. It might be said that a supervening tort is not one of the ordinary vicissitudes of life, or that it is too remote a possibility to be taken into account, or that it can properly be disregarded because it carries its own remedy. None of these formulations, however, is entirely satisfactory. The fact remains that the principle of full compensation requires that a just and practical solution should be found. In the event that damages against two successive tortfeasors fall

Negligence 223

to be assessed at the same time, it would be highly unreasonable if the aggregate of both awards were less than the total loss suffered by the plaintiff. The computation should start from an assessment of that total loss. The award against the second tortfeasor cannot in fairness to him fail to recognize that the plaintiff whom he injured was already to some extent incapacitated. In order that the plaintiff may be fully compensated, it becomes necessary to deduct the award so calculated from the assessment of the plaintiff's total loss and award the balance against the first tortfeasor. If that be a correct approach, it follows that, in proceedings against the first tortfeasor alone, the occurrence of the second tort cannot be successfully relied on by the defendant as reducing the damages which he must pay.

Notes

Jobling is similar to *Barnett* in that the defendant was not liable for the ultimate result (complete physical incapacity and death, respectively) even though he was negligent. As I have mentioned earlier, the question is "would the plaintiff have suffered the injury 'but for' the defendant's negligence?"; that is, if Mr. Jobling would have become completely incapacitated even if Associated Dairies were not negligent (this is known as the "crumbling skull rule" and I will discuss this below), then the latter will not be liable. Relying on expert evidence, the court concluded that Mr. Jobling would have become wholly disabled even if he was not injured in January 1973, and therefore, Associated Dairies was not liable for the complete incapacity, but was liable for the initial injury whereby Mr. Jobling's earning capacity was reduced by 50%.

It is, however, important to understand that since Mr. Jobling's complete incapacity was caused by spondylotic myelopathy, which was congenital, and therefore, would have happened anyway, Associated Dairies was not liable. Nonetheless, the court added that had his complete incapacity been caused by another tortious act (and not by his congenital disorder) by another party, or by Associated Dairies, then they would have been liable for that injury. As in, Associated Dairies' negligence injured Mr. Jobling's back, which reduced his earnings by 50%, and for their negligence, Associated Dairies were liable. However, if someone else's negligence (e.g. failing to mop up a slippery floor at a grocery store Mr. Jobling visited) injured Mr. Jobling, which completely incapacitated him, then the second party, whose negligence caused him to fall at the grocery store, will be liable for the second injury. Essentially, liability will be shared between the negligent defendants for the injuries they caused.

For example, imagine you went to Yellow Box Cafe in Banani, Dhaka, for coffee with your friends. While entering the store, you slip on oil, fall, and injure your lower back. For this injury, you can bring an action against Yellow Box under negligence for their failure to either, (a) clean up the oil-spill, or (b) warn visitors of the slippery floor. Unfortunately, a week later, while waiting in line at a bank to deposit cash, you sustain a gunshot

224 *Negligence*

wound to your lower back, which paralyses you from the waist down.[134] Experts conclude that had you not injured your lower back at Yellow Box, then the gunshot would not have paralysed you. However, simply because the injury at Yellow Box weakened you does not mean they will be liable for the eventual paralysis because that was caused by a separate tortious (and criminal, but it is up to the victim to elect how he wishes to proceed) act, and it is the shooter that will be liable for the paralysis.[135]

The shooter, however, cannot disclaim liability for your paralysis by contesting that he did not know of your weak back. While his argument is cogent (e.g. you would not have become paralysed had you been stronger), it is untenable, as the court will use the thin-skull, or eggshell skull, rule, which was originally propounded in *Vosburg v Putney*,[136] to impose liability on the shooter. The essence of this common law doctrine is that you must "take your victim as you find him."[137] As in, if you punch someone in the chest using little to no force, but it breaks their sternum because that person suffers from osteogenesis imperfecta, which is commonly known as "brittle bone disease," your defence that you did not know of his pre-existing condition, and therefore, are not guilty of the aggravated injury, such as the broken sternum, will be indefensible and you will be liable for the entire injury. In the words of Justice Kennedy in *Dulieu v White & Sons*,[138]

> If a man is negligently run over or otherwise negligently injured in his body, it is no answer to the sufferer's claim for damages that he would have suffered less injury, or no injury at all, if he had not had an unusually thin skull or an unusually weak heart.

To simplify, we already know that a person is liable for the injury he intentionally or negligently causes another (let us call this the "initial injury").[139] The thin skull rule takes liability one step further and adds that while a person is liable for the initial injury, he will be liable for all subsequent injuries and results if it is caused by the initial injury, and no *novus actus interveniens* breaks the chain of causation. That is to say, so long as a new act does not injure the plaintiff, the defendant that caused the initial injury will be liable for the ultimate result, and it does not matter that he did not know of the plaintiff's infirm condition.

Let us revisit the example of Yellow Box Cafe. Based on what we now know about the thin-skull rule, it is reasonable to conclude that the cafe will not be liable for the paralysis because there was *novus actus interveniens* (e.g. the gunshot wound) between the initial injury and the paralysis, which broke the chain of causation. Therefore, Yellow Box is liable only for the initial injury and the shooter is liable for the paralysis even though he did not know you were weakened by an earlier injury. The thin-skull rule also means that if you have a weak lower back and you slip on the floor at Yellow Box because of their negligence, which, due to your already weakened back, paralyses you from your waist down, then the cafe will be liable for the subsequent paralysis.[140]

Negligence   225

Table 5.1 Thin-Skull and Eggshell Skull Rule

Initial Injury	Thin-Skull Rule	Crumbling Skull Rule
The event that injures the plaintiff	A natural, or non-natural, infirmity the plaintiff has that is aggravated by the initial injury	Perhaps a congenital disorder and one that would have happened anyway – with or without the initial injury
Defendant is liable for the initial injury	Defendant is liable for the aggravated injury (ultimate consequence) if it is *caused* by the initial injury.	Defendant is *not* liable for the ultimate consequence because it is something that would have happened anyway – with or without the initial injury

Source: Author

In *Jobling*, the thin-skull rule was not applied not because the court disregarded the doctrine, but because Alexander Jobling would have become completely incapacitated anyway. As in, his injury (falling on his back) did not cause or exacerbate spondylotic myelopathy. For example, and again, if you suffer from osteogenesis imperfecta, it is reasonably foreseeable that a punch to your sternum may break it, which would probably not happen to a person without the condition. Let us assume that one has punched you and your sternum broke, and that within a week of this incident, you have been diagnosed with lung cancer. The punch to your sternum caused it to break because of your brittle bones, and for this, the batterer will be liable (application of the thin-skull rule) and it does not matter whether he knew of your weakness. However, the punch to your sternum did not cause or exacerbate your lung cancer, and therefore, the batterer will not be liable for it. As in, you would have developed lung cancer anyway, and the punch is not connected to it (crumbling skull rule), and therefore, the batterer is liable only for the broken bone. Similarly, Mr. Jobling's fall inside Associated Dairies' meat shop did not fully incapacitate him; rather, it only reduced his earnings by 50%. He would have become wholly unfit for work anyway. That is to say, even if he was not injured at work. Therefore, Associated Dairies was liable only for the initial injury because it did not cause the ultimate result.

Wright v Cambridge Medical Group[141]

In April 1998, Ms. Wright's daughter, who was 11 months old, contracted chickenpox. On 9 April, she developed a high temperature and tachycardia, and was admitted to South Cleveland Hospital (hereinafter "Hospital"). On 12 April, she was discharged. However, sometime between 9 April and 12 April, and unbeknownst to the doctor, Ms. Wright's daughter was afflicted with *streptococcus pyogenes*, which is a bacterial infection that seeded in her proximal femur (the part of the hipbone closest to the trunk of her body) leading to osteomyelitis (an infection of the bone) on 13 or 14 April.

On 14 April, Ms. Wright noticed that her daughter's health was deteriorating, and therefore, took her to see Dr. Winter who advised Ms. Wright that if her daughter's condition does not improve overnight, then she should

226   *Negligence*

bring her back the following day. On 15 April, Ms. Wright realized that her daughter's condition was "considerably worse," as she was feverish, lethargic, and suffering from diarrhoea. She contacted Dr. Phellas, who, unfortunately, made no arrangements to see the patient.

Expert evidence suggests that the bacteria seeded in the patient's femur on 15 or 16 April developing into a sympathetic effusion, which became infected by 17 or 18 April (still unbeknownst to doctors). This exacerbated her condition whereby her hands and feet swelled and turned blue. Greatly concerned, Ms. Wright's sister spoke to Dr. Robertson at 7:30 pm on 17 April, who saw the patient at 8:30 pm on the same day, and immediately referred her to the paediatrics unit at the Hospital. The patient then went through a series of doctors who prescribed different antibiotics, and ultimately on 21 April, Dr. Hampton realized that she was not moving her hip and ordered an ultrasound, which revealed septic arthritis. Then, in the early hours of 22 April, an arthrotomy (an incision into the joint) was carried out to surgically drain the bacteria. However, by this time, the osteomyelitis and septic arthritis led to the separation and destruction of her bone plate, which, *inter alia*, rendered her hip permanently unstable and restricted her movement.

On behalf of her daughter, Ms. Wright brought proceedings against Dr. Phellas under negligence for his failure to refer her to the Hospital, alleging that had he done so, she probably would not suffer permanent injuries. Dr. Phellas, however, contended that even if he had done so, the hospital would have delayed diagnosing the problem anyway, and therefore, he should not be held liable. Holding Dr. Phellas liable, the court said,

> As well as making good the conceded fact that the defendants were negligent on 15 April, the expert evidence established that, had she been referred to the Hospital by Dr. Phellas on 15 April, and had the Hospital then treated her properly with appropriate antibiotics, the claimant would very probably have made a full recovery without the need for any surgery. The evidence also demonstrated that, when she was actually referred to the Hospital, on the evening of 17 April, she would have made a full recovery if she had been treated promptly with the appropriate antibiotics, although she may well also have required the arthrotomy and surgical drainage which she underwent. [...]
>
> After considering the factual and expert evidence relating to the treatment which the claimant received after she was admitted to the Hospital on 9 April, and, more importantly, 17 April, the [Trial] Judge concluded [...] that, although the defendants were negligent in not referring the claimant to the Hospital on 15 April, this negligence caused the claimant no loss, as, even if she had been admitted to the Hospital then, she would not have been treated properly, so that she would, in any event, have suffered the permanent damage. [...]
>
> I would mention the following. It was common ground between the experts that infection in the hip is "not notably difficult to diagnose or

Negligence 227

to treat" [...] Dr. Rudd said that the claimant had received "substand-ard care," that the absence of a consultant visit on 18 and 19 April infringed "standard practice across the country," and that the failure to examine her bones and joints was "a breach of duty of care by the registrar and the consultant." Professor Pollard described the claimant's treatment as "inadequate," and said that a full septic screening should have been undertaken at once on her admission, and that immediate and consistent administration of a broad spectrum antibiotic treat-ment was clearly appropriate: neither occurred. Dr. Conway, another consultant paediatrician, described the claimant as having received "inadequate" care, that the hospital diagnosis on 18 April was "not reasonable," that the decision to treat her with ciprofloxacin was "not justified [...] inadequate and illogical," and that her symptoms "should have suggested the probability of sepsis." [...]

[The defendants'] argument is that the defendants' breach of duty was in having referred the claimant to the Hospital later than they should have done, but not too late to be treated, and that, as a result, the damages she should recover from the defendants should be for the loss she suffered from having been referred later than she should have been, not for having been referred too late for her condition to have been remedied.

It seems to me that this argument raises two questions. The first is whether, on a fair view of the facts, the defendants' negligence was a cause of, or, to put it another way, significantly contributed to, the claimant's permanent injury. The second question is whether that injury was, to use the traditional expression, too remote, or, to put it in more modern terms, whether that injury fell outside the scope of the defend-ants' duty. [...]

So far as causation is concerned, although it may very well have been that, had it been a party, the Hospital would have been held to be more to blame than the defendants, I would reject the contention that the defendants' admitted negligence did not contribute to the claimant's permanent injury. The defendants' case to the contrary [...], has obvi-ous attraction. However, it should be examined critically, because of the obvious point that, where there are successive tortfeasors, it cannot be right that each can avoid liability by blaming the other.

Accordingly, where there are successive tortfeasors, the contention that the causative potency of the negligence of the first is destroyed by the subsequent negligence of the second depends very much on the facts of the particular case. In many cases where there are successive acts of negligence by different parties, both parties can be held responsible for the damage which ensues, so that the issue is not which of them is liable, but how liability is to be apportioned between them. The mere fact that, if the second party had not been negligent, the damage which subsequently ensued would not have occurred, by no means automatically exonerates the first party's negligence from being causative of that damage. [...]

228 *Negligence*

I do not consider that the Hospital's failure to treat the claimant properly once she was admitted on 17 April was of such significance that it justifies a finding that the defendants' negligence was not causative of the claimant's injury – or indeed a finding that it broke the chain of causation between the defendants' negligence and the claimant's injury. It was not such an egregious event, in terms of the degree or unusualness of the negligence, or the period of time for which it lasted, to defeat or destroy the causative link between the defendants' negligence and the claimant's injury. It took the Hospital less than three days more than it should have taken to make the right diagnosis, and to administer the right treatment. But it took the defendants a little over two days more than it should have done to refer the claimant to the Hospital. Further, it should have been apparent to the defendants that the claimant's condition on 15 April was deteriorating, and that, if treatment was delayed, it would increase the long term risk to her health: the evidence established that it was notorious that ill children can deteriorate fast. [...]

On the agreed evidence of the experts, if the claimant had been first treated with the right antibiotics on 16 April, it "would probably have prevented progress [of the infection]"; on 17 April it would "possibly" have done so; but, if such treatment had only started on 18 April, "it is unlikely to have had an effect in the absence of surgical drainage," and if it had started on 19 April, "it would have had no effect without surgical drainage"; They also agreed that, if surgical drainage had been effected on 17 April, the claimant would be likely to have had "a normal hip"; if it been done on 18 April, there "may have been residual articular cartilage damage", but only "a low risk of AVN [sc. avascular necrosis] and growth disturbance"; if the drainage had occurred on 19 April, there was "an increasing risk of articular cartilage damage, AVN and growth disturbance"; whereas, if drainage had been delayed until 20 April, such damage, necrosis and disturbance had become inevitable. [...]

It would seem to be an affront to justice if a doctor could escape liability by contending that, if he had not been negligent as alleged, the same damage would have occurred because he would have subsequently committed a different act of negligence. However, moral outrage and instinctive reaction are not always the safest of guides to legal principle. A sounder basis for the proposition may be the principle that a party cannot rely on his own wrong: in such a case a doctor would be seeking to rely on his own wrong, even if it is a hypothetical notional or contingent wrong. [...]

Accordingly, it seems to me that, in a case where a doctor has negligently failed to refer his patient to a hospital, and, as a consequence, she has lost the opportunity to be treated as she should have been by a hospital, the doctor cannot escape liability by establishing that the hospital would have negligently failed to treat the patient appropriately,

Negligence 229

even if he had promptly referred her. Even if the doctor established this, it would not enable him to escape liability, because, by negligently failing to refer the patient promptly, he deprived her of the opportunity to be treated properly by the hospital, and, if they had not treated her properly, that opportunity would be reflected by the fact that she would have been able to recover damages from them.

Notes

At the outset, this case must be distinguished from *Barnett*. In both cases, since the doctor did not see the patient, they were liable in negligence. However, in *Barnett*, Dr. Banerjee's failure to see William Barnett *did not cause* his death; rather, he would have died *even if* Dr. Banerjee saw and treated him. In *Wright*, however, the victim would not have been so severely injured had Dr. Phellas saw her on 15 April. As in, not seeing her on 15 April delayed her treatment by two days, which means her treatment would probably have begun two days earlier and this would have considerably reduced her chances of sustaining injuries. According to expert evidence, had Dr. Phellas seen the patient, as a competent doctor, he would have referred her to the Hospital forthwith, and treatment would begin immediately thereafter.[142] However, as Dr. Phellas did not see Ms. Wright, her daughter's treatment was delayed, which significantly increased her chances of injury; in other words, his negligence *caused* the injury. Thence, the question is "would Ms. Wright's infant daughter have been injured 'but for' Dr. Phellas' negligence?" No, and therefore, he was held liable.

Dr. Phellas, however, contended that even if he referred the victim to the Hospital, doctors would probably not have been able to diagnose her condition timely, and therefore, she would have been injured anyway. Let us use another example and I will later revisit his defence.

Imagine you are in a remote village in Bangladesh where there is only a walk-in clinic that can help with minor health problems, such as fevers. One day, you visit the doctor complaining of a cough. He determines that you have a congested chest and prescribes antibiotics. While you finish the course of the medicine, your condition aggravates and approximately twenty days later, you go to the clinic at 8:00 pm to see the doctor, who is not available because he is at a family dinner. You contact him on his cellphone and he tells you that it is late and he will see you tomorrow morning. Unfortunately, he sees you two days later and refers you to a hospital in the city. After eight days and multiple failed attempts in identifying the problem, the hospital finally diagnoses you with lung cancer and begins chemotherapy immediately. The hospital tells you that had you come a day earlier, your life expectancy would have increased by 10 years. For the failure to see you at night or the following day, the doctor at the village can be held liable in negligence. As in, his failure to treat you forthwith delayed you receiving treatment, which *caused* you to lose (or, not gain) 10 years of your life. Additionally, he cannot disclaim liability by contending that even if he had

230   *Negligence*

referred you to the hospital earlier, they would have delayed diagnosing the problem, and beginning treatment, anyway.[143]

Similarly, Dr. Phellas cannot disclaim liability by saying that even if he had seen Ms. Wright's daughter on 15 April, the hospital would not have been able to diagnose her problem immediately, and therefore, she would have been injured anyway. Because he did not see her on 15 April (or, your doctor at 8:00 pm), he *caused* her to receive treatment late, which *caused* her irreparable harm (or, losing 10 years from your life expectancy), and therefore, the doctor will be found liable.[144] However, what happens when there is more than one probable cause of the plaintiff's injury? Will the plaintiff be barred if he cannot definitively prove which defendant caused his injury?

5.8 Material contribution

McGhee v National Coal Board[145]

James McGhee was employed by the National Coal Board (hereinafter "NCB") where he had been working for many years. He was responsible for emptying pipe kilns, where working conditions were hot and dusty, and therefore, Mr. McGhee would sweat profusely. After work, he would ride his bicycle back home and shower, as the NCB did not have cleaning facilities.

On 30 March 1967, he was told to clean brick kilns, where the condition was hotter and dustier than pipe kilns. Then, on 2 April 1967, he experienced extensive irritation on his skin, and soon thereafter, he saw a doctor who referred him to a dermatologist. He was diagnosed with dermatitis. For the injury he suffered, he brought an action against the NCB under negligence for their failure to provide showering facilities. Finding for Mr. McGhee, the court said,

> The medical witnesses are in substantial agreement. Dermatitis can be caused, and this dermatitis was caused, by repeated minute abrasion of the outer horny layer of the skin followed by some injury to or change in the underlying cells, the precise nature of which has not yet been discovered by medical science. If a man sweats profusely for a considerable time the outer layer of his skin is softened and easily injured. If he is then working in a cloud of abrasive brick dust, as this man was, the particles of dust will adhere to his skin in considerable quantity and exertion will cause them to injure the horny layer and expose to injury or infection the tender cells below. Then in some way not yet understood dermatitis may result. If the skin is not thoroughly washed as soon as the man ceases work that process can continue at least for some considerable time. This man had to continue exerting himself after work by bicycling home while still caked with sweat and grime, so he would be liable to further injury until he could wash himself thoroughly. Washing is the only practicable method of removing the danger

of further injury. The effect of such abrasion of the skin is cumulative in the sense that the longer a subject is exposed to injury the greater the chance of his developing dermatitis: it is for that reason that immediate washing is well recognized as a proper precaution. [...]

> It has always been the law that a pursuer succeeds if he can [show] that fault of the defender caused or materially contributed to his injury. There may have been two separate causes but it is enough if one of the causes arose from fault of the defender. The pursuer does not have to prove that this cause would of itself have been enough to cause him injury. [...]

First, it is a sound principle that where a person has, by breach of duty of care, created a risk, and injury occurs within the area of that risk, the loss should be borne by him unless he shows that it had some other cause. Secondly, from the evidential point of view, one may ask, why should a man who is able to show that his employer should have taken certain precautions, because without them there is a risk, or an added risk, of injury or disease, and who in fact sustains exactly that injury or disease, have to assume the burden of proving more: namely, that it was the addition to the risk, caused by the breach of duty, which caused or materially contributed to the injury? In many cases of which the present is typical, this is impossible to prove, just because honest medical opinion cannot segregate the causes of an illness between compound causes. And if one asks which of the parties, the workman or the employers should suffer from this inherent evidential difficulty, the answer as a matter in policy or justice should be that it is the creator of the risk who, *ex hypothesi*, must be taken to have foreseen the possibility of damage, who should bear its consequences. [...]

> [W]here an injury is caused by two (or more) factors operating cumulatively, one (or more) of which factors is a breach of duty and one (or more) is not so, in such a way that it is impossible to ascertain the proportion in which the factors were effective in producing the injury or which factor was decisive, the law does not require a pursuer or plaintiff to prove the impossible, but holds that he is entitled to damages for the injury if he proves on a balance of probabilities that the breach or breaches of duty contributed substantially to causing the injury.

Athey v Leonati[146]

Jon Athey was an auto-body repairman and a manager at Budget Rent-A-Car who had a history of back problems since 1972. In February 1991, he was involved in a car accident, which was caused by the negligence of the other driver. He was taken to the hospital, examined, and released because he did not suffer any major injuries. However, within a few days, he began experiencing pain and stiffness in the neck. His doctor prescribed physiotherapy and chiropractic treatments, which ultimately led him on the way to recovery.

232 *Negligence*

Then, in April 1991, Mr. Athey was involved in another car accident, which, again, was due to the negligence of the other driver. Fortunately, he did not suffer any major injuries this time as well, and his doctor told him to continue physiotherapy and chiropractic treatments. Nonetheless, he did not partake in duties that required heavy labour, but continued to do lights tasks and his managerial work.

Since he was demonstrating improvement, his doctor suggested that he resume his regular exercise routine, and therefore, Mr. Athey went to a health club. While stretching, and before beginning his workout, he heard and felt a "pop" in his back and began experiencing excruciating pain. He went home immediately. However, he was unable to get out of bed the following day and was transported to a hospital by an ambulance, where he was admitted for three weeks.

The doctor diagnosed Mr. Athey's problem as a disc herniation on his lower back, which was ultimately treated by surgery and physiotherapy. Since the result was "good, but not excellent," Mr. Athey was forced to find a managerial position at an alternative company, which paid less than his previous employer, where he would not be required to do heavy physical duties. Therefore, Mr. Athey brought proceedings against the negligent drivers for his injuries, and particularly, alleged that the disc herniation was caused by the collisions and not by his pre-existing condition. Finding for Mr. Athey, the court said,

> Causation is established where the plaintiff proves to the civil standard on a balance of probabilities that the defendant caused or contributed to the injury [...]
>
> The general, but not conclusive, test for causation is the "but for" test, which requires the plaintiff to show that the injury would not have occurred but for the negligence of the defendant [...]
>
> The "but for" test is unworkable in some circumstances, so the courts have recognized that causation is established where the defendant's negligence "materially contributed" to the occurrence of the injury [...] A contributing factor is material if it falls outside the *de minimis* range [...] The causation test is not to be applied too rigidly. Causation need not be determined by scientific precision; as Lord Salmon stated in *Alphacell Ltd v Woodward*, [...] and as was quoted by Sopinka J [...], it is "essentially a practical question of fact which can best be answered by ordinary common sense." Although the burden of proof remains with the plaintiff, in some circumstances an inference of causation may be drawn from the evidence without positive scientific proof.
>
> It is not now necessary, nor has it ever been, for the plaintiff to establish that the defendant's negligence was the sole cause of the injury. There will frequently be a myriad of other background events which were necessary preconditions to the injury occurring. To borrow an example from Professor Fleming [...], a "fire ignited in a wastepaper basket is [...] caused not only by the dropping of a lighted match, but

Negligence 233

also by the presence of combustible material and oxygen, a failure of the cleaner to empty the basket and so forth." As long as a defendant is part of the cause of an injury, the defendant is liable, even though his act alone was not enough to create the injury. There is no basis for a reduction of liability because of the existence of other preconditions: defendants remain liable for all injuries caused or contributed to by their negligence.

This proposition has long been established in the jurisprudence. Lord Reid stated in *McGhee v National Coal Board* [...]

It has always been the law that a pursuer succeeds if he can shew that fault of the defender caused or materially contributed to his injury. There may have been two separate causes but it is enough if one of the causes arose from fault of the defender. The pursuer does not have to prove that this cause would of itself have been enough to cause him injury. [...]

The essential purpose and most basic principle of tort law is that the plaintiff must be placed in the position he or she would have been in absent the defendant's negligence (the "original position"). However, the plaintiff is not to be placed in a position better than his or her original one. It is therefore necessary not only to determine the plaintiff's position after the tort but also to assess what the "original position" would have been. It is the difference between these positions, the "original position" and the "injured position", which is the plaintiff's loss. [...]

The respondents argued that the plaintiff was predisposed to disc herniation and that this is therefore a case where the "crumbling skull" rule applies. The "crumbling skull" doctrine is an awkward label for a fairly simple idea. It is named after the well-known "thin skull" rule, which makes the tortfeasor liable for the plaintiff's injuries even if the injuries are unexpectedly severe owing to a pre-existing condition.

The so-called "crumbling skull" rule simply recognizes that the pre-existing condition was inherent in the plaintiff's "original position." The defendant need not put the plaintiff in a position better than his or her original position. The defendant is liable for the injuries caused, even if they are extreme, but need not compensate the plaintiff for any debilitating effects of the pre-existing condition which the plaintiff would have experienced anyway.

The "crumbling skull" argument is the respondents' strongest submission, but in my view it does not succeed on the facts as found by the trial judge. There was no finding of any measurable risk that the disc herniation would have occurred without the accident, and there was therefore no basis to reduce the award to take into account any such risk. [...]

Future or hypothetical events can be factored into the calculation of damages according to degrees of probability, but causation of the injury must be determined to be proven or not proven. This has the following ramifications:

234   *Negligence*

1   If the disc herniation would likely have occurred at the same time, without the injuries sustained in the accident, then causation is not proven;

2   If it was necessary to have both the accidents and the pre-existing back condition for the herniation to occur, then causation is proven, since the herniation would not have occurred but for the accidents. Even if the accidents played a minor role, the defendant would be fully liable because the accidents were still a necessary contributing cause;

3   If the accidents alone could have been a sufficient cause, and the pre-existing back condition alone could have been a sufficient cause, then it is unclear which was the cause-in-fact of the disc herniation. The trial judge must determine, on a balance of probabilities, whether the defendant's negligence materially contributed to the injury.

Notes

From *McGhee* and *Athey*, we must understand that there are certain situations, albeit infrequent, where the "but for" test is somewhat impracticable. For example, recall from earlier that as you entered Yellow Box Cafe with your friends, you slipped on oil and injured your lower back. While you want compensation from Yellow Box, what if they try to disclaim liability on the grounds that they did not spill the oil? As in, the oil found on the floor was tested and determined to be coconut oil that is used for treating hair, which Yellow Box does not keep in-store. Camera footage reveals that an unidentified person spilled the oil and left hurriedly without informing them and that is why Yellow Box could not clean the area. While it is true that you probably would not have injured your back "but for" the spilled oil, since Yellow Box's negligence (e.g. failure to clean the spilled oil) *materially contributed* to your injury, they will be held liable even though they did not spill the oil; that is, Yellow Box cannot disclaim liability by shifting blame to another reasonable source of the injury.[147]

Think of it this way – almost all injuries can have a myriad of causes, and therefore, denying compensation to the victim from one of the negligent parties, simply because the other is unknown, would be incompatible with the purpose of tort law. For example, to borrow Professor Fleming's illustration, a match dropped into a basket can ignite a fire because the person who lit the match did not extinguish the flame before discarding it, or because the person who was supposed to clean the basket did not do so.[148] If the plaintiff can identify who lit and subsequently discarded the matchstick, but cannot identify who was supposed to clean the basket, it would be unjust to deny him compensation from the person he is able to identify (the one who lit and subsequently discarded the matchstick) because this person's negligence *materially contributed* to the plaintiff's injury.

Similarly, a ceiling fan may fall on someone and injure him because of either (a) the electrician's negligence in installing the fan, or (b) the cleaner's negligence in applying too much force when cleaning it. Likewise, a fire on

Negligence 235

a grill at a restaurant can transform into a conflagration and injure, or kill, customers and staff, which may have been caused by either (a) the negligence of the person responsible for cleaning it, thereby allowing grease to accumulate, or (b) the chef who saw the excess grease, did not clean it, and ignited the grill, which resulted in the fire.

All of this to say that the doctrine of material contribution recognizes that there could be multiple factors with many negligent parties that injure the plaintiff. If the plaintiff is able to identify *one* negligent party and can demonstrate that his negligence *materially contributed* to the plaintiff's injury, then the negligent actor will be liable for all of the plaintiff's injury even if his misconduct was only one of the factors that injured him. For example, in *McGhee*, Mr. McGhee was able to prove that NCB's failure to provide cleaning facilities *materially contributed* to him developing dermatitis, and therefore, NCB was held liable. Essentially, as we will see in numerous other cases, the plaintiff is only required to prove that of the multiple causes, the defendant's misconduct *materially contributed* to his injury, and so long as this is proven, the defendant will be found liable.[149]

Blackstock v Foster[150]

In January 1957, Mr. Blackstock was seated in his car, which was stationary. Mr. Foster drove his vehicle negligently and collided with Mr. Blackstock's car. Due to the collision, Mr. Blackstock was thrown forward and his chest struck the steering wheel with veritable force and he suffered other minor injuries. However, since the accident, it has been discovered that he has an inoperable malignant growth in his chest (under his ribs). Expert evidence suggests that Mr. Blackstock probably had a teratoma, which is a rare condition, in his chest before the accident. However, no doctor testified that the teratoma became malignant *because of* the blow to the chest. Nonetheless, for the injuries suffered, Mr. Blackstock brought an action against Mr. Foster. Finding in favour of Mr. Foster, the court said,

> We are of the opinion that the evidence which we have outlined above could not justify the inference that it was more probable than not that there was a causal connection between the blow and the malignancy of the growth. It is obvious from the evidence that, in the present state of medical and scientific knowledge, little is known of the causes of malignant growths and if medical science is unable to supply the necessary link between such a growth and a blow in the region of it, it is not for a layman to do so. If he does, he seems to us to enter the realm of speculation. As was said by Dixon J [...] in *Adelaide Stevedoring Co Ltd v Forst*:
>
> > Tempting as it always is, particularly in matters of bodily health, to argue from a sequence of external events, such reasoning is justified only when positive knowledge or common experience supplies some adequate ground for believing that the events are naturally associated.

236　*Negligence*

Notes

Blackstock is the paradigm example of the crumbling skull rule. We see that Mr. Blackstock had a benign teratoma before the accident and that it became malignant afterwards. However, what could not be proven was whether the accident *caused* the tumour to become malignant. As in, while Mr. Blackstock had a natural infirmity, or a thin-skull, simply harbouring a weakness is not sufficient to impose liability on the negligent actor unless the misconduct *caused*, or *materially contributed* to, the condition to aggravate. In other words, as I have mentioned earlier, for the thin-skull rule to apply, the condition precedent is that the negligent act causes, or materially contributes to, the plaintiff's natural infirmity to exacerbate.

However, if the misconduct is not connected to the ultimate result, then the crumbling skull rule applies and the defendant will not be found liable. That is to say, since the plaintiff would have suffered his fate anyway, the defendant will not be guilty.[151] Essentially, what must be proven is that the negligent act *caused*, or *materially contributed* to, the aggravation of the plaintiff's natural weakness.

5.9 Factual uncertainty

Sindell v Abbott Laboratories[152]

Between 1941 and 1971, two hundred drug companies manufactured diethylstilboestrol (hereinafter "DES"), which is a synthetic oestrogen that was prescribed to pregnant women to prevent miscarriages. In 1947, the Food and Drug Administration (hereinafter "FDA") authorized the use of DES as a miscarriage preventative. However, it was on an experimental basis and companies were required to provide cautionary labels to that effect. In 1971, the FDA instructed manufacturers to stop producing and marketing DES and to warn physicians and the public that it should not be used by pregnant women because of the risk it poses to their unborn children.

Research demonstrates that DES can cause cancerous vaginal and cervical growths, which is called adenocarcinoma and manifests after 10 or 12 years, in daughters exposed to it before birth if their mothers ingest the drug during pregnancy. DES can also cause adenosis, which are precancerous vaginal and cervical growths that can spread to other areas of the body. The treatment for adenosis is cauterization, surgery, or cryosurgery, and women who suffer from this condition must be monitored by biopsy or colposcopy biannually, which are extremely painful.

Oddly, manufacturers did not adhere to the direction of the FDA and marketed DES on an unlimited basis rather than as an experimental drug. Therefore, Judith Sindell was exposed to DES when her mother was pregnant and now has a malignant bladder. She also has adenosis and must frequently be monitored by biopsy or colposcopic examination to ensure it does not turn malignant. Ms. Sindell, for herself and on behalf of other women similarly affected, brought proceedings against five of the largest

Negligence 237

manufacturers of DES under negligence for their failure to warn pregnant women of the possible risks. Finding in her favour, the court said,

> We begin with the proposition that, as a general rule, the imposition of liability depends upon a showing by the plaintiff that his or her injuries were caused by the act of the defendant or by an instrumentality under the defendant's control. The rule applies whether the injury resulted from an accidental event [...] or from the use of a defective product. [...]
>
> There are, however, exceptions to this rule. Plaintiff's complaint suggests several bases upon which defendants may be held liable for her injuries even though she cannot demonstrate the name of the manufacturer which produced the DES actually taken by her mother. [...]
>
> Plaintiff places primary reliance upon cases which hold that if a party cannot identify which of two or more defendants caused an injury, the burden of proof may shift to the defendants to show that they were not responsible for the harm. [...]
>
> In *Summers [v Tice]*, the plaintiff was injured when two hunters negligently shot in his direction. It could not be determined which of them had fired the shot that actually caused the injury to the plaintiff's eye, but both defendants were nevertheless held jointly and severally liable for the whole of the damages. We reasoned that both were wrongdoers, both were negligent toward the plaintiff, and that it would be unfair to require plaintiff to isolate the defendant responsible, because if the one pointed out were to escape liability, the other might also, and the plaintiff-victim would be shorn of any remedy. In these circumstances, we held, the burden of proof shifted to the defendants, "each to absolve himself if he can." [...] We stated that under these or similar circumstances a defendant is ordinarily in a "far better position" to offer evidence to determine whether he or another defendant caused the injury. [...]
>
> Here [...] the circumstances of the injury appear to render identification of the manufacturer of the drug ingested by plaintiff's mother impossible by either plaintiff or defendants, and it cannot reasonably be said that one is in a better position than the other to make the identification. Because many years elapsed between the time the drug was taken and the manifestation of plaintiff's injuries she, and many other daughters of mothers who took DES, are unable to make such identification. [...] Certainly there can be no implication that plaintiff is at fault in failing to do so – the event occurred while plaintiff was *in utero*, a generation ago.
>
> On the other hand, it cannot be said with assurance that defendants have the means to make the identification. In this connection, they point out that drug manufacturers ordinarily have no direct contact with the patients who take a drug prescribed by their doctors. Defendants sell to wholesalers, who in turn supply the product to physicians and

238   Negligence

pharmacies. Manufacturers do not maintain records of the persons who take the drugs they produce, and the selection of the medication is made by the physician rather than the manufacturer. Nor do we conclude that the absence of evidence on this subject is due to the fault of defendants. While it is alleged that they produced a defective product with delayed effects and without adequate warnings, the difficulty or impossibility of identification results primarily from the passage of time rather than from their allegedly negligent acts of failing to provide adequate warnings. [...]

It is important to observe, however, that while defendants do not have means superior to plaintiff to identify the maker of the precise drug taken by her mother, they may in some instances be able to prove that they did not manufacture the injury-causing substance. In the present case, for example, one of the original defendants was dismissed from the action upon proof that it did not manufacture DES until after plaintiff was born.

Notes

Unfortunately, *Sindell* had multiple defendants and Judith Sindell was not able to identify which defendant harmed her. Using the doctrine of material contribution, the court concluded that so long as (1) the plaintiff is able to identify the cause of her injury, but (2) cannot identify the particular defendant who injured her, but (3) can identify a group of defendants who have materially contributed to her injury, then the group of defendants will be held liable.[153] It is important to understand that manufacturers did not warn physicians or patients about the risk of adenocarcinoma and adenosis from ingesting DES even though the FDA mandated it. Therefore, their failure to warn physicians or patients amounts to negligence.[154] Furthermore, since a warning was not provided, physicians prescribed DES to patients on an unlimited basis, and Judith Sindell's mother was one of the women who took the drug, which ultimately injured her. This means that the manufacturers' negligence materially contributed to Judith Sindell's injury, and because she was able to identify the group of people whose actions materially contributed to her injury, the court held the entire group liable.

Recall from *Ybarra* that Joseph Ybarra could not identify which particular doctor, or nurse, injured him while he was unconscious, and therefore, every doctor and nurse that had control of his body was held liable under the doctrine of *res ipsa loquitur*.[155] As in, there was no reasonable way Mr. Ybarra could have proven which particular doctor injured him, as he was unconscious. Thence, the injury itself is evidence of negligence. Similarly, though not the same, it is reasonable to hold that since DES was manufactured between 1941 and 1971, and since Judith Sindell's mother was injured during that time, all of the manufacturers that produced the drug between 1941 and 1971 are held liable because it is impossible for Judith Sindell to prove which particular company produced the drug her mother ingested. Essentially, even in cases of factual uncertainty, so long as the plaintiff is

Negligence 239

able to prove that a person's negligence caused, or materially contributed to, his injury, then, even if he cannot identify a particular defendant, but is able to identify a group of defendants, the group will be held liable, as to disallow recovery would run afoul the purpose of tort law.

Additionally, it is important to note that factual uncertainty does not relate to causation, but in who the particular negligent party is. That is to say, if Ms. Sindell could not demonstrate that she developed a malignant bladder and adenosis because her mother ingested DES, then the court would absolve the manufacturers because guilt has not been proven. As in, causation must always be proven and if there is a scintilla of doubt regarding whether the defendant caused the injury, then he will not be held liable as the plaintiff has not met his burden of proving the defendant's guilt.

Cook v Lewis[156]

On 11 September 1948, Robert Lewis went hunting for blue grouse and deer with his brother, John Lewis, Dennis Fitzgerald, David Cook, John Wagstaff, and Mr. Akenhead near Quinsam Lake on Vancouver Island. They were using a dog, which belonged to Mr. Akenhead, to guide them. Mr. Cook, Mr. Akenhead, and Mr. Wagstaff were walking next to each other with Mr. Fitzgerald and the dog slightly ahead of them. Mr. Fitzgerald, and the dog, stopped at a clump of trees because he saw Robert and John Lewis hiding behind it. He pointed towards the trees and called out a warning. While Mr. Cook, Mr. Akenhead, and Mr. Wagstaff heard the call, they did not hear what he said, and thought he meant there were grouse behind the clump of trees.

Shortly after Mr. Fitzgerald's call, a covey of blue grouse flew up. Mr. Akenhead and Mr. Cook fired at the birds simultaneously, but unfortunately, a bullet struck Robert Lewis in the face and he lost an eye. For his injury, Mr. Lewis brought an action against Mr. Akenhead and Mr. Cook under negligence for their failure to ensure no hunters were present in the direction of their shot. However, Mr. Akenhead contends it was not his bullet that struck Mr. Lewis, and therefore, he should not be held liable. Mr. Cook also submits the same argument. Holding both parties equally liable, the court said,

> A cause may be said to be an operating element which in *de facto* cooperation with what may be called environment is considered the factor of culpability in determining legal responsibility for damage or loss done to person or property. But in that determination the practical difficulty turns on the allocation of elements to the one or other of these two divisions of data. In considering the second and third possibilities in this case, the essential obstacle to proof is the fact of multiple discharges so related as to confuse their individual effects: it is that fact that bars final proof. But if the victim, having brought guilt down to one or both of two persons before the court, can bring home to either of them a further wrong done him in relation to his remedial right of

240 *Negligence*

making that proof, then I should say that on accepted principles, the barrier to it can and should be removed. [...]

What, then, the culpable actor has done by his initial negligent act is, first, to have set in motion a dangerous force which embraces the injured person within the scope of its probable mischief; and next, in conjunction with circumstances which he must be held to contemplate, to have made more difficult if not impossible the means of proving the possible damaging results of his own act or the similar results of the act of another. He has violated not only the victim's substantive right to security, but he has also culpably impaired the latter's remedial right of establishing liability. By confusing his act with environmental conditions, he has, in effect, destroyed the victim's power of proof.

The legal consequence of that is, I should say, that the onus is then shifted to the wrongdoer to exculpate himself; it becomes in fact a question of proof between him and the other and innocent member of the alternatives, the burden of which he must bear. The onus attaches to culpability, and if both acts bear that taint, the onus or *prima facie* transmission of responsibility attaches to both, and the question of the sole responsibility of one is a matter between them. [...]

The risks arising from these sporting activities by increased numbers of participants and diminishing opportunity for their safe exercise, as the facts here indicate, require appropriate refinements in foresight. Against the private and public interests at stake, is the privilege of the individual to engage in a sport not inherently objectionable. As yet, certainly, the community is not ready to assume the burden of such a mishap. The question is whether a victim is to be told that such a risk, not only in substantive right but in remedy, is one he must assume. When we have reached the point where, as here, shots are considered spent at a distance of between 150 feet and 200 feet and the woods are "full" of hunters, a somewhat stringent regard to conduct seems to me to be obvious. It would be a strange commentary on its concern toward personal safety, that the law, although forbidding the victim any other mode of redress, was powerless to accord him any in its own form of relief. I am unable to assent to the view that there is any such helplessness. [...]

[I]f under the circumstances of the case at bar the jury, having decided that the plaintiff was shot by either Cook or Akenhead, found themselves unable to decide which of the two shot him because in their opinion both shot negligently in his direction, both defendants should have been found liable.

Notes

Similar to *Sindell*, the common law principle is clarified and further entrenched by *Cook* – the plaintiff does not need to identify, with scientific precision, which of the multiple defendants injured him. That is to say, so long as the plaintiff (1) points to a group of negligent parties, and (2)

Negligence   241

demonstrates that his injury was *caused by* their negligence, then all of the negligent parties will be held liable, even if that means one, or the preponderance, of them is not guilty.[157]

Recall that the purpose of tort law is to compensate the victim for his injury by placing him in the position he would have been in had the tort not been committed. Therefore, it would be grossly incorrect, and an affront to tort law, to deny him compensation simply because he is unable to pinpoint who the specific negligent actor is, even though he is able to demonstrate that a group was responsible. As in, the need to compensate the victim outweighs the injustice of imposing liability on an otherwise innocent party who has become liable by virtue of association.

For example, in *Fairchild v Glenhaven Funeral Services Ltd*, Arthur Fairchild worked for two consecutive employers. Unfortunately, he developed mesothelioma, and succumbed to it, when he was exposed to asbestos at both places of work because of his employers' negligence. However, what his wife, Judith Fairchild, could not prove was which exposure (whether from employer one or two) led to the cancer. Nonetheless, the court said that since it is proved that the exposure to asbestos caused cancer, it is just that both parties are held equally liable even if it cannot be proven which exposure caused the cancer.[158] Furthermore, the court outlined six points, which, if met, allows the plaintiff to collect compensation from both, or multiple, defendants:

1. If the plaintiff is employed by two employers at different times; and
2. Both employers owed a duty of care to the plaintiff; and
3. Both employers breached their duty of care they owed the plaintiff; and
4. The plaintiff sustains an injury because of the breach of the duty of care; and
5. Other causes of the injury can be eliminated; and
6. The plaintiff cannot prove when the injury occurred or which party was responsible, then he is allowed to collect damages from both, or multiple, parties.[159]

Using the aforementioned six points, we can see how the facts of *Cook*, though the plaintiff was not an employee of the defendants, can be plugged into the Fairchild Equation to hold both parties liable. As in, (1) Mr. Lewis was associated, and neighbours, with Mr. Cook and Mr. Akenhead (the converse is equally true); (2) therefore, Mr. Cook and Mr. Akenhead owed a duty of care to Mr. Lewis; (3) both of them breached that duty of care by discharging their firearms; (4) Mr. Lewis was injured *because* Mr. Cook and Mr. Akenhead breached their duty of care; (5) the type of injury Mr. Lewis suffered (gunshot wound to the face) was the type or character of harm that was reasonably foreseeable; and (6) since Mr. Lewis could not prove whether the bullet that injured him was fired from Mr. Cook or Mr. Akenhead's gun, both of the negligent parties were held equally liable.

242 *Negligence*

Again, it is important to understand that the factual uncertainty was not whether the defendants' negligence caused the plaintiff's injury, but in *who the negligent actor was*, as Mr. Lewis was unable to establish who, of the two parties, injured him. Nonetheless, since both Mr. Cook and Mr. Akenhead fired their guns, they were both held equally liable. This also means that if Mr. Lewis was unable to prove that a bullet fired by either Mr. Cook or Mr. Akenhead injured him, then neither party would be liable. For example, let us assume that both men fired their guns, but that Mr. Lewis was injured because a Black Widow Spider bit him. For this injury, neither party that fired their guns would be liable, as the cause of the injury was not their negligence, but was an act independent of it.

Kingston v Chicago Northwestern Railway Company[160]

On 30 April 1925, sparks from Chicago Northwestern Railway Company (hereinafter "Northwestern Railway") ignited a fire at the northwest of the plaintiff's property, which was near Northwestern Railway's Bonita track. Strangely, a fire of unknown origin also burned near the northeast of the plaintiff's property. The two fires united at about 940 feet away from the plaintiff's property and destroyed logs, timber, and poles that were on his land. For the damage sustained to his property, the plaintiff seeks compensation from Northwestern Railway. However, Northwestern Railway contends that since they did not create the fire on the northeast and as it is of unknown origin, they should not be fully liable. Finding for the plaintiff, the court said,

> It is settled in the law of negligence that any one of two or more joint tortfeasors, or one of two or more wrongdoers whose concurring acts of negligence result in injury, are each individually responsible for the entire damage resulting from their joint or concurrent acts of negligence. This rule also obtains "where two causes, each attributable to the negligence of a responsible person, concur in producing an injury to another, either of which causes would produce it regardless of the other, [...] because, whether the concurrence be intentional, actual, or constructive, each wrongdoer, in effect, adopts the conduct of his co-actor, and for the further reason that it is impossible to apportion the damage or to say that either perpetrated any distinct injury [...] that can be separated from [...] the whole. The whole loss must necessarily be considered and treated as an entirety." [...]
>
> From our present consideration of the subject we are not disposed to criticize the doctrine [...] which exempts from liability a wrongdoer who sets a fire which unites with a fire originating from natural causes, such as lightning, not attributable to any human agency, resulting in damage. It is also conceivable that a fire so set might unite with a fire of so much greater proportions, such as a raging forest fire, as to be enveloped or swallowed up by the greater holocaust, and its identity destroyed, so that the greater fire could be said to be an intervening

Negligence 243

or superseding cause. But we have no such situation here. These fires were of comparatively equal rank. If there was any difference in their magnitude or threatening aspect, the record indicates that the northeast fire was the larger fire and was really regarded as the menacing agency. At any rate there is no intimation or [...] suggestion that the northeast fire was enveloped and swallowed up by the northwest fire. We will err on the side of the defendant if we regard the two fires as of equal rank.

According to well settled principles of negligence, it is undoubted that if the proof disclosed the origin of the northwest fire, even though its origin be attributed to a third person, [...] the railroad company, as the originator of the northeast fire, would be liable for the entire damage. There is no reason to believe that the northwest fire originated from any other than human agency. It was a small fire. It had traveled over a limited area. It had been in existence but for a day. For a time it was thought to have been extinguished. It was not in the nature of a raging forest fire. The record discloses nothing of natural phenomena which could have given rise to the fire. It is morally certain that it was set by some human agency.

Now the question is whether the railroad company, which is found to have been responsible for the origin of the northeast fire, escapes liability because the origin of the northwest fire is not identified, although there is no reason to believe that it had any other than [...] human origin. An affirmative answer to that question would certainly make a wrongdoer a favourite of the law at the expense of an innocent sufferer. The injustice of such a doctrine sufficiently impeaches the logic upon which it is founded. [...] Where one who has suffered damage by fire proves the origin of a fire and the course of that fire up to the point of the destruction of his property, one has certainly established liability on the part of the originator of the fire. Granting that the union of that fire with another of natural origin, or with another of much greater proportions, is available as a defence, the burden is on the defendant to show that by reason of such union with a fire of such character the fire set by him was not the proximate cause of the damage. No principle of justice requires that the plaintiff be placed under the burden of specifically identifying the origin of both fires in order to recover the damages for which either or both fires are responsible.

Notes

In *Kingston*, Northwestern Railway was liable for all of the damage to the plaintiff even though their negligence ignited only one of the two fires, which eventually united with another fire of unknown origin and collectively destroyed the plaintiff's property. This is because, as I have mentioned earlier, it would be unjust to deny the injured party a remedy simply because he cannot identify the source of the second fire. Therefore, if it can be proven that one party's negligence caused the type and character of injury the plaintiff suffered, which means the injury was reasonably foreseeable,

244   *Negligence*

then the defendant who has been identified to be negligent will be fully liable.

From *Sindell* and *Cook*, we learn that if the plaintiff cannot identify the particular defendant whose negligence injured him, but can identify a group of defendants, then all of the negligent parties will be held liable. From *Kingston*, however, we learn that if the plaintiff can identify only one negligent party whose misconduct is an element of the aggregate injury, and cannot identify the other defendants, then the negligent party that the plaintiff has identified will be liable for all of the injury the plaintiff sustained.

For example, imagine you have spilled nearly 500 millilitres of oil on a tiled-floor, which you did not clean or warn others by placing a cautionary sign. About ten meters away, someone else spilled approximately two litres of oil, which eventually merged with the oil you spilled earlier. If a person slips, falls, and injures himself on the oil, then you and the other negligent party will be liable because it is reasonably foreseeable that a slippery floor can cause a person to lose balance and injure himself. However, if the plaintiff can only identify you and does not know who spilled the other two litres of oil, he will be able to seek compensation from you, and you cannot disclaim liability by saying there was another negligent party and he should be held liable as well. Nonetheless, would the defendant be liable if there are multiple causes of the plaintiff's injury?

Wilsher v Essex Area Health Authority[161]

On 15 December 1978, Martin Wilsher was born nearly 3 months prematurely and weighed 1.2 kilograms. In the first few weeks of his life, Mr. Wilsher suffered from the kinds of health risks that beleaguer premature babies, of which the greatest danger was death by brain damage because his incompletely developed lungs could not supply oxygen to the brain. While he is alive and currently 10 years old, he suffers from a problem common to premature babies, retrolental fibroplasia (hereinafter "RLF"), which is an incurable condition of the retina that has caused total blindness in one eye and impaired vision in the other. Therefore, he has brought proceedings against the Essex Area Hospital Authority, which is responsible for overseeing the Princess Alexandra Hospital, where Mr. Wilsher was born, under negligence, alleging that his RLF was caused by a profusion of oxygen because proper skill was not used in managing his oxygen supply.

Mr. Wilsher's case is primarily predicated on the negligent treatment he received in the first 38 hours after his birth. When monitoring the partial pressure of oxygen (hereinafter "PO_2") in the arterial blood of a premature baby, it is standard practice to insert a catheter into the umbilical artery and pass it to the aorta. This allows PO_2 to be measured in two ways: firstly, there is an electronic sensor at the tip of the catheter, which is connected to a monitor outside the patient's body, that provides an accurate reading of the PO_2; and secondly, close to the sensor in the catheter, an aperture collects blood samples at regular intervals to check the monitor's calibration and adjust it if required. It is standard practice to administer an X-ray to

Negligence 245

check the location of the sensor once the catheter is inserted. Unfortunately, Mr. Wilsher's catheter was inserted into a vein, instead of an artery, and therefore, the sensor and the aperture were wrongly located inside the heart and not the aorta. This meant that the sample was of arterial and venous bloods, instead of pure arterial blood, which provided false readings of PO_2 levels in the arterial blood. The doctors who saw the X-ray failed to notice this mistake. Nonetheless, finding in favour of the hospital, the court said,

> There was in the voluminous expert evidence given at the trial an irreconcilable conflict of opinion as to the cause of Martin's RLF. It was common ground that a sufficiently high level of PO_2 in the arterial blood of a very premature baby, if maintained for a sufficiently long period of time, can have a toxic effect on the immature blood vessels in the retina leading to a condition which may either regress or develop into RLF. It was equally common ground, however, that RLF may occur in premature babies who have survived without any artificial administration of oxygen and that there is evidence to indicate a correlation between RLF and a number of other conditions from which premature babies commonly suffer (e.g. apnoea, hypercarbia, intraventricular haemorrhage, patent ductus arteriosus, all conditions which afflicted Martin) although no causal mechanisms linking these conditions with the development of RLF have been positively identified. However, what, if any, part artificial administration of oxygen causing an unduly high level of PO_2 in Martin's arterial blood played in the causation of Martin's RLF was radically in dispute between the experts. There was certainly evidence led in support of the plaintiff's case that high levels of PO_2 in general and, more particularly, the level of PO_2 maintained when the misplaced catheter was giving misleadingly low readings of the level in the arterial blood were probably at least a contributory cause of Martin's RLF. If the judge had directed himself that it was for the plaintiff to discharge the onus of proving causation on a balance of probabilities and had indicated his acceptance of this evidence in preference to the contrary evidence led for the authority, a finding in favour of the plaintiff would have been unassailable. That is why it is conceded by counsel for the authority that the most he can ask for, if his appeal succeeds, is an order for retrial of the causation issue. However, the burden of the relevant expert evidence led for the authority, to summarize it in very general terms, was to the effect that any excessive administration of oxygen which resulted from the misplacement of the catheter did not result in the PO_2 in the arterial blood being raised to a sufficiently high level for a sufficient length of time to have been capable of playing any part in the causation of Martin's RLF. One of the difficulties is that, underlying this conflict of medical opinion, there was not only a profound difference of view about the aetiology and causation of RLF in general but also a substantial difference as to the inferences which were to be drawn from the primary facts, as ascertained from the clinical

246   *Negligence*

notes about Martin's condition and treatment at the material time and amplified by the oral evidence of Dr. Wiles, the senior house officer in charge, as to what the actual levels of PO_2 in Martin's arterial blood were likely to have been during a critical period between 10 pm on 16 December when Martin was first being administered pure oxygen through a ventilator and 8 am the next morning when, after discovery of the mistake about the catheter, the level of oxygen administration was immediately reduced.

Notes

Wilsher is in harmony with the cases we have discussed in this section, but it must be distinguished from *Sindell* and *Cook*. In those cases, the cause of the injury was identified (DES and gunshot wound respectively), but which particular defendant was negligent was not (200 parties and two parties respectively). Nonetheless, since the plaintiffs were able to prove that the defendants' negligence *caused* their injury, all of the defendants were held liable. However, in *Wilsher*, Mr. Wilsher could not prove that his RLF was *caused by* the hospital's negligence, as there were multiple causes of RLF and negligently administering oxygen was only one of them. In order to understand this better, I will contrast *Wilsher* from *Sindell* and *Cook*.

In *Sindell*, Judith Sindell would not have suffered the injury "but for" the defendants' negligence. As in, since the defendants manufactured and sold DES as a miscarriage preventative drug without warning physicians and customers of its attendant risks, Judith Sindell suffered permanent injuries when her pregnant mother took the drug. That is to say, had the defendants been more careful, Judith Sindell would not have sustained injuries. Therefore, while she could not prove which of the 200 pharmaceutical companies manufactured the drug her pregnant mother ingested that ultimately caused her injuries, she was able to prove that the cause of her injuries was DES.

In *Cook*, Mr. Lewis would not have lost an eye "but for" Mr. Cook and Mr. Akenhead's negligence in firing their guns. However, and similar to *Sindell*, Mr. Lewis could not prove whose bullet, whether fired from Mr. Cook or Mr. Akenhead's firearm, injured him. Nonetheless, since he was able to prove that his injury was caused by the bullet fired by either Mr. Cook or Mr. Akenhead, both parties were held equally liable.

Wilsher, however, is materially different. Here, the doubt is not about *which negligent party* injured the plaintiff; rather, it is about *what caused the injury*. As in, since there were multiple causes of the RLF – e.g. apnoea, hypercarbia, intraventricular haemorrhage, patent ductus arteriosus – and excess oxygen was one of them, Mr. Wilsher could not prove that the doctor's negligence caused his injury. As in, even if the plaintiff cannot prove *which defendant* caused the injury, he must nevertheless prove that the defendant's misconduct *caused* his injury either using the "but for" or material contribution test.[162] As was said in *Resurface Corp v Hanke*,[163]

Much judicial and academic ink has been spilled over the proper test for causation in cases of negligence. [...]

First, the basic test for determining causation remains the "but for" test. This applies to multi-cause injuries. The plaintiff bears the burden of showing that "but for" the negligent act or omission of each defendant, the injury would not have occurred. Having done this, contributory negligence may be apportioned, as permitted by statute.

However, in special circumstances, the law has recognized exceptions to the basic "but for" test, and applied a "material contribution" test. Broadly speaking, the cases in which the "material contribution" test is properly applied involve two requirements.

First, it must be impossible for the plaintiff to prove that the defendant's negligence caused the plaintiff's injury using the "but for" test. The impossibility must be due to factors that are outside of the plaintiff's control; for example, current limits of scientific knowledge. Second, it must be clear that the defendant breached a duty of care owed to the plaintiff, thereby exposing the plaintiff to an unreasonable risk of injury, and the plaintiff must have suffered that form of injury. In other words, the plaintiff's injury must fall within the ambit of the risk created by the defendant's breach. In those exceptional cases where these two requirements are satisfied, liability may be imposed, even though the "but for" test is not satisfied, because it would offend basic notions of fairness and justice to deny liability by applying a "but for" approach.

5.10 Remoteness

As we have learned in the previous section, if the defendant's misconduct does not *cause* the plaintiff's injury, then he will not be held liable. This segues perfectly into remoteness, and that is, if the plaintiff's injury is not "reasonably foreseeable," or is not of a "type or character" that can be said to result from the defendant's negligence, then the injury did not happen "but for" the defendant's negligence, or he did not materially contribute to the plaintiff's injury, and therefore, the defendant will not be held liable. Thence, moving forward, after reading each case, please ask yourself, (1) whether the plaintiff would have suffered the injury "but for" the defendant's misconduct (or whether the defendant materially contributed to the plaintiff's injury), and (2) whether the injury was "reasonably foreseeable."

Overseas Tankship (UK) Ltd v Morts Dock & Engineering Co Ltd[164]

Morts Dock & Engineering Company Ltd (hereinafter "Morts") owned and operated the Sheerlegs Wharf, which is a dock in Sydney, Australia, where they carried on ship building, ship repairing, and general engineering work. In October and November of 1951, Morts was working on a vessel (the Corrimal), and for this purpose, was using electric and oxyacetylene welding equipment. Approximately 600 feet away, on the northern shore of the harbour, the Wagon Mound, which was chartered by demise[165] by Overseas Tankship (UK) Ltd (hereinafter "Tankship"), was discharging gasoline

248   *Negligence*

products and taking in bunkering oil from 9:00 am 29 October to 11:00 am 30 October.

In the early hours of 30 October, a large quantity of bunkering oil spilled onto the bay because of the negligence of Tankship's employees, and by 10:30 am on the same day, the oil had come near Sheerlegs Wharf. When the Manager at Morts became aware of this, he instructed employees to stop all welding activities. He then asked the Manager at Caltex Oil Co whether they could safely carry on welding. A few hours later, he decided that it was safe to do so because he was told, and coupled with his own belief, that furnace oil was not flammable since it was in water. He nevertheless instructed his employees to take safety precautions so that flammable material does not fall into the water.

At about 2:00 pm on 1 November, a fire, which developed into a conflagration, caused considerable damage to Sheerlegs Wharf and the Corrimal. Evidence was adduced that there was a cotton rag in the water near Sheerlegs Wharf and molten metal, from welding carried on at the wharf, fell on it, which sparked and ignited a fire. Morts brought an action under negligence against Tankship for the damage they suffered, which they won in lower court and on appeal. However, Tankship then appealed to the Judicial Committee of the Privy Council, which found in their favour and said,

> There can be no doubt that the decision of the Court of Appeal in *Polemis* plainly asserts that, if the defendant is guilty of negligence, he is responsible for all the consequences, whether reasonably foreseeable or not. The generality of the proposition is, perhaps, qualified by the fact that each of the lords justices refers to the outbreak of fire as the direct result of the negligent act. There is thus introduced the conception that the negligent actor is not responsible for consequences which are not "direct", whatever that may mean. It has to be asked, then, why this conclusion should have been reached. The answer appears to be that it was reached on a consideration of certain authorities, comparatively few in number, that were cited to the court. Of these, three are generally regarded as having influenced the decision. The earliest in point of date was *Smith v London & South Western Ry Co*. In that case, it was said that,
>
>> [...] when it has been once determined that there is evidence of negligence, the person guilty of it is equally liable for its consequences, whether he could have foreseen them or not [...]
>
> Similar observations were made by other members of the court. Three things may be noted about this case: the first, that, for the sweeping proposition laid down, no authority was cited; the second, that the point to which the court directed its mind was not unforeseeable damage of a different kind from that which was foreseen, but more extensive damage of the same kind; and the third that so little was the mind of the court directed to the problem which has now to be solved that no one of the seven judges who took part in the decision thought it

Negligence   249

necessary to qualify in any way the consequences for which the defendants were to be held responsible. It would, perhaps, not be improper to say that the law of negligence as an independent tort was then of recent growth, and that its implications had not been fully examined. [...]

In *Sharp v Powell*, the defendant's servant, in breach of the *Metropolitan Police Act, 1839*, washed a van in a public street and allowed the waste water to run down the gutter towards a grating leading to the sewer, about twenty-five yards off. In consequence of the extreme severity of the weather, the grating was obstructed by ice, and the water flowed over a portion of the causeway and froze. There was no evidence that the defendant knew of the grating being obstructed. The plaintiff's horse, while being led past the spot, slipped on the ice and broke its leg. The defendant was held not to be liable. The judgment of Bovill CJ is particularly valuable and interesting. He said [...]

> No doubt one who commits a wrongful act is responsible for the ordinary consequences which are likely to result therefrom; but, generally speaking, he is not liable for damage which is not the natural or ordinary consequence of such an act, unless it be shown that he knows, or has reasonable means of knowing, that consequences not usually resulting from the act are, by reason of some existing cause, likely to intervene so as to occasion damage to a third person. Where there is no reason to expect it, and no knowledge in the person doing the wrongful act that such a state of things exists as to render the damage probable, if injury does result to a third person it is generally considered that the wrongful act is not the proximate cause of the injury, so as to render the wrongdoer liable to an action.

Here all the elements are blended "natural" or "ordinary consequences", "foreseeability", "proximate cause". What is not suggested is that the wrongdoer is liable for the consequences of his wrongdoing whether reasonably foreseeable or not, or that there is one criterion for culpability, another for compensation. It would, indeed, appear to their Lordships that, unless the learned chief justice was making a distinction between "one who commits a wrongful act" and one who commits an act of negligence, the case is not reconcilable with *Polemis*.

Enough has been said to show that the authority of *Polemis* has been severely shaken, though lip-service has from time to time been paid to it. In their Lordships' opinion, it should no longer be regarded as good law. It is not probable that many cases will for that reason have a different result, though it is hoped that the law will be thereby simplified, and that, in some cases at least, palpable injustice will be avoided. For it does not seem consonant with current ideas of justice or morality that, for an act of negligence, however slight or venial, which results in some trivial foreseeable damage, the actor should be liable for all consequences, however unforeseeable and however grave, so long as they can be said to be "direct." It is a principle of civil liability, subject only

250 *Negligence*

to qualifications which have no present relevance, that a man must be considered to be responsible for the probable consequences of his act. To demand more of him is too harsh a rule, to demand less is to ignore that civilized order requires the observance of a minimum standard of behaviour. This concept, applied to the slowly developing law of negligence, has led to a great variety of expressions which can, as it appears to their Lordships, be harmonized with little difficulty with the single exception of the so-called rule in *Polemis*. For, if it is asked why a man should be responsible for the natural or necessary or probable consequences of his act (or any other similar description of them), the answer is that it is not because they are natural or necessary or probable, but because, since they have this quality, it is judged, by the standard of the reasonable man, that he ought to have foreseen them. Thus it is that, over and over again, it has happened that, in different judgments in the same case and sometimes in a single judgment, liability for a consequence has been imposed on the ground that it was reasonably foreseeable, or alternatively on the ground that it was natural or necessary or probable. The two grounds have been treated as conterminous, and so they largely are. But, where they are not, the question arises to which the wrong answer was given in *Polemis*. For, if some limitation must be imposed on the consequences for which the negligent actor is to be held responsible – and all are agreed that some limitation there must be – why should that test (reasonable foreseeability) be rejected which, since he is judged by what the reasonable man ought to foresee, corresponds with the common conscience of mankind, and a test (the "direct" consequence) be substituted which leads to nowhere but the never ending and insoluble problems of causation.

Notes

This case overturned *Re Polemis and Furness, Withy & Co, Ltd*, where the court said that a negligent actor is liable for all damage resulting directly from his negligence even if the damage was not reasonably foreseeable.[166] While the facts of the two cases are similar, it is of paramount importance to understand why liability was not imposed in *The Wagon Mound* even though Tankship's employees were negligent.

There was sufficient evidence to demonstrate that the large quantity of bunkering oil would not have spilled "but for" the negligence of Tankship's employees. If *Polemis* was followed, then Tankship would have been found liable for the resulting damage.[167] However, in *The Wagon Mound*, the court asked whether the defendant could "reasonably foresee" that his negligent conduct could cause the kind of injury the plaintiff suffered, and concluded that the injury complained of (e.g. destruction by fire) was not reasonably foreseeable from the negligence in question (e.g. spillage of oil).

If oil is spilled in water, the kind of injury that is reasonably foreseeable is contamination of the water, which may kill marine life, or if that water is used for irrigation, the crops that come into contact with that water. However, a fire would not start "but for" *novus actus interveniens*. As in, if oil spilled and it went over to Sheerlegs Wharf, and its Manager stopped welding-work, then molten metal from welding would not have fallen into the water and a fire would not ignite. Furthermore, it is important to note that molten metal did not drop into the water and ignite a fire; rather, it fell on a cotton rag, which was already in the water, due to no fault of Tankship, and then started the fire. In simpler terms, if oil was left at Sheerlegs Wharf without the cotton rag and welding stopped, then there was a high probability that a fire would not ignite. That is to say, oil, left alone, does not fortuitously ignite but for a new act, which, in this case, was the welding carried on by Morts.

Oil is different from hay or matchsticks, which, in dry weather, can naturally spark and ignite a fire even if they are left alone. For example, imagine you own a parcel of land in Bagmara, Rajshahi. You construct a small bungalow, without sufficient ventilation, to store hay on your land, but near the contiguous boundary with your neighbour. If the hay ignites and destroys your neighbour's property, you will be held liable for the damage because it is reasonably foreseeable that hay, without proper ventilation, can spark a fire even if it is left alone.[168] This is materially different from oil, which would not ignite a fire unless done so by some other act.

Let us use another example. Imagine you spilled oil on a tiled-floor and did not place any cautionary signs warning others of the spill. If someone slips on the oil, falls, and injures himself, you will be liable because it is reasonably foreseeable that a person will fall and injure himself on an oily surface as oil can render a tiled-floor slippery.[169] However, what is not reasonably foreseeable is the oil fortuitously igniting a fire and destroying the building.[170]

Overall, and in reference to *The Wagon Mound*, this means that if the type of injury (the destruction of the Corrimal and Sheerlegs Wharf by fire) is not "reasonably foreseeable" from the negligent conduct (spilling bunkering oil into the water), then the defendant is not liable. As in, there must be a nexus between the two, which is the proximate cause, or *causation*. If this connection does not exist, then the defendant cannot be held liable and it does not matter how negligent his conduct truly was because the type of injury the plaintiff suffered is not the natural result of the kind of negligent conduct in question.[171]

Smith v Leech Brain & Co Ltd[172]

William John Smith worked as a galvanizer at Glaucus Iron Works, Poplar, England, which was owned by Leech Brain & Co Ltd (hereinafter "Leech Brain"). His job was to dip articles into, first, hydrochloric acid, and then into a tank containing molten metallic zinc and flux, whose temperature could be as high as 400°C. If the articles were large, they were lowered into the tanks with an overhead crane, which was operated by their employees, and one of them was Mr. Smith, from a position behind a sheet of corrugated iron.

On 15 August 1950, William was operating an overhead crane, and as he was lowering a large article, a piece of molten metallic zinc or flux struck and burned his lower lip even though he was behind the sheet of corrugated

252 *Negligence*

iron. The burn was treated immediately. However, the place where the burn had been (on his lip) began to get larger and ulcerate, and therefore, he consulted a doctor who referred him to another hospital. At this hospital, it was diagnosed that the burn developed into cancer, which was treated with radium needles and was able to destroy primary growth. Soon thereafter, secondary growth occurred, and while William received approximately six or seven operations, he died from cancer on 14 October 1953.

His wife, Mary Emma Smith, seeks damages from Leech Brain under negligence for their failure to provide more protective gear to their employees operating the overhead crane. However, Leech Brain contends that since Mr. Smith worked in the gas industry from 1926 to 1935, he was more susceptible to cancer, which is not their fault. Therefore, for this reason, Leech Brain claims they are only liable for the initial injury and not its sequela. Finding Leech Brain entirely liable, the court said,

> For my part, I am quite satisfied that the Judicial Committee in *The Wagon Mound* did not have what I may call, loosely, the "thin skull" cases in mind. It has always been the law of this country that a tortfeasor takes his victim as he finds him. It is unnecessary to do more than refer to the short passage in the decision of Kennedy J in *Dulieu v White & Sons* [...] where he said:
>
> > If a man is negligently run over or otherwise negligently injured in his body, it is no answer to the sufferer's claim for damages that he would have suffered less injury, or no injury at all, if he had not had an unusually thin skull or an unusually weak heart.
>
> It is true that, if one takes the wording in the advice given by Viscount Simonds in *The Wagon Mound* and applies it strictly to such a case as this, it could be said that they were dealing with this point. But, as I have said, it is, to my mind, quite impossible to conceive that they were, and, indeed, it has been pointed out that they disclose the distinction between such a case as this and the one which they were considering, when they comment on *Smith v London & South Western Ry Co* Lord Simonds, in dealing with that case in *The Wagon Mound* [...] said this:
>
> > Three things may be noted about this case: the first, that, for the sweeping proposition laid down, no authority was cited; the second, that the point to which the court directed its mind was not unforeseeable damage of a different kind from that which was foreseen, but more extensive damage of the same kind [...]
>
> In other words, Lord Simonds is clearly there drawing a distinction between the question whether a man could reasonably anticipate a type of injury, and the question whether a man could reasonably anticipate the extent of injury of the type which could be foreseen. The Judicial Committee were, I think, disagreeing with the decision in *Re Polemis* that a man is no longer liable for the type of damage which he could

Negligence 253

not reasonably anticipate. The Judicial Committee were not, I think, saying that a man is only liable for the extent of damage which he could anticipate, always assuming the type of injury could have been anticipated. That view is really supported by the way in which cases of this sort have been dealt with in Scotland. Scotland has never, as far as I know, adopted the principle laid down in *Re Polemis*, and yet I am quite satisfied that they have throughout proceeded on the basis that the tortfeasor takes the victim as he finds him.

In those circumstances, it seems to me that this is plainly a case which comes within the old principle. The test is not whether these defendants could reasonably have foreseen that a burn would cause cancer and that Mr. Smith would die. The question is whether these defendants could reasonably foresee the type of injury which he suffered, namely, the burn. What, in the particular case, is the amount of damage which he suffers as a result of that burn, depends on the characteristics and constitution of the victim. Accordingly, I find that the damages which the plaintiff claims are damages for which these defendants are liable.

Notes

From *Smith*, we must understand two things. First, Leech Brain was held liable under negligence because the protection they provided to their employees operating the overhead crane was insufficient. Recall from *Bolton*, *Latimer*, and *Tomlinson*, which all relied on the Hand Formula, that a person is not required to eliminate the risk of injury, but is only required to diminish it.[173] This means that Leech Brain was not under a duty to stop its employees from using the overhead crane, for if this were so, their business would come to a grinding halt. They were, however, required to diminish the risk of injury, which the court said was insufficient, as the sheet of corrugated iron was not large enough. Rather, since the temperature of the molten metal could be as high as 400° Celsius, Leech Brain should have provided protective headgear so that not even a fleck of molten metal, from a splash or otherwise, comes into contact with a person's face.

It is a natural, or a reasonably foreseeable, consequence that molten metal could burn someone. Since the injury William Smith suffered was a burn that was caused by molten metal striking his lip, it is of a type that was reasonably foreseeable. As in, he did not contract a frostbite or influenza or COVID-19 from coming into contact with molten metal; rather, as a galvanizer, who handles material with extremely high temperatures, one of the kinds of injuries he could suffer was a burn, which is the type of injury he sustained.

Essentially, as I have mentioned earlier, nearly every product, or activity, carries risks that are reasonably foreseeable.[174] For example, *inter alia*, double or triple A batteries left on the floor can cause one to trip and fall; a can of aerosol placed in direct sunlight can cause it to explode; during sky-diving, one's parachute may inexplicably not open; and oil left on a surface

254 *Negligence*

can cause one to slip and fall. If any of the enumerated happens, then the defendant can be held liable as the injury the plaintiff has suffered is reasonably foreseeable and can be said to have been caused by the negligence of the defendant.

However, take the example of the skydiver, who is a civilian, and is, therefore, strapped to an instructor. Imagine that the parachute opens, but a falcon pecks a hole into it. They eject from the damaged parachute and open their reserve parachute. At approximately 300 feet from the ground, that same falcon pecks another hole into their second parachute. Unfortunately, both of them tumble to the ground, break both of their ankles, and severely injure their lower backs. For this injury, the company that took the skydiver up for the jump would not be liable because the injury is of a type that was not reasonably foreseeable. As in, this injury happened because of the falcon and not due to the negligence of the company. If, however, the parachute did not open, then the company who took the skydiver up for the jump could be liable for any subsequent injuries he sustains, as (1) the company was negligent in overseeing whether the parachute was packed properly so that it could be deployed on command, and (2) the injury the skydiver sustained is of a type that is reasonably foreseeable (or, is the natural result of the parachute not opening).

Second, and more importantly, Leech Brain contended that while they were negligent, they should not be held liable for William's cancer because he worked in the gas industry for 9 years and that would have made him more susceptible to cancer anyway. Essentially, Leech Brain's argument was that the injury William suffered (the burn on his lip due to the negligence of Leech Brain) was too remote and unconnected to the ultimate result (death because of cancer that developed from the burned lip). That is to say, the cancer was not reasonably foreseeable. To this end, they relied heavily on *The Wagon Mound*, but it was to no avail.

In *The Wagon Mound*, Lord Simonds said,

> Three things may be noted about this case: the first, that, for the sweeping proposition laid down, no authority was cited; the second, that the point to which the court directed its mind was not unforeseeable damage of a different kind from that which was foreseen, but more extensive damage of the same kind [...]

The court, in *Smith*, interpreted the above passage and said,

> Lord Simonds is clearly there drawing a distinction between the question whether a man could reasonably anticipate a type of injury, and the question whether a man could reasonably anticipate the extent of injury of the type which could be foreseen.

As in, the question is, "was the injury of a type that was reasonably foreseeable," and if so, then the defendant will be liable for the outcome – whatever it may be.

Recall from earlier the thin-skull rule, which was originally propounded in *Vosburg*, and says that the defendant must "take [his] victim as [he] find[s] him." Therefore, even if Mr. Smith was infirm and the ultimate result (e.g. death by cancer) was not reasonably foreseeable from the initial injury (burn to the lip), the defendant will nevertheless be held liable for it.[175] As in, all that is required is that the plaintiff prove that the defendant's negligence caused his initial injury, and if the initial injury causes more harm than was reasonably foreseeable because of the plaintiff's infirmity, then the defendant will be held fully liable for the ultimate result even if he was unaware of the plaintiff's weak constitution.[176]

Stephenson v Waite Tileman Ltd[177]

Mr. Stephenson worked as a steeplejack at Waite Tileman Limited (hereinafter "Tileman"). On 15 March 1965, during work, he was resetting the wire-rope system of a crane because it began to de-strand. As in, small sections of main strands broke off, which made it frail and fragile and was capable of seriously injuring someone. Unfortunately, while Mr. Stephenson was working, the rope broke free from its sheave and cut the back of his right hand. He immediately washed the wound with cold water and covered it with a plaster.

However, within a few days, his arm began to swell and he developed a fever, and therefore, he was admitted to a hospital. While his fever and swelling subsided, he developed debilitating symptoms, which made him unable to look after himself, as he began experiencing severe headaches and loss of balance. Furthermore, he cannot concentrate and walks with the help of a stick. Mr. Stephenson brought proceedings against Tileman under negligence. Finding in his favour, the court said,

> It is the broad contention of the appellant that a correct application of the decision in *The Wagon Mound (No 1)* [...] to the circumstances of the present case involves no more than that the initial injury to the appellant's hand had to be a kind of injury which was reasonably foreseeable by the respondent. That it was so foreseeable is (as I have already stated) not in dispute. In effect Mr. Thomas submitted that all the subsequent consequences of the initial injury should be regarded as going only to the extent of the damage suffered by the appellant and not to the kind of that damage. Mr. Casey on the other hand, contended that a proper application of *The Wagon Mound* involved a consideration of the ultimate consequences of the initial injury and a comparison of those consequences with the type of consequence which an ordinary prudent employer ought to have regarded as a real possibility flowing from a wound or scratch inflicted by the sprags of the wire rope. He argued that the answer to this question must be one of fact and degree for the jury and not a question of law and that the jury could well take the view that the consequences of this particular injury were such as to have gone beyond a mere matter of extent of the injury and to have reached a stage where they became different in kind. [...]

256 *Negligence*

As is well known, *The Wagon Mound (No 1)* was not a case of damages claimed for bodily injury. Fuel oil had been negligently discharged from a ship in Sydney Harbour. There was therefore a foreseeable risk of damage by pollution. However the damage which was claimed was damage caused by fire resulting from the fuel oil being set alight while floating on the water. There was a finding of fact by the trial Judge that the defendant did not know and could not reasonably be expected to have known that the fuel oil was capable of being set afire when spread on water. [...]

As a result of the three cases it is now quite clear that the rule of foreseeability of damage is concerned only with foreseeability of a real risk of injury of a kind (or class or character) which embraces the actual damage in suit. Although the broad basis of the rule is that it would be unjust to hold a wrongdoer liable for damage of a kind which he could not reasonably foresee, nevertheless the rule accepts the position that there are many matters of detail which nobody could predict but for which the wrongdoer nevertheless remains liable. These details may occur either in an unforeseeable concatenation of circumstances which lead up to the occurrence of damage of the foreseeable kind or they may consist of unpredictable details going to the extent or severity of the damage. To this extent then the general language used in the judgment in *The Wagon Mound (No 1)* is clearly to be read with some qualification and in particular perhaps the sentence [...] "Who knows or can be assumed to know all the processes of nature?" in so far as that sentence may imply that a wrongdoer can in no circumstances be held responsible for the operation of unpredictable natural causes.

It would seem to me that if the principle of the eggshell skull cases is still part of English law, then it must follow both on grounds of logic and practical policy that the principle of new risk created by injury must also be part of the law. It would be illogical to allow recovery in respect of disease latent in the plaintiff's body but activated by physical injury and at the same time to deny recovery in respect of illness caused by an infection entering the plaintiff's system as the result of a wound. On the more practical side, it may in any given case be quite impossible to decide in which category a particular consequence of an accident lies. Thus in the case of the present appeal, it is common ground that an infection entered the appellant's system through the wound caused by the wire rope. It is not however possible to say whether the virus was of an unusually virulent kind against which the appellant put up a normal resistance or whether the virus was one to which the appellant was unusually susceptible. [...]

I now summarize my conclusions:

1. In cases of damage by physical injury to the person the principles imposing liability for consequences flowing from the pre-existing special susceptibility of the victim and/or from new risk or susceptibility created by the initial injury remain part of our law.

Negligence   257

2. In such cases the question of foreseeability should be limited to the initial injury. The tribunal of fact must decide whether that injury is of a kind, type or character which the defendant ought reasonably to have foreseen as a real risk.

3. If the plaintiff establishes that the initial injury was within a reasonably foreseeable kind, type or character of injury, then the necessary link between the ultimate consequences of the initial injury and the negligence of the defendant can be forged simply as one of cause and effect – in other words by establishing an adequate relationship of cause and effect between the initial injury and the ultimate consequence.

Notes

Similar to *Smith*, the court in *Stephenson* held Tileman liable for all subsequent injuries Stephenson suffered because of Tileman's negligence in allowing the rope to precipitate into such disrepair. This means that Tileman would not have been found negligent had they repaired the rope earlier. As Stephenson was a steeplejack, the kind of injury he could sustain was manifold (e.g. falling from the scaffolding or injuring himself while working under insufficient lighting), and one of those injuries could be from the rope grazing his skin, and if that happened with sufficient force, it may lacerate him. Unfortunately, that is the kind of injury Stephenson suffered, which means it was reasonably foreseeable. Therefore, since the injury that Stephenson suffered was "within a reasonably foreseeable kind, type or character of injury," then the defendant, in this case, Tileman, will be found liable for its ultimate result.

There is, however, a crucial difference between *Smith* and *Stephenson*. In *Smith*, William Smith's injury (e.g. burned lip because of hot molten metal striking it) aggravated because of his "thin skull". That is to say, he was susceptible to developing cancer because he worked in the gas industry between 1926 and 1935. In *Stephenson*, however, there was no evidence that Stephenson suffered from a thin skull, but Tileman was nonetheless fully liable because the initial injury exposed the plaintiff to new kinds of risks.[178] As in, the wound can make the plaintiff more susceptible to contracting viruses and infections, and therefore, the defendant is fully liable. To further explain, even though Stephenson did not suffer from a thin skull, holding the defendant liable for the wound, because it can expose the plaintiff to new kinds of risk, is consonant with the thin-skull rule.[179]

Hughes v Lord Advocate[180]

On 8 November 1958, workers employed by the Post Office uncovered a manhole, which was about 9 feet deep, to access underground telephone cables on Russell Road, Edinburgh, Scotland. They used a ladder to descend into the manhole and the area above it was covered by a weather tent (a tarpaulin). As it began to get dark, the workmen placed four paraffin lamps

258   *Negligence*

on the corners of the tent. Shortly after 5:00 pm, they went on a tea-break for approximately fifteen minutes. Before leaving, however, they brought the ladder out of the manhole and placed it outside the tent.

Hughes, who was 8 years old, and David Leishman, who was Hughes' uncle and 10 years old, were walking down Russell Road, and noticed the tent. Since it was unguarded, they brought one lamp and the ladder inside the tent. Each boy grabbed one end of the ladder and began swinging it. Then, Hughes stumbled on the lamp and knocked it into the manhole, which produced a violent explosion that shot flames 30 feet up into the air, causing Hughes to fall into the manhole and sustain severe injuries from burns. He then brought an action against the Post Office under negligence. Finding for Hughes, the court said,

> In a word, the Post Office had brought on the public highway apparatus capable of constituting a source of danger to passers-by and in particular to small, and almost certainly inquisitive, children. It was therefore their duty to see that such passers-by, "neighbours" [...] were, so far as reasonably practicable, protected from the various obstacles, or (to children) allurements, which the workmen had brought to the site. It is clear that the safety precautions taken by the Post Office did not in this instance measure up to Lord Atkin's test.
>
> The only remaining question appears to be whether the occurrence of an explosion such as did in fact take place in the manhole was a happening which should reasonably have been foreseen by the Post Office employees. [...]
>
> It true that the duty of care expected in cases of this sort is confined to reasonably foreseeable dangers, but it does not necessarily follow that liability is escaped because the danger actually materializing is not identical with the danger reasonably foreseen and guarded against. Each case must depend on its own particular facts. For example (as pointed out in the opinions), in the present case the paraffin did the mischief by exploding, not burning, and it is said that, while a paraffin fire (caused, e.g. by the upsetting of the lighted lamp or otherwise allowing its contents to leak out) was a reasonably foreseeable risk so soon as the pursuer got access to the lamp, an explosion was not. To my mind the distinction drawn between burning and explosion is too fine to warrant acceptance. Supposing the pursuer had on the day in question gone to the site and taken one of the lamps, and upset it over himself, thus setting his clothes alight, the person to be considered responsible for protecting children from the dangers to be found there would presumably have been liable. On the other hand, if the lamp, when the boy upset it, exploded in his face, he would have had no remedy, because the explosion was an event which could not reasonably be foreseen. This does not seem to me to be right. I think that in these imaginary circumstances the danger would be a danger of fire of some

Negligence 259

kind, e.g. setting alight to his clothes or causing him bodily hurt. If there is a risk of such a fire as that I do not think that the duty of care prescribed in *Donoghue v Stevenson* is prevented from coming into operation by the presence of the remote possibility of the more serious event of an explosion.

Notes

As we already know, a person is not required to eliminate the risk of injury, but is only required to diminish it. In *Hughes*, since the Post Office did not extinguish the paraffin lamps, the court held that they did not diminish the risk of injury, and therefore, they were negligent.[181] More importantly, though, we must understand why they were liable for the burns that Hughes suffered from the explosion resulting from the paraffin lamp falling into the manhole.

It is important to distinguish this case from *The Wagon Mound*. In that case, Tankship was not held liable for the destruction of Sheerlegs Wharf and Corrimal, even though Tankship's employees were negligent and spilled a large quantity of oil, which ultimately ignited a fire and destroyed the aforesaid, because the fire was not reasonably foreseeable; that is, and as I have previously mentioned, oil left alone does not fortuitously ignite, but does so only when a new act intervenes (e.g. someone tossing a lit match onto the oil). However, the same cannot be said about an unextinguished paraffin lamp.

A paraffin lamp, similar to a candle, uses fire to emit light. Reading that sentence, a reasonable person is supposed know that if the lamp comes into contact with nearly anything, with the exception of, *inter alia*, water, glass, and steel, it can ignite a fire. That is to say, it was reasonably foreseeable that the lamp may light, or spread, a fire if it touches something else. However, and interestingly, in *Hughes*, the lamp was accidentally knocked into the manhole by Hughes, which caused the violent explosion; as in, had Hughes not been playing with the ladder inside the tent, then he probably would not have been injured, which means it was not the fault of the Post Office. Here, we must distinguish between injuries that happen *vis major* and injuries that are a natural result of one's negligence.

For example, if you are driving through Gulshan Avenue during a tempest, and a sign that prescribes the speed limit falls on your windshield and shatters it, you cannot bring an action against the government for the loss you have suffered, because the cause of the damage was *vis major*, or in other words, by a superior force. As in, the sign fell on your windshield due to gale winds, which is a force of nature, and not because of the negligence of the government in installing it. However, if the sign falls on your windshield and inexplicably ignites a fire that damages your vehicle, and it is later discovered that the government failed to remove a protective film from the sign, which was heavily doused with petroleum, then you can bring an action against the government under negligence. As in, even though the sign fell on your vehicle by natural causes, it would not have

260   *Negligence*

ignited a fire had the government removed the petroleum-doused protective film.

In *Hughes*, while the boy inadvertently knocked the paraffin lamp into the manhole, it could have been just as likely that a wind did the same. In either case, the Post Office would have been liable (if someone sustained injuries, and in this case, Hughes did) because even if the lamp fell by natural reasons, it could have caused an explosion that injured someone else.[182] That is to say, because the employees did not extinguish the paraffin lamps, they were not as careful as they should have been. Furthermore, the kind of injuries Hughes sustained was of the "type or character" that was reasonably foreseeable; as in, a paraffin lamp left unextinguished can ignite a fire, which actually happened, and it is from this fire that Hughes suffered severe injuries.

Doughty v Turner Manufacturing Co Ltd[183]

Mr. Doughty worked at Turner Manufacturing Company Limited (hereinafter "Turner Manufacturing"). During work, he went to the heat-treatment department, which contained two baths of cauldrons, to deliver a message to the foreman. Each cauldron was approximately 3 feet 10 inches high and contained an internal space of 18 inches by 31 inches. Two upright electrodes were lowered by chains into the baths, which contained cyanide powder – turning the powder into a viscous molten liquid with a temperature of 800°C.

In order to preserve the temperature of the liquid inside the cauldrons, two covers, which were made by a compound of asbestos and cement, were placed side-by-side over the cauldrons. Unfortunately, a workman accidentally knocked a cover into the cauldron, which disappeared into the molten liquid. After about a minute and a half, the liquid erupted and injured Mr. Doughty and others.

The asbestos and cement covers were bought from reputable manufacturers and have been used in England and the United States for over 20 years. Nonetheless, for his injuries, Mr. Doughty brought an action against Turner Manufacturing. Finding against him, the court said,

> In the present case the evidence showed that nobody supposed that an asbestos cement cover could not safely be immersed in the bath. The learned judge took the view, which counsel for the plaintiff concedes was correct, that if the defendants had deliberately immersed this cover in the bath as part of the normal process, they could not have been held liable for the resulting explosion. The fact that they inadvertently knocked it into the bath cannot of itself convert into negligence that which they were entitled to do deliberately. In the then state of their knowledge, for which the learned judge, rightly on the evidence, held them in no way to blame, the accident was not foreseeable. In spite of counsel for the plaintiff's able argument I am of opinion that they cannot, therefore, be held liable for negligence.

Negligence 261

The evidence showed that splashes caused by sudden immersion, whether of the metal objects for which it was intended or any other extraneous object, were a foreseeable danger which should be carefully avoided. The falling cover might have ejected the liquid by a splash and in the result it did eject the liquid, though in a more dramatic fashion. Therefore, he argues, the actual accident was merely a variant of foreseeable accidents by splashing. It is clear, however, both by inference and by one explicit observation, that the learned judge regarded splashes as being in quite a different category. Moreover, according to the evidence it seems that the cover never did create a splash: it appears to have slid into the liquid at an angle of some 45 degrees and dived obliquely downwards. Further, it seems somewhat doubtful whether the cover falling only from a height of four or six inches, which was the difference in level between the liquid and the sides, could have splashed any liquid outside the bath. And when (if ever) the plaintiff was in the area in which he could be hit by a mere splash (apparently the liquid being heavy, if splashed, would not travel further than a foot from the bath) the cover had already slid into the liquid without splashing. Indeed, it seems from the plaintiff's evidence that when he first came on to the scene the cover was already half in and half out of the liquid. On broader grounds, however, it would be quite unrealistic to describe this accident as a variant of the perils from splashing. The cause of the accident, to quote Lord Reid's words [from *Hughes*], was "the intrusion of a new and unexpected factor". There was an eruption due to chemical changes underneath the surface of the liquid as opposed to a splash caused by displacement from bodies falling on to its surface.

[Lord Justice Diplock concurred and added:]

The use of a cover made of this material presents, it is now known, two risks of injury to persons in the vicinity of the furnace. The first risk, which it shares with any other solid object of similar weight and size, is that if it is allowed to drop on to the hot liquid in the bath with sufficient momentum it may cause the liquid to splash on to persons within about one foot from the bath and injure them by burning. The second risk is that if it becomes immersed in a liquid, the temperature of which exceeds 500° C, it will disintegrate and cause an under-surface explosion which will eject the liquid from the bath over a wide area and may cause injury by burning to persons within that area.

The former risk was well-known (that was foreseeable) at the time of the accident; but it did not happen. It was the second risk which happened and caused the plaintiff damage by burning. The crucial finding by the learned judge, in a characteristically laconic judgment, was that this was not a risk of which the defendants at the time of the accident knew, or ought to have known. This finding, which was justified by the evidence and has not been assailed in this appeal, would appear to lead logically to the conclusion that in causing, or failing to prevent, the immersion of the cover in the liquid, the defendants, by their servants,

262   *Negligence*

were in breach of no duty of care owed to the plaintiff, for this was not an act or omission which they could reasonably foresee was likely to cause him damage. [...]

There is no room today for mystique in the law of negligence. It is the application of common morality and common sense to the activities of the common man. He must take reasonable care to avoid acts or omissions which he can reasonably foresee would be likely to injure his neighbours; but he need do no more than this. If the act which he does is not one which he could, if he thought about it, reasonably foresee would injure his neighbour it matters not whether he does it intentionally or inadvertently. The learned judge's finding, uncontested on appeal, that in the state of knowledge as it was at the time of the accident the defendants could not reasonably have foreseen that the immersion of the asbestos cement cover in the liquid would be likely to injure anyone, must lead to the conclusion that they would have been under no liability to the plaintiff if they had intentionally immersed the cover in the liquid. The fact that it was done inadvertently cannot create any liability, for the immersion of the cover was not an act which they were under any duty to take any care to avoid.

Notes

Imagine a two-litre bucket that is filled with water. If something is dropped into it, it is reasonably foreseeable that the water may splash outside the bucket. Now, instead of water, imagine molten liquid that is approximately 800°Celsius inside the bucket. Again, if an item is dropped into it, the molten liquid may splash outside the bucket. This means that the type and character of injury that is reasonably foreseeable, from an item dropping into liquid, is from a splash. However, Doughty was injured not from the splash, but from the molten liquid erupting as a result of the asbestos and cement cover falling into the cauldron. This means that the injury Doughty sustained from the negligent conduct (e.g. inadvertently knocking the asbestos and cement cover into the cauldron) was not reasonably foreseeable. As in, even though an employee was negligent and knocked a cover into the cauldron, since Doughty's injury was not a direct result of the type and character of injury that was reasonably foreseeable, Turner Manufacturing was not liable.

In 1964, when this incident happened, companies and scientists did not know that the asbestos and cement cover could, if submerged in the molten liquid, erupt and injure others nearby. However, shortly after this incident, an experiment conducted by Imperial Chemical Industries Limited demonstrated that any cover made of asbestos and cement, immersed into molten liquid over 500° Celsius, can cause an eruption. This means that if a similar situation were to happen today, the employer would be liable because it is his duty to remain abreast scientific developments that affect his trade; or, in other words, use a compound that will not erupt if dropped into hot molten liquid today.[184]

Negligence   263

Palsgraf v Long Island Railroad Company[185]

On 24 August 1924, Helen Palsgraf, a 40-year-old woman, was at the East New York train station with her two daughters to head to Rockaway Beach. As they waited, a train pulled in, allowed passengers to disembark and board, and then began moving again. At this time, two passengers ran towards the moving train and one boarded without incident. However, the second passenger (whose identity is not known), was carrying a package, whose content was not visible, and as he leapt onto the train, it seemed as though he was going to lose balance and fall onto the platform. Therefore, a guard on the platform pushed him in while a crew member on the train pulled him inside. Unfortunately, this dislodged the package the passenger was carrying, which caused it to fall on the platform, and since it contained fireworks, it exploded.

Helen Palsgraf was more than 10 feet away from the place of the incident. Nonetheless, either the force of the explosion or the commotion of people panicking caused a tall, coin-operated scale to fall on her, which caused her, and several others, bruises. For the injuries she sustained, Ms. Palsgraf brought an action against the Long Island Railroad Company for their negligence in pushing, and pulling, a passenger inside a moving train. Finding against her, the court said,

> The conduct of the defendant's guard, if a wrong in its relation to the holder of the package, was not a wrong in its relation to the plaintiff, standing far away. Relatively to her it was not negligence at all. Nothing in the situation gave notice that the falling package had in it the potency of peril to persons thus removed. Negligence is not actionable unless it involves the invasion of a legally protected interest, the violation of a right. [...] If no hazard was apparent to the eye of ordinary vigilance, an act innocent and harmless, at least to outward seeming, with reference to her, did not take to itself the quality of a tort because it happened to be a wrong, though apparently not one involving the risk of bodily insecurity, with reference to someone else. [...]
>
> A different conclusion will involve us, and swiftly too, in a maze of contradictions. A guard stumbles over a package which has been left upon a platform. It seems to be a bundle of newspapers. It turns out to be a can of dynamite. To the eye of ordinary vigilance, the bundle is abandoned waste, which may be kicked or trod on with impunity. Is a passenger at the other end of the platform protected by the law against the unsuspected hazard concealed beneath the waste? If not, is the result to be any different, so far as the distant passenger is concerned, when the guard stumbles over a valise which a truck-man or a porter has left upon the walk? The passenger far away, if the victim of a wrong at all, has a cause of action, not derivative, but original and primary. His claim to be protected against invasion of his bodily security is neither greater nor less because the act resulting in the invasion is a wrong to another far removed. In this case, the rights that are said to have been violated,

264   *Negligence*

the interests said to have been invaded, are not even of the same order. The man was not injured in his person nor even put in danger. [...]

The argument for the plaintiff is built upon the shifting meanings of such words as "wrong" and "wrongful," and shares their instability. What the plaintiff must show is "a wrong" to herself, *i. e.*, a violation of her own right, and not merely a wrong to someone else, nor conduct "wrongful" because unsocial, but not "a wrong" to anyone. We are told that one who drives at reckless speed through a crowded city street is guilty of a negligent act and, therefore, of a wrongful one irrespective of the consequences. Negligent the act is, and wrongful in the sense that it is unsocial, but wrongful and unsocial in relation to other travellers, only because the eye of vigilance perceives the risk of damage. If the same act were to be committed on a speedway or a race course, it would lose its wrongful quality. The risk reasonably to be perceived defines the duty to be obeyed, and risk imports relation; it is risk to another or to others within the range of apprehension [...] This does not mean, of course, that one who launches a destructive force is always relieved of liability if the force, though known to be destructive, pursues an unexpected path. [...] Some acts, such as shooting, are so imminently dangerous to anyone who may come within reach of the missile, however unexpectedly, as to impose a duty of prevision not far from that of an insurer. [...] Negligence is not a tort unless it results in the commission of a wrong, and the commission of a wrong imports the violation of a right, in this case, we are told, the right to be protected against interference with one's bodily security. But bodily security is protected, not against all forms of interference or aggression, but only against some. One who seeks redress at law does not make out a cause of action by showing without more that there has been damage to his person. If the harm was not willful, he must show that the act as to him had possibilities of danger so many and apparent as to entitle him to be protected against the doing of it though the harm was unintended. [...]

The law of causation, remote or proximate, is thus foreign to the case before us. The question of liability is always anterior to the question of the measure of the consequences that go with liability. If there is no tort to be redressed, there is no occasion to consider what damage might be recovered if there were a finding of a tort.

Notes

In *Palsgraf*, the court said that the acts of the guard on the platform (e.g. pushing the passenger inside a moving train) and the crew member on the train (e.g. pulling the same passenger inside the moving train) were wrongful, but it was not *negligent*.[186] As in, and for example, these actions happen not infrequently in Bangladesh, and during the act, if a parcel is dropped by a passenger, which explodes and injures another, the people helping the passenger on board will not be liable so long as the package is not visibly dangerous. To further explain, if it were visible that the passenger boarding

Negligence 265

the train was carrying a grenade, then the ones who helped him board a moving train could be held liable, as they placed others nearby in an unreasonable and foreseeable risk of harm.[187] However, if a passenger is carrying a parcel, whose content is not readily identifiable because it is inside a valise, and if the parcel is subsequently dropped (due to someone pushing the passenger onto the train) and explodes, which injures someone nearby, then liability cannot be imposed on the person pushing the passenger onto the train because he had no knowledge that the passenger was carrying a grenade, or other explosive devices, in his bag.

Let us consider another example. Imagine that you have gone to a concert with two of your friends in Dhaka. It is packed. In order to find a better view, the three of you begin walking towards the south entrance of the concert hall. Unfortunately, you trip on an exposed wire, and in order to prevent yourself from falling, you grab onto a stranger's jacket, which dislodges a grenade from inside his jacket pocket, causing it to explode and severely injure ten spectators. You will not be liable for the injuries because a reasonable person is not supposed to think, or know, that another person is carrying a grenade in his jacket pocket. As in, even though you may have injured others by your negligence, the type of harm caused was not reasonably foreseeable, and therefore, is too remote to ascribe liability.

Bradford v Kanellos[188]

At approximately 10:30 am on 12 April 1967, Roderick and Elizabeth Bradford, who were husband and wife, were having breakfast at Astor Delicatessen & Steak House, which is a restaurant operated by Gus Kanellos and Pete Stamatio. While seated at the counter, a flash fire occurred on the grill because of the restaurant's failure to properly clean it, thereby permitting a substantial amount of grease to accumulate. Nonetheless, the grill was equipped with an advanced fire extinguisher, which started manually to extinguish the fire. Since the fire did not last long and extinguished almost immediately, it did not damage anything. However, the extinguisher made a hissing noise when operated, which prompted an unidentified customer to shout that there was a gas leak and that an explosion was imminent. This caused people to panic and run from the restaurant, which resulted in Elizabeth Bradford being knocked down from her chair and injuring herself. Thence, for the injuries she suffered, Elizabeth brought an action against Kanellos and Stamatio for the restaurant's negligence in not properly cleaning the grill. Finding for the restaurant, the court said,

> By unanimous decision, the Court of Appeal allowed the appeal of the present respondents. Schroeder J.A., who delivered the judgment of the Court, said:
>
> > The practical and sensible view to be taken of the facts here leads fairly to the conclusion that it should not be held that the person guilty of the original negligence resulting in the flash fire on the grill ought reasonably to have anticipated the subsequent intervening act

266 *Negligence*

or acts which were the direct cause of the injuries and damages suffered by the plaintiffs.

[...] I agree with the decision of the Court of Appeal. The judgment at trial found the respondents to be liable because there had been negligence in failing to clean the grill efficiently, which resulted in the flash fire. But it was to guard against the consequences of a flash fire that the grill was equipped with a fire extinguisher system. This system was described by the Chief of the Kingston Fire Department, who was called as a witness by the appellants, as, not only an approved installation, but one of the best.

This system, when activated, following the flash fire, fulfilled its function and put out the fire. This was accomplished by the application of carbon dioxide on the fire. In so doing there was a hissing noise and it was on hearing this that one of the customers exclaimed that gas was escaping and that there was danger of an explosion, following which the panic occurred, and the appellant wife was injured.

On these facts it is apparent that her injuries resulted from the hysterical conduct of a customer which occurred when the safety appliance properly fulfilled its function. Was that consequence fairly to be regarded as within the risk created by the respondents' negligence in permitting an undue quantity of grease to accumulate on the grill? The Court of Appeal has found that it was not and I agree with that finding.

Notes

By now, we are well aware that nearly every product, or activity, carries risks that are reasonably foreseeable, and that the risk from fire is injury by burns.[189] In *Bradford*, was there a fire? Yes. Did someone suffer an injury? Yes, Mrs. Bradford. Did the fire cause the type of injury to Mrs. Bradford that is its natural consequence? No. To further explain, it is indisputable that the restaurant was negligent, which was their failure to properly clean the grill, thereby allowing a substantial amount of grease to accumulate, and this resulted in a fire. However, the fire did not injure Mrs. Bradford; rather, her injury was caused by an unidentified person knocking her down as he, or she, was leaving the restaurant in a hurry.[190] This means that even though the restaurant was negligent (failure to properly clean the grill), Mrs. Bradford's injury (being knocked from her chair and hurting herself) was not connected to their negligence, and therefore, the type and character of injury she sustained was not reasonably foreseeable. Essentially, her case would lie against the one who knocked her down from her seat, and not Kanellos or Stamatio.

Urbanski v Patel[191]

Shirley and Stanley Firman are married, have three kids, and live on a 240-acre farmland in Gimli, Manitoba, Canada. In April 1975, Mrs. Firman consulted Dr. Ramanbhai Patel and Dr. Sunilkumar Patel (collectively and hereinafter "doctors") and decided that she would undergo a tubal ligation

Negligence   267

because she did not want to have any more kids. She also mentioned that she occasionally experienced abdominal discomfort (nothing specific or disabling), which her doctors surmised was an ovarian cyst. Therefore, her doctors said that during the operation, they would explore her abdomen and, if they find a cyst, they would remove it. On 17 April 1975, Mrs. Firman submitted to the procedure. During the operation, on the left lower quadrant of her abdomen, the doctors found a cyst and excised it. She was released from the hospital on the same day. However, she was admitted to the Emergency Department of the Health Sciences Centre in Winnipeg on 19 April 1975. At this point, it was confirmed that the cyst the doctors removed (two days earlier) was a kidney that was ectopic, and therefore, mistakenly identified as an ovarian cyst.

Human beings have two kidneys that serve the vital task of cleansing the body of impurities by draining them out of the blood-system. While a person can function relatively well with one kidney (as opposed to two), Mrs. Firman only had one kidney, which may have been a congenital defect (and perhaps why she occasionally experienced abdominal discomfort). Without proper renal function, impurities interfere with the blood's ability to distribute nutrients and oxygen to other organs and its accumulation can become fatal. Therefore, on 20 April 1975, Mrs. Firman was placed on a dialysis machine, which imitates the function of a kidney.

There are two remedies to renal failure. First, the patient can be connected to a dialysis machine, which, however, is not a complete answer; and second, a kidney taken from another person can be engrafted, which is the long-term solution. Nonetheless, it is important to find a kidney that closely matches the donee's body to minimize the risk of rejection. In such complex cases, "rejection" almost always means death of the donee, whose body is shocked from the introduction of the foreign tissue.

As the search for a kidney continued, Mrs. Firman's father, Victor Urbanski, volunteered to donate one of his kidneys to his daughter. On 8 May 1976, the procedure was completed. Unfortunately, on 11 May 1976, Mrs. Firman's body showed symptoms of rejection, and therefore, the donated kidney had to be removed and she was reconnected to a dialysis machine, as it would take time to locate another donor, and even if one was found, sufficient time would have to pass before another procedure could be carried out as she developed antibodies.

For their injuries, Mrs. Firman and Mr. Urbanski brought proceedings against the doctors under negligence. Holding the doctors liable, the court said,[192]

> In testifying before me, Dr. Thomson spoke of 123 kidney transplants in Winnipeg alone; both he and Dr. Fenton spoke of the many thousands performed in the United States and Europe. [...] [C]ertainly I think it can fairly be said, in light of today's medicine, kidney transplant is an accepted remedy in renal failure. Certainly defendants here can hardly be heard to deny its "foreseeability," in the dictionary sense of that word.

268   *Negligence*

In other terms, the transplant, surely, must be viewed as an expected result, something to be anticipated, as a consequence of the loss of normal kidney function.

The world of medicine has progressed beyond the ratio in *Sirianni* [*v Anna*], so that, given the disaster which befell Shirley Firman, it was entirely foreseeable that one of her family would be invited, and would agree, to donate a kidney for transplant, an act which accords, too, with the principle developed in the many "rescue" cases.

American jurisprudence perhaps anticipated our own in this field, Mr. Justice Cardozo's classic remarks in *Wagner v International Railway* [...] being penned in 1921. From that judgment, [...]

> Danger invites rescue. The cry of distress is the summons to relief. The law does not ignore these reactions of the mind in tracing conduct to its consequences. It recognizes them as normal. It places their effects within the range of the natural and probable. The wrong that imperils life is a wrong to the imperilled victim; it is a wrong also to his rescuer [...] The risk of rescue, if only it be not wanton, is born of the occasion. The emergency begets the man. The wrongdoer may not have foreseen the coming of a deliverer. He is accountable as if he had.

In 1935, with *Haynes v Harwood* [...], Greer, LJ, accepted the American rule as stated by Professor Goodhart [...]

> In accurately summing up the American authorities [...] the learned author says this [...] 'The American rule is that the doctrine of the assumption of risk does not apply where the plaintiff has, under an exigency caused by the defendant's wrongful misconduct, consciously and deliberately faced a risk, even of death, to rescue another from imminent danger of personal injury or death, whether the person endangered is one to whom he owes a duty of protection, as a member of his family, or is a mere stranger to whom he owes no such special duty.' In my judgment that passage not only represents the law of the United States, but I think it also accurately represents the law of this country.

[...] And so, defendants, I find, are answerable to Victor Urbanski.

Notes

It is easy to understand that since the doctors were negligent in removing Mrs. Firman's kidney, which was ectopic, thinking it was an ovarian cyst, they were liable to her. The more complex issue, however, is understanding why they were liable to Mr. Urbanski who voluntarily donated his kidney to his daughter. Again, the question that must be answered is "did the doctors' initial negligence (removing Mrs. Firman's kidney in the mistaken belief that it was an ovarian cyst) cause injury to Mr. Urbanski (being deprived of one of his kidneys because he donated it to his daughter) of a type or character that was reasonably foreseeable'?"

Negligence 269

Recall from *ter Neuzen* that if the issue before the courts is technical and requires special knowledge, such as medicine or engineering, then it is the industry, and not the courts, that will determine the correct standard of care, unless the standard itself is "fraught with obvious risks."[193] *Urbanski* is an ornately complex case, and therefore, the court relied on expert evidence from doctors and concluded that the only realistic way to save a person without kidneys is by engrafting a kidney from another person; or in simpler terms, one must donate his kidney and that donated kidney must be implanted in the recipient's body.[194] This means that Mr. Urbanski did exactly what experts said is the correct treatment. Therefore, this also means that the injury Mr. Urbanski suffered (donating his kidney) was a reasonably foreseeable consequence of the doctors' negligence (excising a kidney in the mistaken belief that it was an ovarian cyst). As in, had the doctors not been negligent in excising Mrs. Firman's kidney, then Mr. Urbanski would not have suffered an injury, and since his injury was the result of the initial negligence (removing Mrs. Firman's kidney), the doctors were held liable.

From *Urbanski* and *Haynes*, it is important to understand that if the rescuer is injured as a result of the initial negligence, then the negligent actor is also liable for the rescuer's injuries.[195] For example, imagine a lake inside a public park that does not have any signs specifying the shallow and deep ends, or signs prohibiting diving. It is 45° Celsius and you are seated on a park chair having ice cream. You see that one visitor approaches the lake, opens his t-shirt, climbs a nearby tree, and dives in. You expect that he will reemerge in approximately 15 seconds, but after about 25 seconds, a lifeless body emerges surrounded by a pool of blood. Without hesitation, you run towards the water to save the injured diver, and as you bring him out of the water, you lose balance on a slippery surface (on-shore, but near the water), fall on your back, and dislocate a disc on your spinal cord. Both of you are subsequently treated for your injuries. While the diver can claim compensation from the city for their negligence (e.g. failure to prohibit diving or post signs of shallow and deep ends), you can also bring an action against the city for your dislocated disc because it is reasonably foreseeable that one may run into the water to save an injured swimmer, and if the rescuer is injured in the act of rescue, then his injury will be held to have been caused by the initial negligence.[196]

Using similar facts, let us consider a slightly different scenario. As you brought the injured diver on shore and called emergency services, an untamed dog bit your left thigh, for which you required nine stitches. Here, the city will not be liable for your injury because it is not connected to the initial negligence (e.g. failure to prohibit diving or post signs of shallow and deep ends). That is to say, the dog could have bitten you even if you were seated on the park chair. However, in the previous example, it is more probable than not that you would not have sustained an injury had you not tried to save the injured diver. To further explain, losing balance and falling on a slippery surface was part of the act of rescue, which would probably not have happened had you remained seated on the park chair; whereas, being bitten by the dog was not, which could have happened even if you were seated on the park chair.

270 *Negligence*

Rajkot Municipal Corp v Manjulben Jayantilal[197]

Mr. Jayantilal lived in Padadhari, Gujarat, India, and worked in the city of Rajkot, Gujarat, India. On 25 March 1975, as he was walking on the sidewalk to work, a road-side tree fell on him, which injured his head and other parts of his body. He was hospitalized. However, he subsequently succumbed to his injuries. Mr. Jayantilal's wife then brought an action against Rajkot Municipal Corporation under negligence for failing to maintain trees that they planted. Finding for the defendant, the court said,

> In determining the legislative intent, the Court is required to consider three factors, viz., the context and the object of the statute, the nature and precise scope of the relevant provisions and the damage suffered not of the kind to be guarded against. The object of the Act is to promote facilities of general benefit to the public as a whole in getting the trees planted on road-sides, the discharge of which is towards the public at large and not towards an individual, even though the individual may suffer some harm. [...]
>
> According to the learned counsel, the liability in tort which arose in Common Law has been evolved by the courts in England but law has not been well developed in our jurisdiction. In Common Law, there existed duty of foreseeability, proximity, just and reasonable cause and policy. Attempts have been made to identify general theory of liability in tort consistent with causation, fairness, reciprocity and justice, balancing conflicting interests as well as economic efficiency. [...] In this case, we are concerned with negligence on the part of the appellant-Corporation in maintaining the trees on the road-sides. The principle evolved by the courts in England is that a reasonable foresight of harm to persons whom it is foreseeable or is likely to harm by one's carelessness is essential. For the plaintiff to succeed in an action for negligence the plaintiff requires to prove that (i) the defendant is under a duty to take care; (ii) the burden of proof owed by the plaintiff has been discharged by the proof of breach of duty; and (iii) the breach of the duty of care is the cause for damage suffered by the plaintiff. [...]
>
> Appellant-Corporation owes a duty of care in common law. The trees and streets vest in the Corporation. It was its responsibility, therefore, to maintain the trees. The Corporation should have the foresight that trees, if neglected to be maintained properly, could cause injury to passers-by. The findings recorded by the courts below that the appellant has committed breach of duty of care are a finding of fact. From the breach of the duty of care, the entitlement to damages arises to the respondents due to the death of Jayantilal. [...]
>
> In the absence of statutory law or established principles of law laid by this Court or High Courts consistent with Indian conditions and circumstances, this Court selectively applied the common law principles evolved by the courts in England on grounds of justice, equity and good conscience [...]. Common law principles of tort evolved by the

Negligence   271

courts in England may be applied in India to the extent of suitability and applicability to the Indian conditions. Let us consider and evolve our principles in tune with the march of law in their jurisprudence of liability on tort. [...]

Local authority, when it exercises its public law function, generally owes no private law duty of care. Duty of care must be owed to a person or class of persons to which the plaintiff belongs and must be to avoid causing particular type of injury or damage to his person or property. [...]

It is now [a] well-settled legal position by court pronouncements in England that a public authority may be subject to common law duty of care when it exercises a statutory power or when there exists a statutory duty. The principle is that when a statutory power is conferred, it must be exercised with reasonable care so that if those who exercise their power could, by reasonable precaution, prevent any injury which has been occasioned and was likely to be occasioned by their exercise and the damage for negligence may be recovered. [...]

Public authority is under a duty of care in relation to decisions which involve or are directed by financial, economic, social or political factors or constraints, in that behalf, the duty of care stands excluded or any action that is merely the product of administrative direction etc. may not provide causation for damages, but when the performance of the duty, though couched with discretion, is enjoined on the statutory authority, the question whether the power, if exercised with due care, would have minimized, rather prevented or avoided the damage sustained by the plaintiff, requires to be examined. [...]

The exercise of power/omission must have been such that duty of care had arisen to avoid danger. Foreseeability of the danger or injury alone is not sufficient to conclude that duty of care exists. The fact that one could foresee that a failure of the authority to exercise a reasonable care would cause loss to the passers-by itself does not mean that such a duty of care should be imposed on the statutory authority. The statutory authority exercises its public law duty or function. [...] It would always cause heavy financial burden on the statutory authority. If the duty of maintaining constant vigil or verifying or testing the healthy condition of trees at public places with so many other functions to be performed, is cast on it, the effect would be that the authority would omit to perform statutory duty. [...]

It is seen that when a person uses a road or highway, under common law one has a right to passage over the public way. When the defendant creates by positive action any danger and no signal or warnings are given and consequently damage is done, the proximate relationship gets established between the plaintiff and the defendant and the causation is not too remote. Equally, when the defendant omits to perform a particular duty enjoined by the statute or does that duty carelessly, there is proximity between the plaintiff-injured person and the defendant in performance of the duty and when injury occurs or damage is

272 *Negligence*

suffered to person or property, cause of action arises to enable the plaintiff to claim damages from the defendant. But when the causation is too remote, it is difficult to anticipate with any reasonable certainty as ordinary reasonable prudent man, to foresee damage or injury to the plaintiff due to causation or omission on the part of the defendant in the performance or negligence in the performance of the duty. [...]

In a developing society it is but obligatory on every householder, when he constructs [a] house and equally for a public authority to plant trees and properly nurture them up in a healthy condition so as to protect and maintain the eco-friendly environment. [...] It is difficult to lay down any set standards for proof thereof. Take for instance, where a hanging branch of a tree [...] is gradually falling on the ground. The statutory/local authority fails to take timely action to have it cut and removed and one of the passers-by dies when the branch/tree falls on him. Though the injured or the deceased has contributed to the negligence for the injury or death, the local authority etc. is equally liable for its negligence/omission in the performance of the duty because the proximity is anticipated. Suppose a boy not suspecting the danger climbs or reaches the falling tree and gets hurt, the defendant would be liable for tort of negligent. The defect is apparent. Negligence is obvious, proximity and neighbourhood anticipated and lack of duty of care stands established. The plaintiff, in common law action, is entitled to sue for tort of negligence. The authority will be liable to pay the damages for omission or negligence in the performance of the duty.

Notes

From *Rajkot*, we should understand two things. Firstly, as I have elucidated in this section, if the injury is too remote (which is what happened in this case), then the party, even though he was negligent, cannot be held liable. Secondly, and more importantly, government does not owe a private duty of care to individuals, especially when it is concerned with *policy* decisions, which are dictated by financial, economic, social, or political factors. However, government can be liable if the injury-causing incident arises out of an *operational* decision.[198]

For example, let us assume that the government has constructed a two-kilometre bridge. While they are supposed to inspect the bridge biannually, due to budget cuts, they only have the wherewithal to inspect it once per year. Imagine that the government inspected the bridge on 1 January, determined that minor work was necessary, and carried out the work to the appropriate standard. However, on 8 August, the bridge collapsed and killed nearly 200 people. Had the government inspected the bridge again in June, then it is not unlikely that the bridge would *probably not* have collapsed because they may have found and fixed the defect. Nonetheless, since the government could not inspect the bridge due to financial constraints, this means that it was a *policy* decision, which *prima facie* tells us that they are excluded from liability.

Negligence 273

Imagine a slightly different scenario. While the government inspected and found a defect on 1 January, it carried out the repair work perfunctorily, and as a result, the bridge collapsed 2 months later and killed nearly 200 people. For this, the government may be held liable because their negligence was at the *operational* level. That is to say, instead of properly repairing the bridge, they did so half-heartedly, which endangered the lives of everyone who used the bridge.

5.11 Defences

Recall from the previous chapter that the extent of a person's liability could be reduced, or he could be exonerated absolutely. As in, even if he is negligent (his conduct fell below the standard of care expected of a reasonable person), his misconduct causes injury to another, and the kind of injury the plaintiff suffers is reasonably foreseeable, the defendant's liability could nevertheless be reduced if it can be demonstrated that the plaintiff contributed to his own injury, or that he voluntarily accepted the risks associated with the activity.

5.12 Contributory negligence

Froom et al v Butcher[199]

On 19 November 1972, Harold Froom was driving home to Hertfordshire with his wife beside him and his daughter seated at the back. Their car, a Jaguar, was fitted with seatbelts for the front seats, but Mr. and Mrs. Froom were not wearing them. Mr. Froom was carefully driving at 30 to 35 miles per hour on a two-way road. Unfortunately, a vehicle driven by Brian Butcher, approaching from the opposite direction, collided head-on with Mr. Froom's vehicle. Mr. Froom, his wife, and his daughter were injured in the collision. Mr. Froom was pushed up against the steering column, broke his finger, suffered abrasions to his head and bruises to his chest, and broke a rib. Fortunately, the injuries were not severe and Mr. Froom went to work the following day. Nonetheless, for the injuries they all suffered, Mr. Froom and his family brought proceedings against Mr. Butcher under negligence. Apportioning liability between Mr. Froom and Mr. Butcher, the court said,

> Negligence depends on a breach of duty, whereas contributory negligence does not. Negligence is a man's carelessness in breach of duty to *others*. Contributory negligence is a man's carelessness in looking after *his own* safety. He is guilty of *contributory* negligence if he ought reasonably to have foreseen that, if he did not act as a reasonable prudent man, he might hurt himself [...]
> In these seat belt cases, the injured plaintiff is in no way to blame for the accident itself. Sometimes he is an innocent passenger sitting beside a negligent driver who goes off the road. At other times he is an innocent driver of one car which is run into by the bad driving of another car

274 *Negligence*

which pulls out on to its wrong side of the road. It may well be asked: why should the injured plaintiff have his damages reduced? The accident was solely caused by the negligent driving by the defendant. Sometimes outrageously bad driving. It should not lie in his mouth to say: "You ought to have been wearing a seat belt." That point of view was strongly expressed in *Smith v Blackburn* [...] by O'Connor J. He said:

> The idea that the insurers of a grossly negligent driver should be relieved in any degree from paying what is proper compensation for injuries is an idea that offends ordinary decency. Until I am forced to do so by higher authority, I will not so rule.

I do not think that is the correct approach. The question is not what was the cause of the accident. It is rather what was the cause of the damage. In most accidents on the road the bad driving, which causes the accident, also causes the ensuing damage. But in seat belt cases the cause of the accident is one thing. The cause of the damage is another. The *accident* is caused by the bad driving. The *damage* is caused in part by the bad driving of the defendant, and in part by the failure of the plaintiff to wear a seat belt. If the plaintiff was to blame in not wearing a seat belt, the damage is in part the result of his own fault. He must bear some share in the responsibility for the damage and his damages fall to be reduced to such extent as the court thinks just and equitable. [...]

Seeing that it is compulsory to fit seat belts, Parliament must have thought it sensible to wear them. But it did not make it compulsory for anyone to wear a seat belt. Everyone is free to wear it or not, as he pleases. Free in this sense, that if he does not wear it, he is free from any penalty by the magistrates. Free in the sense that everyone is free to run his head against a brick wall, if he pleases. He can do it if he likes without being punished by the law. But it is not a sensible thing to do. If he does it, it is his own fault; and he has only himself to thank for the consequences.

Much material has been put before us about the value of wearing a seat belt. It shows quite plainly that everyone in the front seats of a car should wear a seat belt. Not only on long trips, but also on short ones. Not only in the town, but also in the country. Not only when there is fog, but also when it is clear. Not only by fast drivers, but also by slow ones. Not only on motorways, but also on side roads. [...]

The case for wearing seat belts is so strong that I do not think the law can admit forgetfulness as an excuse. If it were, everyone would say: "Oh, I forgot." In order to bring home the importance of wearing seat belts, the law should say that a person who fails to wear it must share some responsibility for the damages.

Thus far I have spoken only of the ordinary run of cases. There are, of course, exceptions. A man who is unduly fat or a woman who is pregnant may rightly be excused because, if there is an accident, the strap across the abdomen may do more harm than good. But, apart from such cases, in the ordinary way a person who fails to wear a seat

Negligence 275

belt should accept some share of responsibility for the damage – if it could have been prevented or lessened by wearing it. [...]

The share of responsibility whenever there is an accident, the negligent driver must bear by far the greater share of responsibility. It was his negligence which caused the accident. It also was a prime cause of the whole of the damage. But insofar as the damage might have been avoided or lessened by wearing a seat belt, the injured person must bear some share. [...]

Everyone knows, or ought to know, that when he goes out in a car he should fasten the seat belt. It is so well known that it goes without saying, not only for the driver, but also the passenger. If either the driver or the passenger fails to wear it and an accident happens – and the injuries would have been prevented or lessened if he had worn it – then his damages should be reduced.

Notes

The principle of contributory negligence is that if your negligence contributes to your own injury, then you will be partially liable. That is to say, the damages you would have otherwise been able to recover from the defendant will be reduced.[200] The objective of this is to make sure everyone in society, and not just the defendant, is careful so as not to injure another.

For example, imagine you are at a university in Dhaka, Bangladesh, to deliver a guest lecture. At the end of your lecture, you receive a phone call from your wife telling you that she is going into labour and that you should immediately meet her at Evercare Hospital. Therefore, you quickly say goodbye and run towards the gate where your vehicle is parked. Unfortunately, while running, you slip on oil on the floor and injure your lower back. Video footage reveals that you slipped on oil, which had a yellowish colour, spilled on a white-tiled floor. While the university can be held liable in negligence for their failure to post a "wet floor" sign, their liability will be reduced because evidence demonstrates that had you not been running, you would probably have seen the oil and avoided it. In fact, the same footage shows that students in the area changed the direction of their walk, thereby avoiding the slippery floor. This means that your injury was caused by, (1) the university's failure to post a "wet floor" sign, and (2) your failure to notice a yellowish substance on a white floor. As in, while the university will be liable for their negligence, their liability will be reduced and you will be partially blamed because you were not as careful as you should have been.[201]

Essentially, contributory negligence tells us that if the injured party could have done something to minimize his injury, he should have done so. This means, *inter alia*, not wearing a hard helmet at a construction site amounts to contributory negligence; falling inside a manhole because the city did not cordon the area, but illuminated it, albeit insufficiently, amounts to contributory negligence if the manhole was visible from a reasonable distance;[202] and diving into the shallow side of a swimming pool even if there are no signs prohibiting diving and no diving board, but there are signs stipulating

276   Negligence

which side is shallow, amounts to contributory negligence, for which the defendant's liability shall be reduced.[203]

5.13 *Volenti Non Fit Injuria*

Lambert v Lastoplex Chemicals Co[204]

Edison Lambert bought two one-gallon cans of Supremo W-200, which is a fast-drying lacquer sealer manufactured by Lastoplex Chemicals Co Ltd (hereinafter "Lastoplex"), from Barwood Sales (Ontario) Ltd. He was going to use it to seal a parquet floor that he was installing in the recreation room of his home, which he co-owned with his wife, Elizabeth Lambert. The recreation room, which was 600 square feet, was in the basement of his home. The basement had a recreation room, a furnace and utility room to the east, which was separated from the recreation room in part by a plywood wall, and in part by a fireplace, and stairs at the southwest wall leading up to the next level

At about 9:00 am on 3 June 1967, Mr. Lambert removed all of the furniture from the recreation room, swept its floors, and opened windows at the northwest and southeast walls. Then, at about 10:00 am, he began applying the sealer – working from east to west. Before application, he read the following three labels on the can: (1) a rectangular-shaped label provided information about its drying time and also said "Caution inflammable! Keep away from open flame!"; (2) a diamond-shaped label stipulating, "KEEP AWAY FROM FIRE, HEAT AND OPEN-FLAME LIGHTS", "CAUTION", "LEAKING Packages Must be Removed to a Safe Place," and "DO NOT DROP"; and (3) another rectangular-shaped label, which cautioned users in four languages, and the English version said, "CAUTION, INFLAMMABLE – Do not use near open flame or while smoking. Ventilate room while using." Unfortunately, at about 11:00 am, when he was nearly done with five-sixths of the floor, he noticed a line of flame advancing towards him from the east. He dropped his roller applicator, ran up the stairs, but before he could reach safety, there was an explosion, which burned him and destroyed the recreation room.

For the injuries he sustained and the damage to their property, Mr. and Mrs. Lambert brought proceedings against Lastoplex under negligence for their failure to provide clearer warnings of the danger of sparks. Finding in their favour, the court said,

> The evidence disclosed that a lacquer sealer sold by a competitor of the respondent contained on its label a more explicit warning of danger in the following terms: "DANGER – FLAMMABLE," "DO NOT SMOKE. ADEQUATE VENTILATION TO THE OUTSIDE MUST BE PROVIDED. ALL SPARK-PRODUCING DEVICES AND OPEN FLAMES (FURNACES, ALL PILOT LIGHTS, SPARK-PRODUCING SWITCHES, ETC.), MUST BE ELIMINATED, IN OR NEAR WORKING AREA."

Negligence   277

A comparison of the cautions on the two competing products shows that the labels of the respondent did not warn against sparks, or specifically against leaving pilot lights on in or near the working area. In neither case was any point made of the rapid spread of vapours from the products. [...]

Manufacturers owe a duty to consumers of their products to see that there are no defects in manufacture which are likely to give rise to injury in the ordinary course of use. Their duty does not, however, end if the product, although suitable for the purpose for which it is manufactured and marketed, is at the same time dangerous to use; and if they are aware of its dangerous character they cannot, without more, pass the risk of injury to the consumer.

The applicable principle of law according to which the positions of the parties in this case should be assessed may be stated as follows. Where manufactured products are put on the market for ultimate purchase and use by the general public and carry danger (in this case, by reason of high inflammability), although put to the use for which they are intended, the manufacturer, knowing of their hazardous nature, has a duty to specify the attendant dangers, which it must take to appreciate in a detail not known to the ordinary consumer or used. A general warning, as for example, that the product is inflammable, will not suffice where the likelihood of fire may be increased according to the surroundings in which it may reasonably be expected that the product will be used. The required explicitness of the warning will, of course, vary with the danger likely to be encountered in the ordinary use of the product.

In my opinion, the cautions on the labels affixed to the container cans of Supreme W-200 lacked the explicitness which the degree of danger in its use in a gas-serviced residence demanded. A home owner preparing to use that lacquer seal could not reasonably by expected to realize by reading the three cautions that the product when applied as directed gives off vapours to such a degree as likely to create a risk of fire from a spark or from a pilot in another part of the basement area.

Notes

"*Volenti non fit injuria*" is a common law doctrine and is Latin for "to a willing person, no injury is done." This means that if a person knowingly and willingly places himself in a position of danger, then he cannot subsequently recover compensation for the injuries. Therefore, in *Lambert*, the real issue was whether Mr. Lambert deliberately and willingly placed himself in the course of harm.

From *Donoghue*, we know that a manufacturer owes a duty of care to the ultimate consumer.[205] Therefore, Lastoplex was legally bound to inform its consumers, and in this case, Mr. Lambert, of the attendant risks of its products. While Lastoplex notified Mr. Lambert of the risks of Supremo W-200, the information provided was insufficient. Evidence showed that a competitor's product's notice was more explicit and warned of fires that could be

278   *Negligence*

ignited by "spark-producing switches," which the Supremo W-200 did not. This means that it is imperative that a manufacturer informs the consumer of *all* attendant risks and the notice must also be conspicuous; that is, in order for *volenti non fit injuria* to apply, the injured party must be cognizant of *all of the concomitant risks* associated with the product or activity.[206]

For example, imagine you bought a canister of aerosol and, after use, placed it near a window in your room. After the canister has been exposed to sunlight for nearly 72 hours, it exploded and injured you. If the manufacturer of the aerosol did not either, (a) provide a warning that it should be kept away from direct sunlight, or (b) provided a warning, but it was inconspicuous, then you can hold the manufacturer liable because you did not know of the risk of keeping the aerosol in direct sunlight. That is to say, you were not aware of the risk of explosion, and therefore, you could not knowingly accept its consequences.

However, and interestingly, while the manufacturer can be liable in negligence, they can also allege contributory negligence on your part for keeping the canister of aerosol under direct sunlight. As of 2020, it is common knowledge that, *inter alia*, aerosols, fragrances, cellphones, and power-banks should not be kept under direct sunlight, and if you elect to not adhere to this recommendation, then you are also liable in negligence for your own injury.

There is, however, an exception to the doctrine. Recall from *Haynes* that Harwood alleged contributory negligence on the part of Mr. Haynes, who deliberately interposed himself in danger when trying to save a woman and a group of children from the might of the horse.[207] However, the court said that a person who, in the course of rescue, injures himself cannot be held to waive his right to seek compensation from the original negligent party. Therefore, as I had mentioned earlier, if you try to save a drowning person from a public lake, and, in the course of rescue, you injure yourself, you can seek compensation from the city so long as the drowning victim was also injured as a result of the city's negligence because *volenti non fit injuria* does not apply.

Let us now consider a different example. Imagine you are jogging on the roads of Mirpur DOHS when a car hits you from the back. Can the motorist allege *volenti non fit injuria* or contributory negligence on the grounds that since you were jogging on the road and that it is probable that a vehicle may hit you, you cannot seek compensation because you have impliedly consented to such contact? The answer depends on four factors. Firstly, were there sidewalks? Secondly, if there were sidewalks, were you jogging on the sidewalk? Thirdly, were you jogging during the day or night? Lastly, if during the night, were you wearing clothes and shoes capable of reflecting light?

Even if there was a sidewalk and you were jogging at night and not wearing clothes and shoes capable of reflecting light, the motorist will nevertheless be liable in negligence (or, depending on evidence, intentional tort).[208] However, his liability can be reduced if he was driving within the speed limit[209] and because you should have been more careful by wearing clothes

Negligence 279

and shoes that can reflect light, which can alert other motorists of your presence, or you should have jogged during the daytime.[210] Nonetheless, since the driver collided with you from the back, he had the "last clear chance" to prevent the accident, which he did not, and therefore, his liability will be significantly more than yours.[211] More importantly, though, simply because you are jogging on the road, as there are no sidewalks, does not mean you have impliedly consented to being struck by motor vehicles,[212] but it does mean that you should have exercised more caution. Similarly, simply because you board an airplane does not mean you consent to it crashing and injuring or killing you; or, when you visit a barber, it does not mean you consent to him injuring you with his scissors; or, when you have an electrician install a ceiling fan in your room, it does not mean that you consent to it becoming loose and falling on you and injuring you even if there is a probability that it may happen.[213]

Notes

1 See generally Percy H Winfield, "The History of Negligence in the Law of Torts" (1926) 42:2 L Q Rev 184.

2 John G Fleming, *The Law of Torts*, 9th ed (Sydney: LBC Information Services, 1998) at 113 [Fleming].

3 It is worth noting that in the 18th century, though rare, the earliest form of what we now call "tortious negligence" were found with innkeepers, carriers, surgeons, and lawyers because they held themselves out as competent to pursue their profession. Therefore, they were expected to conform to a standard of reasonable skill and proficiency, at *ibid*.

4 *Ibid* at 114.

5 *Ibid*; Also see Ernest J Weinrib, *Tort Law: Cases and Materials*, 4th ed (Toronto: Emond Montgomery Publications Limited, 2014) at 49–50 [Weinrib].

6 Fleming, *supra* note 2 at 115–116. Also see R F V Heuston & R A Buckley, *Salmond and Heuston on the Law of Torts*, 19th ed (London: Sweet & Maxwell, 1987) at 214–216 [Heuston & Buckley].

7 See Allen M Linden & Bruce Feldthusen, *Canadian Tort Law*, 9th ed (Markham, ON: LexisNexis Canada Inc, 2011) at 113–115 [Linden & Feldthusen].

8 *Vaughan v Menlove*, [1835–42] All ER Rep 156, [1837] 132 ER 490 [*Vaughan*].

9 See generally Oliver W Holmes Jr, *The Common Law* (Boston: Little, Brown & Co, 1881) at 77–110.

10 In 1935, it was Lambert Adolphe Jacques Quetelet, who was a Belgian mathematician and sociologist, who first introduced the concept of *l'homme moyen*, which is French for the "average man," in this book *Sur l'homme et le développement de ses facultés and Du systeme social et des lois qui le régissent*. Two years later, it was imported into the common law world through *Vaughan* and continues to be used heretofore; See generally, Sandra Caponi, "Quetelet, the average man and medical knowledge" *SciELO* (2013), online: SciELO https://www.scielo.br/scielo.php?pid=S0104-59702013000300830&script=sci_arttext&tlng=en. [17/03/2021].

11 However, see *Mansfield v Weetabix Ltd*, [1998] 1 WLR 1263, [1997] Lexis Citation 2009 [*Mansfield*], where the court took into consideration that Mr.

280 Negligence

Tarleton did not know that his brain malfunctions when his blood sugar is low, and said, "The standard of care that Mr. Tarleton was obliged to show was that which is expected of a reasonably competent driver. He did not know and could not reasonably have known of his infirmity which was the cause of the accident. Therefore he was not at fault. His actions did not fall below the standard of care required."

12 *McHale v Watson*, [1966] 115 CLR 199, 39 ALJR 459 [*McHale*].

13 The age of majority, which is the age at which a person is considered an adult, in Bangladesh is 18 years, at *The Majority Act*, 1875 (Bangladesh), Act No IX of 1875, s 3.

14 I note here that *The Penal Code*, 1860 (hereinafter "*Penal Code*") and *The Children Act*, 2013 (hereinafter "*Children Act*") should be read in tandem.

First, pursuant to section 82 of the *Penal Code*, a child's action does not merit criminal liability if he is under the age of 9. This is supplemented by section 44(1) of the *Children Act*, which proscribes the arrest of a child under the age of 9 even if he has committed a crime that would otherwise have warranted detention if the crime had been committed by an adult. Essentially, this means that if a child under the age of 9 stabs (intentionally or otherwise) another with a knife, the child will not be held criminally responsible. However, if the child is between the ages of 9 and under 12, then criminal responsibility would be contingent upon his ability to appreciate the consequences of his actions. Strangely, the *Penal Code* is silent regarding the treatment of offenders between the ages of 12 and under 18, at *The Penal Code*, 1860 (Bangladesh), Act No XLV of 1860, s 82.

Second, section 4 of the *Children Act* stipulates that a "child" is anybody under the age of 18, which fills the lacuna of the *Penal Code* (in reference to how persons aged between 12 and under 18 are to be treated). Section 59 establishes Child Development Centres, where children found guilty are housed (unless diverted under section 48 or the child is charged as an adult due to the heinous nature of the offence, which is permitted under section 33(1)) and section 33(1) interdicts the imposition of a sentence of life imprisonment and death upon a child, at *The Children Act*, 2013 (Bangladesh), Act No XXIV of 2013, ss 4, 33(1), 48 and 59.

Overall, the pith and substance of the enumerated provisions of the *Penal Code* and the *Children Act* is that a child is not to be charged as an adult unless exigent circumstances arise (see main body of text).

15 See Mayo Moran, *Rethinking the Reasonable Person* (Oxford: Oxford University Press, 2003) at 64–69.

16 See generally James Fleming Jr, "The Qualities of the Reasonable Man in Negligence Cases" (1951) 16:1 Mo L Rev 1 [James Fleming].

17 *McErlean v Sarel et al.*, [1987] OJ No 873, 61 OR (2d) 396 at paras 53–54.

18 *Rozell v Rozell*, [1939] 281 NY 106, 22 NE 2d 254 [*Rozell*]; Also see *R v Hill*, [1986] 1 SCR 313, [1986] SCJ No 25, where it was said at para 78, "Accordingly, it has been determined that the standard of care applicable to children is only partially objective in that it must be adjusted incrementally in accordance with the age of the child in question [...] At some point, of course, there must be a cut-off so that the fully objective standard of the ordinary person can operate. Until this point is reached, it stands to reason that the reduced legal standard of responsibility to which children are held is reflected in the semi-objective standard of the ordinary thirteen year old, fourteen year old, etc."

19 *Children Act, supra* note 14 at s 33(1).

20 *R v W (RE)*, [2006] OJ No 265, 205 CCC (3d) 183, CarswellOnt 344 [*W (RE)*]; Section 110(1) of the *Youth Criminal Justice Act* proscribes the publication of a young person's name that is being dealt with under the Act. As in, if

Negligence 281

a young person, which is a person between the ages of 12 and under 18 in Canada, is charged under the said legislation, his name cannot be published, and therefore, I shall refer to him as "minor," at *Youth Criminal Justice Act*, SC 2002, c 1, s 110(1) [*YCJA*].

21 Section 39(1) of the *YCJA* stipulates, "A youth justice court shall not commit a young person to custody under section 42 (youth sentences) unless,

(a) The young person has committed a violent offence;

(b) The young person has failed to comply with non-custodial sentences;

(c) The young person has committed an indictable offence for which an adult would be liable to imprisonment for a term of more than 2 years and has a history that indicates a pattern of either extrajudicial sanctions or of findings of guilt or of both under this Act or the Young Offenders Act, chapter Y-1 of the Revised Statutes of Canada, 1985; or

(d) In exceptional cases where the young person has committed an indictable offence, the aggravating circumstances of the offence are such that the imposition of a non-custodial sentence would be inconsistent with the purpose and principles set out in section 38," at *YCJA*, *ibid* at s 39(1).

Alternatively, section 33(1) of the *Children Act* provides, "Notwithstanding anything to the contrary contained in any other law, no child shall be sentenced to death, imprisonment for life, or imprisonment," at *Children Act*, *supra* note 14 at s 33(1). Please also see earlier for the exception, which is commensurate with section 39(1) of the *YCJA*, to this instruction.

22 Also see Himaloya Saha & Saquib Rahman, "Juvenile Delinquents and the *Children Act*" *The Daily Star* (24 January 2017), online: The Daily Star https://www.thedailystar.net/law-our-rights/juvenile-delinquents-and-the-children-act-1350073. [17/03/2021].

23 It is important to note that the question in criminal law differs from that of tort law because, in the former, the person being tried has the probability of losing his freedom, and therefore, the standard of proof is significantly higher – beyond a reasonable doubt. However, in tort law, the standard of proof is "balance of probabilities" and the usual remedy is paying damages to the victim; thence, the question asked in tort law, which is a civil offence, is different from that of criminal law.

24 *Ryan et al v Hickson et al*, [1974] 55 DLR (3d) 196, 7 OR (2d) 352.

25 See Allen M Linden, *Canadian Negligence Law*, 3rd ed (Toronto: Butterworths, 1974) at 33–34.

26 Children under the age of 9 cannot be arrested or detained, at *Children Act*, *supra* note 14 at s 44(1). However, remember that this speaks to criminal law, and therefore, tort litigation would remain unaffected so long as the child is not required to be detained (as in, he does not lose his freedom) and that the victim only seeks monetary compensation.

27 James Fleming, *supra* note 16 at 1; Also see Fleming, *supra* note 2 at 118–119.

28 Alan D Miller & Ronen Perry, "The Reasonable Person" (2012) 87:2 NYUL Rev 323 at 325–326 [Miller & Perry].

29 As in, the average human being is not infallible and whether he was negligent depends on his conduct at the time it was engaged in the impugned activity, and not with the benefit of hindsight that the person ought to have been more careful, see generally *Rzeszewski v Barth*, [1944] 324 III App 345, 58 NE 2d 269.

30 Leon Green, *Judge and Jury* (Kansas City, USA: Vernon Law Book Co, 1930) at 180 [Green]; See generally Warren Seavey, "Negligence – Subjective or Objective" (1927) 41:1 Harv L Rev 1 [Seavey].

282 Negligence

31 James Fleming, *supra* note 16 at 5; Also see James Fleming Jr & John Dickinson, "Accident Proneness and Accident Law" (1950) 63:5 Harv L Rev 769.

32 See *Green v Atlanta Charlotte Air Line Railway Company et al.*, [1925] 131 SC 124, 126 SE 441, where it was said at 133, "The foundation of liability for negligence is knowledge or, what is deemed in law to be the same thing, opportunity, by the exercise of reasonable diligence to acquire knowledge, of the peril which subsequently results in injury, coupled with a legal duty owed to the person injured to exercise the care of the man of ordinary sense and prudence to prevent the existence of the conditions or the occurrence of the event, to which the injury is alleged to be traceable."

33 In *Hope v Full Brook Coal Co*, [1896] 3 AD 70, 38 NYS 1040, it was said at 1043, "An essential element of negligence is a knowledge of facts which render foresight possible, and the circumstances necessary to be known before the liability for the consequences of an act or omission will be imposed must be such as would lead a prudent man to apprehend danger."

34 See *Doherty v Arcade Hotel*, [1943] 170 Ore 374, 134 P 2d 118.

35 James Fleming, *supra* note 16 at 6; Also see Miller & Perry, *supra* note 28 at 330–335.

36 For example, in *Smithline v Hadigrian*, [1942] 34 NYS 2d 509, NY Misc LEXIS 1537, the plaintiff witnessed the janitor washing the stairs on his ascent, and therefore, when he fell on the stairs soon thereafter on his descent, he was also held contributorily negligent (more on this later), as he had knowledge that the floor was going to be wet.

37 For example, in *Davis v Boston MRR*, [1900] 70 NH 519, 49 All 108, it was held that the plaintiff, who knew from previous experience that the train's engine would be sent to the roundhouse, was negligent in failing to look behind him while crossing the tracks. However, also see *Mansfield*, *supra* note 11.

38 See *Belcher v City of San Francisco*, [1945] 69 Cal App 2d 457, 158 P 2d 996, where it was held that the municipality was not negligent in failing to warn the plaintiff the dangers of descending down the stairs (onto a sidewalk) when a veritable wind was blowing, as a reasonable person is expected to know that the circumstances dictate that more care, than is usual, is, or would be, required; Also see *Oran v Kraft-Phenix Cheese Corp*, [1944] 324 Ill App 463, 58 NE 2d 731, where it was held that the driver was negligent in failing to notice a large reflector on the bicycle, as a reasonable person is expected to see the obvious.

However, in *Johnson v Rulon*, [1950] 363 Pa 585, 70 A 2d 325, the court accepted, and subsequently propounded, the theory of "attention arresters," which are attractive displays (e.g. menu on the wall, new clothes on a mannequin, and other analogous grounds) that have the capacity to divert one's attention, and said that it could be considered in determining whether the plaintiff was negligent in failing to see a dangerous condition that he otherwise would have had the attractive display not been in sight.

39 James Fleming, *supra* note 16 at 7–8; Also see William L Prosser, *Handbook of The Law of Torts*, 4th ed (St. Paul, Minnesota: West Publishing Co, 1971) at 149–166 [Prosser].

40 In *Coppins v Jefferson*, [1905] 126 Wis 578, 105 NW 1078, it was said that forgetting an obstruction on the highway created a presumption of negligence.

In *Ramos v Service Bros*, [1931] 118 Cal App 432, 5 P 2d 623, it was said at 435, "One who works at a dangerous vocation, or one who voluntarily places himself in a position of danger, cannot close his eyes to such danger or momentarily forget a known danger, but is required to exercise a *quantum* of care that is commensurate with such danger as may be known to him. And if

Negligence 283

he momentarily forgets such known danger or closes his eyes to such danger, and is thereby injured, and the proximate cause of his injury is his forgetfulness of such danger, or his failure to make reasonable use of his faculties under such circumstances, he cannot recover for the injury."

41 In *Williams v Ballard Lumber Co*, [1906] 41 Wash 338, 83 P 323, since the plaintiff, who was working under machinery, was startled by its starting, his forgetfulness was excused; *Weare v Fitchburg*, [1872] 110 Mass 334 (anxiety due to being summoned home to attend to children); *Houston v Town of Waverly*, [1932] 225 Ala 98, 142 So 80 (mother distracted by her son on a bicycle).

42 *Brown v Swift & Co*, [1912] 91 Neb 532, 136 NW 726 (plaintiff should have known that a wheeled vehicle would roll down an incline); *Huntingburgh v First*, [1896] 15 Ind App 552, 43 NE 17 (a loose plank can tip when stepped on); *Lexington & E R Co v White*, [1918] 182 Ky 267, 206 SW 467 (plaintiff is supposed to know that smoke excreted by a train engine inside a tunnel can cause suffocation); *Evansville v Blue*, [1937] 212 Ind 130, 8 NE 2d 224 (11-year-old boy should have known that he could drown in water and it was not the city's responsibility to guard the pool against such perils); *Gates v Hoston & M Railroad*, [1926] 255 Mass 297, 151 NE 320; Also see James Fleming, *supra* note 16 at 9.

43 *Missouri P R Co v Vinson*, [1938] 196 Ark 500, 118 SW 2d 672, where it was said at 503, "Every man will be presumed to know more about his own strength and to be better informed as to his ability to lift, than is a stranger; and every manual task, however menial, requires the exercise of some intelligence upon the part of those who undertake to perform it."

In *Jennings v Tacoma R & M Co*, [1893] 7 Wash 275, 34 P 937, the plaintiff, who was an employee at Tacoma Railway and Motor Company, was unable to recover damages from his employer when he injured himself trying to squeeze through an opening of three and a half inches wide. The court said at 278,

No sane man is expected to act on an assumption which he knows to be false. It is a man's duty to exercise common sense when in the employment of a master, as well as any other time. The master has a right to rely upon the servant doing this. It is contended by the respondent that the company ought to have notified him of this danger. We think the company had a right to presume that no caution was necessary to a person of ordinary prudence and intelligence; that it is not a reasonable supposition that any man of ordinary size will attempt to force himself through a space three and one-half inches in width between a moving car and a brick wall. The company had a right to suppose that the smallest imaginable modicum of prudence would suggest to the man to let go when he came to the wall. If the space had been wider at the entrance and had narrowed as it progressed, or anything about it had been hidden or concealed, it would have been different, but such was not the case.

In *Hesse v National Casket Co*, [1901] 66 NJL 652, 52 A 384, though the 16-year-old boy cut his hand on a saw, he was unable to recover damages from his employer, as it was presumed that he should have known the bench, on which he was standing, would tip if he moved too far from the centre of gravity.

44 *Baltimore v Thompson*, [1937] 171 Md 460, 189 A 822 (fog is likely to impair vision); *Brune v De Benedetty*, [1924] 261 SW 930, 1924 Mo App LEXIS 487. In fact, very few cases (for example, see *Linnehan v Sampson*, [1879] 126 Mass 506, 1879 Mass LEXIS 306) "have held that when an abnormal individual who lacks the experience common to the particular community comes into it, as in the case of the old lady from the city who comes to the farm

284 Negligence

without ever having learned that a bull is a dangerous beast, the standard of knowledge will still be applied, and it is the individual who must conform to the community, rather than vice versa." At Prosser, *supra* note 39 at 160.

45 *Femling v Star Publishing Company*, [1938] 195 Wash 395, 84 P 2d 1008 (children's recklessness); *Wellman v Fordson Coal Company*, [1928] 105 W Va 463, 143 SE 160 (children's interest in dangerous objects, such as explosives); *Agdeppa v Glougie*, [1945] 71 Cal App 2d 463, 162 P 2d 944 (children's propensity to wander into the streets).

46 *Keys v Alamo City Baseball Co*, [1941] 150 SW 2d 368, 1941 Tex App LEXIS 308 (while this case concerns a spectator being injured by a batted ball at a baseball stadium, it can relate to cricket – or any other sport – in the sense that there is a probability of spectators being injured depending on where they are seated in the arena and the nature of the sport).

47 *Le Vonas v Acme Paper Board Company*, [1944] 184 Md 16, 40 A 2d 43 (electrical wires and lines carrying electricity are dangerous); *Dillenberger v Weingartner*, [1900] 64 NJL 292, 45 A 638 (Maggie Dillenberger, the plaintiff, should have known that revolving fans are dangerous); *Comanche Duke Oil Co v Texas Pacific Coal & Oil Co*, [1927] 298 SW 554, 1927 Tex App LEXIS 1436 (such as explosives); however, the reasonable person is not required to recognize the identity of explosives, at *Parrot v Wells*, [1872] 82 US 524, 21 L Ed 206 (this case is often referred to as the "*Nitro-Glycerine Case*"); *Parton v Phillips Petroleum Co*, [1937] 231 Mo App 585, 107 SW 2d 167 (flammable properties of kerosene); *Burnett v Amalgamated Phosphate Co*, [1938] 96 F 2d 974, 1938 US App LEXIS 3606 (flammable properties of gasoline); *Murphy v Pere Marquette Railroad Co*, [1914] 183 Mich 435, 150 NW 122 (the danger of boarding a train); *McIntyre v Pope*, [1937] 326 Pa 172, 191 A 607 (the inexorable result of overcrowding a driver's seat is diminished control of automobile); *McMillen v Steele*, [1923] 275 Pa 584, 119 A 721 (inherent danger of firearms); *Osborn v Leuffgen*, [1942] 381 Ill 295, 45 NE 2d 622 (alcohol can impair judgment).

48 *Faulkinbury v Shaw*, [1931] 183 Ark 1019 39 SW 2d 708 (the occupier is liable to the visitor if the injury stems from a danger known to the former, but not the latter); *Gobrecht v Beckwith*, [1926] 82 NH 415, 135 A 20 (landlord is liable for the installation of a gas water heater in the tenant's bathroom, which depleted the supply of oxygen and subsequently injured the tenant by carbon monoxide poisoning); *Central of Georgia R Co v Robertson*, [1919] 203 Ala 358, 83 So 102 (derailment of a train is *prima facie* evidence of negligence); *Carter v Yardley & Co*, [1946] 319 Mass 92, 64 NE 2d 693 (manufacturer is liable for using ingredient in perfume that caused the user to suffer a second degree burn from use).

49 *Gould v Slater Woolen Co*, [1888] 147 Mass 315, 17 NE 531.

50 *Grant v Australian Knitting Mills Ltd*, [1935] All ER Rep 209, 105 LJPC 6 [*Grant*]; Additionally, the reasonable person is supposed to be cognizant of the law. If otherwise, his defence that he did not know the law is untenable; see *Dow v Brown*, [1939] 193 So 239, 1939 La App LEXIS 506; *Mazza v Greenstein*, [1948] 82 Ohio App 145, 80 NE 2d 216; *Rodgers v Cox*, [1944] 130 Conn 616, 36 A 2d 373.

51 James Fleming, *supra* note 16 at 15; Also see Fleming, *supra* note 2 at 120–125.

52 *Borgstede v Waldbauer*, [1935] 337 Mo 1205, 88 SW 2d 373.

53 *Louisville & Nashville Railroad Co v Perry's Administrator*, [1917] 173 Ky 213, 190 SW 1064; *Donathan v McConnell*, [1948] 121 Mont 230, 193 P 2d 819; *Vigneault v Dr. Hewson Dental Co*, [1938] 300 Mass 223, 15 NE 2d 185; Moreover, in *M/S Islamia Automatic Rice Mills Ltd v Bangladesh Shilpa Rin Sangstha et al.*, [1998] 23 BLD 139, the High Court of Bangladesh said,

Negligence   285

"[S]o far [as the lawyer's negligence] relates to giving legal [advice] or doing other paper work not connected with litigation, he is liable in negligence. He owes a duty of care to his client [...] This [...] is founded on the principle that a person who undertakes to do work which requires special skill holds himself out as having that skill; the lack of it then becomes blameworthy."

54   Seavey, *supra* note 30 at 20–28; Also see *McHale*, *supra* note 12 and my subsequent notes for a more thorough understanding of this issue.

55   See *Holland v Pitocchelli*, [1938] 299 Mass 554, 13 NE 2d 290 and *Goff v Hubbard*, [1927] 217 Ky 729, 290 SW 696.

56   Fleming, *supra* note 2 at 125.

57   *McLaughlin v Griffin*, [1912] 155 Iowa 302, 135 NW 1107 (disability); *Balcom v Independence*, [1916] 178 Iowa 685, 160 NW 305 (disability); *Armstrong v Warner Brothers Theatres Inc*, [1947] 161 Pa Super 385, 54 A 2d 831 (a 75-year-old woman is supposed to be more vigilant due to her age); *Keith v Worcester and Blackstone Valley Street Railway Co*, [1907] 196 Mass 478, 82 NE 680 (the standard of care expected of a near-sighted woman is the same as a woman with perfect vision, but the former ought to exercise greater vigilance than the latter).

58   *Henderson v Public Transport Commission of New South Wales*, [1981] 37 ALR 29, 56 ALJR 1 (a person's defective peripheral vision means he should take extra care to look sideways).

59   In *Foy v Winston*, [1900] 126 NC 381, 35 SE 609, the court said that a blind man, who fell into a ditch, was supposed to exercise more caution than a man with full possession of his faculties; In *Marks' Adm'r v Petersburg Railroad Co*, [1891] 88 Va 1, 13 SE 299, the court held that a woman, who was blind in one eye, was contributorily negligent for failing to take greater care than would otherwise be required of the reasonable person.

60   In *Lobert v Pack*, [1939] 337 Pa 103, 9 A 2d 365, it was said at 107, "He must have done that which he ought not to have done or omitted that which he ought to have done, as a conscious being endowed with a will [...] Nowhere in cases dealing with the subject of torts do we find the suggestion that a person should be held responsible for injuries inflicted during periods of unconsciousness."

61   In *Diamond State Telephone Co v Hunter*, [1941] 41 Del 336, 21 A 2d 286, the court held that the act of falling asleep while operating a motor vehicle created a rebuttable presumption of negligence. Furthermore, the court said at 340, "Sleep does not ordinarily come upon one unawares, and by watching for indications of its approach, or heeding circumstances which are likely to bring it about, one may either ward it off or cease an activity capable of danger to others or to their property [...] As I have stated before, the act of falling asleep while driving an automobile raises a presumption of negligence against that party; however, this is a presumption only, and can be rebutted by evidence showing that the defendant as a careful and cautious man could not have foreseen that he was about to fall asleep."

62   *Waters v Pacific Coast Dairy Inc*, [1942] 55 Cal App 2d 789, 131 P 2d 588. Contrast with *Mansfield*.

63   *Geist v Moore*, [1937] 58 Idaho 149, 70 P 2d 403 (the degree of care expected of a voluntarily intoxicated person is the same as a person not intoxicated); Also see *Remmenga v Selk*, [1948] 150 Neb 401, 34 NW 2d 757.

64   See *McHale, supra* note 12 and subsequent discussion; Also see Fleming, *supra* note 2 at 126–127 and *Tucker v Tucker*, [1956] SASR 297 (again, a 16-year-old driver being treated like an adult).

65   *Seattle Electric Co v Hovden*, [1911] 190 F 7, 1911 US App LEXIS 4426; *Johnson v St. Paul City Railway Co*, [1897] 67 Minn 260, 69 NW 900.

66   *Bolton v Stone*, [1951] 1 All ER 1078, 59 LGR 32 [*Bolton*].

286 Negligence

67 *United States v Carroll Towing*, [1947] 159 F 2d 169, 1947 US App LEXIS 3226, at 173 [*Carroll Towing*]; Also see *Agni v Wenshall (in re City of New York)*, [2008] 522 F 3D 279, 2008 US App LEXIS 6416.

68 For example, in *McCarty v Pheasant Run, Inc*, [1987] 826 F 2d 1554, 1987 US App LEXIS 11047, the court said at 1556, "There are various ways in which courts formulate the negligence standard. The analytically (not necessarily the operationally) most precise is that it involves determining whether the burden of precaution is less than the magnitude of the accident, if it occurs, multiplied by the probability of occurrence (The product of this multiplication, or "discounting," is what economists call an expected accident cost). If the burden is less, the precaution should be taken. This is the famous "Hand Formula" announced in *United States v Carroll Towing Co* [...] an admiralty case, and since applied in a variety of cases not limited to admiralty."

69 See Richard A Posner, *Tort Law: Cases and Economic Analysis* (Toronto: Little, Brown & Co, 1982) at 1–2.

70 See generally Richard A Posner, "A Theory of Negligence" (1972) 1:1 J Leg Stud 29 at 29–34 [Posner].

71 *Miller v Jackson*, [1977] 3 All ER 778, [1977] QB 966 [*Miller*].

72 See Posner, *supra* note 70.

73 *Latimer v AEC Ltd*, [1953] 2 All ER 449, 51 LGR 457 [*Latimer*].

74 Stephen G Gilles, "On Determining Negligence: Hand Formula Balancing, the Reasonable Person Standard, and the Jury" (2001) 54:3 Vand L Rev 813 at 822–831.

75 See *Levesley v Thomas Firth and John Brown Ltd*, [1953] 2 All ER 866, [1953] 1 WLR 1206.

76 *Tomlinson v Congleton Borough Council*, [2003] 3 All ER 1122, 2003 UKHL 47 [*Tomlinson*]; Distinguish this case from *Risk v Rose Bruford College*, [2013] All ER (D) 92 (Dec), [2013] EWHC 3869 (QB).

77 Also see *Edwards v Sutton London Borough*, [2016] All ER (D) 90 (Oct), [2016] EWCA Civ 1005.

78 *Appleby v Erie Tobacco Co*, [1910] OJ No 64, 22 OLR 533.

79 *The TJ Hooper*, [1932] 60 F 2d 737, 1932 US App LEXIS 2592.

80 Since I have already spent a lot of time delineating the Hand Formula, here, I shall abstain. Nonetheless, it is important to note that the court imposed liability (though this language was not used) because the burden of taking precautions (B), which were equipping the tugboats with radio receiving sets, was significantly lower than the probability of occurrence (P) and the gravity of the loss (L).

81 This reasoning is similar to *Froom et al v Butcher*, [1975] 3 All ER 520, [1975] 3 WLR 379 [*Froom*], where the court held the injured driver, who was not at fault, contributorily negligent for his injuries for driving without a seatbelt on even though he was not required by law to wear them in England in 1975. I will discuss this case in greater detail below in Section 5.12.

82 *ter Neuzen v Korn*, [1995] 3 SCR 674, [1995] SCJ No 79 [*ter Neuzen*].

83 It is worth noting that, in October 1983, Dr. Mascola published a letter in the *New England Journal of Medicine* suggesting that sexually transmitted diseases (hereinafter "STD") *may* be transmitted through AI. Evidence suggests that Dr. Mascola was perhaps the first person in the world to express concern about said risk. However, though the journal was prestigious, its readership was highly limited and Dr. Korn, including the preponderance of doctors in Canada, did not read this letter.

84 Fleming, *supra* note 2 at 353.

85 *Swan v Salisbury Construction Co Ltd*, [1966] 2 All ER 138, 1 WLR 204 and *Bellizia v Meares*, [1971] VR 641.

Negligence 287

86 *The Road Transport Act,* 2018 (Bangladesh), Act No XLVIII of 2018, s 52, which stipulates, "In case of injury, or death due to injury, caused by a motor vehicle accident, the injured person or, as the case may be, the person nominated by his heirs, may seek compensation from the Financial Assistance Fund constituted under section 53 or, as required by the Board of Trustees will incur costs." [*RTA*].

This legislation has originally been promulgated in Bengali and was translated by me. Therefore, in the event my translation is incorrect, I am providing the original text as reference: "কোনো মোটরযান হইতে উদ্ভূত দুর্ঘটনার ফলে কোনো ব্যক্তি আঘাতপ্রাপ্ত বা ক্ষতিগ্রস্ত হইলে বা আঘাতপ্রাপ্ত হইয়া মৃত্যুবরণ করিলে, উক্ত ক্ষতিগ্রস্ত ব্যক্তি বা, ক্ষেত্রমত, তাহার উত্তরাধিকারীগণের পক্ষে মনোনীত ব্যক্তি ধারা ৫৩ এর অধীন গঠিত আর্থিক সহায়তা তহবিল হইতে ট্রাস্টি বোর্ড কর্তৃক নির্ধারিত ক্ষতিপূরণ বা, প্রযোজ্য ক্ষেত্রে, চিকিৎসার খরচ প্রাপ্য হইবেন।"

87 *Baker v Market Harborough Industrial Society Ltd,* [1953] 1 WLR 1472, 97 Sol Jo 861 [*Baker*]; Also see *Chaproniere v Mason*, [1905] 21 TLR 633.

88 Stanley Schiff, "A Res Ipsa Loquitur Nutshell" (1976) 26:4 UTLJ 451 at 451 [Schiff]; Furthermore, he adds at 451–452, "Upon rational analysis of why 'the thing speaks for itself' in the trial of a negligence action, at least two propositions should be clear: Even if the plaintiff introduces no evidence tending to demonstrate the precise cause of his injury, if the injurious event he alleges is of such factual nature that, in the ordinary course of things known to reasonable men, it would probably not have occurred if defendant had acted according to the applicable duty of care, the trier of fact may infer by common reasoning from the fact of the injurious event itself that something done by defendant in violation of that duty caused plaintiff's injury. And, since injurious events involved in litigation may vary infinitely in their factual nature, the strength of the justifiable inference in any particular trial always depends upon the probabilities of the defendant's negligent conduct in the proved situation weighed on the trier's scales of experience."

89 *Children Charity Bangladesh Foundation v The Government of Bangladesh*, [2017] 5 CLR 278 (HCD) [*Children Charity*]. Also see Farhana Helal Mehtab & Ali Mashraf, "Decoding *Children's Charity Bangladesh (CCB) Foundation v Government of Bangladesh*: The First Ever Public Law Compensation Case in Bangladesh and the Way Forward" (2019) 4:2 BiLD LJ 9, which can also be found at https://bildbd.com/wp-content/uploads/2019/10/BiLD-Law-Journal-42-9-31.pdf. [17/03/2021].

90 In *Scott v London and St. Katherine Docks Co*, [1865] 3 H & C 595, it was said at 600, "There must be reasonable evidence of negligence. But where the thing is shewn to be under the management of the defendant or his servants, and the accident is such as in the ordinary course of things does not happen if those who have the management use proper care, it affords reasonable evidence, in the absence of explanation by the defendants, that the accident arose from want of care."

91 See William L Prosser, "The Procedural Effect of Res Ipsa Loquitur" (1936) 20:3 Minn L Rev, where the author highlights what kinds of inferences a court is allowed to draw and mentions that the burden of proof is never shifted on the defendant; Also see Schiff, *supra* note 88 at 452 where the author says, "The conclusion that the evidence introduced by the plaintiff at the trial warrants the label *res ipsa loquitur* does not change the ordinary allocation of the burden of persuasion. To succeed in the action the plaintiff must still persuade the trier of fact that the defendant caused the plaintiff's injury by some conduct in violation of the applicable duty of care."

92 *Ybarra v Spangard et al.*, [1944] 154 P 2d 687, 25 Cal 2d 486 [*Ybarra*].

93 As Fleming, *supra* note 2 said at 358, "The principal function of the maxim is to prevent injustice which would result, if a plaintiff were invariably compelled to prove the precise cause of the accident and the defendant's

288 *Negligence*

responsibility for it, even when the facts bearing on these matters are at the outset unknown to him and often within the knowledge of the defendant."

94 For example, in *Fontaine v British Columbia (Official Administrator)*, [1998] 1 SCR 424, [1997] SCJ No 100, the court said at paras 19–20 that, "For *res ipsa loquitur* to arise, the circumstances of the occurrence must permit an inference of negligence attributable to the defendant. The strength or weakness of that inference will depend on the factual circumstances of the case. [...] As the application of *res ipsa loquitur* is highly dependent upon the circumstances proved in evidence, it is not possible to identify in advance the types of situations in which *res ipsa loquitur* will arise. The application of *res ipsa loquitur* in previous decisions may provide some guidance as to when an inference of negligence may be drawn, but it does not serve to establish definitive categories of when *res ipsa loquitur* will apply. It has been held on numerous occasions that evidence of a vehicle leaving the roadway gives rise to an inference of negligence. Whether that will be so in any given case, however, can only be determined after considering the relevant circumstances of the particular case."

95 As was said by KM Stanton, *The Law of Tort* (London: Sweet & Maxwell) at 76, "*Res ipsa loquitur* only operates to provide evidence of negligence in the absence of an explanation of the cause of the accident. If the facts are known, the inference is impermissible and it is the task of the court to review the facts and to decide whether they amount to the plaintiff having satisfied the burden of proof which is upon him."

96 Also see *Byrne v Boadle*, [1863] 159 ER 299, [1861–1873] All ER Rep Ext 1528 and *Fitzpatrick v Cooper*, [1935] 54 CLR 200, 9 ALJR 343.

97 *Donoghue v Stevenson*, [1932] All ER Rep 1, [1932] SC (HL) 31 [*Donoghue*].

98 See R F V Heuston, "*Donoghue v Stevenson* in Retrospect" (1957) 20:1 Modern L Rev 1 [Heuston].

99 *Winterbottom v Wright*, [1842] 11 LJ Ex 415, 10 M&W 109 [*Winterbottom*]. The court said, "Here the action is brought simply because the defendant was a contractor with a third person; and it is contended that thereupon he became liable to everybody who might use the carriage. If there had been any ground for such an action, there certainly would have been some precedent of it; but with the exception of actions against innkeepers, and some few other persons, no case of a similar nature has occurred in practice. [...] There is no privity of contract between these parties; and if the plaintiff can sue, every passenger, or even any person passing along the road, who was injured by the upsetting of the coach, might bring a similar action. Unless we confine the operation of such contracts as this to the parties who entered into them, the most absurd and outrageous consequences, to which I can see no limit would ensue. Where a party becomes responsible to the public, by undertaking a public duty, he is liable, though the injury may have arisen from the negligence of his servant or agent. So, in cases of public nuisances, whether the act was done by the party as a servant, or in any other capacity, you are liable to an action at the suit of any person who suffers."

100 *Mullen v Barr & Co*, [1929] SC 461 [*Mullen*].

101 For example, Professor John Fleming observed, "In short, recognition of a duty of care is the outcome of a value judgment, that the plaintiff's invaded interest is deemed worthy of legal protection against negligent interference by conduct of the kind alleged against the defendant. In the decision whether or not there is a duty, many factors interplay: the hand of history, our ideas of morals and justice, the convenience of administering the rule and our social ideas as to where the loss should fall. Hence, the incidence and extent of duties are liable to adjustment in the light of the constant shifts and changes in community attitudes [...] In 1842, Lord Abinger foresaw, that "the most absurd

Negligence 289

and outrageous consequences, to which I can see no limit, would ensue," if it should ever be held that a party to a contract was under a duty to anyone but the promisee. This standpoint, based on the fear of impeding industrial development, has long since given way to a policy of making negligent manufacturers, repairers and others shoulder the accident losses incidental to their activities. Here, the advent of insurance and a more realistic appreciation of the methods available for the distribution of losses have led to an enormous widening of the field of duty." At John G Fleming, *The Law of Torts*, 8th ed (Sydney: Law Book Co, 1992) at 139.

102 As the High Court Division of the Supreme Court of Bangladesh said in *Catherine Masud et al v Kashed Miah et al*, [2016] 67 DLR 523, "[T]he time has come for us to review the law of tort and consider whether [it] should be incorporated in Bangladesh law so that claims arising from negligence, be it medical or otherwise, are properly dealt with [...] We feel [that the] time has come for us to recognize the concept of duty of care, the applicable standard of care owed which would be instrumental in determining whether there has been negligence."

103 See here *Clay v A J Crump & Sons Ltd*, [1963] 3 All ER 687, [1964] 1 QB 533.

104 See Heuston, *supra* note 98 at 11–17.

105 *Dobson (Litigation Guardian of) v Dobson*, [1999] 2 SCR 753, [1999] SCJ No 41 [*Dobson*].

106 *Ibid* at paras 25 and 27.

107 See *Cooper v Hobart*, [2001] 3 SCR 537, [2001] SCJ No 76; This test comes from *Kamloops v Nielson*, [1984] 2 SCR 2, [1984] SCJ No 29, which the Supreme Court of Canada adopted from *Anns v Merton London Borough Council*, [1977] 2 All ER 492, [1978] AC 728; Furthermore, in *Tremblay v Daigle*, [1989] 2 SCR 530, [1989] SCJ No 79, the Supreme Court of Canada said that a foetus is not a person and that legal personality begins at birth and ends at death.

108 Shortly afterwards, the Canadian province of Alberta promulgated the *Maternal Tort Liability Act*, SA 2005, c M-7.5 [*MTLA*]; Also see Kristin Ali, "Defining the Standard of Prenatal Care: An Analysis of Judicial and Legislative Responses" (2007) 1 McGill JL & Health 69 for an interesting and engaging discussion on whether the statute would be able to withstand a section 7 *Charter* challenge. I anticipate that if a similar legislation were enacted in Bangladesh, it would also withstand a section 32 *Constitution*, which guarantees the right to life and personal liberty, challenge, at *The Constitution of the People's Republic of Bangladesh* (Bangladesh), Act of 1972, s 32.

109 *MTLA, ibid* at s 4.

110 *MTLA, ibid* at s 5.

111 It is also important to note that section 5 of the *MTLA* limits the mother's liability to the "amount of insurance money payable under contracts of automobile insurance." This means that even if the child (a foetus at the moment of the injury) has suffered an injury worth $10,000, if the mother's insurance policy is $3,000, the child will only be able to recover the insured amount. As in, the mother is not properly liable and will not pay any money out of her own pocket for her child's injury.

112 *Penal Code, supra* note 14 at s 312.

113 This is why the term "menstrual regulation" is used in Bangladesh and permits a woman to terminate her pregnancy within 10 weeks of her last menstrual cycle. See generally Susheela Singh et al, "The Incidence of Menstrual Regulation Procedures and Abortion in Bangladesh" (2012) 38: 3 Int'l Pers Sexual & Rep Health 122; also see Anika Rahman, Laura Katzive, & Stanley Henshaw, "A Global Review of Laws on Induced Abortion" (1998) 24:2 Int'l Fam Plan Pers 56.

290 Negligence

However, I will not opine on whether abortion should be legalized in Bangladesh, as that is beyond the ambit of this book. Nonetheless, it is worth noting that a woman who is raped, and consequently impregnated, cannot get an abortion unless the pregnancy endangers her health, which is preposterous.

114 *Duval et al v Seguin et al*, [1972] 2 OR 686, [1972] OJ No 781 [*Duval*]; Also see *Keys v Mistahia Regional Health Authority*, [2001] AJ No 461, 291 AR 97.

115 See generally Percy H Winfield, "The Unborn Child" (1942) 8:1 Cambridge LJ 76.

116 For example, in *Montreal Tramways Co v Léveillé*, [1933] SCR 456, [1933] 4 DLR 337 [*Montreal Tramways*], a 7-month pregnant woman was descending from a tram, when, due to the negligence of the tram's operator, she was thrown from the car and injured. Two months later, she gave birth to a female child with club feet, which was attributed directly to the accident. A lawsuit was filed against the company, which was eventually appealed to the Supreme Court of Canada, and the court said that a child who suffered injuries *en ventre sa mere* could recover compensation from a third party, as it is in his benefit to do so.

117 *Renslow v Mennonite Hospital*, [1976] 40 Ill App 3d 234, 1976 Ill App LEXIS 2748 [*Renslow*]. Also see *Renslow v Mennonite Hospital*, [1977] 67 Ill 2d 348, 1977 Ill LEXIS 328.

118 *Dietrich v Northampton*, [1884] 138 Mass 14, 1884 Mass LEXIS 4. Mr. Justice Holmes said at 16, "For, apart from the question of remoteness, the argument would not be affected by the degree of maturity reached by the embryo at the moment of the organic lesion or wrongful act. Whereas Lord Coke's rule requires that the woman be quick with child, which, as this court has decided, means more than pregnant, and requires that the child shall have reached some degree of quasi independent life at the moment of the act. [...] If these general difficulties could be got over, and if we should assume, irrespective of precedent, that a man might owe a civil duty and incur a conditional prospective liability in tort to one not yet in being, and if we should assume also that causing an infant to be born prematurely stands on the same footing as wounding or poisoning, we should then be confronted by the question raised by the defendant, whether an infant dying before it was able to live separated from its mother could be said to have become a person recognized by the law as capable of having a *locus standi* in court, or of being represented there by an administrator."

119 *Allaire v St. Luke's Hospital*, [1900] 184 Ill 359, 56 NE 638. However, Mr. Justice Boggs provides a cogent argument in dissent, saying, "A fetus in the womb of the mother may well be regarded as but a part of the bowels of the mother during a portion of the period of gestation; but if, while in the womb, it reaches that prenatal age of viability when the destruction of the life of the mother does not necessarily end its existence also, and when, if separated prematurely and by artificial means from the mother, it would be so far a matured human being as that it would live and grow, mentally and physically, as other children generally, it is but to deny a palpable fact to argue there is but one life, and that the life of the mother. Medical science and skill and experience have demonstrated that at a period of gestation in advance of the period of parturition the fetus is capable of independent and separate life, and that though within the body of the mother it is not merely a part of her body, for her body may die in all of its parts and the child remain alive and capable of maintaining life when separated from the dead body of the mother. If at that period a child so advanced is injured in its limbs or members and is born into the living world suffering from the effects of the injury, is it not sacrificing truth to a

Negligence 291

mere theoretical abstraction to say the injury was not to the child but wholly to the mother?"

120 *Bonbrest v Kotz*, [1946] 65 F Supp 138, 1946 US Dist LEXIS 2712.

121 *Amann v Faidy*, [1953] 415 Ill 422, 114 NE 2d 412. In this case, the child was born alive, but died thereafter due to the injuries he suffered *in utero*. However, it is important to note that Canadian courts understood the requirement of permitting a child, who was injured *in utero*, to hold a third party liable back in 1933, at *Montreal Tramways, supra* note 116.

122 *Rodriquez v Patti*, [1953] 415 Ill 496, 114 NE 2d 741; also see John Brantley, "Wrongful Birth: The Emerging Status of a New Tort" (1976) 8:1 St Mary's LJ 140.

123 See generally Philippe Nonet & Philip Selznick, *Law & Society in Transition: Toward Responsive Law* (New Brunswick, NJ: Transaction Publishers, 2001); Also see Steven Vago et al, *Law and Society* (New York, NY: Routledge, 2018).

124 *Penal Code, supra* note 14 at ss 300 and 494.

125 *Haynes v G Harwood & Son*, [1934] All ER Rep 103, [1935] 1 KB 146 [*Haynes*].

126 Harry Street, *The Law of Torts* (London: Butterworths, 1955) at 154.

127 See generally P QR Boberg, "Reflections on the *Novus Actus Interveniens* Concept" (1959) 76:3 SALJ 280.

128 *La Lievre v Gould*, [1893] 1 QB 491, 57 JP 484, at 2. Causation has plagued scholars and courts more than any other topic in tort law; see grand monograph by the authors at HLA Hart & Tony Honoré, *Causation in the Law*, 2nd ed (London: Clarendon Press, 1985). As Professor Fleming has said, "Every event or occurrence is the result of many conditions that are jointly sufficient to product it." At Fleming, *supra* note 2 at 219.

129 *Barnett v Chelsea & Kensington Hospital Management Committee*, [1968] 1 All ER 1068, [1969] 1 QB 428 [*Barnett*].

130 See Fleming, *supra* note 2 at 550–662; Also see Kenneth Abraham, "Self-Proving Causation" (2013) 99:8 Va L Rev 1811. Nonetheless, the "but for" test does not need to be proven with scientific precision, at *Athey v Leonati*, [1996] 3 SCR 458, [1996] SCJ No 102 at para 16 [*Athey*].

131 See generally Patrick Kelley, "Proximate Cause in Negligence Law: History, Theory, and the Present Darkness" (1991) 69:1 Wash ULO 49; Also see Clarence Morris, "Duty, Negligence and Causation" (1952) 101:2 U Pa L Rev 189.

132 See Linden & Feldthusen, *supra* note 7 at 120–132, Prosser, *supra* note 39 at 236–290, and Fleming, *supra* note 2 at 218–227.

133 *Jobling v Associated Dairies Ltd*, [1981] 2 All ER 752, [1982] AC 794 [*Jobling*].

134 These facts are similar to *Baker v Willoughby*, [1969] 3 All ER 1528, [1970] AC 467, which *Jobling* eventually overturned.

135 Additionally, the shooter will not be able to disclaim liability for your paralysis on the grounds that he did not know that you were already infirm from a previous injury. This is known as the thin-skull, or eggshell skull, rule and I will delineate this when discussing *Smith v Leech Brain & Co Ltd*, [1961] 3 All ER 1159, [1962] 2 QB 405 *infra* [*Smith*].

136 *Vosburg v Putney*, [1893] 86 Wis 278, 56 NW 480 [*Vosburg*]. In that case, George Putney, a 12-year-old boy, kicked Andrew Vosburg, who was a 14-year-old boy, in the shin. While the kick would have hardly injured a healthy child, Vosburg was not absolutely healthy and it aggravated his tibia infection, which resulted in Vosburg's leg being amputated. Even though Putney did not know of Vosburg's pre-existing condition, he was held liable for all of the damage following the initial injury.

292 *Negligence*

Also see *Stoleson v United States*, [1983] 708 F 2d 1217, 1983 US App LEXIS 27489 and *Jordan v Atchison Topeka & Santa Fe Railway Co*, [1991] 934 F 2d 225, 1991 US App LEXIS 10880.

137 Alfred Aman Jr., "The Earth as Eggshell Victim: A Global Perspective on Domestic Regulation" (1993) 102:8 Yale LJ 2107 at 2107 [Aman]; See generally Francis Glorieux et al, "Osteogenesis Imperfecta Type VI: A Form of Brittle Bone Disease with a Mineralization Defect" (2002) 17:1 J Bone Miner Res 30.

138 *Dulieu v White & Sons*, [1900–3] All ER Rep 353, [1901] 2 KB 669, at 359.

139 Please keep in mind that if it is claimed that the injury was caused by negligence, then it will be necessary for the plaintiff to prove a standard of care, that the defendant owed the plaintiff a duty of care, that the duty the defendant owed the plaintiff was breached, that the injury was a proximate cause of the negligent act, and that the injury from the negligent conduct was not remote and that the injury was of a type that was reasonably foreseeable (more on this in the following section).

140 Pursuant to section 299 of the *Penal Code*, criminal law in Bangladesh also recognizes the thin skull rule. The relevant portion of the provision states, "Whoever causes death by doing an act with the intention of causing death, or with the intention of causing such bodily injury as is likely to cause death, or with the knowledge that he is likely by such act to cause death, commits the offence of culpable homicide. […] Explanation 1. A person who causes bodily injury to another who is labouring under a disorder, disease or bodily infirmity, and thereby accelerates the death of that other, shall be deemed to have caused his death." At *Penal Code, supra* note 14 at s 299.

141 *Wright v Cambridge Medical Group*, [2011] EWCA Civ 669, [2012] 3 WLR 1124 [*Wright*].

142 Expert evidence also established that had Dr. Phellas seen the patient and not referred her to the Hospital, then he still would have been negligent because a competent doctor, viewing the patient's condition, would have referred her to the Hospital anyway.

143 See *Gregg v Scott*, [2005] 4 All ER 812, [2005] UKHL 2.

144 See generally E Wayne Thode, "Indefensible Use of the Hypothetical Case to Determine Cause in Fact" (1968) 46:4 Tex L Rev 423.

145 *McGhee v National Coal Board*, [1972] 3 All ER 1008, [1973] 1 WLR 1 [*McGhee*].

146 *Athey, supra* note 130.

147 Also see *Faulkner v Keffalinos*, [1971] 45 ALJR 80.

148 Fleming, *supra* note 2 at 219.

149 For example, see Gillian Demeyere, "The Material Contribution Test: An Immaterial Contribution to Tort Law: A Comment on *Briglio v. Faulkner*" (2000) 34:1 UBC L Rev 317 and Dennis Klimchuk & Vaughan Black, "A Comment on *Athey v. Leonati*: Causation, Damages and Thin Skulls" (1997) 31:1 UBC L Rev 163 where the authors state that proving cause-in-fact is a "complex area" of the law [Klimchuk & Black]; Also see Richard W Wright, "Causation, Responsibility, Risk, Probability, Naked Statistics, and Proof: Pruning the Bramble Bush by Clarifying the Concepts" (1988) 73:5 Iowa L Rev 1001.

150 *Blackstock v Foster*, [1958] SR (NSW) 341 (SC), 1958 75 WN (NSW) 393 [*Blackstock*]. Also see Weinrib, *supra* note 5 at 236–237.

151 Klimchuk & Black, *supra* note 149 at 165–168.

152 *Sindell v Abbott Laboratories*, [1980] 26 Cal 3d 588, 1980 Cal LEXIS 151 [*Sindell*].

153 See Richard Epstein, *Modern Products Liability Law* (Westport, Connecticut: Quorum Books, 1980) at 159–160 for his criticism of *Sindell*.

Negligence   293

154 However, see *Abel v Eli Lilly & Co*, [1984] 418 Mich 311, 343 NW 2d 164, where the court said at 172–173, "Perhaps the most fundamental, and arguably the most important, factual difference between *Summers [v Tice]* and this case is that in *Summers* each defendant was negligent toward the sole plaintiff; each could have caused the injury to the plaintiff although only one in fact did so. Here, the plaintiffs do not even claim that each of the defendants was negligent toward each of the plaintiffs. Therefore, each of the defendants in this case could not have caused injury to each of the plaintiffs. Stated differently, in *Summers*, each defendant was negligent toward *the* plaintiff; here, each defendant was negligent toward *a* plaintiff, but each defendant was not negligent toward *each* plaintiff. Thus, all defendants were not negligent toward each plaintiff, and each defendant could not have caused each plaintiff's injury." Contrast this case with *Hymowitz v Eli Lilly & Co*, [1989] 73 NY 2d 487, 539 NE 2d 1069.

155 *Ybarra, supra* note 92.

156 *Cook v Lewis*, [1951] SCR 830, [1951] SCJ No 28 [*Cook*].

157 See Wex S Malone, "Ruminations on Cause-in-Fact" (1956) 9:1 Stan L Rev 60 at 73 where he says, "All rules of conduct, irrespective of whether they are the product of a legislature or are a part of the fabric of the court-made law of negligence, exist for purposes. They are designed to protect *some* persons under *some* circumstances against *some* risks. Seldom does a rule protect every victim against every risk that may befall him, merely because it is shown that the violation of the rule played a part in producing the injury. The task of defining the proper reach or thrust of a rule in its policy aspects is one that must be undertaken by the court in each case as it arises."

158 If we assume that the cancer was caused by the exposure to asbestos by the second employer, then this means that the first employer is innocent, but is nevertheless liable. The opposite assumption is true as well.

159 *Fairchild v Glenhaven Funeral Services Ltd*, [2002] 3 All ER 305, [2003] 1 AC 32 at para 2.

160 *Kingston v Chicago Northwestern Railway Company*, [1927] 191 Wis 610, 1927 Wisc LEXIS 108 [*Kingston*].

161 *Wilsher v Essex Area Health Authority*, [1988] 1 All ER 871, [1988] AC 1074 [*Wilsher*].

162 Also see *Snell v Farrell*, [1990] 2 SCR 311, [1990] SCJ No 73 and *Leigh v London Ambulance Service NHS Trust*, [2014] EWHC 286 (QB), [2014] All ER (D) 201 Feb.

163 *Resurface Corp v Hanke*, [2007] 1 SCR 333, [2007] SCJ No 7 at paras 20, 21, 24 and 25.

164 *Overseas Tankship (UK) Ltd v Morts Dock & Engineering Co Ltd*, [1961] 1 All ER 404, [1961] 2 WLR 126. This case is commonly known as *The Wagon Mound (No 1)*, which I shall refer to as "*The Wagon Mound*".

165 "Chartered by demise" means that the ship and the crew of the Wagon Mound was under the complete control of Overseas Tankship. As in, it is as if Overseas Tankship owned the Wagon Mound.

166 *Re Polemis and Furness, Withy & Co, Ltd*, [1921] All ER Rep 40, [1921] 3 KB 560. In this case, Polemis and Boyazides were shipowners, who chartered a ship to Furness, Withy & Company Ltd (hereinafter "Furness"). Due to rough waters, leakage from the cargo caused gas vapours to form below deck. When the ship reached port, Furness hired stevedores to unload the goods, and one of them knocked down a plank, which created a spark, ignited a fire, and damaged the entire ship. Polemis and Boyazides sought compensation from Furness, but Furness contended that the damage was not reasonably foreseeable. However, the court ruled against Furness and said that a negligent actor

294   *Negligence*

is liable for all damage resulting directly from his negligent conduct even if the damage was not reasonably foreseeable.

167   Martin Davies, "The Road from Morocco: *Polemis* through *Donoghue* to No-Fault" (1982) 45:5 Modern L Rev 534 at 535–542 where he argues that *Polemis* was required at that time given the social context.

168   See *Vaughan, supra* note 8.

169   See *Latimer, supra* note 73.

170   For an influential formulation of the duty, breach of that duty, and the consequences for which the defendant is liable, see *South Australia Asset Management Corp v York Montague Ltd*, [1996] 3 All ER 365, [1997] AC 191.

171   See generally Fleming, *supra* note 2 at 239–245.

172   *Smith, supra* note 135.

173   *Bolton, supra* note 66; *Latimer, supra* note 73; *Tomlinson, supra* note 76.

174   Green, *supra* note 30.

175   *Vosburg, supra* note 136; Also see Aman, *supra* note 137.

176   For example, in *Cotic v Gray*, [1981] 33 OR (2d) 356, 124 DLR (3d) 641, Nediljko Cotic suffered injuries in a car accident because of the negligence of the defendant. Before the accident, he suffered from severe depression and neurotic behaviour, and after the accident, it developed into a terrible psychotic one. Sixteen months after the accident, he committed suicide. Mr. Cotic's wife wanted compensation (under the then *Fatal Accidents Act*, which has since been replaced by the *Family Law Reforms Act*) for his death from the defendant, who accepted liability for the accident, but denied it for his death, claiming that it was not reasonably foreseeable. However, using the thin-skull rule, the court imposed liability on the defendant saying that he must take his victim as he finds him (a subsequent appeal to the Supreme Court of Canada was denied, see *Cotic v Gray*, [1983] 2 SCR 2.

177   *Stephenson v Waite Tileman Ltd*, [1973] 1 NZLR 152 [*Stephenson*]; Also see Heuston & Buckley, *supra* note 6 at 598–614

178   See generally Douglas Payne, "Foresight and Remoteness of Damage in Negligence" (1962) 25:1 Modern L Rev 1; also see R Dias, "Remoteness of Liability and Legal Policy" (1962) 20:2 Cambridge LJ 178.

179   Also see *Corrie v Gilbert*, [1965] SCJ No 19, [1965] SCR 457 and *Winteringham v Rae et al*, [1965] OJ No 1149, [1966] 1 OR 727.

180   *Hughes v Lord Advocate*, [1963] 1 All ER 705, [1963] AC 837 [*Hughes*].

181   Since I have already done so above innumerable times, I will eschew a discussion of the Hand Formula in the main text. However, keep in mind that it would not cost the employees considerable resources to extinguish the paraffin lamps.

182   Also see *Jobling, supra* note 133 and its subsequent discussion to understand *novus actus interveniens*.

183   *Doughty v Turner Manufacturing Co Ltd*, [1964] 1 All ER 98, [1964] 1 QB 518.

184   See James Fleming, *supra* note 16 at 5–15; Also see Robert Keeton, *Legal Cause in the Law of Torts* (Columbus: Ohio State University Press, 1963) at 49–60.

185   *Palsgraf v Long Island Railroad Company*, [1928] 248 NY 339, 1928 NY LEXIS 1269 [*Palsgraf*].

186   See Warren A Seavey, "Mr. Justice Cardozo and the Law of Torts" (1939) 48:3 Yale LJ 390.

187   See generally Ernest J Weinrib, "The Passing of *Palsgraf*" (2001) 54:3 Vand L Rev 803.

188   *Bradford v Kanellos*, [1974] SCR 409, [1974] RCS 409 [*Bradford*]. For the decision of the Court of Appeal, see *Bradford v Kanellos*, [1970] OJ No 1790, [1971] 2 OR 393.

189   See, for example, *Hughes, supra* note 180.

Negligence 295

190 Also see *Martin v McNamara Construction Company Limited*, [1955] OJ No 569, [1955] OR 523.

191 *Urbanski v Patel*, [1978] MJ No 211, 84 DLR (3D) 650 [*Urbanski*].

192 Here, I am only concerned with the court's opinion in reference to Victor Urbanski's claim. However, please see *ibid* at paras 30–96 to read the court's opinion and on the damages awarded to Mr. and Mrs. Firman.

193 However, in *The TJ Hooper*, it was held that the courts determine industry standards and whether its practices are in conformity with what is expected of a reasonable person.

194 *Urbanski, supra* note 191 at paras 17–19.

195 See Haynes, *supra* note 125; See generally Peter F Lake, "Recognizing the Importance of Remoteness to the Duty to Rescue" (1997) 46:2 DePaul L Rev 315.

196 See *Wagner v International Railway Company*, [1921] 232 NY 176, 1921 NY LEXIS 490; Also see John G Fleming, "Remoteness and Duty: The Control Devices in Liability for Negligence" (1953) 31:5 Can Bar Rev 471 at 480–493.

197 *Rajkot Municipal Corp v Manjulben Jayantilal*, [1997] 9 SCC 522 [*Rajkot*].

198 See, for example, *Swinamer v Nova Scotia (Attorney General)*, [1994] 1 SCR 445, [1994] SCJ No 21.

199 *Froom, supra* note 81.

200 Also see *Davies v Swan Motor Co (Swansea) Ltd*, [1949] 1 All ER 620, [1949] 2 KB 291. Previously, contributory negligence barred one from recovering any damages, see *Butterfield v Forrester*, [1809] 103 ER 926, [1809] 11 East 60.

201 See Fleming, *supra* note 2 at 302–306.

202 *Bourgoin v Leamington (Municipality)*, [2006] OJ No 1474, [2006] OTC 351; Also see Heuston & Buckley, *supra* note 6 at 573–576.

203 See *Biletski v University of Regina*, [2019] SJ No 193, 2019 SKCA 44; See Lewis Klar, *Tort Law*, 5th ed (Toronto: Carswell, 1996) at 549–554 for a summary of cases on seatbelts in Canada; Also see Patrick Atiyah, *Accidents, Compensation and the Law*, 2nd ed (London: Weidenfeld and Nicolson, 1975) at 135–139 where he argues that the doctrine of contributory negligence should be abolished for personal injury claims, but should remain in cases of property damage.

204 *Lambert v Lastoplex Chemicals Co*, [1971] SCJ No 132, [1972] SCR 569 [*Lambert*].

205 *Donoghue, supra* note 97.

206 See Charles Warren, "Volenti Non Fit Injuria in Actions of Negligence" (1895) 8:8 Harv L Rev 457.

207 *Haynes, supra* note 125.

208 See *Penal Code, supra* note 14 at s 338A, which stipulates, "Whoever causes grievous hurt to any person by driving any vehicle or riding on any public way so rashly or negligently as to endanger human life, or the personal safety of others shall be punished with imprisonment of either description for a term which may extend to [two years], or with fine, or with both." Also see *RTA, supra* note 86 at ss 52–62.

209 *Pelletier v Ontario*, [2013] OJ No 5271, 2013 ONSC 6898.

210 *Bradley v Bath*, [2010] BCJ No 24, 2010 BCCA 10; Also see *Lloyd (Litigation Guardian of) v Rotter*, [2003] OJ No 5064, [2003] OTC 1064.

211 *Davies v Mann*, [1842] 10 M&W 547.

212 *Dube v Labar*, [1986] SCJ No 29, [1986] 1 SCR 649.

213 See generally Fleming, *supra* note 2 at 327–345, Heuston & Buckley, *supra* note 6 at 556–561, and Prosser, *supra* note 39 at 439–457.

296 *Negligence*

References

Legislation

Maternal Tort Liability Act, SA 2005, c M-7.5
The Children Act, 2013 (Bangladesh), Act No XXIV of 2013
The Constitution of the People's Republic of Bangladesh (Bangladesh), Act of 1972
The Majority Act, 1875 (Bangladesh), Act No IX of 1875
The Penal Code, 1860 (Bangladesh), Act No XLV of 1860
The Road Transport Act, 2018 (Bangladesh), Act No XLVIII of 2018
Youth Criminal Justice Act, SC 2002, c 1

Caselaw

Abel v Eli Lilly & Co, [1984] 418 Mich 311, 343 NW 2d 164
Agdeppa v Glougie, [1945] 71 Cal App 2d 463, 162 P 2d 944
Agni v Wenshall (in re City of New York), [2008] 522 F 3D 279, 2008 US App LEXIS 6416
Allaire v St. Luke's Hospital, [1900] 184 Ill 359, 56 NE 638
Amann v Faidy, [1953] 415 Ill 422, 114 NE 2d 412
Anns v Merton London Borough Council, [1977] 2 All ER 492, [1978] AC 728
Appleby v Erie Tobacco Co, [1910] OJ No 64, 22 OLR 533
Armstrong v Warner Brothers Theatres Inc, [1947] 161 Pa Super 385, 54 A 2d 831
Athey v Leonati, [1996] 3 SCR 458, [1996] SCJ No 102
Baker v Market Harborough Industrial Society Ltd, [1953] 1 WLR 1472, 97 Sol Jo 861
Baker v Willoughby, [1969] 3 All ER 1528, [1970] AC 467
Balcom v Independence, [1916] 178 Iowa 685, 160 NW 305
Baltimore v Thompson, [1937] 171 Md 460, 189 A 822
Barnett v Chelsea & Kensington Hospital Management Committee, [1968] 1 All ER 1068, [1969] 1 QB 428
Belcher v City of San Francisco, [1945] 69 Cal App 2d 457, 158 P 2d 996
Biletski v University of Regina, [2019] SJ No 193, 2019 SKCA 44
Bellizia v Meares, [1971] VR 641
Blackstock v Foster, [1958] SR (NSW) 341 (SC), 1958 75 WN (NSW) 393
Bolton v Stone, [1951] 1 All ER 1078, 59 LGR 32
Bonbrest v Kotz, [1946] 65 F Supp 138, 1946 US Dist LEXIS 2712
Borgstede v Waldbauer, [1935] 337 Mo 1205, 88 SW 2d 373
Bourgoin v Leamington (Municipality), [2006] OJ No 1474, [2006] OTC 351
Bradford v Kanellos, [1970] OJ No 1790, [1971] 2 OR 393
Bradford v Kanellos, [1974] SCR 409, [1974] RCS 409
Bradley v Bath, [2010] BCJ No 24, 2010 BCCA 10
Brown v Swift & Co, [1912] 91 Neb 532, 136 NW 726
Brune v De Benedetty, [1924] 261 SW 930, 1924 Mo App LEXIS 487
Burnett v Amalgamated Phosphate Co, [1938] 96 F 2d 974, 1938 US App LEXIS 3606
Butterfield v Forrester, [1809] 103 ER 926, [1809] 11 East 60
Byrne v Boadle, [1863] 159 ER 299, [1861–1873] All ER Rep Ext 1528
Carter v Yardley & Co, [1946] 319 Mass 92, 64 NE 2d 693
Catherine Masud et al v Kashed Miah et al, [2016] 67 DLR 523

Negligence   297

Central of Georgia R Co v Robertson, [1919] 203 Ala 358, 83 So 102

Chaproniere v Mason, [1905] 21 TLR 633

Children Charity Bangladesh Foundation v The Government of Bangladesh, [2017] 5 CLR 278 (HCD)

Clay v A J Crump & Sons Ltd, [1963] 3 All ER 687, [1964] 1 QB 533

Comanche Duke Oil Co v Texas Pacific Coal & Oil Co, [1927] 298 SW 554, 1927 Tex App LEXIS 1436

Coppins v Jefferson, [1905] 126 Wis 578, 105 NW 1078

Cook v Lewis, [1951] SCR 830, [1951] SCJ No 28

Cooper v Hobart, [2001] 3 SCR 537, [2001] SCJ No 76

Corrie v Gilbert, [1965] SCJ No 19, [1965] SCR 457

Cotic v Gray, [1981] 33 OR (2d) 356, 124 DLR (3d) 641

Cotic v Gray, [1983] 2 SCR 2

Davies v Mann, [1842] 10 M&W 547

Davies v Swan Motor Co (Swansea) Ltd, [1949] 1 All ER 620, [1949] 2 KB 291

Davis v Boston MRR, [1900] 70 NH 519, 49 All 108

Diamond State Telephone Co v Hunter, [1941] 41 Del 336, 21 A 2d 286

Dietrich v Northampton, [1884] 138 Mass 14, 1884 Mass LEXIS 4

Dillenberger v Weingartner, [1900] 64 NJL 292, 45 A 638

Dobson (Litigation Guardian of) v Dobson, [1999] 2 SCR 753, [1999] SCJ No 41

Doherty v Arcade Hotel, [1943] 170 Ore 374, 134 P 2d 118

Donoghue v Stevenson, [1932] All ER Rep 1, [1932] SC (HL) 31

Donathan v McConnell, [1948] 121 Mont 230, 193 P 2d 819

Doughty v Turner Manufacturing Co Ltd, [1964] 1 All ER 98, [1964] 1 QB 518

Dow v Brown, [1939] 193 So 239, 1939 La App LEXIS 506

Dube v Labar, [1986] SCJ No 29, [1986] 1 SCR 649

Dulieu v White & Sons, [1900–3] All ER Rep 353, [1901] 2 KB 669

Duval et al v Seguin et al, [1972] 2 OR 686, [1972] OJ No 781

Edwards v Sutton London Borough, [2016] All ER (D) 90 (Oct), [2016] EWCA Civ 1005

Evansville v Blue, [1937] 212 Ind 130, 8 NE 2d 224

Fairchild v Glenhaven Funeral Services Ltd, [2002] 3 All ER 305, [2003] 1 AC 32

Faulkinbury v Shaw, [1931] 183 Ark 1019 39 SW 2d 708

Faulkner v Keffalinos, [1971] 45 ALJR 80

Femling v Star Publishing Company, [1938] 195 Wash 395, 84 P 2d 1008

Fitzpatrick v Cooper, [1935] 54 CLR 200, 9 ALJR 343

Fontaine v British Columbia (Official Administrator), [1998] 1 SCR 424, [1997] SCJ No 100

Foy v Winston, [1900] 126 NC 381, 35 SE 609

Froom et al v Butcher, [1975] 3 All ER 520, [1975] 3 WLR 379

Gates v Hoston & M Railroad, [1926] 255 Mass 297, 151 NE 320

Geist v Moore, [1937] 58 Idaho 149, 70 P 2d 403

Grant v Australian Knitting Mills Ltd, [1935] All ER Rep 209, 105 LJPC 6

Gregg v Scott, [2005] 4 All ER 812, [2005] UKHL 2

Gobrecht v Beckwith, [1926] 82 NH 415, 135 A 20

Goff v Hubbard, [1927] 217 Ky 729, 290 SW 696

Gould v Slater Woolen Co, [1888] 147 Mass 315, 17 NE 531

Green v Atlanta Charlotte Air Line Railway Company et al, [1925] 131 SC 124, 126 SE 441

Haynes v G Harwood & Son, [1934] All ER Rep 103, [1935] 1 KB 146

298   *Negligence*

Henderson v Public Transport Commission of New South Wales, [1981] 37 ALR 29, 56 ALJR 1

Hesse v National Casket Co, [1901] 66 NJL 652, 52 A 384

Holland v Pitocchelli, [1938] 299 Mass 554, 13 NE 2d 290

Hope v Full Brook Coal Co, [1896] 3 AD 70, 38 NYS 1040

Houston v Town of Waverly, [1932] 225 Ala 98, 142 So 80

Hughes v Lord Advocate, [1963] 1 All ER 705, [1963] AC 837

Huntingburgh v First, [1896] 15 Ind App 552, 43 NE 17

Hymowitz v Eli Lilly & Co, [1989] 73 NY 2d 487, 539 NE 2d 1069

Jennings v Tacoma R & M Co, [1893] 7 Wash 275, 34 P 937

Jobling v Associated Dairies Ltd, [1981] 2 All ER 752, [1982] AC 794

Johnson v Rulon, [1950] 363 Pa 585, 70 A 2d 325

Johnson v St. Paul City Railway Co, [1897] 67 Minn 260, 69 NW 900

Jordan v Atchison Topeka & Santa Fe Railway Co, [1991] 934 F 2d 225, 1991 US App LEXIS 10880

Kamloops v Nielson, [1984] 2 SCR 2, [1984] SCJ No 29

Keith v Worcester and Blackstone Valley Street Railway Co, [1907] 196 Mass 478, 82 NE 680

Keys v Alamo City Baseball Co, [1941] 150 SW 2d 368, 1941 Tex App LEXIS 308

Keys v Mistahia Regional Health Authority, [2001] AJ No 461, 291 AR 97

Kingston v Chicago Northwestern Railway Company, [1927] 191 Wis 610, 1927 Wisc LEXIS 108

La Lievre v Gould, [1893] 1 QB 491, 57 JP 484

Lambert v Lastoplex Chemicals Co, [1971] SCJ No 132, [1972] SCR 569X

Latimer v AEC Ltd, [1953] 2 All ER 449, 51 LGR 457

Le Vonas v Acme Paper Board Company, [1944] 184 Md 16, 40 A 2d 43

Leigh v London Ambulance Service NHS Trust, [2014] EWHC 286 (QB), [2014] All ER (D) 201 Feb

Levesley v Thomas Firth and John Brown Ltd, [1953] 2 All ER 866, [1953] 1 WLR 1206

Lexington & E R Co v White, [1918] 182 Ky 267, 206 SW 467

Linnehan v Sampson, [1879] 126 Mass 506, 1879 Mass LEXIS 306)

Lloyd (Litigation Guardian of) v Rotter, [2003] OJ No 5064, [2003] OTC 1064

Lobert v Pack, [1939] 337 Pa 103, 9 A 2d 365

Louisville & Nashville Railroad Co v Perry's Administrator, [1917] 173 Ky 213, 190 SW 1064

Mansfield v Weetabix Ltd, [1998] 1 WLR 1263, [1997] Lexis Citation 2009

Marks' Adm'r v Petersburg Railroad Co, [1891] 88 Va 1, 13 SE 299

Martin v McNamara Construction Company Limited, [1955] OJ No 569, [1955] OR 523

Mazza v Greenstein, [1948] 82 Ohio App 145, 80 NE 2d 216

McCarty v Pheasant Run, Inc, [1987] 826 F 2d 1554, 1987 US App LEXIS 11047

McErlean v Sarel et al, [1987] OJ No 873, 61 OR (2d) 396

McGhee v National Coal Board, [1972] 3 All ER 1008, [1973] 1 WLR 1

McHale v Watson, [1966] 115 CLR 199, 39 ALJR 459

McIntyre v Pope, [1937] 326 Pa 172, 191 A 607

McLaughlin v Griffin, [1912] 155 Iowa 302, 135 NW 1107

McMillen v Steele, [1923] 275 Pa 584, 119 A 721

Miller v Jackson, [1977] 3 All ER 778, [1977] QB 966

Missouri P R Co v Vinson, [1938] 196 Ark 500, 118 SW 2d 672

Negligence 299

Montreal Tramways Co v Léveillé, [1933] SCR 456, [1933] 4 DLR 337

M/S Islamia Automatic Rice Mills Ltd v Bangladesh Shilpa Rin Sangstha et al, [1998] 23 BLD 139

Mullen v Barr & Co, [1929] SC 461

Murphy v Pere Marquette Railroad Co, [1914] 183 Mich 435, 150 NW 122

Oran v Kraft-Phenix Cheese Corp, [1944] 324 Ill App 463, 58 NE 2d 731

Osborn v Leuffgen, [1942] 381 Ill 295, 45 NE 2d 622

Overseas Tankship (UK) Ltd v Morts Dock & Engineering Co Ltd, [1961] 1 All ER 404, [1961] 2 WLR 126

Palsgraf v Long Island Railroad Company, [1928] 248 NY 339, 1928 NY LEXIS 1269

Parrot v Wells, [1872] 82 US 524, 21 L Ed 206

Parton v Phillips Petroleum Co, [1937] 231 Mo App 585, 107 SW 2d 167

Pelletier v Ontario, [2013] OJ No 5271, 2013 ONSC 6898

R v W (RE), [2006] OJ No 265, 205 CCC (3d) 183, CarswellOnt 344

Rajkot Municipal Corp v Manjulben Jayantilal, [1997] 9 SCC 522

Ramos v Service Bros, [1931] 118 Cal App 432, 5 P 2d 623

Re Polemis and Furness, Withy & Co, Ltd, [1921] All ER Rep 40, [1921] 3 KB 560

Remmenga v Selk, [1948] 150 Neb 401, 34 NW 2d 757

Renslow v Mennonite Hospital, [1976] 40 Ill App 3d 234, 1976 Ill App LEXIS 2748

Renslow v Mennonite Hospital, [1977] 67 Ill 2d 348, 1977 Ill LEXIS 328

Resurface Corp v Hanke, [2007] 1 SCR 333, [2007] SCJ No 7

Risk v Rose Bruford College, [2013] All ER (D) 92 (Dec), [2013] EWHC 3869 (QB)

Rodgers v Cox, [1944] 130 Conn 616, 36 A 2d 373

Rodriquez v Patti, [1953] 415 Ill 496, 114 NE 2d 741

Rozell v Rozell, [1939] 281 NY 106, 22 NE 2d 254

Ryan et al v Hickson et al, [1974] 55 DLR (3d) 196, 7 OR (2d) 352

Rzeszewski v Barth, [1944] 324 Ill App 345, 58 NE 2d 269

Scott v London and St. Katherine Docks Co, [1865] 3 H & C 595

Seattle Electric Co v Hovden, [1911] 190 F 7, 1911 US App LEXIS 4426

Sindell v Abbott Laboratories, [1980] 26 Cal 3d 588, 1980 Cal LEXIS 151

Smith v Leech Brain & Co Ltd, [1961] 3 All ER 1159, [1962] 2 QB 405

Smithline v Hadigrian, [1942] 34 NYS 2d 509, NY Misc LEXIS 1537

Snell v Farrell, [1990] 2 SCR 311, [1990] SCJ No 73

South Australia Asset Management Corp v York Montague Ltd, [1996] 3 All ER 365, [1997] AC 191

Stephenson v Waite Tileman Ltd, [1973] 1 NZLR 152

Stoleson v United States, [1983] 708 F 2d 1217, 1983 US App LEXIS 27489

Swan v Salisbury Construction Co Ltd, [1966] 2 All ER 138, 1 WLR 204

Swinamer v Nova Scotia (Attorney General), [1994] 1 SCR 445, [1994] SCJ No 21

ter Neuzen v Korn, [1995] 3 SCR 674, [1995] SCJ No 79

The TJ Hooper, [1932] 60 F 2d 737, 1932 US App LEXIS 2592

Tomlinson v Congleton Borough Council, [2003] 3 All ER 1122, 2003 UKHL 47

Tremblay v Daigle, [1989] 2 SCR 530, [1989] SCJ No 79

Tucker v Tucker, [1956] SASR 297

United States v Carroll Towing, [1947] 159 F 2d 169, 1947 US App LEXIS 3226

Urbanski v Patel, [1978] MJ No 211, 84 DLR (3D) 650

Vaughan v Menlove, [1835–42] All ER Rep 156, [1837] 132 ER 490

Vigneault v Dr. Hewson Dental Co, [1938] 300 Mass 223, 15 NE 2d 185

Vosburg v Putney, [1893] 86 Wis 278, 56 NW 480

300 *Negligence*

Wagner v International Railway Company, [1921] 232 NY 176, 1921 NY LEXIS 490

Waters v Pacific Coast Dairy Inc, [1942] 55 Cal App 2d 789, 131 P 2d 588

Weare v Fitchburg, [1872] 110 Mass 334

Wellman v Fordson Coal Company, [1928] 105 W Va 463, 143 SE 160

Williams v Ballard Lumber Co, [1906] 41 Wash 338, 83 P 323

Wilsher v Essex Area Health Authority, [1988] 1 All ER 871, [1988] AC 1074

Winterbottom v Wright, [1842] 11 LJ Ex 415, 10 M&W 109

Winteringham v Rae et al, [1965] OJ No 1149, [1966] 1 OR 727

Wright v Cambridge Medical Group, [2011] EWCA Civ 669, [2012] 3 WLR 1124

Ybarra v Spangard et al, [1944] 154 P 2d 687, 25 Cal 2d 486

Secondary Material: Books

Atiyah, Patrick, *Accidents, Compensation and the Law*, 2nd ed (London: Weidenfeld and Nicolson, 1975)

Epstein, Richard, *Modern Products Liability Law* (Westport, Connecticut: Quorum Books, 1980)

Fleming, John G, *The Law of Torts*, 8th ed (Sydney: Law Book Co, 1992)

Fleming, John G, *The Law of Torts*, 9th ed (Sydney: LBC Information Services, 1998)

Green, Leon, *Judge and Jury* (Kansas City, USA: Vernon Law Book Co, 1930)

Hart, Herbert L. A. & Honoré, Tony, *Causation in the Law*, 2nd ed (London: Clarendon Press, 1985)

Heuston, Robert F V & Buckley, Richard A, *Salmond and Heuston on the Law of Torts*, 19th ed (London: Sweet & Maxwell, 1987)

Holmes Jr Oliver W, *The Common Law* (Boston: Little, Brown & Co, 1881)

Keeton, Robert, *Legal Cause in the Law of Torts* (Columbus: Ohio State University Press, 1963)

Klar, Lewis, *Tort Law*, 5th ed (Toronto: Carswell, 1996)

Linden, Allen M, *Canadian Negligence Law*, 3rd ed (Toronto: Butterworths, 1974)

Linden, Allen M & Feldthusen, Bruce, *Canadian Tort Law*, 9th ed (Markham, ON: LexisNexis Canada Inc, 2011)

Moran, Mayo, *Rethinking the Reasonable Person* (Oxford: Oxford University Press, 2003)

Nonet, Philippe & Selznick, Philip, *Law & Society in Transition: Toward Responsive Law* (New Brunswick, NJ: Transaction Publishers, 2001)

Posner, Richard A, *Tort Law: Cases and Economic Analysis* (Toronto: Little, Brown & Co, 1982)

Prosser, William L, *Handbook of The Law of Torts*, 4th ed (St. Paul, Minnesota: West Publishing Co, 1971)

Stanton, Keith M, *The Law of Tort* (London: Sweet & Maxwell)

Street, Harry, *The Law of Torts* (London: Butterworths, 1955)

Vago, Steven, Nelson, Adie, Nelson, Veronica & Barkan, Steven E, *Law and Society* (New York: Routledge, 2018)

Weinrib, Ernest J, *Tort Law: Cases and Materials*, 4th ed (Toronto: Emond Montgomery Publications Limited, 2014)

Negligence 301

Secondary Material: Journal Articles

Abraham, Kenneth, "Self-Proving Causation" (2013) 99:8 Va L Rev 1811

Ali, Kristin, "Defining the Standard of Prenatal Care: An Analysis of Judicial and Legislative Responses" (2007) 1 McGill JL & Health 69

Aman Jr, Alfred, "The Earth as Eggshell Victim: A Global Perspective on Domestic Regulation" (1993) 102:8 Yale LJ 2107

Boberg, P QR, "Reflections on the *Novus Actus Interveniens* Concept" (1959) 76:3 SALJ 280

Brantley, John, "Wrongful Birth: The Emerging Status of a New Tort" (1976) 8:1 St Mary's LJ 140

Davies, Martin, "The Road from Morocco: *Polemis* through *Donoghue* to No-Fault" (1982) 45:5 Modern L Rev 534

Demeyere, Gillian, "The Material Contribution Test: An Immaterial Contribution to Tort Law: A Comment on *Briglio v. Faulkner*" (2000) 34:1 UBC L Rev 317

Dias, R, "Remoteness of Liability and Legal Policy" (1962) 20:2 Cambridge LJ 178

Fleming, John G, "Remoteness and Duty: The Control Devices in Liability for Negligence" (1953) 31:5 Can Bar Rev 471

Fleming Jr, James & Dickinson, John, "Accident Proneness and Accident Law" (1950) 63:5 Harv L Rev 769

Fleming Jr, James, "The Qualities of the Reasonable Man in Negligence Cases" (1951) 16:1 Mo L Rev 1

Gilles, Stephen G, "On Determining Negligence: Hand Formula Balancing, the Reasonable Person Standard, and the Jury" (2001) 54:3 Vand L Rev 813

Glorieux, Francis H, Ward, Leanne M, Rauch, Frank, Lalic, Ljiljana, Roughley, Peter J & Travers, Rose, "Osteogenesis Imperfecta Type VI: A Form of Brittle Bone Disease with a Mineralization Defect" (2002) 17:1 J Bone Miner Res 30

Heuston, Robert F. V., "*Donoghue v Stevenson* in Retrospect" (1957) 20:1 Modern L Rev 1

Kelley, Patrick, "Proximate Cause in Negligence Law: History, Theory, and the Present Darkness" (1991) 69:1 Wash ULO 49

Klimchuk, Dennis & Black, Vaughan, "A Comment on *Athey v. Leonati*: Causation, Damages and Thin Skulls" (1997) 31:1 UBC L Rev 163

Lake, Peter F, "Recognizing the Importance of Remoteness to the Duty to Rescue" (1997) 46:2 DePaul L Rev 315

Malone, Wex S, "Ruminations on Cause-in-Fact" (1956) 9:1 Stan L Rev 60

Miller, Alan D & Perry, Ronen, "The Reasonable Person" (2012) 87:2 NYUL Rev 323

Morris, Clarence, "Duty, Negligence and Causation" (1952) 101:2 U Pa L Rev 189

Payne, Douglas, "Foresight and Remoteness of Damage in Negligence" (1962) 25:1 Modern L Rev 1

Posner, Richard A, "A Theory of Negligence" (1972) 1:1 J Leg Stud 29

Rahman, Anika, Katzive, Laura & Henshaw, Stanley, "A Global Review of Laws on Induced Abortion" (1998) 24:2 Int'l Fam Plan Pers 56

Schiff, Stanley, "A Res Ipsa Loquitur Nutshell" (1976) 26:4 UTLJ 451

Seavey, Warren A, "Negligence – Subjective or Objective" (1927) 41:1 Harv L Rev 1

Seavey, Warren A, "Mr. Justice Cardozo and the Law of Torts" (1939) 48:3 Yale LJ 390

302 *Negligence*

Singh, Susheela, Hossain, Altaf, Maddow-Zimet, Isaac, Bhuiyan Hadayeat U, Vlassoff, Michael & Hussain, Rubina, "The Incidence of Menstrual Regulation Procedures and Abortion in Bangladesh" (2012) 38: 3 Int'l Pers Sexual & Rep Health 122

Thode, E Wayne, "Indefensible Use of the Hypothetical Case to Determine Cause in Fact" (1968) 46:4 Tex L Rev 423

Warren, Charles, "Volenti Non Fit Injuria in Actions of Negligence" (1895) 8:8 Harv L Rev 457

Weinrib, Ernest J, "The Passing of *Palsgraf*" (2001) 54:3 Vand L Rev 803

Winfield, Percy H, "The History of Negligence in the Law of Torts" (1926) 42:2 L Q Rev 184

Winfield, Percy H, "The Unborn Child" (1942) 8:1 Cambridge LJ 76

Wright, Richard W, "Causation, Responsibility, Risk, Probability, Naked Statistics, and Proof: Pruning the Bramble Bush by Clarifying the Concepts" (1988) 73:5 Iowa L Rev 1001

Secondary Material: Websites

Caponi, Sandra, "Quetelet, the average man and medical knowledge" *SciELO* (2013), online: SciELO https://www.scielo.br/scielo.php?pid=S0104-5970201300 0300830&script=sci_arttext&tlng=en

Mehtab, Farhana H & Mashraf, Ali, "Decoding *Children's Charity Bangladesh (CCB) Foundation v Government of Bangladesh*: The First Ever Public Law Compensation Case in Bangladesh and the Way Forward" (2019) 4:2 *BiLD LJ* 9

Saha, Himaloya & Rahman, Saquib, "Juvenile Delinquents and the *Children Act*" *The Daily Star* (24 January 2017), online: The Daily Star https://www.thedailystar.net/law-our-rights/juvenile-delinquents-and-the-children-act-1350073

6 Strict liability

As I have mentioned in the fourth and fifth chapters of this book, the early common law was concerned with breaches of the King's peace (or, in other words, intentional torts),[1] and therefore, royal courts assumed jurisdiction.[2] It was not until the 19th century that courts began focusing on the concept of negligence to provide redress to the aggrieved party. Eventually, negligence became the cornerstone of liability in tort law and "no liability without fault" became the motto of a society that was socially and economically changing.[3]

However, as is generally the case in law, this maxim became antiquated and calls emerged to saddle liability even without fault, as public opinion gradually shifted and began focusing on social well-being.[4] As Professor Fleming has said,[5]

> [I]ncreasing consideration is being given to the compensatory aspect of tort law and to the social value of shifting accident losses by widely distributing their cost among those who benefit from the accident producing activity. It is realized that the result of letting accident losses lie where they fall is not only to impoverish the victim but ultimately to throw the loss on the community as a whole, which must in the last resort foot the bill of rehabilitation and income maintenance through taxation.

This is because there are many activities, especially today when our lives have become increasingly mechanized, which place a high toll on life and limb (e.g. driving, manufacturing garments or appliances, and using an elevator). In these situations, the law has one of the following three options: (1) it may prohibit the activity altogether by promulgating legislation (e.g. theft, robbery, and murder); (2) it may allow the activity to continue because of its social utility, but will prescribe conditions under which to operate (e.g. driving requires a licence); or (3) it may tolerate the activity on condition that money is paid regardless of whether it was carried out carelessly, which, essentially, is strict liability.[6]

The hallmark of strict, or "no-fault," liability is that it is imposed on lawful activity, whereby the defendant is held liable because he *caused* harm, but is

DOI: 10.4324/9781003241782-6

304   *Strict liability*

not otherwise blameworthy.[7] That is to say, he was perhaps negligent, but his fault is either minimal or entirely non-existent. For example, the owner of a dog, or any pet, will be liable if it bites and injures another, regardless of whether the animal is *mansuetce naturae* or *ferae naturae*.[8] Furthermore, since the pet has bitten another person, it can be said that it happened because of the owner's negligence because had he been more careful in keeping the animal, then it probably would not have gotten away and bitten another.[9] Notice, however, that the injury was not caused by the person on whom liability is sought to be imposed. Nonetheless, even if his fault is de minimis or entirely non-existent, the reasons for compensating the victim outweigh the reasons for not imposing liability on an otherwise not-guilty defendant.

6.1 The person, himself

Munn & Co v The Sir John Crosbie[10]

The *Sir John Crosbie*, which is a ship, was moored to, and unloading coal at, Munn & Company Limited's (hereinafter "Munn & Co") wharf. Without warning, a tempest blew in and its gale winds began to repeatedly push the ship against the wharf, causing damage to the wharf. Therefore, Munn & Co brought proceedings against the *Sir John Crosbie*. Finding against them, the court said,

> We find no support in the authorities referred to by counsel for the appellant for his submission that a rule of absolute liability applies in a situation of this kind and we have come to the conclusion that, apart from statute (and no statute has been brought to the Court's attention which would have any application to the facts in this case), the responsibility or duty of the defendant ship to take reasonable care to avoid damage to the plaintiff's property, to which it was at the plaintiff's invitation or with its permission moored, was no greater than that which would have been applicable had the ship at the material time been under way. With respect to a ship under way the common law is set out in *River Wear Commissioners v Adamson and Others*, [...] per Lord Blackburn [...], where he says:
>
>> The common law is, I think, as follows: Property adjoining a spot in which the public have a right to carry on traffic is liable to be injured by that traffic. In this respect, there is no difference between a shop the railings or windows of which may be broken by a carriage on the road, and a pier adjoining a harbour, or a navigable river, or the sea, which is liable to be injured by a ship. In either case the owner of the injured property must bear his own loss, unless he can establish that some other person is liable to make it good; and he does not establish this against a person merely by showing that he is owner of the carriage or ship which did the mischief, for that owner incurs no liability merely as owner; but he does

Strict liability   305

establish such a liability against any person who either wilfully did the damage, or neglected that duty which the law casts upon those in charge of a carriage on land, and a ship, or a float of timber, on water, to take reasonable care, and use reasonable skill to prevent it from doing injury, and that this neglect caused the damage; and if he can prove that the person who has been guilty of this negligence stood in the relation of servant to another, and that the negligence was in the course of his employment, he establishes a liability against the master also.

The question to be decided, therefore, is whether the defendant "wilfully did" the plaintiff's damage or whether it "neglected that duty which the law casts upon those in charge of [...] a ship [...] to take reasonable care, and use reasonable skill to prevent it from doing injury, and that this neglect caused the damage; [...]"

In this case, there is no suggestion that the defendant wilfully did the damage. The plaintiff's submission throughout was simply that the defendant master had failed to move the ship from the wharf which in our opinion is in substance an allegation of neglect of a duty to remove her. We have already reached the conclusion that the finding of the learned trial Judge, that the appellant failed to establish that the respondent was guilty of negligence in that respect, must be affirmed. There is, therefore, no liability apart from statute. [...]

In this case, not only was there no allegation in the pleadings, but it was not established, that at any point of time those in charge of the vessel took any steps to preserve the ship at the expense of the wharf. There was evidence that additional bow and stern lines were made fast when the wind was still southeasterly and tending to push the ship away from the wharf but it does not appear that this was done to protect the ship at the expense of the wharf or that in the circumstances of wind and weather then prevailing damage to the wharf was to be expected from further securing the ship in her position. On this point the trial Judge found that it was by no means certain at that time that to ride out the storm at the wharf would necessarily cause damage to the wharf. The defendant ship was there as an invitee and it would not be trespass for her to be pushed by the wind into contact with the wharf. Save on the possible hypothesis that damage to the wharf was to be expected by such pressing there could, as we see it, be no liability arise therefrom, and even if damage were to be expected from the ship remaining there and such a liability could arise it would, in our view, sound in negligence rather than in trespass. On the question of what was reasonably foreseeable, it is not without significance that no action was taken by the plaintiff either to terminate the defendant's invitation to remain moored to its property or to require the ship to leave the wharf. Nor is it established that the ship would not have been held without the additional lines. In fact the additional lines had nothing to

306 *Strict liability*

do with the damage since they had no effect in pressing or even holding the ship against the wharf. In the *Vincent [v Lake Eerie Transportation Co]* case, the damage was caused by pounding, and the renewing of the lines as they chafed or parted held the ship in a position where she could pound against the wharf. Here there is no evidence of renewal of lines to hold the ship in position to press against the wharf after she began to do so, and there is thus no material fact upon which liability might be based beyond that of the master's decision in the circumstances not to move the ship away from the wharf. A decision not to move may be evidence of neglect if in the circumstances there is a duty to move, but it is not in itself an act of trespass.

Notes

To delineate this case, I will illustrate three scenarios. First, imagine you rode your motorcycle to your friend's house at Dhanmondi for dinner. You parked your motorcycle in the garage on the ground floor at an empty space designated for visitors, next to a vehicle owned by the tenant on the third floor. During dinner, a storm with veritable winds began. By the time it subsided, your friend's intercom rang – it was the guard on duty who informs your friend that winds knocked over your motorcycle, which fell on the third-floor tenant's vehicle, broke the headlight, and dented the front bumper. For the damage sustained to his vehicle, he cannot seek compensation from you. Oddly, the tenant's vehicle would not have been harmed "but for" your motorcycle being *knocked over by the wind*, which would not have happened had you not parked your motorcycle at the empty space next to his vehicle. This means there is *causation* between the plaintiff's injury and your conduct (or misconduct). However, similar to *Munn & Co*, you will not be liable for his injury because (1) you are not blameworthy for the result, and more importantly, (2) this happened because of *vis major*, which is a superior force, such as a storm, and not because of anything you did or omitted doing.[11]

Second, let us assume that the parking space for visitors was occupied by another vehicle, and therefore, you parked your motorcycle in front of the third floor tenant's vehicle, instead of at the somewhat empty space about 20 feet away. If the motorcycle is then knocked over by winds, you would be held liable, and the doctrine of *vis major* would not apply because you were not as careful as you should have been, as you parked your motorcycle in front of the third floor tenant's vehicle.[12] As in, although the winds, which knocked over your motorcycle, were an act of God, you should have been more careful and parked your motorcycle 20 feet away, removed from other vehicles, and since you did not, you will be liable. To further explain, *vis major* will exonerate the defendant only if his misconduct, which is otherwise not blameworthy, does not contribute to the plaintiff's injury.

Third, imagine that when you entered your friend's garage, you saw that the parking space for visitors was occupied, and therefore, you parked your motorcycle about 20 feet away, which is an awkward little area where a trashcan and other similar items are kept. During dinner, since you heard the cacophony of thunder and wind, you decided to go downstairs to check whether your motorcycle was safe. Unfortunately, you see that it was knocked over. You also notice that the parking space for visitors is now empty; therefore, you pick up your motorcycle and park it there. You then go back upstairs and finish your dinner. However, as the storm did not dissipate, it knocked over your motorcycle again, which struck the third-floor tenant's vehicle, broke the headlight and dented the bumper. For this incident, you will be liable because your intervention was a significant contributing factor in damaging the tenant's vehicle;[13] that is, had you kept your motorcycle in its original place, and not relocated it to the empty parking space, then the tenant's vehicle would not have been damaged. To further explain, your intervention of picking up your motorcycle and relocating it to the empty parking space contributed to the plaintiff's injury, which would not have happened "but for" this action, and therefore, even though it was ultimately knocked over by *vis major*, you will be liable.[14]

It is important to note the distinction between scenarios one and three. In the first situation, you parked your motorcycle at the space designated for visitors. The motorcycle was then knocked over by a superior force and you will not be found liable because other than properly parking your motorcycle at the allocated space, you did nothing further. However, in the third situation, you saw that the motorcycle was already knocked over by winds, and you picked it up from one location, relocated it next to the tenant's vehicle, which was again knocked over. For this, you will be liable because you intervened in this scenario and it was this intervention (relocating motorcycle to designated parking space) that, in addition to *vis major*, damaged the plaintiff's vehicle. That is to say, had you left it in its original place, liability would not have been imposed on you.[15]

Rylands v Fletcher[16]

John Rylands owned the Ainsworth Mill and, in 1860, commissioned contractors to build a reservoir on his land so that it could supply water to his mill. He played no active part in the construction. In the course of building the reservoir, the contractors learned that it was being constructed on top of an abandoned coal mine, which was improperly filled with soil and debris. They did not inform Mr. Rylands of their discovery. After work was completed and the reservoir filled, on 11 December 1860, it burst and caused damage of £937 to the Red House Colliery, which was a mine owned by Thomas Fletcher. Therefore, Mr. Fletcher brought proceedings against Mr. Rylands. Finding in the former's favour, the court said,

> The question of law, therefore, arises: What is the liability which the law casts upon a person who, like the defendants, lawfully brings on his land something which, though harmless while it remains there, will naturally do mischief if it escapes out of his land? It is agreed on all hands that he must take care to keep in that which he has brought on the land, and keep it there in order that it may not escape and damage

308   *Strict liability*

his neighbour's, but the question arises whether the duty which the law casts upon him under such circumstances is an absolute duty to keep it in at his peril, or is, as the majority of the Court of Exchequer have thought, merely a duty to take all reasonable and prudent precautions in order to keep it in, but no morn. If the first be the law, the person who has brought on his land and kept there something dangerous, and failed to keep it in, is responsible for all the natural consequences of its escape. If the second be the limit of his duty, he would not be answerable except on proof of negligence, and consequently would not be answerable for escape arising from any latent defect which ordinary prudence and skill could not detect. [...]

We think that the true rule of law is that the person who, for his own purposes, brings on his land, and collects and keeps there anything likely to do mischief if it escapes, must keep it in at his peril, and, if he does not do so, he is *prima facie* answerable for all the damage which is the natural consequence of its escape. He can excuse himself by showing that the escape was owing to the plaintiff's default, or, perhaps, that the escape was the consequence of *vis major*, or the act of God; but, as nothing of this sort exists bore, it is unnecessary to inquire what excuse would be sufficient. The general rule, as above stated, seems on principle just. The person whose grass or corn is eaten down by the escaped cattle of his neighbour, or whose mine is flooded by the water from his neighbour's reservoir, or whose cellar is invaded by the filth of his neighbour's privy, or whose habitation is made unhealthy by the fumes and noisome vapours of his neighbour's alkali works, is damnified without any fault of his own; and it seems but reasonable and just that the neighbour who has brought something on his own property which was not naturally there, harmless to others so long as it is confined to his own property, but which he knows will be mischievous if it gets on his neighbour's, should be, obliged to make good the damage which ensues if he does not succeed in confining it to his own property. But for his act in bringing it there no mischief could have accrued, and it seems but just that he should at his peril keep it there, so that no mischief may accrue, or answer for the natural and anticipated consequences. On authority this, we think, is established to be the law, whether the thing so brought be beasts or water, or filth or stenches.

The case that has most commonly occurred, and which is most frequently to be found in the books, is as to the obligation of the owner of cattle which he has brought on his land to prevent their escaping and doing mischief. The law as to them seems to be perfectly settled from early times; the owner must keep them in at his peril, or he will be answerable for the natural consequences of their escape, that is, with regard to tame beasts, for the grass they eat and trample upon, although nor for any injury to the person of others, for our ancestors have settled that it is not the general nature of horses to kick or bulls to gore, but if

Strict liability 309

the owner knows that the beast has a vicious propensity to attack man he will be answerable for that too. [...]

On the other hand, if the defendants, not stopping at the natural use of their close, had desired to use it for any purpose which I may term a non-natural use, for the purpose of introducing into the close that which, in its natural condition, was not in or upon it – for the purpose of introducing water, either above or below ground, in quantities and in a manner not the result of any work or operation on or under the land, and if in consequence of their doing so, or in consequence of any imperfection in the mode of their doing so, the water came to escape and to pass off into the close of the plaintiff, then it appears to me that that which the defendants were doing they were doing at their own peril; and if in the course of their doing it the evil arose to which I have referred – the evil, namely, of the escape of the water, and its passing away to the close of the plaintiff and injuring the plaintiff – then for the consequence of that, in my opinion, the defendants would be liable.

Notes

The essence of *Rylands* is the following:

We think that the true rule of law is that the person who, for his own purposes, brings on his land, and collects and keeps there anything likely to do mischief if it escapes, must keep it in at his peril, and, if he does not do so, he is *prima facie* answerable for all the damage which is the natural consequence of its escape.

[I]f the defendants, not stopping at the natural use of their close, had desired to use it for any purpose which I may term a non-natural use, for the purpose of introducing into the close that which, in its natural condition, was not in or upon it [...] then for the consequence of [its escape and injury to the plaintiff], in my opinion, the defendants would be liable.

In simpler terms, if one brings onto his land something non-natural, then he will be liable for the non-natural substance's subsequent escape and the injury it causes to others' property.

Imagine you own a parcel of land in Baridhara where you have constructed an eight-story residential building with one apartment on each floor. While you live on the sixth floor, every other apartment has been rented to tenants. You have installed a 20,000-litre water tank at the rooftop to supply water throughout the building. The water tank has been maintained in accordance with the manufacturer's guidelines, but it inexplicably explodes, allowing the water to escape and cause extensive damage to the eighth-floor tenant's property and the building next door, which is owned by another individual. Since the water tank has undergone its scheduled maintenance, for the damage it has caused, you will not be liable because even though it is a non-natural substance that you have brought onto your land, it is

310 *Strict liability*

not something that has "increased danger to others" and the water tank is "proper for the general benefit of the community."[17] Essentially, this means that not only must the substance be non-natural, but it must also increase danger to others[18] and its use must not otherwise benefit the community.[19] This, however, renders the test of "non-natural" substance "likely to do mischief if it escapes" difficult to ascertain. For example, is petroleum inside a vehicle or fire used for cooking[20] non-natural and likely to do mischief if it escapes?

In order to meet the test from *Rylands*, which was modified by *Transco*, a two-fold question needs to be asked: (1) is the non-natural substance likely to increase danger to others; and (2) is the non-natural substance so vitally important that it is indispensable to contemporary society so much so that its removal would otherwise incapacitate life?[21] For example, even if water, which is inside a tank and placed on top of a building, increases danger to others nearby, since it is indispensable to contemporary society, its escape would not make the landlord liable so long as he, or one of his agents, was not negligent in its maintenance. However, fire, I surmise, would not be indispensable, as electric stoves, which are safer, are now widely available. Similarly, if someone collects barrels of oil on his land, its escape and subsequent damage to another's property can make the collector liable.

Let us revisit the earlier example of the apartment building you own at Baridhara. Imagine that the tenant of the fourth floor left all of the faucets open and clogged all of the sinks and shower corners, which prevented drainage, thereby allowing water to accumulate and damage the third-floor tenant's property. For this, you will not be liable, as we require water for daily life even though it is a non-natural substance that you brought onto your land. Liability, however, will be imposed on the tenant of the fourth floor because it was his action, and not your negligence or inaction that caused the damage.[22]

It should be noted that *Rylands* is a complex case and courts are still deliberating its interpretation.[23] For example, in *Read v J Lyons & Co Ltd*,[24] Ms. Read, as an employee of the Ministry of Supply, went to inspect the filling of shell cases at the Elstow Ordinance Factory, which was operated by J Lyons & Company Limited (hereinafter "J Lyons"). Unfortunately, and because of the negligence of J Lyons, there was an explosion, which killed another and injured Ms. Read. For her injuries, she brought proceedings against J Lyons under the principle of *Rylands*. Finding in favour of J Lyons, the court said,

> Every activity in which man engages is fraught with some possible element of danger to others. Experience shows that even from acts apparently innocuous injury to others may result. The more dangerous the act the greater is the care that must be taken in performing it. This relates itself to the principle in the modern law of torts that liability exists only for consequences which a reasonable man would have foreseen. One who engages in obviously dangerous operations must be taken to know that if he does not take special precautions, injury to others may

Strict liability 311

very well result. In my opinion, it would be impracticable to frame a legal classification of things as things dangerous and things not dangerous, attaching absolute liability in the case of the former but not in the case of the latter. In a progressive world things which at one time were reckoned highly dangerous come to be regarded as reasonably safe. The first experimental flights of aviators were certainly dangerous, but we are now assured that travel by air is little, if at all, more dangerous than a railway journey.

Accordingly, I am unable to accept the proposition that in law the manufacture of high explosive shells is a dangerous operation which imposes on the manufacturer an absolute liability for any personal injuries which may be sustained in consequence of his operations. Strict liability, if you will, is imposed on him in the sense that he must exercise a high degree of care, but that is all. The sound view, in my opinion, is that the law in all cases exacts a degree of care commensurate with the risk created. It was suggested that some operations are so intrinsically dangerous that no degree of care, however scrupulous, can prevent the occurrence of accidents, and that those who choose for their own ends to carry on such operations ought to be held to do so at their peril. If this were so, many industries would have a serious liability imposed on them. Should it be thought that this is a reasonable liability to impose in the public interest, it is for Parliament so to enact. [...]

The doctrine of *Rylands v Fletcher*, as I understand it, derives from a conception of the mutual duties of adjoining or neighbouring landowners and its congeners are trespass and nuisance. If its foundation is to be found in the injunction *sic utere two ut alienum non laedas*, then it is manifest that it has nothing to do with personal injuries. The duty is to refrain from injuring not *alium* but *alienum*. The two prerequisites of the doctrine are that there must be the escape of something from one man's close to another man's close and that that which escapes must have been brought on the land from which it escapes in consequence of some non-natural use of that land whatever precisely that may mean. Neither of these features exists in the present case. I have already pointed out that nothing escaped from the defendants' premises, and, were it necessary to decide the point, I should hesitate to hold that in these days and in an industrial community it was a non-natural use of land to build a factory on it and conduct there the manufacture of explosives. I could conceive it being said that to carry on the manufacture of explosives in a crowded urban area was evidence of negligence, but there is no such case here and I offer no opinion on the point.

Essentially, *Read* clarifies that in order for strict liability to apply under *Rylands*, there must be an escape of a non-natural substance, which goes to another's land and causes harm. Moreover, the principle cannot be relied upon if the injury is personal or death. Therefore, since the harm-causing activity did not "escape" and injure Ms. Read, as her injury happened on

312 *Strict liability*

the land where the activity was ongoing, damages cannot be claimed unless evidence is adduced that the injury happened due to negligence.

This, however, poses a problem. Imagine you have invited your friend for dinner and are cooking on a fire-top stove. The stovetop explodes, igniting a fire, which injures your friend, destroys his cellphone, and damages two floors of the adjacent building. An investigation reveals that it was not your, or the manufacturer's, fault. Under the principle of *Rylands* and modified by *Read*, your friend would not be able to bring proceedings against you for his injury or the destruction of his cellphone, as firstly, he cannot claim compensation for personal injury, and secondly, the harm-causing event happened on the land where he was standing. Your neighbour, on the other hand, can claim compensation as a non-natural substance that has "increased danger to others" escaped and caused mischief.[25]

As I have mentioned before, the principle of *Rylands* still befuddles and bemuses courts. Nonetheless, George Fletcher provides the following exposition:[26]

> Expressing the standard of strict liability as unexcused, nonreciprocal risk-taking provides an account not only of the *Rylands* and *Vincent* decisions, but of strict liability in general. It is apparent, for example, that the uncommon, ultra-hazardous activities pinpointed by the Restatement are readily subsumed under the rationale of nonreciprocal risk-taking. If uncommon activities are those with few participants, they are likely to be activities generating nonreciprocal risks. Similarly, dangerous activities like blasting, fumigating, and crop dusting stand out as distinct, nonreciprocal risks in the community. They represent threats of harm that exceed the level of risk to which all members of the community contribute in roughly equal shares.
>
> The rationale of nonreciprocal risk-taking accounts as well for pockets of strict liability outside the coverage of the *Restatement's* sections on extra-hazardous activities. For example, an individual is strictly liable for damage done by a wild animal in his charge, but not for damage committed by his domesticated pet. Most people have pets, children, or friends whose presence creates some risk to neighbours and their property. These are risks that offset each other; they are, as a class, reciprocal risks. Yet bringing an unruly horse into the city goes beyond the accepted and shared level of risks in having pets, children, and friends in one's household. If the defendant creates a risk that exceeds those to which he is reciprocally subject, it seems fair to hold him liable for the results of his aberrant indulgence. Similarly, according to the latest version of the *Restatement*, airplane owners and pilots are strictly liable for ground damage, but not for mid-air collisions. Risk of ground damage is nonreciprocal; homeowners do not create risks to airplanes flying overhead. The risks of mid-air collisions, on the other hand, are generated reciprocally by all those who fly the air lanes. Accordingly, the threshold of liability for damage resulting from mid-air collisions is

higher than mere involvement in the activity of flying. To be liable for collision damage to another flyer, the pilot must fly negligently or the owner must maintain the plane negligently; they must generate abnormal risks of collision to the other planes aflight.

Negligently and intentionally caused harm also lend themselves to analysis as nonreciprocal risks. As a general matter, principles of negligence liability apply in the context of activities, like motoring and sporting ventures, in which the participants all normally create and expose themselves to the same order of risk. These are all pockets of reciprocal risk-taking. Sometimes the risks are grave, as among motorists; sometimes they are minimal, as among ballplayers. Whatever the magnitude of risk, each participant contributes as much to the community of risk as he suffers from exposure to other participants. To establish liability for harm resulting from these activities, one must show that the harm derives from a specific risk negligently engendered in the course of the activity. Yet a negligent risk, an "unreasonable" risk, is but one that unduly exceeds the bounds of reciprocity. Thus, negligently created risks are nonreciprocal relative to the risks generated by the drivers and ballplayers who engage in the same activity in the customary way.

If a victim also creates a risk that unduly exceeds the reciprocal norm, we say that he is contributorily negligent and deny recovery. The paradigm of reciprocity accounts for the denial of recovery when the victim imposes excessive risks on the defendant, for the effect of contributory negligence is to render the risks again reciprocal, and the defendant's risk-taking does not subject the victim to a relative deprivation of security.

Thus, both strict liability and negligence express the rationale of liability for unexcused, nonreciprocal risk-taking. The only difference is that reciprocity in strict liability cases is analyzed relative to the background of innocuous risks in the community, while reciprocity in the types of negligence cases discussed above is measured against the background of risk generated in specific activities like motoring and skiing. To clarify the kinship of negligence to strict liability, one should distinguish between two different levels of risk-creation, each level associated with a defined community of risks. Keeping domestic pets is a reciprocal risk relative to the community as a whole; driving is a reciprocal risk relative to the community of those driving normally; and driving negligently might be reciprocal relative to the even narrower community of those driving negligently. The paradigm of reciprocity holds that in all communities of reciprocal risks, those who cause damage ought not to be held liable.

6.2 Vicarious liability

Vicarious liability is a form of strict liability in the sense that one is held liable for no fault of his own, but for the fault of another, and, from its

314　*Strict liability*

origin, it has been intertwined with policy.[27] In early English law, the master was liable for every wrongdoing of his servant, wife, and inanimate objects. This dramatically changed by the 16th century, at which point, the master was liable only for acts he ordered. However, with the slow growth of international commerce and the changing nature of business in the 1700s, the master's liability changed again. People no longer believed that a master could maintain control over all elements of modern industry; thus, two policy considerations emerged to expand vicarious liability. First, there emerged a social interest in allowing a tort victim to seek reparation from a solvent defendant; and second, there emerged the idea that business enterprises should not be unduly burdened.[28] Then, in the 20th century, vicarious liability was expanded to include a broader class of cases with "its basis in a combination of policy considerations," which I shall explain later.[29]

Jones v Hart[30]

Mr. Hart was a pawnbroker, whose servant had taken in, but then lost, Mr. Jones' goods. When the servant was unable to return the goods on Mr. Jones' tender of money, the latter sued Mr. Hart for trover, which is an action for the recovery of the value of property wrongfully taken. Finding in Mr. Jones' favour, the court said,

> The action well lies in this case: If the servants of A, with his cart run against another cart, wherein is a pipe of wine, and overturn the cart and spoil the wine, an action lieth against A. So where a carter's servant runs his cart over a boy, action lies against the master for the damage done by this negligence: and so it is if a smith's man pricks a horse in shoeing the master is liable. For whoever employs another, is answerable for him, and undertakes for his care to all that make use of him.
>
> The act of a servant is the act of his master, where he acts by authority of the master.

Notes

From *Jones*, we should know that the act of the servant amounts to the act of the master, and therefore, the master will be liable for the servant's negligence even if the master was not at fault. Put differently, vicarious liability is imposing liability on *Person A* for the actionable conduct of *Person B*, even though *Person A* is free of fault and blameworthiness. For example, imagine that in your apartment building, which you own, you have employed three guards who do eight-hour shifts. One day, while closing the building's gate, a guard failed to notice a three-year-old child entering the premises, and the gate hit the toddler, which fractured his skull. You were at work during the incident. Though this is in no way your fault, you will nevertheless be held vicariously liable for your employee's negligence. This is because, as was identified by Professor Fleming, there are two fundamental policies lying at the heart of vicarious liability. First, providing a just and practical remedy, and second, the deterrence of future harm.[31] It is important to compensate people that are injured as a result of another's business. As in, "[A] person

Strict liability 315

who employs others to advance his own economic interest should in fairness be placed under a corresponding liability for losses incurred in the course of the enterprise."[32] As I have said multiple times before, at the heart of tort law lies the idea that a person is liable for injuries he causes another, and therefore, should compensate the injured party.[33] Page Keeton said,[34]

> The losses caused by the torts of employees, which as a practical matter are sure to occur in the conduct of the employer's enterprise, are placed upon that enterprise itself, as a required cost of doing business. They are placed upon the employer because, having engaged in an enterprise [...] and sought to profit by it, it is just that he, rather than the innocent injured plaintiff, should bear them.

Inarguably, the principle of holding the master liable for the negligence of his employee is consonant with the purpose of tort law.

Let us refer back to the example of the guard and the toddler. Assume that the child's medical fee is ₺10,000. Your guard may, or may not, be able to pay that amount immediately or at all. However, the purpose of tort law is to compensate one for the injury he has suffered. We know that the child has been injured as a cause of the guard's negligence, and therefore, if he is unable to recover compensation, it runs afoul the objective of tort law. Thence, in order to improve a victim's chance of recovering damages, courts ascribe liability on the master vicariously.[35]

Bazley v Curry[36]

The Children's Foundation (hereinafter "the Foundation") is a non-profit organization that operated two residential care facilities for children between the ages of 6 and 12. Through its employees, the Foundation acted as substitute parents and exercised "total intervention" in all aspects of children's lives, which included caring for them generally and bathing and tucking them into bed.

In April 1966, the Foundation hired Mr. Leslie Charles Curry, who, unbeknownst to the Foundation, was a pedophile, to work in its Vancouver home. In March 1980, someone lodged a complaint against Mr. Curry, and the Foundation investigated and discovered that he was a pedophile and discharged him immediately. He was charged with 18 counts of gross indecency, but died soon thereafter. Nonetheless, for the sexual abuse Patrick Bazley suffered, he seeks damages from the Foundation alleging they are vicariously liable for hiring a pedophile. Finding in his favour, the court said,

> Both parties agree that the answer to this question is governed by the *Salmond* test, which posits that employers are vicariously liable for (1) employee acts authorized by the employer; or (2) unauthorized acts so connected with authorized acts that they may be regarded as modes (albeit improper modes) of doing an authorized act. Both parties also agree that we are here concerned with the second branch of the test. They diverge, however, on what the second branch of the test means.

316   Strict liability

The Foundation says that its employee's sexual assaults of Bazley were not "modes" of doing an authorized act. Bazley, on the other hand, submits that the assaults were a mode of performing authorized tasks, and that courts have often found employers vicariously liable for intentional wrongs of employees comparable to sexual assault.

The problem is that it is often difficult to distinguish between an unauthorized "mode" of performing an authorized act that attracts liability, and an entirely independent "act" that does not. Unfortunately, the test provides no criterion on which to make this distinction. In many cases, like the present one, it is possible to characterize the tortious act either as a mode of doing an authorized act (as the respondent would have us do), or as an independent act altogether (as the appellants would suggest). [...]

Looking at these three general classes of cases in which employers have been held vicariously liable for employees' unauthorized torts, one sees a progression from accidents, to accident-like intentional torts, to torts that bear no relationship to either agency-like conduct or accident. In search of a unifying principle, one asks what the three classes of cases have in common. At first glance, it may seem little. Yet with the benefit of hindsight it is possible to posit one common feature: in each case it can be said that the employer's enterprise had created the risk that produced the tortious act. The language of "furtherance of the employer's aims" and the employer's creation of "a situation of friction" may be seen as limited formulations of the concept of enterprise risk that underlies the dishonest employee cases. The common theme resides in the idea that where the employee's conduct is closely tied to a risk that the employer's enterprise has placed in the community, the employer may justly be held vicariously liable for the employee's wrong. [...]

Vicarious liability has always been concerned with policy [...] The view of early English law that a master was responsible for all the wrongs of his servants (as well as his wife's and his children's) represented a policy choice, however inarticulate, as to who should bear the loss of wrongdoing and how best to deter it. The narrowing of vicarious responsibility with the expansion of commerce and trade and the rise of industrialism also represented a policy choice. Indeed, it represented a compromise between two policies – the social interest in furnishing an innocent tort victim with recourse against a financially responsible defendant, and a concern not to foist undue burdens on business enterprises [...] The expansion of vicarious liability in the 20 century from authorization-based liability to broader classes of ascription is doubtless driven by yet other policy concerns. "[V]icarious liability cannot parade as a deduction from legalistic premises, but should be frankly recognized as having its basis in a combination of policy considerations" [...]

First and foremost is the concern to provide a just and practical remedy to people who suffer as a consequence of wrongs perpetrated by an employee. Fleming expresses this succinctly [...] "a person who employs others to advance his own economic interest should in fairness be placed under a corresponding liability for losses incurred in the course of the enterprise." The idea that the person who introduces a risk incurs a duty to those who may be injured lies at the heart of tort law. As Cardozo CJ stated in *Palsgraf v Long Island R Co* [...], "[t] he risk reasonably to be perceived defines the duty to be obeyed, and risk imports relation; it is risk to another or to others within the range of apprehension." This principle of fairness applies to the employment enterprise and hence to the issue of vicarious liability. While charitable enterprises may not employ people to advance their economic interests, other factors, discussed below, make it fair that they should bear the burden of providing a just and practical remedy for wrongs perpetrated by their employees. This policy interest embraces a number of subsidiary goals. The first is the goal of effective compensation. "One of the most important social goals served by vicarious liability is victim compensation. Vicarious liability improves the chances that the victim can recover the judgment from a solvent defendant." [...]

However, effective compensation must also be fair, in the sense that it must seem just to place liability for the wrong on the employer. Vicarious liability is arguably fair in this sense. The employer puts in the community an enterprise which carries with it certain risks. When those risks materialize and cause injury to a member of the public despite the employer's reasonable efforts, it is fair that the person or organization that creates the enterprise and hence the risk should bear the loss. This accords with the notion that it is right and just that the person who creates a risk bear the loss when the risk ripens into harm. While the fairness of this proposition is capable of standing alone, it is buttressed by the fact that the employer is often in the best position to spread the losses through mechanisms like insurance and higher prices, thus minimizing the dislocative effect of the tort within society. "Vicarious liability has the broader function of transferring to the enterprise itself the risks created by the activity performed by its agents" [*London Drugs*] [...]

The second major policy consideration underlying vicarious liability is deterrence of future harm. Fixing the employer with responsibility for the employee's wrongful act, even where the employer is not negligent, may have a deterrent effect. Employers are often in a position to reduce accidents and intentional wrongs by efficient organization and supervision. Failure to take such measures may not suffice to establish a case of tortious negligence directly against the employer. Perhaps the harm cannot be shown to have been foreseeable under negligence law. Perhaps the employer can avail itself of the defense of compliance with the industry standard. Or perhaps the employer, while complying with the standard of reasonable care, was not as scrupulously diligent as it might feasibly have been. [...]

318   *Strict liability*

Underlying the cases holding employers vicariously liable for the unauthorized acts of employees is the idea that employers may justly be held liable where the act falls within the ambit of the risk that the employer's enterprise creates or exacerbates. Similarly, the policy purposes underlying the imposition of vicarious liability on employers are served only where the wrong is so connected with the employment that it can be said that the employer has introduced the risk of the wrong (and is thereby fairly and usefully charged with its management and minimization). The question in each case is whether there is a connection or nexus between the employment enterprise and that wrong that justifies imposition of vicarious liability on the employer for the wrong, in terms of fair allocation of the consequences of the risk and/or deterrence.

In summary, the test for vicarious liability for an employee's sexual abuse of a client should focus on whether the employer's enterprise and empowerment of the employee materially increased the risk of the sexual assault and hence the harm. The test must not be applied mechanically, but with a sensitive view to the policy considerations that justify the imposition of vicarious liability – fair and efficient compensation for wrong and deterrence. This requires trial judges to investigate the employee's specific duties and determine whether they gave rise to special opportunities for wrongdoing. Because of the peculiar exercises of power and trust that pervade cases such as child abuse, special attention should be paid to the existence of a power or dependency relationship, which on its own often creates a considerable risk of wrongdoing. [...]

In determining the sufficiency of the connection between the employer's creation or enhancement of the risk and the wrong complained of, subsidiary factors may be considered. These may vary with the nature of the case. When related to intentional torts, the relevant factors may include, but are not limited to, the following:

(a) the opportunity that the enterprise afforded the employee to abuse his or her power;
(b) the extent to which the wrongful act may have furthered the employer's aims (and hence be more likely to have been committed by the employee);
(c) the extent to which the wrongful act was related to friction, confrontation or intimacy inherent in the employer's enterprise;
(d) the extent of power conferred on the employee in relation to the victim;
(e) the vulnerability of potential victims to wrongful exercise of the employee's power.

Notes

Let us, again, assume that you own an apartment building where you have employed three guards who do eight-hour shifts. After a guard's shift ended, he got on his motorcycle and as he was riding back home, he hit a pedestrian,

Strict liability 319

which broke the latter's right ankle. For this injury, you will not be vicariously liable because there is a disjunct between (a) the time the guard's misconduct happened, and (b) what the guard was authorized to do. As in, he is authorized, *inter alia*, to open and close the gate, prohibit entrance to some, and guide reversing vehicles out of the garage. If his actions injure another while he is on duty, then the employer will be vicariously liable. However, in this situation, his shift ended, and though he is your employee, you are not answerable for his misconduct because he was heading home and the misconduct did not occur during or under the "scope of employment."[37]

Imagine, however, a different scenario. You have instructed your chauffeur to drop off your cousin to her house. During the journey and due to your chauffeur's negligence, he collided with a tree, which injured your cousin even though she was wearing her seatbelt. For her injuries, your cousin can bring an action against you, holding you vicariously liable for your chauffeur's negligence. While you can try disclaiming liability by asserting that you did not authorize your chauffeur to crash into a tree, you will nevertheless be held liable because he was in the middle of doing something you have authorized.[38] That is to say, the employer will be vicariously liable if (a) the employee injures another while doing something he was authorized to do, or (b) while doing something he was not authorized to do, but what he was doing is so closely connected to authorized acts that it is considered a mode of doing what has been authorized. As in, since you have authorized your chauffeur to drive and since he was on-duty and driving, then you will be liable for the injuries he causes even if the accident-causing injury was not something you explicitly or implicitly authorized.

It is important to notice the distinction between the two scenarios. In the first example, your guard finished his shift and injured someone as he was headed back home. Since his work was done for the day, this means that he is temporarily not under your control, and therefore, he will be blamed for his actions. To further explain, employees who injure others while travelling to and from work are liable and their employer will not be vicariously liable. However, in the second example, your chauffeur was under your command, and therefore, you will be liable for your chauffeur's negligence. Nonetheless, would you be vicariously liable if, instead of crashing into a tree, your chauffeur managed to avoid an almost certain collision with another car, but he then alighted the vehicle and slapped the other driver several times?[39]

It is apodeictic that you did not authorize your chauffeur to slap and punch others on the road, and therefore, the question is "was your chauffeur's action of battering the other driver a mode of doing what he was authorized to do"? Let us consider the five non-exhaustive factors outlined in *Bazley*. Firstly, driving your vehicle does not provide your chauffeur the ability to abuse his power in relation to a stranger. Secondly, punching another driver does not further your aims, and therefore, it cannot be said that he would be more inclined to do so. Thirdly, in the context of Bangladesh, there is friction and confrontation associated with driving. However,

320   *Strict liability*

fourthly, similar to the first factor, since you did not know the other driver, there is no power you gave to your chauffeur over the other driver. Rather, the other driver is unrelated, unconnected, and is a stranger to your business (or, to your chauffeur's duty). Lastly, the other driver was not vulnerable but was an adult who could have defended himself. However, and to now use a different example, what if your chauffeur was transporting your female maid to her house, but took her to a remote location en route and sexually assaulted her?

While your maid can press criminal charges,[40] she can also seek damages under tort law. However, you will not be vicariously liable for your chauffeur's misconduct, as his reprehensible conduct was not authorized, or a mode of doing that which has been authorized, by you. To use the question from *Bazley*, "did your enterprise empower the employee to commit the offence"?

At first glance, it seems as though it was your enterprise (by this, I mean you empowering your chauffeur to transport passengers, whoever they may be, from one location to another) that created the risk of harm, and therefore, was a mode of doing that which has been authorized by you. Nonetheless, it was not, as the five factors from *Bazley* need to be considered. Firstly, you provided an opportunity to your chauffeur to come into contact with your maid. This contact was ephemeral and dropping her off home is not a common activity for your chauffeur. Essentially, this means that you did not increase the risk of harm upon the victim.[41] Secondly, your chauffeur's decision to sexually assault your maid did nothing to further your aims; that is to say, it would not profit your enterprise, and therefore, it cannot be said that it was a mode of doing something that you have authorized. Thirdly, there is no relationship of friction or confrontation between your chauffeur and your maid.[42] Fourthly, segueing from the previous point, this also means that your chauffeur did not exercise any power or authority over your maid. Lastly, your maid was not particularly vulnerable to your chauffeur's transgression. That is to say, while women are more susceptible to sexual assault than men, simply because you asked your chauffeur to drop her off home, which brought your maid into contact with your chauffeur, does not mean that you have increased the risk of harm upon her or made her especially vulnerable to the attack.[43]

However, for example, imagine that you hired another person to learn from your chauffeur and shadow him, which means this person would be spending about 10 hours per day with your chauffeur. If your chauffeur sexually assaults his apprentice, then you would be vicariously liable because you have increased the risk of harm upon the newly hired employee and conferred on your chauffeur great power and authority over him.

Let us understand the difference between the two examples. In the first example, you will not be vicariously liable because, as I have outlined above, you did not empower your employee to commit the offence. This means that the commission of the sexual assault was not brought about by you hiring your chauffeur or asking him to drop your maid off to

Strict liability   321

her home. Rather, if you were held vicariously liable for this misconduct, then it would be similar to imposing liability on you had your chauffeur drove your vehicle to a village and sexually assaulted a woman there who is not known to you.[44] As in, simply because you brought a person into contact with the aggressor, does not mean that you will be liable for his misconduct simply because he is your employee. More, such as the five factors provided in *Bazley*, is required to impose vicarious liability on the employer. Otherwise, this would disproportionately expand the scope of vicarious liability and make employers liable even more independent acts of employees.

In the second example, however, you hired another employee to work under your chauffeur, who was going to spend approximately 10 hours per day with the former. This means that your chauffeur will have authority over him, which gives rise to the possibility of abusing his power. As in, here, not only did you bring the victim in contact with the perpetrator, but you also tacitly facilitated its commission by giving him power over the new employee to your chauffeur. Therefore, you will be held vicariously liable for your chauffeur's misconduct, as your enterprise materially increased the risk of harm upon the victim.[45]

Notes

1 R F V Heuston & R A Buckley, *Salmond and Heuston on the Law of Torts*, 19th ed (London: Sweet & Maxwell, 1987) at 46 [Heuston & Buckley].
2 William L Prosser, *Handbook of The Law of Torts*, 4th ed (St. Paul, Minnesota: West Publishing Co, 1971) at 28; Also see Frederick Pollock & Frederic W Maitland, *The History of English Law before the Time of Edward I*, 2nd ed (London: Cambridge University Press, 1968) at ii.
3 John G Fleming, *The Law of Torts*, 9th ed (Sydney: LBC Information Services, 1998) at 113–114 & 367 [Fleming].
4 *Ibid* at 368.
5 *Ibid*.
6 *Ibid*.
7 See generally Robert E Keeton, "Conditional Fault in the Law of Torts" (1959) 72:3 Harv L Rev 401.
8 *Singh (Litigation Guardian of) v Chini*, [2005] OJ No 5965, 145 ACWS (3D) 5; *Mansuetce naturae* are animals that can be owned, such as dogs and cattle. *Ferae naturae* are animals that have a vicious and fierce propensity, such as snakes and bulls.
9 See *Losee v Buchanan*, [1873] 51 NY 476, 1873 NY LEXIS 563.
10 *Munn & Co v The Sir John Crosbie*, [1967] 1 Ex CR 94 [*Munn & Co*]. Also see Ernest Weinrib, *Tort Law: Cases and Materials*, 4th ed (Toronto: Emond Montgomery Publications Limited, 2014) at 582–584.
11 For more information about *vis major*, see Heuston & Buckley, *supra* note 1 at 372–373.
12 *Vandry v Quebec Railway, Light, Heat and Power Co*, [1916] SCJ No 17, 53 SCR 72.
13 See *Vincent v Lake Eerie Transportation Co*, [1910] 109 Minn 456, 124 NW 221 [*Vincent*], where the court reached the opposite conclusion of *Munn & Co* and imposed liability on Lake Eerie Transportation Company for damaging the plaintiff's wharf because the ship's crew intervened and replaced its ropes in

322   *Strict liability*

order to prevent it from floating away due to the violent tempest. In *Munn & Co*, however, since the defendants did not intervene to fix the ropes to keep the ship docked to the wharf, the plaintiff was unable to recover.

14 For an excellent analysis of *Vincent*, see Francis H Bohlen, "Incomplete Privilege to Inflict Intentional Invasions of Interests of Property and Personality" (1926) 39:3 Harv L Rev 307 at 313–316; Also see Richard A Epstein, "A Theory of Strict Liability" (1973) 2:1 J Leg Stud 151 at 157–160 where he argues that *Vincent* stands for the principle of strict liability. He says at 158, "There is no argument that the conduct of the defendant was 'blameworthy' in any sense. The coercion on him was great, even though not imposed by some human agency. Any person in the position of the defendant's captain would have made the same choice under the circumstances. It is true that he knew that his conduct could damage the dock, but nonetheless the necessity of the situation would serve as an adequate defence against any charge of intentional wrong-doing. Similarly, if the economic conception of negligence is adopted, the same result must be reached once it is admitted that the conduct of the defendant served to minimize the total amount of damage suffered; the expected benefits of further precautions were outweighed by their costs."

15 See *Ploof v Putnam*, [1908] 81 Vt 471, 71 A 188, which, due to the doctrine of necessity, allows one to trespass onto another's land if his life and limb are imperilled.

16 *Rylands v Fletcher*, [1861–73] All ER Rep 1, 33 JP 70 [*Rylands*].

17 *Rickards v Lothian*, [1911–13] All ER Rep 71, [1913] AC 263 at 80 [*Rickards*]; Also see *Transco PLC v Stockport Metropolitan Borough Council*, [2004] 1 All ER 589, [2003] UKHL 61 [*Transco*] and *Smith v Inco*, [2012] OJ No 4225, 2012 ONSC 5094.

See R F V Heuston & R A Buckley, *Salmond and Heuston on the Law of Torts*, 20th ed (London: Sweet & Maxwell, 1992) at 321–322 where it was said,

> Blackburn J's statement, basing liability on the defendant's artificial accumulation of the thing in question, was expressly approved in the House of Lords. But difficulty has arisen because Lord Cairns, probably unconsciously, laid down another principle, distinguishing the natural from the non-natural user of land, and holding that in the latter case only was the liability absolute. This is to substitute a different principle from that adopted by Blackburn J. Its advantage is that it converts a rigid into a flexible rule, and enables the court by determining what is or is not a natural user of land to give effect to its own view of social and economic needs. Its disadvantage is that it has produced a bewildering series of decisions on the meaning of non-natural use. What is the natural use of land? Is it natural to build a house on it, or to light a fire? Is it natural to keep cattle on land? This must be one of the oldest methods of using land, but in Blackburn J's view, it is quite logical to impose strict liability because the cattle have been artificially collected. But in Lord Cairn's view, it is necessary to say that cattle-keeping is non-natural. Again it has been held not be natural to spray crops with herbicide from an aircraft: the activity of destroying weeds is as old as nature itself, but it seems odd today to insist that the hoe should be the only method used.

Also see *Fleming, supra* note 3 at 375–377.

18 *Parker v New Brunswick Power Corp*, [1996] NBJ No 61, [1996] ANB No 61.

19 *Ernst v EnCana Corp*, [2014] AJ No 975, 2014 ABCA 285.

20 See *Musgrove v Pandelis*, [1918–19] All ER Rep 589, [1919] 2 KB 43 and *Jones v Festiniog Railway Company*, [1861–73] All ER Rep Ext 1998, 32 JP 693.

21 See Francis H Bohlen, "Rule in *Rylands v Fletcher*" (1910–1911) 59:5 U Pa L Rev 298 at 300–305.

Strict liability 323

22 *Rickards, supra* note 17. The court said at 81–82, "The provision of a proper supply of water to the various parts of a house is not only reasonable, but has become, in accordance with modern sanitary views, an almost necessary feature of town life. It is recognized as being so desirable in the interests of the community that in some form or other it is usually made obligatory in civilized countries. Such a supply cannot be installed without causing some concurrent danger of leakage or overflow. It would be unreasonable for the law to regard those who install or maintain such a system of supply as doing so at their own peril, with an absolute liability for any damage resulting from its presence even when there has been no negligence. It would be still more unreasonable if, as the respondent contends, such liability were to be held to extend to the consequences of malicious acts on the part of third persons. In such matters as the domestic supply of water or gas, it is essential that the mode of supply should be such as to permit ready access for the purpose of use, and hence it is impossible to guard against wilful mischief. Taps may be turned on, ball cocks fastened open, supply pipes cut, and waste pipes blocked. Against such acts no precaution can prevail. It would be wholly unreasonable to hold an occupier responsible for the consequences of such acts which he is powerless to prevent, when the provision of the supply is not only a reasonable act on his part but probably a duty. Such a doctrine would, for example, make a householder liable for the consequences of an explosion caused by a burglar breaking into his house during the night and leaving a gas tap open."

23 For example, In *Burnie Port Authority v General Jones Pty Ltd*, [1994] 120 ALR 42, [1994] 179 CLR 520, Australia ousted the *Rylands* principle; Also see *Cambridge Water Co Ltd v Eastern Counties Leather Plc*, [1994] 1 All ER 53, [1994] 2 AC 264.

24 *Read v J Lyons & Co Ltd*, [1946] 2 All ER 471, [1947] AC 156.

25 See Richard A Posner, "Strict Liability: A Comment" (1973) 2:1 J Leg Stud 205.

26 George Fletcher, "Fairness and Utility in Tort Theory" (1972) 85:3 Harv L Rev 537 at 547–549 [footnotes omitted]. Also see Guido Calabresi and Jon Hirschoff, "Toward a Test for Strict Liability in Torts" (1972) 81:6 Yale LJ 1055 and Steven Shavell, "Strict Liability versus Negligence" (1980) 9:1 J Leg Stud 1.

27 Fleming, *supra* note 3 at 409–411.

28 *Ibid* at 410. Also see Harold Laski, "The Basis of Vicarious Liability" (1916) 26:2 Yale LJ 105.

29 Fleming, *ibid*; Vicarious liability was previously held to rest on two logical bases: (1) *respondeat superior*, which translates into "let the master answer," was when liability was imputed on the employer simply because he is the employee's superior; and (2) *qui facit per alium facit per se*, where the employer was held vicariously liable for the acts of his employee because the acts were regarded as being authorized by the earlier so that in law the acts of the employee amounted to the acts of the employer, *ibid*; Also see Patrick Atiyah, *Vicarious Liability in the Law of Torts* (London: Butterworth & Co Ltd, 1967) at Chapter 2 [Atiyah]; William Douglas, "Vicarious Liability and Administration of Risk" (1929) 38:5 Yale LJ 584 [Douglas]; *London Drugs Ltd v Kuehne & Nagel International Ltd*, [1992] 3 SCR 299 at 335–336.

30 *Jones v Hart*, [1698] 1 LD RAYM 739, 2 Salk 441.

31 Fleming, *supra* note 3 at 410.

32 Fleming, *ibid*; Also see Alan Sykes, "The Boundaries of Vicarious Liability: An Economic Analysis of the Scope of Employment Rule and Related Legal Doctrines" (1988) 101:3 Harv L Rev 563 [Sykes].

33 Fleming, *supra* note 3 at 3–4; Also see Sykes, *ibid*, Douglas, *supra* note 29, Fleming, *supra* note 3 at 410–415, and Heuston & Buckley, *supra* note 1 at 506–511.

34 Keeton et al, *Prosser and Keeton on The Law of Torts*, 5th ed (St. Paul, MN: West Publishing Co, 1984) at 500.

324 *Strict liability*

35 Bruce Feldthusen, *Torts Tomorrow: A Tribute to John Fleming*, ed by Nicholas Mullany & Allen Linden (Sydney: LBC Information Services, 1998) at 224.
   If you view ৳10,000 as nominal, imagine if this were a bigger disaster and fine. For example, in 2015, British Petroleum was fined $18.7 billion for the Deepwater Horizon oil spill, at Campbell Robertson, John Schwartz & Richard Pérez-Peña, "BP to Pay $18.7 Billion for Deepwater Horizon Oil Spill" *The New York Times* (2 July 2015), online: The New York Times Company https://www.nytimes.com/2015/07/03/us/bp-to-pay-gulf-coast-states-18-7-billion-for-deepwater-horizon-oil-spill.html. [18/03/2021]. Also see Ronen Perry, "The Deepwater Horizon Oil Spill and the Limits of Civil Liability" (2011) 86:1 Wash L Rev 1.
36 *Bazley v Curry*, [1999] 2 SCR 534, [1999] SCJ No 35 [*Bazley*]. [Emphasis removed]; Also see *Jacobi v Griffiths*, [1999] 2 SCR 570, [1999] SCJ No 36.
37 Heuston & Buckley, *supra* note 1 at 521–522.
38 This is known as the "Salmond Test," which is a common law, and commonly used, test in determining vicarious liability, at *ibid*; Additionally, Patrick Atiyah explained that there are three factors to consider when imposing vicarious liability: first, the misconduct or omission is done by a party, but liability is sought to be imposed on another party; second, there is a relationship between the tortfeasor and the defendant; and third, there is a connection between the tortious act, or omission, and the relationship that exists between the tortfeasor and the defendant, at Atiyah, *supra* note 29 at 2.
39 For his action, criminal charges can be filed against your chauffeur under the *The Penal Code*, 1860 (Bangladesh), Act No XLV of 1860, s 350. The relevant portion of the provision stipulates, "Whoever intentionally uses force to any person, without that person's consent, in order to the committing of any offence, or intending by the use of such force to cause, or knowing it to be likely that by the use of such force he will cause injury, fear or annoyance to the person to whom the force is used, is said to use criminal force to that other." Also see s 349, which stipulates, "A person is said to use force to another if he causes motion, change of motion, or cessation of motion to that other, or if he causes to any substance such motion, or change of motion, or cessation of motion as brings that substance into contact with any part of that other's body, or with anything which that other is wearing or carrying, or with anything so situated that such contact affects that other's sense of feeling [...]"
40 Section 375 of the *Penal Code, ibid*, which stipulates,
   A man is said to commit "rape" who except in the case hereinafter excepted, has sexual intercourse with a woman under circumstances falling under any of the five following descriptions:
   Firstly. Against her will.
   Secondly. Without her consent.
   Thirdly. With her consent, when her consent has been obtained by putting her in fear of death, or of hurt. Fourthly. With her consent, when the man knows that he is not her husband, and that her consent is given because she believes that he is another man to whom she is or believes herself to be lawfully married. Fifthly. With or without her consent, when she is under fourteen years of age.
   Explanation: Penetration is sufficient to constitute the sexual intercourse necessary to the offence of rape. [...]"
41 See *EB v Order of the Oblates of Mary Immaculate in the Province of British Columbia*, [2005] 3 SCR 45, [2005] SCJ No 61 at para 48 where it was said, "The respondent provided Saxey with the opportunity to come into contact with the children. Opportunity will often be a question of degree. 'As the opportunity for abuse becomes greater, so the risk of harm increases' [...] The review of previously decided cases shows that opportunity in this case lies at the low end of significance. As put in *Bazley*, '[i]f an employee is permitted or required to be with children for brief periods of time, there may be a small risk of such

harm — perhaps not much greater than if the employee were a stranger' [...] Here, Saxey was not 'permitted or required' to be with the children at all, apart from trips in the motorboat which were supervised by one of the religious brothers or equivalent and occasionally in the bakery."

42 "The respondent did not confer any power on Saxey in relation to the appellant. Despite the loose structure of the school, as discussed by the trial judge, Saxey's position was not one involving regular or meaningful contact with the students. Of course, as the trial judge pointed out, the very fact that Saxey was an adult in a children's school conferred a certain status, but to find that Saxey's status as an 'adult' in the school was sufficient to attract vicarious liability would in practice cross the line into making the employer an 'involuntary insurer'" [...]. At *ibid*.

43 "The students in any residential school are vulnerable and require protection, but it is the nature of a residential institution rather than the power conferred by the respondent on Saxey that fed the vulnerability. In *Bazley*, [...] the Court said that '[i]t must be possible to say that the employer significantly increased the risk of harm by putting the employee in his or her position and requiring him to perform the assigned tasks' [...]. Such a statement cannot fairly be said of the respondent employer in this case." At *ibid*. [Emphasis removed].

44 For example, if you board an Uber and the driver sexually assaults you or engages in other tortious misconduct, Uber Technologies Inc. will not be vicariously liable because Uber is not considered the employer of the drivers, but a service that connects drivers to passengers. See generally Brishen Rogers, "The Social Costs of Uber" (2015–2016) 82 U Chi L Rev Dialogue 85, Agnieszka A McPeak, "Sharing Tort Liability in the New Sharing Economy" (2016) 49:1 Conn L Rev 171, and Benjamin Means & Joseph A Seiner, "Navigating the Uber Economy" (2016) 49:4 UC Davis L Rev 1511.

However, please see *Uber BV and others v Aslam and others*, [2021] All ER (D) 89 (Feb), 2021 UKSC 5, where the Supreme Court of the United Kingdom (hereinafter "UK") held that Uber is the employer of the drivers on its app. Nonetheless, please keep in mind that this ruling only applies to the UK, and since it is a new ruling, we will have to wait and see how other countries rule in the future. Essentially, this means that it may so happen that Bangladesh follows the UK ruling, which would essentially render this footnote of no force or effect.

45 The test developed in *Bazley* has had a reverberating impact throughout the common law world. For example, in *Lister et al v Hesley Hall Ltd*, [2001] 2 All ER 769, [2001] UKHL 22, it was said at paras 27, "My Lords, I have been greatly assisted by the luminous and illuminating judgments of the Canadian Supreme Court in *Bazley*'s case and *Jacobi*'s case. Wherever such problems are considered in future in the common law world these judgments will be the starting point. On the other hand, it is unnecessary to express views on the full range of policy considerations examined in those decisions." Also see *Blackwater v Plint*, [2005] 3 SCR 3, 2005 SCC 58.

References

Legislation

The Penal Code, 1860 (Bangladesh), Act No XLV of 1860

Caselaw

Bazley v Curry, [1999] 2 SCR 534, [1999] SCJ No 35
Blackwater v Plint, [2005] 3 SCR 3, 2005 SCC 58
Burnie Port Authority v General Jones Pty Ltd, [1994] 120 ALR 42, [1994] 179 CLR 520

326   *Strict liability*

Cambridge Water Co Ltd v Eastern Counties Leather Plc, [1994] 1 All ER 53, [1994] 2 AC 264

EB v Order of the Oblates of Mary Immaculate in the Province of British Columbia, [2005] 3 SCR 45, [2005] SCJ No 61

Ernst v EnCana Corp, [2014] AJ No 975, 2014 ABCA 285

Jacobi v Griffiths, [1999] 2 SCR 570, [1999] SCJ No 36

Jones v Festiniog Railway Company, [1861–73] All ER Rep Ext 1998, 32 JP 693

Jones v Hart, [1698] 1 LD RAYM 739, 2 Salk 441

Lister et al v Hesley Hall Ltd, [2001] 2 All ER 769, [2001] UKHL 22

London Drugs Ltd v Kuehne & Nagel International Ltd, [1992] 3 SCR 299

Losee v Buchanan, [1873] 51 NY 476, 1873 NY LEXIS 563

Munn & Co v The Sir John Crosbie, [1967] 1 Ex CR 94

Musgrove v Pandelis, [1918–19] All ER Rep 589, [1919] 2 KB 43

Parker v New Brunswick Power Corp, [1996] NBJ No 61, [1996] ANB No 61

Ploof v Putnam, [1908] 81 Vt 471, 71 A 188

Read v J Lyons & Co Ltd, [1946] 2 All ER 471, [1947] AC 156

Rickards v Lothian, [1911–13] All ER Rep 71, [1913] AC 263

Rylands v Fletcher, [1861–73] All ER Rep 1, 33 JP 70

Singh (Litigation Guardian of) v Chini, [2005] OJ No 5965, 145 ACWS (3D) 5

Smith v Inco, [2012] OJ No 4225, 2012 ONSC 5094

Transco PLC v Stockport Metropolitan Borough Council, [2004] 1 All ER 589, [2003] UKHL 61

Uber BV and others v Aslam and others, [2021] All ER (D) 89 (Feb), 2021 UKSC 5

Vandry v Quebec Railway, Light, Heat and Power Co, [1916] SCJ No 17, 53 SCR 72

Vincent v Lake Eerie Transportation Co, [1910] 109 Minn 456, 124 NW 221

Secondary Material: Books

Atiyah, Patrick, *Vicarious Liability in the Law of Torts* (London: Butterworth & Co Ltd, 1967)

Feldthusen, Bruce, *Torts Tomorrow: A Tribute to John Fleming*, ed by Nicholas Mullany & Allen Linden (Sydney: LBC Information Services, 1998)

Fleming, John G, *The Law of Torts*, 9th ed (Sydney: LBC Information Services, 1998)

Heuston, Robert F V & Buckley, Richard A, *Salmond and Heuston on the Law of Torts*, 19th ed (London: Sweet & Maxwell, 1987)

Heuston, Robert F V & Buckley, Richard A, *Salmond and Heuston on the Law of Torts*, 20th ed (London: Sweet & Maxwell, 1992)

Pollock, Frederick & Maitland, Frederic W, *The History of English Law before the Time of Edward I*, 2nd ed (London: Cambridge University Press, 1968)

Prosser, William L, *Handbook of The Law of Torts*, 4th ed (St. Paul, Minnesota: West Publishing Co, 1971)

Prosser, William L, Keeton, Page, Dobbs, Dan, Keeton, Robert & Owen, David, eds, *Prosser and Keeton on The Law of Torts*, 5th ed (St. Paul, MN: West Publishing Co, 1984)

Weinrib, Ernest J, *Tort Law: Cases and Materials*, 4th ed (Toronto: Emond Montgomery Publications Limited, 2014)

Secondary Material: Journal Articles

Bohlen, Francis H, "Rule in *Rylands v Fletcher*" (1910–1911) 59:5 U Pa L Rev 298

Bohlen, Francis H, "Incomplete Privilege to Inflict Intentional Invasions of Interests of Property and Personality" (1926) 39:3 Harv L Rev 307

Calabresi, Guido and Hirschoff, Jon, "Toward a Test for Strict Liability in Torts" (1972) 81:6 Yale LJ 1055

Douglas, William, "Vicarious Liability and Administration of Risk" (1929) 38:5 Yale LJ 584

Epstein, Richard A, "A Theory of Strict Liability" (1973) 2:1 J Leg Stud 151

Fletcher, George, "Fairness and Utility in Tort Theory" (1972) 85:3 Harv L Rev 537

Keeton, Robert E, "Conditional Fault in the Law of Torts" (1959) 72:3 Harv L Rev 401

Laski, Harold, "The Basis of Vicarious Liability" (1916) 26:2 Yale LJ 105

McPeak, Agnieszka A, "Sharing Tort Liability in the New Sharing Economy" (2016) 49:1 Conn L Rev 171

Means, Benjamin & Seiner, Joseph A, "Navigating the Uber Economy" (2016) 49:4 UC Davis L Rev 1511

Perry, Robert, "The Deepwater Horizon Oil Spill and the Limits of Civil Liability" (2011) 86:1 Wash L Rev 1

Posner, Richard A, "Strict Liability: A Comment" (1973) 2:1 J Leg Stud 205

Rogers, Brishen, "The Social Costs of Uber" (2015–2016) 82 U Chi L Rev Dialogue 85

Shavell, Steven, "Strict Liability versus Negligence" (1980) 9:1 J Leg Stud 1

Sykes, Alan, "The Boundaries of Vicarious Liability: An Economic Analysis of the Scope of Employment Rule and Related Legal Doctrines" (1988) 101:3 Harv L Rev 563

Secondary Material: Websites

Robertson, Cambell, Schwartz, John & Pérez-Peña, Richard, "BP to Pay $18.7 Billion for Deepwater Horizon Oil Spill" *The New York Times* (2 July 2015), online: The New York Times Company https://www.nytimes.com/2015/07/03/us/bp-to-pay-gulf-coast-states-18-7-billion-for-deepwater-horizon-oil-spill.html

Index

abatement: remedy for nuisance 22–24, 35–37, 51–52; *see also* nuisance; remedies

abnormal sensitivity 26–28, 45–46; *see also* nuisance

abortion 205–206; *see also* duty of care

absolute right *see* balancing of rights

abuse of legal procedure: abuse of process 66–67; damage 67–68; *see also* injury; distinguishing malicious prosecution and false imprisonment 68; initiating proceedings 66; lacking grounds 67

accident *see* tort

activity common to adults 170, 173, 175–176; *see also* standard of care

age of majority 169

aircraft *see* false imprisonment; interference with airspace

animals *see* chattel

assault: coupled with threat 65; definition of 64; imminent threat of battery 64; seriousness of threat 64–65

assumption of risk *see* defences

azan 26–27; *see also* nuisance

balance of probabilities *see* tort

balancing of rights 31–34, 37, 45–46, 48–50, 78–79, 108–109; *see also* nuisance

bargaining power *see* consent

battery: consent to treatment 73–75; examples of 69; failure to disclose risks 100; learned intermediary 98–100; no proof of damage 69; *see also* injury; offensive or harmful 69, 87; saving a patient's life 94; teachers 103; *see also* assault; consent

blasphemous language 103; *see also* defences

bodily harm 90; *see also* battery; consent

breach of the King's peace *see* intentional torts

burden of proof *see* criminal law; tort

but for 219–220, 246; *see also* cause in fact

cause in fact: eliminate other causes of injury 229–230; injury but no liability 266; injury happen anyway 236; insufficient protection 253; material contribution 234–235; multiple defendants 238–239, 241–242; multiple factors 234–235; rescuer's injury 268–269; *vis major* 259; *see also* but for; crumbling skull rule; reasonably foreseeable; remoteness; thin-skull rule

cautionary signs *see* negligence

characteristics of a neighbourhood 23–24, 27, 45–46, 187; *see also* nuisance; reasonable care

chattel: dangerous animals 304; movable property 109; *see also* trespass to chattel

childbirth 94; *see also* consent

children *see* reasonable person; standard of care

The Children Act, 2013 170–173; *see also* criminal law

commercial activity 23–24, 42; *see also* nuisance

commercial area *see* nuisance

common law offences 1, 15; *see also* tort

compensation *see* remedies

Index 329

consent: emergency treatment 74; failure to disclose condition 90; implied consent 23, 49–50, 83; knowledge 45–46; lacking choices 86–88; reasonable amount of time 106; reasonableness in seeing ticket 106; revoking consent 91, 94; sports 83–84; vitiation of 84, 87, 90–91; *see also* bodily harm; childbirth; defences; doctrine of necessity; excessive noise; fraudulent misrepresentation; license; mature minor; search warrant; sexual interference

consent form *see* consent

conspiracy: economic injury 129–130; simple conspiracy 130; unlawful means 133

constitutional tort *see* duty of care; tort

contract *see* inducement to breach contract; tort

contributory negligence 275–276; *see also* defences

construction 29–31, 36, 45–46; *see also* nuisance

conversion: asportation is extensively inconsistent 111–112; momentarily losing chattel 111; unable to recover chattel 110–111; *see also* trespass to chattel

corporal punishment *see* battery

criminal law: focus of 3–4; imprisonment 4; insufficient protection 87–88; prosecution of 3; standard of proof 3; *see also The Children Act, 2013; The Penal Code, 1860*

crumbling skull rule 223–225; *see also* battery

damages: in contract 2–3; factors of 51; *see also* remedies

dangerous animals *see* chattel

death *see* cause in fact; injury

deceptive practices: damage 115–117; elements of 113–114; reliance 113–114; sales commendation 113

defective products *see* duty of care; manufacturer's liability

defences: damages reduced 276; force to correct behaviour 102–103; imminence of threat 102; not a family member 102; repelling an attack 101–102; temporal closeness

103; *volenti non fit injuria* 277–279; *see also* blasphemous language; consent; contributory negligence

detinue *see* trespass to chattel

development of tort in Bangladesh 15–16; *see also* tort

dignity of individual 91; *see also* battery

disability *see* negligence; reasonable person; standard of care

distress damage feasant *see* trespass to chattel

doctor's liability *see* battery; consent

doctrine of necessity 106–107, 307; *see also* consent

duty of care: contractual relationship 199–200; government and private duty of care 272; *see also* torts; history of 199–200; pregnant woman 204–206, 211; symbiotic relationship 211–212, 303; ultimate consumer 277–278; abortion; liability to fetus; manufacturer liability; *Maternal Tort Liability Act*; neighbour principle; *novus actus interveniens*

economic harm *see* conspiracy; interference with economic interests

emotional distress *see* nervous shock

employer-employee relationship 314–315; *see also* vicarious liability

end of proceedings 67; *see also* abuse of legal procedure

escape *see* strict liability

excessive noise 42; *see also* consent

exploitation *see* battery; consent; misappropriation of personality

factual uncertainty *see* cause in fact

false imprisonment: complete restriction on liberty 65; confinement 65; difference between aircraft and other vessels 65–66; locking doors and windows 66; partial restriction on liberty 65; voluntarily entering premises 65–66

foetus *see* duty of care; liability to foetus

fraudulent misrepresentation 90–91, 113; *see also* consent; deceptive practices

general deterrence 4; *see also* tort

330 *Index*

halting traffic 49–50; *see also* nuisance
hypothetical scenarios 6, 26–27, 63–67, 73, 79, 81, 86–87, 94, 101–102, 104–110, 113–114, 122, 165, 169, 172–175, 177–178, 181, 186–187, 195, 200, 215, 219–220, 223–224, 229, 243–244, 250–251, 253–254, 259–260, 264–265, 269, 275–279, 306–307, 310, 314–315; *see also* tort

improper market practices *see* conspiracy
inducement to breach contract: existence of contract 135; knowledge of contract 136
infectious diseases 35–36; *see also* nuisance
injunction 24, 45–46; *see also* nuisance; remedies
injurious falsehood *see* interference with economic interests
injury 45–46, 76–77, 108–109, 123–124, 181
intentional torts 50, 132, 238; *see also* abuse of legal procedure; assault; battery; false imprisonment; inducement to breach contract; interference with airspace; interference with chattel; interference with economic interests; interference with land; interference with the person; intimidation; nervous shock; malicious prosecution
interference with airspace: aircrafts 108–109; duration of intrusion 109; *see also* injury; permanent intrusions 108; zone of effective possession 108–109; balancing of rights
interference with bodily integrity 69, 73, 84, 87; *see also* battery
interference with chattel *see* trespass to chattel
interference with economic interests: communication of statement 117; definition of 112–113; malicious intent 117–118; truth of statement 118; *see also* conspiracy; deceptive practices; inducement to breach contract; misappropriation of personality; passing-off
interference with land: definition of 104–105; distinguished from nuisance 20, 41; physical object 104–105; possession of premises 105;

tangibility of object 105; trespass 104; *see also* consent
interference with the person *see* abuse of legal procedure; assault; battery; false imprisonment; malicious prosecution; nervous shock
International Board for Corporate Governance 16–18
intimate relationships *see* consent
intimidation 133–135
intrusion upon seclusion 78–79; *see also* privacy

joint tortfeasors *see* cause in fact; tort

liability to foetus 208–209; *see also* duty of care
license 106; *see also* consent
lex loci delicti see tort

malice 67, 118, 131; *see also* abuse of legal procedure; interference with economic interests
malicious prosecution 66–68; *see also* abuse of legal procedure
manufacturer liability 100, 200–201, 238; *see also* duty of care; negligence
master-servant *see* vicarious liability
Maternal Tort Liability Act 205; *see also* duty of care
mature minor 95; *see also* consent
medical malpractice *see* negligence
medical procedure *see* battery; consent
medical products 99; *see also* battery; consent
medical treatment 91; *see also* battery; consent
mental injury *see* nervous shock
misappropriation of personality: commercial purposes 126; image 126; subject of work 128
misrepresentation *see* consent; deceptive practices
monetary compensation 6–7; *see also* tort
moral blameworthiness *see* strict liability
motive of noisemaker 27; *see also* nuisance
movable property *see* chattel

negligence: concept of 173–174; industrial revolution 164, 303, 314; *see also* cause in fact; duty of

Index 331

care; reasonable care; reasonable
person; remoteness; *res ipsa loquitur*;
standard of care
neighbour principle 200, 208; *see also*
duty of care
nervous shock 76–78
no-fault liability *see* strict liability
non-compensable injuries 5; *see also*
tort
nonconsensual medical treatment 92;
see also battery
non-natural *see* strict liability
novus actus interveniens 214–215, 224,
250, 259–260, 277–279; *see also*
duty of care
nuisance: bad smell 47; basis of liability
21; consent 42; depreciation in value
36; dry fish 22–23; distinguished
from interference with land 20, 42;
duration of injury 46; *see also* injury;
etymology 20; exercising a public
right 47; fear of infection 35; kinds
of 21; Kurmitola Golf Club 41–42,
96; low probability 40–42, 180–182;
material discomfort 22, 33; new smell
24; noise 26–28; no recognizable
medical condition 23; ordinary
comfort 22; property holders 33;
prostitution 36–37; public 47; public
road 48; smell 22–24; solar-power
29–31; vibration 105; who was where
first 26, 105, 181–182; abnormal
sensitivity; azan; characteristics
of a neighbourhood; commercial
activity; construction; halting traffic;
infectious diseases; injunction; motive
of noisemaker; *sahūr*

objective test 166, 169; *see also*
standard of care
objectivity *see* reasonable person

passing-off: casual consumer 123–124;
codification of 1–2; different country
124–126; distinctive features 122;
geographic region 123–126; goodwill
121–122; purpose of trademark 118;
The Trademarks Act, 2009 1, 118,
121–122; unregistered trademark 119
patients *see* consent
The Penal Code, 1860 2–4, 20, 63, 88,
100–101, 169, 205–206, 224–225,
320; *see also* criminal law
The Pornography Control Act, 2012
79; *see also* privacy

preexisting condition *see* cause in fact
pregnancy *see* duty of care
privacy: consent 81; expectation of
privacy in public places 82; fitting
rooms 82; nature of information
81; *see also* intrusion upon
seclusion; social media; telephone
conversations; *The Pornography
Control Act, 2012*
private nuisance *see* nuisance
product liability; duty of care;
manufacturer's liability
provocation; defences
proximate cause; cause in fact
psychiatric illness; nervous shock
public nuisance; nuisance

Rana Plaza 15–16; *see also* tort
reasonable care: diminishing risk of
injury 183–184; education 187;
Hand Formula 180–181, 183–184,
186–187; industry standard
189–190; low probability 40–42,
181; special training 192; *see also*
characteristics of a neighbourhood
reasonable force *see* defences
reasonable person: disability 177–178;
extra caution 177; knowledge of
common things 174–176; knowledge
of danger 174; knowledge of sports
175; knowledge of surroundings
175–176; landlord's appliances
176; liability of a beginner 177;
memory 174–175; moral qualities
173–174; occupier's knowledge
175–176; profiting from business
173–174; scientific advancement
176, 189–190, 192–193, 262, 269;
skill 176–177; subjective elements
176; who he is 173
reasonably foreseeable 250, 253–255,
262, 268–269; *see also* cause in fact
remedies 4–6, 20, 22–24, 27, 35–37,
42, 45–46, 51–52, 111, 123–124,
303; *see also* damages
remoteness 250–251, 266, 272–273;
see also cause in fact; negligence
residential area *see* nuisance
res ipsa loquitur: apportioning liability
195; nature of accident 194;
reasonable explanation of injury 197,
238–239; requirements of 194
right to air and light 29; *see also*
nuisance
risk *see* negligence

332 *Index*

The Road Transport Act, 2018 49, 193; *see also* balancing of rights

Rylands v Fletcher: dangerous thing 309; escapement of 309; non-natural substance 310; stovetop explosion 311–312; *see also* strict liability

sahūr 28; *see also* nuisance
search warrant 107–108; *see also* consent
self-defence *see* defences
sexting *see* privacy
sexual harassment 87–88; *see also* battery
sexual interference 87; *see also* battery; bodily integrity; consent; interference
simple conspiracy *see* conspiracy
slander of goods *see* interference with economic interests
slander of title *see* interference with economic interests
social media 80–81; *see also* privacy
specific deterrence 3–4; *see also* tort
standard of care: characteristics of every individual 166; children 169; exceptional circumstances 171; incapable of seeing risk 169; *see also* activity common to adults; objective test; reasonable person
statute *see* tort
strict liability: clogged sinks 310; rationale of 304; water tank 310; *see also Rylands v Fletcher*; vicarious liability

telephone conversations 80; *see also privacy*
thin-skull rule 2, 224, 254, 257; *see also* cause in fact
tort: civilized forum 7; definition of 1; distinguished from contract law

2–3; distinguished from criminal law 3–4; etymology 1; focus of 4; government liability 76, 272; holding one accountable 6; kinds of conduct 5; objective of 2, 5–7, 135, 164, 178, 195, 214–215, 238–239, 241; protecting a group of people 2; standard of proof 3–4; tortfeasor 1; *see also* common law offences; development of tort in Bangladesh; general deterrence; hypothetical scenarios; monetary compensation; non-compensable injuries; specific deterrence
trademark *see* passing-off
traffic *see* halting traffic; nuisance
trespass *see* interference with land
trespass to chattel: no proof of injury 109–110; refusing to return chattel 110, 112; right to recover chattel 111; when not returning another's chattel is acceptable 112; *see also* conversion; wireless piggybacking

vehicular accidents *see* negligence
vicarious liability: authorizing an act 318–319; factors of 318; history of 313–314; rationale of 8, 314–315; Salmond Test, 319; *see also* employer-employee relationship; strict liability
voluntary assumption of risk *see* defences
voluntary intoxication *see* reasonable person

Wi-Fi *see* trespass to chattel
wireless piggybacking 109–110; *see also* trespass to chattel
workplace injuries *see* negligence

Printed in the United States
by Baker & Taylor Publisher Services